se·lect (si-lekt') *v.* **-lect·ed**, **-lecting**, **-lects**. —*tr.* To choose from among several; pick out, —*intr.* To make a choice or selection. —*adj.* Also **se·lect·ed** (-lek'tid). **1.** Singled out in preference; chosen. **2.** Of special value or quality; preferred. —*n.* One that is select. [Lat. *seligere*, select-: se-, apart+legere, to choose.] —**se·lect'ness** *n.*

SELECT REGISTRY, Distinguished Inns of North America—the premier guide to exceptional travel and lodging for more than 30 years—invites you to find that special place that will make your next trip unforgettable.

Whether you're traveling for business or pleasure, by yourself or with your family, this guidebook will help you locate extraordinary places to stay throughout the U.S. and Canada. And, no matter what the season or the type of property that you find most comfortable, SELECT REGISTRY likely has something for you.

Most importantly, you can rest assured that our member properties have been ***selected*** as among the best for all of the items listed at the top of this page.

In years past, the registry book in the lobby of hotels and inns welcomed guests and provided a connection between innkeepers and travelers. The historical registry "quill"—the original instrument of guest registration—has been incorporated into our Association's graphic identity. "Distinction, choice, preference, and authenticity" establish our members as "the best of the best"—select properties that will exceed your highest expectations when it comes to lodging.

What is a typical SELECT REGISTRY property? That's difficult to say, since our member properties are extremely diverse. Some are in cities and towns; some are nestled in the countryside. They range in size from upscale B&Bs of less than 10 rooms (***not*** home stays) to 70-room unique hotels. Some are historical, and others are contemporary. Many offer full-service dining; all provide exceptional breakfasts and warm hospitality. Spa services, wine lists, nearby shopping, intriguing area attractions and events, the tranquility of the countryside—you can find most anything available at our various member inns. And, whichever SELECT REGISTRY property you choose, you can rest assured that the experience will be of the highest possible caliber. Our independent inspection program and rigorous membership standards provide that assurance to you.

Look for the plaque with the quill on it when you visit our members' inns, and you'll know that you'll be welcomed and treated to something truly extraordinary.

For information online, go to:
www.SelectRegistry.com

In the late 1960s, one man had an interesting idea. A travel writer named Norman Simpson drove throughout North America in a paneled station wagon, identifying unique places that offered exceptional hospitality and what he called, "good honest lodgings, good honest food, and good honest feeling." Hailed as "the Father of Country Inn Travel," Simpson—through his pioneering book, *Country Inns and Back Roads*—introduced an entirely new type of lodging experience to the traveling public.

Thirty years is a long time, and certainly much of what we consider to be routine in the travel industry today is different than in 1972, when Norman Simpson first organized our Association. Airline travel is commonplace. Gasoline is no longer 40 cents a gallon. Women comprise a much greater percentage of business travelers. Extraordinary Bed and Breakfast Inns complement their Country Inn cousins.

And the Association that Norman Simpson started with a handful of New England properties now includes more than 400 of the "finest country inns, B&Bs, and unique small hotels" from California to Nova Scotia.

Simpson was an innovator, and his vision and tireless promotion fundamentally changed the public perception of the Inn in North America. Today, the Association that was his brainchild is alive and well as SELECT REGISTRY—and we still represent the very best the travel industry has to offer.

Independent Innkeepers Association

"Among all the different ratings existing today, the most coveted innkeeping award should be an eager referral from a satisfied guest to a friend planning a trip."

Keith Kehlbeck, Executive Director

The Select Registry Board of Directors

Welcome

You may be asking, "What exactly ***is*** SELECT REGISTRY?" A better question might be, "***Who*** are we?" SELECT REGISTRY is a nonprofit association of independent innkeepers united by a commitment to gracious hospitality and exceptional settings and amenities.

Of the nearly 30,000 properties today that call themselves "inns" or "B&Bs," only a select few qualify to become members of SELECT REGISTRY. Many of us have been part of the Association for years. Others have joined more recently, but we all offer exceptional lodging experiences. We network and refer among each other—providing a spirit of camaraderie and professionalism valued by guests. Each year, we add new members, allowing us to continue to grow as an organization and to better serve the traveling public.

Most importantly, in an increasingly impersonal world, we pride ourselves in the personal hospitality we provide to our visitors. We're proud of our attention to detail and we work each day to make our guest experiences the best they can possibly be.

Our Association's Central Office—in historic Marshall, Michigan, "the City of Hospitality"—is here to assist you, the traveler, with items ranging from Gift Certificates to a suggestion for a SELECT REGISTRY member in your area.

...and ***that's*** essentially what SELECT REGISTRY is all about—helping travelers find special places and encouraging them to return again and again.

Thank you for choosing SELECT REGISTRY and its members as your partners in finding the best places for that special getaway, a more comfortable business trip, or something simply preferable to the ordinary chain or cookie-cutter lodging alternatives that now seem to abound in many destinations. Why ***not*** go for something a little more special this time? Don't you deserve the best?

We hope that you enjoy this complimentary copy of our directory—which is a gift from your hosts. Use it in good health as you travel; we look forward to welcoming you along the way!

Your Select Registry Innkeeper

Virginia • Charlottesville

Prospect Hill Plantation Inn

www.srinns.com/prospecthill
Box 6909, Charlottesville,VA 229
800-277-0844 • 540-967-0844 • Fax 540-967-01
Innkeerer@prospecthill.com

Innkeepers/Owners
The Sheehan family since 1977
Elegant Plantation Country Inn

Mobil ★★★

Award-winning dining and lodging in the 1732 manor house and original 18th century outbuildings and former slave quarters on this historic 50 acre plantation located just 15 miles East of Charlottesville, VA. Romantic 5-course candlelight dining daily. 13 rooms and suites featuring breakfast-in-bed, working fireplaces, double Jacuzzis in most rooms, private balconies, gazebo amidst manicured grounds, and swimming pool in the serenity of the coutryside near Monticello, wineries, and many other historic sites. Selected many times over the past 28 years as one of America's most romantic getaways. Come early for our complimentary pre-dinner wine reception and stroll our arboretum gardens and lawns while smelling the aromas wafting from the kitchen as we prepare the evening meal. MAP Lodging Packages include pre-dinner wine reception, candlelight dinner at table for two, full country breakfast and all gratuities. B&B and other special rates available.

Rooms/Rates
13 rms/suites from $145/$345 sgl B&B, $295/$495 dbl MAP pkgs w/gratuities incl.

Cuisine
Elegant Continental-American cuisine. Wine and snacks on arrival, pre-dinner wine reception, 5-course candlelight dinner, full country breakfast-in-bed (or in dining room). All gratuities included with MAP.

Nearest Airport(s)
Charlottesville Albemarle
Richmond International

Directions
From Charlottesville (15 mi.) E via I-64, exit 136 at Zion Crossroads. From Washington, DC (approx. 100 mi.) I-66 W to Hwy#29 S, to Hwy#15 S to Zion Crossroads. Turn L on Hwy#250 E for 1 mile and L on Poindexter Rd. Inn is 3 mi down on L.

Member Since 1979

Our favorite inn. Fantastic food! Coming every year for 21 years JM, Annapolis, MD Wonderful food! What a GREAT inn! LP, ChevyChase, MD

448 SelectRegistry.com

The guidebook is organized in alphabetical order, by state and province (our Canadian members have a separate section, which begins on page 20). A map of the state or province at the beginning of each section shows the location of each property, relative to major cities and highways. Nearby SELECT REGISTRY properties "just across the border" in neighboring states or provinces are indicated by a small quill symbol and page numbers on the map. For larger map images, go to the SELECT REGISTRY web site, www.SelectRegistry.com.

Generally speaking, properties are grouped within each state or province by travel area. All Mendocino, California properties, for example, are listed together.

For the convenience of our guests, an index of the properties by state and province is provided at the front of the book. At the back of the book, you'll find an alpha-listing of all member properties.

Each SELECT REGISTRY member property is represented with its own page of information in this guidebook. The page includes one or two pictures, a brief description of the experience a guest can expect at that property, and contact information. The innkeepers/owners are listed, and the property is identified by a general type/architectural style descriptor (e.g., "Elegant In-Town Breakfast Inn" or "Rustic Country Inn"). ❶

The Rooms/Rates section gives the number of rooms and pricing structure for the property. ❷ Cuisine describes the food and beverage specialties for which our members are famous. ❸ Directions give you an easy to follow "road map" to reach the property. ❺ Nearest Airport(s) tells you where you might fly in. ❹

Some of our members wish to indicate certain awards or ratings (e.g., AAA, Mobil, DiRōNA, or *Wine Spectator*), and guests will find the appropriate symbols in the sidebar. ❻

For many years, while we were known as the Independent Innkeepers' Association, our logo was a lit lantern, symbolizing "the Shining Light in Hospitality." Founders and members who have been in the Association since the 1970s are identified with that logo. ❼

Many of our inns feature "business friendly amenities," including such things as corporate rates, Internet access, meeting areas, flexible check-in times, and more. If an inn meets at least 12 of 14 criteria we've identified as catering to the business traveler, they will have a briefcase icon at the top of their page. ❽

At the bottom of each page, there is an Amenities and Policies grid—a brief indication of the services each SELECT REGISTRY member property offers its guests. Briefly stated, the icons stand for: ❾

12+ Suitable for Children	Exercise Facilities
Not Suitable for Children	Spa Services
Non-smoking Inn	Reservations by Travel Agents
Handicap accessible guestrooms	Internet Access
Credit cards accepted	Pets Welcome
Corporate/Business Rates	Pool
Conference Facilities	Fireplaces
Wedding Facilities	Whirlpool Tubs

Breakfast Lunch Dinner Wine/Cocktails

Each of our inns has a slightly different mix of food and beverage services. Although these are often described in more detail in the Cuisine section for each inn, we want to give our guests a quick snapshot of what each inn offers in-house. The icons near the top of each page tell you whether the inn serves breakfast, lunch, and/or dinner, and whether or not wine or cocktails are available. ⓫ In many cases, at the very bottom of each page, you'll find a guest quote or some recognition garnered by the property. This tells you something, in particular, for which the property is known. ❿

"I keep the book in my glove compartment. Never travel without it!"

Gift Certificates

The gift of an overnight stay or a weekend at an inn or B&B can be one of the most thoughtful and appreciated gifts you can give your parents, children, or dear friends. Employers are discovering that a gift certificate for a "getaway" is an excellent way of rewarding their employees, while at the same time giving them some much needed rest and relaxation. And "Good Morning America" featured SELECT REGISTRY gift certificates as one of the "most unique gifts" for brides and grooms.

Our gift certificates are valid at any of our more than 400 member properties. We ship certificates daily, **packaged with our Association guidebook and your personal message.** The next time you think about gift-giving, think about our Gift Certificate Program—the perfect gift for that special person.

Order online at: www.SelectRegistry.com
or call: 1-800-344-5244
(269) 789-0393

Loyalty is important!

Because we value our many return guests, for the past several years SELECT REGISTRY has administered a modest frequent traveler reward effort called "The North American Passport Program." Upon sending in a completed passport card (with stamps from three separate visits to a SELECT REGISTRY property), thousands of our guests have received a Passport voucher for use at our member properties. This year, we're in the process of taking our loyalty program to the next level. Introducing...The Golden Quill Club Loyalty Travel Program!

In the back of this book, you'll find a detachable post card that you may now use as a passport *and* a voucher, all rolled into one. Rules and instructions are printed on the card. As you redeem the completed card, you'll be provided with a new one for your next set of visits. If you choose, you'll be added to our e-newsletter recipient list. Most importantly, as an additional reward, you'll be entered in our current "Vacation of a Lifetime" drawing for a multi-inn stay in one of our geographic regions throughout North America. Watch our web site for additional details.

Start collecting Loyalty Rewards today while staying at SELECT REGISTRY inns. We think you'll find that some experiences are worth repeating!

"Select Registry Gift Certificates — a unique gift for brides and grooms."
-Good Morning America

www.SelectRegistry.com
www.innbook.com

It's no secret that we have become an "online" society. Recent statistics indicate that more people than ever in the U.S. and Canada are using computers and the Internet to search for products and services. The digital revolution is here to stay—particularly when it comes to the travel industry. Because of this, SELECT REGISTRY maintains a user-friendly, information-filled central web site for prospective guests.

After you've read our printed guidebook—and for more information on our member properties, log onto our central Association web site, where you'll find thousands of pages of information, as well as links to the home web sites of our individual members. Among other things, you'll find:

- "Find an Inn" search engine
- Descriptions and photos for each of our more than 400 member properties
- Trip Planner itineraries
- Featured inns
- Recipes
- Area attractions
- Specials
- Email post cards (using photos of our inns)
- Online guestbook.

And, you'll be able to:

- Check availability and request a reservation online
- Order a SELECT REGISTRY gift certificate (good at any of our current member properties)
- Sign up for exciting promotions and our e-newsletter
- Take our guest e-survey.

We're proud of our central web site, which is the perfect complement to our unequaled guidebook, now in its 17th Edition. Wherever you travel, carry the book in your briefcase or glove compartment, and log onto www.SelectRegistry.com to find that "special place" for your next business trip or getaway!

"By far, the most attractive, complete directory of top quality inns, B&Bs, and small hotels and resorts on the Internet! Loads of information."

Perhaps the most important distinction that sets a SELECT REGISTRY member apart from other inns or B&Bs is our Quality Assurance Program. **SELECT REGISTRY carries out periodic quality assurance inspections for each of its 408 members.** This program is conducted by an independent consulting firm (not employees of SELECT REGISTRY) that specializes in providing quality assurance evaluations for the hospitality industry. The inspectors arrive unannounced and unidentified, spend the night, and evaluate the inn on a detailed point system, which translates into a pass/fail grade for the inn. Each evaluation is conducted in a fair and unbiased manner, based on the requirements of SELECT REGISTRY and the expectations of guests. Not all inns have what it takes to pass the inspections, and this process provides a guarantee to the traveling public that a SELECT REGISTRY inn is in a class of its own.

No other online directory or organization of innkeepers has a comparable inspection program.

All of our members must achieve and maintain a certain threshold level of excellence, in order to remain in the Association. This year, our guidebook includes four properties which scored a perfect 200 (out of 200) on their most recent Quality Assurance inspection. On their pages, the name of the `inn is in gold, signifying this extraordinary accomplishment.

Although we don't rank our members with diamonds or stars, many of our properties carry the high ratings you'd expect from groups such as AAA, Mobil, *Wine Spectator*, or DiRōNA. All SELECT REGISTRY members strive to be "the best at what we do," and our inspection program helps to maintain the high standards and overall level of guest satisfaction that today's inn traveler has come to expect.

"I could see that all of your guests were being treated like the inspector."

Every year, we add extraordinary new properties to our SELECT REGISTRY directory. The following properties have passed the Association's rigorous quality assurance procedures and have been voted into membership by their peers on our Board of Directors. We recommend them highly to you, along with the other 373 inns in this directory!

"Select Registry keeps adding great new members in places I want to visit!"

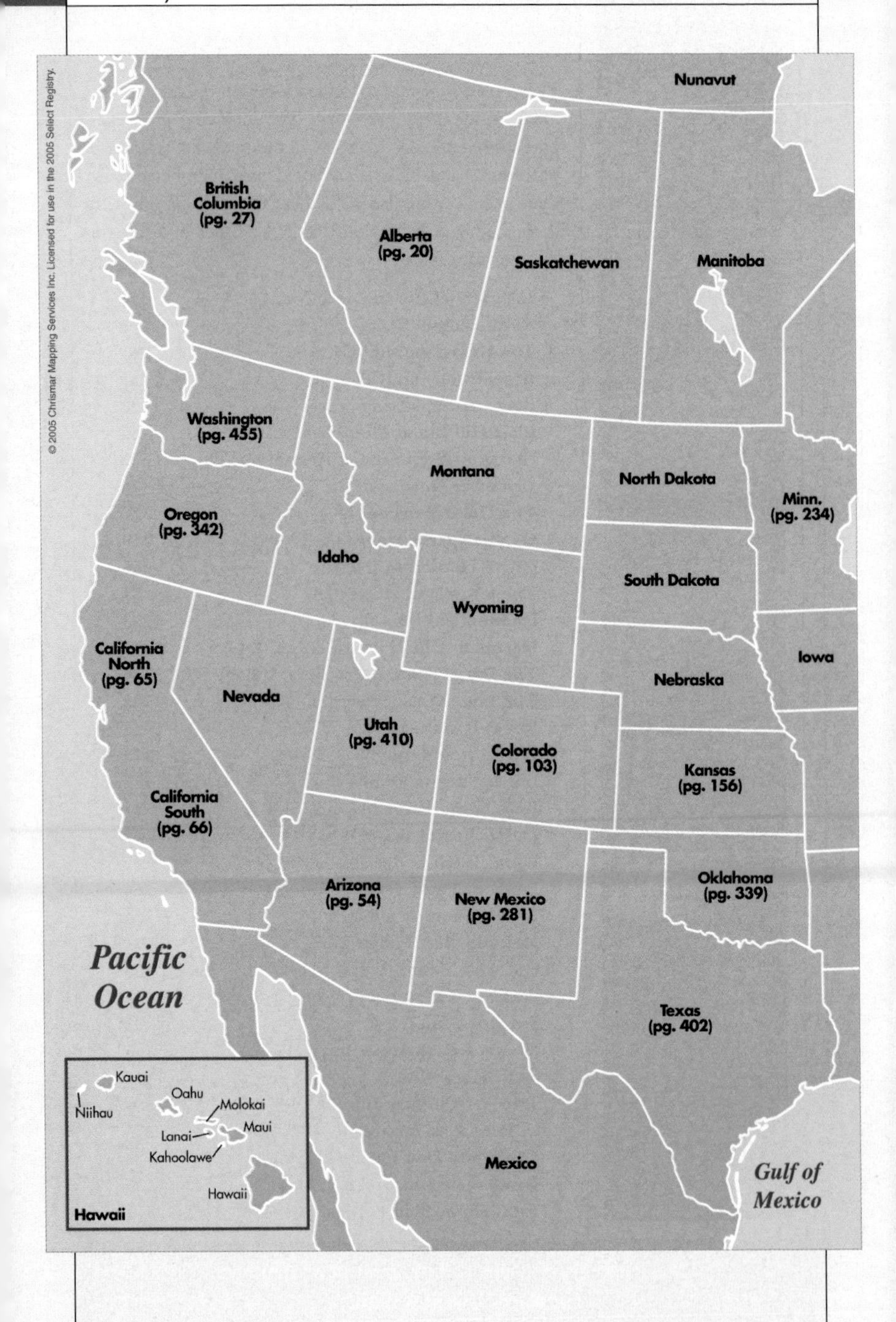
© 2005 Chrismar Mapping Services Inc. Licensed for use in the 2005 Select Registry.
Nunavut
British Columbia (pg. 27)
Alberta (pg. 20)
Saskatchewan
Manitoba
Washington (pg. 455)
Montana
North Dakota
Minn. (pg. 234)
Oregon (pg. 342)
Idaho
South Dakota
Wyoming
California North (pg. 65)
Nevada
Iowa
Nebraska
Utah (pg. 410)
Colorado (pg. 103)
Kansas (pg. 156)
California South (pg. 66)
Arizona (pg. 54)
New Mexico (pg. 281)
Oklahoma (pg. 339)
Pacific Ocean
Texas (pg. 402)
Kauai
Oahu
Niihau
Molokai
Maui
Lanai
Kahoolawe
Hawaii
Hawaii
Mexico
Gulf of Mexico

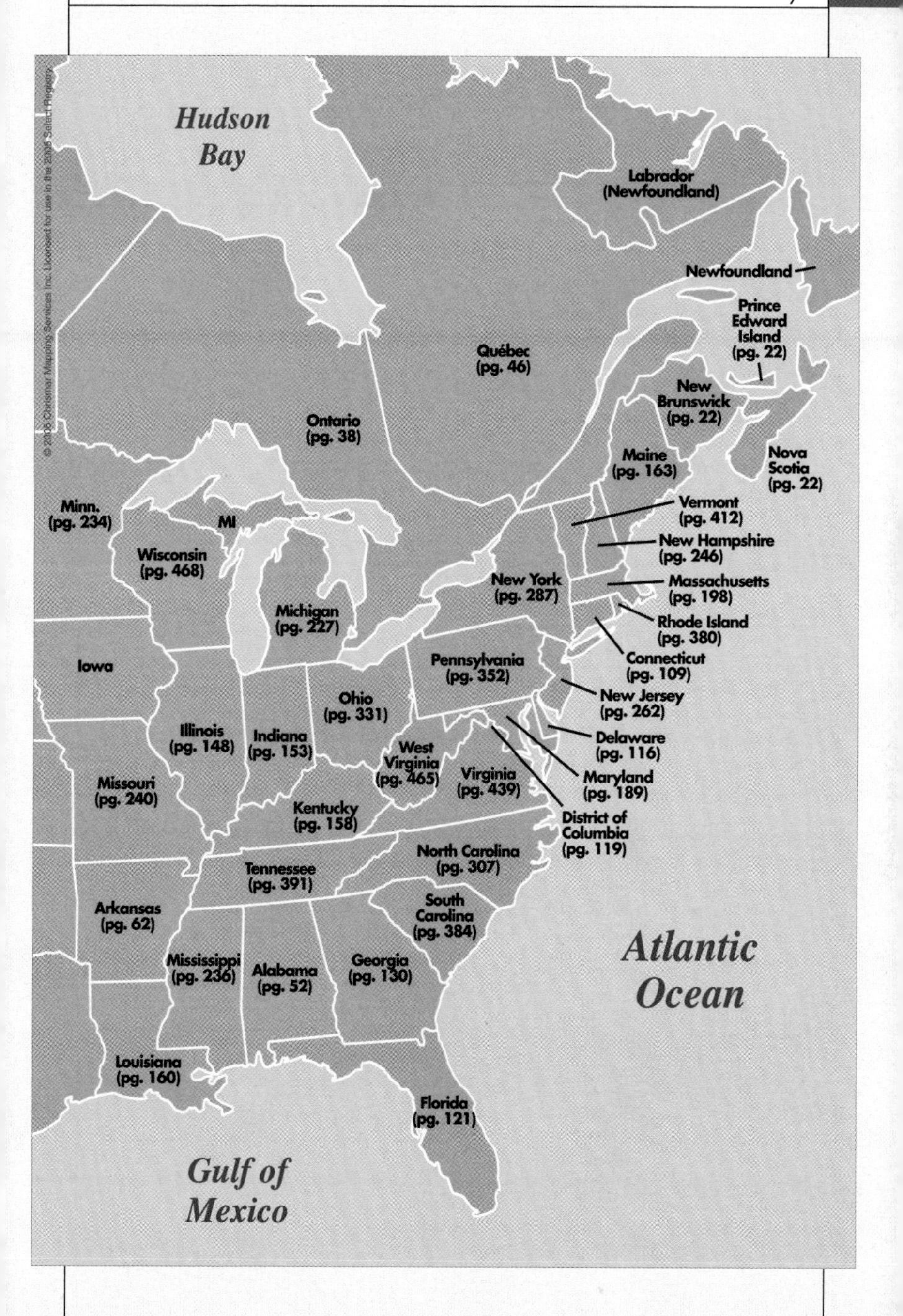
© 2005 Chrismar Mapping Services Inc. Licensed for use in the 2005 Select Registry
Hudson Bay
Labrador (Newfoundland)
Newfoundland
Prince Edward Island (pg. 22)
Québec (pg. 46)
New Brunswick (pg. 22)
Ontario (pg. 38)
Maine (pg. 163)
Nova Scotia (pg. 22)
Minn. (pg. 234)
MI
Vermont (pg. 412)
New Hampshire (pg. 246)
Wisconsin (pg. 468)
New York (pg. 287)
Massachusetts (pg. 198)
Michigan (pg. 227)
Rhode Island (pg. 380)
Connecticut (pg. 109)
Iowa
Pennsylvania (pg. 352)
New Jersey (pg. 262)
Ohio (pg. 331)
Illinois (pg. 148)
Indiana (pg. 153)
Delaware (pg. 116)
West Virginia (pg. 465)
Virginia (pg. 439)
Maryland (pg. 189)
Missouri (pg. 240)
Kentucky (pg. 158)
District of Columbia (pg. 119)
North Carolina (pg. 307)
Tennessee (pg. 391)
South Carolina (pg. 384)
Arkansas (pg. 62)
Atlantic Ocean
Mississippi (pg. 236)
Alabama (pg. 52)
Georgia (pg. 130)
Louisiana (pg. 160)
Florida (pg. 121)
Gulf of Mexico

Index by State

Some of the more common alternatives when it comes to lodging plans are identified in the Rates sections of our inns' pages and below.

B&B Plan: Breakfast included in the rate (a few inns charge for breakfast, but tell you this in their listing). Breakfast might consist of an elegant continental breakfast or a four-course extravaganza.

American Plan (AP): Breakfast, lunch and dinner are included.

Modified American Plan (MAP): Breakfast and dinner included.

European Plan (EP): A guest pays for the room and its amenities, but breakfast, lunch and dinner are billed separately.

Taxes and gratuities: Plans may or may not include service charges, state and local taxes and gratuity. Please ask your Innkeeper in advance about tax and gratuity policies.

Price changes: Please call the Inn to verify all prices and services, which are subject to change during the lifetime of this book.

Cancellation policies: Cancellation policies vary from Inn to Inn and with particular circumstances. A late cancellation often costs the Innkeeper room revenue, and this is why nearly every Inn has a cancellation policy.

Note: Nearly all of our Inns feature individual baths. Those few that have shared baths will tell you.

While Select Registry members share a commitment to quality and hospitality, the type, style and location of our properties can vary dramatically.

Writer: Keith Kehlbeck. Canadian copy: Steve Stafford. Design: Haas-Wittmann Design. Maps: Chrismar Mapping Services, Inc. Production: Online Architecture and Cadmus Media Works. Publisher: Select Registry, Distinguished Inns of North America, Keith Kehlbeck, Executive Director .

We appreciate the photo skills of everyone who contributed to this book. Some member inns have provided photographs without photographic credits, and other images are unidentified. If you're not listed here, we extend our thanks. We will be pleased to publish a credit if it is furnished to Select Registry.

Images/Inns featured in the book: Cover, Tara–A Country Inn, ©Richard Smaltz. Back cover, Stonecroft Country Inn. Pages 101, 123, 125, 146, 193, 199, 203, 207, 225, 258, 260, 266, 269, 271, 275, 276, 280, 284, 288, 289, 320, 322, 333, 364, 382, 383, 421, 425, 431, 435, 437, photos: George W. Gardner Associates. Page 432, photo:Tim Shellmer. Gift certificate photo: Craft Photographic Studio; (page 6) Quebec City, photo: Brad Wittman (page 18), Auberge des Gallant (QUE); (page 18) Galerie Parchemine, photo: © Tourisme Montréal, Stéphan Poulin. Other photo credits available upon request.

Select Registry, Distinguished Inns of North America, P.O. Box 150, 501 E. Michigan Avenue, Marshall, MI 49068. Phone: 269-789-0393. Fax: 269-789-0970.

To assure a safe and happy trip, please call ahead to verify times, prices, Inn policies, etc.

From California to Nova Scotia, SELECT REGISTRY represents the finest inns, B&Bs, and unique small hotels North America has to offer. We are proud to include among our members a number of exceptional Canadian properties. To our Canadian guests, we say, "Our innkeepers stand ready to welcome you during your travels, whether it is to the States or within Canada." To our American guests, we say, "Why not see what Canada has to offer?"

In these uncertain times, when crossing oceans is worrisome, nothing beats the exhilarating feeling of visiting an exciting new country in the security and comfort of your own car. Yes, for many millions of Americans, Canada is just a short drive away—and yet it is a whole new world!

No wonder Americans love to travel to Canada: not only do their U.S. dollars go a lot further there (which means a lot more holiday for the same amount of money), but they also get to choose between a multitude of completely different experiences.

De la Californie à la Nouvelle-Ecosse, le SELECT REGISTRY représente plusieurs auberges, cafés-couettes et petits hôtels des plus distingués en Amérique du Nord. Nous sommes fiers de pouvoir compter parmi nos membres plusieurs des plus beaux établissements canadiens. À tous les voyageurs, canadiens-français, nous vous souhaitons de merveilleux sejours dans les auberges de prestige du SELECT REGISTRY.

"We've experienced all four seasons in Canada—and we can't pick a favorite!"

There are the breathtaking vistas, mountain wildlife, Asian food and totem poles of British Columbia, the "foodie" paradise of the Niagara Peninsula (Canada's Napa Valley) and the Eastern Townships of Quebec, replete with friendly wineries and raw milk cheeses. There are festivals galore, museums, parks and world-class shopping in Toronto and Montreal as well as the fascinating culture of the Province of Quebec where French-Canadians take food and fun very, very seriously. And, never to be forgotten, the bucolic seaside charm and legendary hospitality of Canada's maritime provinces, New Brunswick, Prince Edward Island and Nova Scotia.

Many travelers have experienced all four seasons of the Northland (the winters are sunnier and less cold than you think). Traveling east to west, it would be hard to declare a regional winner. Some Canadians modestly claim to be the most hospitable of innkeepers, and a critic can't easily challenge that assertion.

Superb food, wine and service can be expected at the Canadian inns of the SELECT REGISTRY. Understated luxury, too. But above all, they offer you an exclusive glimpse of the best of Canada: its forests, crystalline lakes, affordable golf and skiing and cosmopolitan, secure and friendly cities. The Northland beckons!

"Unbelievable natural beauty, exceptional food and wine, and our friendly neighbors to the North...perfect!"

Alberta

"Canada's Rocky Mountain Playground"

Famous For: Camping, Wildlife, Skiing and Winter Fun (Lake Louise), Mt. Columbia, Hiking, Kayaking, Canoeing, Banff National Park, West Edmonton Mall, Birding, Bison Olympic Hall of Fame, Calgary Stampede

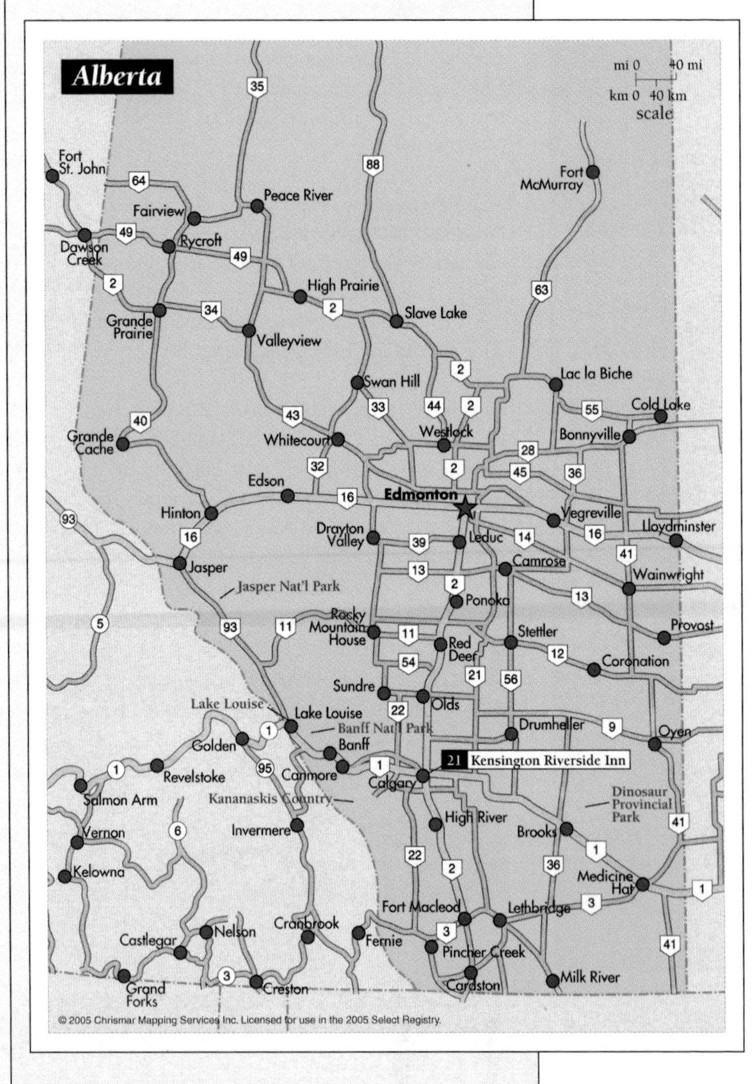

Kensington Riverside Inn

www.srinns.com/kensingtonriverside
1126 Memorial Drive NW, Calgary, AB T2N 3E3
877-313-3733 • 403-228-4442 • Fax 403-228-9608
info@kensingtonriversideinn.com

Innkeepers/Owners
Karen & Bob Brown
Elegant Urban Inn

AAA ◆◆◆◆

Rooms/Rates
19 Guest Rooms. $239/$399 CDN (approx. $195/$325 US). 5 room types featuring fireplaces, balconies, patios or Jacuzzis.

Cuisine
A coffee tray is delivered to your room with the morning newspaper, followed by a gourmet breakfast in our dining room. In the evening, hors d'oeuvres are served in the living room. You'll also find chocolates by the bedside and cookies 24 hours a day. Light meals are available at any time.

Nearest Airport(s)
Calgary International Airport.

Directions
From Downtown: West on 4th Avenue S.W., north on 10th Street S.W., west on Memorial Drive for one block.

In the midst of Calgary's trendy Kensington district, just a short walk from the business centre of town, the Kensington Riverside Inn has made a name for itself as Alberta's only AAA Four Diamond Inn. The Inn is traditional in style and gracious in atmosphere, with 10-foot ceilings, cornices and columns throughout, and a wood-burning fireplace and bar in the living room. Guests are treated to a magnificent view of the Bow River and the downtown skyline, exceptional accommodations, first-class service and amenities galore. Shops, restaurants and a theatre are close by, as well as the Light Rail Transit System, making many of the city's attractions readily accessible. Comfort and convenience are the way in each of the 19 guest rooms, from balconies or patios to gas fireplaces and Jacuzzis, to Egyptian cotton sheets and goose-down duvets. A video and book lending library as well as voice mail and wireless Internet complete the picture. There's lots to do in and around Calgary, and the Canadian Rockies are only an hour away.

Member Since 2005

"The most comfortable stay I've ever had!" - Phoenix, AZ "Perfect as always" - Sunnyvale, CA "An absolutely fabulous & relaxing getaway." Toronto

New Brunswick: "The Picture Province"
Famous For: The Maritimes, Acadia and the Cajuns, forests, Trans-Canada Highway, Fundy National Park

Nova Scotia: "The Land of Evangeline"
Famous For: Cabot Trail, fishing, Cape Breton Highlands, harbours and coves, lobster, Christmas trees, wild blueberries

Prince Edward Island: "The Garden Province"
Famous For: Lighthouses, Confederation Centre of the Arts, Anne of Green Gables, Confederation Bridge

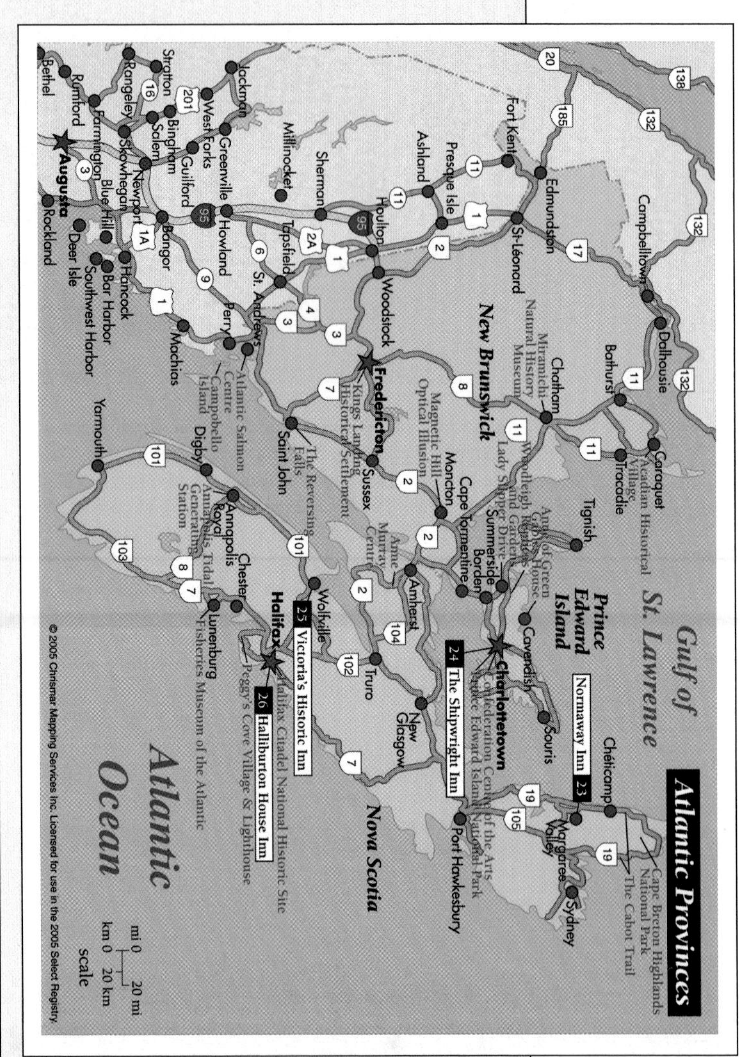

Normaway Inn

www.srinns.com/normaway
Box 138, Margaree Valley, NS, Canada B0E 2C0
800-565-9463 • 902-248-2987 • Fax 902-248-2600
normaway@lincsat.com

Innkeeper/Owner
David M. MacDonald

Traditional Country Retreat/Lodge

Nestled in the hills of the Cape Breton Highlands, near the beginning of the spectacular Cabot Trail, this 250-acre property offers a 1920s inn and cabins, most with woodstove fireplaces and some with Jacuzzis. Enjoy superb food, sincere service, and choice wines. Guests often relax by the fieldstone fireplace after dinner and enjoy films or traditional entertainment nightly. Weekly fiddling concerts in music barn, tennis, hiking trails, biking, salmon and trout fishing. Arrangements for whale watching, sailing and horseback riding. 2900 foot paved air strip adjacent to property. Also, within 10 minutes of the Normaway, a large farm house on a 25 acre river property is available for weekly/daily rental. Many great hiking trails within 25 miles.

Rooms/Rates
9 Rooms, $99/$139 EP;
17 Cabins, $139/$279 EP;
3 Suites, $179/$279 EP; $45-60 per person MAP.

Cuisine
June 15 - October 15.
Dinner 6-9 p.m., Breakfast 7:30-10:00 a.m. Picnic lunches.

Nearest Airport(s)
Sydney (YQY)

Directions
Trans-Canada Hwy. Jct. 7 at Nyanza, N on Cabot Trail 17 mi. Turn off between NE Margaree and Lake-O-Law on Egypt Road; 2 mi. to Inn. From Rte 19, Drive North on Rte 19 Margaree Forks, Turn Right, 10 miles to Egypt Road. Turn Left on Egypt Rd, 2 mi.to Inn.

Member Since 1972

"Normaway Inn offers country fare and does so with flair."
Canadian House and Home

Shipwright Inn B & B

www.srinns.com/shipwright
51 Fitzroy Street, Charlottetown, PEI, Canada C1A 1R4
888-306-9966 • 902-368-1905 • Fax 902-628-1905
innkeeper@shipwrightinn.com

Innkeepers/Owners
Judy & Trevor Pye
Elegant Victorian Breakfast Inn

Enjoy a "Unique Experience" at the award winning Shipwright Inn. This early Victorian, Anne of Green Gables style, historic home was built in 1865 by shipbuilder James Douse. It is located in Olde Charlottetown within a 3 minute walk of historic/cultural sites, waterfront, live theatre, fine dining and shopping. In keeping with the nautical theme antiques and artwork have been lovingly collected for your enjoyment.

All bedrooms have polished pine floors, en-suite bathrooms, some with double Ultra Air Tubs, whirlpools and fireplaces. While savouring a memorable breakfast, beneath the dining-room chandelier, imagine how the rope insignia dinner service must have looked at the captain's table. Safe, free parking, peaceful, comfortable and quiet. We pride ourselves on delivering warm Island hospitality, attentive service and believe in pampering our guests. CanSelect ★★★★★ Star, Frommer's Best on PEI.

Member Since 1999

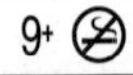

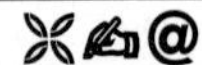

Rooms/Rates
3 Executive suites, 1 Apartment Unit, 5 Premium suites
CDN $135/$279.
Open all year-round.
Off-season rates apply.

Cuisine
Afternoon tea/coffee and cakes. Memorable full served hot breakfast of four courses (if you have the appetite!)

Nearest Airport(s)
Charlottetown Airport - approximately a 10 minute drive.

Directions
From Confederation Bridge : TCH 1 East to the centre of Charlottetown. Turn R on Fitzroy St. go 1.5 blocks. On R before Pownal Street look for lighted red/gold sign with a gold ship model on top.
From Ferry : TCH 1 West, R on Univ Av. L on Fitzroy.

"Exceptional experience! Great restoration and historic feeling. Incredibly beautiful."

Victoria's Historic Inn

www.srinns.com/victoriainn
600 Main Street, Wolfville, NS, Canada B4P 1E8
800-556-5744 • 902-542-5744 • Fax 902-542-7794
victoriasinn@eastlink.ca

Innkeepers/Owners
The Cryan Family
Elegant Victorian Village Breakfast Inn

AAA ◆◆◆

Rooms/Rates
14 Rooms, $128/$195.
2 Suites, $245 CDN B&B.
Open year-round.

Cuisine
Hot breakfast included in room rate. Award-winning restaurants within walking distance. Selection of wines available.

Nearest Airport(s)
Halifax International Airport
1 hour driving distance.

Directions
From Yarmouth: 101 E to exit #11. L off exit ramp. R onto Hwy 1. Just inside town limits on L. From Halifax Airport: Hwy. 102 S towards Halifax to exit 4B onto 101 W and Annapolis Valley (approx 15 min.) Take exit 10. Follow Hwy 1 to town. Located on R after downtown.

The Cryan family has worked tirelessly to achieve the first B&B five-star Canada Select rating in the province. Now perhaps the finest Victorian home in Nova Scotia, the Inn's professionally decorated rooms lend an intimate and first-class atmosphere, all with ensuite baths; some offer double Jacuzzis and fireplaces, with balcony or sweeping view. Travel writers say, "It is the attention to detail and the softly decorated rooms, as well as the sincere care of the innkeepers, that draw people back to Victoria's again and again for peace and relaxation in a pampered environment."

Nestled in the picturesque and historic town of Wolfville, travelers are surrounded by a choice of activities. Hiking trails, scenic vistas, historic sites, award-winning dining, golf and wineries are all minutes away.

Member Since 1998

"Came for one night, stayed five - perfect!"

The Halliburton

www.halliburton.ns.ca
5184 Morris Street, Halifax, NS, Canada B3J 1B3
902-420-0658 • Fax 902-423-2324
information@thehalliburton.com

Manager
Robert Pretty
Elegant In Town Inn

AAA ◆◆◆

Downtown Halifax's boutique hotel. The Halliburton features signature dining and individually appointed guestrooms in a trio of heritage townhouses. Twenty-nine rooms and suites of various sizes, complimentary breakfast, and wireless Internet access. 'Stories' restaurant offers inventive regional cuisine in intimate dining rooms. In the summer months guests enjoy cocktails and light fare in the garden courtyard. In the autumn and winter a crackling fire invites from the cozy library. The Halliburton, was built in 1809 and was home to Sir Brenton Halliburton, the first Chief Justice of the Nova Scotia Supreme Court. More recently, the building housed Dalhousie University's prestigious law school. A short stroll from popular shops, restaurants and the Halifax waterfront. AAA/CAA ◆◆◆ Award Canada Select ★★★★ Award

Rooms/Rates
29 rooms including 4 suites, rates from $140 CDN, plus tax, includes breakfast. Open year-round.

Cuisine
An extensive continental breakfast is served each morning from 7-10. 'Stories' offers relaxed fine dining from 5:30 until 10:00, reservations are recommended. Fine wine, local beer and cocktails are served after 4:00 in the Library or garden courtyard.

Nearest Airport(s)
Halifax International -- CYHZ

Directions
Downtown Halifax, Barrington at Morris Street. Use Hwy #102 from Halifax International Airport or Hwy #103 from Yarmouth.

Member Since 1998

   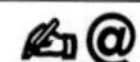 

"The finest food we've had so far, your staff deserve much praise!"

British Columbia

"The Pacific Province"

Famous For: Canadian Rockies, ferries, Vancouver Island, spiral railway tunnels, Butchart Gardens

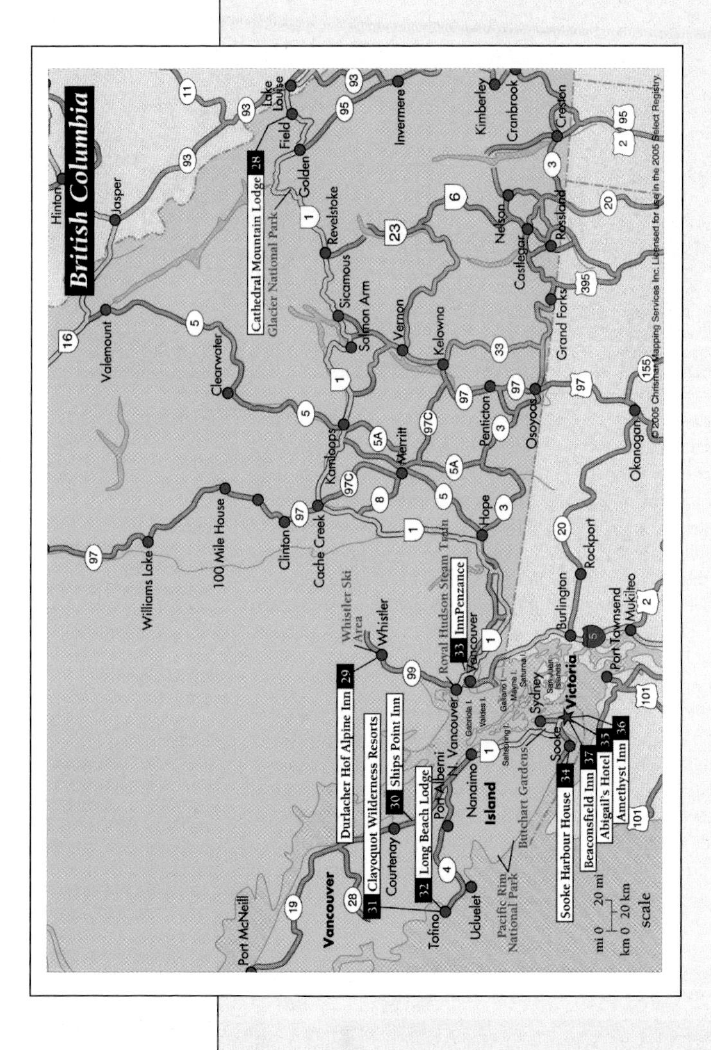

Cathedral Mountain Lodge

www.srinns.com/cathedralmountain
Yoho Valley Road, P.O. Box 40, Field, BC, Canada V0A 1G0
866-619-6442 • 250-343-6442 • Fax (250) 343-6424
info@cathedralmountain.com

Innkeepers/Owners
Nancy Stibbard
General Manager
Craig Chapman
Elegant Rocky Mountain Retreat/Lodge

Imagine your own log cabin in the heart of the Canadian Rocky Mountains; a stocked wood burning fireplace, down duvets, deep soaker bathtub, tranquil sitting areas and a generous private deck with commanding views of the magnificent Rocky Mountains and the glacier fed Kicking Horse River. Wake up to the song of wild birds and the call of an alpine river, to the scent of fresh pine and the beauty of mountain wildflowers. There is no television or telephone to disrupt your mountain escape. Your purpose is to replenish and revive - because tomorrow you can hike, climb, raft, canoe, bike, fish, golf and horseback ride!

From leisurely strolls to day-long expeditions, an endless array of hiking trails are just outside your door. This is an authentic Rocky Mountain retreat surrounded by other-worldly alpine meadows, abundant wildlife, towering peaks and epic waterfalls. Close to the all the attractions and activities of Yoho National Park, Lake Louise and Banff National Park, there is so much to do! Come to Cathedral Mountain Lodge - a place where every day is like no day anywhere else.

Member Since 2003

Rooms/Rates
Rates vary according to season and cabin type. Range $150/$350 USD.

Cuisine
Complimentary continental breakfast is served from 7 - 10 a.m. Lunch and dinner feature a range of entree choices, emphasizing fresh regional ingredients.

Nearest Airport(s)
Calgary International Airport

Directions
Cathedral Mountain Lodge is located 200km (125 miles) from Calgary, Alberta. Travel west on Trans Canada Highway 1. Go past Canmore, Banff and Lake Louise before crossing into B.C. 5 km into B.C., the highway starts a steep descent; at the bottom take a right turn on Yoho Valley Road. This will take you directly to the lodge.

"Dining Room was exceptional. We have travelled for a month up the West coast and this food and service is the best we have had!" - Taylor/Voller, U.K.

Durlacher Hof Alpine Inn

www.srinns.com/durlacherhof
7055 Nesters Rd., Whistler, BC, Canada V0N 1B7
877-932-1924 • 604-932-1924 • Fax 604-938-1980
info@durlacherhof.com

Innkeepers/Owners
Peter & Erika Durlacher

Traditional Mountain Breakfast Inn

AAA ◆◆◆

Rooms/Rates
8 Guest Rooms. Summer $129/$239 CDN. Winter $179/$359 CDN. Ski & Golf packages. 10 days summer, 30 days winter cancellation policy, min. German spoken, Canada Select Inn ★★★★ 1/2.

Cuisine
Dinners offered in Winter on selected evenings. Special culinary events in Spring and Fall. Complimentry Old Country Breakfast Buffet and afternoon refreshments. Outdoor Tea Parties in Summer. Lounge Licensed.

Nearest Airport(s)
Vancouver International 2.5 hrs.

Directions
75 miles/125 kilometres N of Vancouver on Hwy 99 (approx. 2 hours). 7 traffic lights on Hwy 99 from the 'Whistler Welcome' sign to Nesters.

Nestled in the spectacular Coast Mountains of British Columbia lies Whistler Resort, home to the Durlacher Hof, an enchanting mountain retreat. Durlachers' reputation as Whistler's most welcoming and generous innkeepers is legendary. The Hof serves up the complete authentic Austrian experience from ornate exterior trimmings to the Kaiserschmarren served at breakfast. Painstaking attention to detail is evident in the cozy guest lounge and the immaculate pretty rooms all with mountain views, goose-down duvets, luxury linens and ensuite baths with jacuzzi. Durlacher Hof is part of a place that mixes old world charm with romance and a natural beauty with inviting warmth and hospitality. The natural setting of Whistler offers a bounty of outdoor activities, a quaint village, which hosts art, culture events, and intriguing shops along with a wide spectrum of international cuisine. Host location of the 2010 Winter Olympics and Paralympics.

Member Since 1998

"Breakfast 'par excellence.' Upon first site, we knew Durlacher Hof would be our official return destination. We feel refreshed & refueled. Memorable."

Ships Point Inn

www.srinns.com/shipspoint
7584 Ships Point Road, Fanny Bay, BC, Canada V0R 1W0
877-742-1004 • 250-335-1004 • Fax 250-335-1014
info@shipspointinn.com

Proprietors
Pamela and Gary Entwistle
Innkeeper
Karen MacGruther

Traditional Waterside Breakfast Inn

AAA ◆◆◆

A serene bayside hideaway at the tip of historic Ships Point peninsula, Vancouver Island. This intimate inn, nestled between cedars and pristine shore, is a favorite for romantic getaways. Each distinctively appointed room offers a glorious view of the bay, where seals and otters cavort, eagles soar on gentle breezes, and ferries pass in the distance. Manicured English gardens with gazebo and outdoor hot tub complete the setting. Enjoy a shoreline walk to watch oyster farmers harvesting their crops, or stroll up the beach to George Sawchuck's Woodlife Gallery, a unique exhibit of forest art. Visit Fanny Bay Bird Sanctuary, or ride the 10-minute ferry to Denman Island, home of artisan studios and fine art galleries. Experience Mount Washington Ski resort or the 18-hole championship golf course at Crown Isle Resort. This Canada Select four and a half star property offers gentle pampering and world-class amenities. Excellent local restaurants and a year-round calendar of festivals and events make Ships Point Inn an irresistible travel destination.

Member Since 2002

  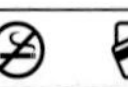    

Rooms/Rates
6 Rooms,$135/$185 CDN. Kings/Queens, all with bay views and ensuite baths. Open year-round.

Cuisine
Four-course gourmet breakfast offered: Fresh fruit juices, fresh-baked bread or muffins, egg dish of the day, locally produced sausage/fresh oysters, international coffees, teas.

Nearest Airport(s)
Comox

Directions
From Victoria, take Hwy. 1 N to Nanaimo. Hwy. 1 becomes Hwy. 19. Proceed toward Campbell River for 65 km. (36 mi.) Turn R on Cook Creek Rd. (exit 87). Turn L at Old Island Hwy.(19-A). Go 5 km. (3 mi.) Turn R onto Ships Point Rd., then 2 km. (1.5 mi.) to end of road.

"Thank you for creating such a haven. Everything is magical at this delightful Inn."

General Managers
John and Adele Caton
Luxury
Wilderness Oceanside Resort

Clayoquot Wilderness Resorts & Spa

www.srinns.com/clayoquot
380 Main Street, Tofino, BC, Canada V0R 2Z0
888-333-5405 • 250-726-8235 • Fax 250-725-2681
info@wildretreat.com

Two ultra-luxurious resorts and a beautiful new spa located in the Clayoquot Sound Biosphere Reserve on Vancouver Island. A 16-room floating resort and spa at Quait Bay and the Wilderness Outpost at Bedwell River; a 21st-Century-safari style enclave of 16 opulently furnished prospector style guest tents, plus dining, games, library lounge and spa tents. Both resorts offer super natural adventure including saltwater and freshwater fishing, whale and bear watching, horseback riding, hot springs, kayaking, canoeing, hiking, mountain biking, sailing and naturalist tours. *Conde Naste Traveler* magazine calls the resorts "rusticating luxury," *Spa* magazine calls the new Spa the "quintessential natural retreat." *Cowboys and Indians* magazine says, "Bedwell Outpost gets every exquisite detail right." Canada Select ★★★★; Unique Inns.

Rooms/Rates
Both resorts offer 3,4,7 night packages. Eco-Adventure or Spa Packages include deluxe accom, guided activities, spa treatments, all meals, snacks, beverages incl alcohol, water transfers, Vancouver-Tofino return airfare. Quait Bay Eco-Adventure and Spa Pckgs from $933 USD pp per day. Wilderness Outpost Pckgs from $1288 USD pp per day.

Cuisine
Chef May's modern & natural local cuisine is eclectic and ever-changing. Seafood is the anchor for his specialties and attention is paid to special requirements.

Nearest Airport(s)
Local: Tofino
International: Vancouver

Directions
One hour flight from Vancouver, BC

Member Since 2003

"Civilization is so much more enjoyable when experienced here in the wild."
— *Vancouver Sun*

Long Beach Lodge Resort

www.srinns.com/longbeachlodge
P.O. Box 897, 1441 Pacific Rim Highway, Tofino, BC V0R 2Z0
877-844-7873 • 250-725-2442 • Fax 250-725-2402
info@longbeachlodgeresort.com

Experience the natural beauty, exceptional amenities and handcrafted gourmet cuisine at our luxurious beachfront resort on the West Coast of Vancouver Island. Our relaxed and inspirational coastal setting offers a perfect escape from your everyday responsibilities. Choose between accommodation in our beachfront Lodge with spectacular oceanviews or retreat to one of our tranquil, fully equipped, two bedroom Rainforest Cottages with private outdoor patios and hot tubs. You will begin to relax as soon as you enter the Lodge Great Room with its massive granite fireplace and its Douglas fir post and beam construction. Sink into an overstuffed chair, put your feet up, and gaze out at the sandy beach with the crashing surf to the lighthouse beyond. You will appreciate the attention to detail that has been lavished on each of our guest rooms, including luxurious bath amenities, fleece bathrobes, cozy duvets, decadent chocolates and waterproof rain jackets for those rainy day beach walks!

Member Since 2005

Owner
Timothy Hackett
General Manager
Carly Hall

Luxury Beachfront Resort

AAA ◆◆◆

Rooms/Rates
41 Lodge Rms $169/$529 CDN.
20 Cottages $259/$429 CDN
Seasonal.

Cuisine
The Resort's dining room is a relaxed, informal space where the emphasis is placed on fresh food, superior service & meticulous attention to detail. Our chef captures the intricate flavours of sea, field & forest with his inventive & memorable gourmet cuisine.

Nearest Airport(s)
Tofino Airport, 10km

Directions
Take Highway 1 North from Victoria past Nanaimo. Turn west, onto Highway 4 at the Qualicum Beach/Port Alberni exit and follow signs. The drive will take approximately 4.5 hours. Direct flights available from Vancouver and Seattle.

"Sitting in the Great Room listening to some great music and watching the sunset was one of my top ten magical moments."

Inn Penzance

www.srinns.com/innpenzance
1388 Terrace Avenue, North Vancouver, BC, Canada V7R 1B4
888-546-3327 • 604-988-1378 • Fax 604-688-8812
penzanceme@westendguesthouse.com

Innkeeper/Owner
Evan Penner and Ron Cadarette

Elegant & Whimsical Breakfast Inn

Rooms/Rates
Garden view room, $125/$175 CDN; 2 enchanting cottages, New Orleans Suite for families, Caribbean Cottage in garden for honeymooners, $185/$250 CDN, DBL. Extra person $19 CDN. Open year-round.

Cuisine
Full breakfast prepared; afternoon refreshments available.

Nearest Airport(s)
Vancouver International

Directions
From Vancouver take Georgia St through Stanley Park, across the Lions Gate Bridge R on Marine Dr, L on Capilano Rd for one mile, R on Paisley Rd, R on Philip Ave. R on Woods Drive, L on Terrace Ave., and '1388'.

Romantic, restful, peaceful, seclusion far from the madding crowd. This elegant country inn is set off by an award-winning English Garden surrounded by virgin forests. The Inn features three beautifully decorated, charming rooms with queen beds, private baths and garden views. The Caribbean Cottage, accessible by a foot bridge which crosses a small creek. A hammock is nestled behind the giant rhodo trees offering peace filled quiet moments in the shade. Perfect for a couple on their honeymoon. The New Orleans Suite is romantic and dramatic and is suitable for a small family stay with a loft bed for two. Both suites have soaker tubs and fireplaces. The Silk Road Room offers a superb view of the garden and two beds. Various spots in the woods are available to our guests to walk through or to ponder the meaning of life. We are pet friendly with aged pets on premises and the occasional ducks in the pond!

Member Since 1999

"A romantic Vancouver Bed and Breakfast in a secluded garden setting."

Sooke Harbour House

www.srinns.com/sookeharbour
1528 Whiffen Spit Road, Sooke, BC, Canada V0S 1N0
800-889-9688 • 250-642-3421 • Fax 250-642-6988
info@sookeharbourhouse.com

Innkeepers
Sinclair and Frederique Philip

Elegant/Romantic
Oceanfront Retreat/Inn

Cozy and enchanting, Sooke Harbour House was rated, "Second Best Country Inn in the World" by Gourmet Magazine and "One of the World's Top Ten Hotels" by *Travel + Leisure*. Its restaurant specializes in West Coast Canadian cuisine, especially seafood, and much of its produce comes from the Inn's organic gardens. The rooms feature stunning ocean views, wood burning fireplaces, original art, and soaker or Jacuzzi tubs. Some offer steam showers for two. Step onto your private balcony, the perfect location for watching sea lions, river otters, seals and eagles play. Activities include: kayaking, whale watching, cycling and fishing.

Rooms/Rates
28 Guest Rooms from $215/$295 U.S. (low/high) Incl. breakfast. Incl. lunch during high season. Gourmet, Spa, and Romance Getaway Packages available. Open year-round.

Cuisine
Re-awaken your taste buds to the pleasures of fresh, local, seasonal culinary creations. Wine pairings from our cellar, one of the 95 best in the world, add to the adventure.

Nearest Airport(s)
Victoria, BC

Directions
23 miles W of Victoria. Take Hwy. 1 north to exit 14. Turn right onto Hwy.14 to Sooke. Turn left 2 miles past Sooke's third traffic light onto Whiffen Spit Road. We're at the end of the road, on the beach.

Member Since 2003

Canada Select 5 Star Rating "Bliss defined." - 2003 Guest

Innkeeper/Owner
Ellen Cmolik
General Manager
Marion Hansen

Elegant In Town
Breakfast Inn

AAA ◆◆◆

Abigail's Hotel

www.srinns.com/abigails
906 McClure Street, Victoria, BC V8V 3E7
800-561-6565 • 250-388-5363 • Fax 250-388-7787
innkeeper@abigailshotel.com

Rooms/Rates
23 Rooms. $119/$409 CDN. Honeymoon Suites, King beds, fireplaces, double Jacuzzi tubs. Charming Sunflower and Country rooms, Queen beds with soaker tubs or shower. Seasonal discounts available. Open year-round, reservations available 24 hrs.

Cuisine
Our famous gourmet breakfast included with every stay. Complimentary evening appetizers are available every night in our fireside library.

Nearest Airport(s)
Victoria International Airport.

Directions
From Airport S on Hwy 17, L on Fort St., R on Vancouver St. and R on McClure St. From Downtown E on Fort St., R on Vancouver St. and R on McClure St.

Intimate, elegant, exclusive… Abigail's delivers 'Romance and the City' with its heritage ambiance and modern conveniences, located in a peaceful cul de sac in downtown Victoria. Each luxurious room has antique furnishings, cozy down duvets, and fresh flowers; most rooms have wood-burning fireplaces and jetted tubs. To enhance your experience, enjoy breakfast in bed or select from Celebration, Spa, Golf and Wine-Tasting Packages. Abigail's Hotel is rated five stars by Canada Select and has recently won several awards, including Victoria's best small hotel" by Frommers for the past four years. The "#1 B&B-Best of the City" in the Victoria News Group readers' poll for 2000-2004.

Member Since 2000

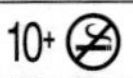

"Lovely rooms, great food, and warm caring staff...a wonderful romantic get-away. The breakfast was delicious and the staff were friendly at all times."

Amethyst Inn at Regents Park

www.srinns.com/amethystinn
1501 Fort Street, Victoria, BC, Canada V8S 1Z6
888-265-6499 • 250-595-2053 • Fax 250 595-2054
innkeeper@amethyst-inn.com

Innkeepers/Owners
Karl and Grace Sands
Elegant Victorian In Town Breakfast Inn

AAA ◆◆◆

Amethyst Inn at Regents Park is a heritage jewel and Victoria's most historically significant Inn. An award winning 1885 Victorian Mansion, which retains many original architectural features and is furnished with antiques. The preferred Inn for guests celebrating special occasions and cozy retreats. Comfortable, romantic, individually appointed accommodations offer a king or queen bed and sitting area with a fireplace. Bathrooms offer luxurious two person Jacuzzi Spa Tubs, deep soaking tubs or claw foot tubs. Mornings begin with coffee service followed by an elegant full breakfast. Enjoy visiting in the Parlor in the evening and gracious hospitality. The Inn is surrounded by heritage estates, beautiful gardens and tree lined streets. Conveniently located in the heart of Victoria and walking distance to Craigdarroch Castle, Antique Row and central to attractions. Concierge service for city and Butchart Garden tours, dining reservations, whale watching, golf and nature exploring.

Best Breakfast in Canada 2005 *Inn Traveler.*

★★★★★ Canada Select.

Member Since 2003

Rooms/Rates
16 romantic rooms and suites. $199/$399 CDN ($110/$330 US) Anniversary, Wedding, Elopement, Honeymoon, Spa & Sightseeing Packages. Seasonal Discounts. Open year-round. King or Queen beds, ensuite baths, two-person jacuzzi Spa tubs, fireplaces.

Cuisine
Enjoy morning coffee and an elegant full breakfast. Organic, farm fresh and seasonal as available. Dining Room tables are set with linen, fine china and crystal.

Nearest Airport(s)
Victoria Int'l (YYJ) - 20 miles

Directions
HWY17 (Douglas St): L on Fort, R on St Charles
INNER HARBOUR: L on Government, R on Fort, R on St Charles. Free on-site Parking.

"We have traveled far and wide and never enjoyed an experience as delightful as Amethyst Inn. Our stay was one of those 'Beautiful Memories' that will last."

Beaconsfield Inn

www.srinns.com/beaconsfield
998 Humboldt St., Victoria, BC, Canada V8V 2Z8
888-884-4044 • 250-384-4044 • Fax 250-384-4052
info@beaconsfieldinn.com

Innkeepers/Owners
Bob and Dawna Bailey
Elegant Edwardian In Town Breakfast Inn

AAA ◆◆◆

Rooms/Rates
Nine elegant rooms: 5 Deluxe Rooms, $129/$295 CDN ; 4 Suites, $229/$359 CDN. Open year-round.

Cuisine
Full breakfast, English style afternoon tea, evening sherry.

Nearest Airport(s)
Victoria International

Directions
From North: Hwy. 17 to City Centre, L on Humboldt St.; From Inner Harbor: Government St. N to Humboldt St. turn R for 4 blocks.

An Award-winning 1905 Edwardian manor located four blocks from Victoria's Inner Harbor, the Beaconsfield is the ultimate in charm, luxury and romance. Enjoy antiques, Oriental carpets, stained glass windows, fresh flowers, feather beds and down comforters, fireplaces, and Jacuzzis in most every room. The Beaconsfield Inn is situated on a quiet, tree-lined street a short 10 minute walk from shopping, restaurants and attractions. Indulge in a lovely English style afternoon tea, evening sherry hour, night time cookies and full breakfasts. *The Beaconsfield Inn has been awarded a ★★★★★ rating from Canada Select.*

Member Since 1994

"The Beaconsfield is...the standard by which we judge all others...," *Special Places*

Ontario

"The Heartland Province"

Famous For: Wine country, Niagara Falls, Toronto, the Shaw Festival, forests, lakes

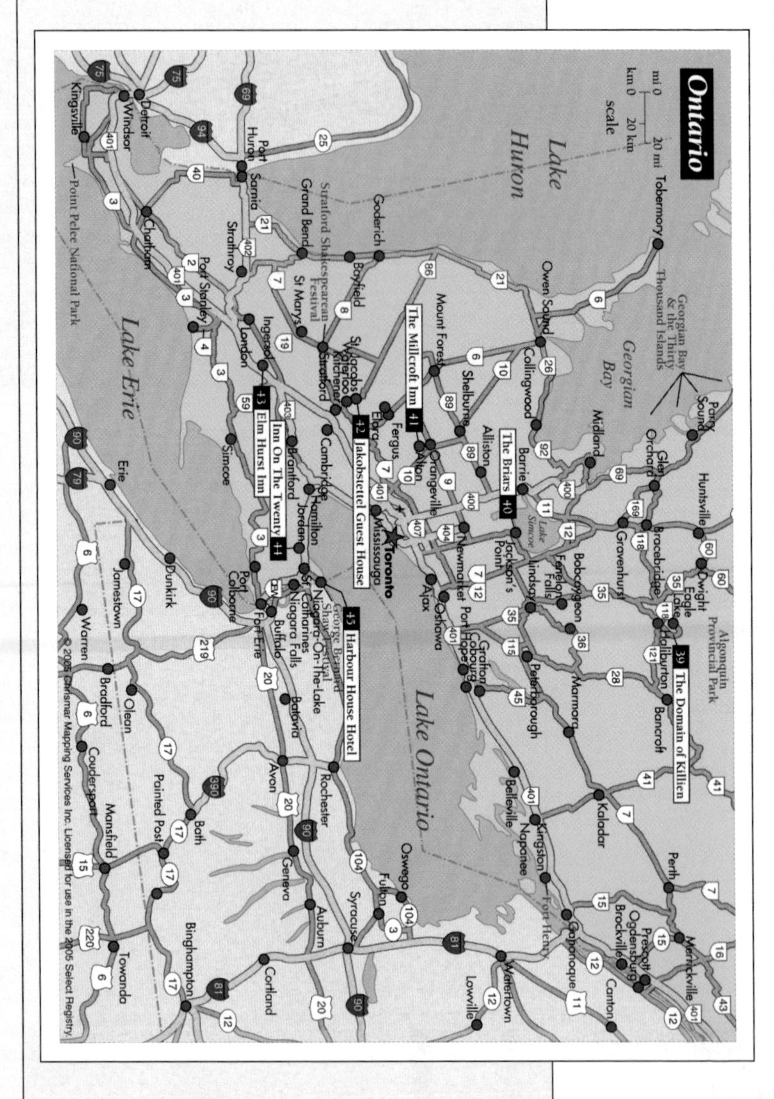

Innkeeper/Owner
Jean-Edouard de Marenches

Traditional Waterside Inn

Domain of Killien

www.srinns.com/domainofkillien
P.O. Box 810, 1282 Carroll Road
Haliburton, ON, Canada K0M 1S0
800-390-0769 • 705-457-1100 • Fax 705-457-3853
killien@bellnet.ca

Rooms/Rates
5 Rooms, $162/$198 CDN PP MAP; 1 Suite; 6 Chalets, $159/$224 CDN PP MAP. Open year-round.

Cuisine
Breakfast and dinner. Picnic lunches available. Liquor served.

Nearest Airport(s)
Stanhope Airport

Directions
From Toronto Hwy 404 N to Davis Dr, R to 48 to 35 N, 35 N to Minden, 121 R, N to Haliburton L, W on 118, R (N) on Harburn Rd 12 km to Carroll Rd.

At the south tip of Algonquin Park, a charming inn rests on a quiet bay amidst a 5000-acre private estate of lakes, forest and rugged hills: the Domain of Killien. You can enjoy a morning game of tennis, a fly-fishing outing or later, an afternoon sail or a quiet paddle. Or you can simply Master the Art of Doing Nothing... beautifully. Summer or winter, guests have exclusive access to our hiking or nordic ski trails and to a day-cabin on a remote lake. Whatever you did today, warm and comfortable inn rooms and lakeside chalets welcome you back. Dining at the Domain is an experience to savour. Fine wines complement delicate flavours created by our team of chefs from France. The inn's full breakfast includes freshly-baked croissants and other house specialties. Year round, the Haliburton Highlands are a photographer's dream.

Member Since 1995

12+   

"You come to the Domain to master the Art of doing nothing...beautifully."
Jean-Edouard

The Briars

www.srinns.com/briars
55 Hedge Rd., R.R. #1, Jackson's Point, ON, Canada L0E 1L0
800-465-2376 • 905-722-3271 • Fax 905-722-9698
www.briars.ca

Innkeepers/Owners
The Sibbald Family

Traditional Waterside Resort

With its lush gardens, gracious accommodation, memorable dining and warm hospitality, The Briars is the perfect destination for any occasion. Guests enjoy rooms or suites in the inn with views of the gardens and lake, or private lakeside cottages. This spacious property features an incredible variety of recreation. Discover championship golf, nature walks, tennis and boating. The Briars Spa provides luxurious treatments, a solarium pool, sauna, whirlpool and exercise room. In winter there's also cross-country skiing and horse-drawn sleigh rides. The Briars is situated on Lake Simcoe just an hour from Toronto. Nearby there's antiquing, shopping, fishing and southern Ontario's many attractions. An Ontario Heritage property. Member Ontario's Finest Inns and Premier Spas of Ontario.

Rooms/Rates
46 rooms $129 - $209 CDN, pp AP; 4 Suites & Cottages $149 - $249 CDN, pp AP. Open year-round.

Cuisine
All meals are included in your visit. Dining features fresh herbs and fruits from the inn's gardens. Luncheons can be packed for excursions. Light meals and entertainment are also available in Drinkwaters Lounge and on the patio. Saturday evening features a dinner dance.

Nearest Airport(s)
Toronto Pearson Int'l

Directions
From Toronto: 404(N) to Davis Dr., R.(E) 6 mi. to 48; L.(N) 15 mi. to Sutton; L on High St., follow signs to Jackson's Point & Briars. From west of Toronto: take ETR 407 to 404.

Member Since 1980

"The surroundings, comforts and amenities, happy and pleasant staff - outstanding!"

The Millcroft Inn & Spa

www.srinns.com/millcroftinn
55 John Street, Alton, ON, Canada L0N 1A0
800-383-3976 • 519-941-8111 • Fax 519-941-9192
millcroft@millcroft.com

Innkeeper
Wolfgang Stichnothe
Traditional Country Inn and Spa 

AAA ♦♦♦♦

Rooms/Rates
52 Rooms, from $235/$325 CDN per person ($178/$250 US funds** may vary due to rate of exchange). B&B; packages available, Golf nearby. 4 Diamonds from CAA/AAA. All season.

Cuisine
Continental cuisine available for breakfast, lunch & dinner. 4 Diamonds CAA/AAA. Extensive selection of wines & spirits.

Nearest Airport(s)
Pearson International (YYZ)

Directions
From Toronto: Hwy. 401W to Hwy. 410N to Mayfield Rd., W (L) to Hwy. 10 N (Hurontario) to Caledon, L on Hwy. 24 (Charleston Sideroad) 3 km to Peel Regional Road 136 (Main Street), then R (3 km), follow to stop sign, then L on Queen Street in Alton.

Just 40 minutes from Toronto, the unparalleled refinement and a tranquil location amid the rolling Caledon Hills make the Millcroft Inn & Spa the Definitive Country Retreat. The inn's serene surroundings and historic charm provide a balm for the city-weary. Its riverside setting, fifty-two beautiful guestrooms (some with a fireplace, a Jacuzzi or a private outdoor hot-tub) and one hundred acres of wooded trails combine with the appeal of four-diamond cuisine and vintage wines in a warmly appointed dining room for an extraordinary getaway experience. The full-service Millcroft Spa, Centre for Well-Being pampers guests with a broad range of treatments, including hydrotherapy and massage, and features fine European products. Whether you choose to read by the lounge's wood-burning fireplace, hike a sun-dappled wooded trail, or relax in the Spa, the Millcroft is ready to make your next escape the best yet. Visit the website or call for more details.

Member Since 1995

"Hospitality, fine dining and its country setting make the Millcroft a perfect getaway!"

Jakobstettel Inn

www.srinns.com/jakobstettel
16 Isabella St., St. Jacobs, ON, Canada N0B 2N0
800-431-3035 • 519-664-2208 • Fax 519-664-1326

Innkeepers
Ivan McQuillan
Steven D. Haney
Traditional Victorian Village Breakfast Inn

This Victorian Inn has style—with casual hospitality. This property of five treed acres is two blocks from the main street. Steps away in a visitor's village, are fabulous shops (the best in fashion, artifacts, specialty foods, unique gifts and antiques), excellent dining choices, and theatre. During your stay enjoy the lounge with pool table or the exercise area. Take a dip in our heated pool, hot tub and sauna. Perhaps you'll take a refreshing stroll along the Trans Canada Trail. Staff is available to help in planning activities such as canoeing on the Grand, horseback riding, golf, hiking, sleigh rides, touring the countryside, and discovering the local history. Meetings can be arranged in our newly renovated conference facility.

Rooms/Rates
10 Rooms, $250 per night. This includes a hot buffet breakfast and a complimentary massage. Open year-round.

Cuisine
A hot buffet breakfast is included. Lunch and dinner served to groups only when pre-arranged.

Nearest Airport(s)
Kitchener-Waterloo Regional Airport

Directions
From Hwy. 401 exit Hwy. 8 W to Kitchener then Hwy. 85 N through Waterloo, choose Rd. 15 or Rd. 17 exit; in St. Jacobs turn W on Albert St.

Member Since 1995

"Awesome renovations, we love your classic new look!"

Innkeepers/Owners
Pat Frey and Giacomo Negro

Traditional Victorian Country Inn

AAA ◆◆◆

Elm Hurst Inn

www.srinns.com/elmhurstinn
415 Harris Street, P.O. Box 123, Ingersoll, ON, Canada N5C 3K1
800-561-5321 • 519-485-5321 • Fax 519-485-6579
info@elmhurstinn.com

Rooms/Rates
39 Inn Rooms (QN or 2 DB beds) $175 CDN; 3 Fireplace Rooms (KG bed) $199 CDN; 2 Executive Suites (KG bed) $225 CDN; 3 Jacuzzi Rooms (KG or QN bed) $225 CDN; includes country breakfast buffet.

Cuisine
Victorian Restaurant, licensed, private rooms, patio, award winning cuisine for breakfast, lunch and dinner.

Nearest Airport(s)
London International Airport is located 30 minutes away.

Directions
90 min west of Toronto, ON and 30 min east of London, ON, on Hwy. 401 (exit 218) at Hwy. 19.

The country Inn is nestled amongst century-old maple trees on 37 acres of land with walking trails, flowing creek and pond. Our spacious guest rooms are uniquely decorated with picturesque views some including a fireplace or Jacuzzi tub. Rooms include breakfast, movie channel, coffee makers & other amenities. Choose room service or dine in the Victorian Mansion. The Elm Hurst Inn is an ideal setting for any occasion. Enjoy our full-service Aveda spa, sauna, steam room and whirlpool. We are perfectly situated 30 min from Stratford or 2 hrs from Detroit. Enjoy golf, X-country skiing, great shopping, sight-seeing and nearby tourist attractions.

Member Since 1996

 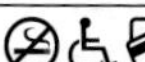   

"Service was excellent and the food was great. We are already planning to come back."

Inn on the Twenty

www.srinns.com/innonthetwenty
3845 Main Street, Jordan, ON, Canada L0R 1S0
800-701-8074 • 905-562-5336 • Fax 905-562-0009
info@innonthetwenty.com

Innkeeper/Owner
Helen Young

Elegant Contemporary Village Inn

AAA ◆◆◆◆

This is the heart of Ontario's wine country! Renovated winery buildings boast twenty-seven suites, all with fireplaces and Jacuzzi tubs; antiques and unique art abound. The Inn is located in a charming village with artisans and antique shops. Great golf, walking and bicycling opportunities as well as the sophistication of Niagara's famous Shaw Theatre and the not-to-be-missed Falls. Our restaurant, On the Twenty, is a DiRoNA award winner and a leader in regional cuisine. Cave Spring Cellars, one of Canada's most prestigious wineries is our partner. Our full service Spa enhances any stay. The wine route beckons!

Member Since 1998

Rooms/Rates
27 Suites, 7 two-story, 20 one-level, 5 with private garden. $194/$308 US (exchange approximate) $223/$355 CDN Open year-round.

Cuisine
On the Twenty is a DiRoNA Award restaurant with regional focus. Private Dining Rooms available for up to 135. Ontario wines and beers. Full bar. Cave Spring Cellars Winery on site. Tours and tastings available daily.

Nearest Airport(s)
Buffalo, Toronto

Directions
QEW Hwy. to Victoria Avenue (Vineland Exit 57). L off the Service Road, S to Regional Road 81 (King Street). Turn L and go through the valley; first L at top of the hill onto Main Street. 5 minutes from QEW.

A Triple A, Four Diamond Restaurant and Inn.

Innkeepers/Owners
Susan Murray
General Manager
Timothy Taylor

Elegant Waterside
Breakfast Inn

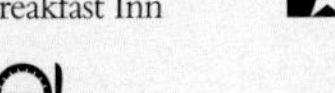

AAA ♦♦♦♦

Harbour House Hotel

www.srinns.com/harbourhouse
Box 760, 85 Melville Street
Niagara-on-the-Lake, ON, Canada L0S 1J0
866-277-6677 • 905-468-4683 • Fax 905-468-0366
inquire@harbourhousehotel.ca

Rooms/Rates
Deluxe Rooms and Riverview Suites from $199 CDN. Packages and seasonal rates available.

Cuisine
Harbour House features a classic European-style buffet breakfast, an afternoon wine and cheese sampling and cookies at bedtime. A shuttle service is available for dozens of local restaurants.

Nearest Airport(s)
Buffalo, 45 min; Toronto, 60 min.

Directions
Queen Elizabeth Way (QEW) to Exit #38—Route #55. Turn right on East-West Line to Niagara Pkwy. Left on the Niagara Pkwy to Wellington St. Right on Wellington to Ricardo St. Right 1/2 block.

Harbour House is a wonderful blend of intimacy, quality, personality, professionalism, sensuous comfort and attention to every detail. Overlooking the Niagara River and within walking distance of the Shaw Festival, many intriguing shops and more than a dozen fine restaurants, Harbour House is just a short drive from the wonder of Niagara Falls, Niagara's world class wineries and dozens of top-flight golf courses. Perched beside Niagara-on-the-Lake's pretty yacht harbour, Harbour House has been designed in the spirit of maritime life in the 1880s—elegant simplicity, quality finishes, carefully selected antiques and unique accents. Each bedroom and suite offers whirlpool baths, fireplaces and much more. Harbour House captures the flavour of historic Niagara. Member of Ontario's Finest Inns and CAA/AAA Four Diamond.

Member Since 2003

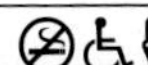

"Simply Elegant...an oasis of luxury in the heart of historic Niagara."

Quebec

"La Belle Province"

Famous For: St. Lawrence Seaway, French culture, maple syrup, winter sports, apples, camping

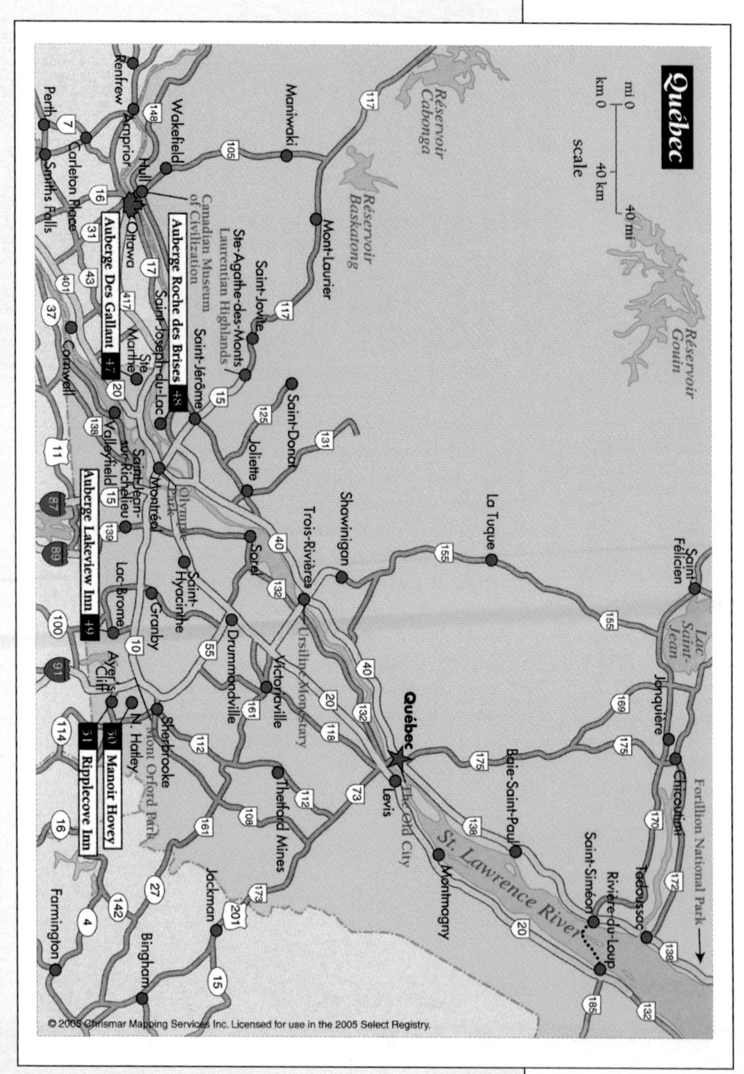

Innkeepers/Owners
Linda and Gerry Gallant
Elegant Mountain Resort

Auberge des Gallant (The Gallant Inn)

www.srinns.com/desgallant
1171 St - Henry Rd., Ste-Marthe, Rigaud
QUE, Canada J0P 1W0
800-641-4241 • 450-459-4241 • Fax 450-459-4667
info@gallant.qc.ca

Rooms/Rates
25 Rooms with wood-burning fireplace & balcony, From $125 CDN/$99 US, MAP pp. for a country room and $150 CDN/$120 US, MAP pp. for a honeymoon suite. Open year-round.

Cuisine
Breakfast, lunch, gourmet 5 course dinner, Sunday brunch. Extensive wine list and liquor.

Nearest Airport(s)
Montreal, Trudeau, 30 miles.

Directions
Between Montreal and Ottawa, Rte. 40 W, Exit 17, Left on Rte. 201, 3 miles & Right on St-Henri 5 miles.

Garden lovers will enjoy this romantic inn nestled in the heart of a bird and deer sanctuary. Enjoy award-winning French cuisine and wine list, as our attentive staff cater to your every whim! Elegant spacious rooms with real wood-burning fireplace and balcony overlook our five acres of beautifully appointed gardens, which in summer attract a multitude of birds and butterflies, while winter promises sleigh rides, cross country skiing and down hill skiing. Fall foliage is at its best in October, and our maple sugar shack with its 11,000 taps is open from late February to the end of April for traditional maple meals. Maple syrup is available all year round!

Member Since 1998

12+

"We loved the decor!!! Staff and food were excellent!" Doug & Pauline Panter
"Very friendly, warm, professional. Excellent food and service." B. Willet

La Roche des Brises

www.srinns.com/larochedesbrises
2007, rue Principale, St-Joseph-du-Lac, QUE J0N 1M0
450-472-2722 • Fax 450-473-5878
info@rochedesbrises.com

Innkeeper/Owner
Gina Pratt

Elegant Country Inn

The Inn is located on the outskirts of Montreal overlooking rolling hills, orchards and our vineyard with a spectacular view of Montreal. Beautifully decorated with antiques, the Inn has been awarded the Five Sun top rating by Quebec Tourism for the Laurentians. Our rooms all have King size beds and private baths and air conditioning. We also offer our guests the luxury of hot stone and grape seed massage in a relaxing ambiance. The Inn has its own pool and is close to beautiful Lake of Two Mountains. And if you take a little stroll through the vines and experience our charming fine dining restaurant or wine tasting room, revealing our renowned award winning wines, you shall feel the true nature and magic of this unique ambiance. Location: Downtown Montreal is located 30 minutes away by car or commute by train to avoid traffic. "Auberge Roche des Brises" offers a unique lodging experience in a country setting, close to the heart of Montreal.

Rooms/Rates
5 suites, $120/$180 CDN double occupancy. Open February through December 31.

Cuisine
Elegant full breakfast included. Award winning fine dining with a french twist. World wines available. Roche des Brises winery on site. Tours and tasting available daily.

Nearest Airport(s)
Dorval/Pierre Eliot Trudeau Airport, 50 minutes

Directions
From South: Highway 13 North to Highway 640 West, Exit 2 Left on "Chemin Principal" for 4.7 km

Member Since 2005

Award winning Gold Medal of the Laurentians Tourist Association.

Innkeeper
Chris Voutsinas
Historic Victorian Village Inn

AAA ♦♦♦♦

Auberge Lakeview Inn

www.srinns.com/aubergelakeview
50, rue Victoria, Knowlton, Brome Lake
QUE, Canada J0E 1V0
800-661-6183 • 450-243-6183 • Fax 450-243-0602
info@aubergelakeviewinn.com

Rooms/Rates
24 rooms, 4 studios, from $126CDN/$105US, MAP, pp. (gratuities included) AAA/CAA 4 diamond rating. Open year-round.

Cuisine
Dine by candle-light in our elegant Victorian dining room where flavours of French cuisine are enhanced by an outstanding wine and Port cellar and be pampered by our "Traditional European Service." Linger over cocktails in an authentic English pub or in our garden-terrace by our heated swimming pool.

Nearest Airport(s)
Montreal Airport

Directions
Go North on I-91 to the Canada Border. Go North on QUEBEC AUT.55 to QUEBEC AUT. 10. Take exit 90 and follow signs to Auberge Lakeview Inn.

History... Romance... Elegance... Step thru the front door and go back 131 years in history as you enter the romantic, Victorian atmosphere of one of Quebec's most celebrated Inns. Imagine lodging and dining where Sir Wilfrid Laurier, Sir Robert Borden and the Right Hon. Arthur Meighen, former Prime Ministers of Canada, stayed. The "Lakeview Inn," built in 1874 by loyalists, is now an historic multi-award winning antique-filled Victorian Inn. Enjoy the visual splendour and ambiance of yesteryear with all of today's comforts including central air-conditioning. Beautifully decorated with antiques and hand-carved turn-of-the-century furnishings. Browse in local antique shops and boutiques. Enjoy a variety of water and summer activites. Our BUSINESS CENTRE combines a relaxed atmosphere, secretarial services, audio-visual equipment, data lines and teleconferencing. For business meetings, receptions or whatever the occasion, our facilities can accomodate from five to 225 persons.

Member Since 2002

"Lakeview Inn is the most exciting four-season destination for business, leisure, relaxation, and romance..."

Manoir Hovey

www.manoirhovey.com
Lake Massawippi, 575 Hovey Road
North Hatley, QUE, Canada J0B 2C0
800-661-2421 • 819-842-2421 • Fax 819-842-2248
innkeeper@manoirhovey.com

Innkeepers/Owners
Steve, Kathryn, and Jason Stafford

Elegant Waterside Resort Inn

AAA ◆◆◆◆

This gracious manor was built as a private estate by a wealthy Atlanta industrialist in 1900 and modeled after George Washington's Mount Vernon. The site is spectacularly nestled on 25 acres of prime lakeshore amidst celebrated English gardens and birch forest. Most of the lakeside rooms (among Quebec's most luxurious) offer combinations of fireplaces, Jacuzzis, canopy beds, and balconies. They are also equipped with Frette towels, two bathrobes, Aveda bath products, WiFi, CD player and nightly turn-down service. The Manor is also renowned for its cuisine and personalized service (2004 double gold medal winner for best restaurant and best wine list in Quebec). The addition of two small beaches, heated pool, water sports, clay tennis, massage room, X-country ski trails, skating, and many other year round recreational facilities on site (INCLUDED in the MAP rates) have made this inn an international destination in itself. We're only 25 minutes from Vermont, four hours from Boston and six and a half hours from New York City en route to Montreal and Quebec City.

Member Since 1973

Rooms/Rates
40 luxurious year-round rooms, mostly on the lake (US $94/$250 MAP/person/day). Many fireplaces, balconies, jacuzzis and canopy beds.

Cuisine
Breakfast, lunch, dinner, cream teas. 2004 Gold Medal winner for both gastronomy and for best wine list in all of Quebec. Triple 5 Stars for cuisine, decor and service in Quebec's "Voir" Restaurant Guide. Lakeside lunches, garden cocktails, historic pub.

Nearest Airport(s)
Montreal

Directions
VT I-91 to Canadian border. Continue on Rte 55N for 29 kms to N. Hatley exit 29. Follow Rte 108 E and Manoir Hovey signs to the Inn (9 kms). Only 25 minutes from VT.

"Wow! Most deserving of your 5 stars. Quality far surpasses other inns. A perfect 10! Hovey certainly lived up to its reputation. The food is to die for."

Innkeepers/Owners
Debra and Jeffrey Stafford

Elegant Victorian Waterside Resort

AAA ◆◆◆◆

Ripplecove Inn

www.srinns.com/ripplecove
700 Ripplecove Road, Lake Massawippi
Ayer's Cliff, QUE, Canada J0B 1C0
800-668-4296 • 819-838-4296 • Fax 819-838-5541
info@ripplecove.com

Rooms/Rates
35 Rooms, Suites and Cottages, US $105/$240MAP/person/day including dinner, breakfast and service. All rooms offer TV, TEL, A/C and designer decor Most rooms offer fireplace, private lakeview balcony and whirlpools

Cuisine
Four Diamond Award cuisine in our Victorian dining room & lakeside terrace. 6000 bottle wine cellar and pub.

Nearest Airport(s)
Pierre E Trudeau Montreal

Directions
From New England take I-91 N to the Canadian border then follow Rte. 55 N to exit 21. Follow signs to Inn which is 3 miles from exit 21. Distances: Montreal 1.5 hrs, Boston 3 hrs, New York 6 hrs.

Since 1945 Ripplecove Inn has been chosen by sophisticated travelers from around the world to get away from it all in an atmosphere of romance, privacy, refined service and luxury. The Inn resides on a beautifully landscaped 12 acre peninsula alive with English gardens, and century-old pines. This year marks our 60th anniversary and a recent expansion in 2004 is now fully complete. New for 2005, ten additional luxurious rooms and a full service Spa have been added offering massage, hydro therepy, facials and a four season outdoor Jacuzzi tub. A private beach, boating, biking, tennis, heated outdoor pool and lake cruises are also all on site! Rated as one of Quebec's top 10 best places to dine, our victorian diningroom and lakeside terrace offer refined cuisine and vintage wines accompanied by the strains of live piano music and sterling silver service. American visitors don't forget; a Canadian exchange rate of 20% means extra value for you!

Member Since 1995

"One of the most beautiful Inns we have ever stayed at! Keep up the good work!"

"Heart of Dixie"

Famous For: Cotton, Steel, Antebellum Mansions, Confederate Capital (1861), Azalea Trail, U.S. Space and Rocket Center

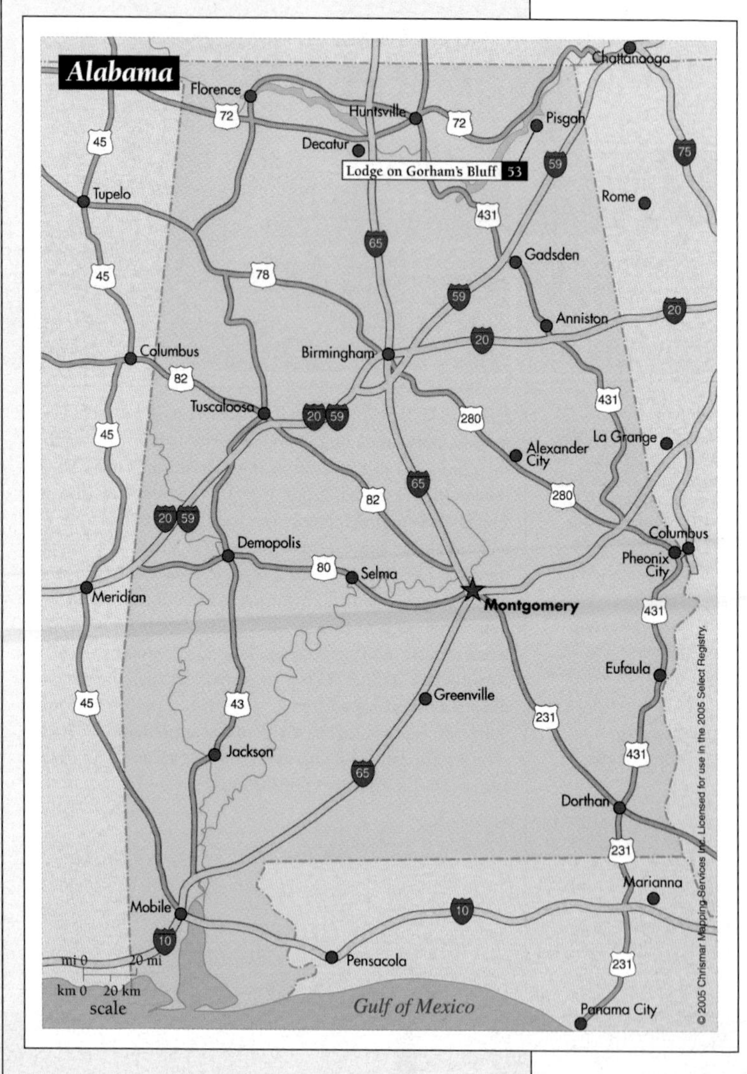

Innkeeper
Diane McGee
Traditional Country Retreat/Lodge

Lodge on Gorham's Bluff

www.srinns.com/gorhamsbluff
101 Gorham Drive, Gorham's Bluff, Pisgah, AL 35765
256-451-VIEW • 256-451-8439 • Fax 256-451-7403
reservations@gorhamsbluff.com

Rooms/Rates
6 Rooms. $150/$350 per evening, double occupancy. Breakfast is included. Tax and service charge is additional.

Cuisine
A regionally inspired four-course gourmet meal, prepared with only the freshest locally grown ingredients, is served in the candle lit dining room each evening. Fresh flowers, fine linens and flawless service enhance the romantic experience. Guests may reserve a gourmet picnic lunch if desired. Reservations are required for dinner and lunch. Additional charges will apply.

Nearest Airport(s)
Chattanooga, TN

Directions
Directions available on website and from the innkeeper by request.

The Lodge on Gorham's Bluff is perched high on the bluffs overlooking the Tennessee River Valley. Although the atmosphere is one of mannered Southern charm, the daily routine is low-key and casual dress is encouraged. Furnished in an elegant, traditional country style the Lodge and Cottage suites are appointed with antiques, CD/DVD players, in-room snacks, luxurious his/her bathrobes, fine Egyptian cotton linens, feather mattresses, down pillows and remote-controlled fireplaces. Generously sized windows and multiple sets of French doors and private balconies bring the mountain-high views indoors. Amenities include hiking trails, biking, fishing, bird watching, pool, fitness center and seasonal events. *Southern Living* Magazine rated Gorham's Bluff as the most romantic destination in Alabama for the April 2005 issue.

Member Since 2003

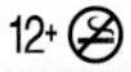

"Gorham's Bluff smoothes the wrinkles of my soul." Ms. Polk, Lexington, KY
"Beautiful room, glorious food, marvelous view!" Beth and Steve, Birhimingham, AL

Arizona

"Grand Canyon State"

Famous For: Grand Canyon, Painted Desert, Petrified Forest, Copper Mines, Gila Monster, Lake Mead (largest manmade lake in the world), Tombstone (Wyatt Earp's fight at the OK Corral), Cliff Dwellings

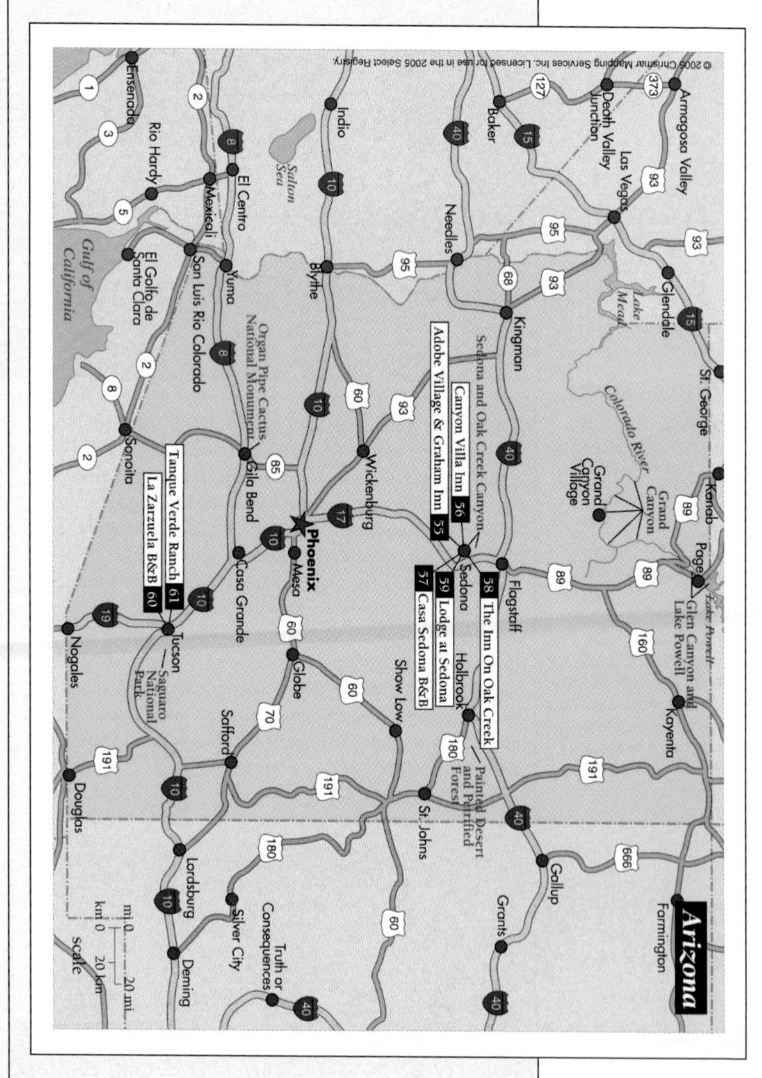

Adobe Village Graham Inn

www.srinns.com/adobevillage
150 Canyon Circle Drive, Sedona, AZ 86351
800-228-1425 • 928-284-1425 • Fax 928-284-0767
info@sedonasfinest.com

Innkeepers/Owners
Stuart & Ilene Berman
Elegant Southwestern Village Breakfast Inn

AAA ◆◆◆◆

This world renowned Inn has received the AAA Four Diamond Award of Excellence for the past 9 years. Acclaimed for its stunning red rock views and located within walking distance of dining, shopping, art galleries, hiking and biking trails, and in view of Bell Rock, the most photographed monument in Sedona. All guests receive gourmet breakfast, hot afternoon hors d'oeuvres, and evening pastries, complimentary use of Internet Center, mountain bikes and hiking packs, swimming pool and in-ground jetted spa. Received 5 star award "Best Bed & Breakfast Inn in North America."

Rooms/Rates
7 Rooms in main inn $169/$599. 4 Luxury Casitas $389/$469. Spacious and distinctive theme rooms with fireplaces, Jetted tubs, TV/VCRs, CDs.

Cuisine
Full, gourmet breakfast. Afternoon hors d'oeuvres, evening pastries. Casitas have bread makers allowing guests to come in to the aroma of fresh-baked bread each day. Guests are welcome to bring their own spirits.

Nearest Airport(s)
Phoenix Sky Harbor International

Directions
From Hwy 179, turn W onto Bell Rock Blvd. Drive two blocks passing the first Canyon Circle Drive. You will see us on the R, on the corner of Bell Rock Blvd. and Canyon Circle Drive. You're home.

Member Since 2000

 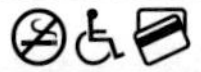  

"...from the red rocks to the stained glass window in our casita, every detail is perfect."

Canyon Villa Bed & Breakfast Inn

www.srinns.com/canyonvilla
125 Canyon Circle Drive, Sedona, AZ 86351
800-453-1166 • 928-284-1226 • Fax 928-284-2114
canvilla@sedona.net

Innkeepers/Owners
Les & Peg Belch

Elegant Village Inn

AAA ◆◆◆◆

A past recipient of the elite "Best U.S. Bed and Breakfast" award from Harper's *Hideway Report*, this custom built B&B Inn provides guests with spectacular bedside views of the Red Rocks of Sedona. Themed intimate guest rooms open through arched French doors onto private balconies and lush garden patios. Rooms include cable TV, phone, radio, CD player, and some have gas-log fireplaces. Ceramic baths include jetted tubs and luxurious lounge robes. Guests relax daily in the warm Arizona sun by the on-premises pool, hike desert trails from the premises, and stargaze cool evenings by firelight. Recommended by Frommers, Fodors, Conde-Nast Johansens and Mobil travel guides. One of only six Arizona B&Bs listed in Zagat Survey's 2005 "Top U.S. Hotels, Resorts, & Spas." Awarded AAA Four Diamond Award of Excellence for past 13 years.

Member Since 1995

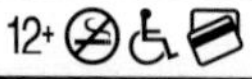

Rooms/Rates
11 Rooms. Red Rock View Rooms $219/$304. Limited-View room $189. Ceramic private baths with jetted tubs & many with fireplaces.

Cuisine
Gourmet breakfast, afternoon refreshments, and evening hors d'oeuvres included. Coffee, tea, and original light deserts are available throughout the entire evening in the dining area. Guests welcome to bring their own spirits.

Nearest Airport(s)
Phoenix

Directions
From I-17, use Exit 298 and go N on SR 179 for 8 mi. L on Bell Rock Blvd. After 1 block turn R on Canyon Circle Dr. The Inn is on the R. Please call for directions if arriving from SR 89-A.

"One night is too short to stay in a place as wonderful as this. The views are spectacular."

Casa Sedona Inn

www.srinns.com/casasedona
55 Hozoni Drive, Sedona, AZ 86336
800-525-3756 • 928-282-2938 • Fax 928-282-2259
casa@sedona.net

Innkeepers/Owners
Robert & Donna Marriott

Elegant Adobe Style In Town B&B Inn

Mobil ★★★
AAA ◆◆◆◆

Rooms/Rates
16 rooms, $185/$290. Each room is unique in its personality with styles from Cowboy to Lace and features amenities such as gas fireplaces, King or Queen beds, private baths, soft robes, Jacuzzi tubs, TV/VCR's, CD players and private balconies.

Cuisine
Full gourmet breakfast. Late afternoon hor d'ouevres, beverages and homemade cookies. Guests are welcome to bring their own alcoholic beverages.

Nearest Airport(s)
Phoenix Sky Harbor

Directions
From Hwy. 89A, turn north onto Tortilla Drive then left at the first stop sign (Southwest Drive). Take an immediate right onto Hozoni Drive.

Extraordinary Views!! At the base of Sedona's highest Red Rock peak is Casa Sedona, an adobe style inn designed by a protégé of Frank Lloyd Wright featuring sun terraces with awe-inspiring 180-degree views, a large garden patio and fountains and recipient of the AAA 4-Diamond Award of Excellence for 9 years. Guests enjoy the tranquil ambiance of the inn, beautifully landscaped grounds, evening appetizers, a hot tub for stargazing and bountiful breakfasts served in the garden or fireside. Exclusive in its location, Casa Sedona is a mere three miles from the towns center making it the perfect quiet respite from the city, yet only minutes from fine restaurants and shops. Luxury, elegance, privacy and exceptional cuisine in an unparalled setting have guests returning "home" time after time. Featured by The Travel Channel on its "Best of the Best" series.

Member Since 2004

"The surroundings are spectacular, the garden relaxing and the stars are so bright each night from the balcony. Thanks for the memories."

The Inn on Oak Creek

www.srinns.com/innonoakcreek
556 Hwy. 179, Sedona, AZ 86336
800-499-7896 • 928-282-7896 • Fax 928-282-0696
theinn@sedona.net

Owner/ Manager
Jim Matykiewicz
Elegant Contemporary
Waterside Bed & Breakfast Inn

Mobil ★★★
AAA ◆◆◆◆

Initially built in 1972 as an art gallery, then totally refurbished and transformed in 1995, the Inn perches on a bluff overlooking Oak Creek, one of Arizona's premier year-round spring-fed streams. Within easy walking distance are Sedona's best art galleries, boutique shops, several fine restaurants and Tlaquepaque shopping village. Yet, almost as close, are National Forest trails that will take you to the heart of red rock country. So while the guests are constantly surprised that an Inn so centrally located in Sedona can offer such privacy and relaxation, the luxurious AAA Four Diamond accommodations, professional staff, and culinary delights are what really please them.

Member Since 2001

Rooms/Rates
9 Rooms, $195/$290 DBL; 1 Suite, $295, $20 each add'l. person. All rooms feature private marble baths, whirlpool tubs, gas fireplaces, TV/VCR/HBO, Cable, data ports, luxurious bathrobes, hairdryers, phones. Creekside rooms have decks with dramatic VIEWS. Full conceierge service.

Cuisine
Full gourmet breakfast, afternoon beverages, cookies and hors d'oeuvres included in price. Guests are welcome to bring their own adult beverages. All served creekside during warm weather. Five Star food!

Nearest Airport(s)
Flagstaff (30 min.), Phoenix (2.5 hrs.)

Directions
In Sedona proper on Hwy. 179 just 0.4 mile S of the intersection of Hwy 179 and Hwy 89A.

"This is the way all B&Bs ought to be. You've thought of everything. Thank you! Thank you!"

The Lodge at Sedona

www.srinns.com/lodgeatsedona
125 Kallof Place, Sedona, AZ 86336
800-619-4467 • 928-204-1942 • Fax 928-204-2128
Info@LODGEatSEDONA.com

Proprietors
Ronald & Shelley Wachal

Elegant Arts & Crafts Village Breakfast Inn

Mobil ★★★

"Romance and intrigue, comfort & luxury, beauty and character, escape & adventure - the Lodge at Sedona has it all" AZ News. Elegant Mission/Arts & Craft estate set on 3 acres of grand seclusion in the very heart of Sedona. Awarded Top 10 Inns in US by Forbes.com, Best B & B's by Phoenix Magazine. Recommended by *Small Elegant Hotels, Historic Lodging Directory, Bon Appetite, Fodors.com,* and Frommer's. Spectacular red rock views, sculpture gardens, fitness center priviledges & pools, fountains and a magical labyrinth. Artful King suites with fireplaces, jetted tubs, large decks, stereo TV, CD, DVD. "The Lodge at Sedona is one of the most romantic inns in Arizona," AZ Foothills Magazine.

Rooms/Rates
14 rooms & suites, $160/$325 B & B; most with fireplaces, jetted tubs, view decks, stereo TV/DVD.

Cuisine
Professional five course breakfast with Sedona Gold Coffee, Lodge Granola & Fresh OJ. Sunset appetizers, spring water & snacks all day. Complimentany wine setups provided. Conferences & receptions catered.

Nearest Airport(s)
Phoenix (PHX)

Directions
Located at 125 Kallof Place in West Sedona. Kallof Place, south off Hwy 89A, is 2 mi. west of Hwy 179, a block W of Mountain Shadows Dr. or a block E of Coffee Pot Dr. in the heart of Sedona. Refer to the map on our website.

Member Since 2003

"The Lodge at Sedona - A Luxury Bed & Breakfast Inn, is a grand setting for receptions."

La Zarzuela, A Bed and Breakfast Inn

www.srinns.com/lazarzuela
455 No. Camino de Oeste, Tucson, AZ 85745
888-848-8225 • 520-884-4824 • Fax 520-903-2617
stay@zarzuela-az.com

Innkeepers/Owners
Clifford Aberham & Lew Harper

Pauline Spurgiesz
Southwestern Villa Bed & Breakfast

Imagine that you have a very well-to-do friend, with very good taste, who owns a large, private villa in the Tucson Mountains (think carefree). This friend, being a very good friend, offers you the use of the villa and its staff, who have been instructed to do anything your heart desires: arrange flights, limos, massages, dinner, whatever - anything to make you blissfully happy. That's La Zarzuela, "the operetta," in a nutshell. The Frank Lloyd Wright-inspired architecture resonates Southwestern culture, with scored concrete floors and walls painted in vibrant hues. With five lovely casitas, La Zarzuela is small enough to provide you the personal level of service we are committed to, yet large enough for the vacationer to meet new people, if you wish.

Rooms/Rates
5 Rooms. $250/$295. Accommodations all with private facilities, TV,VCR,DVD,CD Player, Coffee Maker, Hairdryer, and Frig.

Cuisine
Fresh coffee is ready at 7:00am, and breakfast is served from 8:00am-8:30am. Breakfast is a gourmet, full course meal including: baked breads, fruit, fresh homepade pastries and a hot baked dish. Teas from Harrods of London, England.

Nearest Airport(s)
Tucson International Airport

Directions
Located in the mountains off Gates Pass and only 10 minutes from downtown Tucson's historical Presidio District and Convention Center.

Member Since 2004

"Exemplary, there simply are no superlatives big enough for the music, the beauty, the food and hospitality. A profoundly wonderful experience."

Tanque Verde Ranch

www.srinns.com/tanqueverde
14301 East Speedway, Tucson, AZ 85748
800-234-3833 • 520-296-6275 • Fax 520-721-9426
dude@tvgr.com

Innkeepers/Owners
Robert and Rita Cote

Traditional Southwestern Country Ranch

Founded on a Spanish land grant in 1868 in the spectacular Sonoran Desert, Tanque Verde Ranch has evolved into one of the Southwest's most complete vacation destinations. A 4-star quality resort, it maintains the cowboy traditions & spirit unique to this western cattle ranch. Sonoran-style with adobe walls, high saguaro rib ceilings, beehive fireplaces and mesquite corrals, the Ranch setting provides expansive desert & mountain views. The facilities are just as remarkable, with 140 horses, tennis courts, indoor/outdoor pools, saunas, spa, guided hiking, mountain biking, nature programs, children's program, outdoor BBQ's, breakfast rides & more, in a casual relaxed atmosphere!

Rooms/Rates
Nightly rates include room accommodations, three meals a day & all of the wonderful ranch activities! The Ranch offers 51 charming rooms and 23 spacious suites, is open year round and has three rate seasons. Rates vary by room type & number of people.

Cuisine
In addition to the activities, three delicious meals are included in the rate! Meals are served daily from 8:00-9:00am, 12:00-1:30pm and 6:30-8:00pm. 4-star quality, fully licensed.

Nearest Airport(s)
Tucson International

Directions
From Tucson, east on Speedway Blvd. to the dead-end, in the Rincon Mountain foothills.

Member Since 1970

Voted one of The Top Ten Family Resorts in North America by The Travel Channel, March 2003!

Arkansas

"The Land of Opportunity"

Famous For: Natural Hot Springs, The Ozarks, Waterfalls, Diamonds, Oil, Aluminum.

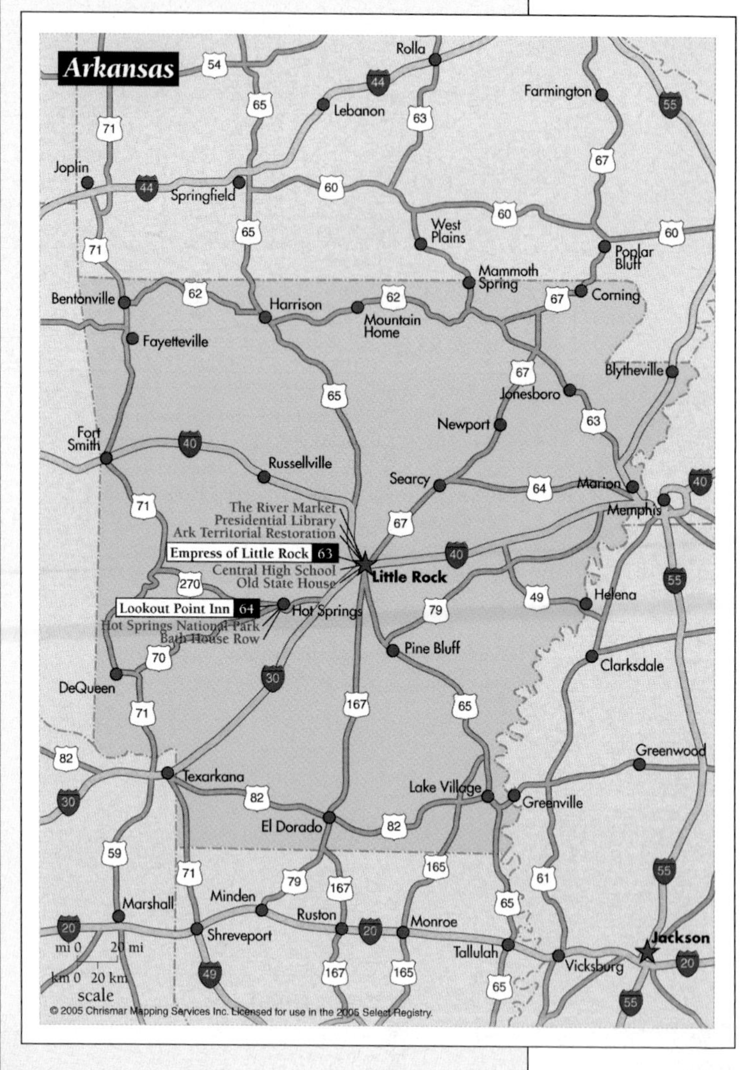

Innkeepers/Owners
Robert Blair and Sharon Welch-Blair

Small Luxury Hotel and Breakfast Inn

Mobil ★★★★
AAA ◆◆◆◆

The Empress of Little Rock

www.srinns.com/TheEmpress
2120 Louisiana Street, Little Rock, AR 72206
877-374-7966 • 501-374-7966 • Fax 501-375-4537
Email: hostess@theempress.com

Rooms/Rates
8 Rooms, 3 Spa Suites, 3 Mini-Suites, $125/$265 Featherbeds/Cable/DSL/Jacuzzi/Fireplaces

Cuisine
Gourmet two-course breakfast by candlelight served 'Before the Queen' with formal Victorian pomp and circumstance—silver, china, and a bow-tied 'butler.' Plethora of excellent restaurants available. Complimentary liqueur.

Nearest Airport(s)
Little Rock

Directions
From I-30, take I-630 W. Exit Main St. L on Main to 22nd St. R on 22nd-1 block. From Airport: I-440 W to I-30 E to I-630. Follow above directions. I-430: I-430 to I-630. Take Center St. exit thru light to Main to 22nd St.

Visit the most Victorian of Bed & Breakfasts, the Award-Winning EMPRESS OF LITTLE ROCK SMALL LUXURY HOTEL, for an adventure far from the cares of today! Central Arkansas' only AAA Four Diamond Bed & Breakfast. Named Best of the Best by the *Arkansas Democrat Gazette* consecutively since 1998. Winner of the Great American Home Award; the coveted Arkansas Henry Award for Heritage. Named one of the Top 25 Inns in the South by the *National Geographic Traveler*, referred to by Delta *Sky Miles Magazine* as the "Grand Dame of the Ozarks." Watch for us on HGTV: "If Walls Could Talk"; "Porches" and "Homes Across America." Experience a sample taste of the "forgotten experience." The Empress of Little Rock!!

Member Since 2001

6+ 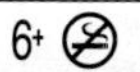    

"In over 80 countries on 6 continents, The Empress is the very best B&B we have ever visited."

Lookout Point Lakeside Inn

www.srinns.com/lookoutpoint
104 Lookout Circle, Hot Springs, AR 71913
866-525-6155 • 501-525-6155 • Fax 501-525-5850
innkeeper@lookoutpointinn.com

Innkeepers/Owners
Kristie and Ray Rosset
Waterside Breakfast Inn

A true sanctuary for body, mind and soul--Lookout Point is a slice of paradise. This newly constructed Arts & Crafts inn is located on the soothing waters of beautiful Lake Hamilton in the low lying Ouachita Mountains. Experience an exceptional inn, with a fine attention to detail as its hallmark. Understated luxury invites relaxation, romance, and rejuvenation. The magnificent gardens with waterfalls and meditation labyrinth are perfect for small, intimate weddings. Canoe the bay, watch the birds, nap in the hammock, or soak in the nearby historic Hot Springs bathhouses. The well-stocked library and video collection, puzzles, and board games enhance the experience of simplifying life. Come relax, feast, and play!

Member Since 2005

Rooms/Rates
10 rooms, $150/$265. Corporate weekday rates available. All rooms overlook the gardens/waterfalls and Lake Hamilton.

Cuisine
Fresh and hearty breakfast included, plus afternoon homemade dessert with wine and tea. Complimentary snack bar with coffee/tea available. Famous Hot Springs bottled mineral water in every room.

Nearest Airport(s)
Little Rock, 60 miles

Directions
From East: I-30 to US 270 (exit 98B) to AR Hwy 7. South on 7 3.5 miles. Left on Lookout Point, to stop sign; right on Lookout Circle. From West: I-30 to AR Hwy 7 (exit 78). N 24.5 miles. Right on Central Terrace to top of hill.

"This is one of the loveliest inns anywhere! Rarely does an inn 'have it all' and 'do it all' in such a special way."

California, North

"The Golden State"

Famous For: Spanish Missions, Gold Rush, Golden Gate Bridge, Wine Country, Citrus, Giant Sequoia Redwoods, Hollywood, Disneyland, Lake Tahoe, Sierra Nevada, Yosemite National Park, Big Sur, Earthquakes, and Death Valley

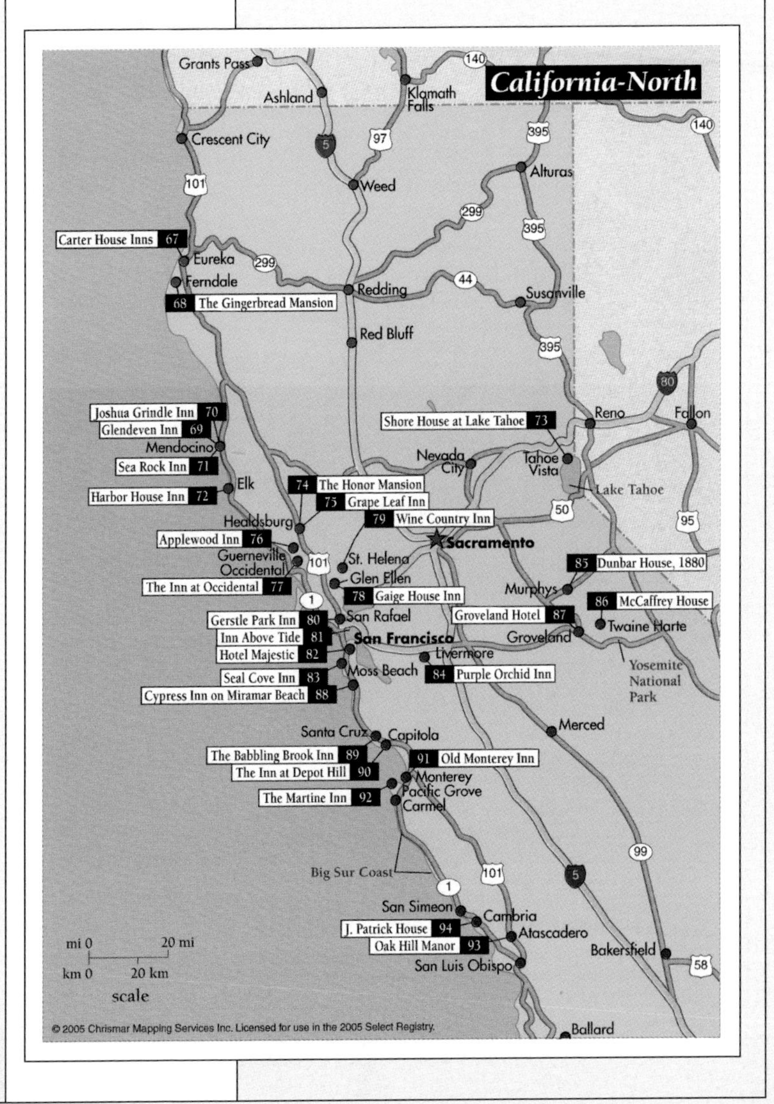

California, South

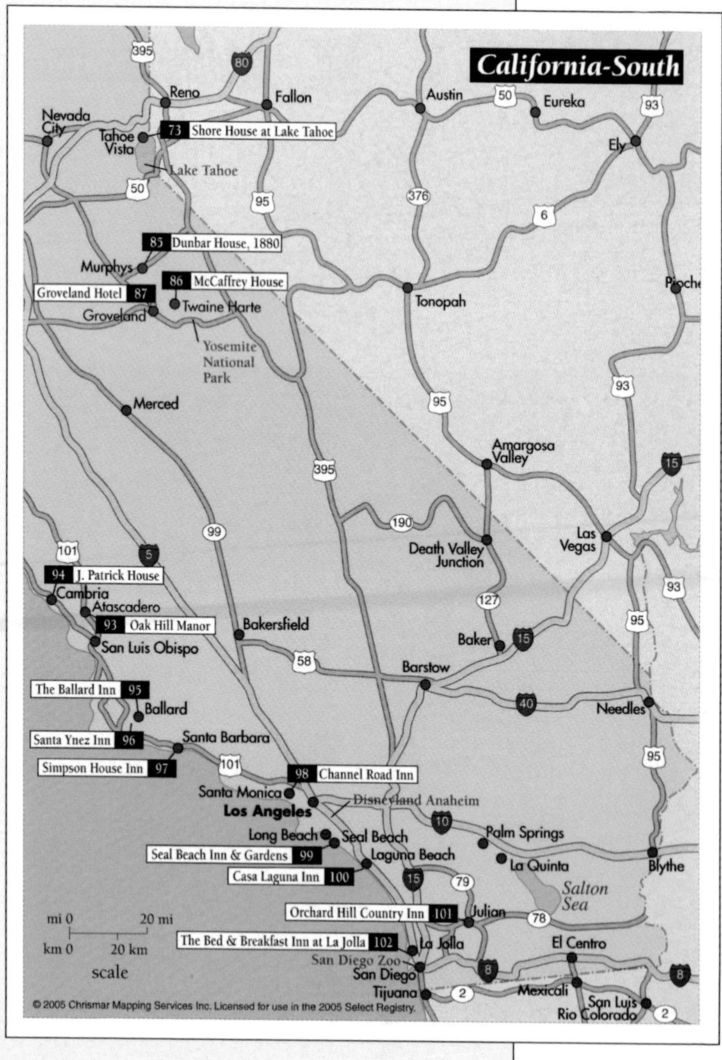

Carter House Inns

www.srinns.com/carterhouse
301 L Street, Eureka, CA 95501
707-444-8062 • 707-445-1390 • Fax 707-444-8067
reserve@carterhouse.com

Innkeepers/Owners
Mark and Christi Carter

Elegant Victorian
In Town Inn

AAA ◆◆◆◆

Rooms/Rates
7 Rooms, $155/$350 B&B,
2 Suites, $275/$595 B&B.
Open year-round.

Cuisine
Full service award-winning restaurant open nightly, full breakfast. Full bar, wine shop—3,880 wine selections.

Nearest Airport(s)
Eureka-Arcata Airport is 16 miles north of Eureka.

Directions
From Highway 101 heading South turn right on L Street. From Highway 101 heading North turn left on L Street. The hotel is located on the corner of 3rd & L Street.

Located on the northern border of Eureka's historic Old Town, The Carter House Inns and Restaurant 301 have been welcoming travelers to The Redwood Empire with world-class accommodations and cuisine since 1981. An enclave of four unique, magnificent Victorians perched alongside Humboldt Bay, we greet our guests with a special brand of hospitality imbued with the friendly, easy-going style of the North Coast. Our AAA Four Diamong-rated accommodations and service are unparalleled; our cuisine and wine list, award-winning. Restaurant 301 is one of only 89 dining establishments worldwide to hold a *Wine Spectator* Grand Award.

Member Since 2003

"I'll never forget my stays at the Carter House Inns."
Lora Finnegan, *Sunset* Magazine

Gingerbread Mansion Inn

www.srinns.com/gingerbreadmansion
400 Berding Street, P.O. Box 1380, Ferndale, CA 95536
800-952-4136 • 707-786-4000 • Fax 707-786-4381
innkeeper@gingerbread-mansion.com

Innkeepers/Owners
Vince & Sue Arriaga and Robert & Juli McInroy

Elegant Victorian Village Breakfast Inn

Mobil ★★★
AAA ◆◆◆◆

Exquisitely turreted and gabled, the Gingerbread Mansion Inn is truly a visual masterpiece. Located in the Victorian village of Ferndale, the Inn is surrounded by lush English gardens. Featuring two of the West Coast's most luxurious suites—the 'Empire Suite' and 'Veneto.' Garden views, and old-fashioned tubs and fireplaces for fireside bubble baths are featured. Amenities include a morning tray service, full gourmet breakfast, afternoon tea, turn-down service with bedside chocolates, bathrobes. Near the Giant redwood parks and ocean beaches.

Rooms/Rates
11 rooms and suites, $150/$400. All private baths; many luxurious with clawfoot tubs and fireplaces as big as bedrooms. Office hours 7:00 a.m. to 7:00 p.m. Open year-round.

Cuisine
Full gourmet breakfast with hot entree, side dish, and many other items. Afternoon tea service. Complimentary port served in four premium suites. Wine and champagne available.

Nearest Airport(s)
Arcata Airport

Directions
101 4-1/2 hours N of S.F. Ferndale exit, 5 miles to town, L at Bank, 1 block to Inn. From Oregon, 20 minutes S of Eureka. Ferndale exit.

Member Since 1988

Conde Naste Johansen's 2001
"North America Inn of Year"

Proprietors
Sharon Williams & Higgins

Elegant Country Breakfast Inn

AAA ◆◆◆

Glendeven Inn

www.srinns.com/glendeven
8205 North Highway One, Little River, CA 95456
800-822-4536 • 707-937-0083 • Fax 707-937-6108
innkeeper@glendeven.com

Rooms/Rates
6 rooms, 4 suites in the inn: $145/$275 B&B; K & Q beds; 2 people per room. Ocean view luxury cottage: $320/$410 (up to 4 people, including children) EP Open year-round.

Cuisine
Delicious homemade, hot country breakfasts are brought to your room to begin the day. Informal early evening gatherings in the Farmhouse living room with wine & hors d'oeuvres. Coffee, teas and homemade cookies always available in the living room.

Nearest Airport(s)
Sacramento, Oakland and San Francisco

Directions
From San Francisco: Hwy 101 N to Hwy 128 W to Hwy 1 N; then 8.2 miles

Unwind at a tranquil, 1867 country estate on a headland meadow above Little River, minutes south of historic Mendocino Village.

Glendeven Inn blends the best of the Mendocino coast: gracious accommodations of a first-class inn, ocean views and a contemporary art gallery.

The heart of Glendeven is a beautifully restored New England-style farmhouse surrounded by ever-flowering gardens.

Guest quarters provide undisturbed luxury, combining tasteful antiques, comfortable furniture, featherbeds and fine art.

All accommodations feature well lighted reading areas, and most include wood burning fireplaces, private decks and stirring views of the ocean.

Member Since 2002

"Dreamy ... I give it '5 Pillows' ... no wonder Glendeven rhymes with Heaven!"

Joshua Grindle Inn

www.srinns.com/joshuagrindle
P.O. Box 647, 44800 Little Lake Road, Mendocino, CA 95460
800-474-6353 • 707-937-4143 • Fax 775-243-6930
stay@joshgrin.com

Proprietors
Charles & Cindy Reinhart

Traditional Victorian Village Bed & Breakfast Inn

Mobil ★★★
AAA ◆◆◆◆

Experience Mendocino at its best. Our welcoming home sits atop a two-acre knoll overlooking the village and ocean. Park and forget about your car, as galleries, shops, restaurants and hiking trails are just a short stroll away. Tastefully decorated, comfortable, and exceptionally clean rooms await you. Charles and Cindy and our friendly staff will attend to your every need, and serve a full gourmet breakfast. Enjoy chatting with fellow guests over evening refreshments in our parlor, or escape to a private, quiet nook in our gardens. Relax on our front veranda and watch the whales spout in the distance. Recommended by prestigious Andrew Harper's *Hideaway Report*.

Member Since 1996

Rooms/Rates
10 Rooms Main House, Cottage, Water Tower, $160/$259 B&B. Ocean view luxury Grindle Guest House (2 bdrm) $250/$400 (EP).

Cuisine
Full gourmet breakfast specializing in fresh local ingredients. The highly regarded Cafe Beaujolais is just a two-block stroll from the Inn. Wineshop on premises with selection of premium Mendocino wines. Complimentary wine in room & Cream Sherry in Parlor.

Nearest Airport(s)
Little River Airport
San Francisco International
Oakland International

Directions
From San Francisco, take Hwy. 101 N to Hwy. 128 West to Hwy. 1 N. From Hwy. 1 turn west onto Little Lake Road. First driveway on your right.

"The hospitality, food, service, & property are among the best we have experienced."

Sea Rock Inn

www.srinns.com/searockinn
11101 Lansing Street, PO Box 906, Mendocino, CA 95460
800-906-0926 • 707-937-0926
innkeeper@searockinn.com

Innkeepers/Owners
Andy and Susie Plocher

Contemporary Country Seaside Inn

AAA ◆◆◆

Rooms/Rates
10 Suites, 4 Rooms. $179/$395.

Cuisine
Guests enjoy an attractive breakfast buffet with daily changing quiche, hard boiled eggs, yogurt, fresh pastries, juices, fruit and more. Upon check in to the room, guests may relax with a complimentry split of fine local wine.

Nearest Airport(s)
SFO or Oakland, 3 1/2 hrs

Directions
From SF area take Hwy 101 north to Hwy 128 West (scenic) at Cloverdale-Turn right onto Hwy 1 at ocean & go north (scenic) 10 mi to Mendocino. Turn left on Little Lake Rd & make a right on Lansing - inn is 1/3 mi ahead on right.

One of the few inns in Mendocino with ocean views from every hillside accommodation, The Sea Rock Inn beckons with crashing surf and inviting firelit rooms. From your suite or cottage you will experience the true beauty of the Mendocino Coast with spectacular panoramic views of the ocean and dramatic rocky cliffs of the Mendocino Headlands State Park. The setting is perfect for a memorable getaway. Hand hewn wood treatments accent luxuriously comfortable coastal contemporary design and appointments of virtually every amenity imaginable. Stroll through colorful gardens, curl up by the fire or relax on your deck and watch the sunset from your private oceanview cottage or suite. Hiking trails abound nearby, as does ocean and river kayaking, canoeing and many other outdoor actvities. Gourmet dining is a short walk or minute's drive away, and the charming village of Mendocino is a National Historic Register community laden with special shops and attractions. Great rooms, stunning views and nice people...The Sea Rock Inn.

Member Since 2005

"Sipping wine-relaxing fireside in our room watching waves crash on the shore...authentic and special inn...we'll cherish all the great memories forever."

Harbor House Inn by the Sea

www.srinns.com/harborhouseinn
P.O. Box 369, 5600 S. Highway, Elk, CA 95432
800-720-7474 • 707-877-3203 • Fax 707-877-3452
innkeeper@theharborhouseinn.com

Innkeeper/Owner
Sam Haynes
General Manager
Jennifer Monnier

Elegant Country Inn

Built in 1916, the Harbor House is at the throne of the Redwood Empire, standing vigil on a cliff overlooking Greenwood Cove with its spectacular rock formations and powerful surf. Pathways meander through magnificent seaside gardens and lead to the private beach below. The drama continues throughout the Inn's ten guest rooms, its stately sitting room, and breathtaking ocean-view dining room. Refurbished with luxury in mind, the Inn features antique and classic appointments throughout. Creative California cuisine, fresh daily. *Wine Spectator* 'Award of Excellence.' Prix-fixe four-course dinner included. Distinctive lodging, fine dining and timeless luxury; only three hours from San Francisco.

Rooms/Rates
10 Rooms (6 in Main House, 4 Cottages) $300/$475 MAP. Open year-round.

Cuisine
Dramatic ocean-view dining. Full breakfast and highly rated 4-course gourmet dinner included in rates. Extensive wine cellar featuring local and international selections.

Nearest Airport(s)
Santa Rosa, San Francisco

Directions
From San Fancisco take 101 N, in Cloverdale take Hwy. 128 W to Hwy. 1, S 5 miles to Elk.

Member Since 1975

"This inn has it all: views, elegant rooms, and meals that alone make the trip worthwhile."

Shore House at Lake Tahoe

www.srinns.com/tahoe
7170 North Lake Blvd., P.O. Box 499, Tahoe Vista, CA 96148
800-207-5160 • 530-546-7270 • Fax 530-546-7130
innkeeper@shorehouselaketahoe.com

Innkeepers/Owners
Barb & Marty Cohen
Mountain Waterside
Breakfast Inn & Spa

Rooms/Rates
9 King or Queen Rooms, $190/$290. Each room has a gas log fireplace, custom-built log beds, down comforters, featherbeds and TVs. All private baths, most with whirlpool tubs.

Cuisine
Award-winning gourmet breakfasts, wine and appetizers served daily in lakefront dining room or in lakeside gardens. Walk to extraordinary lakefront restaurants.

Nearest Airport(s)
Reno International

Directions
Take Hwy 80E from San Francisco or 80W from Reno. Take Exit 188B onto Hwy 267 towards Kings Beach and North Lake Tahoe. Turn R on Hwy 28 (N Lake Blvd.). Go 3/4 mile to the Shore House at 7170 N Lake Blvd.

The Shore House is the ultimate romantic getaway on the shore of spectacular Lake Tahoe. Surrounding decks offer fabulous views of the pristine lake and mountains. Relax in the large outdoor lakefront hot tub. Enjoy fine lakefront restaurants, art galleries, and casinos close by. This winter wonderland offers downhill and x-c skiing at 29 resorts, ice skating, snowmobiling, sleigh rides. Summer activities include spectacular hiking, biking, golf, rafting, parasailing, and lunch cruises on the Shore House 36' cabin cruiser, *Lady of the Lake*. Rent kayaks right from the Shore House. Intimate lakefront weddings are our specialty. Enjoy romantic couples' massage packages in the spa overlooking the Lake and Mountains.

Member Since 2000

"The views, the hospitality, the breakfasts, who could ask for more?"

The Honor Mansion

www.srinns.com/honormansion
14891 Grove Streeet, Healdsburg, CA 95448
800-554-4667 • 707-433-4277 • Fax 707-431-7173
innkeeper@honormansion.com

Owners
Steve & Cathi Fowler
General Manager
Kelly Barba

Luxury Resort Inn

A Resort Inn...let us pamper you! Built in 1883, this luxuriously comfortable Resort awaits your arrival. Imagine "World-class" amenities and service with hometown hospitality. Spa Services, Pool, Tennis, PGA Putting Green, Bocce, Competition Croquet lawn, Decks, Fountains and Walking Gardens, situated on more than three acres of landscaped grounds, yet a pleasant walk to the downtown square which is replete with terrific shops, bakeries and restaurants. The perfect "special" occasion get-away. Romantic and private. Located in Healdsburg at the confluence of the world-renowned wine growing appellations of Dry Creek, Alexander and Russian River Valleys, with over 100 wineries. Come enjoy our passion for this incredible area and discover some of our boutique wineries, as well as those that have been here for over 100 years. Our fully trained concierge staff is at your service. Plan day trips, picnics, get that special "private" wine tour in some of the world's best wineries right in our back yard. You will never want to leave!

Member Since 1998

Rooms/Rates
13 Rooms, $190/$550, two people per room. King & Queen beds, fireplaces, soaking tubs, garden spa tubs, private decks, room service menu, full turn down service.

Cuisine
Full gourmet breakfast multiple seatings, as well as room service menu, complimentary evening wine and appetizers, sherry, cappuccino machine, & bottomless cookie jar.

Nearest Airport(s)
Oakland and San Francisco

Directions
From the South: Take Hwy 101 North to Healdsburg. Take the Dry Creek exit to the R for 1 block, turn R on Grove St. We are the first white picket fence on the R. From the North: Take Hwy 101 South to the Dry Creek exit; go L.

"Far more than 'First Class'-it's more like 'World Class.'"

Innkeepers/Owners
Richard & Kae Rosenberg

Luxury Wine Country Inn

Grape Leaf Inn

www.srinns.com/grapeleafinn
www.grapeleafinn.com, 539 Johnson Street, Healdsburg, CA 95448
866-433-8140 • 707-433-8140 • Fax 707-433-3140
info@grapeleafinn.com

Rooms/Rates
12 Rooms. $200/$350.

Cuisine
Breakfast is an exquisite culinary experience, not just another morning meal. From your 1st cup of freshly ground coffee,to the four-course gourmet breakfast,created from the freshest local produce and herbs grown in our gardens,--all are prepared with imaginative flair by the owners/chefs to create a delicious start to your day. Join us nightly in our "Speakeasy" wine cellar, hidden behind a bookcase, for award-winning local wines and cheeses.

Nearest Airport(s)
SFO and OAK

Directions
See our website for directions from anywhere.

Surrounded by century-old evergreens and lush award-winning gardens, this luxury wine country Inn is tucked away on a quiet historic street, a short walk from fine shops and restaurants. A ten minute drive takes you to more than 104 world-class wineries and the most picturesque countryside imaginable. This highly acclaimed B&B combines the gracious hospitality of a country inn with meticulous service, fine cuisine and 12 luxurious accommodations. Stylish, contemporary decor paired with timeless antiques meld to create the best of California Wine Country style. The relaxing ambience, attentive staff, and its unmistakable romance have made this B&B one of the most sought after small luxury inns in the Wine Country. The 12 rooms, most with king beds, have TV, DVD, CD, Internet wireless service, plush, down bedding and fine pressed linens. Many rooms have fireplaces and phones. Most baths offer two-person spa tubs, and one has a two-person steam shower and Japanese soaking tub. All have Frette linens and Aveda bath amenities.

Member Since 2004

"The Wine Country's beautiful Grape Leaf Inn combines the luxury and amenities of a chic boutique hotel with the romantic charm of a B&B."

Applewood Inn

www.srinns.com/applewood
13555 Hwy 116, Guerneville, CA 95446
800-555-8509 • Fax 707-869-9170
stay@applewoodinn.com

Innkeepers/Owners
James Caron & Darryl Notter

Historic California Premier Inn

A gently sloping valley guarded by towering Redwoods in the heart of Sonoma's Russian River Valley is home to Applewood Inn and its acclaimed restaurant. Splashing fountains and whimsical statues add texture to the terraced courtyard and gardens that separate the tiled roofed and stuccoed villas of this gracious Mediterranean complex. The old-world atmosphere of a "Gentleman's Farm" is evoked in lovingly maintained orchards and kitchen gardens that supply the restaurant through the Summer and early Fall. Applewood's cooking school housed in the sunny kitchen of Belden House, offers intimate wine country cooking classes and field trips to neighboring farms. Day spa services add a touch of indulgent pampering. Located within a short drive of the Sonoma coast and Armstrong woods.

Member Since 2004

Rooms/Rates
19 Rooms. $185/$345.

Cuisine
The Zagat rated, 4 1/2 star restaurant @ Applewood offers Mediterranean inspired wine country fare paired with an award winning Sonoma County wine list. The inn's romantic dining room features two fireplaces and lovely views over a garden courtyard and towering redwoods. A popular dining spot for locals. Advanced reservations suggested.

Nearest Airport(s)
San Francisco

Directions
Hwy. 101 North from San Francisco to the River Road exit past Santa Rosa. West on River Road 15 miles to traffic signal @ Guerneville. Turn left at signal, cross Russian River & proceed 1/2 mile to the inn.

"The inn's restaurant is a marvel...The wine list is a particular joy."
- *Wine Spectator*

Inn at Occidental of Sonoma Wine Country

www.srinns.com/innatoccidental
3657 Church Street, P.O. Box 857, Occidental, CA 95465-0857
800-522-6324 • 707-874-1047 • Fax 707-874-1078
innkeeper@innatoccidental.com

Innkeepers/Owners
Jerry & Tina Wolsborn
Elegant Village
Breakfast Inn

Mobil ★★★
AAA ◆◆◆◆

According to *The Wine Spectator*, "One of the Top Five Wine Country Destinations." The antiques, original art and decor provide charm, warmth and elegance exceeded only by the hospitality you experience. "Tops our List as the Most Romantic Place to Stay" is what *Bride and Groom* said of the featherbeds, down comforters, spa tubs for two, fireplaces and private decks. The gourmet breakfast and evening wine and cheese reception add to a memorable experience. Excellent boutique wineries, nearby Armstrong Redwoods State Reserve, Russian River, the dramatic coast and scenic drives along country backroads make for a great destination. Hiking, biking, horseback riding and golfing nearby. All reasons why *AAA VIA* says of The Inn "The Best Bed-and-Breakfast in the West." An *Andrew Harper* Recommendation.

Rooms/Rates
3 Suites, 13 Rooms: Fireplaces, Spa Tubs, Decks $199/$329, 2 BR Home $625.

Cuisine
Full gourmet breakfast. Local wines, cheeses and hors d'oeuvres nightly. NIghtly sweets. Concierge service. Wonderful dining nearby. Special Functions: Wedding, Corporate Retreat, Wine Seminar/Dinner.

Nearest Airport(s)
San Francisco (SFO) or Oakland (OAK)

Directions
From San Francisco (101-N) exit at Rohnert Park/Sebastopol. Take 116-W for 7.4 mi to Sebastopol. Turn left onto Bodega Hwy for 6.4 mi, turn Right onto Bohemian Hwy thru town of Freestone for 3.7 mi to Occidental. At 4-way stop, turn right to Inn's parking.

Member Since 1995

"Simply everything you want at a Country Inn" – *Recommended Country Inns.*
"Great to be back!! Just as beautiful as the last time."

Gaige House Inn

www.srinns.com/gaigehouse
13540 Arnold Drive, Glen Ellen/Sonoma, CA 95442-9305
800-935-0237 • 707-935-0237 • Fax 707-935-6411
gaige@sprynet.com

Innkeepers
Ken Burnet and Greg Nemrow
Manager
Sue Burnet

Elegant Village Breakfast Inn

Mobil ★★★

In June, 2000, The Gaige House Inn was named the #1 B&B in America by *Travel + Leisure* magazine. Similarly, the Arts and Entertainment (A&E) channel honored the inn as one of the 'top 10 most romantic getaways in the world.' Only one hour from San Francisco, the inn is in the heart of Napa/Sonoma Wine country. Gently influenced Asian decor helps create a sophisticated, yet comfortable environment. Breakfasts are 'outrageously good,' according to *Random House's Guide to The Wine Country.* Relax by the pool, or walk to nearby restaurants. In-room/outdoor spa treatments! Noting all of this, *Frommer's* calls The Gaige House the 'Best B & B in Wine Country.'

Rooms/Rates
23 Rooms and Suites $175/$575 B&B; most with fireplace, Jacuzzis and decks, TV, phone, and AC. 4 Cottages off-site. Open year-round.

Cuisine
Professional chef gourmet breakfasts served w/Peet's Coffee and fresh-squeezed juice. Evening wine service w/light appetizers. Complimentary water and snacks all day. Walk to four excellent restaurants for dinner.

Nearest Airport(s)
San Francisco, Sacramento

Directions
From San Fran: RT 101N to RT 37 exit. Follow Rt 37 to RT 121 exit. Follow RT 121N to RT 116. Take right-hand exit onto Arnold Drive/Glen Ellen. Proceed N and pass through village of Glen Ellen.

Member Since 1998

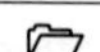

The 2003 thru 2005 ZAGAT Hotel Survey rated us Number One in Wine Country.

Innkeeper
Jim Smith

Traditional Country Inn

The Wine Country Inn

www.srinns.com/winecountryinn
1152 Lodi Lane, St. Helena, CA 94574
888-465-4608 • 707-963-7077 • Fax 707-963-9018
romance@winecountryinn.com

Rooms/Rates
20 Rooms 4 Suites 5 luxury cottages. Rates are $185/$550 Off-season and $210/$595 Harvest Season. All rates include a full buffet breakfast and wine social in the afternoon; off-season mid-week discounts are available. Open year-round.

Cuisine
Fresh fruit, juices, home-made granola and nut-breads compliment an innovative egg dish as well as fun bagel bar. Family-recipe appitizers with great local wines in afternoon.

Nearest Airport(s)
Sacramento

Directions
From San Francisco take I-80 (E) to Hwy. 37 follow signs to Napa (Hwy. 29N) 18 miles N to St. Helena. 2 miles N to Lodi Lane R on Lodi 1/3 mile.

For thirty years, three generations of Ned and Marge Smith's family have been welcoming guests to their little slice of Heaven. The Inn is a tranquil and hidden oasis in the heart of America's center for fine wine and eclectic dining. The antique-filled rooms, lush gardens, sun-drenched pool and star-canopied hot tub make it hard for guests to leave, but for those that do, the Smiths and their staff are eager to use their local knowledge to arrange truly memorable days of sampling the finest the area has to offer. At the end of the day guests gather with the innkeepers to compare experiences over more great wine and tables laden with home-made appetizers.

Member Since 1978

"This stay was simply outstanding. The facilities are wonderful and the staff has been great!!"

Gerstle Park Inn

www.srinns.com/gerstlepark
34 Grove St., San Rafael, CA 94901
800-726-7611 • 415-721-7611 • Fax 415-721-7600
innkeeper@gerstleparkinn.com

Owners
Jim & Judy Dowling

Elegant Village
Bed & Breakfast Inn 

Mobil ★★★
AAA ◆◆◆

Located 20 min. N. of San Francisco and 30 min S. of the wine country, the Inn was once the site of a English-style estate built in 1895. Situated on 2 1/2 acres in a quiet and historic neighborhood, giant cedar, oak and redwood trees lend ample shade to terraced gardens and green lawns. In the evening, relax on the veranda during wine hour, play croquet, or pick fruit from the orchard. Also, hike in the woods that border the estate. In the morning, enjoy a full hot breakfast to order at your leisure on the veranda or in the breakfast room. Spacious guest rooms are plush in comfort and color, with fine fabrics, antiques, parlor areas and private decks or patios with beautiful views. Gerstle Park Inn is perfectly located for exploring all of the San Francisco Bay Area. There is nothing like this in Marin County!

Member Since 1998

Rooms/Rates
12 Rooms, 4 with Jacuzzi tubs; Cottages and Carriage House Suites with kitchens $179/$245. Open year-round. Meeting facilities up to 20 people conference style.

Cuisine
Accommodations include full hot breakfast to order during a 2-hour period. Wine hour in the evening and 24 hour kitchen privileges which include cookies, snacks, fruit, sodas, juice, tea and coffee.

Nearest Airport(s)
SFO-San Francisco, & OAK-Oakland A.P., 45 min.

Directions
Hwy-101, Exit Central San Rafael, West on 4th St, L.on D St., R.on San Rafael Ave, L.on Grove St. 34 Grove St.

"In two words 'Comfortable Elegance' discribes the Inn. It is a quiet private retreat that soothes the soul; like being in the wine country yet so close."

Inn Above Tide

www.srinns.com/innabovetide
30 El Portal, Sausalito, CA 94965
800-893-8433 • 415-332-9535 • Fax 415-332-6714
stay@innabovetide.com

General Manager
Mark Flaherty

Luxury Seaside
Boutique Hotel

AAA ♦♦♦♦

Rooms/Rates
29 Rooms. $270/$895.

Cuisine
Coffee & tea is available 24/7. Elegant expanded continental breakfast (room service available). Daily sunset wine & cheese reception

Nearest Airport(s)
SFO / 21 mi
Oakland / 27 mi

Directions
From SF Airport: Take Hwy 101 North to Hwy 380 West to Hwy 280 North. Take the 19th Ave exit & follow 19th Ave North to Golden Gate Bridge. Once across the bridge, take the Alexander Ave exit. Follow Alexander Ave into downtown Sausalito (Alexander Ave becomes Bridgeway as water approaches) Go 1/2 block past first stoplight and turn right on El Portal. Inn is at end of El Portal

There are hundreds of hotels around San Francisco Bay, but only one actually on the water. Every room and suite has an unparalleled panoramic view of San Francisco Bay. Spectacular views, stylish new design throughout and a romantic atmosphere make this luxury boutique hotel a delight to discover. The 29 rooms and suites feature every conceivable amenity including private decks, fireplaces, TV/VCR/DVDs with in-house DVD library, phones, personal voicemail, complimentary in-room wi-fi Internet access, CD players, Hermes amenities, European linens, down comforters, robes, hairdryers, binoculars, in-room honor bar, full evening turn down service, complimentary shoe shine, room service breakfast, sunset wine and cheese, concierge, warm and capable 24/7 staffing to meet every need and valet parking. On your private deck - work via wi-fi, enjoy an ocean side massage, glass of wine or room service breakfast with the ever-changing scenery of the Bay at your feet. Guests rave about this truly memorable experience. Andrew Harper recommended.

Member Since 2004

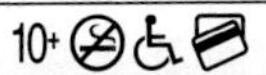
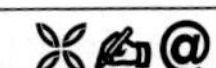

"There is no finer view of San Francisco...No Swiss inn could offer more personal service. This is my favorite hotel of all time...stunning & fantastic."

Hotel Majestic

www.srinns.com/hotelmajestic
1500 Sutter Street, San Francisco, CA 94109
800-869-8966 • 415-441-1100 • Fax 415-673-7331
info@thehotelmajestic.com

General Manager
Catherine Nelson

Elegant Edwardian
In Town Hotel

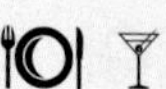

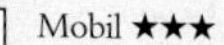

Mobil ★★★

The romance and elegance of a bygone era in San Francisco thrive at the Hotel Majestic. Enjoy the Edwardian architecture and turn of the century elegance of this 1906 earthquake survivor. European antiques and gracious service are a part of your visit in this century old landmark home. Graceful high ceilings and fine detailed molding are visible throughout the building. Many rooms, and all suites, have marble fireplaces, large bay sunny windows, canopied beds, and feather pillows. Relax in the lobby by the fireplace with one of many daily newspapers or enjoy complimentary wine and hors d'oeuvres in the late afternoon. The Hotel Majestic is convenient to the Performing Arts Center, cable cars, and many cultural centers in the city. Cocktails are served in the Avalon Bar, home of an extensive collection of rare Asian butterflies. Guests may access the Internet via high speed wireless connection in the lobby and guest rooms. A laptop computer is available for guest use in the lobby.

Rooms/Rates
32 Rooms $115/$150, 17 Jr. Suites $175/$195, 9 Suites $195/$250

Cuisine
The Dining Room, serves a delicious Continental Breakfast buffet each morning. The Avalon Bar, which features delicious speciality cocktails and wines from nearby Sonoma & Napa also serves a bar menu from 5p - 9p nightly.

Nearest Airport(s)
SFO

Directions
From North: Hwy. 101 over B to Lombard St. R on Van Ness Ave. to Sutter R. From South: Hwy. 101 to SF exit 9th St. Cross Market St.; it becomes Larkin. L on Sutter. From East: On Bay Bridge, exit 9th St. Cross Market. It becomes Larkin. L on Sutter.

Member Since 2002

"Ambiance of an elegant turn of the century hotel with great furnishings and absolutely meticulously clean rooms. Impeccable service from the staff."

Innkeepers/Owners
Karen Brown Herbert & Richard Craig Herbert
Traditional Village Breakfast Inn

AAA ◆◆◆◆

Seal Cove Inn

www.srinns.com/sealcove
221 Cypress Ave., Moss Beach, CA 94038
800-995-9987 • 650-728-4114 • Fax 650-728-4116
Innkeeper@Sealcoveinn.com

Rooms/Rates
2 Suites, 8 Guestrooms, $215/$325. All have fireplaces and TV with VCR. Open year-round except a few days at Christmas.

Cuisine
A full breakfast is served in the dining room or a freshly baked continental is offered in the guest rooms. Complimentary wake-up coffee outside your door in the morning and wine & hors d'oeuvres in the evening.

Nearest Airport(s)
San Francisco Airport is 30 minutes from the Inn.

Directions
From Hwy. 101 or 280 take Hwy. 92 W to Half Moon Bay. Travel N from Half Moon Bay 6 miles on Hwy. 1, turn W on Cypress Ave towards the ocean.

Spectacularly set amongst wildflowers and bordered by towering cypress trees, Seal Cove Inn looks out to the ocean over acres of county park. Owned by travel writer Karen Brown and her husband, Rick, the inn is an oasis where you can enjoy secluded beaches, explore tidepools, watch frolicking seals, and follow the tree-lined path tracing the windswept ocean bluffs. Each bedroom is its own private haven with a cozy fireplace and doors opening onto a private deck or patio with views to the distant ocean. Country antiques, lovely watercolors, rich fabrics and grandfather clocks all create a perfect romantic ambiance. Nearby the Inn are the world famous Maverick Surfing Waves, Elephant Seals of Ano Nuevo, majestic coastal Redwood Trees and shopping in the hamlet of Half Moon Bay. The attractions of San Francisco are a mere 30 minutes away. Guests enjoy day trips to Napa/Sonoma and Carmel/Monterey which are 1 1/2 to 2 hours distant.

Member Since 1998

 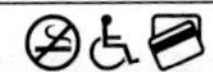   

"Seal Cove is truly a special place as are you and your staff. We felt so welcome."

Purple Orchid Inn, Resort & Spa

www.srinns.com/purpleorchid
4549 Cross Road, Livermore, CA 94550
800-353-4549 • 925-606-8855 • Fax 925-606-8880
info@purpleorchid.com

Owner
Karen Hughes
Guest Service Manager
Heidi Farah

Elegant Country Resort

This distinctive South Livermore Valley Inn offers soaring eagles, singing meadowlarks and the rush of the waterfall - all minutes from the freeway, but miles away in your mind. Our concierge will assist you with reservations for dinner, meeting/conference space or wedding receptions. Located in America's oldest award winning wine country, this elegant estate surrounds your senses with flowers, acres of vinyards and olive orchards. The tranquility will massage your mind with relaxing images of your luxury suite, private jacuzzi tubs in all guest rooms, a leisurely full breakfast, 18 holes of championship golf, a soak in the poolside hot tub, followed by the spa treatment of your choice. Don't forget to enjoy the hors d'oeuvre wine reception and our Estate Grown olive oil tasting nightly!

Rooms/Rates
4 Rooms $150/$195; 4 Suites/Retreats $225/$260; 2 Patio Suites, $360/$380. FP/TV/VCR/Voicemail, concierge service until 8:00pm, Q/K beds,views from all rooms, Always open.

Cuisine
Homemade pastries,fresh fruit,full gourmet made-to-order breakfast, Spa & Supper Club Food theater;Local dining

Nearest Airport(s)
Oakland Intl: I880 S to I238 E, becomes I580 E, see directions below.

Directions
From SF Intl:Take Hwy 101 S ~5 mi to Hwy 92E to I880 N ~5 mi to I580 E ~25 mi to exit S Vasco Rd until it ends at Tesla Rd. Turn L on Tesla Rd ~2 mi. Turn L on Cross Rd. The Inn is on the L

Member Since 2000

 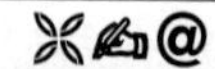 

"Better than a cruise and no sea sickness! We felt like a prince and princess."

Innkeepers/Owners
Arline and Richard Taborek
General Manager
Anita Miller

Traditional Village Breakfast Inn

AAA ◆◆◆◆

Dunbar House, 1880

www.srinns.com/dunbar
271 Jones Street, Murphys, CA 95247
800-692-6006 • 209-728-2897 • Fax 209-728-1451
innkeep@dunbarhouse.com

Rooms/Rates
3 Rooms, $190/$240; 2 Suites, $250/$260. TV,DVD,data ports, phone,refrigerators, fireplaces,spa baths, down comforters, Q or K beds, AC.

Cuisine
Appetizer plate and bottle of wine await in each guest's room. Candlelit breakfast endowed with edible flowers served in dining room by the fire, in the rose garden, or in the privacy of the guest's room.

Nearest Airport(s)
Sacramento Airport

Directions
From San Francisco: 580 E to Tracy to 205 E to 99 N to Stockton, exit on Hwy. 4 E (Farmington exit), to Angels Camp. 49 S to Hwy. 4 E again. 9 miles to Murphys. L at Main St. L at Jones St.

Arrive at the Inn and begin a visit with history. Located two hours east of San Francisco, between Lake Tahoe and Yosemite, in the Sierra foothills. Murphys remains much the same as it was during the Great Gold Rush. The village is just steps across the bridge over Murphys Creek, and offers fine dining, galleries, wineries, seasonal events, and live theatre. Water fountains and birdhouses abound in the lovingly tended historic rose garden, surrounded by a white picket fence with many private sitting areas. A suite may offer such indulgences as an English towel warmer, balcony in the trees, fine linen, stereo system, champagne and a whirlpool bath for two.

Member Since 2001

"Comfortable & elegant with fabulous food in a gracious setting. We'll be back soon!"

McCaffrey House

www.srinns.com/mccaffreyhouse
23251 Highway 208, P.O. Box 67, Twain Harte, CA 95383
888-586-0757 • 209-586-0757 • Fax 209-586-3689
innkeeper@mccaffreyhouse.com

Innkeeper/Owner
Michael & Stephanie McCaffrey

Natural Grand Mountain Home

Mobil ★★★
AAA ◆◆◆◆

Pure elegance...in a wilderness setting. This AAA Four Diamond Inn is a delightfully warm and charming three-story country home nestled in the quiet forest hollow of the High Sierras - near Yosemite National Park. Guestrooms are artfully decorted and feature handmade Amish quilts, fire stoves, private bath, TV/VCR, CD players plus exquisite views. McCaffrey House was designed and built by your hosts, Michael and Stephanie McCaffrey. They had one essential theme in mind - warmth and comfort. General gathering areas are spacious and tastefully decorated, with a large collection of furniture and art acquired by Michael and Stephanie during their travels. All appointments have such a welcoming touch that they extend an invitation to come often and stay a while.

Member Since 2004

Rooms/Rates
8 Rooms. $140/$175

Cuisine
Awaken to the aroma of fresh brewed coffee - imported from Costa Rica. Relax in the beautifully decorated dining room for a full country breakfast, prepared by Stephanie McCaffrey, a master of the culinary arts. Enjoy the warmth of friendship along with views of the pristine forest, diverse birds and wildlife, rays of sunshine or snowflakes in flight.

Nearest Airport(s)
Sacramento Airport

Directions
McCaffrey House is located 11 miles east of Sonora and one-half mile above the East Twain Harte exit on Highway 108. 3 hour drive from San Francisco; 2 from Sacramento; 3 from Monterey.

"McCaffrey House - set off the main road, among trees that reached halfway to heaven ... you could leave the windows open and hear the trees whisper. It's a great place!" Al Martinez, columnist - Los Angeles Times

Innkeepers/Owners
Peggy and Grover Mosley
Victorian Country Inn

Mobil ★★★
AAA ◆◆◆

Groveland Hotel

www.srinns.com/grovelandhotel
18767 Main Street, P.O. Box 289, Groveland, CA 95321
800-273-3314 • 209-962-4000 • Fax 209-962-6674
guestservices@groveland.com

Rooms/Rates
17 Rooms. Decadent Suites: $225
Truly Decadent Suites: $265/$275
Really Nice Rooms: $135
Extremely Nice Rooms: $145/$155
Luxury Rooms: $165/$175
Rates are for 2 guests. Additional guests: $25
Pets Welcome - $10/pet per night includes Treats, use of Bowls and Granny blanket.

Cuisine
Guest Breakfast Buffet, Lunch for Groups and Full Service Dining, open to the public. Full Service Saloon and Wine List.

Nearest Airport(s)
Approximately 2.5 hours from Sacramento (SAC), San Francisco (SFO) or E45.

Directions
Located East of San Francisco, and South of Sacramento, on Highway 120.

Drive to Yosemite 24/7 - take a picnic and great bottle of wine from our restaurant. We have it all – Tuolumne Whitewater Rafting, a US Top 10 River, over 100 species of wildflowers, hiking, golf, tennis, stables, swim at Rainbow Pool or discover God's Bath on the Clavey River. Four seasons - Spring, with songbirds, incredible flowers and North America's tallest waterfall. Summer's roses, hydrangeas, lavender and balmy evenings to herald Fall's brilliant color and crispness in the air. Winter temps suggest hot cider, cozy fireplaces, toboggans, snowshoes and skis. Lots of wildlife - deer, squirrel, possum, skunk, raccoon, fox, coyote, cougar, and an occasional bear. Feathered species offer a wide variety of birds, and an occasional eagle. *Country Inns* Magazine named it one of the US Top 10 Inns, and *Sunset* Magazine called it 'One of the West's Best Inns.' Romantic parlour dining with fireplace, music, fresh flowers and candlelight. Upscale linens surround your warm, snuggly bed. We provide the ambience – you create the memories! A perfect venue for weddings, receptions, family reunions, company parties, etc. Our Conference Room for 15 people, has a 1900 Belgian conference table. Full service business amenities and free wireless access.

Member Since 2005

"Most Comfortable Bed I've EVER slept in." - Bill Bruzy - *New Texas* Magazine
"The cuisine is exquisite." - Elizabeth Kennedy - *SF Chronicle*

Cypress Inn on Miramar Beach

www.srinns.com/cypressmiramar
407Mirada Road, Half Moon Bay, CA 94019
800-83-BEACH • 650-726-6002 • Fax 650-712-0380
CypressInn@innsbythesea.com

Manager
Dave Rooker

Contemporary Waterside Breakfast Inn

This contemporary beach house is just steps from a five-mile stretch of white sand beach. Breathtaking ocean views, a palette of colors from the sea, sky, and earth, Mexican folk art and hand-carved wooden animals contribute to the colorful celebratory embrace of nature. Natural Pine and wicker furniture, saltillo-tiled floors, dramatic skylights and gentle seabreezes create a peaceful serenity. Fall asleep listening to the soothing sounds of the ocean. The 'Beach House,' behind the main Inn, has four luxurious rooms named after area beaches. Newly built are 6 more beautiful oceanfront rooms in the 'Lighthouse' addition. Some rooms with two-person tubs.

Rooms/Rates
17 Rooms $180/$375 (K,Q,T featherbeds); 1 Suite $350/$420. Most have decks with full ocean view, fireplaces, TV & phone.

Cuisine
Complimentary full gourmet breakfast cheerfully brought to your room at requested time or join others in the dining room. Evening wine and hors d'oeuvres and homemade dessert served fireside in the lobby. Conferences catered.

Nearest Airport(s)
San Francisco International

Directions
One-half hour drive S of San Francisco off Hwy 1 between Princeton Harbor and Half Moon Bay. From Hwy 1 take Medio towards the ocean. Last building on the L, on Miramar Beach.

Member Since 2000

"Peaceful elegance, view and sound of the waves are magical, unspoiled simplicity."

Babbling Brook Inn

www.srinns.com/babbling
1025 Laurel Street, Santa Cruz, CA 95060
800-866-1131 • 831-427-2437 • Fax 831-427-2457
BabblingBrook@innsbythesea.com

Manager
Claire De Vos

Traditional Contemporary
In Town Breakfast Inn

AAA ◆◆◆

Rooms/Rates
13 Rooms, $179/$295. All rooms with fireplace, TV, phone. Some with 2-person tubs. Calm Season rates: $129/$205. Open year-round.

Cuisine
Complimentary full country breakfast, afternoon tea and cookies, evening wine and cheese. Wine, champagne and non-alcoholic beverages available.

Nearest Airport(s)
San Jose, San Francisco

Directions
Hwy17 take exit to Hwy1(N) continue on Mission St to L on Laurel 1.5 blocks down hill on R. From (S) on Hwy1, turn R on Laurel 1.5 blks on R.

Cascading waterfalls, a meandering brook, and a romantic garden gazebo grace an acre of gardens, pines and redwoods surrounding this urban Inn, yet it is close to dining, shops, Pacific Garden Mall, and the beach/boardwalk. Built in 1909 on the foundation of a 1790 gristmill and 2000-year-old Indian fishing village, it's on the National Register of Historic Places. Rooms in Country French decor with some jet bathtubs, private entrances, and decks overlooking the gardens and babbling brook. All rooms have fireplaces. The gazebo is popular for weddings. The newest addition, the Artists Retreat, has a large deck with recessed hot tub overlooking the beautiful gardens and brook.

Member Since 1990

"Cascading waterfalls, a meandering brook and a romantic garden gazebo grace an acre of gardens, pines and redwoods surrounding this secluded urban inn."

Inn at Depot Hill

www.srinns.com/depothill
250 Monterey Ave., Capitola-by-the-Sea, CA 95010
800-572-2632 • 831-462-3376 • Fax 831-462-3697
DepotHill@innsbythesea.com

Manager
Claire DeVos

Elegant Greek Revival
Waterside Breakfast Inn

Mobil ★★★★
AAA ◆◆◆◆

Near a sandy beach in a quaint, Mediterranean-style resort, this award-winning Inn was named one of the top 10 Inns in the country. A decorator's delight, upscale rooms resemble different parts of the world: Cote d' Azur, a chic auberge in St. Tropez; Paris, a romantic French hideaway; Portofino, an Italian coastal villa; Kyoto, classic Japanese; and Sissinghurst, a traditional English garden room, to name a few. All rooms have Fireplaces, TV/VCR, stereos, phones and modem connections, robes, featherbeds, fresh roses, and in-room coffee/tea. Most have private hot tubs in private garden patios. Complimentary gourmet breakfast, wine with hors d'oeuvres, and homemade desserts.

Rooms/Rates
12 Rooms $230/$385. Calm Season $185/$275

Cuisine
Full gourmet breakfast cheerfully delivered to your room, at the time you request, or dine with others in the dining room or patio. Afternoon wine & hors d'oeuvres; evening Port/Sherry/tea and homemade dessert. All complimentary, prepared by our chef. Seltzer with syrups and other non-alcoholic beverages available.

Nearest Airport(s)
San Jose

Directions
From Hwy. 1 exit Park Ave., turning towards the ocean for 1 mile. L on Monterey Ave & immediately L into Inn's driveway (on corner of Park & Monterey). Look for white columns & flags (weather permitting).

Member Since 1992

"The epitome of elegance, romance and comfort."
McCormack Publishing

Old Monterey Inn

www.srinns.com/monterey
500 Martin Street, Monterey, CA 93940
800-350-2344 • 831-375-8284 • Fax 831-375-6730
omi@oldmontereyinn.com

Innkeeper/Owner
Patricia Valletta

Elegant In Town Inn

AAA ♦♦♦♦

Rooms/Rates
Cottage, 3 Suites & 6 Rooms w/sitting areas - fireplaces, spa tubs, pvt. baths, feather beds, DSL, TV/VCR, TEL. $270/$450. Open year-round.

Cuisine
Evening wine and hors d'oeuvres. Extaordinary restaurants nearby. Port and fresh fruit...

Nearest Airport(s)
Monterey Airport - 10 min.
San Jose Airport - 1 hr. 15 mins.
SFO - 2 hrs. 30 mins.

Directions
SOUTH on Hwy 1: exit Soledad-Munras Ave, cross Munras Ave, R on Pacific. Go about 1 mile, L on Martin St. NORTH on Hwy 1: exit Munras Ave, L to Soledad, R on Pacific, L on Martin. Continue on Martin St 1 long block, Inn is on the R.

'The level of service and accommodations here would rival most any inn or hotel we've visited,' says *The San Francisco Chronicle.* Set amidst an acre of spectacular gardens on a quiet, oak studded Monterey hillside, the Old Monterey Inn exudes romance and warmth. The 1929 half-timbered English Tudor Inn's rooms all overlook the uniquely beautiful gardens. Inside, guests find the attention to detail, which is the hallmark of the Inn--memorably fluffy featherbeds and 24-hour access to mineral waters, juices, tea and coffee. A full gourmet breakfast is served bedside or in our Heritage dining room, or, weather permitting, in our gardens. The owners imbue every element with the extra touches that help the Inn achieve near perfection. Recommended by prestigious Harper's *Hideaway Report* and Conde Nast Gold List.

Member Since 1993

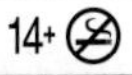

"Old Monterey Inn: elegance, comfort & room decors that read like poetry" - Discovery Magazine "Voted one of California's Top 10 Inns" - ILoveInns.com

Martine Inn

www.srinns.com/martine
255 Oceanview Boulevard, Pacific Grove, CA 93950
800-852-5588 • 831-373-3388 • Fax 831-373-3896
don@martineinn.com

Innkeeper/Owner
Don Martine
General Manager
Lori Anderson

Elegant Victorian Waterside Breakfast Inn

Mobil ★★★
AAA ◆◆◆

Just blocks from Monterey's bustling Cannery Row lies a 24-room Victorian villa that *Bon Appetit* considers "one of the 8 best B&Bs in historic homes" and *Conde Nast Traveler* calls a "spectacular place for a romantic getaway." Welcome to the Martine Inn, built in the 1890s as a lavish private residence just 90 minutes south of San Francisco. Today it's a meticulously renovated resort steps from the water's edge, where every fixture and furnishing is an authentic Victorian-era antique, and every room, many with fireplaces, claw foot tubs and/or ocean views, has its own name and unique decor. Two sitting rooms afford priceless views of the bay, and other inn extras include a library, piano, game room replete with a 1917 nickelodeon, spa and Don Martine's collection of vintage MG autos. Miles of coastal hiking and biking are accessible literally at the inn's front door. All the attractions of California's magnificent Monterey Peninsula are nearby, including the Monterey Bay Aquarium, Monarch butterfiles, and Point Pinos Lighthouse.

Member Since 1992

Rooms/Rates
24 Rooms, 4 Suites. $135/$360.

Cuisine
Morning brings a full breakfast on a background of silver, crystal and lace, while evening presents wine and hot hors d'oeuvres. Group lunches and dinners prearranged from 20 to 50, Victorian dinners up to 12 courses.

Nearest Airport(s)
Monterey - 5 miles
San Jose - 70 miles

Directions
Hwy 1 to Pebble Beach Pacific Grove exit. Turn on to Hwy 68 toward Pacific Grove. Stay in R lane on Forest Ave. at the water turn R on Ocean View Blvd turn R at 255 Ocean View Blvd.

"One of the 10 Most Romantic Inns in the U.S." - *Vacations* Magazine "It's the kind of place where starry eyed young lovers dream of getting married." - *San Francisco Magazine*

Innkeepers/Owners
Maurice and Risë Macaré

Elegant European B&B

Oak Hill Manor

www.srinns.com/oakhillmanor
12345 Hampton Court, Atascadero, CA 93422
866-625-6267 • 805-462-9317 • Fax 805-462-0331
macare@oakhillmanorbandb.com

Rooms/Rates
8 Suites, $155/$275

Cuisine
Enjoy full breakfast choices including Eggs Benedict, Orange French Toast, Swiss quiche, Greek Omelette or Zuchini Pancakes.

Nearest Airport(s)
San Luis Obispo County Airport, 30 minutes

Directions
Oak Hill Manor is located halfway between San Francisco and Los Angeles. Take Highway 101 to the Santa Barbara Road exit. Turn East on Santa Barbara Road and drive approximately 1/2 mile passing the Nazarene Church on the left and two stop signs. Turn right at our sign onto Hampton Court. Oak Hill Manor is the large Tudor estate on the hill.

Oak Hill Manor Bed and Breakfast estate sits graciously on an oak studded hill with a sunset view of the Santa Lucia Mountains and our newly planted Zinfandel vineyard. Eight elegant suites, each styled after a different European country decor, await you. Fireplaces, whirlpool tubs and private decks enhance the ambiance of many suites. Enjoy a quiet conversation in the parlor; play a game of pool or darts in the pub; read a book in the library; enjoy a beautiful sunset; relax on your balcony; share a bottle of champagne; or pamper yourself with a massage. We offer the opportunity to escape from your busy life, relax and unwind, renew your spirit, and enjoy all the charm and beauty the Central Coast has to offer. Relax in our Lincoln Town Car stretch limo as you visit the Paso Robles Wine Country or the Edna Valley Wine Trail. Hike or bike the many trails available in San Luis Obispo County; tour Hearst Castle; shop for antiques or just enjoy the ambiance and hospitality of our European styled B&B. Rediscover your Joie de Vivre!

Member Since 2005

"You have thought of every detail for comfort and pleasure ... truly a treasure that we will always remember!" "...the best B&B we have ever stayed at..."

J. Patrick House Bed & Breakfast Inn

www.srinns.com/jpatrickhouse
2990 Burton Drive, Cambria, CA 93428
800-341-5258 • 805-927-3812 • Fax 805-927-6759
jph@jpatrickhouse.com

Innkeepers/Owners
Ann O'Connor and John Arnott

Log Home & Carriage House Breakfast Inn

Mobil ★★★
AAA ◆◆◆

Country Elegance in Accommodations: Cambria's original - and still the finest - Bed and Breakfast Inn, nestled in the tall Monterey pines above Cambria's charming east village. As you enter the front door of this enchanting log home, the warmth of its embrace will welcome you. The aroma of freshly baked cookies, homemade granola, breads and muffins will transport you to a magical place. The main log home has one guest suite. Stroll through the passion vine covered arbor to the charming carriage house with seven additional "exquisitely appointed" guest rooms. Indulge in wine and hor d'oeuvres in the evening and "killer" chocolate chip cookies and cold milk before bedtime. Each morning a delicious full breakfast is served in the light-filled Garden Room. Enjoy exemplary guest services.

Rooms/Rates
8 Rooms. $165/$205

Cuisine
Enjoy a full gourmet breakfast in our Garden room. Fresh fruit, homemade granola, fresh plump raisins and delicious yogurt for starters. Main entrees such as, Vegetable strata, Blintzes with Raspberry Sauce, Chili Corn Soufflé and Stuffed French Toast with pure Maple syrup to name a few, change daily. Wine and hors d' oeuvres are served in the early evening and killer chocolate chip cookies and milk at bedtime.

Nearest Airport(s)
San Luis Obispo Airport

Directions
Midway between Los Angeles and San Francisco on the Central Coast of California. 6 Miles from Hearst Castle.

Member Since 2003

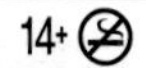   

"Best On the West Coast and One of the Top 15 B&B/Country Inns."
Inn Traveler Magazine

Innkeepers/Owners
Budi & Chris Kazali
General Manager
Christine Forsyth

Elegant Country Inn

AAA ◆◆◆◆

The Ballard Inn

www.srinns.com/ballardinn
2436 Baseline Avenue, Ballard, CA 93463
800-638-2466 • 805-688-7770 • Fax 805-688-9560
innkeeper@ballardinn.com

Rooms/Rates
15 Rooms, $215/$305. Closed Christmas Eve & Christmas Day.

Cuisine
French-Asian cuisine.

Nearest Airport(s)
Santa Barbara

Directions
From Hwy. 101, take Solvang exit, follow Route 246 E through Solvang to Alamo Pintado; turn L. Drive 3 miles to Baseline Ave. turn R. The Inn is on your R.

Voted one of America's Top Ten Most Romantic Inns, our comfortably elegant 4 diamond Country Inn is nestled among vineyards and orchards in the charming township of Ballard. Each of the 15 rooms posesses its own special charm and character reflecing local history. Many of our rooms have fireplaces, creating an especially romantic retreat. Borrow our bicycles and take one of our picnic lunches for an adventurous tour of the Santa Barbara wine country. A tasting of local wines, hors d'oeuvres and a full breakfast are included in your stay. The acclaimed Ballard Inn Restaurant features French-Asian cuisine in an intimate dining room complete with a magnificent marble fire place. It is open to the public Wednesday-Sunday.

Member Since 1993

The West's Best Small Inns/Sunset Magazine
Top 10 Most Romantic Inn/American Historic Inns

Santa Ynez Inn

www.srinns.com/santaynezinn
3627 Sagunto St., Santa Ynez, CA 93460
800-643-5774 • 805-688-5588 • Fax 805-686-4294
info@santaynezinn.com

Innkeeper/Owner
Douglas Ziegler
General Manager/
Innkeeper
Rick Segovia

Victorian Breakfast Inn

Our Wine Country Getaway awaits in 14 individually decorated rooms and junior suites. Accommodations feature unique antiques, queen or king-sized beds with Frette linens, remote-controlled gas fireplaces and whirlpool tubs in deluxe marble baths. Most rooms offer a private balcony or patio to savor the beauty and serenity of the Santa Ynez Valley.

Take advantage of all that Santa Barbara County has to offer, from wine tasting and antique shopping, to Glider rides and Jeep tours. There's something for everyone in Santa Ynez. After a day of Southern California sightseeing adventures, you may wish to unwind in the heated outdoor whirlpool, lounge on the sundeck, or take a leisurely stroll through the gardens of the Inn. Whatever your needs--whether you wish to arrange for wine tasting tours, shopping, dining, glider rides, bicycle rentals or transportation--our concierge service is eager to assist you.

Member Since 2004

Rooms/Rates
Standard Queen $265, Garden King $275, Deluxe Queen $315, Superior King $325, Deluxe King $365, Deluxe Double Queen $365, Junior Suite $425.

Cuisine
Full Gourmet breakfast, Evening Wine & Hors d'oeuvres and Evening Desserts.

Nearest Airport(s)
Santa Barbara Airport

Directions
From the North: Take 101 South to Highway 246. Take 246 East (left) to the town of Santa Ynez and turn left on Edison and right on Sagunto. From the South: Take 101 North to Highway 154. Take 154 over the San Marcos Pass to Highway 246 and make a L onto 246. R on Edison and R on Sagunto.

"What a delight to find one such a quality country Inn with such charm. We will return!"

Owners
Glyn & Linda Davies
Managing Partner
Janis Clapoff

Elegant Victorian
Bed & Breakfast Inn

AAA ◆◆◆◆◆

Simpson House Inn

www.srinns.com/simpsonhouse
121 East Arrellaga Street, Santa Barbara, CA 93101
800-676-1280 • 805-963-7067 • Fax 805-564-4811
reservations@simpsonhouseinn.com

Rooms/Rates
6 Main House and 1 Garden Room $235/$475.
4 Old Barn Rooms $585/$615.
4 Garden Cottages $595/$605.
Open year-round.

Cuisine
Full vegetarian breakfast. Afternoon dessert tea. Mediterranean hors d'oeuvres buffet with local wine tasting each evening.

Nearest Airport(s)
Santa Barbara

Directions
From San Francisco - Mission St. exit, L. Anacapa St., R. Arrellaga St., L; From Los Angeles - Garden St. exit, R. Gutierrez St., L. Santa Barbara St., R. Arrellaga St., L.

This elegantly restored 1874 Historic Landmark Victorian Estate is the only Five Diamond Bed and Breakfast Inn in North America. The Inn is secluded within an acre of beautifully landscaped English gardens, yet just a five-minute walk from the historic downtown, restaurants, shopping, theater and a pleasant walk to the beach. Guestrooms and Cottages feature antiques, fine art and Oriental rugs. Fireplaces and whirlpool tubs are available. We serve a delicious full gourmet breakfast, to your room, in the gardens or our dining room. Afternoon dessert tea and lavish evening Mediterranean hors d'oeuvres and wine tasting are not to be missed. Additional complimentary amenities include full access to the Athletic Club a short distance from the Inn, bicycles, English croquet and a city Trolley tour. Our Concierge can arrange spa treatments in your guest room, tours of the wine country, whale watching or a host of other activities.

Member Since 1993

"The staff and Inn completely exceeded our expectations. We had a beautiful stay!"

Channel Road Inn

www.srinns.com/channelroad
219 W. Channel Road, Santa Monica, CA 90402
310-459-1920 • Fax 310-454-9920
info@channelroadinn.com

Owner
Susan Zolla
Innkeeper
Christine Marwell
Traditional Colonial
In Town Breakfast Inn

Mobil ★★★
AAA ◆◆◆

A surprise by the beach in the eclectic Los Angeles neighborhood of Rustic Canyon, the Channel Road Inn provides the comfortable elegance of a restored 1915 Santa Monica home and the timeless pleasure of a seashore retreat. Guests enter through the original polished oak doors. The living room is furnished in period antiques and arranged to highlight the Batchelder tiles surrounding the fireplace. The Inn's guest rooms and suites feature blue water or garden views, some with fireplaces or whirlpool tubs, others with sunny decks. All offer fine white linens and upscale amenities. Some of the city's best dining, shopping, and entertainment venues are within minutes of the Inn.

Member Since 2002

Rooms/Rates
14 rooms and suites; $225/$375.

Cuisine
Delicious hot breakfasts served buffet style or brought to your room or patio when you desire. Informal early evening gatherings with wine & hors d'oeuvres. Tea, lemonade and cookies.

Nearest Airport(s)
Los Angeles International (LAX)

Directions
From the #405 Freeway N or S, take the 10 Freeway W to Pacific Coast Hwy N. (becomes the coast highway going N when it meets the ocean). Continue N 1.8 mi. to stoplight for West Channel Road and Chautauqua - both streets come off the coast highway. Make a very hard R onto West Channel and proceed one block to 219 W. Channel Road; the Inn is the big blue house on the L.

"Please bottle whatever you do so I can remember the Channel Road Inn always."

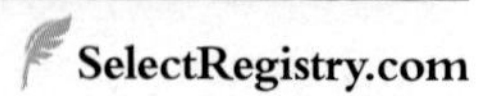

Innkeepers/Owners
Marjorie Bettenhausen Schmaehl & Harty Schmaehl

Elegant Waterside Inn

Mobil ★★★
AAA ◆◆◆

The Seal Beach Inn & Gardens

www.srinns.com/sealbeachinn
212 5th Street, Seal Beach, CA 90740
800-HIDEAWAY • 562-493-2416 • Fax 562-799-0483
hideaway@sealbeachinn.com

Rooms/Rates
23 Rooms. $140/$230; Penthouse $399. Includes lavish breakfast and evening tea, fresh flowers, fruit baskets, all day refreshments, robes, phones. Many rooms have fireplaces, Jacuzzis, skylights.

Cuisine
Lavish breakfasts w/Belgian waffles, quiche, fresh fruit platters, inn-made granola, breads, pastries, gourmet teas/coffee. Evening tea/light supper spread. Chocolate chip cookies. Walk/drive to many fine nearby restaurants. Inn dinners by advance arrangement.

Nearest Airport(s)
Long Beach, LAX, John Wayne

Directions
N or S 405 Freeway, exit Seal Beach Blvd. L 3 mi to Pacific Coast Hwy. R on PCH. L on 5th St, 2 blocks.

Internationally honored elegant Country Inn one block from Southern California beaches, in a charming seaside village. Caring staff, artistic, handsome, world class rooms and suites. Exquisite Tearoom, brass chandeliers, oriental carpets, fireplaces, Jacuzzis, fine art, flowers, pool, library, intimate garden nooks; a warm welcome to classic Mediterranean ambience. Brick courtyard, blue canopies, stately fountains, ornate antique streetlamps. The Inn radiates peaceful historic charm. Minutes from live theatre, museums, malls, golf, sports venues, harbor cruises, Disneyland, Universal Studio, Hollywood, Knotts, Old Town shops, pier, marina, Newport, Huntington, Long Beach.

Member Since 1981

 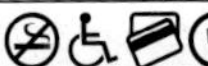   

"Serenity is The Seal Beach Inn. Magical, quaint, fabulous, relaxing. A celebration of life."

Casa Laguna Inn

www.srinns.com/casalaguna
2510 South Coast Highway, Laguna Beach, CA 92651
800-233-0449 • 949-494-2996 • Fax 949-494-5009
innkeeper@casalaguna.com

Innkeepers/Proprietors
Paul Blank & Francois Leclair

Historic Oceanview Breakfast Inn

AAA ◆◆◆

Voted "Best B&B in Orange County" for eight consecutive years by the OC Register. Terraced on a hillside amid tropic gardens and flower-splashed patios, the historic Casa Laguna Inn exudes an ambiance of bygone days when Laguna Beach was developing its reputation as an artists' colony and hideaway for Hollywood film stars. The mission style inn set below towering palms framing views of the blue Pacific invites you to slow your pace to that of another, less hurried era. The magnificent Palm Court and the ocean-view pool deck will enchant you with fountains and rare Catalina tiles. Two lovely beaches are a few minutes walk from the hotel.Victoria Beach offers a long stretch of white sand while Moss Point offers tide pools and coves. One and a half miles south of Main Beach, the inn is a short distance from the boutiques, pottery shops, and galleries for which Laguna Beach is famous. A Casa Laguna Spa treatment is an excellent way to enhance your stay at Casa Laguna. Guests are pampered, rejuvenated and renewed.

Member Since 2004

Rooms/Rates
15 Rooms, 5 suites and a Cottage: $160/$550. All rooms are air-conditioned and feature a nine-layer, deluxe bed, CD and DVD players. Some with private patios, jetted tubs and/or fireplaces.

Cuisine
Full gourmet breakfast and afternoon wine and hors d'oeuvres are included. Laguna Beach offers a variety of fine dining.

Nearest Airport(s)
Orange County - John Wayne, SNA

Directions
From I-5 N: Exit CA-1/Camino Las Ramblas to Beach Cities. Keep left at the fork; merge to CA-1/PCH for 6.7 miles. From I-5 S or I-405 S: Exit CA-133 S to Laguna Beach for 9 miles, then left onto CA-1/PCH for 1.75 miles.

"The perfect getaway! A charming and relaxing retreat. Marvelous setting with wonderful staff."

Innkeepers/Owners
The Straube Family
Traditional Village
Retreat/Lodge

Mobil ★★★
AAA ◆◆◆◆

Rooms/Rates
Cottage Rooms: $285,
Lodge Rooms: $205, Suite: $425.
Discounts midweek (R)

Cuisine
Full breakfast, afternoon hors d'oeuvres included, dinner served on selected nights, picnic lunches available. Excellent selection of beer & wine.

Nearest Airport(s)
San Diego International

Directions
60 mi. NE of SD. IS 15 north to Scripps Poway Pkwy, turn right (East). Approx. 12 mi, left on Hwy 67 (North). Hwy 67 becomes Hwy 78 in Ramona and continues straight into Julian through Santa Ysabel (22 mi.) In Julian, at the four way stop sign, continue straight. Orchard Hill Country Inn is up one block on the left.

Orchard Hill Country Inn

www.srinns.com/orchardhill
2502 Washington St., P.O. Box 2410, Julian, CA 92036
800-716-7242 • 760-765-1700 • Fax 760-765-0290
information@orchardhill.com

Orchard Hill Country Inn is reminiscent of America's great national park lodges. Secluded, this award-winning premiere inn is nestled in the heart of the Julian Historic District. Featuring hilltop vistas, a mountain spring, colorful native gardens and hiking trails leading to abandoned gold mines and vistas. Bicycles available. Julian is renown for birding, star gazing, hiking and nearby desert wildflower preserves. Cottages with porches have abundant amenities, TV/VCR, fireplaces; most have whirlpools. Our comfortable rooms and warm hospitality will delight you. Orchard Hill provides the ultimate in relaxation, memorable dining and is wonderfully romantic.

Member Since 1998

   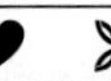  

Top 9 western lodges - *Sunset* Magazine
"Perfection is now more than a word."

The Bed & Breakfast Inn at La Jolla

www.srinns.com/innatlajolla
7753 Draper Avenue, La Jolla, CA 92037
800-582-2466 • 858-456-2066 • Fax 858-456-1510
bed+breakfast@innlajolla.com

Innkeeper/Owner
Marilouise Micuda

Historic Village
Breakfast Inn

This elegant historical inn is drenched in sunlight, draped in brilliant bouganvillia and kissed by mild ocean breezes. Located in one of the most beautiful seaside villages in the world, it is only steps to the best beaches and snorkeling in California, as well as the finest shops, restaurants, art galleries, and museums. The inn is central to the main attractions of San Diego, such as the Stephen Birch Aquarium, Sea World, Old Town, Wild Animal Park, and Mexico. After a fun-filled day, return to the peaceful respite of the inn, where, lulled by the melodious garden fountain and surrounded by lush greenery, you will have time to reflect and relax and savor the good life.

Member Since 2002

Rooms/Rates
14 Rooms $179/$359; 1 Suite $399. Rooms are deluxe, elegant cottage-style rooms with fresh flowers and fruit. Open year round.

Cuisine
Full candlelit breakfast. Gourmet entrees served with fresh fruit, muffins, scones, homemade granola topped with honey and vanilla-laced yogurt, rich coffee and exotic teas.

Nearest Airport(s)
San Diego International

Directions
From the South: I-5 N; exit La Jolla Parkway to Torrey Pines Rd. west, R on Prospect Place to Draper Ave., L on Draper. From the North: I-5 S; exit La Jolla Village Dr. West, L on Torrey Pines Rd., R on Prospect Place to Draper, L on Draper.

"Delighted we switched from the Hilton!"

Colorado

"The Centennial State"

Famous For: Gold Rush, Mile-High City, Mesa Verde, Cliff Dwellings, Rocky Mountains, Skiing, and Hiking

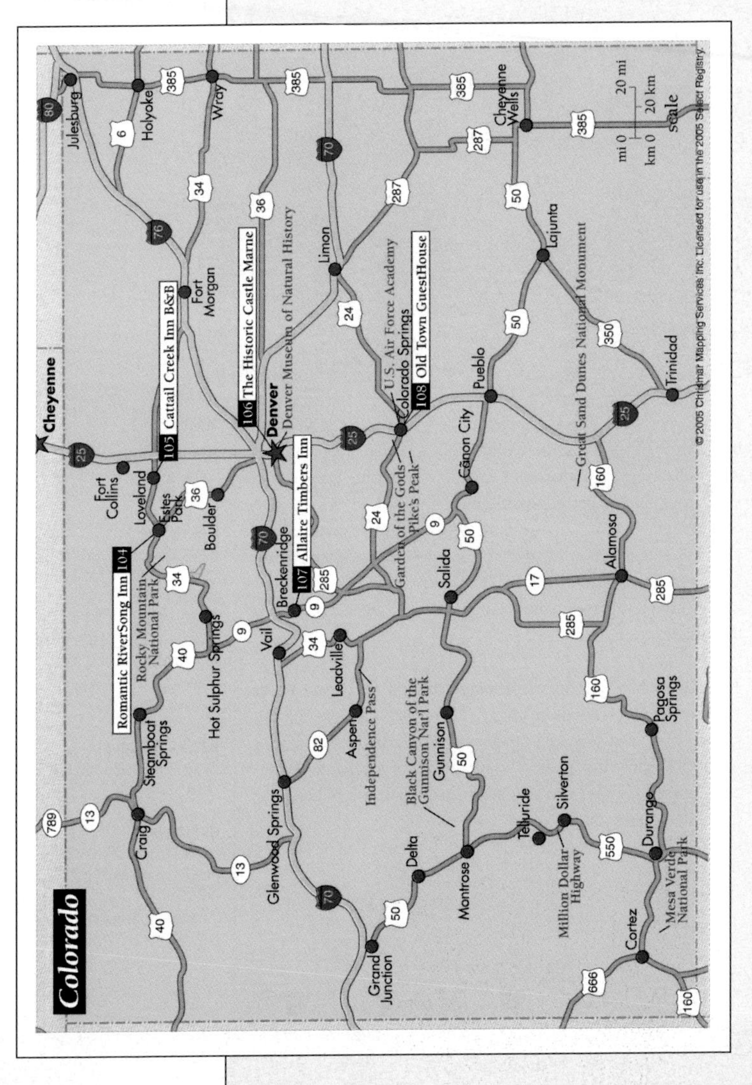

Romantic RiverSong Inn

www.srinns.com/romanticriversong
P.O. Box 1910, Estes Park, CO 80517
970-586-4666 • Fax 970-577-1336
romanticriversong@earthlink.net
www.romanticriversong.com

Innkeepers/Owners
Sue & Gary Mansfield

Traditional Mountain Retreat/Lodge

Mobil ★★★

Once every three days a couple chooses Romantic RiverSong Inn as their hideaway in the Colorado Rockies to elope. The inn is secluded on 27 wooded acres with towering Blue Spruces and Ponderosa pines, quiet ponds, hiking trails and tree swings. With only ten guest rooms, the inn has achieved a marvelous balance with its luxurious rooms (radiant heated floors, jetted tubs for two by a crackling fire) and nature. These lovely rooms are merely background to the mountain melodies of songbirds and a rushing mountain stream.

After a great hike in Rocky Mountain National Park come home to a relaxing "streamside massage." Then, later that evening enjoy our own chef prepared candlelight dinner by fireside. It's the warm hospitality that makes the memories of Romantic RiverSong linger long after you've gone from this little bit of heaven in the Colorado mountains.

Member Since 1987

Rooms/Rates
4 Rooms, $150/$175 B&B; 5 Cottage Suites, $225/$295 B&B. Tubs for 2; and marvelous packages online.

Cuisine
Evening dining is reserved for the first four couples that sign up for a marvelous five-course dinner by fireside. The tables are set with fine china and bone handle silver service on white lace linens, while softly in the background the sounds of jazz classics soothe your soul.

Nearest Airport(s)
Denver International, 1 hour & 45 minutes

Directions
Hwy 36 through Midtown of Estes, Hwy 36 to Mary's Lk Rd; L at Mary's Lk Rd; Go 1 bk Cross bridge. Turn R immediately; take country road to the end.

"Mountain Rose room was perfect for my husband's romantic surprise. Our room was the perfect choice to view the sunset over the snow-capped mountains!"

Innkeepers/Owners
Sue and Harold Buchman

Contemporary In Town Breakfast Inn

Mobil ★★★

Cattail Creek Inn B&B

www.srinns.com/cattailcreek
2665 Abarr Drive, Loveland, CO 80538
800-572-2466 • 970-667-7600 • Fax 970-667-8968
info@cattailcreekinn.com

Rooms/Rates
8 Rooms $115/$210. The inn's eight guest rooms have distinctive individual features and are situated for optimal privacy. Open year-round.

Cuisine
Full gourmet breakfast, snacks. B&B liquor license.

Nearest Airport(s)
Denver International Airport (most major carriers)

Directions
I-25 to exit 257B to US Hwy. 34 (W). Go (W) on US 34 for 6 miles to Taft. Turn R (N) on Taft and go 3/4 mile to 28th. Turn L on 28th and go one block to Abarr Drive. Turn L on Abarr Drive. Follow Abarr Dr (S)to the inn.

You will sense the feeling of casual elegance and warmth the minute you enter the grand foyer of this luxurious inn. From the finely crafted cherry woodwork, the golden-glazed hand-plastered walls to the fine art and the world-class bronze sculpture, this unique inn is truely an artistic experience! Located on the seventh tee box of the Cattail Golf Course, guests have peaceful views of Lake Loveland and majestic views of the Rocky Mountains. The Inn is across the lagoon from Columbine Art Gallery and is within walking distance to Benson Sculpture Park.

Member Since 2000

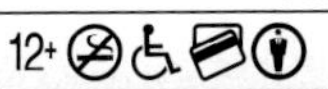

"Nothing Short of Heaven!! We've never been so relaxed nor felt so comfortable."

The Historic Castle Marne Inn

www.srinns.com/castlemarne
1572 Race Street, Denver, CO 80206
800-92-MARNE • 303-331-0621 • Fax 303-331-0623
info@castlemarne.com

Denver's grandest historic mansion, listed on the National & Local Historic Registers. Built in 1889, features handhewn lavastone exterior, hand-rubbed woods, balconies, four-story tower and stained glass Peacock Window. It all blends beautifully with period antiques and family heirlooms to create a charming Victorian atmosphere. Relax in the English garden beside the bubbling fountain. Full gourmet breakfast served in the original Dining Room. Complimentary Afternoon Tea served in the Parlour. Whirlpool spas and private outdoor hot tubs. Lunch & Private candlelight dinners by reservation. In Denver's Wyman Historic District. Near Museum of Nature and Science, Zoo, Botanic Gardens. Five minutes from Downtown and Cherry Creek Shopping area. Walking distance to many restaurants. Wedding and Honeymoon packages available. Small weddings and elopements a specialty. The AIA says, "Castle Marne is one of Denver's great architectural legacies." Free Parking. WIFI. Business meeting space.

Member Since 1991

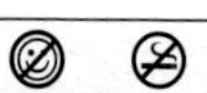

Innkeepers/Owners
The Peiker Family
Diane, Jim, Melissa, and Louie

Elegant Victorian
In Town Breakfast Inn

Mobil ★★★
AAA ◆◆◆

Rooms/Rates
9 Rooms, $105/$260
2 Suites with Jacuzzi tubs.
3 Rooms with private hot tubs for two.

Cuisine
Full gourmet breakfast
Elegant Private 6 course Dinners
Afternoon Tea and Luncheons

Nearest Airport(s)
Denver International

Directions
From DIA, Pena Blvd. To I-70 W to Quebec. L to 17th Ave. R to York St. L to 16th Ave. R 4 blocks to Race St. From mountains, I-70 E, R onto 6th Ave.Frwy(US 6) E to Josephine St. L to 16th Ave. L to Race St. From Colo Spgs, I-25 N exit R onto University Blvd N, R on 16th Ave. to Race St. From Cheyenne, I-25 S, exit R on Park Ave. R on Broadway, L on 17th Ave. R on Race St. one block to 16th Ave.

Winner of 2004 Condé Nast Johansens Top 3 Inns on the North American continent. "... they pay impeccable attention to details that excite the senses."

Innkeepers/Owners
Sue Carlson and Kendra Hall

Contemporary Western-Rustic Mountain Breakfast Inn

Mobil ★★★

Allaire Timbers Inn

www.srinns.com/allairetimbers
9511 Hwy. 9, South Main Street, P.O. Box 4653
Breckenridge, CO 80424
800-624-4904 Outside CO • 970-453-7530 • Fax 970-453-8699
info@allairetimbers.com

Rooms/Rates
8 Lodge Rooms, 2 Suites
$145/$400.

Cuisine
Hearty breakfast of homemade breads and sweets, fresh juices and fruits, the Inn's special recipe granola and changing menu of hot entrees. Evenings enjoy fresh baked cookies and seasonal herbal iced tea or hot citrus cider.

Nearest Airport(s)
Denver International

Directions
From Denver, I-70 West to exit 203. Hwy. 9 South to Breckenridge, through town past the traffic light at Boreas Pass Road (gas station on right). Take next Right, bear right into private parking lot.

This contemporary log B&B is the perfect Rocky Mountain Hideaway. Located on a tree filled bluff at the south end of historic Main Street, the Allaire Timbers offers 10 guest rooms, each with private bath and deck. Two elegant suites offer a special touch of romance with private hot tub and fireplace. Relax by a crackling fire in the log and beam Great Room. Enjoy the serenity of the tiled sunroom. Retreat to the reading loft, or unwind in the outdoor hot tub with spectacular mountain views. Just steps from downtown Victorian Breckenridge with its many and varied restaurants and shops. Access to the ski area and Breckenridge Riverwalk arts/music amphitheatre via the Free Ride town bus system. Featured in Arrington's Inn Traveler and CNN's Travel Guide.

Member Since 1995

"Hospitality, comfort and culinary magic."
Washington Post

Old Town Guest House

www.srinns.com/oldtownguesthouse
115 South 26th Street, Colorado Springs, CO 80904
888-375-4210 • 719-632-9194 • Fax 719-632-9026
Luxury@OldTown-GuestHouse.com

Innkeepers/Owners
Kaye and David Caster

Elegant In Town Breakfast Inn

AAA ◆◆◆◆

The three-story brick guesthouse, built as a B&B, is in perfect harmony with the 1859 period of the surrounding historic Old Town. The urban Inn offers upscale amenities for discerning adult leisure and business travelers. The foyer elevator allows the entire Inn to be accessible. The soundproof, uniquely decorated guestrooms have private porches overlooking Pikes Peak. Relax on the umbrella-covered patio for afternoon wine and hors d'oeuvres. The innkeepers are Pikes Peak area concierges. The elegance and hospitality of the Guest House was awarded AAA's Four Diamond Award for Excellence. Distinctive Inn of Colorado.

Rooms/Rates
8 Rooms, $99/$225, Corporate rates available, Private hot tubs, steam showers, fireplaces, TV/VCR, phones, wireless Internet, A/C, International videoconferencing in private conference room. Open year-round. Attractions: Pikes Peak, Garden of the Gods, Air Force Academy, Olympic Training Center, hiking, biking, fishing, Jeep & horse trips.

Cuisine
Evening wine and hors d'oeuvres, full sit-down breakfast.

Nearest Airport(s)
Colorado Springs

Directions
From I-25, exit 141 going West to 26th St. North on 26th, proceed 2 1/2 blocks, turn right into B&B's private parking lot.

Member Since 2001

"We loved being able to walk to 100 boutiques, galleries, and restaurants."

Connecticut

"The Constitution State"

Famous For: Inventors (Charles Goodyear, Elias Howe, Eli Whitney, Eli Terry), Inventions, Watchmaking, Typewriters, Insurance, Submarines

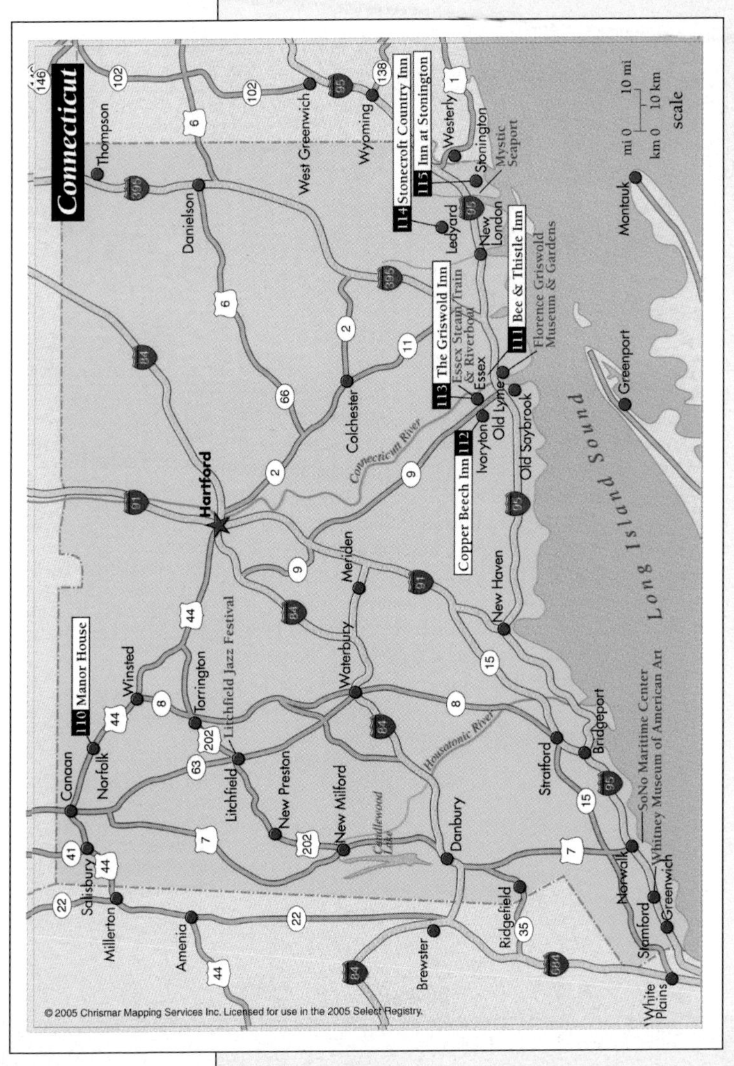

Manor House

www.manorhouse-norfolk.com
69 Maple Avenue, Norfolk, CT 06058
Toll Free 866-542-5690 • Fax 860-542-5690
innkeeper@manorhouse-norfolk.com

Innkeeper/Owner
L. Keith Mullins
Innkeeper/Manager
Lisa T. Auclair

Village Breakfast Inn

Surround yourself by Victorian Elegance in this 1898 Tudor Estate described by Gourmet as "Quite Grand", and designated "Connecticut's Most Romantic Hideaway" by the Discerning Traveler. Featured in National Geographic Traveler, Good Housekeeping's "Best Weekend Getaways", and listed as one of the top 25 Inns by American Historic Inns. All rooms offer views of the spacious grounds and perrenial gardens, are furnished with period antiques, and luxurious down comforters. Savour a full breakfast in the elegant dining room, relax by the barronial fireplace in the living room, or read a book in the library, all adorned with Tiffany windows and architectual detail. Located at the foot of the Berkshires, travlers can enjoy an array of outdoor activities, shopping, summer theatre, and music festivals.

Rooms/Rates
8 Rooms, 1 Suite, $110/$235. Four rooms offer wood or gas fireplaces, 3 with whirlpools, and two with private balconies.

Cuisine
Full country breakfast. Complimentary coffee, hot or iced tea, and hot chocolate available all day, glassware and refrigerator also available.

Nearest Airport(s)
Bradley International

Directions
NYC: I-84 E to exit for Rte. 8 N in Waterbury. At terminus of highway in Winsted take Rte. 44W R to Norfolk. Boston: I-84 W to exit for Rte. 4 Farmington to Rte. 179 to Rte. 44W to Norfolk.

Member Since 2000

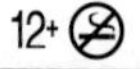

"Connecticut's Most Romantic Hideaway"
The Discerning Traveler

Chef and Proprietors
Philip and Marie Abraham
Innkeeper/Sommelier
Jeffrey T. Hamill
Traditional Village Inn

Bee and Thistle Inn

www.srinns.com/beeandthistle
100 Lyme Street, Old Lyme, CT 06371
800-622-4946 • 860-434-1667 • Fax 860-434-3402
innkeeper@beeandthistleinn.com

Rooms/Rates
11 Rooms, $130/$239; All private baths, AC, 1 with fireplace; Full breakfast with hot entrees included; Seasonal midweek rates, packages with area attractions available.

Cuisine
Contemporary American "menu worthy of nobility." As "if Laura Ashley had married Julia Child." -*Zagat.* Intimate spaces offer candle-lit dining overlooking gardens with live jazz duo on Friday, harp on Saturday. Member of Sommelier Society of America.

Nearest Airport(s)
Hartford (BDL)
Providence (PVD)

Directions
I-95 S exit 70 turn R off ramp to 3rd house on L – I-95N L off ramp to 2nd light, turn R to end of road, turn L, 3rd house on L

This lovely 1756 Inn is located along the Lieutenant River in the Historic District of Old Lyme, neighboring the Florence Griswold Museum - Home of American Impressionism. Its English gardens, sunlit porches, fireplaces, beautifully carved staircase, canopied and 4-poster beds, artisanal quilts and furnishings reflect a gracious lifestyle. Widely commended for its cuisine and wine list, it has been voted the Best Restaurant and "Most Romantic Place to Dine in Connecticut" for over a decade by readers of *Connecticut Magazine.* Once again the 2005 *Yankee Magazine* Connecticut Editor's Choice, "The inn is a perennial favorite, thanks not only to the old-fashioned hospitatlity and outstanding American cuisine but also to its well-earned reputation as one of Connecticut's most romantic spots along the shore."

Member Since 1984

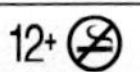

"I am grateful to your staff for all that you did to help this be a wonderful memory."

The Copper Beech Inn

www.srinns.com/copperbeech
46 Main Street, Ivoryton, Essex, CT 06442
888-809-2056 • 860-767-0330 • Fax 860-767-7840
info@CopperBeechInn.com

Proprietors
Ian S. Phillips
Barbara C. Phillips

Elegant Country Hotel

Mobil ★★★★
AAA ◆◆◆◆

Selected as *"The Best Country Inn"* in Connecticut by the readers of *Connecticut Magazine*, for the past two years, the Copper Beech Inn is minutes from the Connecticut River and Long Island Sound, and is just a 2-hour drive from either New York or Boston. Lovingly restored over the past three years, the period antiques, Oriental rugs, and richly textured fabrics bring comfort and classic European sophistication to this grand estate. Elegant guest rooms & suites with oversize beds feature Italian marble bathrooms and air-jet thermo-masseur tubs. The highly acclaimed AAA ◆◆◆◆ restaurant was named the *"Best Overall"* in the state by the readers of *Connecticut Magazine* in 2005. It features extraordinary food and a *Wine Spectator* award-winning wine list with over 400 selections. Andrew Harper's *Hideaway Report* selected the inn as one of the *"The Best in New England"* and, *The New York Times* said in a recent review "The Copper Beech Inn is a lovely example of what Americans look for in a three or four-star country inn ... the wine list is pretty spectacular ... the dining experience always marvelous."

Member Since 2003

Rooms/Rates
13 Rooms including 2 suites $150/$395 Full Breakfast. Open Year-Round. All w/private baths.

Cuisine
French with a contemporary flair. Select from an extraordinary menu and 400 selection award-winning wine list. "Worth the 2-hour drive from New York & Boston alone" *Boston Magazine.* "Crystal sparkles, silver shines, Oriental rugs glow on polished floors, antiques & masses of fresh flowers set the scence for the flawlessly elegant dining" *Connecticut Magazine.*

Nearest Airport(s)
Hartford 45 mins
Boston 2 hours
New York 2 hours

Directions
I-95 to Exit 69 to Route 9. Exit 3. Left off ramp. 1.5 mi on Left.

"Everything was perfect, from the warm hospitatity to the gorgeous flowers to the delicious food to the charming service."

The Griswold Inn

www.srinns.com/griswold
36 Main Street, Essex, CT 06426
860-767-1776 • Fax 860-767-0481
griswoldinn@snet.net

Innkeeper/Owner
Douglas Paul
General Manager
Alan A. Barone

Traditional Village Inn

Rooms/Rates
Seasonal Rates. 14 Guest Rooms, $100/$220 B&B;
16 Suites $160/$370 B&B.
Open year-round.

Cuisine
Complimentary continental breakfast for inn guests. Lunch, dinner, Sunday Hunt Breakfast. Authentic American Cuisine featuring New England favorites and inspired originals served in historic inn dining rooms. "Small" plates served in Wine Bar. Full service, award-winning Tap Room.

Nearest Airport(s)
Hartford's Bradley Airport - 1 hour
Boston, JFK

Directions
I-91 S to exit 22 S (left-hand exit). Rte. 9 S to exit 3 Essex. I-95 (N&S) to exit 69 to Rte. 9 N to exit 3 Essex. Two hours from New York and Boston.

This 1776 landmark is located in the "storybook" village of Essex, selected as the Best Small Town in America. The Connecticut River Valley, in which Essex is situated, has been designated one of the world's "Last Great Places" by the Nature Conservancy. Mere steps from the Connecticut River, the Inn's connection with the sea is apparent throughout. Filled with brass bells and binnacles, the 'Gris' also houses a renowned maritime art collection. In its historic Tap Room you'll find a long-standing tradition of sea chanteys, banjo and more: live entertainment nightly. The Inn also includes a stunning Wine Bar featuring a small plate menu concept and an extensive selection of wines. Riverboat cruises, antiquing, hiking, museums and historic homes are just outside the door, while Mystic Seaport and Aquarium, Goodspeed Theatre, Foxwoods and Mohegan Sun casinos and entertainment complexes are within easy reach.

Member Since 1974

"The hospitable 'Gris' retains a place of honor as an American treasure."

Stonecroft Country Inn

www.srinns.com/stonecroft
515 Pumpkin Hill Road, Ledyard, CT 06339
800-772-0774 • 860-572-0771 • Fax 860-572-9161
innkeeper@stonecroft.com

Relax in quiet country elegance on an 1807 sea captain's six-acre estate, only ten minutes from Mystic Seaport, Foxwoods and Mohegan Sun casinos. Ancient stone walls and lush green lawns surround the Inn, consisting of The Main House, a sunny Georgian colonial, and The Grange, our recently converted 19th century barn. Romantic guestooms feature French, English and American country decor, with fireplaces, whirlpools and heated towel bars, television and internet access. Pamper yourself with an on-site massage, and savor an exquisite dinner fireside in our elegant granite-walled restaurant or the candlelit garden terrace. Open year-round.

Member Since 2002

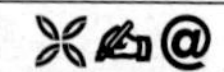

"Dreamy, cozy, luxurious."
Zagat Food Rating 27

Owners
Joan R. & Lynn E. Egy

Elegant Country Inn

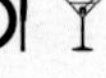

Rooms/Rates
4 Rooms Main House: AC, 3 with fireplace; 4 Deluxe Rooms Grange: AC, gas fireplace, TV, 2-person whirlpool; 2 Suites Grange: AC, gas fireplace, TV, bidet, 2-person whirlpool, walk-in shower. All rooms $200/$400. King, Queen beds.

Cuisine
Full country breakfast included. Dinner in the Grange Dining Room or on the terrace with contemporary American cuisine. Classical guitarist plays Monday and Saturday nights. Full service bar and extensive wine list.

Nearest Airport(s)
TF Green (Providence)

Directions
I-95 N: Exit 89, L off ramp, straight 3.75 miles. I-95 S: Exit 89, R off ramp, straight 3.5 miles.

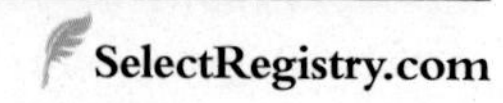

Innkeeper/Owner
William Griffin
General Managers
Susan Irvine
Anne Starzec

Historic Village
Breakfast Inn

Inn at Stonington

www.srinns.com/innatstonington
60 Water Street, Stonington, CT 06378
860-535-2000 • Fax 860-535-8193
www.innatstonington.com

Rooms/Rates
18 Rooms. Seasonal rates $135/$435. Open Year Round.

Cuisine
Continental breakfast served. Fresh baked breakfast breads, asst muffins, bagels,croissants, fresh fruit.

Nearest Airport(s)
T.F. Green, Prov. RI

Directions
North on I-95 Exit 91 turn right at the bottom of ramp. Proceed 1/2 mile and turn left on North Main St. Proceed to stoplight & cross US Rt. 1. At 1st stop turn left. At next stop, take a right onto Water St. Proceed over bridge, bear left and travel approx. 6/10 ths of a mile to 60 Water St. South on I-95, turn left at bottom of ramp. Use same dir. as above.

Named by *Travel + Leisure* as Inn of the Month, this newly constructed 18 room inn is located in the heart of Stonington Borough, one of the last untouched and 'historic' villages in New England. Relax in the privacy of your room, snuggled in front of your fireplace or take a luxurious bath in the soaking Jacuzzi tub. Public rooms include a top floor sitting room overlooking the Harbor, intimate bar with adjoining breakfast room, a cozy living room, and a well equipped gym. During the day stop by one of the local wineries, visit downtown Mystic, or simply take a stroll down Water Street and enjoy the specialty shops and some of the finest antiques in the area. Each evening join us for complimentary wine and cheese before walking to dinner at one of four fabulous restaurants in the village. Area attractions: small beach within walking distance, Mystic Seaport, Mystic Aquarium, Mohegan Sun and Foxwood Casinos, Watch Hill beaches. Come see what *CT Magazine* and *Coastal Living* consider one of New England's most romantic Inns.

Member Since 2005

14+    

"There's surely more than one kind of romance in this world, but Stonington Village – and The Inn at Stonington – seem to have most of them covered."

Delaware

"The First State"

Famous For: Historic Brandywine Valley—Museums and Gardens, Du Pont Family Mansions, Beaches, Fishing, Wildlife, Farmland, Bird-watching, Nascar races, and No-sales-tax shopping.

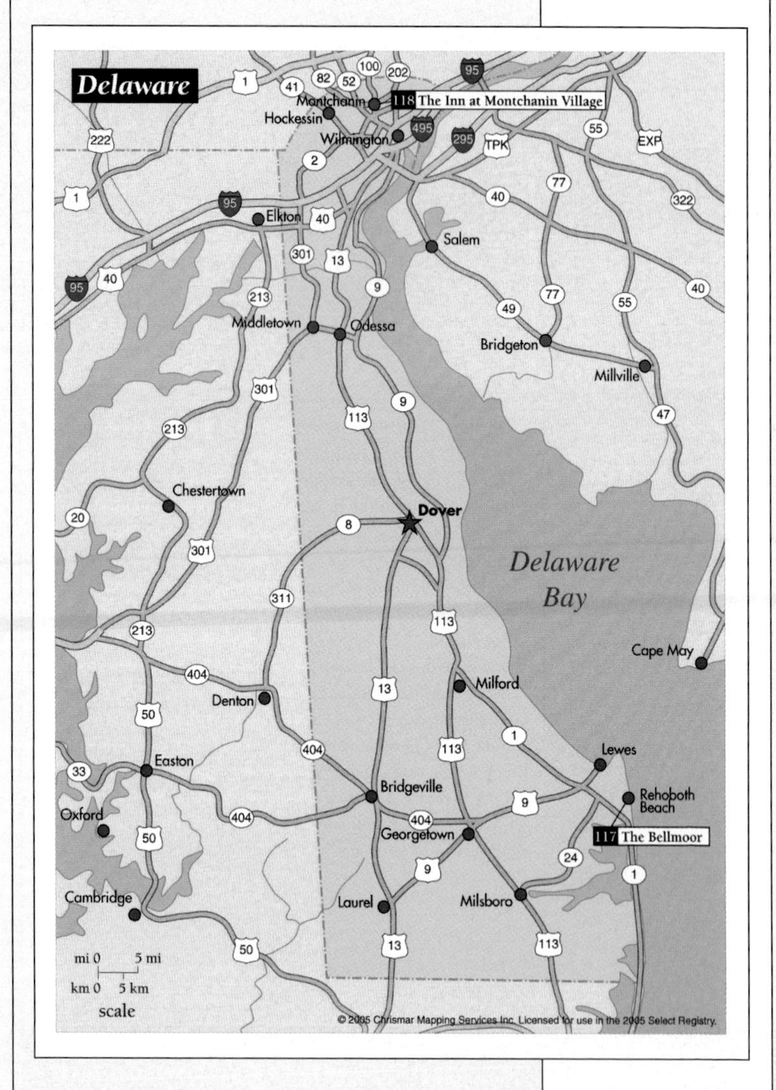

Proprietors
Moore Family
General Manager
Chad Moore
Elegant In-Town
Breakfast Inn

The Bellmoor

www.srinns.com/bellmoor
6 Christian Street, Rehoboth Beach, DE 19971
800-425-2355 • 302-227-5800 • Fax 302-227-0323
info@thebellmoor.com

Rooms/Rates
55 rooms, $105/$395 B&B. 23 suites, $150/$550 B&B; suites include marble bath, fireplace, whirlpool, wet bar. Adult concierge floor available. Rates change seasonally. Packages available, see website or call. Open Year Round.

Cuisine
Full country breakfast in Garden Room or in garden. Afternoon refreshments. 24 hour coffee service. Many fine dining options within walking distance. Entire property non-smoking.

Nearest Airport(s)
Philadelphia

Directions
Downtown Rehoboth Beach, residential setting 2 blocks from the ocean. See website or call for detailed directions.

Quiet moments in the garden...sunrise on the beach...the crackle of the fire in the Jefferson Library...a leisurely walk to unique boutique shopping and fine dining restaurants...a favorite book in the Sunroom. Our newly expanded Day Spa offers over 30 services to restore and rejuvenate body and spirit. Whether you choose a sea-weed wrap, hot stone pedicure or a soothing springtime facial, you can leave the world behind and experience refined relaxation and well-being. Additional complimentary services: concierge, bellman, high speed Internet access, wireless access on first floor and in garden, guest computer room, two pools, hot tub, fitness room. Enjoy complete relaxation in our beautifully appointed accommodations of unsurpassed comfort combining the warm, residential feel of a B&B with the efficient, professional service of a small European hotel.

Member Since 2004

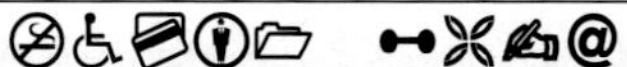

"...like visiting the seaside manor of a longtime friend."

The Inn at Montchanin Village

www.srinns.com/montchanin
Rte 100 & Kirk Road, P.O. Box 130, Montchanin, DE 19710
800-269-2473 • 302-888-2133 • Fax 302-888-0389
inn@montchanin.com

Innkeeper/Owner
Dan and Missy Lickle
General Manager
Jacques Amblard
Elegant Village Inn

Mobil ★★★

Listed on the National Historic Register, it was once a part of the Winterthur Estate and was named for Alexandria de Montchanin, grandmother of the founder of the Du Pont Gunpowder Company. One of the few remaining villages of its kind, the settlement was home to laborers who worked at the nearby Du Pont powder mills. In eleven carefully restored buildings dating from 1799 to 1910, there are 28 richly furnished guest rooms and suites appointed with period and reproduction furniture. The Inn's renowned Krazy Kat's Restaurant, once the village blacksmith shop, is known as much for its creative cuisine as its whimsical décor. Krazy Kat's and The Inn are rated Mobil ★★★★.

Member Since 2002

Rooms/Rates
The 28 elegant rooms and suites from $169 to $375. Marble baths, nightly turndown, New York Time daily newsppaper and imported linens. Open year-round.

Cuisine
Krazy Kat's Restaurant is part of the Inn. Eclectic continental cuisine, specializing in local ingredients. Private dining rooms available for groups of 10-40.

Nearest Airport(s)
Philadelphia International

Directions
From I-95 N or S: Exit 7 (Delaware Ave.). Follow Rte. 52 N (Pennsylvania Ave.) for 2.2 miles. Turn R onto Rte. 100 N, continue through 2 traffic lights. At the 3rd light, make a R, then a quick L into the parking lot. (Registration in barn).

"...from the gardens, to the elegant rooms, to the antiques and imported linens-no detail has been missed."

"The Nation's Capital"

Famous For: The White House, the Capitol, Arlington Cemetery, Cherry Festival, the Smithsonian, Washington Monument

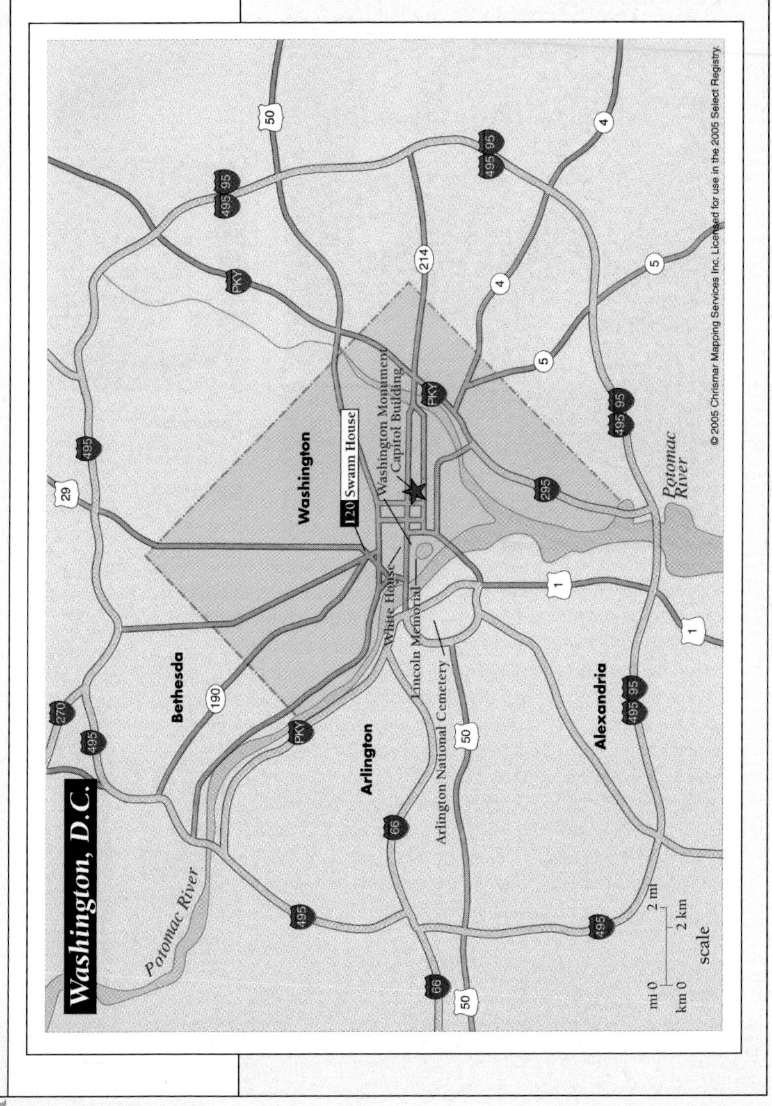

Swann House

www.srinns.com/swannhouse
1808 New Hampshire Ave. N.W., Washington, DC 20009
202-265-4414 • Fax 202-265-6755
stay@swannhouse.com

Innkeepers/Owners
Mary & Richard Ross
General Manager
Rick Verkler

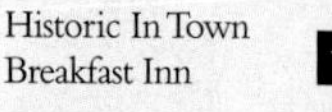

AAA ◆◆◆

Elegantly situated in the Dupont Circle Historic District, Swann House shines among its neighboring embassies and stately Victorian homes. Nearby you will find dozens of colorful shops, restaurants, and galleries. We invite you to sip sherry by the fire and savor the ambiance of our 1883 Richardson Romanesque gem. Our sitting rooms, verandas and pool, all graciously appointed for your comfort, beckon you to unwind. Cozy fireplaces, flower-filled balconies and Jacuzzi bathtubs enhance several of our unique guestrooms, and all offer luxurious down featherbeds, cable TV and telephones with voice mail and data port. Named 'Best B&B in Washington' by *Frommer's* every year since 1999. Voted "Top 10 Most Romantic Inn" in the country -*American Historic Inns* and "Top 10 Urban Inn" -*Forbes*

Member Since 2002

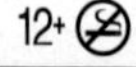  

Rooms/Rates
7 Rooms $150/$325; 2 Suites $195/$325. Each room is unique; all private baths, 5 with fireplace, 2 Jacuzzis. Open year-round.

Cuisine
Deluxe continental breakfast daily with gourmet entree on weekends, afternoon refreshments, evening sherry, dozens of fine restaurants within walking distance. Elegant venue for private parties, weddings, receptions, meetings and retreats.

Nearest Airport(s)
Reagan National (DCA)

Directions
Centrally located, just 12 blocks N of the White House. From Dupont Circle, take New Hampshire Ave. N. Swann House is on the W side, just N of S St., on the corner of Swann.

"Beautiful place, delightful and helpful people and a location that is as good as it gets!""Wonderful service and charm! We didn't want to leave the room!"

Florida

"The Sunshine State"

Famous For: Disney World, Busch Gardens, St. Augustine (the oldest city in U.S., founded 50 years before Plymouth), Florida Keys, Everglades, Space Shuttles, Beaches, Alligators, Oranges, Grapefruit, Wildlife

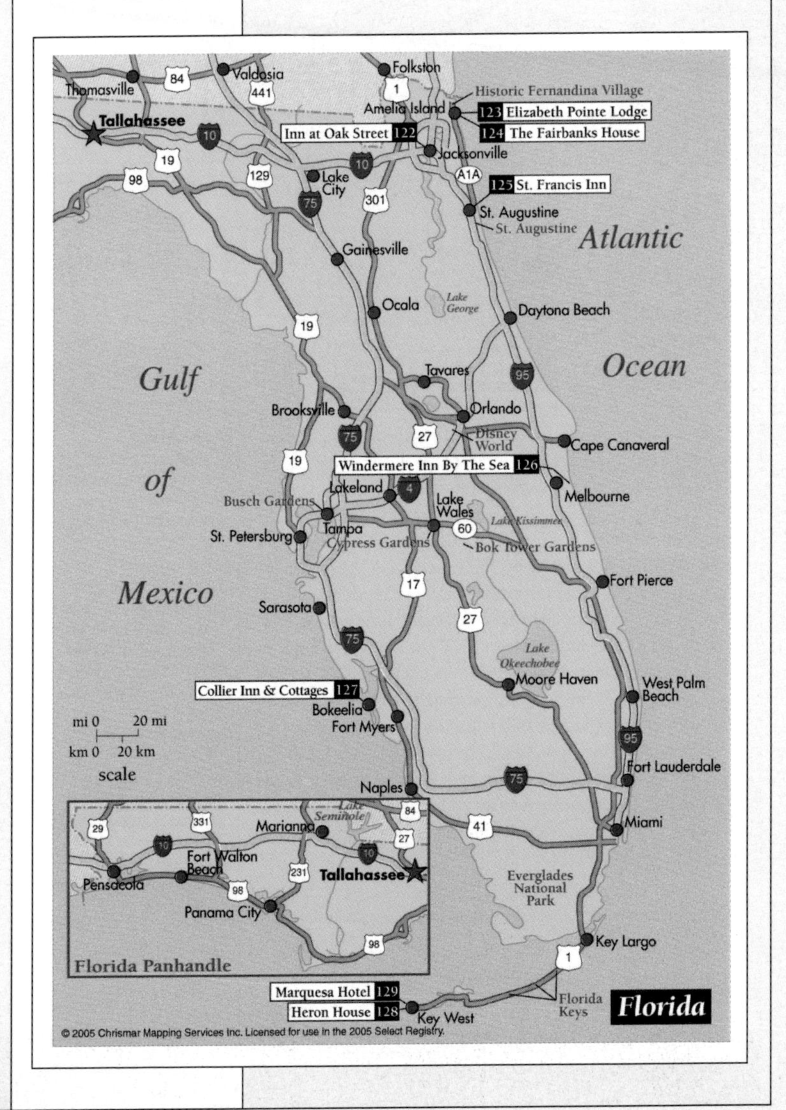

The Inn at Oak Street

www.srinns.com/innatoakstreet
2114 Oak Street, Jacksonville, FL 32204
904-379-5525 • Fax 904-379-5525
innatoakstreet@yahoo.com

Proprietors
Tina Musico & Robert Eagle
Historic Urban Inn

Bordering downtown Jacksonville, the Inn is located in the Riverside National Register Historic District, one of the most diverse collections of historic residential architecture in Florida. The Inn provides luxurious accommodations and superb amenities in the heart of this beautiful neighborhood, just steps from the St. Johns River. Built in 1902, and meticulously renovated by the owners, the Inn offers a vibrant and stylish interior in an urban historic environment. Spacious guestrooms, elegantly furnished, provide modern comforts including flat screen TV with DVD/CD player and wine refrigerator. Business travelers enjoy wireless Internet while lounging on the wraparound porch, while leisure guests relax with massage in our tranquil spa room. Indulge in our complimentary wine hour, full gourmet breakfast and 24-hour coffee bar. Experience local boutiques, outstanding eateries and art museums, or enhance your stay with a variety of our special packages. Our personal service, fine details and amenities make your visit a memorable one.

Member Since 2005

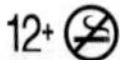    

Rooms/Rates
6 guestrooms. $100/$165. Open year-round. Feature flat screen TV with DVD, wine refrigerator, plush robes. 3 rooms with spa tubs and balconies, 1 room with fireplace.

Cuisine
Full gourmet breakfast included. Complimentary wine hour and 24 hour coffee bar. We offer a variety of Special Packages which include menu selections for dining at the Inn.Excellent dining within walking distance and a short drive.

Nearest Airport(s)
Jacksonville International Airport

Directions
15 minutes from airport. From 95 N, take Margaret Street exit, make a right onto Oak Street and the Inn is one block down on left.

"A Jewel in Jacksonville...rooms combine comfort with couture."
Travel + Leisure

Elizabeth Pointe Lodge

www.srinns.com/elizabethpointe
98 South Fletcher Avenue, Amelia Island, FL 32034
888-757-1910 • 904-277-4851 • Fax 904-277-6500
info@elizabethpointelodge.com

Innkeepers/Owners
David and Susan Caples

Traditional Waterside Inn

AAA ◆◆◆

Rated "One of the 12 best waterfront inns" in America, the Pointe sits overlooking the Atlantic Ocean. Focusing on individualized attention, the inn is Nantucket "shingle style" with an oversized soaking tub in each bath, fresh flowers, morning newspaper, full seaside breakfast and a staff that wants to exceed your expectations. Light food, dessert, and room service available 24 hours. Only a short bike ride to the historic seaport of Fernandina. Horseback riding, tennis, golf and sailing nearby.

Rooms/Rates
24 Rooms, $175/$350 B&B; 1 Cottage, $350 B&B. Open year-round.

Cuisine
A complete and tended buffet breakfast in the Sunrise Room or outside on the deck overlooking the ocean. A light fare menu available 24 hours. Complimentary social hour each evening at 6 p.m. Wine and beer available. Our culinary staff welcomes special dietary requests.

Nearest Airport(s)
Jacksonville International
Approximately 35 minutes away.

Directions
From I-95 take exit 373 and follow Route A1A to Amelia Island. Our address on A1A is 98 S. Fletcher Avenue, on ocean side.

Member Since 1998

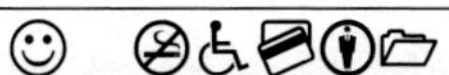

"The ideal place for a waterside escape."
Country Inns Magazine

The Fairbanks House

www.fairbankshouse.com
227 South 7th Street, Amelia Island, FL 32034
888-891-9880 • 904-277-0500 • Fax 904-277-3103
email@fairbankshouse.com

Innkeepers/Owners
Bill & Theresa Hamilton

Elegant Victorian In Town Breakfast Inn

Featured in *The Best Romantic Escapes in Florida* and built in 1885, Fairbanks House is an 8000 sq. ft. Italianate villa rising above a quiet Victorian village on Amelia Island. Surrounded by soaring magnolias and live oaks with dripping Spanish moss, the mansion, cottages and pool rest on a strikingly landscaped acre where guests enjoy a serene 100% smoke-free stay. Rooms are elegantly furnished with period antiques and romantic reproductions. Numerous upscale amenities are designed for a carefree getaway, honeymoon or vacation. King beds, Jacuzzis, bikes, beach gear, Romance Packages, and full concierge service are but a few examples of our attention to detail. Close to secluded beaches and 1100 acre park. Ask for details on seasonal specials and Girls Just Wanna Have Fun Getaways.

Rooms/Rates
6 Rooms, 3 Cottages, 3 Suites, $180/$395 B&B. Open year-round.

Cuisine
Sumptuous gourmet breakfast served in our formal dining room, or on piazzas and patios amid our hidden gardens by the pool. Lively daily social hour with beverages, hot and cold hors d'oeuvres. Three minute walk to casual cafes, taverns and fine-dining restaurants.

Nearest Airport(s)
Jacksonville, FL

Directions
Use exit 373 from I-95 and follow the signs for Fernandina Beach along Highway A1A, 200 East. After bridge go 3.3 miles to Cedar. L onto Cedar and R onto 7th. 25 minutes from JAX, FL airport, 15 minutes from I-95.

Member Since 1998

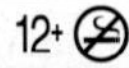

"Your packages are so creative - they make trip-planning simple. Love your social hours!"

St. Francis Inn

www.srinns.com/stfrancisinn
279 St. George Street, St. Augustine, FL 32084
800-824-6062 • 904-824-6068 • Fax 904-810-5525
info@stfrancisinn.com

Innkeepers/Owners
Joe and Margaret Finnegan
Historic In Town Bed & Breakfast Inn

AAA ◆◆◆

Rooms/Rates
12 Rooms. $119/$239; 4 Suites $139/$239; 2-bedroom Cottage $229/$299. Free parking, health club access, attractions discounts. Explore the Old City steps away. Special packages & ala carte extras, too.

Cuisine
Homemade breakfast entrees, fresh pastries and more, served in our dining room, your room, balcony or courtyard! Appetizers & beverages at social hour; evening sweets; homemade cookies.

Nearest Airport(s)
St. Johns County (SGJ); Jacksonville Internat'l

Directions
I-95 to exit 318 St. Augustine SR16, to US 1, south to King St, go L. 2/3 mi to St. George St, turn R. Inn is 3 blocks on L, park on R.

Come visit the past! Antique filled rooms & suites, fireplaces, kitchenettes, jacuzzis, balconies, walk to everything. This historic Inn overflows with hospitality, set in a lush walled courtyard on brick paved streets with horse drawn buggys. It's a treasure within the Old City, but modern comforts abound! Enjoy a swimming pool, gourmet Southern breakfasts, bikes, social hour, evening sweets, beach privileges, VCR, wi-fi access, courtesy local transportation. Our tropical Florida setting provides endless outdoor activity, plus sightseeing, historic landmarks, cultural events and special celebrations. Many theme packages enhance your stay, with history, romance or adventure.

Member Since 2002

"It's great to choose your room or suite with all of them pictured on www.stfrancisinn.com!"

Windemere Inn By The Sea

www.srinns.com/windemereinn
815 S. Miramar Avenue (A1A), Indialantic, FL 32903
800-224-6853 • 321-728-9334 • Fax 321-728-2741
stay@windemereinn.com

Innkeeper
Elizabeth G. Fisher
Luxury Oceanfront B&B

AAA ◆◆◆

Imagine ... a luxury, ocean front bed & breakfast, only an hour east of Orlando. Guest rooms and suites are furnished with antiques and fine linens, most with ocean views, some with balconies, porches, whirlpool tubs or TVs. Start each morning with a full, gourmet breakfast, enjoy pastries and sherry at "tea time." Windemere is the ideal spot for your corporate retreat, small wedding, honeymoon or special getaway, for watching a rocket launch form Kennedy Space Center, or witnessing sea turtles nest and hatch. The grounds have several gardens, including herbs for cooking. The central point is a lily pond alive with marine plants and animals. Sit on our Beachside Pergola and watch dolphins and surfers play in the waves, or the moon rise. We have private beach access, and provide beach gear. Windemere is 45 minutes south of Kennedy Space Center, an hour east of Orlando and 10 minutes from Historic Downtown Melbourne with shopping, arts and entertainment and casual and fine dining.

To view rooms please visit www.windemereinn.com.

Rooms/Rates
7 Guest Rooms. $120/$250. 2 two bedroom suites $280 and $400. AAA and pre-registered corporate discounts offered. Open year round.

Cuisine
Start each morning with the sunrise over the Atlantic, and a full gourmet breakfast. A fruit course is followed by alternating sweet and savory dishes. Home made pasteries and desserts served at "tea time" daily. We are able to cater to most dietary needs upon request.

Nearest Airport(s)
Melbourne Int'l 15 minutes, Orlando Int'l 1 hour

Directions
I-95, exit #180 (Hwy. 192) east to A1A, right/ south 1/4 mile on left/ocean side.

Member Since 2005

"Our stay far exceeded our expectations. You made our 12th Anniversry very special. We will be back before our 13th." Ron & Valerie Carl, Palm Bay, FL.

Collier Inn & Cottages

www.srinns.com/collierinn
P.O. Box 640, Bokeelia, FL 33922
888-735-6335 • Fax 239-283-0290
www.useppa.com
collierinn@useppa.com

Innkeeper
Vince Formosa

Historic Waterside Inn

Steeped in tradition, the Collier Inn is one of the finest private retreats ever operated in Florida. Located on a pristine island adjacent to the famed fishing of Boca Grande, the resort has been catering to a select clientele for over 100 years. The modern history began with the opening of the famed "Tarpon Inn" in 1898. This early facility was the home to Chicago Street Car magnate, John M. Roach. Early in the 20th century, the property was purchased by Baron G. Collier, and his home today serves as the Collier Inn. Guest accommodations are elegant and reflect the expectations of distinguished travelers of another time. Amenities abound!

Rooms/Rates
14 Elegant Rooms and Suites $140/$400 w/Cont. Breakfast. Each room individually decorated, all with private baths and sitting areas. Pool, tennis, croquet, water sports & more.

Cuisine
Dining varies from poolside to the elegant tradition of the Collier Dining Room. Fresh fish, daily specials, and traditional Island meals are an event! The Inn Bar offers a retreat to share the lore with guests and Useppa Club members.

Nearest Airport(s)
Fort Myers

Directions
The Collier Inn is located on Useppa Island and is accessed by private boat or scheduled launch from Pine Island.

Member Since 2003

"One of the top 25 true island retreats in the world." —Conde' Naste Traveler

Heron House

www.srinns.com/heronhouse
512 Simonton Street, Key West, FL 33040
888-265-2395 • 305-294-9227 • Fax 305-294-5692
heronkyw@aol.com

The Heron House is located on Simonton Street in the Historic District of Old Town Key West, only one block from the main street known as Duval. The Heron House is a 23-room small romantic Inn, comprised of three historical conch-style homes. An elegantly tiled swimming pool is nestled between two of the homes. Luxuriously landscaped, Heron House features an orchid nursery, as well as exotic tropical plants. Centrally located, the Heron House provides easy access to numerous restaurants and beaches. Winner of *American Bed & Breakfast Association* 4-Crown award.

Member Since 2002

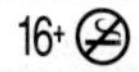    

Proprietors
Roy and Christina Howard
General Manager
Jeffrey Brannin
Historic In Town Inn

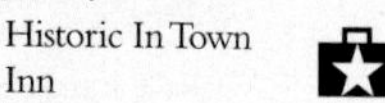

AAA ◆◆◆◆

Rooms/Rates
23 Rooms, $129/$369; 3 poolside, 3 Premium Poolside, 4 Garden, 7 Deluxe Garden, 4 Garden Terrace Junior, and 2 Honeymoon Junior Suites. Newly renovated, designer furnished, AC, phones, color cable TV.

Cuisine
Poolside expanded continental breakfast; wine and cheese served nightly before sunset.

Nearest Airport(s)
Key West International Airport

Directions
Take Truman Ave (US 1) S. Head W on Simonton St. The Heron House is on the S side, between Southard and Fleming.

"Unique...rich and luxurious; an orchid lover's paradise!"

Innkeeper/Owner
Carol Wightman
Owners
Richard Manley and Erik DeBoer

Elegant Greek Revival In Town Hotel

AAA ◆◆◆◆

The Marquesa Hotel

www.srinns.com/marquesahotel
600 Fleming St., Key West, FL 33040
800-869-4631 Reservations Only • 305-292-1919
Fax 305-294-2121
info@marquesa.com

In the heart of Key West's Historic District, the Marquesa Hotel and Cafe is a landmark 120-year-old home, restored to four-diamond status. Floor-to-ceiling windows, large bouquets of flowers, two shimmering pools and lush gardens are Marquesa trademarks. Rooms and suites are luxurious with private marble baths, bathrobes, and fine furnishings. Located one block from Duval Street for shops, galleries, restaurants and night life. *The Miami Herald* rated it as one of Florida's top 10 Inns, and *Zagat's* rated it 17th in the U.S.A. Named an "Orvis-Endorsed Lodge" for fishing expeditions.

Rooms/Rates
14 Rooms, $175/$320; 13 Suites, $270/$430. Open year-round.

Cuisine
Poolside or room service dining for breakfast; fine dining in Cafe Marquesa with an inventive and delicious menu. Excellent wine list.

Nearest Airport(s)
Key West International Airport 3 miles

Directions
US 1, R on N Roosevelt Blvd, becomes Truman Ave. Continue to Simonton, turn R, go 5 blks to Fleming. Turn R. Hotel on R.

Member Since 1991

"Bravo! Beautifully appointed, gorgeous setting, accomodating and knowledgeable staff."

Georgia

"The Peach State"

Famous For: Stone Mountain, Okefenokee Swamp, Live Oak Trees, Islands, Beaches, Peaches, Historic Savannah

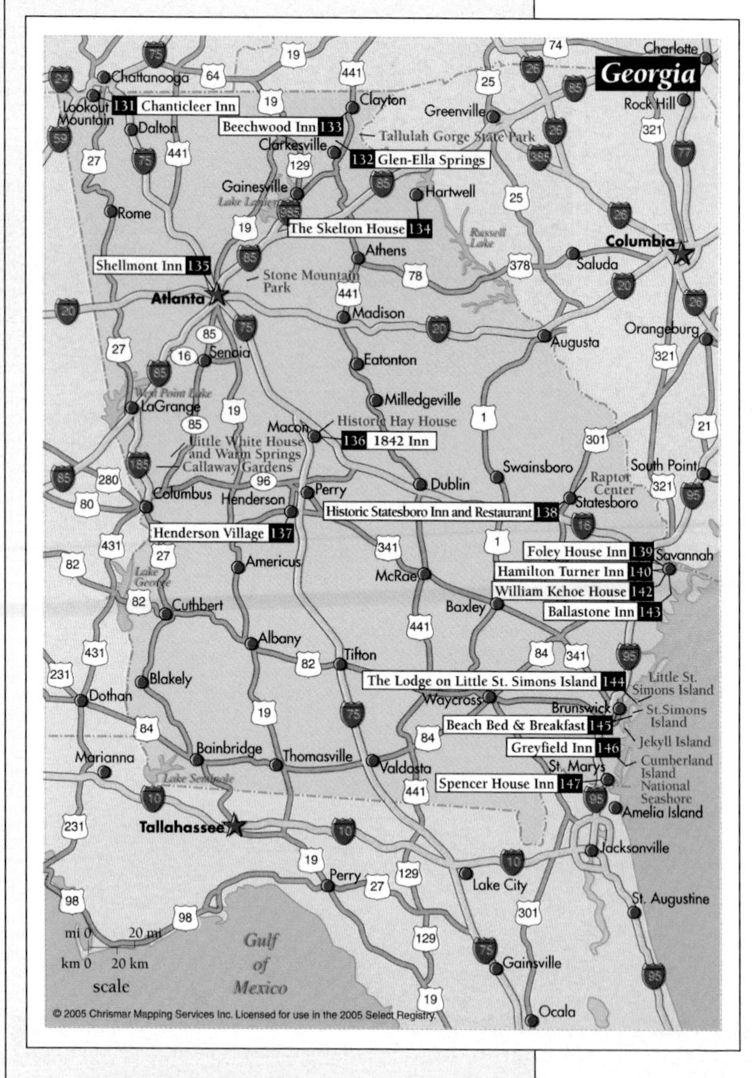

Innkeepers
Kirby & Judy Wahl
Historic Mountain Top Breakfast Inn

Chanticleer Inn

www.srinns.com/chanticleer
1300 Mockingbird Lane, Lookout Mountain, GA 30750
866-777-7999 • 706-820-2002 • Fax 706-820-7976
info@stayatchanticleer.com

Rooms/Rates
$100/$275 per night includes full breakfast. Rooms have a king, queen, or two queen beds. Rates are based on room size and amenities such as whirlpool tub. Suites are available.

Cuisine
Breakfast is freshly prepared each day. We recommend local restaurants for lunch and dinner. We also host weddings, conferences, & meetings, see www.meetat-grandview.com.

Nearest Airport(s)
Chattanooga

Directions
From Chattanooga take Broad Street South to Lookout Mountain and follow the signs to Rock City. From I-24 take the Lookout Mtn. exit and follow the signs to Rock City.

THIS HISTORIC INN combines the ambiance of yesteryear with the comfort and amenities of today. Built in 1927, Chanticleer Inn offers 17 luxurious guest rooms each decorated with antiques and classic fabrics. Nestled among gardens and stone walkways, the cottage rooms have modern conveniences and some extras such as private patio, fireplace, or Jacuzzi. Perfect for romance, relaxation, sightseeing, business, or weddings, the Chanticleer Inn caters to each guest with gracious hospitality. Located high atop Lookout Mountain near all Chattanooga attractions, Chanticleer Inn is convenient yet tranquil. Guests enjoy our National Parks, waterfalls, golf, shops, spas, and many nearby restaurants.

Member Since 2003

"You are such wonderful hosts! This was so relaxing. We cannot wait to return. Thank you."

Glen-Ella Springs

www.srinns.com/glen-ella
1789 Bear Gap Rd, Clarkesville, GA 30523
888-455-8886 • 706-754-7295 • Fax 706-754-1560
info@glenella.com

Innkeepers/Owners
Barrie & Bobby Aycock

Rustic Mountain Inn

Wander down the gravel road at the southernmost tip of the Blue Ridge Mountains and discover the peaceful setting of Glen-Ella Springs Country Inn. Listen to the birds sing while you rock on the porch. Stroll around the extensive perennial and herb gardens, and eighteen acres of meadow bordered by Panther Creek. Relax by the massive stone fireplace in our century-old inn, a rare example of the traditional small hotels that once dotted the North Georgia Mountains. Relish the comfort of the inn's tasteful décor. Savor the outstanding food, from bountiful country buffet breakfasts to elegant dinners. The constantly changing menu in our award-winning restaurant, named one of Georgia's Top Ten Dining Destinations in 2004, guarantees a memorable dining experience in an atmosphere of casual elegance. Spend leisurely days fishing world class trout streams, hiking numerous scenic trails, boating on nearby rivers and lakes, or exploring charming historic villages filled with fine art and crafts by local artisans.

Member Since 1990

Rooms/Rates
16 Rooms, $140/$265 B&B.
Open year-round.

Cuisine
Bountiful country breakfasts. Dinner by reservation from a constantly changing menu of upscale southern-American cuisine prepared by our professional staff, guaranteeing a memorable dining experience. Guests may bring their own spirits.

Nearest Airport(s)
Greenville, SC or Atlanta, GA

Directions
At the edge of the Blue Ridge Mtns, 90 miles north of Atlanta. 3 miles off 4-lane US 441 between Clarkesville & Clayton; Go west on T. Smith Rd. at mile marker 18, then N. on Historic Old 441. Take the first left on Orchard Rd., then follow the signs.

"Delicious food, beautiful scenery, fine hospitality."
"God smiles on Glen-Ella."

Innkeepers/Owners
Gayle and David Darugh

Elegant Rustic Mountain Inn

Beechwood Inn

www.srinns.com/beechwoodinn
P.O. Box 429, 220 Beechwood Dr, Clayton, GA 30525
866-782-2485 • 706-782-5485 • Fax 706-782-7644
david-gayle@beechwoodinn.ws

Rooms/Rates
2 rooms, 4 suites $139/$159 B&B. Private baths. Open year-round. Complimentary afternoon appetizers and wine.

Cuisine
Beechwood Bountiful Breakfast daily. 5 course Prix Fixe dinners with wine on most Saturdays, advance reservations needed. Extensive wine list. Visit our website for information on gourmet wine events, winetastings and special weekend packages.

Nearest Airport(s)
Atlanta, GA. and Asheville, NC each 90 minutes.

Directions
In Clayton, Georgia, at the intersection of Highways 441 and 76, turn east on 76. Go one tenth of a mile turn left on Beechwood Drive. Follow inn signs up Beechwood Drive.

Georgia's premier wine country inn provides rustic elegance in a romantic setting overlooking the historic town of Clayton. The Inn was voted "Number One Inn in North America for a Weekend Escape - 2005." Filled with antiques and primitives, yet warm and inviting, Beechwood Inn is altogether homey and comfortable. Food and wine enthusiasts will want to experience wine weekend packages and culinary events, when celebrated winemakers and chefs from around the world collaborate to expand guests' epicurean horizons. Nearby mountains, trails and rivers offer activities and experiences for a lifetime of memories. Explore mountain villages, raft the Chattooga River, hike to a waterfall or drive along bucolic country lanes. History buffs will want to visit the Foxfire Museum. Close to three mountain golf courses. Everyone will enjoy relaxing in our 100 year old gardens with a good book and a glass of wine. Romantic guest rooms have fine linens, robes, private porches or balconies, fireplaces, wonderful views, and cozy privacy.

Member Since 2005

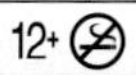   

"Innkeepers Dave & Gayle Darugh will make you so glad you visited. We consider a trip to the Beechwood Inn one of life's finest pampering experiences."

The Skelton House

www.srinns.com/skeltonhouse
97 Benson Street, Hartwell, GA 30643-1991
877-556-3790 • 706-376-7969 • Fax 706-856-3139
t.skeltonhouse@comcast.net

Innkeepers/Owners
Ruth and John Skelton

Historic Village
Breakfast Inn

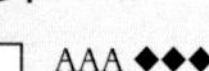

AAA ◆◆◆

The Skelton House is an 1896 National Register Victorian Inn, located in the historic downtown area of the small town of Hartwell. The charm, grace and hospitality of the original Skelton family and their grand home has been retained by today's generation of Skeltons as their home, restored in 1997, enjoys its new life as The Skelton House. Wrap yourself in luxury while enjoying the beauty of the Victorian period joined with the comfort and elegance today's discerning guests expect. Enjoy the beautiful Victorian parlor, the sunny morning room, the cozy receiving room, the spacious dining room, or one of the many porches and balconies. Located only 13 miles South of I-85 in the NE corner of GA. Less than 2 hours from the metro Atlanta area or 1 hour from the local Greenville/Spartanburg airport. The perfect getaway for vacationers and business travelers alike. Come experience what many believe to be the ultimate in Southern Hospitality!

Rooms/Rates
7 Guestrooms, $100/$135. Antiques, Cable TV w/HBO, phones w/dataports, room thermostats, ceiling fans, queen beds, private baths w/hairdryers. Discounts available.

Cuisine
Creative full service hot breakfasts made with the best seasonal and local ingredients. Nearby casual dining with a lunch and dinner menu of southern regional cuisine and a full service bar. Closed Monday.

Nearest Airport(s)
Greenville, SC (GSP) 60 mi.

Directions
I-85 to GA exit 177. 13 miles S on GA Hwy. 77 to Hartwell. Turn R at 5th traffic light onto Carter St. Look for us on the immediate L. past the Presbyterian Church.

Member Since 2001

"Thank you for the time to just 'Be'. No agenda. No timetable. Everything was wonderful!!"

Shellmont Inn

www.srinns.com/shellmontinn
821 Piedmont Ave. N.E., Atlanta, GA 30308
404-872-9290 • Fax 404-872-5379
innkeeper@shellmont.com

Innkeepers/Owners
Ed and Debbie McCord
Traditional Victorian
In Town Breakfast Inn

Mobil ★★★
AAA ◆◆◆

The Shellmont Inn is an impeccably restored 1891 National Register mansion in Midtown Atlanta's theatre, restaurant and cultural district. The Inn is a treasure chest of stained, leaded and beveled glass, intricately-carved woodwork and hand-painted stenciling. Guest rooms are furnished with antiques, oriental rugs and period wall treatments. Wicker-laden verandas overlook manicured lawns and gardens—including a Victorian fishpond. The experience is unforgettable. National Register of Historic Places Property. City of Atlanta Landmark Building. Recipient of Mayor's Award for Excellence for Historic Preservation.

Rooms/Rates
5 Rooms;
Standard Rooms $125/$175;
Whirlpool Suites $160/$200;
Carriage House $175/$275.
Open year-round.

Cuisine
Full gourmet breakfast, complimentary beverages, fresh fruit basket, evening chocolates, evening turn-down service. Fully licensed and inspected. Atlanta's smallest Historic Hotel.

Nearest Airport(s)
Hartsfield-Jackson International
8 miles

Directions
From airport, I-75/85 N, exit 248-C (International Blvd), turn L at 2nd traffic light (Ellis St), turn R at next traffic light (Piedmont Ave). Go N 1 1/4 mile. Located at the intersection of Piedmont Avenue and 6th. Street on the R.

Member Since 1994

"A jewel in the heart of Atlanta. Southern hospitality at its finest. Exquisite!"

1842 Inn

www.srinns.com/1842inn
353 College Street, Macon, GA 31201
800-336-1842 • 478-741-1842 • Fax 478-741-1842
management@1842inn.com

Innkeeper
Nazario Filipponi

Elegant In Town
Breakfast Inn

Mobil ★★★★
AAA ◆◆◆◆

The 1842 Inn boasts 19 luxurious rooms and public areas tastefully designed with fine English antiques, tapestries and paintings. A quaint garden courtyard and garden pool greet guests for cocktails or breakfast. Nightly turndowns, shoeshines and fresh flowers enhance many other gracious grand hotel amenities. Rooms available with whirlpool tubs and fireplaces. High level of service. Valet parking on request. Considered 'One of America's Top 100 Inns in the 20th Century' by the International Restaurant & Hospitality Rating Bureau.

Rooms/Rates
19 Guest Rooms, $109/$230 B&B. (Rates subject to change without notice.) Open year-round.

Cuisine
Full breakfast and hors d'oeuvres included. Dinner in nearby private club. Full service bar.

Nearest Airport(s)
Macon, Atlanta

Directions
Exit 164 on I-75 turn L fm N; R fm S go to College St; turn Left; Inn is 2 blks on left.

Member Since 1994

Zagat top 50 US Inns and Resorts.

General Manager
Heather Bradham

Traditional Victorian Country Resort

AAA ◆◆◆◆

Henderson Village

www.srinns.com/hendersonvillage
125 South Langston Circle, Perry, GA 31069
888-615-9722 • 478-988-8696 • Fax 478-988-9009
info@hendersonvillage.com

Rooms/Rates
24 Rooms/Suites $175/$350. Cottages are elegantly rustic; houses are subtly refined. Office hours are 7 a.m. to 10 p.m. EDT.

Cuisine
Excellent a la carte breakfast, lunch and dinner menu, hot country breakfast, homemade pastries, fruit; room service available. Full bar and extensive wine list.

Nearest Airport(s)
Atlanta International

Directions
I-75 to Exit 127; Hwy. 26 W 1 mile. Henderson Village is at the crossroads of GA Hwy. 26 and US Hwy. 41. 40 miles south of Macon, 10 miles south of Perry.

Authentic Southern Hospitality awaits, with twelve historic homes beautifully restored and relocated to create a most charming country resort with thousands of acres to relax, unwind and recuperate in traditional southern style. Delight in our gourmet restaurant voted 'The absolute best dining experience in Georgia,' by *Georgia Trend* Magazine. Unwind as you ride horses alongside the cotton fields and through our pecan orchards. Test your skills shooting sporting clays or spend a lazy day in the sun fishing for bass. Rejuvenate your spirit with massage and an afternoon by the pool. Henderson Village is a rare find. Top Ten Most Romantic Inn for 2003.

Member Since 2002

"This is my kind of country living!
Great food, great service, great place, thank you."

Historic Statesboro Inn and Restaurant

www.statesboroinn.com
106 S. Main Street, Statesboro, GA 30458
800-846-9466 • 912-489-8628 • Fax 912-489-4785
frontdesk@statesboroinn.com

Innkeepers/Owners
Tony & Michele Garges; Melissa (daughter) and John Armstrong

Traditional Victorian
In Town Inn

A 1905 historic Victorian oasis where porches, rockers, and gardens adorned with small tranquil ponds are blended with gracious Southern hospitality. Our style is eclectic yet comfortable, with furnishings from three generations and a small pub adds a European feel. Our service is attentive, just right for that relaxing get away. Our spacious banquet room fronted with a Southern style brick veranda makes the Inn a natural setting for that special occasion or executive retreat. While you are at the Inn, visit the Georgia Southern Botanical Garden, or see birds of prey at the Raptor Center. Attend a show or tour exhibits at the Averitt Arts Center. History and antiques are also a treat. Small pets under 20lbs. are welcome.

Rooms/Rates
15 Rooms, 1 two-room Suite, $85/$130 B&B. Open year-round.

Cuisine
Homemade treats await your arrival, and a hearty country breakfast is complimentary for guests. Enjoy our Sunday buffet of traditional southern cooking. Catering available. Please call for special holiday meals and Sunday brunch schedules.

Nearest Airport(s)
Savannah International Airport

Directions
From Savannah: I-16 W to Exit 127 (Rt. 67) to Statesboro to 301N (Main St.); From Atlanta, I-75S to Macon I-16E to exit 116, (301N) to Statesboro. (Do NOT take 301 bypass).

Member Since 1998

"THE STATESBORO INN IS WONDERFUL: Thank you for making our trip great......highy reccomended."

Foley House Inn

www.foleyinn.com
14 West Hull Street, Chippewa Square, Savannah, GA 31401
800-647-3708 • 912-232-6622 • Fax 912-231-1218
info@foleyinn.com

Innkeepers/Owners
Beryl W. and Donald G. Zerwer
Elegant Italianate
Historic District

Mobil ★★★
AAA ◆◆◆◆

Rooms/Rates
18 Rooms $230/$355. Closed Christmas Day.

Cuisine
Complimentary gourmet breakfast, afternoon tea with sweets,and hors d'oeuvres with complimentary wine in the evening...all prepared by our critically-acclaimed chef. Treats w/ turndown service. Premium wines & champagnes for sale by the bottle or glass at any time. Short walk to fine restaurants.

Nearest Airport(s)
Savannah/Hilton Head International

Directions
From I-95 to I-16 to end at Montgomery St. Right at 2nd light onto Oglethorpe St., R onto Bull St., R onto Hull St. 1st red brick building on R. Beautiful Chippewa Square is our front yard.

An upscale AAA 4-diamond Southern B&B with a European appeal. Common areas & guest rooms decorated with British period decor and stunning architecture. Gas fireplaces in most rooms; canopied and four-poster beds. Some rooms with oversized Jacuzzi baths and private balconies. Enjoy a complimentary gourmet breakfast, afternoon tea with sweets, and hors d'oeuvres with wine in the evening...all prepared by our critically-acclaimed chef. Our concierge will make dinner and tour reservations. Amazingly short walk to restaurants, theatres, antique stores, art galleries, etc. from this perfectly central location. Some rooms have private balconies overlooking historic Chippewa square, the site where "Forrest Gump" was filmed eating chocolates and waiting for the bus. Our park-like setting leads to Bull Street and one of the most historic walks in America. All the luxor of the 1800s without sacrificing modern conveniences. Wireless internet connections and spa services are available complete with a fitness room.

Member Since 1998

12+ 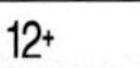   

"One of the top ten romantic inns in all of North America!"
- *Vacation* Magazine

Hamilton Turner

www.hamilton-turnerinn.com
330 Abercorn Street, Savannah, GA 31401
888-448-8849 • 912-233-1833 • Fax 912-233-0291
info@hamilton-turnerinn.com

Innkeepers/Owners
Jane & Rob Sales
Victorian Parkside
Historic Mansion

AAA ◆◆◆◆

"Historically, the talk of the town," the photogenic Hamilton-Turner Inn is the quintessential Savannah society mansion. With stylish comforts and chic Southern hospitality reminiscent of the Savannah 400 era, the inspiring Mid-Victorian, Second Empire architecture woos travelers to the "hip and historic" manor on the park (circa 1873). The culture-rich walking vacation begins from the low key, high style of relaxation at the inn with a lazy stroll (or brisk walk) from the prestigious garden park of Lafayette Square -- one of the hallmark convivial spaces of the world-famous planned city. Unpretentious luxuries include imaginative family fun; romantic honeymoon or getaways, business travel-with-leisure retreat; Savannah destination weddings; full house reservations; and last minute macro vacation packages. Leisure in the slowed Southern pace. Featured in *Esquire, Conde' Nast Traveler*, and *Country Discoveries*.

Member Since 2003

Rooms/Rates
Seventeen rooms from $175 per night, double occupancy. King, double queen, queen, and double twin beds. Carriage house offers 3 clustered rooms. ADA & pet friendly lodging.

Cuisine
Complimentary cuisine features the signature "dessert beings at breakfast" ... afternoon wine with hors d'oeuvres, bedtime brandy or port and a sweet surprise; plus, playful child friendly menus.

Nearest Airport(s)
Savannah-Hilton Head International Airport

Directions
I-16 East to Savannah. Exit on Montgomery St. Right on Liberty St. Right on Abercorn St. to Lafayette Square. The Cathedral is on the same square.

"Stay at the Hamilton Turner and enjoy the magical views of Lafayette Square." - *Southern Living.* "...a step back to a more gracious era."

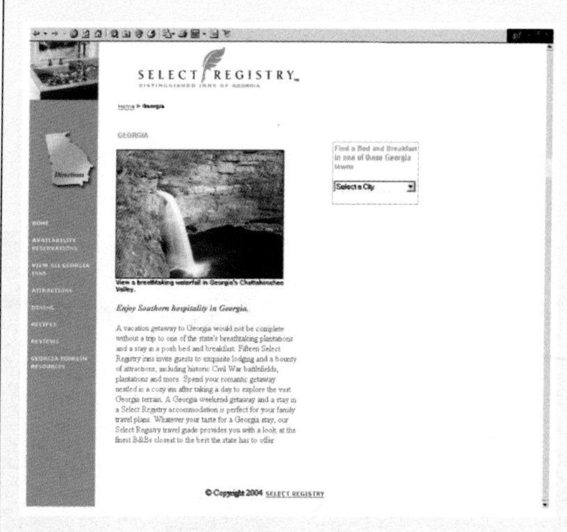

SELECT REGISTRY members are found across North America, and we're eager to give you many different types of tools to find the destination you're seeking.

In order to better serve our guests, many of whom search online geographically and travel regionally, SELECT REGISTRY has created Internet portals for each of the 48 states and provinces where we currently have member properties.

These portals—such as the one for Georgia—contain links to our members' pages, information on local activities and attractions, area room availability for our inns, inn reviews, dining and recipes, and state and city tourism links—all in one place.

Georgia's portal can be found at: www.bbselectregistry.com/georgia.

Visit the state or provincial portal of your choice by logging on at www.bbselectregistry.com/ (state or province name), or check out the content-filled central association web site at www.SelectRegistry.com today!

www.bbselectregistry.com/ (state or province name)

Kehoe House

www.srinns.com/kehoehouse
123 Habersham Street, Savannah, GA 31401
800-820-1020 • 912-232-1020 • Fax 912-231-0208
info@kehoehouse.com

Owner
Kessler Collection
Innkeeper
Sarah Hartman

Historic In Town
Breakfast Inn

The Inn, built in 1892 in the Renaissance Revival style, is one of Savannah's most distinctive landmarks and a perfect venue for a luxury Bed & Breakfast Inn. It enjoys a prime location on Columbia Square in the Historic District. Antiques, oriental carpets, and intriguing art accent the gracious and inviting décor. Generous guestrooms are distinctively decorated from romantic to stately. Verandahs and private balconies are favorite outdoor retreats. For your convenience the Inn offers complimentary private parking and elevator service to all floors. You'll be welcomed at the Inn by an attentive staff dedicated to serving you in the true tradition of Southern hospitality. The recent renovation and refurbishment enhanced the interior and guestrooms, which now reflect a sense of Southern hospitality, history and romance with gilded mirrors, opulent fabrics and antique chandeliers.

Rooms/Rates
13 guestrooms- Low Season $249/$379, High Season $299/$429. Special Packages, Wedding/Meeting Space. Each guestroom features all-white queen or king-size bedding with contrasting colors, armoire, wireless high-speed Internet access, stereo CD player, color televisions and exquisite private bath with unique accoutrements.

Cuisine
Gourmet made-to-order breakfast, afternoon tea service, and evening hors d'oeuvres with wine. Coffee and tea available 24 hours.

Nearest Airport(s)
Savannah Airport

Directions
I-95 to I-16 to end at Montgomery. Right on Liberty, left on Habersham to Columbia Square.

Member Since 2003

"We have never had such a lovely time. The house is beautiful and the staff is fantastic!"

Ballastone Inn

www.srinns.com/ballastoneinn
14 East Oglethorpe Avenue, Savannah, GA 31401
800-822-4553 • 912-236-1484 • Fax 912-236-4626
inn@ballastone.com

Innkeepers/Owners
Jennifer and Jim Salandi
Historic In Town Luxury Hotel

AAA ◆◆◆◆

Rooms/Rates
16 Rooms. Double occupancy $215/$395. Selection includes courtyard, deluxe, and superior rooms, plus luxury suites which overlook the lush garden.

Cuisine
An elegant, personally prepared "table for two," made-to-order breakfast, afternoon high tea enjoyed with fragrant antique linens, pre-dinner gourmet hors d'oeuvres, and private bar with premium liquors and boutique wines. Smoking is permitted out-of-doors.

Nearest Airport(s)
Savannah-Hilton Head International

Directions
East on I-16 to Savannah. Exit on Montgomery St. R on Oglethorpe Avenue to Drayton Street. U-turn L around the median to the Inn.

This classic patriarch of Savannah's historic bed and breakfast mansions intrigued Andrew Harper sufficiently to earn his prestigious 2005 "Hideaway of the Year" Grand Award. *MONEY* named the intimate Italiante mansion among its top six great romantic getaways. Guests are invited to "escape" ... for an embellished Savannah vacation to yesteryear, a romantic honeymoon destination, or a chic holiday getaway. The small luxury hotel awaits with around-the-clock concierge for service and security, elevator to access the entire mansion, antique hotel bar, table for two privacy, lush courtyard garden, designer decor and the Southern ambiance of 16 unique luxury hotel rooms. Actor Paul Newman wrote, "... a delightful slice of the Old South." Escape to Ballastone ... and Savannah, a first-class travel destination experience. "Is not this the true romantic feeling - not to desire to escape life, but to prevent life from escaping you?" -- Thomas Wolfe, quoted in Andrew Turnbull's *Thomas Wolfe* (1968).

Member Since 2005

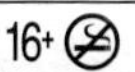

"If there was a hall of fame for bed and breakfasts, Ballastone would be at the top." -- North Carolina guests. "A splendid oasis!" -- England guests.

The Lodge on Little St. Simons Island

www.srinns.com/lodgeonlittlestsimons
P.O. Box 21078, Little St. Simons Island, GA 31522-0578
888-733-5774 • 912-638-7472 • Fax 912-634-1811
Lodge@LittleStSimonsIsland.com

General Manager
Joel Meyer

Private Island Getaway

Nature prevails on this pristine Georgia island where 10,000 acres are shared with no more than 30 overnight guests at a time. Accessible only by boat, Little St. Simons Island unfolds its secrets to those eager to discover a bounty of natural wonders. Seven miles of shell-strewn beaches meet acres of legendary moss-draped live oaks, glistening tidal creeks, and shimmering salt marshes to provide an unparalleled setting for a host of activities and total relaxation. Guests enjoy interpretive tours, birding, canoeing, kayaking, fishing, bicycling and horseback riding. Creature comforts include gracious accommodations, delicious regional cuisine and Southern hospitality.

Rooms/Rates
Open year-round. Children of all ages welcome May - Sept, children over 8 years Oct - Apr. All inclusive rates 11 Rooms $450/$675; 2 Suites $1100/$1200; Full House $1650/$2500; Exclusive Full Island $7700/$8000 - See website for SPECIALS!

Cuisine
Delicious regional cuisine served family-style. 3 meals daily. Snacks, personal picnics, oyster roasts, crab boils, cocktail cruises and beach picnics.

Nearest Airport(s)
Brunswick, GA (BQK)
Savannah, GA (SAV),
Jacksonville, FL (JAX)

Directions
Accessible only by boat with departures twice daily from St. Simons Island.

Member Since 1993

"Great getaway, perfect balance of seclusion and comfort, relaxation and activity."

Beach Bed & Breakfast

www.srinns.com/beachbb
907 Beachview Drive, St. Simon's Island, GA 31522
912-634-2800 • 912-638-5042 • Fax 912-634-4656
reservations@beachbedandbreakfast.com

Innkeeper/Owner
Joe McDonough
Waterside Resort
B&B

Rooms/Rates
7 Suites, $240/$500. Southern breakfast served at your ocean-front table each morning along with Capt Joe's internationally famous fresh fruit bowl.

Cuisine
Delightful full breakfast served on an oceanfront deck.

Nearest Airport(s)
Brunswick

Directions
Take exit 38 (I-95) towards US17 Brunswick. Take US17 S and turn L onto St. Simons Causeway (Torres Causeway). As you come off the last bridge, take R at traffic light. Go to yield sign and turn L onto King's Way. Go straight thru 2 traffic lights, then .4 mi. Turn R onto 5th Street around the 90 degree curve, and 2nd unit on the left.

The Beach Bed & Breakfast is a beautiful 13,000 square feet oceanfront Spanish-Mediterranean villa. Its seven suites are furnished with exquisite décor and detail. Guests can take advantage of ocean-front decks for a hot served breakfast, pool, Jacuzzi and home theatre, and the property is perfectly located within walking distance of ten of the island's best restaurants. In-Suite Complimentary beverages and snacks are an added bonus, along with complimentary bicycles and local airport pickup. Site-seeing tours, golf, tennis, boating, fishing and dinner boat tours are available through the B&B. A full-service staff awaits your arrival. 10 top Romantic Inns.

Member Since 2003

"The St. Simon's Suite would make the most discerning mermaid come in from the sea and stay ashore!" "Absolutly the Best."

Greyfield Inn

www.srinns.com/greyfieldinn
Post Office Box 900, Fernandina Beach, FL 32035
Cumberland Island, GA 32035
888-243-9238 • 904-261-6408 • Fax 904-321-0666
seashore@greyfieldinn.com

Innkeepers/Owners
The Ferguson Family

Traditional Colonial
Waterside Retreat/Lodge

This turn-of-the-century Carnegie mansion is on Georgia's largest and southernmost coastal island. Miles of trails traverse the island's unique ecosystems along with a beautiful, undeveloped white sand beach for shelling, swimming, sunning and birding. Exceptional food, lovely, original furnishings, and a peaceful, relaxing environment provide guests with a step back into another era. Overnight rate includes an island outing with our naturalist, bicycles and kayaks for exploring the island, round-trip boat passage on our private ferry, and meals.

Rooms/Rates
16 Rooms, $395/$575 AP.
Open year-round.

Cuisine
Hearty southern breakfast, delightful picnic lunch, gourmet dinner. Full bar; wine, beer, liquor, cocktail hour with hors d'oeuvres.

Nearest Airport(s)
Jacksonville, Florida

Directions
I-95 to Highway A1A (Exit 373) to Amelia Island. 14.8 miles to Centre St. Turn left and go to waterfront. Meet at Dock 3 at the "Lucy R. Ferguson/Greyfield" sign. Call for parking instructions.

Member Since 1982

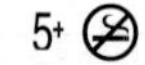    

"We took away memories that will last a lifetime...we felt right at home."

Spencer House Inn

www.spencerhouseinn.com
200 Osborne Street, St. Marys, GA 31558
877-819-1872 • 912-882-1872 • Fax 912-882-9427
info@spencerhouseinn.com

Innkeepers/Owners
Mary and Mike Neff
Victorian Era Historic Village B&B Inn

Spencer House Inn, built in 1872, is located in the heart of the St. Marys Historic District within walking distance to restaurants, shops, museums and the ferry to Cumberland Island National Seashore. We can make your ferry reservation and pack a picnic lunch for you as you head off for your adventure on a beautiful, undeveloped and pristine barrier island - the beach was voted "one of the best wild beaches" by *National Geographic Traveler* magazine. You'll enjoy relaxing in the cypress rockers on the Inn's verandahs. For your convenience, the Inn has an elevator. Walk to the waterfront park, fishing pier, boat ramp & new marsh walk. Take a leisurely stroll around our historic village. There are 2 championship golf courses nearby. Okefenokee Wildlife Refuge is 45 minutes away. The beaches of Jekyll, St. Simons and Amelia Islands are a short drive. We are 9 miles east of I-95 by the St. Marys River on the Georgia/Florida border.

Rooms/Rates
14 rooms $100/$185. Rates subject to change. All private baths. Elevator and outside ramp. Open year-round.

Cuisine
Full buffet breakfast. Picnic lunches available. Walk to restaurants for lunch and dinner. Guest refrigerator. Afternoon iced tea, coffee and homemade treats.

Nearest Airport(s)
Jacksonville, FL

Directions
On Georgia/Florida border. From I-95 take Georgia Exit 3, turn left at stop light and travel 9 miles east on Highway 40 which becomes Osborne Street. The Inn is on the left at the corner of Osborne & Bryant Streets. Ample parking & lobby entrance are on Bryant Street.

Member Since 2003

 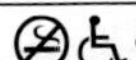  

"Your hospitality is outstanding, we're already looking forward to our next stay."

"The Prairie State"

Famous For: Hogs, Pigs, Cattle, Electronics, Chemicals, Manufacturing, Ancient Burial Mounds, Lake Michigan, Chicago "Windy City", Sears Tower, Wrigley Building

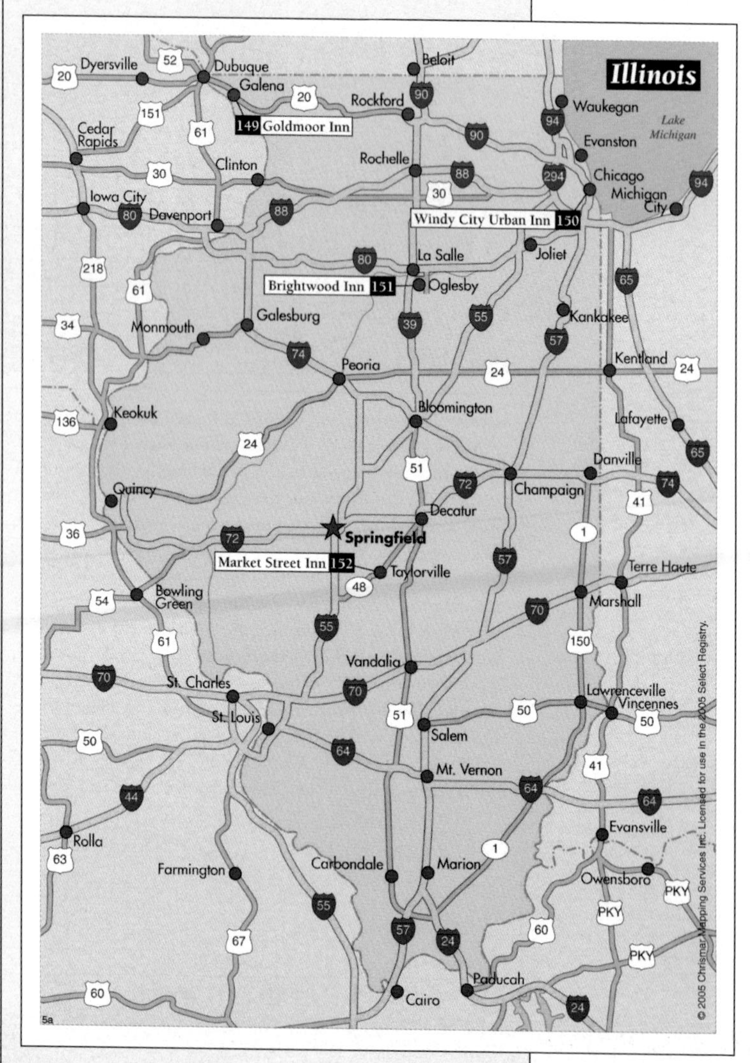

Goldmoor Inn

www.srinns.com/goldmoor
9001 Sand Hill Road, Galena, IL 61036
800-255-3925 • 815-777-3925 • Fax 815-777-3993
goldmoor@galenalink.com

Innkeepers/Owners
Patricia and James Goldthorpe
Traditional Country Inn

Rooms/Rates
4 Suites $215/$275, 3 Cottages $275/$345, 2 Cabins $255/$295, 2 Rooms $135/$165. Open year round.

Cuisine
Full gourmet breakfast served 8:30-10:00 overlooking Mississippi River, or in your choice of great room dining or free room service. Homebaked cookies in your accommodation. Custom catering for groups or wedding receptions.

Nearest Airport(s)
Dubuque, IA, 25 minute drive.

Directions
Six miles South of Galena on Blackjack Road to Sand Hill Road: follow the blue and white tourism signs on Blackjack Road. Turn on Sand Hill and the Inn is 1/4 mile down on the left.

Contemporary luxury country Inn atop a bluff overlooking the Mississippi River, 6 miles south of historic Galena. The Goldmoor features the perfect setting for small weddings, romantic getaways, anniversaries, and honeymoons. Our grand deluxe suites and cottages, and log cabins feature fireplaces and whirlpools, some even overlooking the Mississippi. We pamper you with first-class amenities such as European terry robes,the finest linens, heated towel bars in each bath,VCR/DVD stereo systems with Bose surround sound,TVs with digital satellite systems and multi-line phones with modem hook-ups and free long distance. Complimentary mountain bikes and a full gourmet breakfast with free room service. Top rated Inn in Illinois, from 1993 to present by ABBA.

Member Since 2001

"This was the perfect spot. We loved it! We'll be back next year."
S&J MN. (Ask us for more.)

Windy City Urban Inn

www.srinns.com/windycity
607 West Deming Place, Chicago, IL 60614
877-897-7091 • 773-248-7091 • Fax 773-529-4183
stay@windycityinn.com

Owners
Mary and Andy Shaw
Contemporary In Town Breakfast Inn

Welcome to a slice of life in the 'city of big shoulders.' A Victorian mansion on a quiet tree-lined street near Lincoln Park and the lake. Where the music is from the Chicago Symphony and South King Drive. The rooms are named after Chicago authors with the class of Saul Bellow, the populism of Studs Terkel and the hot romance of Nelson Algren and Simone DeBeauvoir. And where you can choose from guest rooms in the main house or apartment suites in a coach house behind an ivy covered courtyard garden. Your hosts guarantee a comfortable night's rest, a phlethora of restaurant, entertainment and sightseeing recommendations, and a truly Midwestern experience.

Rooms/Rates
4 Rooms, $245/$545 (3 Q, 1 K, 2 w/Jacuzzi); 3 suites, $225/$355. (kitchen, fireplace, Jacuzzi, Q & K beds). Open year-round.

Cuisine
Buffet breakfast in main house. Snacks and beverages. Terrific variety of restaurants in walking distance.

Nearest Airport(s)
Midway and O'Hare

Directions
Via I-90/I-94: Exit at Fullerton. E 1 1/2 miles to Halsted. N/L 1 light to Wrightwood. E/R to dead end at Clark. S/R 1 block to Deming. W/R 1 1/2 blocks to Inn. Parking 2515 N Clark St. Via Lake Shore Drive: Exit Fullerton. W 1/2 mile to Clark. N/R 1/4 mile to Deming. W/L to the Inn.

Member Since 2001

"A great sleep, terrific breakfast and the ambiance of walking along a tree-lined street in Lincoln Park...an oasis in the busy-ness that defines Chicago."

Innkeepers/Owners
Jo and John Ryan
General Manager
Kevin Ryan

Traditional Country Inn

Brightwood Inn

www.srinns.com/brightwood
2407 N. IL Rt. 178, Oglesby, IL 61348
888-667-0600 • 815-667-4600 • Fax 815-667-4727
brtwood@starved-rock-inn.com

Rooms/Rates
7 Rooms, $115/$210; 1 Suite, $225/$250. Each of the eight rooms features its own unique personality and style. All rooms have gas fireplace, private bath and TV/VCR/DVD. Open year-round.

Cuisine
Full breakfast with room. Dinner Thurs-Sun. Elegant dining 5-course meal, advanced reservation required. Beer, wine and liquor. Simple suppers offered Mon-Wed. Lunch totes available.

Nearest Airport(s)
Midway Airport/Chicago

Directions
From I-80 take exit 81, go S on IL Rte 178 for 6 miles. Inn will be on R side. From I-39 take Tonica exit. Go R second stop sign take L on IL Rte 178. Follow for 3 miles, Inn on L side.

Newly constructed in 1996 and nestled on 14 acres of meadow within the confines of Matthiessen State Park, the Brightwood Inn was designed to resemble a vintage farmhouse complete with a veranda and rocking chairs. The Inn will provide you with a romantic, peaceful and luxurious stay amid the beauty of nature. All rooms have TV/VCR & DVD and phones with modem hookup. Six rooms have large Jacuzzi tubs and three have private balconies. Starved Rock State Park and the I&M Canal are located just two miles north. Intimate dining room with seasonally adjusted menu features herbs fresh-picked from our garden. The entire inn is smoke-free and pets are not allowed.

Member Since 2000

"Where do we start? AMAZING! the food, atmoshpere, a perfect romantic getaway."

Market Street Inn

www.srinns.com/marketstreet
220 E. Market Street, Taylorville, IL 62568
800-500-1466 • 217-824-7220 • Fax 217-824-7229
jhauser@chipsnet.com

Innkeepers/Owners
Myrna & Joseph Hauser
Historic In Town Breakfast Inn

Rich in architectural detail, this romantic 1892 Queen Anne Victorian jewel boasts six original fireplaces and mantels, ornate woodwork, fretwork over pocket doors and beveled glass windows. Sit by the parlor fireplace and feast your eyes upon the antiques, semi-antiques and Oriental rugs to appreciate the blend of history, luxury, charm and hospitality. In the main inn, the grand oak staircase beckons one to unwind in one of the guest rooms--each with delightfully different decor. Our Carriage House has two rooms, including a King Grand Deluxe with two fireplaces, a wet bar, a double whirlpool and a separate shower. Modern amenities include central air, private baths--most with double whirlpool tubs/showers, fireplaces, cable TV, in-room phones and wireless DSL. At day's end stroll through the perennial gardens to view over 200 hostas. Then relax in the gazebo of the Victorian wrap-around porch with wine or soft drink. Lincoln Library and sites are 30 minutes away. Lincoln Prairie Bike Trail is six blocks away. Golfing and skydiving.

Member Since 2002

Rooms/Rates
$109/$375. 8 Rooms, $109/$375. 2 King Jr. Suites w/dbl whirlpools, some w/fireplaces. 2 Queen standard rooms w/fireplaces. Handicap Suite. Open year-round. Packages available.

Cuisine
Full hearty candlelight breakfast served daily. Complimentary wine served each evening and hors d'oeuvres on weekends. Complimentary: coffee, tea, soda & bottled water. Fine dining 2 blocks away.

Nearest Airport(s)
Springfield Airport

Directions
3.5 hrs. from Chicago. I-55 to Springfield: Rt. 29 S to Taylorville; R on Walnut, L on Market. From Decatur: Rt. 48 W to Taylorville, L on Walnut, L on Market. 90 minutes from St Louis: I-55 north, exit 63 onto Rt. 48 go 25 miles, exit L at 1 mile sign for Taylorville; R on Market.

"Peaceful! I lost all sense of time while soaking in the hot tub just talking for 2 1/2 hours."

Indiana

"The Hoosier State"

Famous For: Farmlands, Cornfields, Wildflowers, Indiana Dunes National Lakeshore, Indianapolis 500

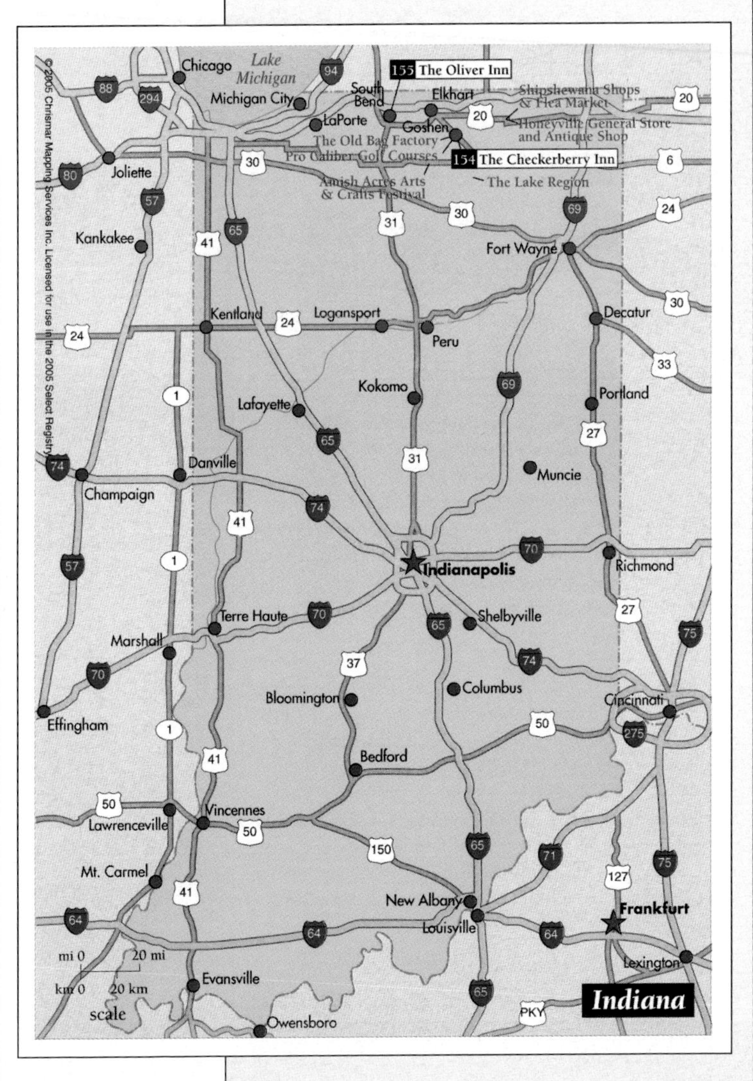

The Checkerberry Inn

www.srinns.com/checkerberryinn
62535 County Rd. 37, Goshen, IN 46528
574-642-4445 • 574-642-0191 • Fax 574-642-0198
reservations@checkerberryinn.com

Innkeepers/Owners
Karen Kennedy and Kelly Graff

Elegant Georgian Country Inn

AAA ◆◆◆

Rated one of the ten best inns nationwide by Inn Review, featured in many national travel magazines, and the only inn and restaurant in Indiana to be featured in Patricia Schultz's *New York Times* best-selling book, "1,000 Places to See Before You Die." Nestled in the center of a 100-acre private wooded estate in the heart of Amish country, the Inn offers breathtaking views of unspoiled countryside, Amish buggies clip-clopping by, glorious gardens and sunflower fields from individually decorated rooms and luxurious suites.

Amenities include in-room spa services, private wooded walking trail, outdoor pool, tennis & croquet courts, and a spacious library opening to our lovely back courtyard, ideal for weddings (up to 150), business meetings & retreats (up to 50).

Excellent bistro restaurant with full bar features live entertainment on most Friday nights. Just two hours from downtown Chicago and three hours north of Indianapolis, the Checkerberry Inn is an oasis of calm in a hectic world, and a perfect weekend escape.

Member Since 1990

Rooms/Rates

11 Rooms, $100/$155 B&B; 3 Suites, $120/$325 B&B Single (corporate) rate: $95. All rooms have private baths, satellite TV, VCRs, coffee makers, blowdryers & high-speed internet. Suites also feature Jacuzzis, CD players & refrigerators.

Cuisine

Continental+ breakfast included with rooms. Upscale chef-owned restaurant, Citrus, an American Bistro serves dinner Tues–Sat. Full bar.

Nearest Airport(s)

South Bend Regional Airport (SBN)

Directions

IN Toll Road: Exit 107. Turn right onto SR 13, go south (10 mi) to "T" intersection at SR 4. Right onto SR 4 to first left, CR 37. Inn is one mile down on right.

"Kudos to Karen & Kelly for providing exquisite dining & a peaceful, first-class paradise in the middle of the heartland."- Steve Buscemi, NYC

Innkeepers/Owners
Richard and Venera Monahan
Victorian In Town Breakfast Inn

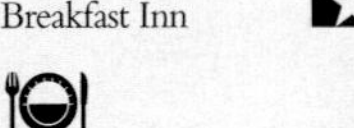

The Oliver Inn

www.srinns.com/oliverinn
630 W. Washington Street, South Bend, IN 46601
888-697-4466 • 574-232-4545 • Fax 574-288-9788
oliver@michiana.org

Rooms/Rates
9 Rooms $130/$195, 1 Suite, King/Queen beds, A/C, telephone, hairdryers, cable TV. Some with fireplace, balcony, or whirlpool tub. Football and special event rates higher.

Cuisine
Full candlelight breakfast with live piano music. Complimentary drinks and snacks from Butler's Pantry. Dine at Tippecanoe Place Restaurant in the Studebaker Mansion right next door.

Nearest Airport(s)
South Bend (SBN)

Directions
From the North: Indiana Toll Road (I-80/90), exit 77, S at light on 31/933, 2 miles to R on Washington St. From the South: N on Hwy 31 into downtown South Bend, L on Washington.

The Oliver Inn Bed & Breakfast offers a 'turn-of-the-century' feeling with all of today's important amenities. Experience Victorian elegance in this historic mansion surrounded by a lush acre of manicured gardens, gazebo and lawn swings. Nine beautiful rooms in main house, private baths, double whirlpools, A/C, fireplaces, CD players, hairdryers, luxurious robes. Enjoy candlelight breakfast by the fire to live piano music and complimentary snacks, gourmet coffees and soft drinks from the Butler's Pantry. For dinner, stroll next door to Tippecanoe Place Restaurant in the Studebaker Mansion. Come discover why The Oliver Inn was voted the Michiana area's 'Best Bed & Breakfast' and why Steve Thomas from 'This Old House' stays at The Oliver Inn. Experience the ultimate in relaxation, luxury and serenity in our newly renovated Carriage House Suite. Two bedrooms, two baths, jetted marble shower, double whirlpool tub, living room with fireplace and entertainment center, screened in porch and full kitchen stocked with goodies.

Member Since 2000

"We haven't been this relaxed in a long time; warm and gracious hospitality; lovely décor."

Kansas

"The Sunflower State"

Famous For: "Home on the Range," Wild West, Dodge City, Buffalo, Agriculture, Aircraft Manufacturing, Sunflowers, Grain, Great Plains

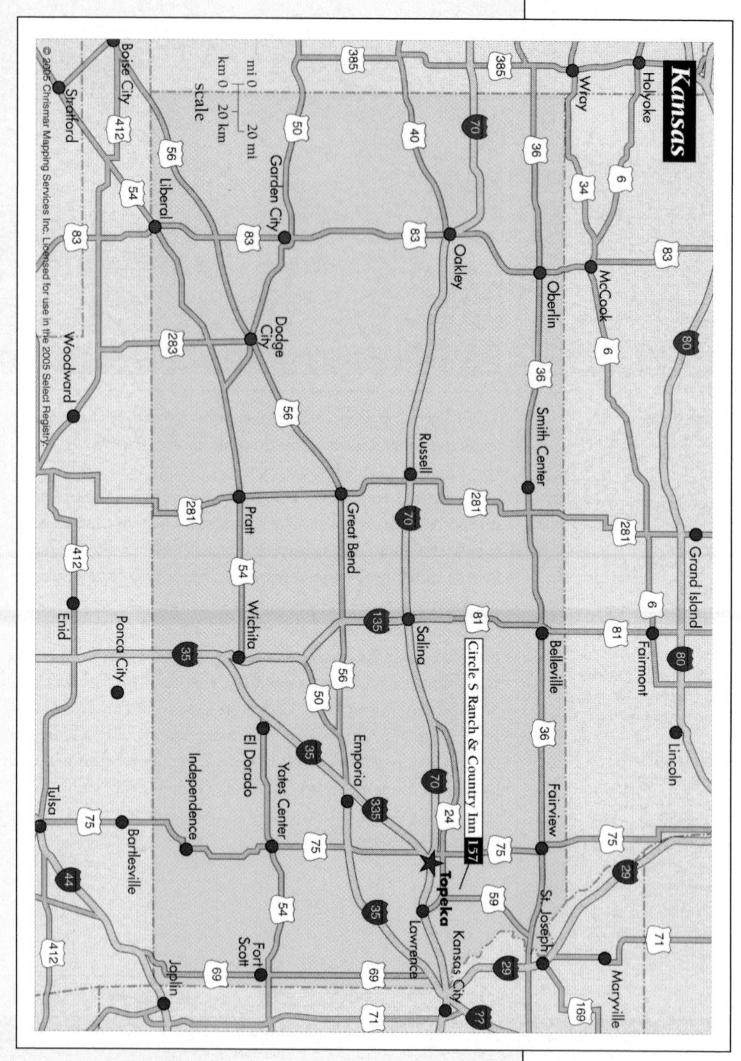

Circle S Ranch & Country Inn

www.srinns.com/circlesranch
3325 Circle S Lane, Lawrence, KS 66044
800-625-2839 • 785-843-4124 • Fax 785-843-4474
circlesinn@aol.com

Innkeepers/Owners
Mary and Jack Cronemeyer

Rustic Country Inn 

AAA ◆◆◆

Rooms/Rates
8 rooms, $155-$175/$215. 4 Suites, $215/$245. Unique decor;rooms available with whirlpool tubs and fireplaces.All rooms have robes,phones,and sitting areas. Hot tub.

Cuisine
Hearty country style breakfast, with soft drinks, bottled water, guest refrigerator, and ice. Dining schedule varies seasonally, with many items coming from our kitchen garden. Fine wines, beer and liquors available.

Nearest Airport(s)
Kansas City International Airport

Directions
From Kansas City: I-70 W toward Topeka. Exit at East Lawrence exit 204. R on 59 Hwy. NW for 3 miles. R on CR-1045 N for 5.5 miles. R on 35th St. E for 2 miles.

Nestled amid 1,200 acres of gently rolling hills fifty minutes west of Kansas City, is a place where visitors can experience a rare vestige of the once vast tallgrass prairie.The Circle S Ranch, owned and operated by Mary's family since the 1860s, offers a romantic retreat where couples' favorite pastime is connecting with one another and nature. Each of the elegantly rustic country inn's uniquely-themed guestrooms feature gracious comforts, luxurious amenities, air conditioned with sweeping views of the prairie landscape where buffalo still roam. Conference and Wedding facilities are available in our Party Barn, Conference Room, or Great Room. Open Year round. You can reserve a room at a moment's notice, and online reservations are accepted. Voted best Inn in the U.S. by bedandbreakfast.com, and one of the 'Top 15 B&B/Inns' for business travelers by *Arrington's Bed and Breakfast Journal*. Best in the Midwest 2003. We also recieved an award for Best for Honeymoon/Anniversary in Arrington's *Inn Traveler* 2005 Book of Lists.

Member Since 2002

"There is something magical...with its serene surroundings. You can't help relaxing..."

Kentucky

"The Bluegrass State"

Famous For: Horses, Kentucky Derby, Tobacco Farms, Fine Bourbon, Lakes, Hardwood Forests, Daniel Boone Bluegrass music, "My Old Kentucky Home"

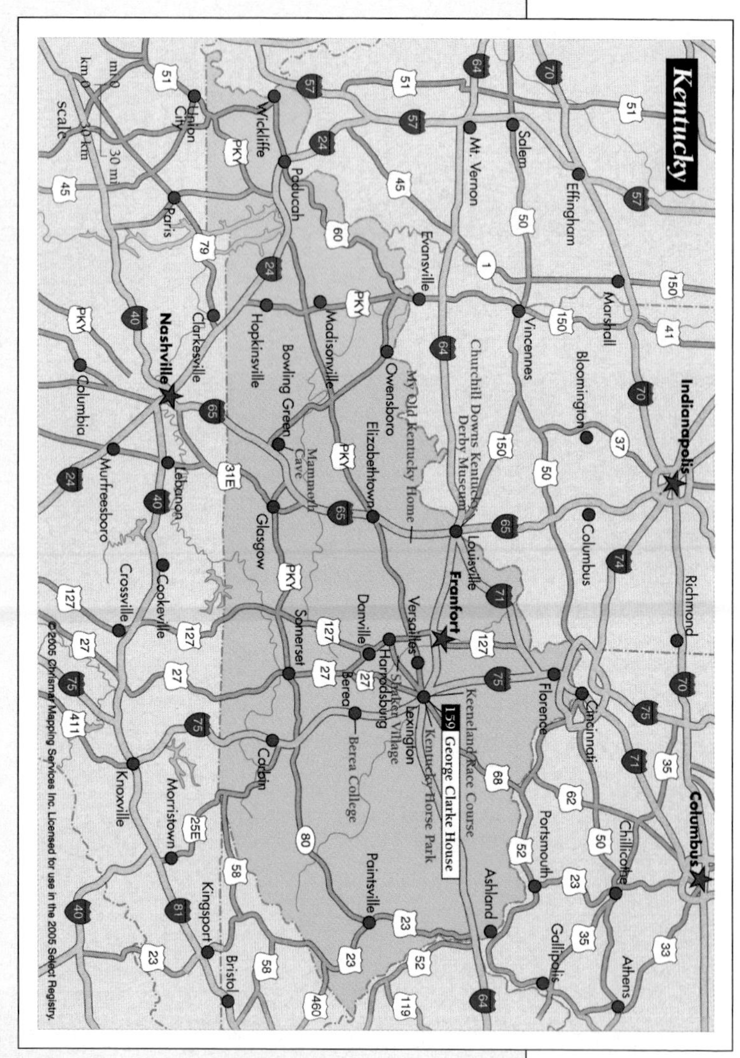

Proprietress
Kathryn L. Bux
Historic Urban Bed & Breakfast

George Clarke House

www.srinns.com/georgeclarke
136 Woodland Ave., Lexington, KY 40502
866-436-1890 • 859-254-2500
jeeves@georgeclarkehouse.com

Rooms/Rates
4 Rooms. All guest rooms have fireplaces, private baths (some with whirlpool tubs), and queen or king beds. High Season: $169/$299 Low Season: $135/$259. Resident cats greet you upon arrival.

Cuisine
Breakfasts are sumptuous affairs. Delicacies such as crême brûlée French toast, waffles with Grand Marnier strawberries, or Crab Cakes Benedict are served on delicate china with gleaming silver and sparkling crystal.

Nearest Airport(s)
Bluegrass Airport - 5mi from GCH

Directions
Located in historic, residential downtown neighborhood. Specific driving directions provided upon reservation.

In Victorian times, George Clarke was a prominent Lexingtonian, whose house reflected his reputation as a builder and a gentleman. If he were to visit today, he would feel right at home, unwinding in the glow of a gas fireplace, and perhaps enjoying the antics of the resident cats before retiring to his room. After relaxing in the period tub with its whirlpool bath, he might enjoy a snack or a complimentary refreshment before sinking into his luxurious four-poster bed. In the morning he would enjoy a gourmet breakfast served, in appropriate attire, on china with silver and crystal. He might also explore the life of Lexington today, with downtown restaurants and shops close-by. Come visit us at George's house -- it's a trip into the past, with the amenities of the present. Jeeves, the butler, is in service most weekends. We're listed in Haunted Inns of America, so you never know whom you might meet.

Member Since 2005

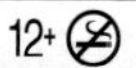

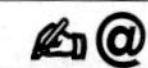

"This is one of the finest historic preservations of a private home in the state of Kentucky."

Louisiana

"The Pelican State"

Famous For: Mardi Gras, Dixieland Jazz, French Quarter, Bayou, Crayfish, Pirates, Creole, Cajun Cooking, Salt (#1 salt-producing state), Rice, Sugar, Oil, Gas

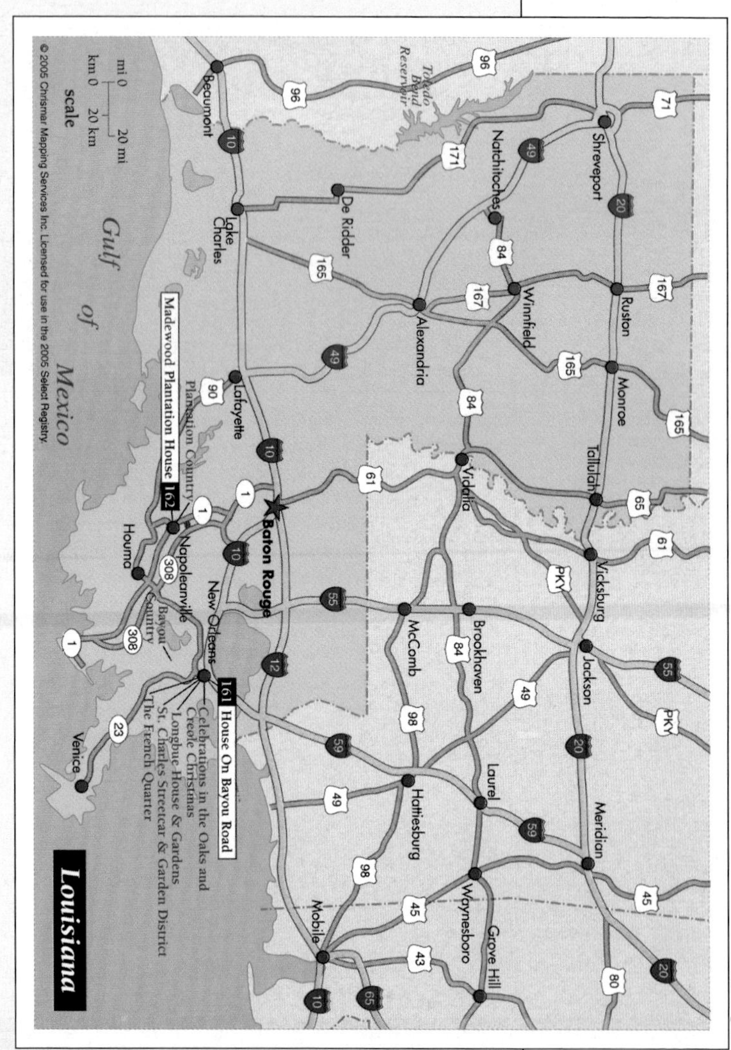

Innkeeper/Owner
Cynthia Reeves
General Manager
Karon Hale

Historic In Town
Breakfast Inn

House on Bayou Road

www.srinns.com/bayou
2275 Bayou Road, New Orleans, LA 70119
800-882-2968 • 504-945-0992 • Fax 504-945-0993
hobr@hobr.nocoxmail.com

Rooms/Rates
4 Rooms, 4 suites $145/$310. Jacuzzis and fireplaces, rooms individually decorated with antique and designer touches.

Cuisine
Mini-bars in rooms stocked with beer, soft drinks, juices. Breakfast is served poolside and features Louisiana favorites, such as Eggs Benedict and Pan Perdu, among others.

Nearest Airport(s)
Louis Armstrong International (MSY), 8 miles

Directions
From W: Take I-10 to Metaire Rd Exit. L on City Park Ave. to Carrollton. L on Carrollton, R on Esplanade. 1/4 mile to L on Tonti. Immediate L on Bayou Rd. The inn is on the R of the first block

Circa 1798. Romantic guest rooms, gourmet cuisine and two acres of grounds await guests at this Creole plantation home. Built as the main house to an Indigo plantation, the lush surroundings are a distraction from city life. Yet this restful inn is just a few blocks from the historic French Quarter.The guest quarters are appointed with fine linens and elegant furnishings. Breakfast is a 'don't miss' event, served poolside. Our fun and delicious hands-on cooking classes are taught in the historic house kitchen. The attentive staff is ready to help plan a memorable stay with lots of 'inside info.' Restaurant Indigo accepts reservations Tuesday through Sunday. This beautiful award-winning restaurant features contemporary Louisiana cuisine served inside or on the veranda. Together, Indigo and House on Bayou Road create a captivating oasis from which to tour New Orleans.

Member Since 2002

12+  

"The Inn creates a good balance between genuine, unpretentious hospitality, gracious service and an atmosphere that is elegant and down to earth."

Madewood Plantation House

www.srinns.com/madewoodplantation
4250 Highway 308, Napoleonville, LA 70390
800-375-7151 • 985-369-7151 • Fax 985-369-9848
madewoodpl@aol.com

Owners
Keith and Millie Marshall
Manager
Christine Gaudet
Traditional Southern Country Inn

Madewood Plantation House offers elegant accommodations in a homelike atmosphere. The National Historic Landmark is lovingly maintained by its longtime staff, who provide the relaxed atmosphere for which Madewood is noted. Guests enjoy antique-filled rooms and canopied beds along with a house-party ambiance that includes a wine and cheese hour prior to a family-style candlelit dinner prepared by Madewood's cooks.

Selected one of the top 12 Inns by *Country Inns* magazine, featured in *National Geographic Traveler* and named by *NGT* in 1999 as one of the top 54 inns in US, *Travel Holiday* magazine and *Time* magazine. French spoken.

Rooms/Rates
6 Rooms; 2 Suites, $259/$289 double occupancy. Seasonal package rates MAP (Dinner, Breakfast). Open year-round, except Thanksgiving, Christmas and New Year's Eves and Days.

Cuisine
Wine and cheese hour. Candelit Southern/Cajun dinner served with other guests in plantation dining room. Full service liquor. Full plantation breakfast.

Nearest Airport(s)
Ryan Airport - Baton Rouge

Directions
I-10 W. from New Orleans to exit 182, Cross Sunshine Bridge and follow LA Hwy 70 to Spur 70, then L on LA Hwy 308, 2.2 miles past Napoleonville.

Member Since 1993

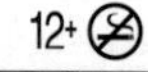

The "Queen of the Bayou"

Maine

"The Pine Tree State"

Famous For: Lobsters, Lighthouses, Rocky Coastlines, Potatoes, Pines, Ports, Paper

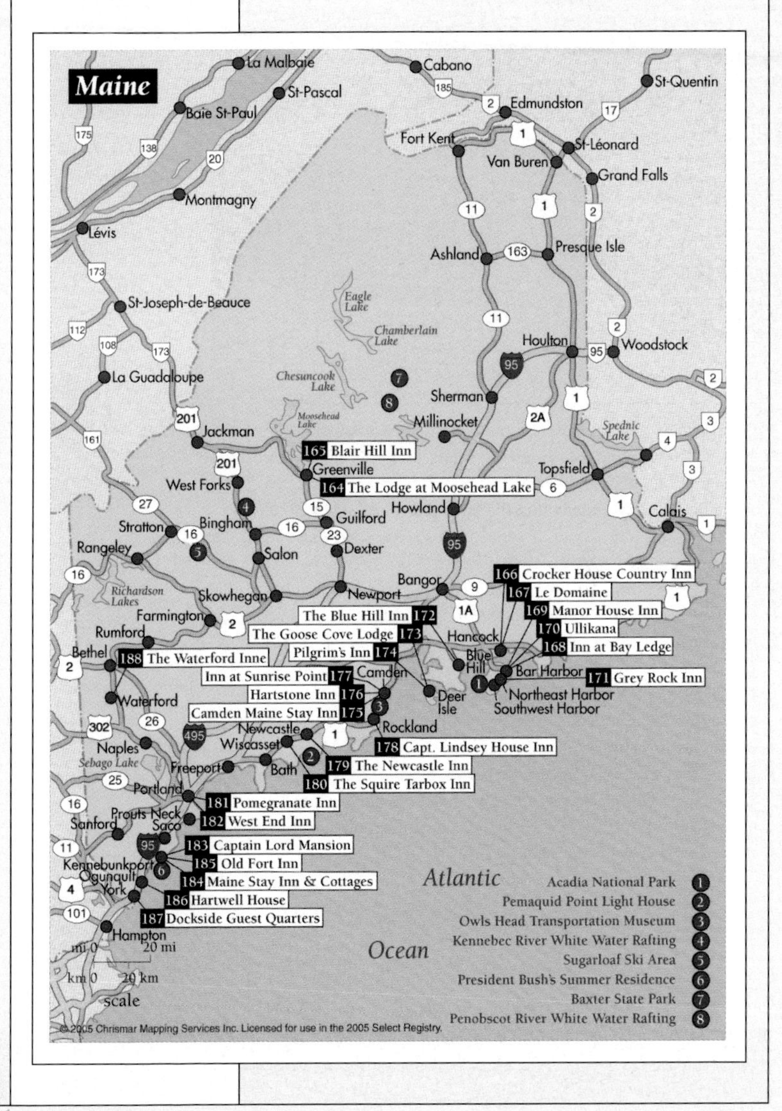

Lodge at Moosehead Lake

www.srinns.com/mooseheadlake
Upon Lily Bay Road, Box 1167, Greenville, ME 04441
800-825-6977 • 207-695-4400 • Fax 207-695-2281
innkeeper@lodgeatmooseheadlake.com

Owners
Sonda and Bruce Hamilton

Traditional Country Retreat/Lodge

Overlooking the broad waters and islands of Moosehead Lake and the surrounding mountains the views from all but 1 guest room are absolutely breathtaking. Comfort and pampering is assured by the lodge combining the amenities of a luxury hotel with the casual intimacy of a Country Inn. Each accommodation in the main lodge includes a hand carved 4 poster bed, Jacuzzi, TV/VCR, air-conditioning and gas fireplace create a private haven. Guests often prefer the expansive pleasures of the great room with its massive stone fireplace or the 136 ft. veranda overlooking the lake which provides captivating sunsets. Join us in the Lakeview dining room where culinary excellence, attentive service, exquisite views, and impressive ambiance, mesh to create an extraordinary dining experience. 2005 Grand Award winner in the Andrew Harper's Hideaway report listing the Worlds top 24 captivating hideaway hotels and resort. Inland Maine's only AAA 4 diamond. 2004 Winner of the "Most Outstanding Inn in North America" by Conde Naste Johansen.

Member Since 1995

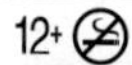
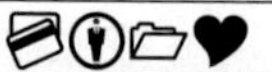

Rooms/Rates
5 Rooms, $205/$375;
3 Suites, $325/$475 B&B.
Open year around.

Cuisine
Full Breakfast with starter buffet. In season-dinner served nightly except Tuesday, Wednesday and Thursday. Off season-dinner served Friday and Saturday nights. 24-hour pantry. Full liquor license and impressive wine list.

Nearest Airport(s)
Bangor

Directions
I-95 to Newport, 7N to Dexter, 23N to Guilford, 15N to Greenville. 1.5 hrs drive from Bangor airport 2 1/2 hrs. from Portland & 4 1/2 hrs. from Boston.

"We loved it all-beyond expectations. Innkeepers so awesome! The Lodge is Magnificent!"

Blair Hill Inn at Moosehead Lake

www.srinns.com/blairhillinn
351 Lily Bay Road, Greenville, ME 04441
207-695-0224 • Fax 207-695-4324
info@blairhill.com

Innkeepers/Owners
Dan and Ruth McLaughlin
Historic Victorian Country Manor

Rooms/Rates
8 Beautiful Guest Rooms. $250/$425.

Cuisine
A lavish breakfast is served each morning. Dinner, a Top Ten culinary delight of Maine, is served Fri.& Sat. from mid-June to mid-Oct. Fresh, wood-grilled seafood, produce from the inn's own gardens and greenhouse, jazz & Caribbean music, and brilliant lake views create that special vacation evening. End with a cocktail on the veranda at sunset and it's as it should be, you're living life large!

Nearest Airport(s)
Bangor International

Directions
95N to Newport; 7N to Dexter; 23N to Guilford; 15N to Greenville. 1.5 hours from Bangor, 2.5 from Portland, 4.5 from Boston.

It's a thrilling sight rising up from the hillside atop massive stone walls as if a jewel set upon a pedestal. This historic country manor will take your breath away. Its unsurpassed location provides an astounding display of nature's brilliance. The seemingly endless mountaintops, the rich colors of the sky and the crystal blue waters of Moosehead Lake will leave you without words. With a perfect balance of warmth and elegance, its style and grace breathe an uncommon air. The relaxed atmosphere, together with service that speaks thoughtfully to your needs, will set you instantly at ease. It is truly a one of-a-kind property. This formerly private 9,000 square foot estate has been restored to perfection. Grand and exceptionally spacious, it offers beautiful guest rooms and baths, fine amenities, award-winning dining, summer evening concerts and 15 serene acres of gardens, woodlands, and ponds. Sitting on the broad porch as the sun sets across the lake, you'll realize that this is the hidden gem you've been looking for.

Member Since 2005

10+ 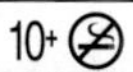   

"Thank you for preserving such Royal Magnificence! Few hotels can boast such beauty, inside and out. Our dinner was the culinary high point of our trip."

Crocker House Country Inn

www.srinns.com/crocker
967 Point Road, Hancock Point, ME 04640
877-715-6017 • 207-422-6806 • Fax 207-422-3105
info@crockerhouse.com

Innkeepers/Owners
Richard and Elizabeth Malaby
Traditional Country Inn

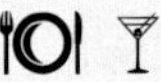

The Crocker House Country Inn is tucked away on the peninsula of Hancock Point. Its quiet, out of the way location, fine cuisine and individually appointed guest rooms, all combine to make the Crocker House a refreshing and memorable destination. The restaurant, open to the public, continues to draw guests from distant places for its extraordinary cuisine and live piano on Friday and Saturday nights. A three-minute walk to Frenchman Bay and public moorings. An ideal location for wedding receptions, family reunions and small business retreats. Pet friendly. Wireless.

Rooms/Rates
11 Rooms, $110/$160 in-season, $85/$120 off-season B&B. Late April until New Year's Day. MAP available-off season.

Cuisine
Breakfast and dinner. Wine list and full bar. Classic continental cuisine with a downeast flair. Extensive use made of organic and indigenous products.

Nearest Airport(s)
Bar Harbor - 17 miles
Bangor - 42 miles

Directions
If you are travelling N on Rt. 1 proceed to Ellsworth. If you are travelling N on US 95 proceed to US 395 in Bangor. Follow US 395 to the end. Take Rt 1A 23 miles to Ellsworth. From Ellsworth go 8 miles N on U.S. Rt. 1, turn R on Point Road. Continue 5 miles to Inn on R.

Member Since 1987

"Don't really have the right words to thank you for our stay. Your staff is incredible!"

Owner/Chef
Nicole Purslow

Beth Clarke Bean

Elegant Village Inn

Le Domaine

www.srinns.com/ledomaine
P O 519, Hancock, ME 04640
800-554-8498 • 207-422-3395
nicole@ledomaine.com

Rooms/Rates
3 Rooms, 2 Suites $200/$285.
June 10 to October 16.

Cuisine
Renowned French restaurant named 'One of the Best Restaurants in the World for Wine' by *Wine Spectator* magazine. French provencal cooking using the finest of Maine's seafood, local produce and choicest meats.

Nearest Airport(s)
Bar Harbor/Trenton 20 minutes.

Directions
Located on U.S. Rte 1, in Hancock, ME. Just 10 min. E of Ellsworth, 45 min. from Bangor. From I-95 in Bangor, take I-395, follow signs to Ellsworth. From Bar Harbor Airport or Cat Ferry from Nova Scotia, take Rte. 3 N to Ellsworth, then U.S. Rte.1 E.

The colorful, sun-soaked atmosphere of Provence surrounds you when you step into Le Domaine. The scent of lavender and fresh flowers, French furnishings, cheerful prints, antiques and art create a truly unique atmosphere. There are many delights to savor... breakfast overlooking the garden, the elegant dining room, selecting from Nicole's dinner offerings, studying our award-winning list of French wines, the waft of wonderful aromas, delectable desserts. However you choose to spend your days - at a concert, hiking in Acadia National Park or shopping for treasures in this lively area of Coastal Maine - Le Domaine makes any visit truly memorable.

Member Since 2002

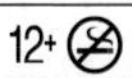

"Le Domaine was a unique experience that transported me back to my days in Provence. Now it is a happily anticipated destination when visiting Maine."

Inn at Bay Ledge

www.srinns.com/bayledge
150 Sand Point Road, Bar Harbor, ME 04609
207-288-4204 • Fax 207-288-5573
bayledge@downeast.net

Innkeepers/Owners
Jack and Jeani Ochtera
Elegant Rustic Waterside Breakfast Inn

Mobil ★★★
AAA ◆◆◆

Amidst the towering pines, The Inn at Bay Ledge literally clings to the cliffs of Mt. Dessert Island, which is locally and aptly referred to as "The Eden of New England." The veranda, appointed with comfy wicker, overlooks the spectacular coastline and is extremely inviting. Guests may enjoy a swim in our pool, relax in a hammock or take a stroll along our private beach. The elegant bedrooms compliment the style of the inn which was built in the 1900s and possesses an upscale country ambiance. Beautifully decorated with antiques, all rooms are unique with views of Frenchmen Bay. King and queen beds are covered with designer linens, down quilts and feather beds. Our new Summer Cottage sits just 25 feet from the cliff's edge!

Rooms/Rates
8 rooms, $100/$275 low season; high season $150/$375.
4 cottages $125/$375 low season; high season $175/$475.
All rooms are king or queen with private baths. Inn rooms have bay view. Cottages enjoy a pine view. Summer Cotage has bay view.

Cuisine
Full gourmet breakfast served in the sunroom over looking the bay. Enjoy afternoon tea and refreshments on the porch.

Nearest Airport(s)
Bar Harbor 15 minutes, Bangor 1 hour, Portland 3 hours

Directions
From the head of the island follow Rt. 3 for 5 miles. L onto Sand Point Road. The inn will be on the L over looking the bay.

Member Since 2002

"We don't want to leave-Can't wait to return. This is one of the prettiest places on earth!"

Innkeepers/Owners
Stacey and Ken Smith

Traditional Village Breakfast Inn

Mobil ★★★
AAA ◆◆◆

Manor House Inn

www.srinns.com/manorhouseinn
106 West Street, Bar Harbor, ME 04609
800-437-0088 • 207-288-3759 • Fax 207-288-2974
manor@me.acadia.net

Rooms/Rates
18 Rooms/Suites $135/$275 B&B. Off-season $77/$185. Open April - November.

Cuisine
Full breakfast and afternoon tea.

Nearest Airport(s)
Hancock County Airport; Trenton, Maine, 20 miles

Directions
As you approach Bar Harbor on Route 3, turn Left onto West Street. Manor House Inn will be 3 blocks down, on the right.

Built in 1887 as a 22-room mansion, Manor House Inn has been authentically restored to its original splendor and is now on the National Register of Historic Places. The moment you step into the front entry a romantic Victorian past becomes the present. Enjoy comfort, convenience, and privacy while staying within easy walking distance of Bar Harbor's fine shops, restaurants and ocean activities. Each morning wake up to a delicious home-baked breakfast such as baked stuffed blueberry French toast. Then spend your day exploring Acadia National Park.

Member Since 1998

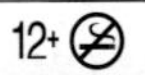

"Delightfully peaceful and charming!"

Ullikana & A Yellow House

www.srinns.com/ullikana
15 The Field, Bar Harbor, ME 04609
207-288-9552 • Fax 207-288-3682

Innkeepers/Owners
Helene Harton and Roy Kasindorf

Traditional In Town Breakfast Inn

Ullikana, a secluded, romantic haven, overlooking the harbor, and our sister Inn, A Yellow House, only steps away, are two of the few remaining cottages from the 1800s in Bar Harbor. Only a minute walk from the center of town, our quiet location offers a haven of hospitality. Watch the lobster boats in the harbor from the garden or the patio, where sumptuous breakfasts are served. Relax in the casual elegance of these historic Inns, where art is an important part of our decor. We invite you to share the history and hospitality of Ullikana and A Yellow House with us.

Rooms/Rates
16 Rooms, high season: $150/$285; low season: $100/$225. All our rooms have king or queen beds. All have private baths. Some have porches overlooking harbor. Some rooms have fireplaces.

Cuisine
We serve a full breakfast on our patio, looking out on the water. Also we have afternoon refreshments on the patio.

Nearest Airport(s)
Bangor Airport
Bar Harbor Airport

Directions
Rte 3 to Bar Harbor. L onto Cottage St. R onto Main St. L after Bar Harbor Trust Company building. Take gravel road towards water.

Member Since 2000

"When in Bar Harbor, I always stay at Ullikana!" (Roy's Mom)

Innkeepers/Owners
Janet, Karl & Adam Millett

Elegant Country Breakfast Inn

Grey Rock Inn

www.srinns.com/greyrock
Harbourside Road, Northeast Harbor, ME 04662
207-276-9360 • Fax 207-276-9894

This beautifully situated mansion on seven acres overlooks the harbor lighthouse and outer islands off Mt. Desert. Built in 1910 as a private residence, Grey Rock has been a gathering place, hosting many of the famous families that built their homes in NE Harbor. With warmth and charm, Grey Rock offers elegant rooms that are pleasingly decorated. To assure your pleasure and relaxation, fireplaces are featured throughout the public rooms and in many of the bedrooms. Grey Rock is a seven-minute walk to the picturesque village of NE Harbor with its quaint old-fashioned shops and to our marina, a popular yachting basin. Elegant, Cottage style, country inn with breakfast.

Rooms/Rates
7 Rooms, 1 Suite, May to June 20, $110/$275. July thru October, $165/$375.

Cuisine
Breakfast only; 110 restaurants on this island. We make reservations for you. Guests are welcome to bring their own spirits. We supply ice and glassware. Afternoon Tea.

Nearest Airport(s)
Bangor International

Directions
Follow RT 198 on Mount Desert Island. We are the first property bordering the National Park as you approach the Village.

Member Since 1998

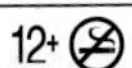

"Maine Coast Living at its Best!"

The Blue Hill Inn

www.srinns.com/bluehill
40 Union Street, P.O. Box 403, Blue Hill, ME 04614
800-826-7415 • 207-374-2844 • Fax 207-374-2829
mary@bluehillinn.com

Innkeepers/Owners
Mary & Don Hartley

Traditional Federal Village Breakfast Inn

The small village of Blue Hill wraps around the head of Blue Hill Bay and is centrally located for exploring Acadia National Park, Deer Isle, Castine, and the Blue Hill Peninsula. The beauty of the area's rugged coastlines, blueberry barrens, pine trees, crystal blue waters, lobster buoys, lighthouses, and small villages is complemented by fine arts, crafts, and food. Evening skies are brilliant with stars. The multi-chimneyed, clapboarded Inn is situated in the historic district and is a short walk to the harbor, Kneisel Chamber Music Hall, Blue Hill Mountain, art and antique galleries. The circa 1830 hostelry retains many original features with fireplaces, gleaming 19th Century floors, and antique furnishings contributing to an intimate atmosphere. After a day of hiking, boating, birdwatching, or gallery hopping, guests return for a perfect pot of tea and pastries in the garden. Hors d'oeuvres are served before dinner; down comforters, turn-down service, and cappuccino service await after dinner. Guest rooms have airconditioning for those warmer days.

Member Since 1994

Rooms/Rates
11 Rooms, $138/$195 B&B; Cape House luxury suite, $225/$285 B&B. Fpls, AC. Inn opened mid-May to Oct 31. Cape House available as self-catering Nov-May - $165. 7% tax additional.

Cuisine
Multi-course breakfasts with several entrees, afternoon refreshments, evening hors d'oeuvres. Locally grown organic produce and Maine seafood featured. Wine Dinners in May & October. Fine Wines list with 100 selections.

Nearest Airport(s)
Bangor International

Directions
From S, ME I95N to I295N to Augusta. 3E to Bucksport, 15S to Blue Hill. Right at Inn's road sign to 177E to Inn. From W 2E to 95N to 15S to 177E.

"Stay here if you enjoy antiques, warm hospitality, and classic New England Inns." Maine Handbook.

The Goose Cove Lodge

www.srinns.com/goosecovelodge
Deer Isle, 300 Goose Cove Rd., P.O. Box 40, Sunset, ME 04683
800-728-1963 • 207-348-2508 • Fax 207-348-2624
goosecove@goosecovelodge.com

Innkeepers/Owners
Dom & Joanne Parisi
Rustic Waterside Retreat/ Lodge

Mobil ★★★

Rooms/Rates
22 Cottages,Cabins and Suites: Spring & Fall $111/$368 B&B, Summer $148/$525 B&B. May-Oct. All accommodations have private baths, are comfortably furnished, from rustic Maine to elegant Great North Woods style.

Cuisine
Serving breakfast and fine regional bistro dinner fare in The Point Dining Room. Full bar and wine list.

Nearest Airport(s)
Bangor International

Directions
From Rte 1 N in Bucksport, turn R 1 1/2 miles to Lodge.

Located on Deer Isle and overlooking the majestic beauty of Penobscot Bay sits the secluded paradise of Goose Cove Lodge. Nestled on a gently sloping hillside, the lodge is a highly informal and unhurried place ruled by the restorative rhythms of nature. The setting is one of incomparable natural beauty; the warm hospitality and celebrated cuisine is considered some of the best on coastal Maine. Our guests from all corners of the world treasure the informal, comfortable and rustic accommodations of this pristine property. Goose Cove Lodge offers secluded lodging, sand beaches, superb sailing and sea-kayaking tours, hiking and stargazing parties. Kid Camp during July and August, with off-site horseback riding, golf and tennis lessons available. Weekly guided nature walks and astronomy offered by the naturalist innkeeper. Near Acadia National Park, Haystack Mountain School of Crafts and Opera House Arts, in Stonington, a working fishing village.

Member Since 1981

"I've found heaven on earth. Stay as long as you can afford!" "Any nature lover who's in need of a room would be foolish not to hole up here."

Pilgrim's Inn

www.pilgrimsinn.com
P.O. Box 69, 20 Main Street, Deer Isle, ME 04627
888-778-7505 • 207-348-6615 • Fax 207-348-6615
innkeeper@pilgrimsinn.com

Innkeepers/Owners
Rob and Cathy DeGennaro
Innkeeper/Manager
Marge Chickering

Historic Waterside Country Inn

Overlooking Northwest Harbor and the picturesque millpond, the 1793 colonial is surrounded by the unspoiled beauty of remote Deer Isle in Penobscot Bay. Glowing hearths, colonial colors, pumpkin pine floors, antique furnishings, combined with warm hospitality and gourmet meals in the famous Whale's Rib Tavern have pleased many contented guests. Easy access to Haystack School of Crafts, the busy fishing village of Stonington, Isle au Haut, views of lighthouses and numerous galleries. Day-trips to pleasant coastal villages and Acadia National Park. A kayaking, sailing and hiking paradise. On the National Register of Historic Places. Chosen by Forbes.com as one of the Country's Best B&Bs and by *Discerning Traveler* as a Romantic Getaway. Cottages, perfect for families with children and pets, are open year round. Come as our guest ... leave as our friend.

Member Since 1980

Rooms/Rates
12 Rooms, 3 Cottages and the Loft on 3 acres with 500 ft of water front; $99/$269, B&B. All rooms have water views and private baths. Open May through October; Cottages open year round.

Cuisine
Full Country Breakfast; Afternoon refreshments; and Dinner at the famous Whale's Rib Tavern with a full liquor license and extensive wine list. Casual seaside dining at its best.

Nearest Airport(s)
Bangor International Airport

Directions
I-95 to Augusta, Rte 3 to Belfast, Route 1 N, in Bucksport take Rte 15 S. Go 25 miles, over Deer Isle bridge, go 5 miles to Village, Right onto Main St, Inn on left 200 yds.

"The Inn is splendid and everything was absolutely out of this world, from our room to the meals. A wonderful seaside getaway."

Camden Maine Stay

www.srinns.com/camdenmainestay
22 High St., Camden, ME 04843
207-236-9636 • Fax 207-236-0621
innkeeper@camdenmainestay.com

Innkeepers/Owners
Bob and Juanita Topper

Historic Village
Breakfast Inn

Relaxed, warm, and very friendly the Maine Stay is located in the historic district of one of America's most beautiful seaside villages. A short walk down tree-lined streets brings you to the harbor park, shops and restaurants. Built in 1802, the striking main house, attached carriage house, and four-story barn are outstanding examples of early American architecture and old New England taste and charm. Spacious common areas with an eclectic collection of furnishings and artwork, exquisite guestrooms, and a big country kitchen, enchant and delight. A perfect getaway for any season. Chosen by *Frontgate* as one of *America's Finest Homes*. In the words of *Vacations Magazine*, "Down east hospitality at its very best," and *Frommer's*, "Camden's premier Bed and Breakfast."

Rooms/Rates
8 Rooms, all with private baths, $125/$250. Spacious and tastefully decorated common areas with wood burning fire places. Open year-round.

Cuisine
Full breakfast, which may be taken at our antique harvest table in the dining room or at a table for two on our sun porch overlooking our beautifully landscaped one-acre garden. Tea is served in the afternoon and nearby restaurants offer fine dining and casual harbor settings...lobster at its best.

Nearest Airport(s)
Rockland (RKD); Bangor (BGR); Portland (PWM)

Directions
US Rte 1 (High Street) 3 blocks N of the village.

Member Since 1995

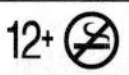

"..like returning home.." (Dr. S. Lewis) "...friendly happy atmosphere.." (P&K Chin)

Camden Maine Hartstone Inn

www.srinns.com/camdenhartstone
41 Elm Street, Camden, ME 04843
800-788-4823 • 207-236-4259 • Fax 207-236-9575
info@hartstoneinn.com

Owners
Mary Jo Brink and Michael Salmon

Elegant 1835 Victorian Mansard Village Inn

Wine Spectator
AWARD OF EXCELLENCE

Built in 1835, the architecturally splendid Hartstone Inn is an enchanting hideaway in the heart of Camden. Surrounded by English gardens and perfectly situated for those who prefer staying in the center of the village, close to good shopping and with easy access to the harbor. The inn's beautifully decorated rooms offer lace canopy beds with fluffy feather duvets, jacuzzi tubs and fireplaces. Elegant china, fine crystal and internationally award-winning cuisine make breakfast and dinner a truly memorable experience. Gourmet getaway packages and cooking class weekends available November-June. Tour our rooms and check availability on our website at www.hartstoneinn.com

Rooms/Rates
6 rooms, 5 suites,$100/$245 B&B. Gourmet Getaway packages and Cooking Class weekends available. Open year- round.

Cuisine
Memorable full breakfast, afternoon cookies and tea, and a five-course gourmet dinner by reservation. Dinner is served Wed.-Sun, July-Oct. (Thurs.-Sun, Nov.-June). Fine wine selection from our cellar list.

Nearest Airport(s)
Bangor or Portland

Directions
US Rt. 1 into Camden, the Inn is on your left as you enter the village from the South.

Member Since 2002

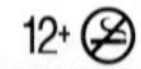

"Blossoming orchids, gourmet cuisine and the attention to detail will bring us back!"

Proprietors/Hosts
Stephen T. & Deanna Tallon
Innkeepers
Joerg & Patty Ross
Elegant Waterside Breakfast Inn

Mobil ★★★
AAA ◆◆◆◆

Inn at Sunrise Point

www.srinns.com/sunrisepoint
PO Box 1344, Camden, ME 04843
207-236-7716
info@sunrisepoint.com

Rooms/Rates
3 rooms $235/$330. 4 cottages $265/$495. Suite $250/$350. Loft $290/$405. Open Mid-April to Mid-November. All accommodations with partial to full ocean views and all with private decks.

Cuisine
Gourmet Breakfast

Nearest Airport(s)
Portland - 80 minutes

Directions
From S I-95 N to Portland. Joins Rte 295 N to Coastal Exit 31 (formely exit 24) at Topsham. Make right from the off-ramp and continue until signs directing you to Rte 1 N to Bath. Follow Rte 1 N through Camden and inn is 4 miles N on right hand side down to water's edge.

A pampering seaside haven, this Andrew Harper Best Hideaways-recommended bed and breakfast inn offers spectacular ocean views and all the luxuries you can expect from a AAA Four-Diamond property. Set within a secluded four-and-a half-acre oceanfront hideaway and just minutes from picturesque Camden. Sleep soundly in the wonderful sea air, comforted by the gentle murmur of waves outside your window. Awaken to the breath-taking sight of the sunrise across Penobscot Bay before enjoying a complimentary gourmet breakfast in the inn's bright conservatory or ocean room. Later, browse in the cherry-paneled library with a glass of fine wine and select a good book. Stay in an elegantly furnished room in the main house, a wonderfully restored 1920s shingle-style Maine summer "cottage," or in one of the beautifully furnished cottages or suite at the water's edge. Perhaps a romantic loft above all of the cottages and high in the trees will let you dream with the birds. A luxurious, romantic and elegant retreat for discerning travelers.

Member Since 2005

"Heaven on Earth! We were lulled to sleep by the sound of waves on Penobscot Bay. Wake up to a gourmet delight each morning. Sheer Luxury! Wonderful!"

Captain Lindsey House Inn

www.srinns.com/captainlindsey
5 Lindsey Street, Rockland, ME 04841
800-523-2145 • 207-596-7950 • Fax 207-596-2758
lindsey@midcoast.com

Innkeepers/Owners
Ken & Ellen Barnes
Co-Manager
Cindy D'Ambrosio

Elegant In Town Inn

AAA ◆◆◆

Located in the heart of Rockland's Historic Waterfront District, this "in-town" inn offers up old world charm with all the modern amenities in a comfortably elegant setting. Antiques and artifacts from around the world grace our spacious guest rooms, cozy parlor and library. Afternoon refreshments are served fireside or outside on our garden terrace and a sumptuous dinner awaits you in our Waterworks Restaurant. Close by you'll enjoy the Farnsworth Art Museum, fine galleries and "Down East" coastal life. Come, relax, and experience your comfort zone.

Rooms/Rates
9 Rooms, $85/$125 off season (Oct 15th to June 1st), $140/$190 in season. Business rates available year-round. Packages available. Open year-round.

Cuisine
Lunch and dinner in our Waterworks Restaurant. Pub favorites, local fare and seafood. Microbrewed beers, wines and spirits.

Nearest Airport(s)
Portland Jetport, Portland, ME
Bangor International

Directions
From Boston: Rte. I- 95 N to Rte. I-295N to Rte. I-95N to exit 28(Coastal Rte. 1) into Rockland, Main St. to L. Summer St (by Ferry terminal), L on Union, 1st L to Lindsey.

Member Since 1998

"Terrific staff! We'll return for our 3rd year in a row, comfortable beds clean bathrooms wonderful country breakfast buffet." The Svendsens Glendale, AZ

The Newcastle Inn

www.srinns.com/newcastleinn
60 River Road, Newcastle, ME 04553
800-832-8669 • 207-563-5685 • Fax 207-563-6877
innkeep@newcastleinn.com

Innkeepers/Owners
Peter and Laura Barclay

Traditional Village Country Inn

A romantic Country Inn located in Maine's Mid-Coast, famous for its beaches, lighthouses and rocky shore. The Inn's living rooms and special sunporch are a quiet, peaceful, and relaxing place from which to enjoy the wonders of Coastal Maine. Overlooking the harbor, the Inn's gardens abound in lupines and other perennials. Renowned for its dinner service, the Inn offers french cuisine with a decidedly New England Flair! Many of the Inn's rooms feature king or queen canopy or four-poster beds, fireplaces, water views, Jacuzzis and other special treats. Winner of the prestigious *Waverly/Country Inns* Magazine Room of the Year Award.

Rooms/Rates
15 Rooms including 4 Suites. 2005 rates: $155/$295 in season $125/$225 off season.

Cuisine
Multi-course breakfast served from 8-9:00 a.m. Innkeeper's Reception at 6:00 p.m. on dinner nights. Exceptional 5-course gourmet dinner by reservation each night except Sunday and Mondays (weekends only in winter season). Extensive wine list.

Nearest Airport(s)
Portland

Directions
Take I-95 North to exit 44, I-295 North. Take Exit 31 and turn right onto Rte 196 heading south. After 2.5 miles, take Route 1 North toward Bath. 7 miles past Wiscasset bridge, turn right on River Rd. Inn is 1/2 mile on the right.

Member Since 1990

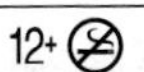    

"Exactly what we dreamed about a Maine Country Inn; comfort, hospitality, and superb food!"

The Squire Tarbox Inn

www.srinns.com/squiretarbox
1181 Main Road, Westport Island, Wiscasset, ME 04578
800-818-0626 • 207-882-7693 • Fax 207-882-7107
squiretarbox@prexar.com

Innkeepers/Owners
Roni and Mario De Pietro

Traditional Colonial Country Inn

Once upon a time, there was a Country Inn conspicuous from all others. After a restoration for your comfort, this colonial farm created an alternate luxury, amidst the splendor of nature. Set within fields, stone walls, and woods, and with kindness to all creatures great and small, pristine barns are filled with gentle animals. The Inn offers you peace and tranquility, away from tourist crowds, but convenient to coastal adventures. Relax on our screened in deck while watching the wild life. Dine leisurely in our 1763 dining room with meals created by our Swiss/owner chef, using all local and home grown organic vegetables. Sleep with the luxury of down duvets and pillows. On the National Register of Historic Places.

Rooms/Rates
11 Rooms, $99/$190 double occupancy. Open April 1 thru' Dec. 31.

Cuisine
A full hot breakfast is served. Fresh goat cheese at the cocktail hour, and chocolate chip cookies all day. A la carte dinner menu is prepared by Mario Swiss/owner chef. Enjoy dining on the deck or in the dining room. We have a full liquor license.

Nearest Airport(s)
Portland Jetport

Directions
I-295 to exit 28/Brunswick; Rt.1 N through Brunswick & Bath; from Bath bridge continue 7 miles on Rt.1; turn R on Rt.144 & take it 8.5 miles, it twists & turns but is well marked; you can't miss us - The Rambling Colonial Farmhouse on R.

Member Since 1974

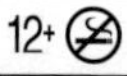   

"Fantastic food. Very friendly caring innkeepers. Beautiful quiet location. Excellent place."

Innkeeper/Owner
Isabel Smiles
General Manager
Chris Monahan

Elegant In Town Breakfast Inn

Pomegranate Inn

www.srinns.com/pome
49 Neal St., Portland, ME 04102
800-356-0408 • 207-772-1006 • Fax 207-773-4426

Portland's beautiful Western Promenade District, an historic residential neighborhood, is the location of this special city inn. It is a small sophisticated hotel which offers a quiet haven from the tensions of travel. The bustle of downtown is forgotten when you step through the Pomegranate's doors. Antiques and modern art abound in the eclectic atmosphere recently featured in the *New York Times, Boston Globe* and *Travel + Leisure* Magazine. For real seclusion, the carriage house offers a first floor guest room with its own private terrace. The main house also has a lovely urban garden. A lot of elegance with a touch of panache.

Rooms/Rates
8 Rooms, 1 Suite, 1 Garden Room, $95/$285 depending on season. Open year-round.

Cuisine
Full, served breakfast included in price. Complimentary wine and tea upon arrival.

Nearest Airport(s)
Portland International Jetport

Directions
Fr. South: I-95N. ex. 44 to I-295N ex. 4 ex. 5 to 22E. R Bramhall St. immediate L Vaughan St. 4th L Carroll St. Inn at intersection Neal and Carroll St. From North: ex. 6A Rte.77 State St. R on Pine L on Neal.

Member Since 1995

"There's a very special place to stay in Portland, Maine...the Pomegrante, a place with a sense of peace and privilege."

West End Inn

www.srinns.com/westend
146 Pine St., Portland, ME 04102
800-338-1377 • 207-772-1377 • Fax 207-772-1377
innkeeper@westendbb.com

Innkeepers/Owners
Dan & Michele Brown
Managers
Pam Bouchard-Nee/ Kate Gonzalez

Elegant In Town Bed and Breakfast

AAA ◆◆◆

Located in the Western Promenade Historic District, this Georgian style brick townhouse is one of a collection of Victorian-era homes, all reflecting a wealth of architectural detail. The comfort and elegance of the West End Inn creates an oasis within the city. A quiet location and six comfortable guestrooms invite an exceptional night's sleep. The sumptuous breakfast is served in the beautiful dining room with its twelve-foot decorative ceilings and afternoon tea in the adjoining library. The residential location provides convenience to the downtown, Arts District and Museums, Public Market, Old Port, Ferry, Civic Center, and Financial District, while offering a refuge and an opportunity for quieter contemplation and a walk on the Promenade. Enjoy city life the Maine way!

Rooms/Rates
6 Rooms Queen/King beds $139/$199, quiet season $89/$129.

Cuisine
Sumptuous full breakfast, afternoon tea, many exceptional restaurants within short walk.

Nearest Airport(s)
Portland International (PWM)

Directions
From South: I-95 exit 44 onto I-295. Exit 6A, Forest Ave South, before first light bear R onto Rte 77, State St, continue up hill cross Congress St (Longfellow statue on your left), immediate R onto Pine St, several blocks corner Neal St and Pine. From North: I-295 to Exit 6A then same directions as above.

Member Since 2004

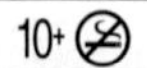

"It is great to find another B&B that is doing things right!"

Captain Lord Mansion

www.srinns.com/captainlord
6 Pleasant Street, P.O. Box 800, Kennebunkport, ME 04046-0800
800-522-3141 • 207-967-3141 • Fax 207-967-3172
innkeeper@captainlord.com

Innkeepers/Owners
Bev Davis and Rick Litchfield

Elegant Federal Village Breakfast Inn

Mobil ★★★
AAA ◆◆◆◆

Rooms/Rates
15 Rooms, $149/$399 B&B; 1 Suite $299/$475 B&B. Open year-round.

Cuisine
Full 3-course breakfast. Afternoon Tea and refreshments. Guests are welcome to bring their own spirits.

Nearest Airport(s)
Portland, ME

Directions
ME Tpke (I-95) to Exit #25. L onto Rte. 35S, go 1.7 mi. to light, cross over Rte.1, bearing R, continue on Rte. 35S/9A for 3.5 miles. At light, turn L onto Rte. 9 E, In Dock Square, @ monument, turn R onto Ocean Ave. Go .3 mile, turn L on Green St. Mansion on 2nd block on L. Parking behind inn.

Enjoy an unforgettable romantic experience here. Your comfort, serenity and intimacy are assured by our location and our large, beautifully appointed guest rooms. Luxurious amenities include oversize four-poster beds, cozy gas fireplaces, stocked mini fridges, CD players, heated marble bathroom floors, several body-jet showers, 9 double whirlpools, as well as fresh flowers, full breakfasts, afternoon refreshments and lots of personal attention. The Inn is situated at the head of a sloping village green, overlooking the Kennebunk River. This picturesque, quiet, yet convenient, location affords a terrific place from which to walk to enjoy the shops, restaurants and galleries in this historic village. AAA-◆◆◆◆

Member Since 1975

2004 Award by America's Historic Inns - Top 10
"America's Most Romantic Inns"

Maine Stay Inn & Cottages

www.mainestayinn.com
34 Maine Street, P.O. Box 500A, Kennebunkport, ME 04046
800-950-2117 • 207-967-2117 • Fax 207-967-8757
innkeeper@mainestayinn.com

Innkeepers/Owners
George and Janice Yankowski

Traditional Victorian Village Breakfast Inn

Mobil ★★★
AAA ◆◆◆

Step back in time to a place where exceptional warmth and hospitality will make your visit to the Southern Maine coast a most memorable experience. Listed on the National Register of Historic Places, the Maine Stay Inn and Cottages at the Melville Walker House offers a charming and comfortable ambiance within the quaint seaside village of Kennebunkport. Choose the Victorian romance of a 19th century Inn Room, or the private intimacy of an English Country Cottage Suite. Relax around a cozy fire or enjoy a double whirlpool Jacuzzi tub. Perfectly located in the quiet residential Historic District, you are just a short stroll along tree-lined streets to the fine shops, galleries and restaurants of Kennebunkport's Dock Square. Sandy beaches and quiet coves provide the tranquility that will soothe your soul.

Member Since 1996

Rooms/Rates
4 Inn Rooms, $109/$219;
2 Inn Suites, $179/$279;
11 Cottage Rooms/Suites, $109/$279. Open year-round.

Cuisine
Awaken to a full New England breakfast served in our dining room or, in summer, on the porch. Guests staying in our charming cottage suites may opt to have their breakfast delivered in a delightful wicker basket. Join us for Afternoon Tea on the sunny porch, or in cooler weather, around a cozy fire.

Nearest Airport(s)
Portland

Directions
ME. Tpke., Exit 25 (formerly Exit 3). L on Rte. 35, 6 mi. to Rte. 9. Turn L on Rte. 9, Go over bridge, thru village to stop sign. Turn R on Maine St. Go 3 blks.

"One of the most relaxing and enjoyable places we have ever stayed."
"We cannot wait to return!"

Innkeepers/Owners
Sheila & David Aldrich
Innkeepers/General Managers
Shana & Tom Hennessey

Elegant Waterside Breakfast Inn

AAA ♦♦♦♦

Old Fort Inn

www.srinns.com/oldfortinn
8 Old Fort Ave., P.O. Box M, KennebunkPort, ME 04046
800-828-3678 • 207-967-5353 • Fax 207-967-4547
info@oldfortinn.com

Rooms/Rates
16 Rooms, $170/$395 B&B.
Open mid-April to mid-December.

Cuisine
Buffet breakfast, fresh fruit, cereals, homemade breads croissants, quiche, waffles, and other hot entrees. Afternoon treats. Guests are welcome to bring their own alcoholic beverages, or special orders may be made.

Nearest Airport(s)
Portland-30 miles

Directions
I-95/Maine Turnpike to Exit 25(Kennebunk exit), turn L on Rte. 35 for 5 1/2 mi. L at light on Rte. 9 for 3/10 mi. R on Ocean Ave. for 9/10 mi. to Kings Hwy@Colony Hotel. Turn L. Follow road to "T" intersection go R up hill to Old Fort Avenue-3/10 mi. Inn on L.

One of Maine's exceptional Country Inns. Tucked away on 15 acres of immaculately maintained grounds and woodlands; the Inn has been described as "sophisticated, elegant, complete tranquility two minutes from the activities of downtown Kennebunkport"★. Just 1 block from the ocean, The Old Fort Inn offers the visiting guest a quiet atmosphere. The antique appointed guest rooms, rich in nostalgic ambience, are located in a turn-of-the-century carriage house of red brick and ocal stone. Done with a meticulous eye for detail, guest rooms are tastefully decorated with wonderful wall coverings and elegent fabrics, with either four-poster or canopy beds and down comforters. Some rooms have fireplaces and Jacuzzis. Amenities include A/C, phones, cable TV, enclosed honor bars, heated tile floors in all baths, a scrumptious buffet breakfast, afternoon treats, heated pool, tennis court and Antique Shop. The Inn is just 1-1/4 miles from the village and 5 minutes from two 18-hole golf courses. ★S. Schatzki-guest

Member Since 1976

"To recommend your Inn to our friends requires only one word, IMPECCABLE." The Somboretz's

Hartwell House Inn & Conference Center

www.srinns.com/hartwell
312 Shore Rd., P.O. Box 1950, Ogunquit, ME 03907
800-235-8883 • 207-646-7210 • Fax 207-646-6032
innkeeper@hartwellhouseinn.com

Owners
James & Trisha Hartwell
Innkeepers
Paul & Gail Koehler

Elegant Village
Breakfast Inn

The romantic Hartwell House Inn, a 16-room inn and conference center, is located in the quaint town of Ogunquit, southern Maine. Open year-round and within easy reach of Boston (1-1/2 hours) and New York City (5 hours), the inn and conference center are steps from the beach, shopping and diverse four-season activities. The Marginal Way, a cliff walk bordering Ogunquit's rugged coastline, is steps from the Inn. Guests can park at the Inn and walk to the sweet village of Ogunquit or Perkins Cove for boating, fishing, boutiques and waterfront lobster dining. The Inn's intimate 36-seat restaurant, S.W. Swan Bistro, is across the street. "Antique Alley," Kittery and Freeport outlet shopping are an easy drive. The dedicated conference center offers private conference rooms accommodating groups from 12 to 75. Outstanding views, state-of-the-art equipment and a customized catering menu create an atmosphere conducive to productive thinking. The Inn offers a romantic site for off-season small weddings and celebrations.

Member Since 1981

Rooms/Rates
16 A/C guest rooms, suites and apartments, some with deck, kitchenette and/or sitting room with sofa bed, $120/$270. Open year-round. Weekly rates available.

Cuisine
Complimentary full gourmet breakfast, afternoon tea with sweets and pastries. The inn's 36-seat restaurant serves French-inspired American Bistro cuisine.

Nearest Airport(s)
Portland International Jetport is 25 miles away.

Directions
From I-95N: exit 7 to Route 1 N. 6.5 miles to R on Bourne Lane. R on Shore Road. 1/4 mile to Inn on R. From I-95S: exit 19, L on Route 109 E. R on Route 1 S to Ogunquit. L on Shore Road, .6 miles to Inn on R.

"Warm, relaxing, beautiful. We can't wait to come back!"
www.hartwellhouseinn.com

Dockside Guest Quarters

www.srinns.com/dockside
P.O. Box 205, Harris Island Rd., York, ME 03909
800-270-1977 • 207-363-2868 • Fax 207-363-1977
info@docksidegq.com

Innkeepers/Owners
The Lusty Family

Traditional Waterside Inn

Mobil ★★★
AAA ◆◆◆

The Dockside captures the essence of Maine with its natural beauty, gracious hospitality, and abundant sights, recreation and activities. Uniquely situated on a private peninsula, each room has a panoramic water view. Accommodations are in the Maine House, a classic 'New England cottage,' furnished with antiques and marine art, and multi-unit buildings at the water's edge. Warmth and charm are found throughout. The Dockside Restaurant boasts a water view from every table. A creative menu specializes in fresh Maine seafood.

Rooms/Rates
19 rooms $95-$198, 6 suites $120-$256. Off & Mid Season. Packages available year-round. EP

Cuisine
Dining on porch, overlooking harbor, a favorite of locals and visitors. Specialties: roast duckling, bouillabaisse, lobster dublin lawyer, grilled salmon maison. Lunch & Dinner are served in the restaurant. Breakfast is available in the Maine House.

Nearest Airport(s)
Manchester, NH

Directions
From I-95 exit at York, ME (exit #7). Go S on Rt 1. First traffic light, turn L on Route 1A. Follow 1A through York Village and turn R on Route 103. Take the 1st L immediately after bridge, follow signs.

Member Since 1975

 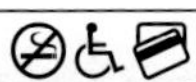   

"The location, serenity and warm hospitality makes this one of our favorites."

The Waterford Inne

www.srinns.com/water
Box 149, 258 Chadbourne Road, Waterford, ME 04088
207-583-4037 • Fax 207-583-4037
inne@gwi.net

Innkeeper/Owner
Barbara Vanderzanden

Traditional Colonial Country Inn

A 19th century farmhouse on a country lane midst 25 acres of fields and woods, distinctively different, a true country inn offering uniquely decorated guest rooms, a charming blend of two centuries - the warmth of early furnishings combined with contemporary comforts. An air of quiet simple elegance pervades the common rooms rich with antiques and art, pewter and primitives. An intimate library with an eclectic collection to appeal to all tastes--travel, nature, history... Step outside to explore the pleasures of country simplicity, to listen to the quiet or the songbirds, to smell the freshness of a summer morning or perhaps the winter fragrance of a woodburning fire. Wander through the gardens which provide a colorful array of flowers and a bounty of fresh fare for your dining table. Return inne-side to pamper your palate with country chic cuisine. The road to the Waterford Inne is traveled by hikers and cyclists, antiquers and skiers, discriminating travelers who delight in the charm and personal attention of a country inn.

Member Since 1979

 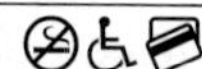   

Rooms/Rates
7 Rooms$100/$150 B&B; 1 Suite, $150 B&B. Open year-round.

Cuisine
Breakfast included. Fine dinners available with advance reservation. Guests are welcome to bring their own spirits.

Nearest Airport(s)
Portland, ME

Directions
From ME Tpke: take Exit 63 to Rt. 26 N for 28 mi. into Norway, then Rt. 118 W for 9 mi. to Rt. 37. Turn L, go 1/2 mi. to Chadbourne Rd. Take immediate R go 1/2 mile up hill. From Conway NH: Rt. 16 to Rt. 302 E to Fryeburg, ME. Rt. 5 out of Fryeburg to Rt. 35 S, continue to left fork onto Rt. 118 E. for approx. 5 miles to Rt. 37. Turn R, go 1/2 mi. to Chadbourne Rd. Turn R.

"The Waterford Inne was one of our inspirations to move to this area! Atmosphere: friendly! We were amazed by the care given to dinners--exquisite!"

Maryland

"The Old Line State"

Famous For: Maryland Crabs, Chesapeake Bay, Ocean City, Atlantic Coast, River Valleys, Rolling Hills, Forests, Appalachian Mountains, Fort McHenry, Tobacco

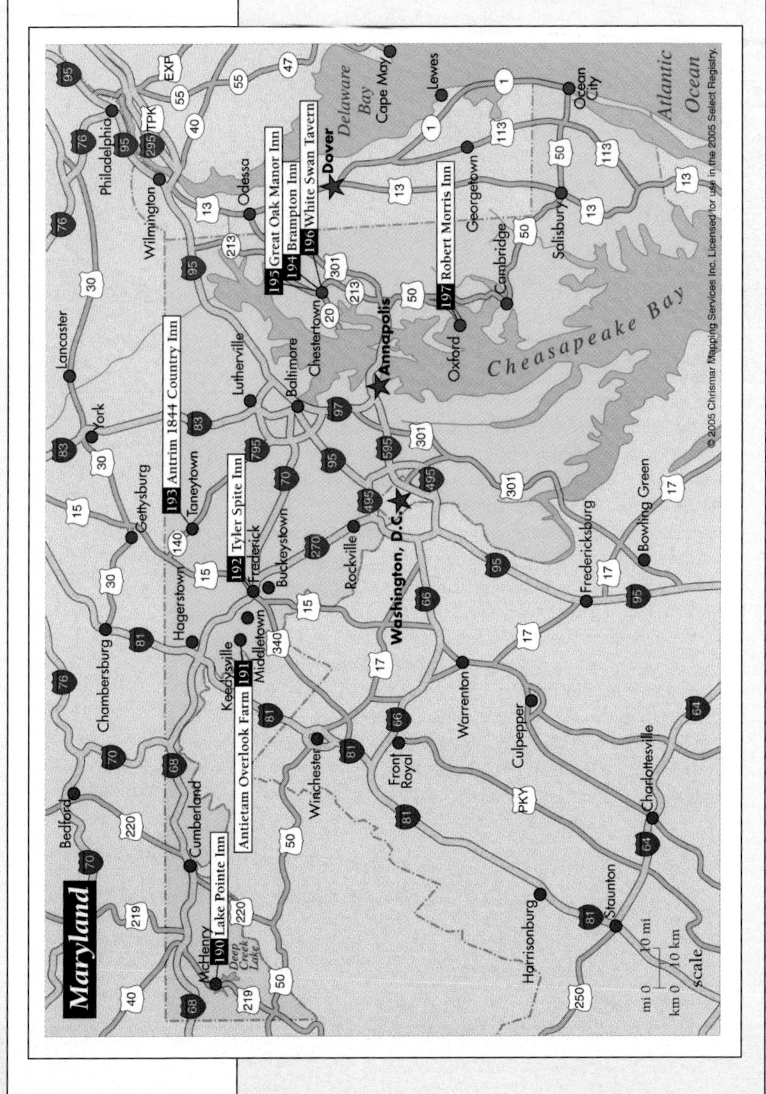

Lake Pointe Inn

www.srinns.com/lakepointe
174 Lake Pointe Drive, Deep Creek Lake, MD 21541
800-523-LAKE • 301-387-0111 • Fax 301-387-0190
relax@deepcreekinns.com

Innkeeper
Caroline McNiece
Traditional Waterside Breakfast Inn

The Lake Pointe Inn decorated in the Arts & Crafts style, embraces you with an exceptionally warm welcome when you enter the chestnut paneled Great Room with it's Mission Style furnishings. Nestled in the Lake Pointe Community, in Western Maryland, the Inn is perched just 13 feet from water's edge. The wraparound porch invites you to relax in a rocking chair, read or watch the waterfowl frolic. It is easy to enjoy Garrett County's 4 season activities while staying at the Inn. Golf, skiing and snowboarding await you at the Wisp Resort, adjacent to the Lake Pointe Community. Tour the area using our complimentary canoes, kayaks and bicycles or hike in the 5 nearby State Parks. The outdoor fireplace, herb garden and hammock provide a perfect haven for private conversation or stargazing. Frank Lloyd Wright's Fallingwater and Kentuck Knob are nearby. Lake Pointe Inn is a perfect getaway in any season for any reason!

Member Since 2000

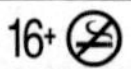    

Rooms/Rates
8 Guest Rooms $158/$249.
2 Suites $209/$259; Some amenities include: Fireplaces, Spa Tubs, Steam Shower, Sauna, CAC, TV/VCR, Bose CD player/alarm (Ipod adaptable), Private Telephone. Massage therapy available. Closed 12/24 & 12/25.

Cuisine
Full breakfast & light hors d'oeuvres included in daily rate; dinners served to Inn guests on 3-day holiday weekends. Meeting space available 8-20 persons.

Nearest Airport(s)
Pittsburgh International

Directions
From I-68 in Western MD, take Rte 219 S for 12.5 mi.; R onto Sang Run Rd; 2 blocks, L onto Marsh Hill Rd., go 1/4 mile; L onto Lake Pointe Dr just past Wisp Resort.

"This is the most relaxing place I have ever been... simply put, EXCEPTIONAL!"

Antietam Overlook Farm

www.srinns.com/antietam
P.O. Box 30, Keedysville, MD 21756
800-878-4241 • 301-432-4200 • Fax 301-432-5230
Reservations@antietamoverlook.com

Innkeepers/Owners
Mark Svrcek and Rudy Novak

Traditional Mountain Country Manor

Our 95-acre mountaintop country manor inn overlooking Antietam National Battlefield has extraordinary views of four states. You will marvel at the hand-hewn timber framing and rough-sawn craftsmanship. Cozy fireplaces, fabulous furnishings and fine crystal create a warm, comfortable atmosphere. In the winter months, guests are invited to spend time in front of the grand fireplace where interesting conversation adds to the warmth. The views are spectacular year round, but in the spring and summer our large "Overlook" porch is wonderful. Spacious suites include fireplaces, sumptuous queen beds, stress relieving bubble baths, and private screened porches. While our seclusion and tranquility are unparalleled, many guests also enjoy visiting the Civil War battlefields at Gettysburg & Bull Run.

Rooms/Rates
6 Suites, $130/$325 B&B. Open year-round. Attractions: Antietam National Battlefield, Harpers Ferry, antiquing, Charlestown horse track, hiking, biking and relaxing. Complimentary beverages, wine & liqueurs.

Cuisine
Unforgettable, three course country breakfast included. Fine dining nearby.

Nearest Airport(s)
Hagerstown airport is about 25 minutes away.

Directions
Located in the Western Maryland Mountains about one hour from Baltimore and Washington, D.C. Call or check on-line for availability and booking. Directions sent with booking confirmation.

Member Since 1992

"Unbelievable food and quiet seclusion...ah!"
Visit on-line at www.AntietamOverlook.com

Tyler Spite Inn

www.srinns.com/tylerspite
112 West Church St., Frederick, MD 21701
301-831-4455 • Fax 301-662-4185

Innkeepers/Owners
The Myer Family

Elegant In Town Breakfast Inn

A romantic 1814 Inn located in the heart of Frederick's Historic District. Spacious, beautifully appointed rooms with 14-foot ceilings, marble fireplaces, oriental carpets, comfortable antique furnishings and paintings captivate our guests who are looking for the ultimate in romanticism. Walled gardens replete with color, entice guests for a leisurely stroll. A stay is complete once you ascend from the carriage block located at the front door for a horse-drawn carriage tour through Frederick's quaint city.

Rooms/Rates
4 Rooms, 1 Suite, $200/$250/$300 B&B. Open year round.

Cuisine
Full breakfast and tea. 20 restaurants 1.5 blocks away.

Nearest Airport(s)
Dulles International, Baltimore (BWI), and Reagan National

Directions
Route 70 to Market St., L on 2nd St., 2 blocks & L on Record St., 2 blocks at corner of Church St.

Member Since 1993

"Personal touches create a mood and ambiance reminicent of a turn-of-the-century resort inn."

Proprietors
Dorothy and Richard Mollett
General Manager
John Vonnes

Elegant Country Inn

Antrim 1844 Country Inn

www.srinns.com/antrim
30 Trevanion Road, Taneytown, MD 21787
800-858-1844 • 410-756-6812 • Fax 410-756-2744
antrim1844@erols.com

Rooms/Rates
29 Guest Rooms and Suites, $160/$375. Open year-round. Activities: Gettysburg, Baltimore & Washington attractions, golfing, antiquing, hiking, biking, swimming, tennis.

Cuisine
Afternoon tea. Evening hors d'ouevres. Elegant 6-course prix fixe dinner $65. Morning wake up tray at your door, plus full country breakfast. Full bar and 1200-selection wine list.

Nearest Airport(s)
Baltimore

Directions
From Wash DC: I-495 to I-270W; 15N to 140E to Taneytown through light; 1 block & bear R on Trevanion Rd. From Balt/BWI: I-695N to I-795W to 140W to Taneytown; L on Trevanion Rd.

One of the most prestigious inns in the country, Antrim 1844 is near Baltimore and Washington, DC, and just 12 miles from historic Gettysburg. Set on 24 acres of rolling Maryland countryside, Antrim's mansion, dependencies and other outbuildings have been restored to their antebellum grandeur. Each guestroom or suite is individually appointed with feather beds and antique furnishings. Fireplaces, Jacuzzis, decks, high speed internet and luxurious baths abound. Expect exquisite dining and incredible wines in an old-world setting. Enjoy outdoor swimming, tennis and croquet amid Antrim's elaborate formal gardens. Golf, historic tour and special getaway packages are also available.

Member Since 1993

"Perfection in every way," "magnificent," "opulent," "superb." *Zagat* Survey

Brampton Inn

www.srinns.com/brampton
25227 Chestertown Road, Chestertown, MD 21620
866-305-1860 • 410-778-1860 • Fax None
innkeeper@bramptoninn.com

Innkeepers/Owners
Danielle and Michael Hanscom
Elegant Country Breakfast Inn

A romantic oasis on Maryland's Eastern Shore, Brampton is a magnificent 1860 National Register Plantation house that sits in serene splendor amid towering trees on 35 acres of lush landscape, forest and fields just outside historic Chestertown, MD. Guest and common rooms are spacious, and feature original floors, windows, doors, and mantles, and are appointed with antiques, oriental rugs and live plants. Whirlpools and wood-burning fireplaces in most guestrooms assure a romantic and comfortable stay. Attention to detail, personal service, and friendly innkeepers will make your visit a relaxed and memorable one. 'Meticulously restored, in a pastoral setting...'The *New York Times*. Chosen as one of the top 12 most romantic B&Bs in the USA by bedandbreakfast.com.

Rooms/Rates
8 rooms, $155/$255; 2 Cottage Suites, $225/$255. Spacious rooms, simple elegance, wood-burning fireplaces, whirlpools. Open year-round.

Cuisine
Full gourmet breakfast with individual table service. Afternoon tea on weekends.

Nearest Airport(s)
Baltimore (BWI)

Directions
0.9 miles outside of Chestertown on Route 20 West.

Member Since 2001

"What a magnificent place this is." "A peaceful and comfortable respite." "Thanks so much."

Great Oak Manor

www.srinns.com/greatoak
10568 Cliff Road, Chestertown, MD 21620
800-504-3098 • 410-778-5943 • Fax 410-810-2517
innkeeper@greatoak.com

Innkeepers/Owners
Cassandra & John Fedas
Waterside Manor House Breakfast Inn 

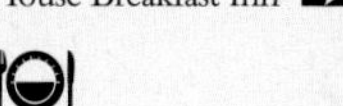

Rooms/Rates
12 rooms, $140/$275. 3 suites, $190/$275. Elegant spacious rooms, fireplaces, gracious public rooms, and the Chesapeake Bay. Open year round. Complimentary 9 hole golf, tennis, and swimming next door.

Cuisine
Complete and Scrumptous Buffet Breakfast. Individual Egg dishes or French Toast daily, "Manor" baked muffins, and always fresh fruits the year round. Afternoon refreshments, snacks, and twenty four hour complimentary coffee, tea, water, and soda.

Nearest Airport(s)
BWI,PHL

Directions
8.5 mi. from High St. Chestertown Rt. 514 N. past pastoral fields until you reach the Chesapeake Bay.

F. Scott Fitzgerald wrote of blue lawns and country houses such is Great Oak Manor. From the estate's walled garden bordered by 65-year old boxwoods and its circular drive on the estate side, to its magnificent view of the Chesapeake Bay and private beach on the water side, this country estate provides the appropriate setting for a relaxing getaway and a weekend of romance. Our guest and public rooms are spacious and beautifully furnished. Built at a time when grandeur was more important than cost, guests are swept away by the majesty of the house. This is a true Manor House with fine details, beautiful furnishings, Orientals, and an 850 volume library to browse. The Manor will meet your every need, with 1200 feet of waterfront on the Cheasepeake Bay, and the most beautiful sunsets on the Eastern Shore of Maryland. Our newest addition, the "Conservatory," which overlooks the Bay, is popular for small business retreats or family reunions.

Member Since 2003

"Gracious, lovely ambiance. Thank you for your peaceful refuge that catered to all of our senses."

White Swan Tavern

www.srinns.com/whiteswan
231 High Street, Chestertown, MD 21620
410-778-2300 • Fax 410-778-4543
info@whiteswantavern.com

Innkeepers/General Managers
Mary Susan Maisel, Wayne McGuire

Elegant In Town Breakfast Inn

The White Swan has been a familiar landmark in Chestertown since pre-revolutionary days. Close to the great Eastern cities, yet quietly nestled in the history of Maryland's eastern shore, the Inn is for those who treasure serene streets, birdsong mornings, impeccable service and the grace of New World tradition. All rooms are elegantly appointed with antiques, reproductions and artwork within a museum quality restoration. Guests enjoy working fireplaces in our common rooms, a lovely garden terrace and meadow, central heat, air conditioning, and off street parking. Experience the historic feeling of this special place. Here, our forefathers and their families gathered to share ideas and to draft a way of life that continues today in the spirit of timeless values. Take a walk to the scenic Chester River waterfront, two short blocks away.

Rooms/Rates
4 Rooms, $140/$180; 2 Suites, $210 & $240. Closed one week in mid-August.

Cuisine
Complimentary Continental breakfast, afternoon tea, fruit basket. Fine restaurants and cafes within walking distance.

Nearest Airport(s)
Baltimore, Philadelphia, Washington

Directions
Rte. 213 to Chestertown. W on Cross St. L on High St. White Swan on R. Ring doorbell. Off street parking in rear off Cannon Street.

Member Since 2001

"A picturesque, delightful, comfortable and tastefully decorated place. We'll be back!"

Innkeeper/Active Owners
Jay Gibson, Wendy & Ken Gibson

Traditional Colonial Waterside Inn

Robert Morris Inn

www.srinns.com/BestCrabCakesOvernight
314 N. Morris St., P.O. Box 70, Oxford, MD 21654
888-823-4012 • 410-226-5111 • Fax 410-226-5744
robertmorrisinn@webtv.net

Rooms/Rates
34 Rooms, $90/$290 EP. $20 off rate w/dinner. Mid-week reduced rates except on holidays.

Cuisine
Apr-Nov, open daily; March weekends only. Breakfast, lunch & dinner. (Breakfast not included in rate). Dining room w/historic murals, rustic tap room, colonial tavern. Full-service bar. Specialty drinks, beer & wine.

Nearest Airport(s)
BWI and National - 1.5 hrs.
Dulles - 2 hrs. 15 mins.

Directions
Hwy 301 to Rte 50 E. Turn R on Rte 322 for 3.4 mi, turn R on Rte 333 for 9.6 mi. 1 hour from Annapolis, 1 1/2 hours from DC, 1 3/4 hours from Baltimore, 2 1/2 hours from Philadelphia. Speed limit in Oxford 25mph and is strictly enforced.

Come to our country romantic (1710) inn and step back in time. Explore the Chesapeake Bay and all the unique things the Eastern Shore of Maryland has to offer. We are indeed the "Land of Pleasant Living." Guests staying overnight can choose between accommodations at our historic Main Inn or Sandaway Lodge where many rooms have porches overlooking the river and beach. We tell guests they have two choices for activities. One, you can take the scenic car ferry across the river for a short-cut to St. Michaels (6 mile drive) and then explore the nearby towns of Tilghman and Easton. We call this doing the loop. Second choice is to find yourself a lounge or adirondak chair at the Sandaway property to linger away the day watching workboats, sailboats, yachts and wildlife go by. After seeing a fabulous sunset just walk up Lovers Lane to the inn for a relaxing dinner. You know James Michener, author of "Chesapeake" use to frequent our inn and wrote the outline for his book in the tavern. He rated our crab cakes the best of any restaurant on the Eastern Shore. We now ship crab cakes nationwide! To order call 1-866-MICHENER (642-4363) April through November. For more information visit www.BestCrabCakes.com

Member Since 1970

"Best crab cakes, great river views, romantic...a walk back into a more relaxed time."

"The Bay State"

Famous For: Pilgrims, Thanksgiving, Salem Witch Trials, Boston Tea Party, Birth of the American Revolution, Minutemen, Freedom Trail, Swan Boats, Cape Cod, Education, Arts, Technology, and Medicine.

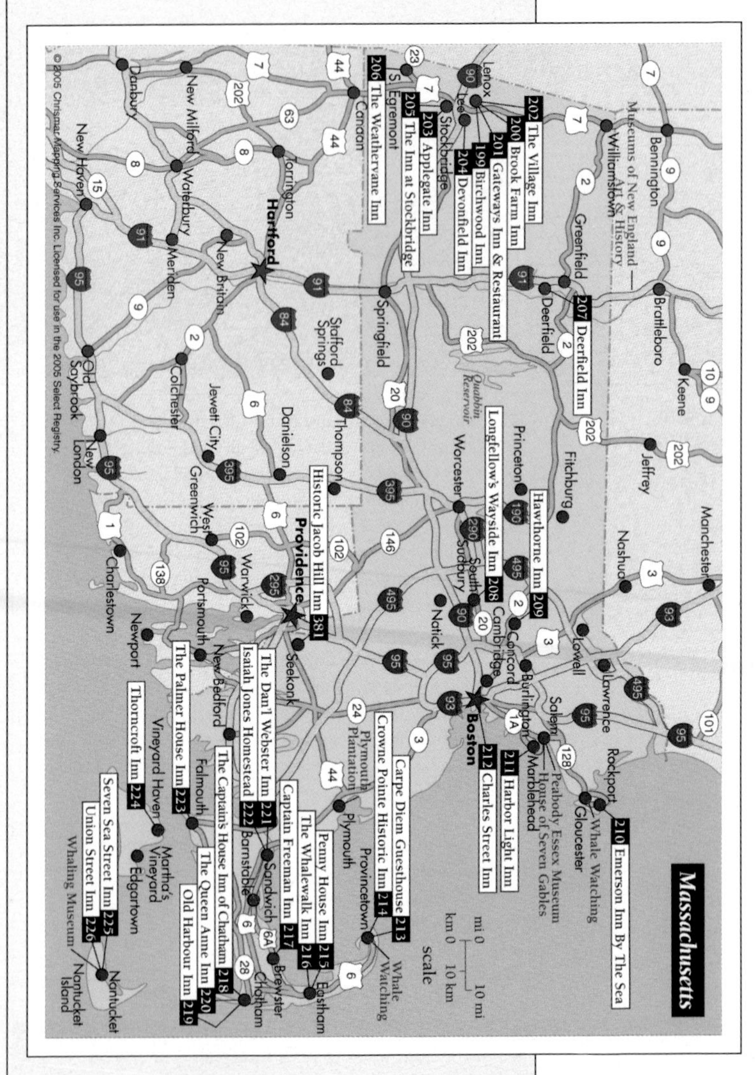

Innkeeper/Owner
Ellen Gutman Chenaux
Historic Colonial
Revival Village

Birchwood Inn

www.srinns.com/birchwood
7 Hubbard Street, P.O. Box 2020, Lenox, MA 01240
800-524-1646 • 413-637-2600 • Fax 413-637-4604
innkeeper@birchwood-inn.com

Rooms/Rates
11 rooms, $115/$275. Rates change seasonally. Distinctly and comfortably decorated guestrooms, 6 with fireplaces and TV, antiques, canopy beds, all with private bath, air-conditioning, hairdrier, outgoing telephone, dataport. Open year-round.

Cuisine
Fireside "best breakfast in New England," featuring seasonal fruit dish, homemade breads, and hot entrée served at individual tables. Afternoon tea with homemade pastries.

Nearest Airport(s)
Albany and Hartford airports

Directions
Mass Pike (I-90), Exit 2, Rte. 20W for 4.5 miles, L at 1st light (183/7A), bear R at monument, up the hill, R on Hubbard.

Experience comfortable country elegance at Birchwood Inn. The oldest home in Lenox has been welcoming friends since 1767. Its tranquil hilltop setting is a short walk from the village's celebrated restaurants, shops and galleries, while year-round culture -- including Tanglewood, the summer home of the Boston Symphony -- and recreation are a stone's throw away. The Colonial Revival mansion's antiques, collectibles, quilts, canopy beds, and nine fireplaces create the idyllic ambience for a romantic getaway. Renown for sumptuous breakfasts and afternoon tea, the inn offers blossoms in stone-fenced gardens in spring, Berkshire breezes and fireflies on the gracious porch in summer, vibrant foliage on the doorstep in autumn, and the welcoming warmth of firesides in winter.

Member Since 2003

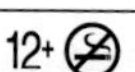

"Wonderfully romantic! Thank you for memories we will cherish forever."

Brook Farm Inn

www.brookfarm.com
15 Hawthorne Street, Lenox, MA 01240
800-285-7638 • 413-637-3013 • Fax 413-637-4751
innkeeper@brookfarm.com

Innkeepers/Owners
Linda and Phil Halpern
Victorian Village Breakfast Inn

Mobil ★★★
AAA ◆◆◆

There is poetry here. Nestled in a wooded glen, Brook Farm, a Victorian inn surrounded by award-winning gardens, is just a short walk to historic Lenox village. Built in 1882, and furnished with antiques, the inn features a library filled with poetry, history and literature, where the sounds of classical music can be heard. Brook Farm is close to Tanglewood and all Berkshire cultural attractions. Your friendly hosts offer gracious hospitality and assistance in planning a memorable Berkshires vacation. The sumptuous buffet breakfasts are unsurpassed. Seasonal activities include downhill and xc-skiing, hiking, antiquing and museum tours. Special winter packages are offered.

Attractions: Tanglewood, Berkshire Theatre Festival, Rockwell Museum, Shakespeare & Co., Hancock Shaker Village, Clark Art Institute.

Rooms/Rates
15 Rooms, $105/$395 B&B. Furnished with antiques, canopy beds. 9 w/fireplaces, some with whirlpool tubs, all with AC, phones. Heated outdoor pool. Open year-round. WIFI access.

Cuisine
Full breakfast and afternoon tea with homemade scones. Well-stocked guest pantry with refrigerators, ice, instant hot water, tea, coffee, hot chocolate, and homemade cookies.

Nearest Airport(s)
Albany, NY and Hartford, CT

Directions
Mass. Tpke. (I-90), exit 2, R on Rte. 20W 5 miles, to L on Rte. 183, 1 mile to Town Hall, sharp L on Old Stockbridge Rd., 2/10 mi then R on Hawthorne Street.

Member Since 2001

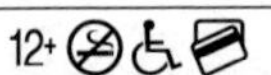

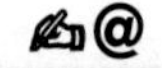

"It's a privilege to stay at Brook Farm--what a find!--and those breakfasts!"

Innkeepers/Owners
Fabrizio and Rosemary Chiariello
Elegant In Town Inn

Gateways Inn

www.srinns.com/gatewaysinn
51 Walker Street, Lenox, MA 01240
888-492-9466 • 413-637-2532 • Fax 413-637-1432
gateways@berkshire.net

Rooms/Rates
11 Rooms, $100/$190; 1 Suite, $230/$350. Many antiques, 4-poster canopy or sleigh beds. Peak season premium apply.

Cuisine
Full breakfast and elegant, yet casual, dining Tuesday-Sunday. After-theatre desserts and light meals available. Open to the general public. Extensive selection of American and Italian wines and a fully-stocked bar.

Nearest Airport(s)
Albany, NY

Directions
From Boston: I-90 W to Lee, exit 2. Turn R on Rte. 20 W.—stay on until intersect Rte. 183 S. Turn L onto Rte.183 S (Walker St.). One mile on R. From New York: Taconic Pkwy. to I-90E, exit 2 Lee (same as above).

Gateways Inn, a turn-of-the-century neoclassical mansion, built for Harley Procter, offers European hospitality in an elegant setting. A relaxing atmosphere, in the center of town. The beauty of Stanford White's staircase and Tiffany-style rose windows enhance the building. Charming rooms each uniquely decorated with antiques, many with fireplaces, with modern amenities including centralized air-conditioning, TV, phones with dataport and voice mail. The aroma of fresh-brewed coffee and warm croissants fills the air each morning, as guests awake to breakfast and to another day of being pampered by the owners and staff. Our award winner Bar offer the largest selection of Single Malt and Grappas in the County and is famous also for special cocktail. After theater, light meals are served until midnight. By request, we can organize balloon trips, massages, personal guided hiking, biking and fly fishing excursions. (One week minimum advance notice needed).

Member Since 2001

"Charming, a little bit of Europe right here. A memorable weekend. We got engaged!"

The Village Inn

www.srinns.com/thevillageinn
16 Church St., P.O. Box 1810, Lenox, MA 01240
800-253-0917 • 413-637-0020 • Fax 413-637-9756
villinn@vgernet.net

Innkeepers/Owners
Billy and Pat Soto

Traditional Village Inn

Mobil ★★★

The Village Inn has welcomed guests since 1771 and over the years has gained a reputation for fine hospitality and exceptional cuisine. The new innkeepers have refurbished the kitchen, dining, and common areas, while maintaining the period charm. Begin your day with gingerbread pancakes or sweet potato hash, enjoy lunch by the gardens, and savor a sumptuous dinner of Shaker-style pot roast or pistachio-encrusted rack of lamb, serenaded by music from our new baby grand piano. Conveniently located in the historic district of Lenox, guest rooms are individually furnished with antiques and reproductions, private baths, many with whirlpool tubs, and feature modern amenities including an extensive video lending library. The Inn welcomes visitors all four seasons, and offers winter/spring packages, cooking classes, mid-week discounts, and off-site catering.

Rooms/Rates
32 Rooms, $79/$285 B&B;
1 Suite, $370/$590 B&B;
Rates change seasonally.
Open year-round.

Cuisine
Breakfast daily, dinner Friday and Saturday (June-Oct). Full bar service in the dining rooms.

Nearest Airport(s)
Albany

Directions
Mass. Tpke. (I-90): Exit 2, Rte. 20 W to Rte. 183 S. Turn L for 1 mi. to R on Church St. & Inn. From Rte. 7: take Rte. 7A to Church St. in Lenox.

Member Since 1977

"Thank you for making my visit absolutely wonderful. Thank you for a wonderful holiday!"

Applegate Inn

www.srinns.com/applegate
279 West Park Street, Lee, MA 01238
800-691-9012 • 413-243-4451 • Fax 413-243-9832
lenandgloria@applegateinn.com

Owners/Innkeepers
Gloria and Len Friedman

Elegant Country Breakfast Inn

AAA ◆◆◆

Once inside the iron gate, the circular drive, lined with lilac bushes reveals this elegant 1920s white-pillared Georgian mansion. It is situated on a 6 acre country estate across the road from a golf and tennis club one-half mile from the historic town of Lee and about 3 miles from Stockbridge. The inn's spacious public rooms are furnished with antiques and antique reproductions. The 11 guest accommodations are uniquely decorated and luxuriously appointed. From the screened porch look beyond the heated swimming pool to the lawns, towering trees and gardens. This is tranquility itself—a relaxing place to rejuvenate while pampered with attentive service, candlelit breakfasts, and wine and cheese served each afternoon. Explore Tanglewood, theater, dance, Norman Rockwell Museum, golf, tennis, hiking, swimming, boating, skiing, antiquing, shopping and other natural and cultural wonders of the Berkshires, or linger at the inn by a roaring fire, rest in a hammock for two under an old apple tree, or stroll the perennial gardens.

Rooms/Rates
5 Rooms $120/$245; 5 Suites $200/$350; 1 Cottage $225/$330. Central AC,TV,VCR,CD, many with fireplaces, jacuzzis, mini-fridge, balconies and patios. One room has a steam shower for two. All have robes, hair dryers, phones, fresh flowers, brandy & chocolate. Gift shop.

Cuisine
Multi-course gourmet candlelit breakfast served on china & crystal. Wine & cheese served in the afternoon. Fruit bowl, cookie jar & guest pantry always available.

Nearest Airport(s)
Albany Intl & Bradley Airports

Directions
I-90 to Exit 2 (Lee); Rte. 20 W to stop sign. Go straight .5 mile on L, across from Greenock Country Club.

Member Since 2002

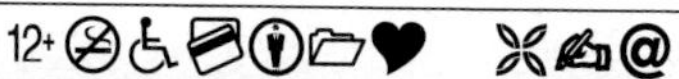
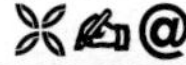

"A lovely place for relaxation and gracious hospitality - a perfect 10!"

Devonfield

www.srinns.com/devonfield
85 Stockbridge Road., Lee, MA 01238
800-664-0880 • 413-243-3298 • Fax 413-243-1360
innkeeper@devonfield.com

Innkeepers/Owners
Jim & Pam Loring
Elegant Federal
Country Breakfast Inn

Devonfield sits amidst 29 beautiful acres overlooking a pastoral meadow shaded by graceful birch trees and towering pines with the rolling tapestry of the Berkshire hills beyond. The 200 year old house has been meticulously cared for and offers guests the relaxed elegance of a British country house. The thoughtfully appointed guest rooms provide air conditioning, cable television/ VCRs, private phones with voicemail, brandy and chocolates. Some rooms also have wood burning fireplaces and Jacuzzis. A heated pool, tennis court, and bicycles offer guests more ways to relax. Devonfield is only minutes away from Tanglewood, Norman Rockwell, Jacobs Pillow, Shakespeare & Co., antiquing and shopping.

Rooms/Rates
6 rooms $110/$245, 3 suites $170/$295, 1 cottage $185/$325. All with private baths, A/C, cable TV/VCR, phones with voice mail, brandy and handmade chocolates.

Cuisine
Early morning coffee and tea. Full gourmet breakfast with candlelight (fireside dining in fall and winter months) and classical music. Soft drinks, cookies, tea and coffee always available in Guest Pantry. Picnic baskets also available for guest use.

Nearest Airport(s)
Bradley International

Directions
I-90 to Exit 2 (Lee); Rt.20 W to stop sign. Go straight through and up hill for 9/10 mile-on left.

Member Since 2003

"Divine is the only word for Devonfield.
The views from every angle are spectacular."

Innkeepers/Owners
Alice & Len Schiller
Manager
Annette Perelli

Elegant Georgian
Village Breakfast Inn

Mobil ★★★
AAA ◆◆◆

The Inn at Stockbridge

www.srinns.com/innatstockbridge
RTE 7N, Box 618, Stockbridge, MA 01262
888-466-7865 • 413-298-3337 • Fax 413-298-3406
innkeeper@stockbridgeinn.com

Rooms/Rates
8 Rooms $140/$275
8 Fireplace and/or Whirlpool Suites $225/$345
Rates vary by room and season.

Cuisine
Gourmet candlelit breakfast. Complimentary wine and cheese. Butlers pantry and complimentary bottled water.

Nearest Airport(s)
Albany, NY
Hartford, CT

Directions
MA Pike to exit 2, W on Rte 102 to Route 7N 1.2 miles to Inn on Rt. From NYC: Saw Mill Pkwy N to Taconic Pkwy N to Rte 23E to MA to Rte 7N past Stockbridge village 1.2 m N. From NJ: NYS Thruway (RT 87N) to exit 17 to Rt 84E to Taconic State Parkway N. Follow above from NY.

Enjoy peaceful charm and elegance in a 1906 Georgian style mansion secluded on 12 acres in Stockbridge, a town described by Norman Rockwell as the best of New England and the best of America. Awaken to the aroma of fresh coffee, stroll the beautiful grounds, take a dip in the heated pool, exercise in the fitness room, relax on the wrap around porch and take time away from the cares of the world. Antiques, collectibles and luxury are very much at home here. Amenities and attention to detail found only in upscale properties for the discriminating traveler await you here. Fireplace and double whirlpool rooms with a private deck are available. Voted by the Discerning Traveler as one of the Most Romantic Inns for 2005.

Member Since 1986

12+

"Wonderful as always. Great hospitality, breakfast and a wonderful time. Loved the poodle Excellent & Elegant Beautiful, comfortable & delicious."

The Weathervane Inn

www.srinns.com/weathervaneinn
17 Main Street, Route 23, South Egremont, MA 01258
800-528-9580 • 413-528-9580 • Fax 413-528-1713
innkeeper@weathervaneinn.com

Innkeepers/Owners
Jeffrey and Maxine Lome

Traditional Federal Village Breakfast Inn

Nestled in the quaint and historic village of South Egremont, this charming landmark Country Inn has been offering gracious hospitality to visitors to the Berkshires for over 18 years. The Lome family invites you to enjoy all the Berkshires has to offer in the comfort of our ten charming and beautifully-appointed guest rooms. We offer a bountiful country breakfast to start your day and a fireside tea for your relaxation after a full day of activities. The Berkshires offer four seasons of cultural and recreational activities including Tanglewood summer stock, historic homes, hiking, skiing and antiquing. Our newly renovated barn offers Yoga, Chikitsa, and Swadhyaya classes. You can also schedule a private Bodywork or Massage session. Please call for more details. Rekindle your romance and get away from it all at the Weathervane.

Rooms/Rates
Guestrooms: $115/$200/night
Suites: $225/$300/night

Cuisine
Full Country Breakfast each morning and afternoon tea. Dinner available to parties of ten or more by prior arrangement. We have a Liquor License and sell and serve a variety of beverages.

Nearest Airport(s)
Albany, NY - 1 hour
Hartford/Bradley, CT - 90 miles

Directions
From NYC: Taconic Pkwy to Rte. 23 E 13 miles to Inn on R. From Mass Tpke: exit 2 to Rte. 102 to Rte. 7 S to Rte. 23 W to Inn on L.

Member Since 1984

"Thank you all very much for your hospitality, thoughtfullness and attention to detail."

Innkeepers
Karl & Jane Sabo
Traditional Village Inn

Mobil ★★★
AAA ◆◆◆

Deerfield Inn

www.srinns.com/deerfieldinn
81 Old Main Street, Deerfield, MA 01342-0305
800-926-3865 • 413-774-5587 • Fax 413-775-7221
info@deerfieldinn.com

Rooms/Rates
23 guest rooms, $181/$248 DBL. Rates include tea and cookies and a full country breakfast. Rates, availability, reservations and seasonal discounts available on our website. Open year-round, except Dec. 24-25.

Cuisine
Award-winning restaurant with French Chef Didier Voisin features foods prepared in classic style, and served with style in our distinctive dining room. A broad range of finely selected American wines complements your dinner.

Nearest Airport(s)
Bradley Field

Directions
FROM NYC: 3.5 hrs. I-91 N to exit 24. Follow signs to Historic Deerfield. FROM BOSTON 2 hrs. I-90 W to Exit 4 & I-91 N to exit 24.

One of the few original country inns in the region, this classic hostelry opened its doors in July 1884, despite a plague of grasshoppers devouring its way across a drought-stricken county! Located along a charming mile-long way known simply as "The Street," the Deerfield Inn is still the centerpiece of Old Deerfield with 11 rooms in the main inn, and 12 in the south wing. A National Historic Landmark, this unspoiled 330-year-old village is a perfect destination for those looking for the real New England. Enjoy Deerfield's farms, museums, events, country walks, friendly folk, and beautiful scenery. Dinner at the Inn is a well-deserved reward after a busy day of touring. We look forward to welcoming you here.

Member Since 1996

"Visiting Deerfield is like stepping back in time.
We love the inn, our home away from home."

Longfellow's Wayside Inn

www.srinns.com/longfellows
72 Wayside Inn Road, Sudbury, MA 01776
800-339-1776 • 978-443-1776 • Fax 978-443-8041
reservations@waysideinn.org

Innkeeper
Robert H. Purrington
18th Century Colonial Country B&B

Step back in time to the Inn that represents the glory of Colonial New England. Licensed since 1716 and immortalized in 1863 by poet Henry Longfellow in his 'Tales of a Wayside Inn,' this Massachusetts Historic Landmark continues today as an Inn, restaurant and museum situated on 130 protected acres. Enjoy antique-filled guest rooms and traditional Yankee fare in any number of our historic dining areas. Stroll the grounds, past our quaint white-steepled chapel, to the water-powered Grist Mill that still produces the flour used in all our baking! Visit our authentic one-room schoolhouse for a lesson on rural education in small-town America, and listen to seasonal fife-and-drum music on warm Wednesday evenings! Museum rooms and other exhibits found throughout the Inn—a unique experience!

Member Since 1967

Rooms/Rates
10 charming, country-style guest rooms with private bath. Single: $96/$120; Double: $122/$155. Private sitting room and breakfast service reserved for house guests only. Many rooms with four-poster bedsteads!

Cuisine
Lunch and dinner served daily in 7 historic dining areas. Traditional Yankee fare served by experienced waitstaff. Open 363 days a year, closed Christmas Day and July Fourth.

Nearest Airport(s)
Boston Logan International

Directions
Located west of Boston, MA. Take Interstate 95 to Rte. 20 west for 11 miles to Wayside Inn Road. From Rte. 495 to Rte. 20 east for 7 miles to Wayside Inn Road.

"Charming." "Exceptional hospitality." "So rustic & quaint—I loved it!" "Great atmosphere!"

Hawthorne Inn

www.srinns.com/hawthorn
462 Lexington Road, Concord, MA 01742-3729
978-369-5610 • Fax 978-287-4949
Inn@ConcordMass.com

Innkeepers/Owners
Gregory Burch and Marilyn Mudry

Traditional Village Breakfast Inn

Mobil ★★★
AAA ◆◆◆

Rooms/Rates
Seven graciously appointed guestrooms offering Canopy or Four-poster Bed. $105/$305. Recognized by *Forbes* Magazine "10 Best Inns of New England."

Cuisine
Breakfast is served each morning, around a convivial common table, on hand-painted Dedham Pottery. Inn guests enjoy a robust selection of fresh-baked breads, breakfast cakes, specialty jams, seasonal fruit offerings and fresh-roasted organic coffee.

Nearest Airport(s)
Logan Airport/Boston

Directions
From Rte 128-95: take exit 30 B (Rte 2A West) for 2.8 miles. Bear Right at fork, go toward Concord for 1.5 miles. Inn is opposite Hawthorne's home.

Just 19 miles from Boston, three rivers wend through a Colonial landscape of Minutemen's fields where lichen-covered walls embrace the homes of Hawthorne, Alcott and Emerson. Under shade of ancient trees you find the Hawthorne Inn an intimate refuge filled with much to share: poetry and literature to entertain and enlighten you, artworks and archaic artifacts that are a wonder to behold, weavings and coverlets to snuggle on a crisp autumn eve and burnished antique furnishings that speak of home and security. Vibrant guestrooms, inspired by a refreshing sense of tradition melded with an artist's whimsy, are highlighted with wonderful colors to rest the soul and warm the heart.

Member Since 1980

"Everything about our stay was wonderful, with beautiful accommodations and gracious hosts."

Emerson Inn By The Sea

www.srinns.com/emersoninn
One Cathedral Avenue, Rockport, MA 01966
800-964-5550 • 978-546-6321 • Fax 978-546-7043
info@EmersonInnByTheSea.com

Innkeepers/Owners
Bruce and Michele Coates
General Manager
Jennifer Messier
Traditional Waterside Inn

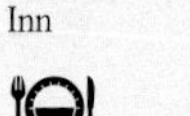

Mobil ★★★
AAA ◆◆◆

Ralph Waldo Emerson called the Inn "Thy proper summer home." Today's guests enjoy the relaxed 19th century atmosphere from our broad oceanfront veranda, but can savor the 21st century amenities of a heated saltwater pool, sauna, room phones, air conditioning, television, private baths and spa tubs. Nearby are hiking trails along the oceanfront, tennis, golf, sea kayaking, scuba diving and the always popular whale watches. Halibut Point State Park features the history of the Rockport Quarries and downtown Rockport is famous for shops and art galleries. The historic Emerson is the ideal ocean front location for weddings, retreats and conferences. "Editors Pick," *Yankee Travel Guide to New England.* And as featured in Zagat's *2005 Top U.S. Hotels, Resorts, and Spas.*

Rooms/Rates
36 Rooms, $95/$350 B&B; Rooms with ocean views, spa tubs, fireplaces. Two Seaside Cottages, each accommodates 8, available for a weekly rental. Open all year.

Cuisine
Award-winning Restaurant. 'Unparalleled ambiance' - *The Boston Globe.* Outdoor oceanfront dining and elegant turn-of-the-century dining room serving breakfast daily; dinner and live music schedules vary by season.

Nearest Airport(s)
Boston Logan International Airport

Directions
Rte. 128 N to traffic light in Gloucester L on Rte.127 to Pigeon Cove. R at our sign on Phillips Ave.

Member Since 1973

"Lovely view of sunrise, comfortable bed, lots of pillows; it was perfectly wonderful."

Harbor Light Inn

www.srinns.com/harborlight
58 Washington Street, Marblehead, MA 01945
781-631-2186 • Fax 781-631-2216
info@harborlightinn.com

Innkeepers/Owners
Peter & Suzanne Conway

Elegant Federal In Town Inn

Mobil ★★★
AAA ◆◆◆

Rooms/Rates
21 Rooms, $125/$195; Suites, $150/$295 B&B. Open year-round.

Cuisine
Breakfast buffet. 7 restaurants within 2 blocks of Inn. Wine & liquor within 2 blocks of Inn.

Nearest Airport(s)
Boston Logan International

Directions
From Boston & airport: take Rt. 1A N to Rt. 129 E to Marblehead. Take first R at Hunneman Caldwell Banker Real Estate, onto Washington St. Follow approx 1/3 mile to Inn.

Winner of numerous national awards for excellence, including *Vacation* magazine's "America's Best Romantic Inns." The Inn offers first-class accommodations and amenities found in the finest of lodging facilities. Elegant furnishings grace these two connected Federalist mansions. Formal fireplaced parlors, dining room and bed chambers, double Jacuzzis, sundecks, patio, quiet garden and outdoor heated pool combine to ensure the finest in New England hospitality. Located in the heart of historic Harbor District of fine shops, art galleries and restaurants.

Member Since 1996

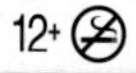

"Impeccable accommodations out done only by the staff and their eagerness to please!"

Charles Street Inn

www.srinns.com/charlesstreet
94 Charles St., Boston, MA 02114
877-772-8900 • 617-314-8900 • Fax 617-371-0009
info@charlesstreetinn.com

Innkeepers/Owners
Sally Deane & Louise Venden

Historic Beacon Hill B&B

A luxury inn located in historic Beacon Hill within blocks of Boston's shopping, touring, and subway stops, the Charles Street Inn offers unique comfort and privacy in nine spacious rooms with elevator access. Each room features a private bath with whirlpool tubs, working marble fireplaces, fresh flowers, BOSE radio/CD player, Cable TV, VCR, DVD, HVAC controls, DSL and Wireless Internet, and Sub-Zero refrigerator. Authentic Victorian-era antiques, king & queen size canopy and sleigh beds, and rich imported linens complete each elegant setting. Relax in front of a fire or enjoy any of the fabulous restaurants that are literally steps from the inn. Recognized among Boston's Best by *Travel + Leisure, Boston Magazine*, and as one of the top 10 romantic inns in the US by America's Historic Inns. Concierge services available.

Member Since 2004

Rooms/Rates
9 Rooms. $225/$425 depending on room, season, and day of the week. Call for rates (US toll-free 877-772-8900) or visit "Reservations" on our web site.

Cuisine
Arrive to sweets, fresh fruit, snacks and refreshments in the lobby and in your room (kitchenette w/dishes, tea kettle, coffee pot and mini-fridge). Then, schedule your in-room breakfast with so many choices we call it "deluxe continental". Or simply walk down the street to discover fine restaurants.

Nearest Airport(s)
Boston

Directions
Find Storrow Drive and take Gov't Ctr Exit. Turn South onto Charles Street and go two blocks.

"A business executive, tired of waiting for elevators in larger chain hotels might find solace here." *Washington Post*

Innkeepers/Owners
Rainer Horn
Jurgen Herzog
Hans van Costenoble

Historic Village
Breakfast Inn

Carpe Diem Guesthouse

www.srinns.com/carpediem
12 Johnson Street, Provincetown, MA 02657
800-487-0132 • 508-487-4242 • Fax 508-487-0138
info@carpediemguesthouse.com

Rooms/Rates
14 rooms and suites, $75/$340. Open year round.

Cuisine
Jurgen's homemade German-style breakfast is famous. The family-size dining table is the meeting point for all guests who like a good cup of coffee, German bread, cakes, Belgian waffles, quiche, omelets or other specials. Afternoon wine & cheese hour and refreshments.

Nearest Airport(s)
Boston & Providence

Directions
Entering Provincetown on Rt. 6 take the second L at the street light. Go down Conwell Street which ends at Bradford Street. Take a R and Johnson Street is your first L.

Seize the day - make your Provincetown stay extraordinary! The Carpe Diem is an intimate Cape Cod Guesthouse and a romantic hideaway combined with luxurious amenities and personal service. Quietly located in the center of town each room is named after a renowned writer, decorated with European antiques and ambience and offers private bath, queen size bed, down bedding, bathrobes and luxury products. Some feature fireplaces, whirlpool tubs, private entrance and/or private patios. Our garden is a green oasis with a heated spa. Let classical music carry you away along a journey of the heart and imagination. Enjoy our homemade gourmet breakfast and join us for our daily Wine and Cheese hour. The common rooms are a great place to relax, read a good book, meet people or chat with new friends. There is a fireplace, video library, complimentary Sherry and Port, a 24-hour coffee station as well as a guest office for those that need to stay connected to the "real" world. And for those who like the excitement of shopping and nightlife, Commercial Street, the pulsating lifeline of Provincetown, is only steps away. Carpe Diem – a magical place on the edge of the continent!

Member Since 2003

"A perfect paradise, it will stay in our memories forever, a wonderful place to wake up in."

Crowne Pointe Historic Inn & Spa

www.srinns.com/crownepointe
82 Bradford Street, Provincetown, MA 02657
877-276-9631 • 508-487-6767 • Fax 508-487-5554
welcome@crownepointe.com

Innkeepers/Owners
David M. Sanford, Thomas J. Walter & Mom
Historic Breakfast Inn & Spa

AAA ◆◆◆◆

A prominent Sea Captain built this historic mansion, which has been fully restored to its 19th Century glory. The inn's stunning Victorian architecture includes two-story wrap around porches complete with turret and harbor views. The *New York Daily News* raves "Five Star Luxury Without the Cost." Revive at our full service on-site Shui Spa featuring many treatments and massage options. Shui Spa offers guests an intimate spa experience. Crowne Pointe is a AAA Four Diamond property located in the center of town. Our signature gourmet hot breakfast and afternoon wine and cheese social are included. Heated in-ground pool, two hot tubs, fireplaces and in-room whirlpools are offered. Spa packages are available. Our restaurant captures our guests with exquisite gourmet cuisine, and our hotel bar is a treasured place to socialize. The finest menu creations from our talented chefs, carefully selected labels from our wine cellar, and excellent service in a charming setting are waiting for you to indulge.

Rooms/Rates
40 Rooms. $110/$465 depending upon season. Min stay req's may apply. Many special packages available, call for details.

Cuisine
The freshest regional ingredients arriving daily, our distinctive full hot breakfasts are unsurpassed. The main selections change daily and special dietary needs are accommodated.

Nearest Airport(s)
Provincetown Airport (PVC) or Boston Logan Airport

Directions
Rt 6 E. 63 m. to Provincetown. Turn L at the 2nd Provincetown exit onto Conwell St. Take Conwell St. to the end and make R onto Bradford St. follow Bradford to 82 Crowne Pointe Inn sits on a bluff.

Member Since 2003

18+   

"Faaaabulous"-Eartha Kitt

Innkeepers/Owners
Margaret & Rebecca Keith

Traditional Village Breakfast Inn

Mobil ★★★
AAA ◆◆◆

Penny House Inn

www.srinns.com/penny
4885 County Rd (Route 6), Eastham, MA 02642
800-554-1751 • 508-255-6632 • Fax 508-255-4893
pennyhouse@aol.com

Rooms/Rates
12 Rooms. Guestrooms $175/$325. Suites $295/$350

Cuisine
Traditional full breakfast with a gourmet flair. Among our specialties: Eggs Benedict, French Toast Croissants and Pecan Waffles with fresh fruit. Special dietary needs accommodated such as Vegetarian, Diabetic or Gluten-free, with advance notice.

Nearest Airport(s)
Boston, MA

Directions
Cross the Cape Cod Canal, take Route 6 towards Provincetown. Go past exit 12, highway ends at a traffic circle, take 2nd exit (Rt6) through 3 traffic lights, exactly 5 miles from circle on left(cnr of Bayside Dr & Rt6) across from St.Aubin's Nursery.

Hidden among the Outer Cape's pristine beauty, is the Penny House Inn. Built in 1690, the original house was subsequently added on to for over 300 years, blending Cape Cod colonial charm with modern conveniences. Guestrooms at the inn are characterized by their own personal charm and amenities. Several rooms are hidden away, perfect for romantic escapes and honeymoons. All rooms have modern private baths, AC, cable TV/VCR and phone. Most guestrooms have fireplaces, while some also have two-person whirlpool tubs and private balconies. For complete pampering our spa offers several services such as massage, Reiki, facials, salt glows, hydrotherapies and mud wraps. A short walk away is a full service health club with indoor tennis. The outdoor heated pool is available Memorial-Labor Day.

Member Since 2003

"A great escape, the perfect stressbuster. A wonderful place to relax & reconnect with my husband. We felt truly pampered." Cary 2005

The Whalewalk Inn and Spa

www.srinns.com/whalewalkinn
220 Bridge Road, Eastham, Cape Cod, MA 02642
800-440-1281 • 508-255-0617 • Fax 508-240-0017
reservations@whalewalkinn.com

Innkeepers
Elaine and Kevin Conlin

Traditional Federal Village Breakfast Inn

AAA ◆◆◆

Abandon every day life. Rekindle your romance and rejuvenate your body and mind. Relax at Cape Cod's most romantic country Inn and Spa. Secluded, but centrally located to all the attractions which make Cape Cod so special. After a gourmet breakfast, walk the "Outer Cape" beaches, listening to the soothing sound of the waves, lapping on Cape Cod Bay or crashing at the National Seashore. At the end of a day on the beach, riding the Rail Trail, kayaking, shopping or museum hopping, restore your inner balance and harmony at The Spa, a very special place with your comfort and exercise regime in mind. Forget the weather; you can pamper your mind and body with a massage or facial package; feel the heat of the dry sauna; or workout in the indoor resistance pool or on the cardiovascular machines. Stay in the luxurious Spa Penthouse or in another of our beautiful accommodations. All rooms are individually decorated, have air-conditioning, TV/VCR, CD players and phones. Come and enjoy our impeccable service and heartfelt hospitality.

Member Since 1993

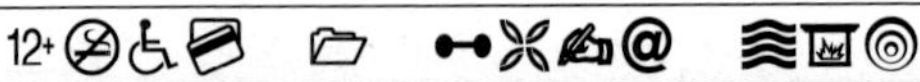

Rooms/Rates
16 rooms and suites, $205/$450 B&B. Open March to December 31.

Cuisine
Full-service gourmet breakfast with fresh home-baked delights and entrees including: Pecan Waffles, Eggs Benedict, Corn Pancakes with Dill Shallot Sauce and Salmon Rosettes, Grand Marnier Oatmeal Pie, Frittata Primavera, and Captain Harding Omelet. There is an hors d'oeuvre hour every evening.

Nearest Airport(s)
Boston, MA
Providence, RI

Directions
Rte. 6 to Orleans Rotary, Rock Harbor Courthouse Exit off Rotary, L on Rock Harbor Road (1/4 mile), R on Bridge Road (1/4 mile). Driving time, Boston or Providence—2 hours.

"We discovered many treasures on the Cape, but none as treasured as The Whalewalk Inn. Another fabulous visit! Thank you for making Cape Cod so memorable."

Innkeepers/Owners
Donna and Peter Amadeo

Elegant Waterside Breakfast Inn

The Captain Freeman Inn

www.srinns.com/captainfreeman
15 Breakwater Road, Brewster, Cape Cod, MA 02631
800-843-4664 • 508-896-7481 • Fax 508-896-5618
stay@captainfreemaninn.com

Rooms/Rates
12 Rooms, 6 w/fireplaces, whirlpool tubs and TV's, $150/$250 B&B. Open year-round.

Cuisine
Full gourmet breakfast, afternoon tea, winter weekend cooking school with wine-tasting and dinner.

Nearest Airport(s)
Providence
Boston Logan International

Directions
From route 6 (Mid Cape Highway) take exit 10 (route 124) toward Brewster. At the end of 124 go Right on Route 6A, then Left on Breakwater. Our driveway is the first one on the Left.

Built just a short stroll from beautiful Breakwater Beach, The Captain Freeman Inn is a lovingly restored Victorian sea captain's mansion furnished with canopy beds and period antiques. Luxury accommodations include fireplace, two-person whirlpool, garden and pool views. Breakfast is served poolside on the wraparound porch overlooking lush perennial gardens. In cooler winter weather you will dine fireside in the garden-view dining room. Bicycles are provided to our guests. Venture out to watch humpback whales at play or bike miles of wooded trails. Return for a glass of wine and a dip in our heated pool. See sunset on Cape Cod Bay. Sail, surf, fish, golf, or rock on our wraparound porch.

Member Since 1998

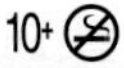    

"A honeymoon made in heaven! We were in awe when we entered our room."

The Captain's House Inn of Chatham

www.captainshouseinn.com
369-377 Old Harbor Rd, Chatham, MA 02633
800-315-0728 • 508-945-0127 • Fax 508-945-0866
info@captainshouseinn.com

Perhaps Cape Cod's finest small Inn, this historic 1839 sea captain's estate on two acres is the perfect choice for a romantic getaway or elegant retreat. Gourmet breakfasts, English afternoon teas, beautifully decorated rooms with king and queen size four-poster beds, fireplaces, seating areas, telephones with data ports, and TV/VCR's; some with whirlpool tubs. Enjoy uncompromising service from our enthusiastic international staff and enjoy the Inn's many gardens and fountains, heated outdoor pool, new fitness centre and spa, and savor the scenic beauty of the historic seafaring village of Chatham with its spectacular views of the ocean.

Member Since 1989

Innkeepers/Owners
Jan and Dave McMaster

Elegant Village
Breakfast Inn

Mobil ★★★
AAA ◆◆◆◆

Rooms/Rates
12 Rooms, $235/$350; 4 Suites, $250/$450 Summer; $185/$250; $225/$295 Winter. All rooms are air conditioned. Open year-round.

Cuisine
Breakfast, poolside lunches, afternoon tea, evening snacks.

Nearest Airport(s)
Providence or Boston

Directions
Rte. 6 (Mid-Cape Hwy) to exit 11(S) Rte. 137 to Rte 28, L approx. 3 miles to rotary. Continue around rotary on Rte. 28 toward Orleans 1/2 mile on L.

"Fantastic service & accommodation. Can't wait to tell our friends."
- L.R., New Zealand

Innkeepers/Owners
Judy & Ray Braz
Village Breakfast Inn

AAA ◆◆◆

Old Harbor Inn

www.srinns.com/oldharborinn
22 Old Harbor Road, Chatham, MA 02633
800-942-4434 • 508 945-4434 • Fax 508 945-7665
info@chathamoldharborinn.com

Rooms/Rates
8 Rooms from $189/$279 in the summer. Rates in the spring and fall shoulder seasons are $169/$249. Winter rates are $129/$199. Minimum stay requirements. Special packages available, please call.

Cuisine
Breakfast of homemade specialties. Coffee,tea, soft drinks and snacks anytime.

Nearest Airport(s)
Barnstable County Airport- Approximately 20 miles

Directions
Rte 6(Mid Cape Hwy)to exit 11 south to Rte 137 3 miles to Rte 28 south approx 3 miles to rotary stay on 28 around rotary We are immediately on right. Please call for directions from Boston, Providence, or New York.

The Inn offers all the amenities that the sophisticated traveler requires, while maintaining an intimate ambiance. Ideally located steps from the major attractions that Chatham offers. Many guests truly enjoy not having to use their cars for several days as they explore the village. Judy, Ray and their knowledgeable staff will offer suggestions for maximizing your leisure activitics. Chatham serves as a centralized base for exploring all of Cape Cod and the islands of Nantucket and Martha's Vineyard. Itineraries for day trips to Sandwich or Provincetown or anywhere in between can be arrainged based on what activities you enjoy the most. Explore the natural beauty of Cape Cod. Discover the breathtaking vistas of the National Seashore. Be pampered at The Old Harbor Inn. Every day you get our best!

Member Since 2004

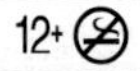

"You have met and exceeded all of our expectations" "Perfection... we will return."

The Queen Anne Inn

www.srinns.com/queenanneinn
70 Queen Anne Road, Chatham Cape Cod, MA 02633
800-545-4667 • 508-945-0084 • Fax 508-945-4884
info@queenanneinn.com

Innkeepers/Owners
Dana and Guenther Weinkopf

Elegant Victorian Country Resort

Welcome to this romantic place of timeless tranquility and complete relaxation. Discover its charm and character of more than 150 years. Find delight in the privacy of your lodgings and the excellent cuisine. Unwind with a relaxing massage in our spa or refresh with a dip in the sparkling heated pool. Soak in your own hot tub while watching the sunset from your balcony or dream in front of a warm fire. Leisurely stroll down the quaint main street, or watch the fishing boats come in. Let us be your home away from home, while discovering Cape-Cod.

Member Since 1981

Rooms/Rates
34 Rooms, $105/$395 B&B. Open year-round. Throughout the year the "Queen Anne" offers a variety of money saving packages and specials. To learn all about them go to our web site or simply call us at 800-545-4667.

Cuisine
Recognized for it's outsanding coastal cuisine by just about every major U.S. and European food critique. Serving a full a la carte breakfast, dinner and snacks by the pool.

Nearest Airport(s)
Hyannis, TF Green, Boston

Directions
Route 6 E to exit 11, L on Rte. 137,go to end of #137 & turn L on the Rte.28 for 3.5 miles to traffic light. Turn R on Queen Anne Rd. Inn is first Right on Queen Anne Rd.

"The inn is fabulous, our room wonderful. The staff great."
Norm & JoAnn Ecker, Woodstock, VT

The Dan'l Webster Inn & Spa

www.srinns.com/danlwebsterinn
149 Main St., Sandwich, MA 02563
800-444-3566 • 508-888-3622 • Fax 508-888-5156
info@danlwebsterinn.com

Innkeeper/Owner
Robert V. Catania
Traditional Colonial Village Inn

Rooms/Rates
53 Traditional/Deluxe/Superior Rooms, $109/$249; 17 Suites, $179/$379. Open year-round. Closed Christmas.

Cuisine
Breakfast, lunch, dinner, & Sunday Brunch. Tavern on premise. Fine & casual dining menus available.

Nearest Airport(s)
TF Green (Providence)

Directions
From Boston, MA: Rte. 3 S to Rte. 6 to exit 2 turn L on Rte. 130 approx. 2 miles–R at fork. Inn will be on L.

This award-winning Inn set in the heart of Historic Sandwich, offers guests the romance of the past with today's conveniences. Canopy and four-poster beds, fireplaces and oversized whirlpool tubs await your arrival. Each guest room and suite has been individually appointed with exquisite period furnishings. The new Spa at The Dan'l Webster offers the ultimate in luxury for Men and Women...from completely organic Body Treatments and relaxing Massages to soothing Facials and more, we will pamper your mind, body and soul! Enjoy a romantic dinner in one of our five distinctive dining rooms, including the renowned Conservatory. Savor delicious award-winning cuisine and creative chef's specials complemented by an acclaimed wine selection, or relax in our casual Tavern at the Inn and enjoy lighter fare and a warm, friendly atmosphere.

Member Since 1994

"The boutique inn is located between heaven, history and the ocean..."

Isaiah Jones Homestead

www.srinns.com/isaiahjones
165 Main Street, Sandwich, MA 02563
800-526-1625 • 508-888-9115 • Fax 508-888-9648
info@isaiahjones.com

Innkeepers/Owners
Cecily Denson and Richard Pratt

Elegant Victorian Village Breakfast Inn

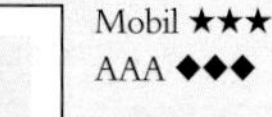

Mobil ★★★
AAA ◆◆◆

Relax in pampered elegance in this 1849 Italianate Victorian Inn. The main house has five exquisitely appointed guest rooms, with private baths, feature queen beds, antique furnishings, oriental carpets, all with fireplaces or glass-front stoves and four with oversize whirlpool tubs. The unique Carriage House has been recently renovated to include two spacious junior suites. Located in the heart of Sandwich village, you are within easy walking distance of many attractions of the Cape's oldest town. Unwind by strolling the meandering garden paths around the goldfish pond, by sitting in comfortable Adirondack chairs that are placed around the well-manicured yard or by relaxing by the original antique-tiled fireplace in the gathering room. A full breakfast, served by candlelight in our cherry-paneled dining room sets a warm tone to start your day. Chosen Editors Choice, *Cape Cod Travel Guide*, Spring, 2005.

Member Since 1989

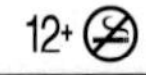   

Rooms/Rates
7 Rooms, $120/$190, includes breakfast. Air conditioned. Open year-round.

Cuisine
Breakfast is served in our cherry paneled dining room. Enjoy a full three-course breakfast of fresh fruit, juices, hot entrees, home-baked scones and coffeecakes, and a 'bottomless' pot of our special blend of coffee.

Nearest Airport(s)
Logan Airport, Boston, MA;
TF Green, Providence, RI

Directions
Rte. 6 (Mid-Cape Hwy.) Exit 2, Left at the end of the ramp onto Rte.130 to the village center. Bear right at the fork, go 2/10 mile, Inn is on the Left - 165 Main.

"All of the little details were wonderful." "Thank you for making our honeymoon very special." "We will never forget such a special place."

Palmer House Inn

www.srinns.com/palmerhouse
81 Palmer Avenue, Falmouth, MA 02540
800-472-2632 • 508-548-1230 • Fax 508-540-1878
innkeepers@palmerhouseinn.com

Innkeepers/Owners
Pat and Bill O'Connell

Elegant Village
Breakfast Inn

AAA ◆◆◆◆

On a tree-lined street in the heart of the Historic District, The Palmer House Inn is an elegant Victorian home. Stained glass windows, rich woodwork, gleaming hardwood floors and antique furnishings create an overall sense of warmth and harmony. Beautiful beaches, quaint shops, ferry shuttles, and excellent restaurants are only a short stroll away. The innkeepers pamper you with meticulous housekeeping, fresh flowers, extra pillows, fluffy robes, fine linens and good reading lights. The Palmer House Inn is the perfect place to stay, in splendid comfort and gracious care.

Rooms/Rates
16 Rooms, $99/$239; 2 Cottage Suites, $185/$299. K,Q,DBL beds, AC, cable TV & phones. Some have whirlpools, fireplaces. Open year-round.

Cuisine
Full gourmet breakfast served with candlelight and classical music. Afternoon and evening refreshments. Early morning coffee.

Nearest Airport(s)
TF Green (Providence)

Directions
After crossing the Bourne Bridge, follow Rte. 28 S for approximately 15 miles. A half-mile past the only traffic light at Jones Road/Ter Heun Drive, Rte. 28 turns left into Falmouth Village. The Inn is on the L just after the turn.

Member Since 2001

"How visually appealing everything is...the decor, the gardens, the porches. We loved it!"

Thorncroft Inn

www.srinns.com/thorncroftinn
460 Main St., P.O. Box 1022, Martha's Vineyard, MA 02568
800-332-1236 • 508-693-3333 • Fax 508-693-5419
innkeeper@thorncroft.com

Proprietors/Innkeepers
Lynn and Karl Buder
Traditional Craftsman Bungalow
Village Breakfast Inn

Mobil ★★★
AAA ◆◆◆◆

Rooms/Rates
14 antique appointed rooms, 10 with working wood burning fireplaces, some with two person whirlpools or private in-room hot tubs. $210/$550 B&B.

Cuisine
Full country breakfast served in two dining rooms at individual tables for two or an ample continental breakfast in bed; Traditional or healthful entrees. Afternoon tea and pastries.

Nearest Airport(s)
Martha"s Vineyard Airport (MVY) 5 miles

Directions
Year-round car & passenger Steamship Authority Ferry at Woods Hole, MA. (508-477-8600) Take left off dock and right at stop sign. Take next right onto Main St. Inn is 1 mile on left.

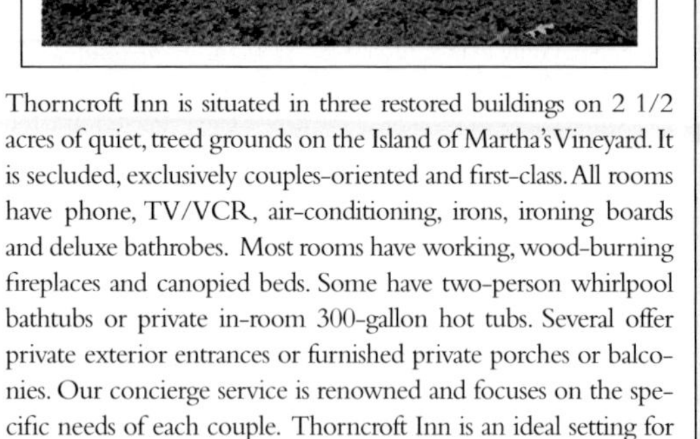

Thorncroft Inn is situated in three restored buildings on 2 1/2 acres of quiet, treed grounds on the Island of Martha's Vineyard. It is secluded, exclusively couples-oriented and first-class. All rooms have phone, TV/VCR, air-conditioning, irons, ironing boards and deluxe bathrobes. Most rooms have working, wood-burning fireplaces and canopied beds. Some have two-person whirlpool bathtubs or private in-room 300-gallon hot tubs. Several offer private exterior entrances or furnished private porches or balconies. Our concierge service is renowned and focuses on the specific needs of each couple. Thorncroft Inn is an ideal setting for honeymoons, anniversaries, elopements, engagements, birthdays or any romantic getaway for couples.

Member Since 1994

"Thorncroft is the kind of place, where we find ourselves falling in love all over again. The perfect place to escape the real world for a time."

Innkeepers/Owners
Matthew and Mary Parker
Assistant Innkeeper
Emily McDowell

Traditional Colonial Village Breakfast Inn

AAA ◆◆◆

Seven Sea Street Inn

www.srinns.com/sevenseastreet
7 Sea Street, Nantucket, MA 02554
800-651-9262 • 508-228-3577 • Fax 508-228-3578
innkeeper@sevenseastreetinn.com

Rooms/Rates
9 Guest Rooms, $99/$269 B&B; 2 Suites, $159/$339 B&B. Seasonal rates.

Cuisine
Expanded Buffet Continental Breakfast served daily. Two seatings, 8 a.m. and 9 a.m. Gourmet coffee, tea, soda, bottled water and homemade cookies available anytime.

Nearest Airport(s)
Nantucket Memorial Airport

Directions
Flights available from Boston, NYC, Providence, & Hyannis. Ferry service from Hyannis to Steamboat Wharf in Nantucket. Less than a 5 minute walk from the wharf to the Inn. Take your 1st right onto South Beach Street then your 2nd left onto Sea Street. The Inn is on the left at 7 Sea Street.

Enjoy Seven Sea Street Inn, a truly charming Nantucket bed and breakfast Inn, where we pride ourselves on the attentive service and elegant accommodations that will make your stay with us a fond memory. Our Inn is distinguished by its beautiful red oak post and beam style, designed and constructed with an authentic Nantucket ambiance in mind. We are the only Inn on the Island which offers guests both a relaxing Jacuzzi Spa and a stunning view of Nantucket Harbor from our Widow's Walk deck. All of our guest rooms are furnished with luxurious Stearns and Foster queen or king mattresses, the worlds finest bedding. Each Main house guest room and suite is furnished with rainshower showerheads, A/C's, high definition TVs, high speed wireless connectivity and a bow box of Nantucket's famous chocolate covered cranberries. Our location, nestled on a quiet tree-lined side street and less than a five-minute walk from Main Street shopping, restaurants, museums and the beach, couldn't be better. Indulge yourself at our lovely Inn this year.

Member Since 1996

"We loved every moment of our stay at your beautiful Inn. Our room was perfect thanks!"

Union Street Inn

www.srinns.com/unionstreetinn
7 Union Street, Nantucket, MA 02554
800-225-5116 • 508-228-9222 • Fax 508-325-0848
unioninn@nantucket.net

Innkeepers/Owners
Deb & Ken Withrow
Elegant Village Breakfast Inn

Nantucket's luxury B&B. "Ken worked in the hotel business, Deborah in high-end retail display, and guests get the best of both worlds. This 1770 house, a stone's throw from the bustle of Main Street, has been respectfully yet lavishly restored. Guests are treated to Frette linens, plump duvets, lush robes and a full gourmet breakfast served on the tree-shaded garden patio."-Fodors.

Professionally decorated in 2005, the inn is ideally located in the heart of the historic village just off Main Street's cobblestones and the harbor. Rooms have air conditioning, cable TV, "fresh" bath amenities and Wi-Fi high speed Internet access. Several rooms have wood burning fireplaces. Nantucket's restaurants, shops, galleries, and museums are a short stroll. Walk or bicycle to Nantucket's beautiful beaches.

Rooms/Rates
12 Rooms. High Season: $275/$445; Shoulder Seasons: $160/$350. Closed November through March.

Cuisine
Full Gourmet Breakfast. Afternoon Treats. Coffee, Tea, Bottled Spring Water always available.

Nearest Airport(s)
Nantucket Memorial Airport-10 minute taxi ride.

Directions
Flights from Boston, NYC, New Bedford & Hyannis. High season from Providence, Washington D.C. & Philadelphia. Ferry service from Hyannis-short walk from ferries.

Member Since 2005

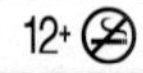

"In a word, lovely. The Union Street Inn has an excellent central location, and the rooms were tastefully decorated and kept very clean."

Michigan

"The Wolverine State"

Famous For: Famous For: Great Lakes (borders on four of the five Great Lakes), Fishing, Swimming, Water Sports, Holland (Tulip Center of America), Cherries, Farmland, Auto Manufacturing

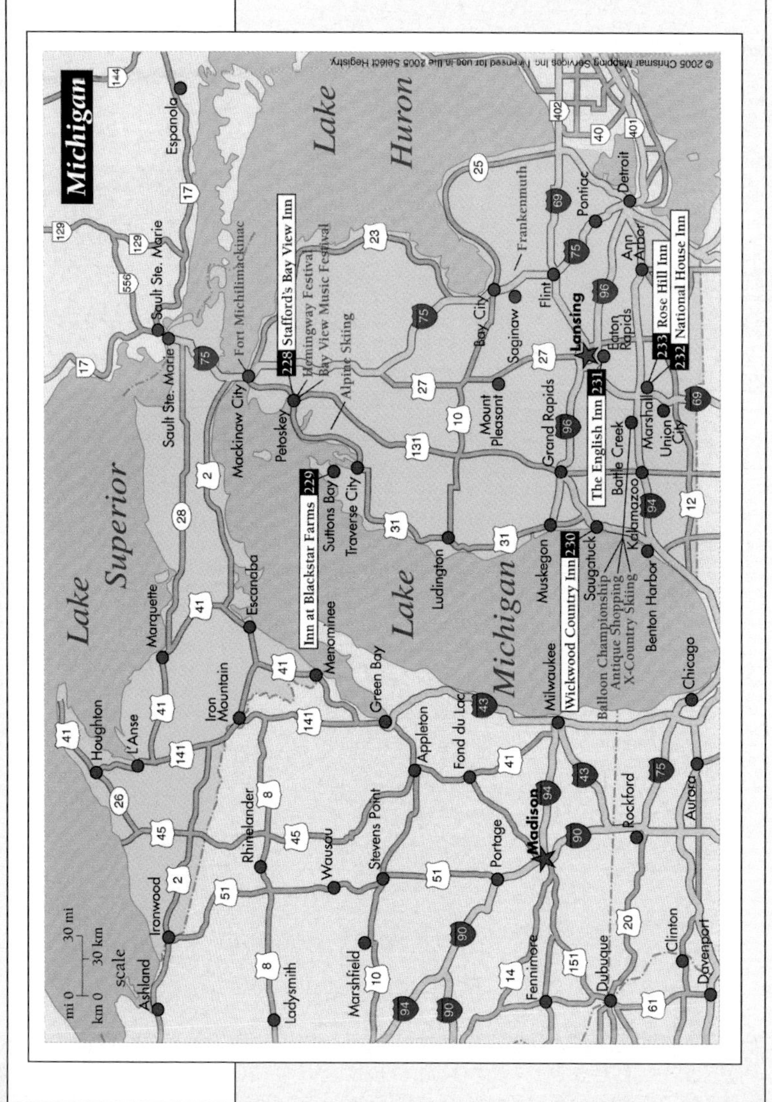

Stafford's Bay View Inn

www.srinns.com/staffordsbay
2011 Woodland Ave., P.O. Box 657, Petoskey, MI 49770
800-258-1886 • 231-347-2771 • Fax 231-347-3413
bayview@staffords.com

Proprietors
Stafford Smith Family
Innkeeper/ General Manager
Dean M. Smith
Traditional Victorian Country Inn

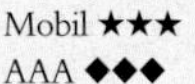

Mobil ★★★
AAA ◆◆◆

"Bay View Inn" was purchased by Stafford and Janice Smith in 1961. Stafford and his family has owned, operated, and lovingly restored, this grand Victorian Country Inn on the shores of Lake Michigan's Little Traverse Bay. Built as a rooming house in 1886 in the Historic Landmark District of Bay View, this Inn sets the standard in country inn dining and gracious service. Each beautifully appointed guest room features a private bath, and individual climate controls. Visitors to the area enjoy summer Chautauqua programs, championship golfing, our September light house tour, fall color tours, winter ski packages, and sleigh rides around the Bay View cottage grounds. Petoskey's Historic Gaslight Shopping District and marina are located nearby. Our inn is an exquisite place to hold weddings, rehearsal dinners, receptions and reunions. Many quiet corners offer a wonderful environment for company meetings and conferences. Landmark Hospitality where yesterday and today come together. Voted 'Michigan's Best Brunch' by *Michigan Living* magazine.

Member Since 1972

Rooms/Rates
21 Rooms, $89/$170;
9 Spa-Fireplace Suites $119/$240;
Bridal Suite $119/$260; B&B, Double Occupancy.

Cuisine
Breakfast & Dinner: May–Oct. and winter weekends. Lunch: Late May –Oct. Sunday Brunch: June-Oct. & Holidays. Visit www.staffords.com for menus, dining schedules and info on full-service, year-round, innkeeper-owned properties nearby.

Nearest Airport(s)
Pellston (PLN) - 17 miles
Traverse (TVC) - 65 miles

Directions
From Detroit: I-75N to Gaylord exit 282, Rte. 32W to US 131N to Petoskey. From Chicago: I-94 to I-196N to US 131N to Petoskey. From the North: I-75S across Mackinac Bridge to Petoskey Exit, US 31S.

"Perfect! The staff-decor-food! The view! Everything at this charming inn is wonderful! Warm caring smiles, yummie cookies, and we love the new color."

Proprietor
Don Coe
Innkeeper
Jill Ryan

Winery Breakfast Inn

Inn at Black Star Farms

www.srinns.com/blackstarfarms
10844 E. Revold Rd., Suttons Bay, MI 49682
877-466-9463 • 231-271-4970 ext. 150
Fax 231-271-6321
innkeeper@blackstarfarms.com

Rooms/Rates
May 27-October 30, 2005:
$200/$350
October 31-May 29, 2006:
$130/$275

Cuisine
Our breakfasts feature fresh fruit and juices, homemade baked goods, a seasonal gourmet entree using local products, and coffee & tea.

Nearest Airport(s)
Cherry Capitol Airport (TVC)

Directions
From Traverse City: Follow M-22 north toward Northport. The Inn will be on your left after about 12 miles. Turn left on Revold Rd. and left again into our driveway. From Cherry Capital Airport: Exit the airport and turn left at the 2nd stoplight - M-72. Follow M-72 to M-22 and proceed as above.

Our year-round Inn is nestled below a hillside of vineyards in the heart of Leelanau Peninsula wine country. Its eight contemporary guestrooms, each with private bath and some with fireplaces and spa tubs, have fine furniture, luxurious linens, and down comforters. Amenities include a bottle of our Red House Wine, cozy robes, and satellite TV/VCR. Sauna and massage services are available. A full gourmet breakfast is prepared for you daily using local seasonal products. You can sample our award-winning wines and spirits at our on site tasting room - also home of the artisanal Leelanau Cheese Co. The farm also features boarding stables and wooded recreational trails that are great in any season. Meetings, reunions and receptions welcomed.

Member Since 2003

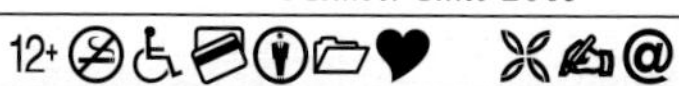

"We celebrate our anniversary here every year. What a perfect place to 'get away,' be pampered, and concentrate on each other."

Wickwood Inn

www.srinns.com/wickwood
510 Butler Street, Saugatuck, MI 49453-1019
800-385-1174 • 269-857-1465 • Fax 269-857-1552
innkeeper@wickwoodinn.com

Innkeepers/Owners
Julee Rosso Miller and Bill Miller

Elegant Colonial Village Breakfast Inn

Travel + Leisure says, "Wickwood is one of America's most romantic Inns, a jewel with delicious food!!" Foodlovers, romantics and art connoisseurs gather at Silver Palate Cookbook author Julee Rosso's Inn in this charming art village on the shores of Lake Michigan. "She changed the way American eats," New York's Newsday compliments. Everyday terrific "surprises" are served including Chocolate Strawberries, lush Evening Hor's d'ouvres, great Champagne Brunch, Biscotti & Vin Santo. This exquisite getaway has a sophisticated décor, stunning artwork, antiques, gazebos and gardens. Guest rooms are appointed with featherbeds, fireplaces, cozy robes, stereos, books and spa secrets. "The décor is breathtaking—the food perfection," raves Zagat. The villages feature one of the "World's Top Ten Beaches," nature and bike trails, antique shops, 50 art galleries, berry and apple orchards, wineries, 150 shops and boutiques, four golf courses, theater, music and film festivals. The Inn is exquisite all year, especially magical at The Holidays.

Member Since 2002

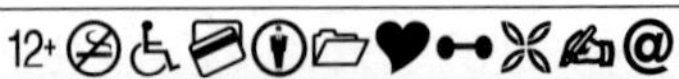

Rooms/Rates
7 traditional rooms, 4 suites with sitting areas, fireplaces & private baths. $155/$355 K & Q or twin beds.

Cuisine
She changed the way America eats—*New York Newsday.* Great eclectic food is evident in a warm complimentary Country Breakfast, daylong Serendipity Sips & Sweets, Candlelight Evening hor's d'ouvres & Brandies & Chocolate finalé.

Nearest Airport(s)
Grand Rapids

Directions
Southwestern Michigan, downtown in Village of Saugtauck on Lake Michigan. Two and one-half hours from Chicago and Detroit. Take I-96 to Exit #36 from the S, Exit #41 from the N on to the Blue Star Highway into Village to Butler Street.

"Every time we visit, now twelve times and counting, we marvel at all of Wickwood's efforts to make our stay ever more memorable during every season."

Innkeepers/Owners
Gary and Donna Nelson

English Tudor Country Inn

AAA ◆◆◆

The English Inn

www.srinns.com/englishinn
677 S. Michigan Rd., Lansing/Eaton Rapids, MI 48827
517-663-2500 • Fax 517-663-2643

Rooms/Rates
10 Rooms, $95/$175 B&B; includes 6 Inn Rooms, Two Cottages include 4 bedrooms w/jacuzzi tubs and fireplaces. Open year-round.

Cuisine
Breakfast w/room, Lunch M-F, Dinner 7 days. Continental-French cuisine, daily chef specials. Specialty of House; Chateaubriand for Two, carved tableside. Authentic English pub. Wine, beer, ale, liquor. Banquet Facilities 15-200+.

Nearest Airport(s)
Lansing Capitol City

Directions
From I-96 in Lansing, take M-99 S (exit 101) 8 mi. From I-94, take M-99(N) 22 mi. Ninety miles W of Detroit, 15 miles S of State Capitol (Lansing), and Michigan State Univ.

A former auto baron's residence, this 1927 Tudor mansion will make you feel as though you've been transported to the English countryside. Perched on a hillside overlooking the Grand River, the Inn is part of a 15-acre estate that includes formal gardens and wooded nature trails. The main house has six well-appointed bedrooms named for English towns or the royal family, a cozy pub, library and a two cottages include 4 bedrooms w/fireplaces and Jacuzzi tubs, common sitting areas. The Inn's award-winning restaurant includes a wine list bestowed with the Award of Excellence by *Wine Spectator.* A perfect setting for get-aways, executive retreats and family gatherings. In addition, a 200-seat, 8000 sq.ft. banquet facility sits adjacent to the main house.

Member Since 1991

"The Inn is a 'magical' place - thanks for the memories!"

National House Inn

www.srinns.com/nationalhouse
102 S. Parkview, Marshall, MI 49068
269-781-7374 • Fax 269-781-4510
innkeeper@nationalhouseinn.com

Innkeeper/Owner
Barbara Bradley

Rustic Village Breakfast Inn

Nestled in the heart of Historic Marshall, National House Inn is Michigan's oldest operating Inn. The first brick building in the county, National House has been restored as a warm, beautifully furnished, hospitable Inn with lovely gardens. Marshall--nicknamed "The City of Hospitality"--has many citations for its 850 19th Century architectural structures, and is included on the National Register of Historic Places, where the Inn is also listed. In 2004, Marshall was chosen as one of 12 distinctive destinations for the National Trust for Historic Preservation, has a prestigious National Historic Landmark District designation and is home to Schuler's Restaurant and the annual fall Historic Home Tour. Come join us for afternoon tea at a turn of the century pace in a turn of the century Inn.

Member Since 1978

Rooms/Rates
15 Rooms, $105/$115 B&B;
2 Suites, $145.

Cuisine
Breakfast, afternoon tea, catered dinners for receptions.

Nearest Airport(s)
Kalamazoo

Directions
I-94 to exit 110 Rte. 27(S) 2 miles to Michigan Ave (SW corner of circle, located in downtown Marshall).

Inn has been featured in the *New York Times* - August 2003 and *Midwest Living* - April 2004

Innkeepers/Owners
Gerald & Carol Lehmann

Historic Italianate Bed & Breakfast

AAA ◆◆◆

Rose Hill Inn

www.srinns.com/rosehillinn
1110 Verona Road, Marshall, MI 49068
269-789-1992 • Fax 269-781-4723
rosehill@cablespeed.com

Rooms/Rates
6 Rooms: $109/$160. Other rates may apply for special events/holidays. Off-season and business rates. Some queen beds and/or fireplaces. Guests may use two parlors, den with fireplace, card room, and billiard room.

Cuisine
Full breakfast is served fireside on Haviland China and includes a hot specialty d'jour, seasonal fruit, juice, yogurt, and home-baked goods. Complementary snacks, coffee/tea, and soft drinks are always available.

Nearest Airport(s)
Kalamazoo

Directions
I94: Exit 110, S. to Mansion St., W. .8 mi. I69: Exit 36, E. to Fountain St., N. 2 blks.

The Rose Hill Inn is an elegant 1860 Victorian mansion, once home of the founder of the American Boy Scouts. Twelve-foot ceilings, tall windows, lovely views, fireplaces, and fine antiques combine to create a mood of tranquility and escape from the modern world. Six guest rooms are decorated in 19th century style with vintage prints, lace curtains, and antique lighting but feature contemporary luxuries like A/C, private baths, cable TV, and internet access. Situated on three acres of landscaped grounds, Rose Hill offers a private swimming pool, tennis court, porches, patios, gardens, and fountains. Located in historic Marshall, Michigan, within walking distance of fine dining, antiques, museums, and shops. The Rose Hill Inn provides a wonderful chance to create a memory.

Member Since 2004

"You are the standard for B&B's. First cabin all the way." "The Rose Hill Inn reminds one of a Tuscan villa." *New York Times* Travel Section

"The Gopher State"

Famous For: Hi-Tech, Grain, Timber, Corn, Sugar Beets, Dairy, Rice, Pillsbury Dough Boy, Twin Cities (St. Paul & Minneapolis), Prairies, Lake Superior, Falls

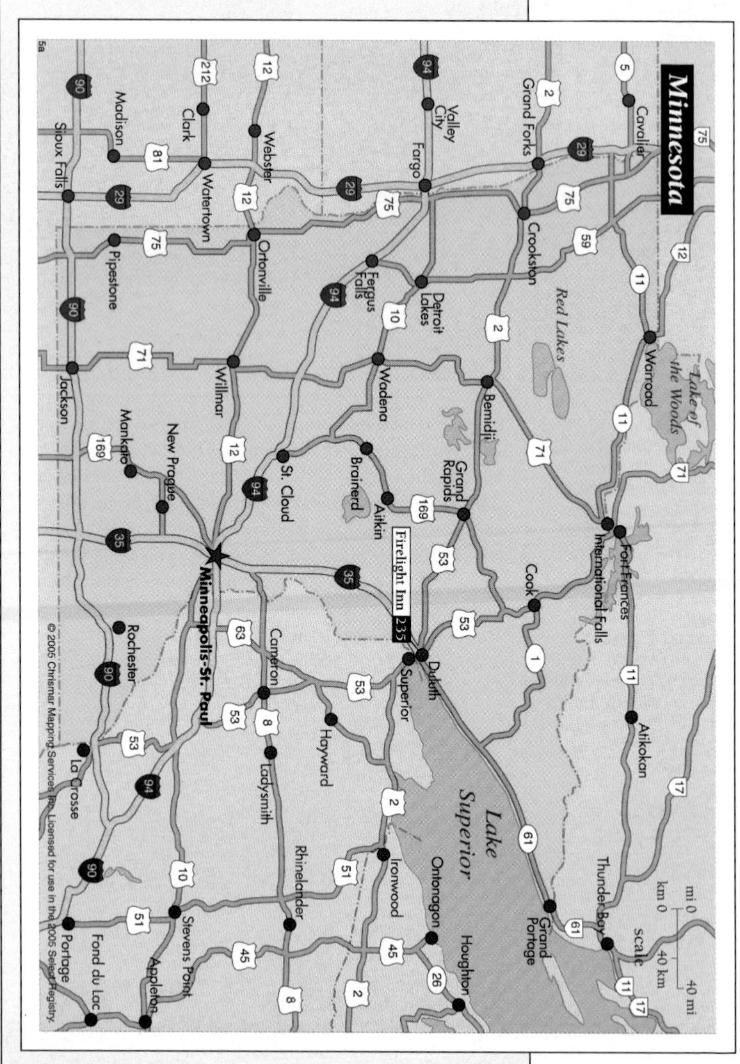

The Firelight Inn on Oregon Creek

www.srinns.com/firelightinn
2211 East Third Street, Duluth, MN 55812
888-724-0273 • 218-724-0272 • Fax 218-724-0304
info@firelightinn.com

Innkeepers/Owners
Jim & Joy Fischer
Elegant In Town Breakfast Inn

Rooms/Rates
5 suites with private bath, fireplace, AC, two person Jacuzzi tub, featherbed, TV/VCR/DVD. Open all year. $179/$279.

Cuisine
Our specialty is delivering your delicious full breakfast in a basket to your suite. Special packages include soup suppers, picnic lunches, gift baskets, flower bouquets, wine selection and champagne.

Nearest Airport(s)
Duluth International.

Directions
From I35 North, exit 21st Ave. East. Left and continue up hill to 4th St. Right turn and travel two blocks to 23rd Ave. East. Right turn to Third St. Another right turn and The Firelight Inn is the second property on your right.

Duluth resides on the tip of the largest freshwater lake in the world--Lake Superior. Over 1,100 vessels slip silently into Canal Park and anchor here each year. The Firelight Inn is located in a historic Duluth neighborhood on a secluded street adjoining Oregon Creek and is a perfect setting for your romantic getaway. In keeping with the history of the mansion which was built in 1910, it has been renovated and furnished in a lasting and timeless traditional style. Comfortable common areas include the Firelight Room pictured above, the formal living room, original butler's pantry and the original glass enclosed front porch overlooking the creek. The Barnum and Brookside Suites with access to an outdoor second floor deck overlooking the creek give beautiful winter views of Lake Superior. In summertime, your breakfast may be enjoyed on the deck listening to the babbling creek. The third floor suites offer spectacular Lake Superior views. Hot stone, seaweed wraps, couples teaching massage and relaxation massage therapy available on site.

Member Since 2003

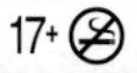

"Everything says luxury--you've thought of every detail--makes it a little piece of heaven!"

"The Magnolia State"

Famous For: Mississippi River, Fertile Soil, Cotton, River Boats, Catfish, Old South, Red Bluff, Civil War Sites, Antebellum Mansions

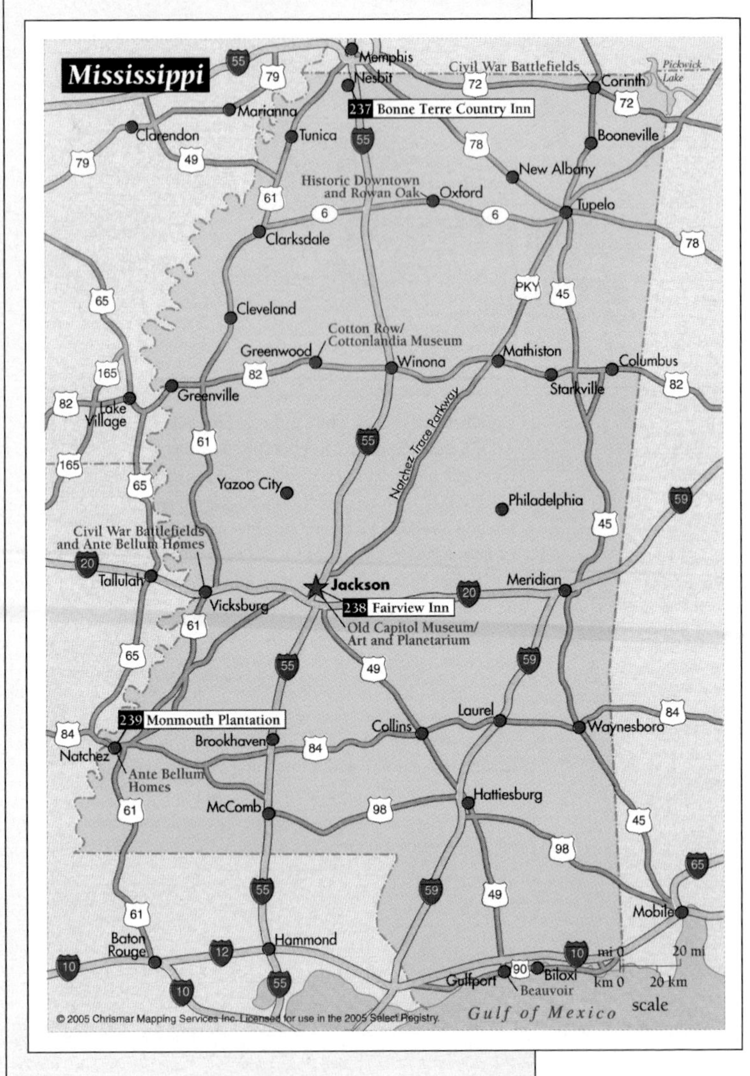

Bonne Terre Country Inn

www.srinns.com/bonneterre
4715 Church Rd. West, Nesbit, MS 38651
662-781-5100 • Fax 662-781-5466
info@bonneterre.com

Innkeepers/Owners
Max and Linda Bonnin

Historic Greek Revival Inn

Rooms/Rates
15 Rooms, $165/$250. Special rates are available for corporate groups and Christian ministers. All rooms are decorated with fine antique décor and include feather beds, fireplaces and whirlpools.

Cuisine
The Bonne Terre Restaurant, the heart of our lovely inn, presents an exquisite fine dining experience for our guests. Our award-winning chefs prepare an array of American Continental cuisine set in an elegant, intimate setting. 16th century French pine doors welcome you.

Nearest Airport(s)
Memphis International

Directions
Just 15 minutes S of Memphis off I-55. Take Church Rd. exit and go W 4.4 miles to Bonne Terre. 3 hours north of Jackson, Miss.

Bonne Terre, French for the "good earth," is a 15-room Country Inn nestled in Nesbit, Mississippi just 15 minutes south of Memphis. The 120 beautifully wooded acres of Mississippi highlands are within a short drive from anywhere in the Mid-South. In our restaurant, a double sided fireplace is a romantic focal point while the indoor veranda paints a beautiful portrait of the woods and Lake Bonnin. Bonne Terre also includes a New England-style Wedding Chapel and gazebo that have created many memorable romantic weddings and Ashley Hall, our grand Colonial Williamsburg-style reception and banquet hall. The premier bed and breakfast property in the Memphis area. Consistently rated #1 in readers polls for both dining and lodging.

Member Since 2003

"It's the most beautiful place I've ever seen.
A romantic, peaceful retreat beyond compare."

Fairview Inn

www.srinns.com/fairview
734 Fairview Street, Jackson, MS 39202
888-948-1908 • 601-948-3429 • Fax 601-948-1203
fairview@fairviewinn.com

Innkeepers/Owners
Carol and William Simmons

Elegant Colonial
In Town Breakfast Inn

AAA ◆◆◆◆

Fairview Inn & Restaurant, located in the Belhaven Historic District of Jackson, Mississippi, offers luxury accommodations with all modern amenities such as high speed internet access and voice mail. Enjoy its well-stocked library, replete with military history and many first editions, its formal garden, flowering magnolia and crepe myrtle trees, and the relaxed ambiance of a two-acre estate on the National Register of Historic Places. Named a Top Inn of 1994 by Country Inns magazine, cited "Southern hospitality at its best" by *Travel + Leisure* 1998, selected by the National Trust for Historic Preservation for inclusion in the 1998 wall calendar featuring Historic Bed & Breakfast Inns and Small Hotels, named a Top Ten Romantic Inn of 2000 by American Historic Inns, featured in Southern Living 2001, winner Conde Nast Johansens "Most Outstanding Inn 2003, North America."

Rooms/Rates
3 Rooms, $115 B&B;
15 Suites, $165/$350 B&B.
Open year-round.

Cuisine
Full breakfast each morning. Fine Dining Thursday-Saturday 5:30 to 9:00 p.m. Sunday Brunch 11:30 a.m. to 2:00 p.m. Banquet and meeting facilities for groups to 100. Wine and liquor available.

Nearest Airport(s)
Jackson International

Directions
I-55 exit 98A on Woodrow Wilson, L at second traffic light at North State, L one block past second traffic light at Fairview St., Inn is first on L.

Member Since 1994

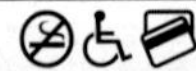

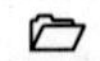

"This is a place to sustain the body and rest the soul." Jane Goodall

Monmouth Plantation

www.monmouthplantation.com
36 Melrose Avenue, Natchez, MS 39120
800-828-4531 • 601-442-5852 • Fax 601-446-7762
luxury@monmouthplantation.com

Owners
Lani & Ron Riches
Elegant In Town Inn 

AAA ◆◆◆◆

Rooms/Rates
17 Rooms, $155/$210; 13 Suites, $190/$380. Open year-round.

Cuisine
Breakfast and dinner, lunch for private parties only. Wine, liquor, and beer.

Nearest Airport(s)
Jackson, Baton Rouge

Directions
E on State Street, 1 mile from downtown Natchez on the corner of John Quitman Parkway and Melrose Avenue.

Monmouth Plantation, a National Historic Landmark (circa 1818), is a glorious return to the Antebellum South, rated "one of the ten most romantic places in the USA" by *Glamour* magazine and *USA Today.* It waits to enfold you in luxury and service. Walk our beautifully landscaped acres. Thirty rooms and suites in the mansion and the seven other historic buildings hold priceless art and antiques while providing every modern comfort. Mornings begin with a delightful complimentary Southern breakfast. Nights sparkle under candlelight during 5-course dinners. *Conde Nast Traveler* 2005 Gold List.

Member Since 1993

Selected by *Travel + Leisure* as among the "500 Greatest Hotels in the World." 2005

Missouri

"The Show-Me State"

Famous For: Center of Continental United States, "Gateway to the West," Livestock, Ozark Plateau, Cottontail Rabbits, Dairy, Corn, Wheat, Cotton, Lead, Zinc, Lime, Cement, Timber, Aircraft, Automobiles, Spacecraft

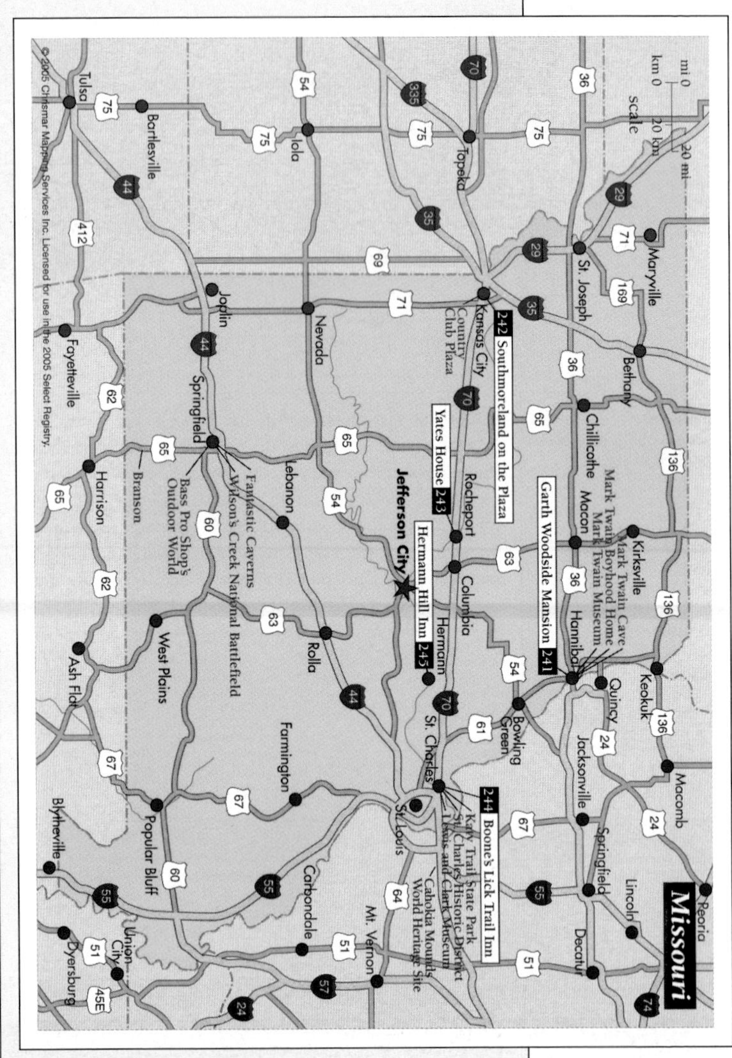

Innkeepers/Owners
Col. (Ret.) John and Julie Rolsen

Traditional Victorian Country Breakfast Inn

Mobil ★★★
AAA ◆◆◆

Garth Woodside Mansion

www.garthmansion.com
11069 New London Road, Hannibal, MO 63401
888-427-8409 • 573-221-2789 • Fax 573-221-9941
innkeeper@garthmansion.com

Rated #1 B&B in Missouri. Step back in time in this beautifully restored 1871 Second Empire Victorian mansion, nestled in 39 acres of gardens, rolling meadows, ponds, and woodlands. Relax among original antiques that fill the parlors, library, sitting and dining rooms. Savor the solitude of natural surroundings or enjoy beautiful architecture including the famed 'flying staircase.' Stretch out on the grand porch or hide away on the romantic second floor balcony. Afternoon treats with tea or your favorite beverage are complimentary upon check-in. Stay where Samuel Clemens opted to be a frequent overnight guest. Cottages provide total privacy. Dine indoors on site at the Woodside Restaurant or in the garden area al fresco with our fresh Missouri Cuisine.

Rooms/Rates
8 Rooms $139/$225; 3 Cottages $279/$395. Original antiques, hypo-allergenic Queen and King feather beds, central heat/air. 2 rooms offer oversized two-person whirlpool tubs. Open all year.

Cuisine
Romantic Dining nestled among the 100+ yr old oak trees. Menu changes nightly, reflecting the daily purchase of the freshest Missouri ingredients available. Finest wines & full bar, too.

Nearest Airport(s)
STL

Directions
From St. Louis: N on SR 61, 75 miles N of I-70. Turn Rt on Warren-Barrett, R on New London. Follow signs. From SR 36 or I-72 S on SR 61, L on Warren-Barrett, R on New London. Follow signs.

Member Since 2001

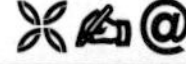

"What an incredible experience....the accommodations were a Victorian lover's treat."

Southmoreland on the Plaza

www.srinns.com/southmoreland
116 East 46th St., Kansas City, MO 64112
816-531-7979 • Fax 816-531-2407
southmoreland@earthlink.net

Innkeepers/Owners
Mark Reichle and Nancy Miller Reichle

Traditional In Town Breakfast Inn

Award-winning Southmoreland's 1913 Colonial Revival styling brings New England to the heart of Kansas City's historic, arts, entertainment, and shopping district - The Country Club Plaza. Business and leisure guests enjoy individually decorated rooms offering decks, fireplaces or Jacuzzi baths. Business travelers find respite at Southmoreland with its rare mix of corporate support services: in-room phones, fax, copier, message center, modem hook-ups, 24-hour access and switchboard. Featured on the Food Channel's "Barbecue with Bobby Flay." Six time winner of Mobil's Four Star Award. Visit us at www.southmoreland.com.

Rooms/Rates
12 Rooms in Main House, $130/$190 Summer, $125/$195 Winter, $235 Carriage House (less $20 SGL.)

Cuisine
Gourmet breakfast served daily. Complimentary afternoon wine & hors d'oeuvres, with hot beverages and sweets served in the evening. Courtyard breakfast BBQ served weekends, Apr-Oct.

Nearest Airport(s)
Kansas City International

Directions
From I-70 or I-29 in downtown KC, take Broadway (S) to Cleaver II Blvd. (47th St.), L on Cleaver II Blvd, L on Main, R on E 46th St. About 1.5 blks down E 46th on the lefthand side. From I-35, take Main St. (S) to E 46th. Make L onto E 46th-down 1.5 blks.

Member Since 1992

"Southmoreland on the Plaza is as restful and alluring a place as I've ever experienced." - *Southern Living* Magazine.

Yates House Bed & Breakfast

www.srinns.com/yateshouse
305 Second Street, Rocheport, MO 65279
573-698-2129
yateshouse@socket.net

Innkeepers/Owners
Conrad and Dixie Yates
Traditional Village Breakfast Inn

Rooms/Rates
5 rooms, $119/$225. 1 suite $239/$269. Corporate rates. Premium quality Queen and King beds. Two jetted tubs. One fireplace. Digital cable/DVD. Wireless DSL. Plentiful outdoor seating in garden areas. Open year-round.

Cuisine
Full, seasonally changing, gourmet breakfast menu with individual table or inroom service. Afternoon cookies and beverage.

Nearest Airport(s)
Columbia Regional Airport, 30 minutes

Directions
I-70 to Exit 115 (Rocheport) at Missouri River Bridge. 2 miles north on BB. Left one block on Columbia Street to 305 Second Street.

Change your pace at this beautiful, Historic Rocheport Bed & Breakfast. Everything you'll need for luxurious and relaxing enjoyment is provided or within easy walking distance. Guest rooms are large, beautifully furnished, and well equipped. All have private, attached baths. Two have Bain-Ultra jetted tubs. A fireplace is located in the spacious Suite. Digital cable TV/DVD, complimentary DVD library, and wireless DSL service provided. Twenty four seat dining/meeting room available and catered for small groups. Individual table or inroom breakfast service provided. Famous for seasonal, gourmet breakfast menu. "Dixie can flat cook," observed *Southern Living* magazine. Within a block of Katy Trail State Park. Photogenic trails, bluffs, tunnels, and Missouri River within short walking distance. Vinyards, winery, shops, and restaurants nearby. Voted "Favorite Day Trip" by readers of the *Kansas City Star*. Fortunately located midway between Kansas City and St.Louis and fifteen minutes from University town of Columbia.

Member Since 2005

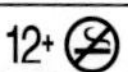

"Unpretentious hospitality, superior breakfasts, and lovely accommodations."

Boone's Lick Trail Inn

www.srinns.com/booneslick
1000 South Main Street, Saint Charles, MO 63301 USA
888-940-0002 • 636-947-7000 • Fax 636-946-2637
innkeeper@booneslick.com

Innkeepers
V'Anne and Paul Mydler, and Venetia McEntire (daughter)

Traditional Federal
In Town Breakfast Inn

Mobil ★★★
AAA ◆◆◆

Explore this 1840's Federal-style inn with antiques where Daniel Boone & Lewis and Clark trekked along the wide Missouri River. In the heart of a colonial village with 100 shops, 30 restaurants, museums & Katy Trail State Park at our door. The old river settlement with its brick street, gas lamps & green spaces, is the start of the Boone's Lick Trail (8 mi. to STL airport & 25 minutes to St. Louis' sights). V'Anne's delicate lemon biscuits, freshest fruits, and hot entrees are served amidst Paul's working duck decoy collection; a perfect escape for new inngoers, return guests and corporate seekers of a different style lodging. Cottage whirlpool suite now available. Mobil ★★★.

Rooms/Rates
4 Rooms, $120/$175; 1 Attic Loft & 1 Master Bedroom, $145/$205. Cottage Whirlpool Suite $195/$275. All private baths. Open year-round. Closed Christmas Day.

Cuisine
Traditional full or continental-plus breakfast served in dining room. Breakfast brought to Attic Loft, Master Bedroom & Cottage for extra fee.

Nearest Airport(s)
STL Int'l - 8 miles

Directions
From downtown St. Louis take I-70 Westbound to exit 229 (St. Charles Fifth St.), Go North 3 blocks to Boone's Lick Rd., Rt. 4 blocks to Main St. Inn on SE corner of Main & Boone's Lick Rd. From I-70 Eastbound exit Fifth St. Go N on Fifth to Boone's Lick Rd.

Member Since 1992

Where you are only a few steps away from history-sleep just 50 yards away from where Lewis and Clark slept.

Innkeepers/Owners
Peggy and Terry Hammer

Luxury Country Inn & Vineyard

AAA ◆◆◆

Hermann Hill Inn & Vineyard

www.srinns.com/hermannhillinn
P.O. Box 555, 711 Wein Street, Hermann, MO 65041
573-486-4455 • Fax 573-486-5373
info@hermannhill.com

Rooms/Rates
8 Rooms, $150/$295 All rooms have king-size oak sleigh bed, fireplace, large whirlpool tub, large separate showers, TV/DVD/VCR.

Cuisine
A full country breakfast with choice of entree served either to your room, or in kitchen, dining room, or outside deck.

Nearest Airport(s)
70 miles west of St. Louis Lambert Airport

Directions
From Exit 175 of I-70, take Hwy 19 south into Hermann, continue south on Hwy 19 to West 6th Street. Turn right on W. 6th Street, then left on Washington Street. At West 10th Street, turn right and go 3 blocks up hill, around sharp right turn and watch for our sign on right.

Enjoy the ultimate country inn experience. We have eight exquisitely appointed staterooms, spectacular views from your own balcony or patio, luxurious private baths with Jacuzzi-style tubs for two, and the privacy and freedom to set your own pace. Sited on a bluff and surrounded by a vineyard, the backdrop for your stay is an ever-changing panorama of Hermann and the Missouri River Valley. Sleep late, have breakfast in bed, walk to a nearby winery, explore a quiet old river town, or simply relax and contemplate the view. Later, as the day wanes, enjoy the late afternoon on your private balcony/patio and revel in the luxury that is Hermann Hill's speciality. The choice is all yours.

Visit us at www.hermannhill.com.

Member Since 2005

"In our many travels together, we have never found a place that was more enjoyable than Hermann Hill."

"The Granite State"

Famous For: Granite, White Mountains, Lakes, Beaches, Prime Primary (The first state to hold presidential primary elections)

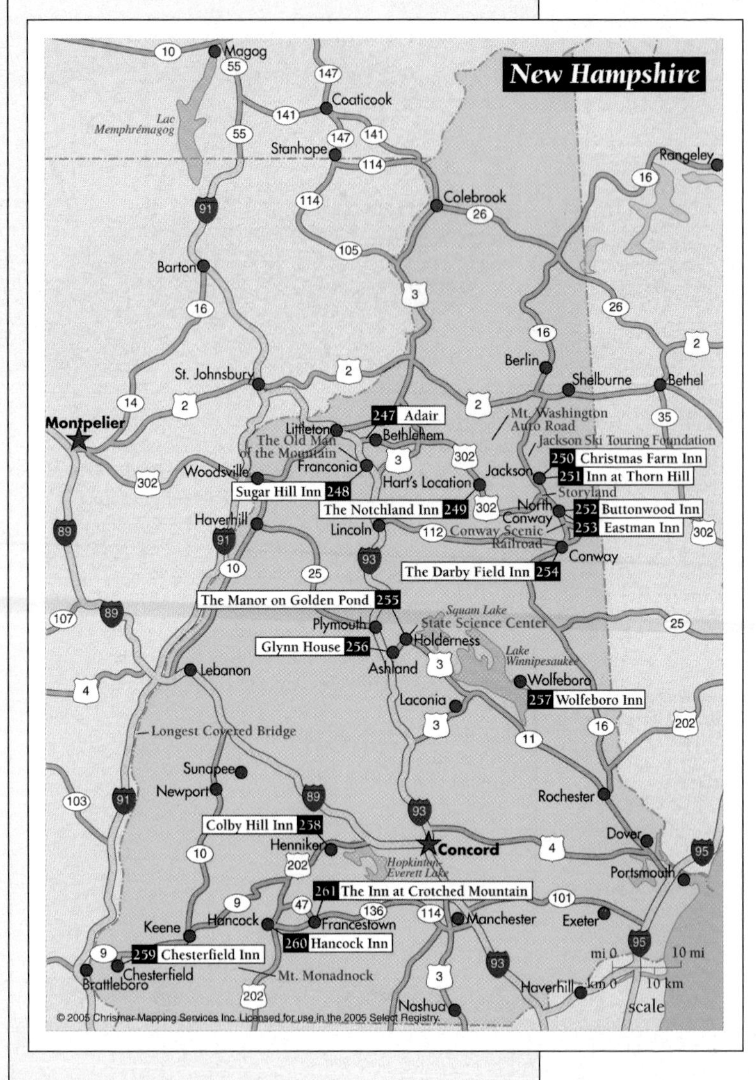

Adair

www.srinns.com/adair
80 Guider Lane, Bethlehem, NH 03574
888-444-2600 • 603-444-2600 • Fax 603-444-4823
innkeeper@adairinn.com

Innkeepers/Owners
Betsy and Nick Young

Elegant Georgian Country Inn

Mobil ★★★
AAA ◆◆◆◆

Get away from it all and unwind at this peaceful country home. Enter a woodland oasis via a long drive bordered by rock walls, stately pines, and white birch. This comfortably elegant inn sits atop a knoll, affording magnificent views of the Presidential Range, and surrounded by sweeping lawns, ponds, perennial gardens, and 200 acres of woods. The Olmstead Brothers originally designed the inn's landscaping with its signature iron gates. Adair serves as an intimate, romantic retreat for adults who wish to relax, observe wildlife and/or take advantage of the nearby White Mountains. The inn's relaxing ambiance and casual dress belie uncompromising attention to detail, highly personalized, warm service, and flavorful food. Adair is within a short drive of Franconia Notch, Mt Washington, Mt Lafayette, The Flume, superb hiking, numerous cross-country venues, and 3 major ski areas. Named a "2005 Top 10 Most Romantic Country Inn/Bed & Breakfast" by American Historic Inns. Deliberately small, naturally quiet.

Rooms/Rates
9 comfortable guest rooms w/ private baths, most with fireplaces and mountain views, several w/ 2-person tubs, $175/$295 B&B gratuity included. Two-week closures possible in Apr & Nov.

Cuisine
Full breakfast, featuring fresh fruit cup, steaming popovers, and hot entree. Afternoon tea with scratch-baked sweets. Fine, new American dining at Tim-bir Alley (W-Su) seasonally. Guests can bring their own spirits. Full set-ups in Tap Room.

Nearest Airport(s)
Manchester, NH. Approx. 95 miles

Directions
From I-93 N or S, take exit 40 onto Rt. 302 E; take sharp L at the Adair sign and follow the signs to the inn. From the E, take Rt. 302 W 3+ miles past Bethlehem and make a R at the Adair sign.

Member Since 1995

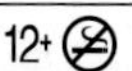 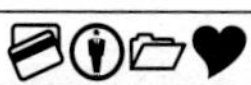  

"Our whole experience here was glorious: the smells, sights, sounds that soothe the soul."

Sugar Hill Inn

www.srinns.com/sugarhill
Scenic Rte. 117, Sugar Hill, NH 03586
800-548-4748 • 603-823-5621 • Fax 603-823-5639
info@sugarhillinn.com

Innkeepers/Owners
Orlo and Judy Coots

Traditional Country Inn

"Romance is virtually guaranteed." *Boston Globe* 2003. This 18th Century classic farmhouse is perched on a hillside on acres of woodlands, rolling lawns and perennial gardens, enhanced by unparalleled views of the White Mountains. Guestrooms are tastefully appointed, several have fireplaces, whirlpool tubs and private decks, all are impeccably kept. Enjoy two spacious common rooms, in-house Spa Room, a large verandah, scrumptious breakfast, afternoon tea, gourmet dining, selected wine list and casual atmosphere. Orlo is a Professional Chef and Judy is a Massage Therapist and Esthetician. With these talents, your stay here is sure to be an unforgettable experience. Also, with abundant outdoor activities, museums, chamber concerts and theatre, your time here will be rewarding.

Member Since 2001

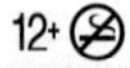    

Rooms/Rates
Classic Rooms $100/$290;
Cottages, $155/$320;
Luxury Rooms, $175/$380.
Open year-round.

Cuisine
Full breakfast and afternoon tea and sweets daily. Dinner Thursday-Sunday by reservations. Wine and liquor available. Nice selection of Port Wine.

Nearest Airport(s)
Manchester Airport - 100 miles.

Directions
From I-93 N or S: Take exit 38, left at bottom of ramp to Rte. 18 N. Travel .5 (1/2) miles L at bridge Rte 117. The Inn is .5 (1/2) miles up the hill on R. From I-91 N or S: take exit 17 onto Rte. 302 E 20 miles on R is Rte. 117. The inn is 8 miles on the L.

"Perfect Getaway. A fantastic location-beautiful rooms-a wonderful time. Great Food."

The Notchland Inn

www.srinns.com/notchlandinn
US Route 302, Hart's Location, NH 03812
800-866-6131 • 603-374-6131 • Fax 603-374-6168
innkeepers@notchland.com

Innkeepers/Owners
Les Schoof and Ed Butler

Traditional Tudor Mountain Country Inn

Rooms/Rates
7 Deluxe Rooms, 6 Suites, 3 Cottages $195/$340, B&B. Open year-round.

Cuisine
5-course distinctive dinners Weds-Sun, hearty country breakfast daily. Fully licensed: wine/spirits/beer. At Notchland, the table is yours for the evening. Dinner is a leisurely affair, taking about 2 hours. $35 per person for in-house guests. $40 Wed, Thur, Sun and $45 Fri, Sat & Holidays for others.

Nearest Airport(s)
Manchester, NH, approximately 125 miles

Directions
Take Rt 93N to exit 35, Rt 3N, go 10 miles to Rt 302, turn R, continue 16.5 miles E on 302 to Inn on R.

Get away from it all, relax and rejuvenate at our comfortable granite manor house, completed in 1862, within the White Mountain National Forest. Settle into one of our spacious guest rooms, individually appointed and each with woodburning fireplaces and private baths. Children and pets are welcome in our newly completed river or mountain view cottages, ranging in size from 1 to 2.5 bedrooms and all with whirlpool baths. A wonderful 5-course dinner and full country breakfast are served in a fireplaced dining room overlooking the gardens. Nature's wonders abound at Notchland. We have 8,000 feet of Saco River frontage on our property and two of the area's best swimming holes! Top off an active day, in any season, with a soak in our wooden hot tub, which sits in a gazebo by the pond. Visit with Abby and Crawford, our Bernese Mountain Dogs. Secluded, yet near to all the Mt. Washington Valley has to offer. Notchland...a magical location.

Member Since 1996

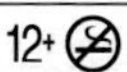

Chosen one of America's 54 Best Inns by *National Geographic Traveler* magazine.

Christmas Farm Inn

www.srinns.com/christmasfarminn
P.O. Box CC Route 16B, Jackson, NH 03846
800-HI-ELVES • 603-383-4313 • Fax 603-383-6495
info@christmasfarminn.com

Proprietors
The Tolley Family
Innkeeper
Tom Spaulding
Traditional Country Inn & Spa

Mobil ★★★
AAA ◆◆◆

AN INN FOR ALL SEASONS. Nestled in the majestic White Mountains on ten breathtaking acres, the Christmas Farm Inn offers a taste of the good life. Accommodations include colonial guestrooms in the main inn, private fireplaced cottages and luxury two-room suites with gas fireplaces, Jacuzzi tubs, private balconies and more....Stroll along our award-winning gardens, swim in the outdoor pool, or soak in the hot tub after a day of cross-country skiing alongside the inn. Enjoy our full service SPA. New American cuisine is featured in the Inn's dining room, complimented by a thoughtful wine list. Conference and intimate wedding settings are available throughout the property.

Rooms/Rates
42 Units, $227/$342 All rates include full breakfast and candle light dinner for two. Taxes and gratuities are additional. Seasonal packages available. Open year-round. Enjoy our all new SPA, opening in June 2004.

Cuisine
Full, cooked-to-order country breakfast, exquisite candlelit dinner, Inn-baked breads and desserts. Mistletoe Pub - full bar available.

Nearest Airport(s)
Portland, ME

Directions
Follow Rte. 16 to Jackson. From Rte. 16 to 16B. Go through covered bridge. 1/2 mi. to school house on R. Keep school house to R and go up hill 1/2 mi. Inn on R.

Member Since 1988

"Magnificent views, great room, excellent food and warm service. This inn has it all!"

Inn at Thorn Hill

www.srinns.com/thornhill
Thorn Hill Road, P.O. Box A, Jackson Village, NH 03846
800-289-8990 • 603-383-4242 • Fax 603-383-8062
stay@innatthornhill.com

Innkeepers/Owners
James & Ibby Cooper
Elegant 19th Century Village Inn

Mobil ★★★
AAA ◆◆◆◆

Rooms/Rates
Main Inn: 4 suites, 15 luxury rooms; Carriage House: 6 North Country rooms; 3 Cottages; Open year round. Breakfast, tea & three-course dinner included. $195/$360. Off Season Spa Packages.

Cuisine
Fine dining room featuring Pacific Rim Cuisine & mountain views. Separate lounge menu. Well stocked bar with over thirty single malt scotches & the wine list has over 1300 selections.

Nearest Airport(s)
Portland, ME

Directions
Boston: I-95 to Spaulding Turnpike Rt.16N to Jackson; Portland: Rt.302 to Rt.16N; Montreal, Canada: Can 55 to I-91/I-93, Exit 40-Rt. 302 to Rt.16N to Jackson. Follow signs to Inn.

Situated grandly on a knoll overlooking Jackson Village and the Presidential Mountains, the Inn offers 25 uniquely decorated guestrooms, suites, and cottages. The recently rebuilt Main Inn features four suites and 12 luxury rooms, all with fireplaces, spa baths, and TV/DVDs, some with steam showers, wet bars, and mountain views. Common areas include a wrap-around porch with views and dining, a lounge in the new turret, library, and spa level. Spa Facilities include an exercise room, sauna, manicure/pedicure and three treatment rooms. Activities are available in all seasons at the Inn and throughout the White Mountains. Outdoor pool, cross-country skiing, and tobogganing at the Inn—hiking, golf, tennis, shopping, skiing, and sleigh rides are all nearby. Only New Hampshire property in *Conde Nast Traveler's* Gold List 2003.

Member Since 1998

"Nobody does it better and we look forward to being in your home again very soon."

The Buttonwood Inn on Mt. Surprise

www.srinns.com/buttonwood
P.O. Box 1817, Mt. Surprise Rd., North Conway, NH 03860
800-258-2625 • 603-356-2625 • Fax 603-356-3140
innkeeper@buttonwoodinn.com

Innkeepers/Owners
Jeffrey and Elizabeth Richards

Traditional Country Breakfast Inn

Enjoy the peaceful surroundings of this 1820's, ten room Inn, hugging the base of Mount Surprise. At Buttonwood, designated "THE MOST PERFECT STAY," Arrington's Inn Traveler Book of Lists, 2004, guests find romance; retreat; family reunions; intimate wedding celebrations; small business meetings, and our holiday shopping packages are all specialties. Air-conditioned Guest-Chambers feature wide pine floors, stenciling, and antiques. Deluxe rooms offer fireplaces, or fireplace and Jacuzzi-for-two. Common living rooms with wood-burning fireplaces welcome you home to afternoon tea and treats. Relax by the outdoor pool, surrounded by memorable perennial gardens while spying on ruby-throated hummingbirds. Revisit favorite hiking trails and ski-slopes, or discover new ones. Plan adventures to the Cog Railway, or the Flume Gorge. Shopping and fine dining are available a few minutes away in Historic Jackson Village and North Conway. Make plans to visit... we'll blend hospitality and laughter especially for you.

Member Since 1999

Rooms/Rates
10 Rooms, $95/$255 B&B. Air-conditioned. Deluxe bed-chambers with fireplaces, fireplace and Jacuzzi-for two.

Cuisine
Full breakfast; different entree daily. Served at individual tables, special dietary requests in advance. Afternoon tea and treats. Fine dining within minutes.

Nearest Airport(s)
Portland, ME - 65 miles
Manchester, NH - 100 miles

Directions
I-95 to Rte. 16 N (Spaulding Tpke.) to North Conway. In North Conway village, at light, turn R on Kearsarge St. At 'T,' bear L. Continue approx. 1.2 miles to stop sign. Straight across intersection, up Mt. Surprise Rd. From N: Rte. 302 S. L to Hurricane Mt. Rd. L to Mt. Surprise Rd.

"We've found The Buttonwood! Perfect! Our little piece of paradise!"

Innkeepers/Owners
Lea Greenwood and Tom Carter
Traditional Village Bed & Breakfast

Eastman Inn

www.srinns.com/eastman
P.O. Box 882, North Conway, NH 03860
800-626-5855 • 603-356-6707 • Fax 603-356-7708
BePampered@eastmaninn.com

Rooms/Rates
14 bedchambers w/private baths,$90/$240. An eclectic mix of antiquity and modern conveniences makes your journey to an earlier time far more comfortable than our ancestors perhaps imagined: deluxe rooms, fireplaces, whirlpool and antique soaking tubs, cable television, telephone, wrap-around porch, lending library.

Cuisine
Breakfast is not traditional country inn fare but a gastronomic adventure with the menu changing daily. Fine dining within minutes.

Nearest Airport(s)
Portland, ME - 60 miles
Manchester, NH - 100 miles

Directions
One-half mile south of Schouler Park in the Village of North Conway on Route 16/302.

Built in 1777 by the Noah Eastman family, the Inn, one of the oldest homes in North Conway, boasts a history rich in tradition in the development of the social and economic growth of the Mt. Washington Valley. The 1930 edition of the New Hampshire Guidebook described the Eastman Inn as "...an all-season house, where hospitality is extended to guests desiring mountain vacations in the quiet comfort of a private home." Seventy-five years later, hospitality remains our priority. Join us for a relaxing, quiet vacation in a home steeped in tradition either for pleasure or on business, and let us treat you to warm, attentive bed and breakfast hospitality in the splendor and style of a bygone era. Relax, enjoy gracious Southern hospitality with New England flair, and ... be pampered!

Winner of the "Best Hospitality" category
2004 Best of BedandBreakfast.com Award

One of the Top Ten Best Overall B&Bs
2004 Best of BedandBreakfast.com Award

Member Since 2004

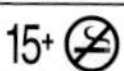

"Tom and Lea have a way of making the 'real world' disappear–we felt peaceful and pampered."

The Darby Field Inn

www.srinns.com/darbyfield
185 Chase Hill Road, Albany, NH 03818
800-426-4147 • 603-447-2181 • Fax 603-447-5726
marc@darbyfield.com

Innkeepers/Owners
Marc & Maria Donaldson

Traditional Full Service Country Inn

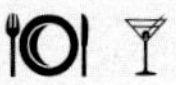

AAA ◆◆◆

Only 6 miles from North Conway, yet right in the middle of nowhere, overlooking the Mt. Washington Valley and White Mountains of New Hampshire, the Darby Field Inn quietly surprises and delights wanderers adventurous enough to leave the beaten path. The Darby Field Inn is much more than just a little bed and breakfast. It is a romantic B&B with fireplace and Jacuzzi rooms and suites, candlelight gourmet dining, sophisticated wine list, moonlit sleigh rides. It's a full service country inn for those looking to relax by the fireplace in the living room, on the mountain-view patio, in the fully stocked sunroom Tavern, in our award winning gardens or by the crystal clear, heated swimming pool. The inn also has private nature trails for x-c skiing, snowshoeing, mountain biking or just walking. And, if that's not enough, how about a nice theraputic massage or a rejuvenating yoga class. Whether you are looking for romance, relaxation or a more active adventure, The Darby Field Inn has it all!

Member Since 1981

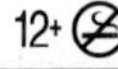

Rooms/Rates
13 Rooms, $130/280 B&B Dbl. Occ; $200/350 MAP Dbl. Occ. before tax and gratuities. Deluxe room/suites, fireplaces, jacuzzi's, A/C & mountain views. Open Year Round.

Cuisine
Country gourmet dining in a casual setting with mountain views. Choose from 130 bottles of fine wines and a fully stocked tavern. Full country breakfast included; served while watching the birds and maybe even a moose!

Nearest Airport(s)
Portland, ME: 60 miles

Directions
One half mile south of Conway Village off Rte.16, turn on to Bald Hill Road. Go up the hill one mile, and turn right onto Chase Hill Rd. Proceed one mile to inn.

"Darby Field Inn was charming and comfortable. A perfect retreat after the rigors of hiking. A wonderful compliment to the magical surroundings. We will send friends."

Innkeepers/Owners
Brian and Mary Ellen Shields

Elegant English Manor Country Inn

AAA ◆◆◆◆

The Manor on Golden Pond

www.srinns.com/manorongoldenpond
Box T, Rt. 3, Holderness, NH 03245
800-545-2141 Reservations • 603-968-3348
Fax 603-968-2116
info@manorongoldenpond.com

Rooms/Rates
25 Rooms $200/$475 B&B for two people per night. Open year-round. Carriage house and cottages open seasonally.

Cuisine
Full Gourmet Breakfast. Afternoon Tea 4-5:00 p.m. each day. Fine Dining New England Cuisine. Ala Carte Menu plus Chef Tasting menu offered. Dinner by reservation. *Wine Spectator* Award of Excellence wine list. Cozy Three Cocks Pub with Piano Bar.

Nearest Airport(s)
Manchester Airport (1 Hour drive)

Directions
I-93, exit 24, E on Rte. 3, proceed for 4.7 mi., turn R at our sign (Less than two hours from Boston.)

A Love Story began at this English Manor House, and continues with each of our guests pampered in our luxuriously appointed suites. Our suites enjoy working fireplace where the fire is always laid, oversized Jacuzzis or Air®baths, and steam showers. Many suites have private decks to enjoy magnificent vistas of Squam Lake and the White Mountains. Guests can enjoy massages in our Spa Treatment Room, a tennis match on our clay tennis court, Lunch beside our outdoor pool, or the tranquility of our private beach on "Golden Pond." Located in the Lakes Region of New Hampshire activities abound no matter what the season for our guests to explore. Guests awaken to our delectable Gourmet breakfasts each morning. English Afternoon tea is served daily for guests to reminisce their day's adventures. Before dinner enjoy a Manor martini in our "Three Cocks Pub" followed by a dinner in our award-winning Van Horn dining room to finish off a perfect day at the Manor. "Best of New England…" Andrew Harper's *Hideaway Report.*

Member Since 1995

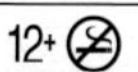

"Everything was wonderful! The Inn is beautiful, as is the view, but the service is what made our experience very special..attention to detail incredible."

Glynn House Inn

www.srinns.com/glynnhouse
www.glynnhouse.com, Ashland, NH 03217
800-637-9599 • 603-968-3775 • Fax 603-968-9415
theglynnhouseinn@aol.com

Innkeepers/Owners
Jim and Gay Dunlop
Historic Village Breakfast Inn

Mobil ★★★
AAA ◆◆◆

Romance amid rural elegance. This beautifully restored 19th Century Inn is located on a quiet tree-lined street in the quaint village of Ashland. Following our gourmet breakfast, relax on our sweeping porches and beautiful gardens. Enjoy a good book by the fire in your room. All rooms offer queen beds, private baths, TV,VCR/DVDs, fireplaces and central A/C. Our eight suites include separate sitting rooms, double whirlpool spas, in-room game boxes, snacks, deluxe amenities and luxurious robes. Centrally located in the heart of the Lakes and White Mountains of New Hampshire, The Glynn House Inn offers seasonal packages including many local activities. In winter, hit the slopes, ride snowmobiling trails, take a snowshoe hike, horsedrawn sleighride or just relax by the fire with your loved one. In spring and summer months, golf at nearby Owl's Nest Golf Club, take a scenic drive, hike the Lakes and mountains, do some great outlet shopping, take a boat tour or swim on famous "On Golden Pond" Squam Lake, and enjoy our many local fine dining spots.

Rooms/Rates
13 Rooms & Suites. High Season 2005 - 5/27/05 - 10/29/05 - $139/$259 per night. Low Season 2005 - 1/1/05 - 5/26/05 & 10/30/05 - 12/31/05 - $139/$229 per night.

Cuisine
The Glynn House Inn offers full, gourmet breakfast each morning including freshly baked goods, fresh fruit and complete hot breakfast. We also offer our guests afternoon refreshments daily.

Nearest Airport(s)
Manchester

Directions
We are located at Exit 24 off I93. Take RTE 3 South and make a left onto Highland Street. The Inn is located 3/4 of mile up on the left.

Member Since 2005

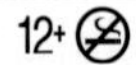

"My husband and I were thrilled with our stay. It was our first time at a B&B, but not our last. Your hospitality made us feel at home! We'll be back!"

Wolfeboro Inn

www.wolfeboroinn.com
90 N. Main Street, P.O. Box 1270, Wolfeboro, NH 03894
800-451-2389 • 603-569-3016 • Fax 603-569-5375
info@wolfeboroinn.com

Innkeepers/Owners
Gary & Hilary Metzger
Historic/Contemporary Village Resort

Nestled on a hill overlooking the eastern shore of Lake Winnipesaukee, the Inn features Wolfe's Tavern, New England as it used to be, with row upon row of pewter mugs hanging from the ceiling. A new addition, built in 1988, includes the 1812 Room, library and guest rooms, many with private balconies affording panoramic views of the lake and waterfront. Relaxing common areas showcase antique country quilts and a fireplaced lobby offers cozy reading nooks. The gazebo and perennial gardens sloping down to our private beach and boat dock add to the enjoyment of our guests. Winnipeasukee Belle, a 65-foot side paddlewheel and a 25-foot Chris Craft are both available for charter.

Rooms/Rates
Winter/Spring $95-$305 B&B
Summer/Fall $185-$315
Packages available.

Cuisine
Wolfe's Tavern and 1812 room serve traditional New England fare, including the finest Angus beef and fresh seafood. Open 7 a.m.-10 p.m. daily, all year. Two fully stocked lounges offer a wide selection of wines and feature 75 varieties of beer. Room service available. Full banquet menus cater functions of up to 250 people.

Nearest Airport(s)
Manchester Airport

Directions
I-93N, exit 15E onto Rte 4E to Epsom, then Rte 28N into Main St, Wolfeboro I-95N to Rte 16 N, then exit 15 onto Rte 11W to Rte 28N in Alton.

Member Since 2003

"The place is fabulous, very relaxing, and the food, especially brunch, was second to none!"

Colby Hill Inn

www.srinns.com/colbyhillinn
3 The Oaks, P.O. Box 779, Henniker, NH 03242
800-531-0330 • 603-428-3281 • Fax 603-428-9218
innkeeper@colbyhillinn.com

Innkeepers/Owners
Cyndi and Mason Cobb

Traditional Elegant
Colonial Village Inn

Mobil ★★★
AAA ◆◆◆

Wine Spectator
AWARD OF EXCELLENCE

Intimate and romantic country inn located in the charming unspoiled village of Henniker. Enjoy romantic touches including down comforters, plush bathrobes, two-person whirlpools, crackling fireplaces and luxurious linens. 14 romantic guest rooms including two intimate suites with period antiques. All guest rooms have private baths, phones & wireless internet access. Award winning candlelight dining nightly overlooking lush gardens, antique barns and gazebo. Bountiful breakfasts and candlelight dinners. Genuine hospitality and central New England location make this an ideal getaway spot. Outdoor pool, lawn chess, cross country & downhill skiing, hiking, biking, and tennis all nearby. *Yankee Magazine* Editor's Pick. *Wine Spectator* Award of Excellence. 90 Minutes North of Boston.

Member Since 1993

Rooms/Rates
14 Guest Rooms, $139/$269 depending on season. Some guest rooms have whirlpools/fireplaces. Gourmet breakfast included.

Cuisine
Full gourmet breakfast including specialties like pumpkin pancakes with warm maple cream. Afternoon cookies. Award-winning romantic candlelight dining with full service bar, fine wines, and spirits. Dinner available nightly for inn guests and public.

Nearest Airport(s)
Manchester

Directions
17 Miles W. of Concord, N.H. 93 N. to 89 N. to Rt. 202/9W (Left exit). Continue on 202/9 & Exit at Rt. 114, Turn L. 1 mile to blinker, turn R, 1/2 mile on Right. 90 min. North of Boston.

"Loved the antiques & attention to detail. So romantic and 'Foodies' will love it."

Innkeepers/Owners
Phil and Judy Hueber
Elegant Colonial Country Inn

Chesterfield Inn

www.srinns.com/chesterfield
Route 9, Box 155, Chesterfield, NH 03443
800-365-5515 • 603-256-3211 • Fax 603-256-6131
chstinn@sover.net

Rooms/Rates
15 Rooms, $150/$295 B&B
2 Suites, $200/$225 B&B.
Open year-round except Christmas Eve and Christmas Day.

Cuisine
Full Country Breakfast cooked to order served daily. Dinner is served Monday through Saturday in our candlelit dining room with sweeping views of the Green Mountains. Room service is available. Wine list and full bar available.

Nearest Airport(s)
Hartford, CT and Boston

Directions
From I-91, take exit 3 to Route 9 E, continue on Route 9 for 2 miles. Turn L onto Cross Road and R into driveway.

Serving since 1787 as a tavern, a farm and a museum, the Inn's guest rooms today are spacious; some with fireplaces, or outdoor balconies, all with private baths, air conditioning, TV, wireless internet access, and telephone. Outside, the meadow overlooks Vermont's Green Mountains. Guests enjoy delicious, innovative cuisine in the candlelit dining room. Chesterfield Inn is a wonderful place to relax in comfortable elegance.

Member Since 1990

Come and rekindle your romance at the Chesterfield Inn.

The Hancock Inn~1789~NH's Oldest Inn

www.srinns.com/hancockinn
33 Main Street, P.O. Box 96, Hancock, NH 03449
800-525-1789 • 603-525-3318 • Fax 603-525-9301
innkeeper@hancockinn.com

Innkeeper/Owner
Robert Short

Traditional Federal Village Inn

Mobil ★★★

Since 1789, the first year of George Washington's presidency, the Inn has hosted rumrunners and cattle drovers, aristocracy, and even a U.S. President. It's seen elegant balls, Concord Coaches, and the first rider of the railroad. Today, the Inn maintains its historic elegance combined with modern day amenities. The town of Hancock, located in the beautiful Monadnock Region of Southern New Hampshire, is considered by many to be one of the prettiest villages in New England, boasting a church with a Paul Revere Bell that rings in each hour, a friendly local general store and many homes that are listed on the National Historic Register. Year-round regional recreation opportunities include hiking, cross country/downhill skiing, swimming, boating and fishing. Visit in any season and find: spring daffodils and real maple sugaring; summer swimming and fishing at Hancock's town beach or music on the village square; fall colors and covered bridges; winter snow...and relaxing by our raging fireplace with a hot toddy!

Member Since 1971

 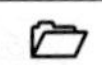  

Rooms/Rates
15 Rooms. $120/$260. Appointed with antiques, TV, phone, AC. 8 with fireplaces, 3 with whirlpools.

Cuisine
Amidst the glow of candles and a flickering fireplace you will dine in Colonial splendor. The recipe for our signature dish, Shaker Cranberry Potroast, was requested by *Bon Appetit.* Full bar with 350 wine selections and many single malts. *Wine Spectator* Award.

Nearest Airport(s)
Manchester Airport

Directions
From Boston: I 93N then 101W to Peterborough. R on 202 to 123. Turn L at stop sign and drive down historic Main Street. From NY: I 91 to Brattleboro. Route 9 toward Keene to 123. Turn R to Hancock.

"Visiting The Hancock Inn is like taking a step back to a kindler, gentler era."

Innkeepers/Owners
John and Rose Perry
Traditional Mountain Breakfast Inn

The Inn at Crotched Mountain

www.srinns.com/crotchedmountain
534 Mountain Rd., Francestown, NH 03043
603-588-6840 • Fax 603-588-6623
perry-inncm@conknet.com

Rooms/Rates
13 Rooms, 3 with fireplaces, $70/$140 B&B. Open year round, except first two weeks in November.

Cuisine
Full breakfast daily. Light fare served in The Winslow Tavern on Saturday. Wine & liquor available.

Nearest Airport(s)
Manchester, N.H.

Directions
From Boston: I-93N 101W to 114N to Goffstown 13S to New Boston 136 W to Francestown 47N 2.5 mi. L onto Mt. Rd 1 mi. From N.Y.: I-91N to Brattleboro Rt. 9E to 31S 47 4.5 mi. R onto Mt. Rd. 1 mi.

This 180 year-old colonial house is located on the northeastern side of Crotched Mountain. An awe-inspiring setting and a spectacular view of the Piscatagoug Valley makes all the difference at this out-of-the-way Colonial Inn. Swimming pool, two clay tennis courts, walking and cx ski trails, vegetable and flower gardens supply food and adornment for tables and rooms. Downhill skiing nearby. Light fare served in The Winslow Tavern on Saturday. John and Rose, who have been operating the Inn since 1973, and their three English Cockers, look forward to welcoming you.

Member Since 1981

"We can't ever thank you both enough for your hospitality and thoughtfulness."

"The Garden State"

Famous For: Princeton University, Battle of Trenton, Atlantic City, Atlantic Coastline, Industry, Menlo Park

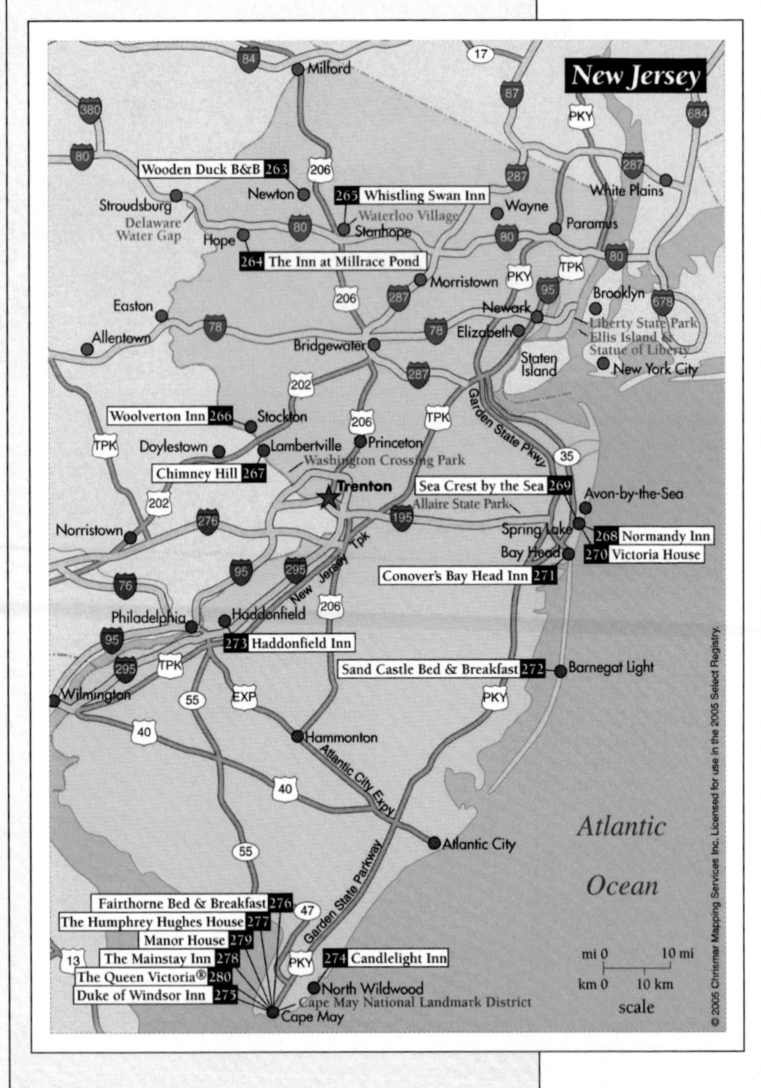

The Wooden Duck B&B

www.srinns.com/woodenduck
140 Goodale Road, Newton, NJ 07860
973-300-0395 • Fax 973-300-0395
woodenduckinn@earthlink.net

Innkeepers/Owners
Bob & Barbara Hadden

Country Colonial Bed & Breakfast Inn

Mobil ★★★

Rooms/Rates
10 rooms, $110/$190 per night/ double Corporate rates Sunday thru Thursday Open all year.

Cuisine
A full country breakfast featuring homebaked breads and muffins, eggs, pancakes, French toast, fresh fruit, juice, tea, coffee and more! Guest pantry features homemade cookies, snacks, fruit, hot and cold beverages. Fine and casual dining nearby.

Nearest Airport(s)
Newark Airport, 45 Miles

Directions
From I-80 take Exit 25, following Route 206 North 7.8 miles to Goodale Road. Turn Right and proceed 1.5 miles through the Kitatinny Valley State Park to The Wooden Duck's driveway (#140) on the left.

An oasis of country pleasures! This mini-estate is nestled on 10 acres adjacent to the 1600 acre Kitatinny Valley State Park, abundant with wildlife and hiking trails. All guestrooms have queen bed, private bath, TV/VCR, telephone, desk, comfortable sitting area. Deluxe rooms have soaking tub for two, fireplace, private outside balcony. Guests are welcome to use the game room with double hearth fireplace, inground pool, complimentary video library. The "Guest Kitchen," with complementary snacks, Barbara's homemade chocolate chip cookies, soda, coffee, and tea, is available 24/7. Nearby are many antique and craft shops, Waterloo Village, NJ Cardinals Baseball, golf, winter and summer sports, horseback riding, cycling. The Wooden Duck is the only B&B in the Northern half of New Jersey rated 3 star by Mobile Travel Guide. Just 75 minutes to Manhattan.

Member Since 2003

"If you like B&B's, you will love this one! Fabulous. Pristine. Impeccable!"

The Inn at Millrace Pond

www.srinns.com/millrace
313 Johnsonburg Road, P.O. Box 359, Hope, NJ 07844
800-746-6467 • 908-459-4884 • Fax 908-459-5276
millrace@epix.net

Innkeepers/Owners
Cordie & Charles Puttkammer

Traditional Colonial Village Inn

The Inn building located on 23 acres was an operating gristmill from 1770 until the early 1950's. Authentically decorated guestrooms with private baths are located in the Gristmill, Millrace House and Stone Cottage suggesting the quiet elegance of Colonial America. Relax in the ambiance of the parlor. Savor romantic candlelight dinners in the fine dining restaurant. Stroll past the mill's antique water wheel and wine cellar into the tavern offering casual midweek dining beside the walk-in fireplace. An 1830s home from the historic Moravian Village of Hope has been restored into the conference center featuring individual meeting rooms along with library, parlor and fitness area. Perhaps a game of tennis on the private court or a hike nearby is in order. The Delaware Water Gap Recreation Area (a National Park) is 13 miles west of the Inn. Excellent antiquing, a vineyard, golf, and skiing are nearby.

Rooms/Rates
17 Guestrooms $135/$175 ($115/$125 Sun-Thurs) Breakfast included Open year-round.

Cuisine
Dinner served Mon-Thurs 6-8 Fri & Sat 5-9 Sunday 4-7:30 Luncheon & dinner for groups~Tavern~Wine/liquor served with meals.

Nearest Airport(s)
Newark International

Directions
From South: 31 to 46W to 519N R at blinker in Hope 1/10M. to Inn. From North, East or West: I-80 exit 12 - 1 mile S on 521 to blinker L 1/10M to Inn.

Member Since 1988

"Peaceful, relaxing, wonderful dining."
"Unique experience; restful weekend at the Inn."

Whistling Swan Inn

www.srinns.com/whistlingswan
110 Main St., Stanhope, NJ 07874
973-347-6369 • Fax 973-347-6379
info@whistlingswaninn.com

Innkeeper
Liz Armstrong
Traditional Victorian Village Breakfast Inn

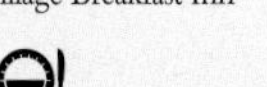

AAA ◆◆◆

Rooms/Rates
7 Rooms, 2 Suites $99/$219. Corporate & Gov't Rates. All with private bath (some w/Jacuzzi), Cable TV/VCR, Wireless Internet, Central AC, some with fireplaces. Open year-round. Special Package & rates available.

Cuisine
Full country buffet breakfast, 24-hour complimentary guest bar.

Nearest Airport(s)
Newark, NJ

Directions
Bus & Train via NJ Transit to Netcong. Take Rte 80W to Exit 27B. Take Route 183N to HESS STATION on right,turn left on MAIN ST. Turn left at KING ST-Inn's parking lot is 2nd driveway on RIGHT. For more directions, visit our website. WATERLOO VILLAGE NEARBY.

Nestled in the Skylands of New Jersey, this graceful 1905 Victorian has been restored to its original splendor and warmth. When you stroll through our garden or breakfast on the veranda you will evoke memories of a time gone by.

Whatever the season, a myriad of activities await you. After a busy day of hiking, biking, kayaking, shopping, or antiquing, relax in a hammock or share pleasant conversations with newfound friends. Enjoy dining at one of the fine area restaurants, some within walking distance. At day's end, snuggle up with your special someone next to a crackling fire. When ready to retire, sink into your queen-sized feather bed, soak in a fabulous two tub Jacuzzi or fall asleep to a movie from our video library.

Perfect for relaxation, romance, adventure, sightseeing, business, or that special party or wedding.

Voted Top Ten "Best Inn in the US" by *Inn Traveler* Magazine.

Member Since 1992

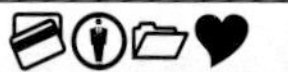

"Every detail has been thought of-wonderful ambiance, friendly hosts, and great food! Perfect! Absolutely the best B&B we've ever visited."

Woolverton Inn

www.srinns.com/woolvertoninn
6 Woolverton Road, Stockton, NJ 08559
888-264-6648 • 609-397-0802 • Fax 609-397-0987
sheep@woolvertoninn.com

Innkeepers/Owners
Carolyn McGavin and Bob Haas

Traditional Village Breakfast Inn

Mobil ★★★★
AAA ◆◆◆◆

Perched high above the Delaware River, surrounded by 300 acres of rolling farmland and forest, The Woolverton Inn provides the seclusion of a grand country estate, yet the activities of New Hope and Lambertville are just five minutes away. Enjoy the glorious setting and relaxed elegance of this 1792 stone manor, while feeling as comfortable as you would at your own home in the country. All guestrooms are unique and thoughtfully decorated; they feature bucolic views, fireplaces, whirlpool tubs and showers for two, private outdoor sitting areas, stocked refrigerators, and Bose CD Wave radios. As recommended by *Travel + Leisure, Country Living,* NBC's *Today in NY* among others.

Rooms/Rates
6 Rooms $135/$295;
2 Suites $225/$325; 5 Cottages $275/$425. Rooms offer featherbeds, fresh flowers, robes, luxury linens, CD Players.

Cuisine
Full gourmet breakfast served by candlelight in our gardens or in bed. Signature Dishes include: apple-cranberry turkey sausage, Pecan Pancakes, homemade cinnamon buns and fabulous cookies.

Nearest Airport(s)
Philadelphia International

Directions
Philadelphia: I-95, exit 1 to Rte. 29 N to Stockton. R on 523 for 2/10 mile, L on Woolverton Rd. NY: I-78 W to exit 29 for 287 S, exit for 202 S for Flemington. Exit Rte. 29 N. Right on 523, L 2/10 mile.

Member Since 2002

"A luxury getaway like no other...thank you for a memorable and romantic Honeymoon! Bravo!"

Owners
Terry Anne & Richard Anderson
Elegant In Town Breakfast Inn

Mobil ★★★
AAA ◆◆◆

Chimney Hill Farm Estate

www.srinns.com/chimneyhillfarm
207 Goat Hill Road, Lambertville, NJ 08530
800-211-4667 • 609-397-1516 • Fax 609-397-9353
info@chimneyhillinn.com

Rooms/Rates
Main Estate House Mon-Thurs $135/$155 Fri-Sun $189/$255. Ol'Barn Inn Suites Mon-Thurs $189/$275 Fri-Sun $289/$395.

Cuisine
Gourmet country breakfast served by candlelight, a guest butler pantry filled with cookies, goodies and sherry. Excellent Resturuants in Lambertville and New Hope.

Nearest Airport(s)
Philadelphia 45 miles
Newark 42 miles

Directions
Phi: I-95N ext1 (Lambertville) to rt. 29N. Travel 7 mi; turn R onto Valley Rd, L on Goat Hill Rd.—1.5 mi on R. NY: I-78W to I-287S to Rt.202S to Rt.179S (Lambertville ex). At traffic light go straight to 2nd L (SWAN St.) Go to 2nd R. (Studdiford St.) to top.

On a country road high in the hills above the charming historic riverside town of Lambertville, New Jersey, sits Chimney Hill Farm Estate & The Ol' Barn Inn. This gorgeous fieldstone house and barn, built in 1820, are surrounded by beautiful fields and gardens. The perfect spot for romantic getaways or corporate retreats, Chimney Hill is only 1/2 mi from the antique-filled towns of Lambertville and New Hope. Known for great country-style hospitality, Chimney Hill Farm Estate provides its guests with comfort and elegance. Featured as the cover for *Country Inns, New Jersey Country Roads* magazines, it is a connoisseur's choice—Come visit!

Member Since 1998

12+    

"We love everything about this lovely Inn! A favorite place with friendly caring Innkeepers and wonderful atmosphere. We will return many times!"

Normandy Inn

www.srinns.com/normandy
21 Tuttle Avenue, Spring Lake, NJ 07762
800-449-1888 • 732-449-7172 • Fax 732-449-1070
normandy@verizon.net

Owners
The Valori Family

Elegant Victorian
Waterside Breakfast Inn

A romantic 19th century inn, the Normandy Inn is on the National Register of Historic Places. Fine antique furnishings adorn this tradionally elegant home which is located just steps from the ocean. Upon visiting the inn, your welcome begins in the spacious double parlors decorated in Victorian splendor. Many guest rooms, each of which are unique, boast cozy fireplaces, Jacuzzis, canopy beds and a peek at the ocean. All rooms include private baths, air conditioning, and telephones. Guests' wake up call is the sound of the ocean as a private table awaits you in the gracious dining room. The Normandy offers a hearty country breakfast, tempting afternoon treats, evening cordials, and prides itself on exceptional service. The Normandy, just 1/2 block to the ocean, is centrally located to cultural and outdoor activities. Mobil and AAA rated, the Normandy makes for the perfect getaway. New York Magazine calls it "an antique-laden dreamworld," your inn for all seasons.

Member Since 1996

Rooms/Rates
18 Rooms, high season $145/$295; quiet season $115/225 2 Suites, high season $395/$375, quiet season $325/$305. Open year-round.

Cuisine
Full gourmet breakfast included and served at your own private table. Sumptuous afternoon treats including seasonal fruits and fresh squeezed juice in the summer, homemeade soups in the quiet season. Evening cordials. Fine dining restaurants located nearby.

Nearest Airport(s)
Newark International

Directions
Garden State Pkwy to exit 98. Follow Route 34 S to traffic circle, 3/4 around to Route 524 E. Take to ocean, turn R onto Ocean Avenue & then first R onto Tuttle. Fifth house on the L.

"Truly a step back in time, this seaside beauty made for the perfect escape!"

Sea Crest by the Sea

www.srinns.com/seacrestbythesea
19 Tuttle Avenue, Spring Lake, NJ 07762
800-803-9031 • 732-449-9031 • Fax 732-974-0403
capt@seacrestbythesea.com

Innkeepers/Owners
Fred & Barbara Vogel

Elegant Victorian
Waterside Breakfast

AAA ◆◆◆

Lovingly restored 1885 Queen Anne Victorian for ladies and gentlemen on seaside holiday. Ocean views, fireplaces, private decks, luxurious linens, DUX beds, whirlpools for two, steam showers, comfort-filled rooms, sumptuous breakfast and afternoon tea, evening cordials. A *Gourmet* magazine "Top Choice." *Philadelphia Magazine says* "Spring Lake's most luxurious inn," one of *Discerning Travelers* top Romantic Inns for 2005. *Victoria Magazine* calls it "a perfect ocean refuge." Barbara and Fred Vogel will pamper you with modern amenities and classic hospitality in an atmosphere that soothes your weary body and soul.

Rooms/Rates
Large Rooms $300-$350;
Suites $350-$495.
All rooms have private baths, whirlpool tubs for two, fireplaces and stocked refrigerators. Open all year.

Cuisine
Full candlelit buffet breakfast and afternoon tea featuring Sea Crest signature specialties, and evening cordials. Fine restaurants and unique dining nearby. First class Concierge service.

Nearest Airport(s)
Newark Liberty-1 hr.

Directions
From NY and North: GS Pkwy to Exit 98. 34 S to first traffic circle. 3/4 around to 524 E. to Ocean, R 1 block. R again to Tuttle Ave. 4th house on L. From South: Rte I-195 to 34 S, then follow above.

Member Since 1993

   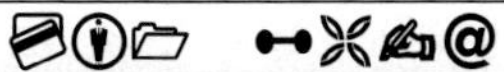 

"We will be returning for another ultimate getaway," Gerry & Ed. "It doesn't get any better than this," Pam Lanier, noted travel expert & guest, April 04.

Victoria House Bed & Breakfast

www.srinns.com/victoriahouse
214 Monmouth Avenue, Spring Lake, NJ 07762-1127
888-249-6252 • 732-974-1882 • Fax 732-974-2132
info@victoriahouse.net

Innkeepers/Owners
Lynne and Alan Kaplan

Elegant Victorian
Waterside B&B Inn

Relax, refresh, renew in our lovingly restored 1882 Queen Anne; the perfect seaside oasis for romantic getaways and business travelers. Enjoy the sea breeze on the veranda or read a book in front of the parlor fireplace. Escape in the distinctive decor of your accommodations; fireplaces, featherbeds, TV/VCRs/DVDs, refrigerator, Jacuzzi for two; all with private baths, air-conditioning, individual temperature control. Stroll our beach boardwalk or around the lake; bicycle our tree-lined streets; or discover a treasure in one of our charming main street shops. Taste our wonderful gourmet breakfasts. Timeless hospitality awaits you. Enjoy our Victorian splendor with modern amenities. A romantic B&B Inn for all seasons. Recently renovated and restored with care. Open all year.

Rooms/Rates
8 beautifully appointed guests rooms: Jacuzzis, Fireplaces, TV/VCR's/DVD's. High Season $199/$379; Low Season $99/$299.

Cuisine
Gourmet-served breakfast with house specialties on the veranda or at tables for two in our dining room. Enjoy afternoon tea and evening cordials & chocolates.

Nearest Airport(s)
Newark, Philadelphia

Directions
From NY, CT, North NJ: GS Pkwy S to ex. 98, to 138E to Rte 35S, 3rd light L Warren Ave. Through next light, turn R on 3rd Ave (Church on L) L on Monmouth Ave. From DC/DE/PA: Rte I-95N/NJ TPKE to 195E to 138E, then follow above dir. NYC/AC 60, Phil 70 miles.

Member Since 1998

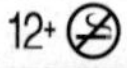

"Best B&B experience at the Shore." "Best Breakfast, my compliments to the chef." "My favorite place to stay."

Owners
The Ramonas Family
Traditional Victorian Village Breakfast Inn

AAA ◆◆◆◆

Conover's Bay Head Inn

www.srinns.com/conoversbay
646 Main Ave., Bay Head, NJ 08742
800-956-9099 • 732-892-4664 • Fax 732-892-8748
innkeeper@conovers.com

Rooms/Rates
12 Rooms, $165/$320 B&B.

Cuisine
Breakfast, afternoon tea.
No alcohol license.

Nearest Airport(s)
Newark Airport

Directions
From NY & North Garden State Parkway exit 98 to Rt 34 South to Rt 35 South to Bay Head from PA & S NJ tpke to S 195 East to Rt 34 South to Rt 35 South to Bay Head.

Discover the antique-filled splendor of Conover's Bay Head Inn, recognized for fine accommodations and hospitality since 1970. Each bed chamber has been uniquely designed for your comfort. Luxurious bed linens are line-dried, starched, and ironed. The aroma of Inn-baked biscuits, muffins or coffee cake and the "feature" of the day will awaken you each morning. Bay Head, with its weathered shingle-style houses, captures the feeling of a late 19th century residential seaside village.

Member Since 1996

"Thank you for making us feel pampered with the wonderful massage, your special linens, a terrific breakfast, but most of all your warm hospitality!"

Sand Castle Bed & Breakfast

www.srinns.com/sandcastle
710 Bayview Avenue, Box 607, Barnegat Light
Long Beach Island, NJ 08006
800-253-0353 • 609-494-6555
info@sandcastlelbi.com

Innkeeper/Owner
Nancy Gallimore
B&B Neo-Victorian Bayfront
Bed & Breakfast Inn

A truly incomparable experience on Long Beach Island! Spacious suites and luxurious rooms with spectacular bay views, all with fireplace, private entrance, private bath some with jacuzzi, A/C, cable TV/VCR/DVD/CD player, in-room telephone with voicemail, current video/DVD movie library, complimentary snacks, 24 hour coffee/tea, soft drinks. Start your day with Nancy Gallimore's sumptuous gourmet breakfast and relaxed hospitality. Enjoy the heated outdoor pool, jacuzzi and exercise room. Take a bike ride or spend a day at our beach, which has been rated one of the top 20 in the USA! The inn provides the bikes and beach gear. Then celebrate a spectacular sunset on the rooftop deck at the end of a relaxing day. This mini-resort is the perfect romantic escape for couples and companions.

Member Since 2003

Rooms/Rates
5 rooms $155/$260 depending on season. 2 suites $235/$395. Open most of the year except December & January. Visit Barnegat Lighthouse,beaches, fishing, bird watching, museum.

Cuisine
Full gourmet breakfast included. Complimentary coffee, tea, snacks, soft drinks available 24 hours. Restaurants next door and within a short drive.

Nearest Airport(s)
Newark Airport

Directions
Garden State Parkway exit 63. Take Route 72 East to end. Left onto Long Beach Blvd. Follow 8 miles to Barnegat Light. At 2nd blinking yellow light make left onto 10th Street. Turn right onto Bayview Ave. Sand Castle is 2 blocks down on right.

"My husband and I travel all over. What elegance, what comfort! We both agree this is the best!"

Innkeepers/Owners
Nancy and Fred Chorpita
Elegant Village Bed & Breakfast

AAA ◆◆◆

Haddonfield Inn

www.srinns.com/haddonfieldinn
44 West End Avenue, Haddonfield, NJ 08033
800-269-0014 • 856-428-2195 • Fax 856-354-1273

Rooms/Rates
9 Rooms. $149/$309, depending on room and day of week.

Cuisine
Full, gourmet breakfast prepared by our chef.

Nearest Airport(s)
Philadelphia International

Directions
From N: NJ turnpike to exit 4. Rt. 73N to 295S. Take exit 30 and follow Warwick Rd to Kings Hwy. L at next light and then R onto West End. From S: 95N to Walt Whitman Bridge. Exit 168(Audubon). L onto Kings Hwy and L onto West End. From W: I-76 to I-676 to Ben Franklin Bridge. Rt. 70E to Cuthbert Blvd (turn R). L onto Park Blvd which becomes West End Ave.

This intimate, elegant hotel in historic Haddonfield is just minutes from Philadelphia and the Cooper and Delaware Rivers. The historic village of Haddonfield offers over 200 unique shops and restaurants. The surrounding areas include countless attractions from aquariums to zoos with art, concerts, history, sports and theatre in-between! Each of our lovely guest rooms has a private bath (many have whirlpools), fireplace, TV, phone with free local calls and voicemail, and wireless Internet access. Enjoy a full, gourmet breakfast served on individual tables adorned with candles and fine linens in our firelit dining room. In the warmer months, enjoy breakfast on the large, wrap-around porch in our beautiful residental neighborhood. Packages and extras include tickets for major sporting events in nearby Philly, fine dining and in-room massage. We specialize in business conferences and retreats with special rates for the business traveler.

Member Since 2005

"What a wonderful place to set up visiting dignitaries!"
"Keeping up the best of B&B traditions."

Candlelight Inn

www.srinns.com/candlelight
2310 Central Avenue, North Wildwood, NJ 08260
800-992-2632 • 609-522-6200 • Fax 609-522-6125
info@candlelight-inn.com

Innkeepers/Owners
Bill and Nancy Moncrief and Eileen Burchsted

Traditional Victorian Village Breakfast Inn

Mobil ★★★

Come visit a unique part of Wildwoods. Enjoy the quiet elegance reminiscent of another era. The Candlelight Inn is a beautifully restored 1905 Queen Anne Victorian home. We offer rooms and suites with private baths, some with double whirlpool tubs and/or fireplaces. Sit on our veranda where cool ocean breezes delight you, relax anytime of the year in our outdoor hot tub, or warm yourself by a roaring fire in our inglenook. Minutes away are spacious beaches, water sports, lighthouses, antiquing, fine dining, nature activities including a zoo, wetlands and birding, golfing, shopping, history, and a fun-filled boardwalk — something for everyone. Cape May County besides having Islands with great Atlantic Ocean beaches has a Naval Air Station Museum, Historic Cold Spring Village, one of the top ten small zoos in the country, and Leaming's Gardens - the largest garden of 'annuals' in the country. The Candlelight is our small piece of the New Jersey Coast that we would like to share with you and your special someone.

Member Since 2001

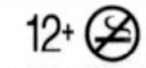   

Rooms/Rates
All rooms have either queen or king beds and all have private baths. 7 Rooms, $95/$175; 3 Suites, $130/$250. Some units have double whirlpool tubs, most have fireplaces, and some have both. Air conditioned. Open year-round.

Cuisine
A 3-course, sit-down breakfast with a choice of entrees and afternoon refreshments.

Nearest Airport(s)
Atlantic City (ACY)

Directions
S-bound: G.S. Pkwy to exit 6; Rte. 147 E; L on 2nd Ave.; R on Central Ave.; go to 24th Ave.; Inn is on R. N-bound: G.S. Pkwy to exit 4 into Wildwood. After bridge, L at 6th light (Atlantic Ave.). L at 24th for 1 block.

"The time spent here was like being 'home away from home,' only better."

Proprietor
Patricia Joyce
Innkeeper/Manager
Julie McElroy

Historic Victorian In Town Breakfast Inn

The Duke of Windsor Inn

www.srinns.com/dukeofwindsor
817 Washington St., Cape May, NJ 08204
800-826-8973 • 609-884-1355 • Fax 609-884-1887
innkeeper@dukeofwindsorinn.com

As you cross the threshold into our expansive foyer, you will immediately sense the romance in this classic Queen Anne Victorian inn. The Duke of Windsor Inn, built in 1896, is among the most authentically restored homes in this historic landmark city. It features a 45-foot tower and a carved oak, open staircase that vaults three stories. The two Tiffany stained glass windows will certainly catch your eye. Renew yourself in the comfort of one of our beautiful guest rooms, furnished with fine antiques, emanating the warmth and elegance of an era gone by. Our location in the heart of the historic district is within a short walking distance to all that Cape May has to offer.

Member Since 2003

Rooms/Rates
10 rooms, $115/$245, all with private baths and air-conditioning. Open year-round. Private parking on the premises.

Cuisine
Included in our rates are scrumptious, gourmet breakfasts served in our grand dining room, and afternoon tea and treats, which can be enjoyed in front of a cozy fire on chilly days, or on our spacious front porch when the weather is warm.

Nearest Airport(s)
Philadelphia

Directions
Garden State Parkway S to the end. Continue straight over bridges, becomes Lafayette St. Turn left at first light. At next light, turn right. Travel 2 blocks on right, 817 Washington St.

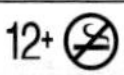

"We had a royal weekend at The Duke of Windsor. It was truly a step back in time."

The Fairthorne

www.srinns.com/fairthorne
111 - 115 Ocean Street, Cape May, NJ 08204
800-438-8742 • 609-884-8791 • Fax 609-898-6129
fairthornebnb@aol.com

Innkeepers Diane and Ed Hutchinson warmly welcome you to their romantic old whaling captain's home. This 1892 Colonial Revival-style Inn features a gracious wraparound veranda where sumptious breakfasts are served on pleasant mornings and stress-relieving rockers offer afternoon relaxation. The Fairthorne is beautifully decorated in period style without being too frilly or formal. Guestrooms are appointed with a seamless blend of fine antiques and contemporary comforts, including air conditioning, mini-fridges and TV/VCR, plus gas log and electric fireplaces and whirlpool tubs in some rooms. Each day Diane and Ed invite you to gather for tasty snacks and fresh-baked cookies.

Member Since 2001

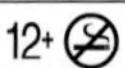   

Innkeepers/Owners
Ed and Diane Hutchinson

Elegant In Town Breakfast Inn

Rooms/Rates
9 Rooms, $140/$275, Antique furnishings, lace curtains, king or queen beds, TVs/VCR, private baths, some fireplaces and whirlpool baths. Open year-round. Closed only Thanksgiving Eve and Day, Christmas Eve and Day.

Cuisine
Full breakfast and afternoon hot tea and coffee on cool days or iced tea and lemonade on summer days. Complimentary sherry. Excellent restaurants a short walk.

Nearest Airport(s)
Phila. & Atlantic City

Directions
Garden State Pkwy S to end; continue straight over bridges, becomes Lafayette St. 2nd light, turn L onto Ocean St. 3rd. block on L—111 Ocean Street.

"I will savor the memory of your hospitality for years to come. Thanks so much!"

The Humphrey Hughes House

www.srinns.com/humphreyhughes
29 Ocean Street, Cape May, NJ 08204
800-582-3634 • 609-884-4428

Owners
Lorraine & Terry Schmidt

Traditional Victorian Village Breakfast Inn

AAA ◆◆◆

Rooms/Rates
10 Rooms. $120/$350 per night, Dbl. Weekday discounts Fall and Spring. All rooms and suites with queen or king beds, TV, Airconditioning.

Cuisine
Delicious and beautifully presented Hot Breakfast (served on the front veranda when weather permits). Elegant Afternoon Tea served in the dining room each day.

Nearest Airport(s)
Atlantic City International

Directions
Take Garden State Parkway South to end. Follow Lafayette Street South. Turn Left at second stop light; Ocean Street. The inn is on your Left, the corner of Ocean and Columbia Streets - only one block from the Ocean.

Nestled in the heart of Cape May's primary historic district, The Humphrey Hughes is one of the most spacious and gracious Inns. Expansive common rooms are filled with beautiful antiques. Relax on the large wraparound veranda filled with rockers and enjoy the ocean view and colorful gardens. Our large, comfortable guest rooms offer pleasant, clean accommodations. All rooms are air-conditioned with cable TV. Our location offers the visitor the opportunity to walk to the beach, restaurants, shops, theatre, concerts, nature trails. A full breakfast and afternoon refreshments are offered daily.

Member Since 1999

"The Inn is so clean and the food is delicious. We will be back soon."

The Mainstay Inn

www.srinns.com/mainstayinn
635 Columbia Ave., Cape May, NJ 08204
609-884-8690 • Fax 609-884-1498
mainstayinn@comcast.net

Proprietors
David & Susan Macrae
Innkeepers
Diane Clark and Kathy Miley
Elegant Victorian Village Breakfast Inn

Mobil ★★★
AAA ◆◆◆

Once an exclusive gambling club, The Mainstay is now an elegant Victorian inn furnished in splendid antiques. Within a lovely garden setting, the Inn and adjacent Cottage feature wide rocker-lined verandas, and large, high-ceilinged rooms which are lavishly but comfortably furnished. The Officers' Quarters is more contemporary with many extras such as whirlpool tubs and fireplaces. The Mainstay is a landmark within a National Historic Landmark town, and is but a short walk to restaurants, shops, theater, concerts, nature trails and beaches.

Rooms/Rates
9 Rooms, $155/$295 B&B; 3 Suites, $165/$325 B&B; 4 Luxury Fireplace Suites, $165/$395. Open year-round; Fireplace suites only Jan. to mid-March.

Cuisine
Breakfast and elegant afternoon tea. Excellent restaurants a short walk away. No liquor license.

Nearest Airport(s)
Atlantic City International 45 minutes away

Directions
Take Garden State Pkwy. (S). In Cape May, Pkwy. becomes Lafayette St. Take L. at light onto Madison Ave. Go 3 blocks, R. at Columbia. Inn on R.

Member Since 1976

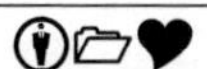

"I want you to know how much I enjoyed may time at The Mainstay Inn. Service, hospitality, and lovely accommodations were far above my expectations!"

Innkeepers/Owners
Nancy & Tom McDonald

Historic Waterside Breakfast Inn

Manor House

www.srinns.com/manorhousecapemay
612 Hughes St., Cape May, NJ 08204
609-884-4710 • Fax 609-898-0471
innkeepr@verizon.net

Rooms/Rates
9 Rooms, $100/$255 B&B;
1 Suite, $150/$295 B&B.
Open year-round.

Cuisine
Bountiful full served gourmet breakfast, creative afternoon refreshments and fresh baked cookies in the evening.

Nearest Airport(s)
Philadelphia

Directions
From Zero-mi. mark on Garden State Pkwy. to Rte. 109 S becoming LaFayette St., turn L. on Franklin for 2 blks to R. on Hughes - 612 Hughes on L.

On a tree-lined residential street in the heart of Cape May's Historic District, Manor House offers guests an exceptionally clean and comfortable turn-of-the-century inn experience. Fluffy robes in the rooms and a generous cookie fairy are but a few of the fun touches found here. Relaxing on the porch, reading in the garden, or roaming the beaches and streets of Cape May occur with little effort. Traditional sticky buns and made-from-scratch full breakfasts and the innkeepers' good humor give the inn its reputation for fine food and character.

Member Since 1991

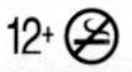

"We had a wonderul time, the food, the atmosphere, the hospitality. We will be back!"

The Queen Victoria®

www.srinns.com/queenvictoria
102 Ocean Street, Cape May, NJ 08204-2320
609-884-8702
reservations@queenvictoria.com

Innkeepers
Doug and Anna Marie McMain

Traditional Victorian Village Breakfast Inn

AAA ◆◆◆

A Cape May tradition since 1980, The Queen Victoria is one of America's most renowned bed & breakfast inns. Two impeccably restored 1880s homes are filled with fine antiques, handmade quilts, and many thoughtful extras. The hospitality is warm and the atmosphere is social. Choose from twenty-one inviting and spacious rooms and suites, all with private bath, AC, mini-refrigerator, and TV. Pamper yourself with a whirlpool tub or gas-log fireplace. For your Victorian enjoyment, rocking chairs fill porches and gardens. A wicker swing carries you back to a quieter time. Bicycles are provided free of charge, as are beach chairs and beach towels. The Queen Victoria is open all year and is located in the center of the historic district, one block from the Atlantic Ocean, tours, shopping, and fine restaurants. Victorian Cape May offers tours, special events, and activities all year including the Spring Music Festival, the Jazz Festival, Victorian Week, and the Food & Wine Festival.

Member Since 1992

Rooms/Rates
15 Rooms: $95/$250. 6 Suites: $140/$480. Weekday discounts Fall, Winter & Spring. Always open. Thanksgiving and Christmas packages.

Cuisine
Rates include generous buffet breakfast & afternoon tea with sweets and savories. Complimentary juices, soft drinks, bottled water, coffee and teas. Fresh fruit always available. Fine dining nearby.

Nearest Airport(s)
Atlantic City

Directions
Garden State Parkway to South end; continue straight over bridges, becomes Lafayette St. 2nd light turn Left onto Ocean St. 3 blocks turn Right onto Columbia Ave. Loading areas for check-in on Right.

"The Queen Victoria is a dream come true! Your hospitality is genuine."

New Mexico

"The Land of Enchantment"

Famous For: Taos, Santa Fe, Pueblos, Adobe, Cliff Dwellings, Carlsbad Caverns (the largest in the world), White Sands National Monument, Ghost Ranch, Ship Rock, Pecos National Historical Park, Pancho Villa State Park, Palace of the Governors (the oldest public building in the country, built in 1610) Desert Flowers, Pottery, Rug-Making, Silver Jewelry, Los Alamos, Uranium.

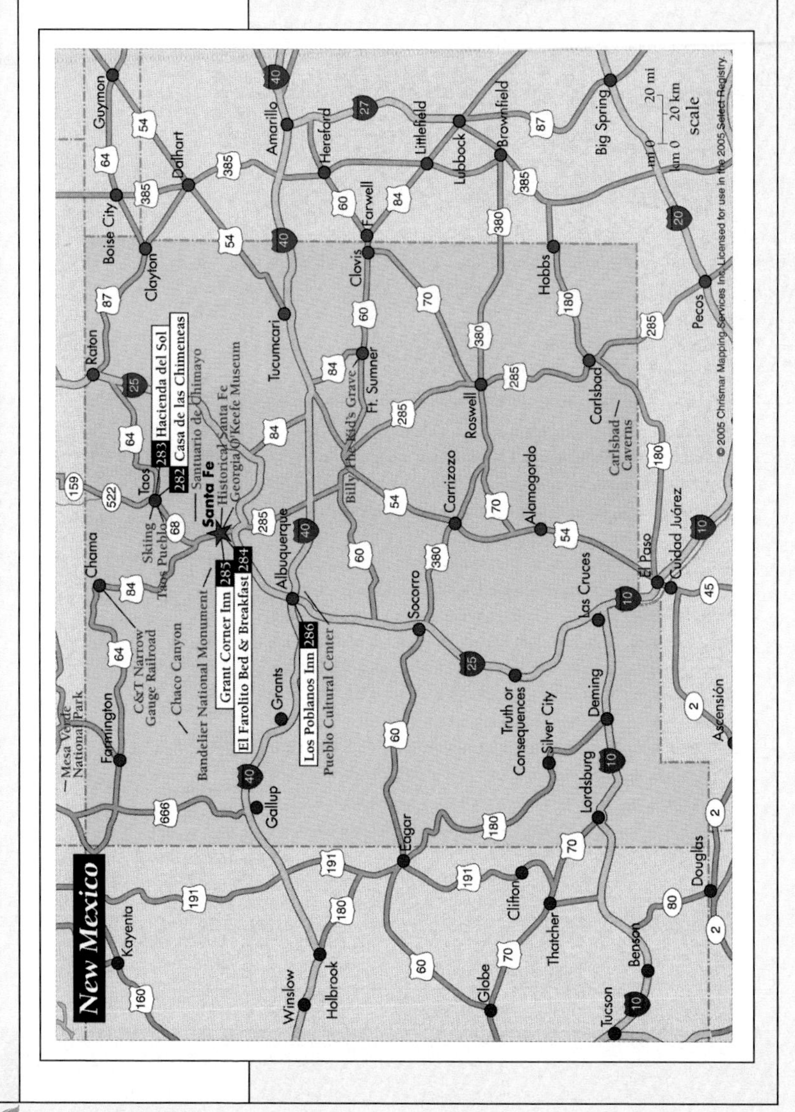

Casa de las Chimeneas

www.srinns.com/casadelaschimeneas
405 Cordoba Road, 5303 NDCBU, Taos, NM 87571
877-758-4777 • 505-758-4777 • Fax 505-758-3976
casa@newmex.com

Innkeeper
Susan Vernon

Traditional Southwestern Village Inn

AAA ◆◆◆◆

Guests to this AAA Four Diamond inn delight in offerings not often found at small properties. The Wellness Spa, complete with workout room, dedicated massage and spa treatment room, sauna and hot tub, entices guests to unwind. An award-winning concierge sees to every guest's need from a menu of possibilities as rich as Taos' multi-cultural history. Special seasonal activities bookable through the inn include hot air ballooning over and into the Rio Grande Gorge, white water rafting, llama trekking, horseback riding, skiing and snowmobiling. A talented kitchen staff prepares two hearty and delicious meals a day. With three scenic byways in Taos County, guests often spend a day enjoying the same views that inspire the many artists that make Taos their home with a lunch packed in a custom backpack. Spectacular gardens, to-die-for accommodations and a perfect location near the Historic Plaza complete the picture. The result: delighted guests who leave with refreshed and renewed spirits, eager to return to Taos' *House of Chimneys*.

Member Since 1998

Rooms/Rates
6 Rooms, $175/$290 B&B;
2 Suites, $325/$615 B&B.
Open year-round.

Cuisine
Three-course breakfast with hot entree, evening buffet supper, complimentary in-room bars with juices, sodas, mineral waters and hot beverages. Optional gourmet picnics.

Nearest Airport(s)
Albuquerque International Sunport, Taos Airport

Directions
From Santa Fe (Hwy. 68): turn R onto Los Pandos, go 1 block & turn R on Cordoba at the four-way stop. The inn is the first L off Cordoba. From Colorado (Hwy 522): turn L on Kit Carson Road, go 1 block & turn R on Montoya. At the four-way stop, go straight. The inn is the first L.

"This, quite possibly, was the most wonderful travel experience we've had. Everything - we do mean everything - was fabulous! Great value for the price."

Innkeeper/Owner
Dennis Sheehan

Southwestern
Bed and Breakfast

Hacienda del Sol

www.srinns.com/haciendadelsol
P.O. Box 177, 109 Mabel Dodge Lane, Taos, NM 87571
866-333-4459 • 505-758-0287 • Fax 505-758-5895
sunhouse@newmex.com

Rooms/Rates
7 Rooms, $115/$325 B&B.
4 Suites, $175/$325 B&B.
Open year round.

Cuisine
Two-course breakfast,with hot entree. Coffee, hot tea and hot cocoa available all day. Afternoon homemade snacks and fruit available. Experience the local's favorite eneregetic bistro, the Trading Post Cafe. The beautiful outdoor patio is a great spot to enjoy the culinary expertise of world renowned Chef Rene Mettler.

Nearest Airport(s)
Albuquerque Airport

Directions
From Santa Fe on Hwy 68: 1 mile north of the Taos Plaza, turn right directly after Southwest Mocassin and Drum onto Mabel Dodge Lane.

The orginal 1804 adobe building once belonged to Mabel Dodge Luhan. This historic Inn has hosted guests such as D.H. Lawrence, Georgia O'Keefe, and Ansel Adams. The Taos Mountain provides a beautiful background to our hacienda which borders 95,000 acres of Taos Pueblo land. Latilla fencing and adobe walls surrounds beautifully landscaped grounds. Though Hacienda del Sol means "House of the Sun" in Spanish, towering cottonwoods, elms, willows and blue spruces shade the hacienda in the summer. Amenities include jacuzzis,outdoor hot tub,wood burning fireplaces and steamrooms. Individually decorated rooms with antiques and hand crafted furniture. Selected by *USA Today* as "One of the 10 most romantic Inns in America."

Member Since 2003

"The best bed and breakfast at 'the edge of Taos desert.'" -Leslie & Mark

El Farolito Bed & Breakfast Inn

www.farolito.com
514 Galisteo Street, Santa Fe, NM 87501
888-634-8782 • 505-988-1631 • Fax 505-989-1323
innkeeper@farolito.com

Innkeepers/Owners
Walt Wyss and Wayne Mainus

Southwestern In Town Breakfast Inn

AAA ◆◆◆

Surround yourself with the richness of Santa Fe's art, culture and history in an authentic adobe compound. The inn offers you award-winning private casitas, showcasing exquisite original Southwestern art and handcrafted furnishings. The rooms are decorated in styles relevant to Santa Fe's rich cultural heritage of native American, Spanish and Anglo inhabitants. Modern amenities also abound including fine linens, rich fabrics, AC, private entrances, TVs, telephones, and in-room coffee service and refrigerators. The Inn is conveniently located in the downtown historic district, a short walk to numerous galleries, shops, museums, fine dining, and the central Plaza. In the warm sunshine, savor a leisurely breakfast on the back portal and relax on your garden patio. In the winter, enjoy a fireside breakfast in the brightly decorated dining room and the coziness of a fireplace in your room. "Most beautifully decorated B&B ever! Great hospitality—great breakfasts!"

Member Since 2001

Rooms/Rates
7 Rooms, $160/$205 ; 1 Suite, $175/$225 . Features: fireplaces (ex. #8) , TV, phones, fine linens, AC, coffee service, and patios. Open all year.

Cuisine
Expanded healthy continental breakfast featuring quality home-baked goods, fresh fruit plate, yogurts, and ample accompaniment. In-room coffee service. World-class fine dining nearby.

Nearest Airport(s)
Santa Fe and Albuquerque

Directions
From Albuquerque: I-25 N, exit 282. St. Francis N to Cerrillos, R on Cerrillos, R at Paseo de Peralta, L at Galisteo to 514. From Taos: S on U.S. 84/285, bear L to downtown, L on Paseo de Peralta, R on Galisteo.

"Quintessential Santa Fe! You create an ambiance that promotes rest and restoration."

Innkeeper/Owner
Louise Stewart
Traditional Colonial
In Town Breakfast Inn

Grant Corner Inn

www.srinns.com/grantcorner
122 Grant Ave., Santa Fe, NM 87501
800-964-9003 • 505-983-6678 • Fax 505-983-1526
gcinn@qwest.net

Rooms/Rates
8 Rooms, $130/$240 B&B; Hacienda, $270/$310 B&B. 10 private baths. Open year-round.

Cuisine
Daily breakfast 8:00-10:30 a.m. Mon.-Sat.; Sunday brunch 8:00 a.m.-2:00 p.m. and complimentary afternoon hors d'oeuvres 5:30-6:30 p.m. included in room rates. Restaurant open to the public for breakfast, brunch, tea, special occasion dinners and catered events.

Nearest Airport(s)
Albuquerque International Sunport; 60 miles

Directions
From Albuquerque, I-25 N exit St. Francis L.(N) 4.5 mi. to R(W) at Alameda. 6 blk., L.(N) on Guadalupe, 2 blk., R.(W) on Johnson, 2 blk., park on L.

This delightful Inn has an ideal location just two blocks from the historic plaza of downtown Santa Fe, among intriguing shops, galleries and restaurants. The world reknowned Georgia O'Keeffe Museum is next door to the Inn. Lush gardens, beautifully appointed guest rooms, fabulous gourmet breakfasts and the gracious hospitality of Louise and her staff make this an experience not to be missed. Inn guests enjoy the flexibility and abundant choices of a full menu, picnic lunch and dinners from the in-house Chef. The restaurant is open to the public daily for breakfast, Sunday brunch, high tea and special occasion dinners. The Inn is especially desirable for small destination weddings. Off street parking is complimentary for house guests.

Member Since 1988

"Incredible breakfast and a wonderfully convenient location for seeing Santa Fe."

Los Poblanos Inn

www.srinns.com/lospoblanos
4803 Rio Grande Blvd. NW, Albuquerque, NM 87107
866-344-9297 • 505-344-9297 • Fax 505-342-1302
info@lospoblanos.com

Innkeepers/Owners
The Rembe Family
Executive Director
Matthew Rembe
Historic Country Estate Inn

Set among 25 acres of lavender fields and lush formal gardens, Los Poblanos Inn is one the most prestigious historic properties in the Southwest. The Inn was designed by the region's foremost architect, John Gaw Meem, the "Father of Santa Fe Style," and is listed on both the New Mexico and National Registers of Historic Places. Guest rooms are in a classic New Mexican style with kiva fire places, carved ceiling beams, hardwood floors, and antique New Mexican furnishings. Guests can relax around the Spanish hacienda-style courtyard or spend hours exploring the property's extensive gardens and organic farm. The buildings feature significant artwork commissioned during the WPA period by some of New Mexico's most prominent artists, including a fresco by Peter Hurd and carvings by Gustave Baumann. Detailed tours highlighting the property's cultural, political, agricultural and architectural history are available to every guest. "One could spend a lifetime at Los Poblanos and never fall out of love." - *Su Casa* Magazine

Member Since 2005

   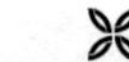  

Rooms/Rates
3 Guest Rooms, 3 Suites, $135/$250. Fireplaces, spa services upon request, wireless internet. Open year-round.

Cuisine
Complimentary gourmet breakfast buffet featuring fresh organic produce and ingredients from our own farm.

Nearest Airport(s)
Albuquerque International Sunport

Directions
From Airport: I-25 N to I-40 W (Gallup Exit 226B). Continue West 3 miles to Rio Grande Exit 157A. Turn right and drive North 3.3 miles to 4803 Rio Grande Blvd. From Santa Fe & Taos: I-25 S to Alameda Exit 233. West on Alameda for 3.2 miles. Left on South Rio Grande Blvd for 3.8 miles to property on right.

"Rough-hewn ceiling beams, Saltillo tiles, and traditional kiva fireplaces give Los Poblanos a cozy, comfortable charm." - *Bon Appétit* Magazine

New York

"The Empire State"

Famous For: Statue of Liberty, Ellis Island, Empire State Building, Times Square, Metropolitan Museum of Art, Central Park, Madison Square Garden, Madison Avenue, Wall Street, Brooklyn Bridge, Catskill Forest, Adirondack Mountains, Finger Lakes, Hudson River, Niagra Falls, Long Island

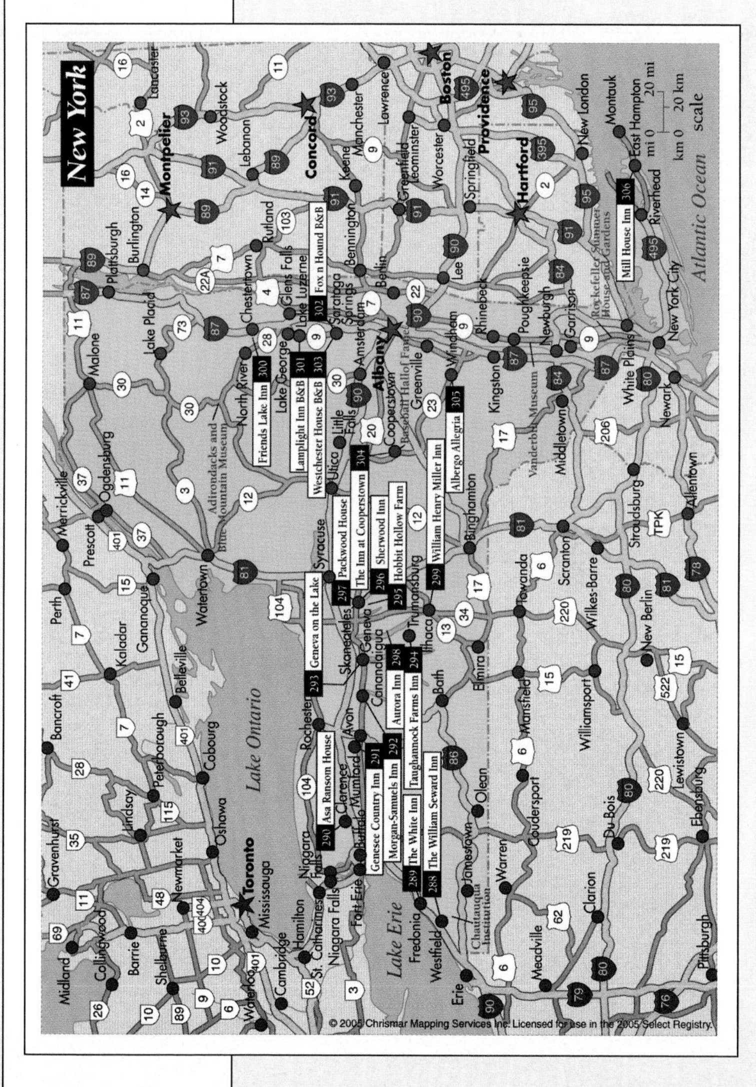

The William Seward Inn

www.srinns.com/williamseward
6645 South Portage Rd., Westfield, NY 14787-9603
800-338-4151 • 716-326-4151 • Fax 716-326-4163
wmseward@cecomet.net

Innkeepers/Owners
Jim & Debbie Dahlberg

Elegant Greek Revival Country Inn

Mobil ★★★
AAA ◆◆◆

Although the cultural and educational offerings of the famed Chautauqa Institution are a major attraction, many travelers come specifically to stay at this 1821 antique-filled Inn for rest and relaxation. With its striking Greek Revival exterior, history, fine dining, gracious accommodations and charming wooded setting, the William Seward Inn provides the base for guests to explore the diverse attraction of the area - wineries, antiquing, outdoor activities, skiing, snowmobiling, Roger Tory Peterson Nature Center, Lucy-Desi Museaum, etc. The Inn is also known for its special weekends - Murder Mystery, International Wine & Gourmet, Cooking, Victorian Christmas and Women's Escape - which consistently attract repeat visit.

Member Since 1992

Rooms/Rates
4 Rooms Double Whirlpool, $170/$195 B&B, 2 Rooms Fireplace, $130/$175 B&B, 8 Rooms $80/$135 B&B. Open year-round.

Cuisine
Dinner available Wednesday-Sunday, by advance reservation with a single seating at 7 p.m. Guests pre-select their appetizer and main entree from our seasonal menu at least one day in advance of dining. The Inn has a selection of fine wines and champagnes.

Nearest Airport(s)
Jamestown, NY - 30 minutes
Erie, PA - 40 minutes

Directions
4 mi. S on Rte 394 from I-90, exit 60. 2.5 hrs. NE of Cleveland, OH; 2.5 hrs. N of Pittsburg, PA; 1.5 hrs. SW of Buffalo, NY; 3 hrs. SW of Toronto, Canada.

"Highlight of our visit was dinner - one of the best we have ever eaten."
T.I., Columbus

Innkeepers/Owners
Robert Contiguglia and Kathleen Dennison

Traditional Victorian
In Town Inn

Mobil ★★★
AAA ◆◆◆

The White Inn

www.srinns.com/whiteinn
52 East Main Street, Fredonia, NY 14063
888-FREDONIA Reservations • 716-672-2103
Fax 716-672-2107
res@whiteinn.com

Rooms/Rates
12 Rooms $69/$119 B&B;
11 Suites, $99/$179 B&B.
Open year-round.

Cuisine
Fine dining ~ American Cuisine. Breakfast, lunch & dinner daily. Cocktails & casual dining in our Lounge. Seasonal outdoor dining. Banquet facilities for up to 150.

Nearest Airport(s)
Buffalo, New York

Directions
NY Thruway (I-90) exit 59. At light, left onto Route 60 (S). At second light, right onto Route 20 (W) (Main Street in Fredonia). Inn is 1.25 miles on right.

Experience The White Inn as described by our guests: "Your attention to detail and the beautiful atmosphere are unbeatable." "The accommodations were excellent, the food superb, the staff delightful." "You helped make our conference a resounding success." "The perfect mix of old-fashioned charm and modern elegance." The White Inn is the focal point of the historic western New York village of Fredonia. Built in 1868 as a private home, the Inn has been receiving guests since 1919. Our beautifully restored guest rooms and public spaces complement our award-winning American cuisine.

Member Since 1989

"No place I've ever stayed is as beautiful and friendly. I love this place."

Asa Ransom House

www.srinns.com/asaransom
10529 Main St. Rt. 5, Clarence, NY 14031
800-841-2340 • 716-759-2315 • Fax 716-759-2791
innfo@asaransom.com

Innkeepers/Owners
Robert Lenz and Abigail Lenz

Traditional Village Inn

Mobil ★★★
AAA ◆◆◆

On the site of the first gristmill built in Erie County (1803), where guests are romanced in the winter by the glowing fireplaces and spacious grounds full of herbs and flowers in the summer. Many rooms have porches or balconies to view the grounds or just relax. Experience world-class cuisine and full country breakfasts with delicious regional accents. Often upon arrival you will find the aroma of fresh pies and breads lingering in the air! Clarence is known throughout the east for its antiques and treasures. Explore the bike trails or visit the nearby Opera House, Erie Canal Cruises, Albright-Knox Art Gallery and much more. Only 28 miles from Niagara Falls.

Rooms/Rates
9 Rooms, $98/$175 B&B; $155/$325 MAP. Closed month of January.

Cuisine
Fine country dining with regional specialties. Fully licensed - NYS Wine award.

Nearest Airport(s)
Buffalo/Niagara

Directions
Traveling E: I-90, exit 49, L on Rte. 78 for 1 mi. to R on Rte. 5 for 5.3 mi. Traveling W: I-90 exit 48A & R on Rte. 77 for 1 mi. to R on Rte. 5 for 10 mi. to Inn.

Member Since 1976

"Our favorite place to stay whenever we travel."

Owner
Fran Pullano
Innkeepers
Kim Rasmussen
Jill Way
Greek Revival
Creekside Inn

Genesee Country Inn Circa 1833

www.srinns.com/geneseecountryinn
948 George Street Box 340, Mumford-Rochester, NY 14511-0340
800-697-8297 • 585-538-2500 • Fax 585-538-9446
room2escapeinn@geneseecountryinn.com

Rooms/Rates
10 rooms - 3 Garden $150/$190, 5 Old Mill Rooms $99/$150, 1 Suite $160/$185.

Cuisine
Full Country Breakfast each morning, tea, coffee available all day.

Nearest Airport(s)
Rochester International Airport

Directions
I-90 Exit 47 to Rte. 19 S. Follow 'Genesee Country Village & Museum' Green signs; turn left onto North Road. Travel 3 miles and turn right onto Rte 36S. At flashing light, turn right onto George St. Go 2 blocks, the Inn is on the right at 948 George St.From I-390 exit 10, Rte 5W to 36N, left at flashing light onto George St.

Step back in time to an era of simple elegance, fine hospitality, and natural beauty. You can escape to our unique water setting with full corporate accommodations like wireless Internet, fax and conference call facilities, while we pamper you with our therapeutic hydro-spa and massage therapy, by appointment. You can hike the grounds or the nearby Nature Center. Fish to your heart's content in our private Spring Creek or visit the famed Oatka. Our Inn, an 1800s plaster-paper mill, boasts extensive gardens and a dynamic waterfall on the seven acres of natural setting. Enjoy the ambience and the bird-watching! The Genesee Country Inn is just remote enough for you to getaway, but close enough to arts and entertainment to keep you coming back! The Inn is a wonderful location for family reunions, corporate events, and intimate weddings. Romance, Spa and fly-fishing packages are available!

Member Since 1988

  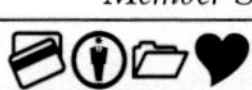  

"A fine Inn indeed. You are on a par with the better country Inns of England."

Morgan-Samuels Inn

www.srinns.com/morgan-samuels
2920 Smith Rd., Canandaigua, NY 14424
585-394-9232 • 585-721-6656 • Fax 585-394-8044
MorSamBBC@aol.com

Innkeepers/Owners
Julie & John Sullivan

B&B Victorian Village
Breakfast Inn

AAA ◆◆◆◆

Travel the 2,000 foot tree-lined drive to the secluded 1810 English style mansion and sense the difference between ordinary and legendary. The Inn sits like a plantation on a rise surrounded by 46 acres. Four patios, trickling waterfall, tenis court, acres of lawn and gardens canopied by 250 noble trees. Three rooms with French doors and balconies, 11 fireplaces. Tea room with stone wall and 16-foot glass windows, pot-bellied stove. Library, common room, large enclosed porch/dining room, four Jacuzzis, outside hot springs spa, museum quality furniture, oil paintings. Recognized as one of the 12 most Romantic Hideaways in the East by Discerning Traveler Magazine.

Member Since 1992

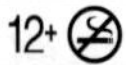   

Rooms/Rates
5 Rooms, $119/$249 B&B;
1 Suite/Lake Villas $199/$395 B&B.

Cuisine
Memorable, extended, candlelit full gourmet breakfast; dinner prix fixe by reservation, special request for eight or more. On day of arrival we serve hot appetizers, fruit, cheeses, and soft beverages served on the Victorian Porch.

Nearest Airport(s)
Rochester International

Directions
I-90 from exit 43 R on 21 to 488; L 1st R on East Ave. to stop. Continue 3/4 mi. to Inn on R. The Inn is located two minutes from Canandaigua Lake.

"We award you two more diamonds making this New York's only 6 Diamond Inn." D.N.

General Manager
William J. Schickel

Elegant Wine Country Resort

AAA ♦♦♦♦

Geneva On The Lake

www.srinns.com/geneva
1001 Lochland Road, Route 14, Geneva, NY 14456
800-3-GENEVA • 315-789-7190 • Fax 315-789-0322
info@genevaonthelake.com

Rooms/Rates
29 Guest Suites (10 with two bedrooms). Open year-round. Many Four-Season Vacation Packages offered for a romantic getaway, honeymoon, gala New Year's and more. From $212 to $1214 per night.

Cuisine
Gourmet cuisine is served with a smile in the warmth of candlelight and live music. Breakfast daily and Sunday Brunch. Lunch On The Terrace in summer.

Nearest Airport(s)
Rochester International

Directions
From the North: NY State Thruway Exit #42 then Rt 14 South 7 miles. From the South or NY City: Rt 17 to Exit #52 then Rt 14 North to Geneva. 1 hour from Rochester, Syracuse or Ithaca Airports.

Experience European elegance and friendly hospitality in the heart of Finger Lakes Wine Country. Amidst an ambiance of Italian Renaissance architecture, classical sculptures, luxurious suites and Stickley furnishings guests from around the world enjoy vacation getaways, family gatherings, weddings and conferences. Rest, relax and surrender yourself to gracious service and breathtaking surroundings. Candlelight dining with live music. A complimentary bottle of wine and basket of fruit are in your suite on arrival and the *New York Times* is at your door each morning. Glorious formal gardens for lawn games, a 70' outdoor pool, a boat-house with dock and moorings. Adjacent are Geneva's charming Historic District and the campus of Hobart and William Smith Colleges, both replete with architectural gems. Enjoy magnificent scenic beauty on the Seneca Lake Wine Trail. Golf is nearby. "The food is extraordinarily good." - *Bon Appetit*. "One of the 10 most romantic inns in the United States." - *American Historic Inns*.

Member Since 2003

6+

"Heavenly!! Thank you (and your wonderful staff) for the grandest stay we've ever had!!"

Taughannock Farms Inn

www.srinns.com/taughannock
2030 Gorge Road, Trumansburg, NY 14886
888-387-7711 • 607-387-7711 • Fax 607-387-7721

Innkeepers/Owners
Susan and Tom Sheridan

Historic Victorian Waterside Inn

AAA ◆◆◆

Relax and enjoy a bygone era at this Victorian country inn. Majestically situated above Cayuga's waters, the inn offers commanding views of the lake. This Finger Lakes wine region landmark, built in 1873, is known for its gracious hospitality, abundant American cuisine, and charming accomodations. In addition to the five rooms in the Main inn that are furnished with antiques, we also have four guesthouses for a total of 22 rooms. Edgewood, the newest of the four, opened in 2004. All 10 rooms, with covered balconies/patios have outstanding views of Cayuga Lake. Four king units feature Jacuzzis. Savor a romantic dinner in the 150-seat fine dining restaurant overlooking the lake. The four-course meal features American cuisine and is complimented by wonderful Finger Lakes wine.

Rooms/Rates
Seasonal rates for all accommodations. Main Inn rooms $80/$165. 3 guesthouses $145/$190 per room. Full cottages $140/$400. Antiques and traditional furnishings.

Cuisine
Expanded Continental breakfast—juice, coffee, fruit, breakfast pastries. 150-seat restaurant. Dinner includes appetizer, salad, entree, dessert. Banquets available.

Nearest Airport(s)
Tompkins Airport

Directions
From Ithaca: Take Rte. 89 N for 9 miles to Gorge Road. Turn L; Inn is on R. From NY State Thruway: Exit 41; Take 318-E to Rte. 5 & 20. Go 1/4 mile; turn R on Rte. 89, S for 34 miles. Inn on R.

Member Since 2002

"This place is magical! The inn, the falls, the lake, the wine! I wish I could live here!"

Proprietor
Noreen Falcone
Property Manager
Julia Bergan
Elegant Country Breakfast Inn

AAA ◆◆◆

Hobbit Hollow Farm

www.srinns.com/hobbithollow
3061 West Lake Road, Skaneateles, NY 13156
800-374-3796 • 315-685-2791 • Fax 315-685-3426
hobbit1@adelphia.net

Rooms/Rates
5 Rooms, $100/$270, elegantly decorated with master-crafted period furniture and antiques. 3 rooms include four-poster beds. Master Suite $250/$270; Lake View $200/$230; Chanticleer $175/$200; Meadow View $150/$170; Twin $100/$120. Open year-round.

Cuisine
Breakfast only. Find excellent dinner and lunches at the Sherwood Inn, Blue Water Grill, and Kabuki.

Nearest Airport(s)
Hancock (Syracuse)

Directions
Located on the West side of Skaneateles Lake on 41A. Route 20 (Genesee Street) to 41A South. In less than 2 miles the stone entrance to Hobbit Hollow Farm will be on the right.

Hobbit Hollow Farm has been painstakingly restored inside and out to recreate the casual comfort of an elegant country farmhouse. Hobbit Hollow serves a full, farm breakfast as part of the room price. Overlooking Skaneateles Lake, Hobbit Hollow Farm is situated on 320 acres of farmland with trails and ponds as well as private equestrian stables. Spend time contemplating the lake on our east verandah. Enjoy afternoon tea or coffee and watch the light play on the water in the soft wash of dusk. Rediscover what it means to be truly relaxed in a setting of tranquility. This is the perfect spot for a quiet, romantic getaway.

Member Since 1998

"From the moment you pass through the stone pillars, you will feel everyday cares lift away."

The Sherwood Inn

www.srinns.com/sherwoodinn
26 West Genesee Street, Skaneateles, NY 13152
800-374-3796 • 315-685-3405 • Fax 315-685-8983
info@thesherwoodinn.com

Owner
William B. Eberhardt
General Manager
Linda B. Hartnett

Traditional Village Inn

Built as a stagecoach stop in 1807, The Sherwood Inn has always been a favorite resting place for travelers. The handsome lobby with fireplace, gift shop, antiques and orientals offers a warm reception. Each room has been restored to the beauty of a bygone era to create a relaxing harmony away from everyday cares. Our newly renovated dining and banquet rooms are able to accommodate groups of all sizes. In addition to our dining rooms, many of our 24 guest rooms overlook beautiful Skaneateles Lake. Fine dining and The Sherwood are synonymous, and we have been recognized by the *New York Times, Bon Appetit, Country Living, Harper's Bazaar* and *New Yorker* magazines. Our extensive menu offers American cooking with a continental touch, accompanied by an impressive wine list.

Rooms/Rates
16 Suites and 8 Rooms, $90/$195. Suites have fireplaces and whirlpool baths. All have private baths, telephones and televisions. We are open year-round.

Cuisine
Our Tavern serves traditional American fare in a relaxed atmosphere. Our Dining Room offers fine dining in an elegant, yet comfortable setting overlooking Skaneateles Lake. Serving Daily.

Nearest Airport(s)
Syracuse (Hancock International)

Directions
From New York Thruway: Exit Weedsport (exit 40) Route 34 S to Auburn. E on Route 20, 7 miles to Skaneateles. From the South: 81 N to Cortland, Route 41 N to Skaneateles Lake, L (west) on Rte. 20 for 1 mi.

Member Since 1979

"The Sherwood has it all...the rooms, the food, the lobby, the village setting... a perfect getaway!"

Proprietor
Michael P. Falcone
Property Manager
Julia Bergan
Contemporary
Village Inn

Packwood House

www.srinns.com/packwoodhouse
14 West Genesee Street, Skaneateles, NY 13152
877-225-9663 • 315-217-8100 • Fax 315-685-8983
info@packwoodhouse.com

Rooms/Rates
19 guest suites. $125/$230
Suites feature a sitting area, desk, cable television, hi-speed internet access, and a kitchenette with microwave, refrigerator and coffee-maker.

Cuisine
Continental breakfast included. Find excellent dinner and lunches at the Sherwood Inn, Blue Water Grill, and Kabuki.

Nearest Airport(s)
Syracuse (Hancock International)

Directions
From New York Thruway: Exit Weedsport (exit 40) Route 34 S to Auburn. E on Route 20, 7 miles to Skaneateles. From the South: 81N to Cortland, Route 41 N to Skaneateles Lake, L (west) on Rte. 20 for 1 mi.

The Packwood House is located in the center of the quaint historic village of Skaneateles on the north shore of Skaneateles Lake, the easternmost of the Finger Lakes. Many of the Packwood's guest suites provide picturesque views of the lake and the village; several feature oversized balconies where guests may sit back and enjoy the view from a unique perspective. The Packwood House is designed to provide all the comforts of home while enjoying the luxury of "getting away." There are many things to see and do, including a scenic boat cruise around the lake, lakeside concerts on summer weekends, and downhill or cross country skiing at nearby trails during the fall and winter months. There is no shortage of activity for guests looking for adventure, and no better place to just sit back, relax and enjoy the scenery.

Member Since 2005

"...comfort and amenities for business or pleasure!"

Aurora Inn

www.srinns.com/aurorainn
391 Main Street/State Route 90, Aurora, NY 13026
866-364-8808 • 315-364-8888 • Fax 315-364-8887
info@Aurora-Inn.com

Innkeeper
Sue Edinger

Historic Village Inn 

  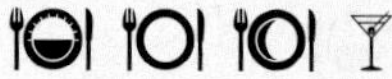

On the shores of Cayuga Lake in the heart of Finger Lakes wine country, the Aurora Inn is a beautiful setting for fine dining, comfortable lodging and special events for all seasons. Elegant décor, fine art and antiques, fireplaces and fresh flowers offer a warm welcome. Its ten luxurious guest rooms are decorated with designer fabrics and furnishings that place an emphasis on comfort. All have well-appointed marble bathrooms with thick towels and terrycloth robes, high-speed Internet access, and flat-panel televisions with DVD players. Most rooms have spacious balconies overlooking the lake or village, and some have inviting fireplaces, deep whirlpool baths, wet bars and other amenities. The Aurora Inn's restaurant is one of the few places in the Finger Lakes to dine outdoors with views of the lake and its spectacular sunsets. Its elegant dining room is warmed by soft music, candlelight and two roaring fireplaces and offers delicious American fare year-round.

Member Since 2005

  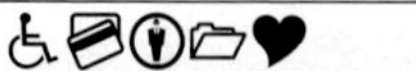  

Rooms/Rates
8 Rooms, 2 Suites. $200/$350 in-season $150/$275 off-season

Cuisine
The Inn serves fine American fare, using the freshest of regional produce. The menu is frequently updated to feature new items throughout the year. Guests enjoy lakeside indoor or outdoor dining for breakfast, brunch, lunch or dinner.

Nearest Airport(s)
Syracuse's Hancock International Airport, 60 miles

Directions
Situated on the east shore of Cayuga Lake on State Route 90, the Aurora Inn is located approx. 30 minutes south of the NY State Thruway (exit 40 or 41). Call for specific directions.

"The Inn is exceptionally well restored, beautifully decorated and staying there was a most gracious experience and of great comfort after a long work day."

Innkeepers/Owners
Lynnette Scofield & David Dier

Victorian In Town Inn

William Henry Miller Inn

www.srinns.com/miller
303 North Aurora Street, Ithaca, NY 14850
877-256-4553 • 607-256-4553 • Fax 607-256-0092
millerinn@cnymail.com

From the time you enter The William Henry Miller Inn, you will find a home rich in architectural detail with stained glass windows, American chestnut woodwork and working fireplaces. Located just off The Commons, the Inn is in the heart of downtown Ithaca. After a bountiful breakfast, spend the day exploring the best of the Finger Lakes. In the evening, while enjoying our homemade desserts, relax in the common areas or on the Inn's comfortable front porch. Visit us for pleasure or business and learn why The *Yankee Magazine* Travel Guide highlights the William Henry Miller Inn as an Editors' Choice, known for "hospitality and attention to detail."

Rooms/Rates
9 rooms King/Queen beds. Rates $115/$210. Private baths; some Jacuzzis and fireplaces. High Speed access. Closed December 24 to January 12.

Cuisine
Breakfast with choice of two main dishes served during a two hour period. Homemade evening dessert and always available coffee and tea. Wonderful restaurants nearby including the world famous Moosewood.

Nearest Airport(s)
Tompkins County (Ithaca) Airport is just ten minutes away.

Directions
Two blocks from The Commons on the northeast corner of Aurora and Buffalo Streets. Ten blocks from Cornell University - one mile from Ithaca College.

Member Since 2003

"We felt truly at home!"

Friends Lake Inn

www.srinns.com/friends
963 Friends Lake Road, Chestertown, NY 12817
518-494-4751 • Fax 518-494-4616
friends@friendslake.com

Innkeepers/Owners
John and Trudy Phillips

Traditional Country Inn

Mobil ★★★
AAA ◆◆◆◆

Experience the comfort and intimate ambiance of this elegantly restored inn, surrounded by the natural beauty of the Adirondacks. Guest rooms feature antiques, fine fabrics, and featherbeds, most with lake views, Jacuzzis and/or fireplaces. Nationally acclaimed cuisine is served daily in the candlelight nineteenth century dining room, complemented by gracious service and a *Wine Spectator* Grand Award-winning wine list. Swim in the lake or the pool, canoe, kayak or fish on Friends Lake. Ski, snowshoe or hike on 32 km. of trails. DiRoNA award of dining excellence.

Rooms/Rates
17 Sumptuous guest rooms, all with private baths and lake or mountain views. Rooms with Jacuzzis or Adirondack Rooms with fireplaces available. Rooms range from $325/$475/couple.

Cuisine
Full country breakfast & candlelight dinner served daily, lunch served on weekends; inquire about conferences, rehearsal dinners, and weddings. Lighter Wine Bar Menu available. Extensive collection of wine.

Nearest Airport(s)
Albany

Directions
I-87 (The Northway) to exit 25, follow Rte. 8W for 3.5 miles, turn L at Friends Lake Rd. Bear R at fork, continue for one mile, then turn R. 8/10ths of a mile to Inn, on the R.

Member Since 1998

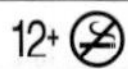

"Ultimate Distinction" Award - *Wine Enthusiast* Magazine

Innkeepers/Owners
Gene & Linda Merlino
Traditional Victorian Village Breakfast Inn

Mobil ★★★
AAA ◆◆◆

The Lamplight Inn Bed & Breakfast

www.lamplightinn.com
231 Lake Ave., P.O. Box 130, Lake Luzerne, NY 12846
800-262-4668 • 518-696-5294 • Fax 518-696-4914
stay@lamplightinn.com

Rooms/Rates
13 Rooms, 12 with fireplaces, 6 with Jacuzzis. 1 is wheelchair accessible. $95/$239—depending on season and type of room. Open year-round. Closed Christmas Eve & Christmas Day.

Cuisine
Memorable full breakfast menu. Wine & beer licensed.

Nearest Airport(s)
Albany, NY

Directions
From the south - NY State Thruway to exit 24 in Albany. After the toll. Take entrance 1N toward Montreal and the Northway (87). Take the Northway to Exit 21 (Lake George/Lake Luzerne). At bottom of ramp make a left on 9N south. Follow 9N south 11 miles. The Inn will be on the right, a block after Lake Luzerne High School.

The Lamplight Inn is in the active Saratoga Springs/Lake George area. It was built in 1890 as a Victorian vacation home of a wealthy playboy/lumberman, on the southern edge of the Adirondack Park. The Inn sits on 10 acres surrounded by towering white pines, just a short walk to crystal-clear Lake Luzerne. The Carriage House includes 4 Jacuzzi/fireplace suites w/TV and private deck & one wheelchair-accessible room w/fireplace, TV and private deck. A romantic getaway—a honeymoon location. Memorable full breakfast. Wine and beer, gift shop. 1992 Inn of the Year—*Laniers-Complete Guide to Bed & Breakfast*. Featured in the 1993 Christmas issue of *Country Inns* Magazine.

Member Since 1996

"Wonderful staff. Beautiful Inn which is kept above my standards. Lots of privacy."
"The Inn looks like a dream Inn should."

Fox 'n' Hound B&B

www.srinns.com/foxnhound
142 Lake Ave., Saratoga Springs, NY 12866
518-584-5959 • Fax 518-584-5959
Innkeeper@FoxnHoundBandB.com

Innkeeper/Owner
Marlena Sacca
Historic Mansion
Bed & Breakfast

AAA ◆◆◆

Visit the historic Saratoga Springs, New York Fox `n Hound Bed and Breakfast. Conveniently located within walking distance from downtown Saratoga shopping, dining, Saratoga Race Course, Skidmore College and Museums. A restored Victorian Mansion with colonial and Queen Ann architectural detail, that offers comfortable elegance with a cosmopolitan flair, European hospitality with the warmth of home, attention to detail found in the finest resorts, and the convenience of in-town location.

MARLENA'S FRITATTA
For complete ingredients, visit www.FoxnHoundBandB.com

Beat 2 eggs per person; add 2 tbsp. sour cream, 1 to 2 tbsp. grated Jarlsburg cheese. You can also add minced fresh basil, parsley if desired. Pour into oven-proof skillet coated with remaining 1/4 cup olive oil, and place on low burner to brown just a bit. Top with some salsa and bake in a 350° oven on middle shelf. The Frittata is done when the center is firm (approximately 15 minutes depending on the amount of eggs used). Cut into wedges and top with a dollop of sour cream and minced fresh basil if desired.

Member Since 2004

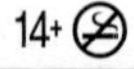   

Rooms/Rates
5 Rooms. $135/$245
$270/$350 racing season.

Cuisine
Guests can expect to find fresh fruit cobblers, fresh baked scones, strudels, muffins, fresh-brewed coffee, an assortment of specially blended teas, and an extensive gourmet breakfast menu that changes daily.

Nearest Airport(s)
Albany International Airport

Directions
I87 take Exit 14 and bear / turn right toward Saratoga Springs. First traffic light take a right onto Henning Ave-Rt. 29. Go approx 1 mile to light go left onto Lake Ave. 1/2 mile on the left (on the corner of Marion Pl. and Lake Ave). Parking is available behind the property.

"A truly special B&B thanks to your warm hospitality. I will enjoy writing about the Fox 'n' Hound- a place I can totally recommend." Katharine Dyson

Owners/Innkeepers
Bob & Stephanie Melvin

Traditional Victorian In Town Breakfast Inn

AAA ◆◆◆

Westchester House Bed & Breakfast

www.srinns.com/westchesterhouse
102 Lincoln Ave., P.O. Box 944, Saratoga Springs, NY 12866
800-579-8368 • 518-587-7613 • Fax 518-583-9562
innkeepers@westchesterhousebandb.com

Rooms/Rates
7 Rooms, King and Queen beds. Customary $115/$225; Special Events $180/$250; Racing Season $250/$445 B&B. Closed December and January.

Cuisine
Full cold breakfast including fruit salad, platter of cold meat and cheeses. A variety of excellent restaurants within easy walk of the Inn.

Nearest Airport(s)
Albany (commercial)

Directions
From the South: 30 mi. N of Albany, I-87 to exit 13N. 4 mi. N to 6th traffic light. R (E) on Lincoln to 102. From the North: I-87 to exit 14. Right on Union Ave .4 mi. to 3rd traffic light. Left (S) on Nelson one block to Lincoln. Right (W) on Lincoln to 102.

Welcome to the Westchester House - Saratoga's hidden jewel. Nestled in a residential neighborhood of tree-lined streets and surrounded by exuberant gardens this enticing Victorian confection combines gracious hospitality, old-world ambiance and up-to-date comforts. Lace curtains, oriental carpets, high ceilings, the rich luster of natural woods, king-or queen-sized beds, tiled baths and luxury linens provide elegance and comfort. The charm and excitement of Saratoga is at our doorstep. After a busy day sampling the delights of Saratoga, relax on the wraparound porch, in the gardens, or in the parlour, and enjoy a refreshing glass of lemonade. Walk to thoroughbred race track, historic districts, downtown, Spa State Park/SPAC. Close to Skidmore College and Saratoga Battlefield.

Member Since 1996

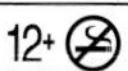

"A little gem that made us feel immediately welcomed. The B&B was immaculate!"

The Inn at Cooperstown

www.srinns.com/innatcooperstown
16 Chestnut Street, Cooperstown, NY 13326
607-547-5756 • Fax 607-547-8779
info@innatcooperstown.com

Innkeepers/Owners
Marc and Sherrie Kingsley

Traditional Village Breakfast Inn

A stay at The Inn at Cooperstown is a special treat. This award-winning historic hotel is ideally situated to enjoy all that Cooperstown offers. The Inn was built in 1874, fully restored in 1985 and is thoughtfully improved upon every year. Spotless rooms are individually decorated with many charming touches. A relaxing atmosphere enables guests to escape the hectic pace of the modern world. After exploring the lovely village of Cooperstown, visitors unwind in rockers on The Inn's sweeping veranda or enjoy the fireplace in a cozy sitting room. Nearby streets are lined with historic buildings, interesting shops and restaurants. The National Baseball Hall of Fame is just two blocks from The Inn. It is a brief trolley ride to experience another century at The Farmers' Museum, where exhibits, a recreated village and costumed staff depict life over 150 years ago. Nearby, the Fenimore Art Museum displays a premier collection of Native American Indian art, American paintings and folk art. The Glimmerglass Opera, beautiful Otsego Lake and many other treasures are located just beyond the village.

Member Since 1998

Rooms/Rates
17 rooms each with private bath, A/C, CD/clock radio, hair dryer, iron, wireless Internet access. Televisions/Phones in sitting rooms. Standard rooms: $99/$187, Suite: $170/$325 B&B. Open year-round.

Cuisine
Continental breakfast, afternoon refreshments, and fine restaurants within walking distance.

Nearest Airport(s)
Albany, NY or Syracuse, NY

Directions
Cooperstown is 70 miles west of Albany. From the south, I-88 to exit 17 to Rte 28N, to 16 Chestnut St. From the west I-90 to exit 30 to Rte 28S, to The Inn. From the southeast, I-87 to exit 21 to Rte 23W to Rte 145 to Rte 20W to Rte 80W to The Inn.

"You clearly understand that a good travel experience comes from attention to detail."

Innkeepers/Owners
Vito and Lenore Radelich
Traditional Victorian Mountain Breakfast Inn

Mobil ★★★
AAA ◆◆◆◆

Albergo Allegria

www.albergoUSA.com
43 Route 296, PO Box 267, Windham, NY 12496-0267
518-734-5560 • Fax 518-734-5570
mail@AlbergoUSA.com

Rooms/Rates
14 Rooms, $73/$189 B&B; 8 Suites, $169/$299 B&B. Guestrooms have down comforters, modern amenities.

Cuisine
Hearty, full gourmet breakfast served each morning. 24-hour guest pantry with complimentary soft drinks, hot beverages and sweets. Afternoon tea served on Saturdays. Dinner restaurants nearby.

Nearest Airport(s)
Albany International Airport - 50 miles North

Directions
I-87 Exit 21 (Catskill). Take Rte. 23 W for 24 miles. L onto Rte. 296. 1/10 mile on L.

Italian for the 'Inn of Happiness,' Albergo Allegria is an 1892 Inn set in the Northern Catskill Mountains. Situated on manicured lawns and country gardens, guests can relax under the 100 year old Oak tree or by the creek that is home to natural wildlife. The Inn's guestrooms offer beauty and history, while the Millenium, Master and Carriage House suites are gracious and inviting with whirlpool and fireplace. A full gourmet breakfast consisting of various frittatas, filled omelettes, Belgian waffles, stuffed French toast, and specialty pancakes are served hot from the kitchen. In addition, a marble side board filled with fresh fruit, homemade muffins, scones, granola and a variety of breads, cereals and juices are offered. Voted '2000 Inn of the Year' by author Pamela Lanier.

Member Since 2001

"This truly is the Inn of Happiness." N.K. of Brooklyn, NY

Mill House Inn

www.millhouseinn.com
31 North Main Street, East Hampton, NY 11937
631-324-9766 • Fax 631-324-9793
innkeeper@millhouseinn.com

Proprietors
Sylvia and Gary Muller
Historic Village
Breakfast Inn

Our historic inn is located in the heart of East Hampton, 'America's most beautiful village.' Surrounded by spectacular ocean beaches, pristine bays, ospreys nesting over sparkling estuaries and mile after mile of quiet country roads, the 'East End' of Long Island is a fisherman's playground, a vintner's paradise & an artist's inspiration. Enjoy foggy mornings, lazy days, blazing sunsets & starry nights. Walk to world-class restaurants, shops, galleries & theatres. Take a scenic drive to all that the Hamptons have to offer – from the fishing boats in Montauk, to the farmers market in Amagansett, quaint antique shops in Sag Harbor, the wineries in Bridgehampton and the magnificent mansions in Southampton! Curl up on our cozy leather sofas, relax in amazingly comfortable Adirondack chairs on our front porch overlooking the Old Hook Windmill, or sneak away for a bit of solitude in our lush gardens. Fine linens, lofty featherbeds, down quilts and pillows, gas fireplaces, oversized glass-walled double marble showers and Serenity Air Baths, a leisurely breakfast our guests proclaim 'simply the best' and our old-fashioned hospitality assure you a memorable stay.

Member Since 2002

Rooms/Rates
10 rooms & suites $200-$875. Queen or King bed/private bath/fireplace. Suites w/foot Serenity Air Baths.

Cuisine
Our guests call Gary's menu "The Breakfast" & there are twenty reasons why! Among them: crayfish & andouille etouffee, house-cured salmon & goat cheese pizza, chicken sausage & wild mushroom hash, "Uncle Shorty's Breakfast" & "the bb&t sandwich."

Nearest Airport(s)
MacArthur Airport (ISP) - 50 miles
East Hampton Airport - 5 miles away takes small corporate jets.

Directions
Rte 495 E to Exit 70. Right on Rte 111 S to end. Left on Rte 27 E. Go approx 30 miles into East Hampton Village. Just past Newtown Lane bear left on North Main St. We are on the left directly across from the windmill.

"Finally a place in The Hamptons where I can be truly comfortable. Gary is an amazing chef...plain breakfast will no longer do. And a good dog fix, too!"

North Carolina

"The Tar Heel State"

Famous For: Blue Ridge Mountains, Smoky Mountains, Outer Banks, Roanoke Island, Cape Hatteras, Kitty Hawk, Tobacco, Textiles, Furniture

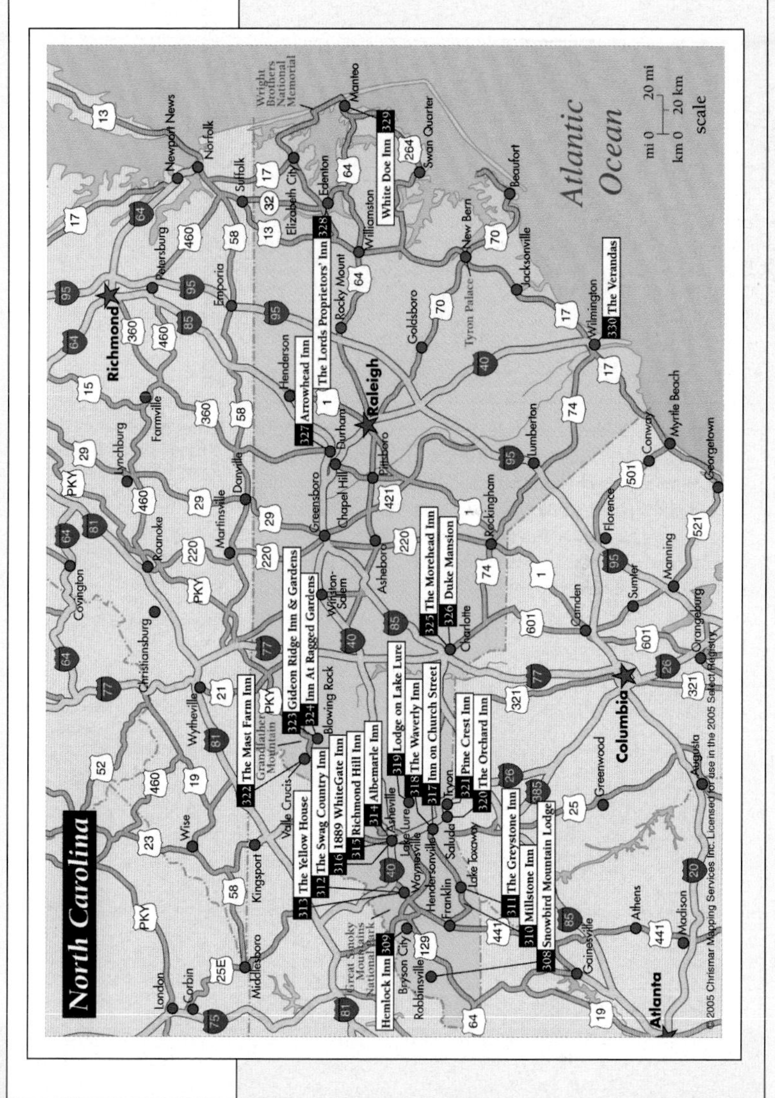

Snowbird Mountain Lodge

www.srinns.com/snowbirdmountain
4633 Santeetlah Rd., Robbinsville, NC 28771
800-941-9290 • 828-479-3433 • Fax 828-479-3473
innkeeper@snowbirdlodge.com

Innkeepers/Owners
Karen & Robert Rankin
Historic Mountain Retreat/Lodge

High up in Santeetlah Gap, on the Southern border of the Great Smoky Mountain National Park, lies this secluded, rustic yet elegant, historic lodge built of stone and huge chestnut logs. The view from the porch is one of the best in the mountains. An excellent library, huge stone fireplaces and award-winning gourmet cuisine make this lodge an exceptional retreat from the pressures of the world. Whether it's fly-fishing, hiking, biking, or just relaxing in front of the fire, we can make your trip to the mountains picture-perfect.

Rooms/Rates
23 Rooms, $175/$300 AP.
In-room fireplaces, whirlpool tubs and steam showers available.

Cuisine
Buffet breakfast, picnic lunch and gourmet dinner.

Nearest Airport(s)
Knoxville, Atlanta

Directions
From Robbinsville take Highway 143 W. 10.5 miles to the Snowbird Mountain Lodge.

Member Since 1973

"...an unspoiled, hidden vacation oasis tucked away in the Southern Appalachians."

Hemlock Inn

www.srinns.com/hemlock
911 Galbraith Creek Road, P.O. Box 2350, Bryson City, NC 28713
828-488-2885 • Fax 828-488-8985
hemlock@dnet.net

Innkeepers/Owners
Mort & Lainey White

Rustic Mountain Inn

AAA ◆◆◆

High, cool, and restful, Hemlock Inn is beautifully situated on 50 wooded acres on top of a small mountain on the edge of the Great Smoky Mountain National Park. There is a friendly informality at meal times around lazy susan tables. Honest-to-goodness home cooked meals are served family style every day. Enjoy a change of pace, a change of scene, and simple pleasures. Get away from schedules as you walk in the Smokies, ride white-water rapids, fish in one of the beautiful streams, ride the Great Smoky Mountain Railroad, or just sit and relax in a rocking chair on our front porch. Ideal for family reunions.

Rooms/Rates
22 Rooms, $174/$196 MAP;
3 Cottages, $180/$237.
Open Year Round

Cuisine
Breakfast, dinner included. Breakfast 8:30 am, daily dinner 6:30 pm Monday - Saturday, and 12:30 Sunday. Genuine home-cooked meals include made from scratch biscuits, rolls and deserts. No alcoholic beverages served.

Nearest Airport(s)
Asheville, NC

Directions
Hwy 74 to exit 69-Hyatt Creek Rd, R on Hyatt Creek 1.5 mi., L on Hwy 19, 1.5 mi to Hemlock Inn sign, turn R at sign, Inn 1 mi on L.

Member Since 1973

"Hemlock Inn is more than a place…it's an attitude."

Millstone Inn

www.srinns.com/millstoneinn
119 Lodge Lane, Cashiers, NC 28717
888-645-5786 • 828-743-2737 • Fax 828-743-0208
office@millstoneinn.com

Innkeepers/Owners
Douglas and Beverly Woock

Elegant Mountain Retreat/Lodge 

Millstone Inn is a true mountain lodge; built as a private home in 1933 with pinewood paneling, exposed beam ceiling and stone fireplace. Guests discover breathtaking views ofWhiteside Mountain and the Natahala National Forest, considered by many to be the finest scenery in North Carolina.The Inn's secluded 20 acres borders a short hiking trail to Silver Slip Falls, the headwaters of the Chattooga River.The Inn`s relaxing mountain atmosphere is enhanced by elegant accomodations and fine dining on Old World Blue Willow china in the Whiteside Mountain Dining Room, making it ideal for a romantic or restful getaway. The 7 guest rooms, 4 suites, and 2 bedroom cottage all have private bathrooms, charming and cheerful ambience, period and antique furnishings, original artwork, and every up to date amenity. All rooms at the Inn have spectacular mountain views, some offer a sitting room, gas fireplace, covered deck, and kitchen. The Millstone Inn has been selected as one of *Country Inns Magazine*`s "12 Best Inns."

Member Since 2003

Rooms/Rates
13 rooms/suites/cottage MAP Plan $285 to $560. Antiques, TV, phone, data port, all rooms have private baths (Rates subject to change without notice). Closed Christmas.

Cuisine
Breakfast, dinner, lite afternoon fare, hors d'oeuvres, complimentary non-alcholic beverages/ snacks included. Elegant fine dining at the Inn's Whiteside Mountian Dining Room offering Classic Contemporary Cusine.

Nearest Airport(s)
Asheville

Directions
The Inn street sign is located 1 mile on Hwy 64 west of center of Cashiers. Turn down Wild River Road and take the second right onto Lodge Lane and the Inn is at the end of the Road.

"Nothing can match this, what a view, what outstanding food, what hospitality."
"Great attention to details!!", "Pure southern comfort."

The Greystone Inn

www.srinns.com/grey
Greystone Lane, Lake Toxaway, NC 28747
800-587-5351 • 828-966-4700 • Fax 828-862-5689
info@greystoneinn.com

Owner
Reg Heinitsh, Jr.
General Manager
Clark E. Lovelace

Historic Mountain Lake Resort

AAA ◆◆◆◆

All of the intimacies of a Four Diamond historic (National Register) inn with the luxurious amenities of a full service resort are combined on North Carolina's largest private mountain lake. Exceptionally romantic, highlights include a pampering spa, championship golf - including Tom Fazio learning center – complimentary at certain times of the year, guided hikes and full lake activities. Afternoon tea and cakes on sun porch and daily champagne cruise on 26-passenger mahogany "Miss Lucy" precede 7-course gourmet meal. Clay tennis courts and fully equipped health and fitness center complement the nearby mountain resort experiences. Modern amenities include Jacuzzi tubs in every room and fireplaces in most. Personal guest recognition and exceptional service are our hallmark.

Rooms/Rates
30 Rooms, $270/$520 MAP; 3 Suites, $405/$605 MAP; Includes boats & most recreational activities. Open year-round, except week days Dec./Mar.

Cuisine
Includes full breakfast, afternoon tea, hors d' oeuvres, & gourmet dinner. Great wine list; liquor available.

Nearest Airport(s)
Asheville Regional

Directions
*From I-40 in Asheville, I-26E, 9mi, Rte 280S 20mi to Brevard, US-64W 20mi to Lake Toxaway Country Club/Greystone Inn sign. Right turn at entrance & gatehouse, proceed 3.5mi to Inn. Specific directions from other locations available on website.

Member Since 1991

Rated one of the best hotels/resorts in the world by both *Travel + Leisure* and *Conde Nast Traveler* magazines.

The Swag Country Inn

www.srinns.com/swagcountryinn
2300 Swag Road, Waynesville, NC 28785
800-789-7672 • 828-926-0430 • Fax 828-926-2036
swaginnkeeper@earthlink.net

Innkeeper/Owner
Deener and Dan Matthews
General Manager
Carolyn Hipps

Rustic Country Inn

The Swag offers the finest hiking and wilderness experience available in the Great Smokies. This country guest house hotel features unique guest rooms with handcrafted interiors, natural materials of handpicked stone, and hand-hewn century-old logs. 250 unspoiled acres next to the Park sit atop our own ridge at 5,000 feet. *Town & Country* says the meals are "sophisticated." A paradise for nature-lovers seeking the finest amenities in a romantic, natural setting. "It is a soul-stirring experience, a welcome respite from the spiral of urgency and distractions of the world in and beyond the valley below." *USA Today* and American Historic Inns in Feb. 2003 named us "One of the ten most romantic retreats."

Rooms/Rates
AP; 12 Rooms $330/$655; 3 Cabins $475/$700; Open late April to mid-November.

Cuisine
A not-to-be-missed hors d'oeuvre hour precedes superb cuisine nightly. All 3 meals are included in the room rate. We are in a dry county. Guests are welcome to bring their own spirits.

Nearest Airport(s)
Asheville

Directions
Via Interstate 40: North Carolina on I-40. Exit #20 onto Hwy. 276 for 2.8 miles. Right on Grindstone Road. At stop sign turn right onto Hemphill Road. Four miles up blacktopped road, left on Swag Road. 2.5 miles up our gravel road to the inn at 5,000 feet.

Member Since 1991

"The Swag is an experience maker. How can you improve upon The Swag?!?"

The Yellow House on Plott Creek Road

www.srinns.com/yellowhouse
89 Oakview Drive, Waynesville, NC 28786
800-563-1236 • 828-452-0991 • Fax 828-452-1140
info@theyellowhouse.com

Innkeepers/Owners
Donna & Stephen Shea

Elegant Mountain
Bed & Breakfast Inn

Mobil ★★★

Rooms/Rates
3 Rooms, 7 Suites, $165-$275.
Open All Year.

Cuisine
Gourmet breakfast each morning served en suite, on private balcony, verandah or dining room depending on accommodation; appetizers each evening. Dinner service Friday and Saturday and most holidays.

Nearest Airport(s)
Asheville (AVL)

Directions
From S, take exit 100 (Hazelwood Ave) off US 23/74. Proceed to the L for 1 1/2 mile on Plott Creek Road. From the N, exit 100 (Hazelwood Ave) from US 23/74, turn R on Eagles Nest Road, L on Will Hyatt, R on Plott Creek Road.

A European-style inn of casual elegance, the 19th century Yellow House accents fine service in a romantic, intimate setting. Located a mile from the lovely mountain community of Waynesville, NC, the inn sits atop a knoll 3,000 feet above sea level, and is surrounded by 5 beautifully landscaped acres of lawns and gardens, with two lily ponds, a footbridge and a deck. The Inn offers three rooms and seven suites, each with luxury linens, private bath, gas fireplace, coffee service, refrigerator and bathrobes; suites also have wet bar and 2-person whirlpool tub. Most accommodations include private balcony or patio. The Yellow House offers a quiet rural setting with piped-in music, and wireless internet hotspot for guests. Minutes from the Blue Ridge Parkway, Great Smoky Mountain National Park, Pisgah National Forest, Cataloochee ski area and Maggie Valley. Close to three mountain golf courses and the Biltmore Estate.

Member Since 1998

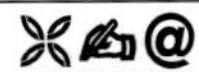

"Our first visit was like a fairy tale. This visit was like a dream come true."

Albemarle Inn

www.srinns.com/albemarle
86 Edgemont Road, Asheville, NC 28801-1544
800-621-7435 • 828-255-0027 • Fax 828-236-3397
info@albemarleinn.com

Innkeepers/Owners
Cathy and Larry Sklar
Elegant In Town Breakfast Inn

AAA ◆◆◆◆

A classic turn-of-the-century Southern mansion on the National Register, the Albemarle Inn offers elegance in a warm and inviting atmosphere. Guests are greeted in the main parlor which glows with recently restored oak wainscoting. An intricately carved staircase leads to period guest rooms, appointed with antiques, fresh flowers, and cozy robes. Morning begins with coffee or tea by the arts & crafts style marble fireplace, followed by a gourmet breakfast on the enclosed, plant-filled sunporch. Late afternoon offers the opportunity to relax on the massive stone veranda overlooking lush gardens while enjoying refreshments and conversation. Near downtown and the Biltmore Estate.

Rooms/Rates
11 Rooms $165/$345, B&B. Elegantly appointed period rooms with claw-foot tubs, fine linens, fresh flowers and turndown service with chocolates. Rooms with whirlpool tub, fireplace or private balcony available. Open year round.

Cuisine
Full gourmet breakfast at private tables, late afternoon refreshments on the veranda, complimentary beverages.

Nearest Airport(s)
Asheville/Hendersonvillle Airport (AVL)

Directions
From I-26 or I-40: to I-240, Exit 5-B (Charlotte St.). Travel 1 mile N on Charlotte St. to Edgemont Rd. Turn R on Edgemont and proceed to the end of the street to the inn.

Member Since 2002

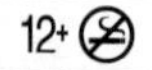  

"Can't imagine a more perfect stay...snuggly robes, dreamy mattresses & mouthwatering menus. Takes breakfast to an entirely new dimension."

Richmond Hill Inn

www.srinns.com/richmondhill
87 Richmond Hill Dr., Asheville, NC 28806
888-742-4550 • 828-252-7313 • Fax 828-252-8726
info@richmondhillinn.com

Innkeeper/Owner
Bland Holland

Elegant Victorian
In Town Inn

Mobil ★★★★
AAA ◆◆◆◆

Rooms/Rates
33 Rooms and 3 Suites, From $205 to $515.

Cuisine
Full breakfast and afternoon tea included. Gabrielle's fine dining in mansion. Extensive wine list & liquor.

Nearest Airport(s)
Asheville Regional Airport

Directions
Take Highway 251 exit on US Highway 19/23, three miles NW from downtown. Follow signs.

Romance is encouraged every moment. The 1889 mansion is perched on a hillside, and each room is uniquely decorated and furnished with antiques. Charming cottages surround a croquet court and feature fireplaces and porch rockers. Each of the spacious rooms in the Garden Pavilion offers beautiful views of the Parterre Garden, waterfall, and mansion. Stroll through gardens by the cascading brook. Relax at afternoon tea in the stately Oak Hall. Read in the library. Savor an exquisite dinner in Gabrielle's, our Four Diamond restaurant, featuring an extensive wine list.

Member Since 1991

Voted Top 3 Country Inns by *Southern Living*

1889 WhiteGate Inn and Cottage

www.srinns.com/whitegateinn
173 East Chestnut Street, Asheville, NC 28801
800-485-3045 • 828-253-2553 • Fax 828-281-1883
innkeeper@whitegate.net

Innkeepers/Owners
Ralph Coffey and Frank Salvo

Historic Breakfast Inn

AAA ◆◆◆

Romance, elegance and tranquility describe the ambiance at the 1889 WhiteGate Inn and Cottage. The Inn is listed on the National Register of Historic Places, and is minutes from the Biltmore Estate and nestled in The Blue Ridge Mountains. Enjoy a special place for your special moments. Sumptuous breakfasts begin your day. Luxurious spa suites with two-person Jacuzzi tubs and fireplaces set the tone for romance. Wander the stunning award winning gardens or stroll to shops and restaurants in Asheville, less than a five-minute walk.

Rooms/Rates
6 Rooms. $170/$340. Separate Cottage with full kitchen, Spa Suites, on site Orchid Greenhouse, Closest Inn to downtown.

Cuisine
Full 3 Course Gourmet Breakfast, Late afternoon refreshments, Complimentary Beverages and Snacks

Nearest Airport(s)
Asheville

Directions
From I-40 or I-26 to I-240 Exit 5B (Charlotte Street) Proceed north on Charlotte; turn LEFT on E. Chestnut Go one block. Turn LEFT onto Central. Turn into the first driveway on the right. Parking is behind the greenhouse in the lower lot.

Member Since 2005

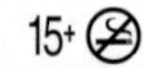     

"It's like waking up to a beautiful dream every morning. A healing place for the mind, body, and soul. The gardens are breathtaking."

Inn on Church Street

www.srinns.com/churchstreet
201 3rd Ave West, Hendersonville, NC 28739
800-330-3836 • 828-693-3258 • Fax 828-693-7263
innonchurch@innspiredinns.com

Innkeepers/Owners
Mike & Rhonda Horton
1920's Art Deco In Town Boutique Hotel

A beautiful mountain inn of distinction, located in the heart of historic downtown Hendersonville and just moments away from mountain adventures, is listed on the National Register of Historic Places. This 1921, three story brick inn has guest rooms graciously decorated in a European Boutique style. Enjoy our innkeepers social and gooey chocolate chip cookies upon arrival, while you relax in the rocking chairs on our wrap around porch. Then celebrate the next morning with the Chef's all natural country breakfast. The perfect getaway for vacationers and business travelers alike.

Rooms/Rates
19 guest rooms $99/$129-$169. 2 suites $250, Juniper House $250.

Cuisine
Experience The Dining Rooms culinary team's award winning Countryside Cuisine, where we marry all natural products and techniques with locally harvested organics. Choose from the Inn's list of over 90 global wines, recent winner of Wine Spectator Award of Excellence in 2004. Relax as our knowledgable staff shows you their southern hospitality for a memorable experience.

Nearest Airport(s)
Asheville Airport

Directions
Hwy 26 to exit 49. Follow to downtown Hendersonville. L on Church St. to the corner of Church and 3rd Ave.

Member Since 2003

"We have traveled and dined around the world, and Inn On Church Streets beautiful decor, fabulous food and award winning wine list make it a must visit!"

The Waverly Inn

www.srinns.com/waverlyinn
783 North Main Street, Hendersonville, NC 28792
800-537-8195 • 828-693-9193 • Fax 828-692-1010
register@waverlyinn.com
www.waverlyinn.com

Innkeepers/Owners
John & Diane Sheiry, Darla Olmstead

Traditional Village Breakfast Inn

Located in the beautiful Blue Ridge Mountains of Western North Carolina, the Inn is a short drive from the Biltmore Estate, Blue Ridge Parkway, Dupont State Forest, Chimney Rock Park, and the Flat Rock Playhouse. Cited in national publications such as The New York Times and Southern Living, we received high praise in Vogue Magazine for our "southern breakfast" with your choice of omelets, french toast, pancakes with real maple syrup, grits, meats, fresh fruit, eggs and egg substitutes. Special touches like 300 count sheets, Egyptian cotton towels, robes, data-ports, wireless internet, and cable TV make our $139-$250 rates a real value. The Inn is within walking distance of the Mast General Store, several fine restaurants, exceptional shopping, and antiquing. Two porches with rocking chairs await you. The New York Times suggests that you "arrive early enough to sit outside and enjoy the descending darkness." "Come experience hospitality as it was meant to be."

Member Since 1991

Rooms/Rates
13 Rooms, $139/$189 B&B;
1 Suite, $195/$250 B&B.
Open year-round. Seasonal and promotional specials appear regularly on our web site at www.waverlyinn.com.

Cuisine
Full breakfast each morning. A wide variety of beverages are available 24 hours a day. Darla's freshly baked delectables each afternoon. Enjoy our evening social hour 5-6 p.m. Guests are welcome to bring their own spirits.

Nearest Airport(s)
Asheville (AVL)

Directions
From I-26, take NC Exit 49B, then U.S. 64W for 2 mi. into Hendersonville. Bear R onto Rte. 25N for 500 yds. Inn is on L at the corner of 8th Ave. & Main St.

"Everything from the delicious full breakfast to the comfortable bed was perfect! We come back every year because of John, Diane, and Darla's hospitality."

Lodge on Lake Lure

www.srinns.com/lakelure
P.O. Box 519, 361 Charlotte Drive, Lake Lure, NC 28746
800-733-2785 • 828-625-2789 • Fax 828-625-2421
info@lodgeonlakelure.com

Innkeepers/Owners
Giselle Hopke
Historic Rustic Mountain Inn

Along the shores of majestic Lake Lure in the Blue Ridge Mountains, you can golf, hike, boat, fish, ride horses, or just lounge and be spoiled at this elegant seventeen-room getaway with fabulous views, stone fireplaces, terraces and distinctive dining. A wonderful combination of an elegant country inn and a casual bed and breakfast, the Lodge is situated on the hillside to afford a sweeping view of the lake and mountains. The Lodge has recently been brilliantly renovated, with much larger guest rooms, fabulous bathrooms and private decks from many of the rooms. During the warmer months, swim, boat and fish from our beautiful lakeside dock.

Rooms/Rates
16 Guest Rooms. $149/$245, based on single or double occupancy. All guest rooms have beautiful private bathrooms and have been individually decorated with country antiques. Many rooms have terraces or balconies overlooking the lake.

Cuisine
Price includes a full breakfast, afternoon coffee, tea and pastries, and evening wine and hors d'oeuvres. On Thursday, Friday and Saturday evenings we serve a full-course dinner by reservation only.

Nearest Airport(s)
Asheville Regional

Directions
The Lodge is located on Lake Lure, just off of Highway 64/74A in scenic Hickory Nut Gorge, 30 miles SE of Asheville.

Member Since 2003

"Exquisite rooms, dining and service have made this our favorite place in the mountains!"

The Orchard Inn

www.orchardinn.com
Highway 176, P.O. Box 128, Saluda, NC 28773
800-581-3800 • 828-749-5471 • Fax 828-749-9805
innkeeper@orchardinn.com

Innkeepers/Owners
Kathy & Bob Thompson
Charley & Robert Thompson

Traditional Mountain Inn

No matter where you start, The Orchard Inn is a perfect destination. Situated on a 12-acre mountaintop with stunning views, this national historic structure has long been a favorite retreat with its wraparound porches and large, inviting living room with stone fireplace. Guest quarters are furnished with period pieces and antiques. Cottages feature fireplaces, whirlpools, and private decks. Enjoy award-winning cuisine while overlooking the gardens, vineyard and mountains. Walk to waterfalls, hike nearby trails, watch the birds, visit Biltmore Estate, Carl Sandburg's home, or local craft galleries, then experience the peace and tranquility of this gracious retreat.

Rooms/Rates
9 Rooms, $139/$189 B&B;
5 Cottages, $169/$395 B&B.
All rooms have private baths, some with whirlpool and steam shower. Open year-round.

Cuisine
A full breakfast is included in room rate. Award-winning cuisine served by reservation Thurs-Sat evenings. Fine wines and beer available. Listed as a 'Food Find' by *Southern Living*.

Nearest Airport(s)
Asheville, NC

Directions
Airports Asheville and Charlotte NC and Greenville SC to Interstate 26. From I-26,take Exit 59 (old Exit 28) Saluda NC, head west up hill 1 mile to Hwy.176. Turn LEFT on Hwy.176, and the Inn will be 1/2 mile on right.

Member Since 1985

"I feel like I'm letting folks in on a special secret when I tell them about this Inn."

Pine Crest Inn

www.srinns.com/pinecrestinn
85 Pine Crest Lane, Tryon, NC 28782
800-633-3001 • 828-859-9135 • Fax 828-859-9136
select@pinecrestinn.com

Owner/General Manager
Carl Caudle

Elegant Mountain Inn

AAA ◆◆◆◆

Rooms/Rates
20 Rooms, $89/$199;
8 Suites, $179/$349. 4 cottages, $139/$559 B&B.

Cuisine
Hot breakfast each day for guests included in rate. The restaurant at Pine Crest Inn offers gourmet American cuisine with regional accents. Award-winning wine collection and full beverage service available every day.

Nearest Airport(s)
Greenville

Directions
From I-26, exit 36 in Columbus, NC to Hwy 108. Follow Hwy 108 to town of Tryon. At intersection of Hwy 108 (Trade St) and New Market Rd. turn L onto New Market Rd. Proceed 1/8 mile to Pine Crest Ln. Turn L onto Pine Crest Ln., follow to Pine Crest Inn.

Nestled in the foothills of the Blue Ridge Mountains since 1917, the Pine Crest Inn is in the heart of North Carolina's Hunt Country. Once a favorite of F. Scott Fitzgerald and Ernest Hemingway, the Inn is listed on the National Register of Historic Places. Crisp mountain air, stone fireplaces, wide verandas and well-manicured grounds create a relaxing atmosphere of casual elegance. The Inn's 35 rooms, suites, and cottages are individually decorated, have cable TV, VCRs, telephones and private baths; most have fireplaces. The Inn's Conference Center combines advanced audio-visual equipment and wireless Internet access with elegant furnishings to provide the perfect place for your executive retreat, seminar or training session. Tea/lemonade and cookies are offered every afternoon, with sherry and port provided to guests in the early evening. AAA Four Diamond award for both the Inn and the restaurant.

Member Since 1991

"We loved the solitude & beautiful flower gardens, but the impeccable service made our stay!"

The Mast Farm Inn

www.srinns.com/mastfarminn
2543 Broadstone Road, P.O. Box 704, Valle Crucis, NC 28691
888-963-5857 • 828-963-5857 • Fax 828-963-6404
stay@mastfarminn.com

Innkeepers/Owners
Kay Hinshaw Philipp and Wanda Hinshaw

Rustic Mountain Inn

The Mast Farm Inn is more than a bed and breakfast, with inn rooms, private getaway cottages, fine dining and great wines, organic gardens, and unique gifts completing our historic country appeal. The key to the Inn's success, however, lies in the exceptionally friendly and caring service offered to lodging and dinner guests alike.

With inspired restoration and continuing care, the Inn continues to welcome guests, as it did over 100 years ago. Choose from 8 guest rooms in our 1880s farmhouse and 7 cottages, some restored from original farm buildings. Cottages range in size from cozy ones suitable for a couple to large ones for up to six guests. All are unique spaces.

The inn's restaurant is celebrated, enjoyed by lodging guests and locals. The service is attentive, yet relaxed and friendly. Enjoy fireside or terrace dining, depending on the season.

The current innkeepers place special emphasis on the environment, creating a "green" inn where recycling, reducing waste, and buying organic produce locally are taken seriously.

Member Since 1988

Rooms/Rates
Eight guest rooms: $145/$250. Seven private cottages: $225/$450.

Cuisine
Full 2-course gourmet breakfast included with lodging. Dinner features fresh, organic delightfully creative cuisine. Dining schedule varies seasonally. Fine wines & beer available. Private parties.

Nearest Airport(s)
Greensboro (GSO) or Charlotte (CLT)

Directions
Boone/Blowing Rock/Banner Elk area. From E & S: turn at V.C. sign on 105 betw Boone & Linville. Inn is 2.5 mi from 105 on Broadstone Rd. From W & N: take 194 from 321/421 west of Boone. In V.C., continue STRAIGHT on Broadstone Rd. to the Inn, 1/4 mile on the right.

"...genuine warmth and hospitality...a unique inn that is wonderfully regional...delightful"

Gideon Ridge Inn

www.srinns.com/gideonridge
202 Gideon Ridge Rd., P.O. Box 1929, Blowing Rock, NC 28605
888-889-4036 • 828-295-3644 • Fax 828-295-4586
Innkeeper@gideonridge.com

Innkeepers/Owners
Cindy & Cobb Milner
Elegant Mountain Inn

Rooms/Rates
10 Rooms, including 3 Deluxe Suites, and 3 Terrace Rooms. 9 rooms have fireplaces. 4 have whirlpools. All rooms B&B. $125/$315. Open year-round.

Cuisine
Full breakfast included, featuring cornmeal pancakes, blueberry-stuffed French Toast or other signature entrees. Afternoon tea with fresh-made shortbread cookies or scones. Dinner served Tu.-Sat. Five course meal with choice of entree. Full wine list.

Nearest Airport(s)
Charlotte; Greensboro

Directions
US 321, 1.5 mi. S of Village of Blowing Rock, turn on Rock Rd. across from Green Park Inn. 1st L on Gideon Ridge Rd. Go to top of the ridge.

Gideon Ridge Inn is ten delightful guest rooms with mountain breezes, French doors and stone terraces. Ceiling fans and wicker chairs. Antiques and good books. Fine breakfasts to linger over. Earl Grey Tea and fresh-baked shortbread cookies to savor. Evening dining with a five-course meal and fine wine list. Bedrooms with warm fireplaces and comfortable sitting areas. Crisp cotton bed linens and well-appointed bathrooms. Suites with whirlpool tubs and massive king beds. And in the library, a piano with a breathtaking view of the mountains. Really...

Guests enjoy hiking and walking, The Blue Ridge Parkway, Golf at nearby clubs and Blowing Rock Village shops.

Member Since 1990

"I always find magical moments at Gideon Ridge Inn... Such elegance and intimacy... The views of the mountains are truly spectacular."

Inn at Ragged Gardens

www.ragged-gardens.com
203 Sunset Drive, Blowing Rock, NC 28605
828-295-9703 • Fax 828-295-6534
innkeeper@ragged-gardens.com

Proprietors
Lee Hyett

Traditional Village Inn

Bordered by a rock wall acre of lush lawn and gardens, is an Arts and Craft style manor whose curb appeal has welcomed guests for a century. Garden theme rooms offering splendid in-room amenities are tailored for guests' comfort; fireplaces, ceiling fans, A/C, whirlpool baths, sitting areas, balconies and patios. Butler pantry refreshments offer tempting delights. Breakfast is served gardenside in the intimate dining room, offering a gourmet breakfast and fresh baked muffins, biscuits, croissants, etc. Not to be overlooked is the Blue Ridge Mountain charm, attentive service and attention to detail of the innkeepers and their staff in this elegant village inn.

Rooms/Rates
4 Rooms, $140/$220; 7 Suites, $185/$310 B&B. Well-appointed interiors, hand-pressed linens, whirlpool baths, fireplaces, AC. Open year-round.

Cuisine
Full breakfast. Butler pantry refreshments. Evening wine/hors d'oeuvres. Fireplaces in two of the rooms.

Nearest Airport(s)
Charlotte/Douglas International

Directions
Turn W at stoplight intersection of Hwy. 321 by-pass & Sunset Dr. Inn 2 blocks on R. Or from village center, 1 block E on Sunset Dr. Inn on L.

Member Since 2001

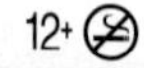   

"Great and grand artistry, creativity, and comfort." "Simplistic elegance." "Welcome warmth."

General Manager
Billy Maddalon
Guest Service Manager
Linda Kiss

Southern Georgian Estate Inn 

AAA ◆◆◆

The Morehead Inn

www.srinns.com/moreheadinn
1122 East Morehead Street, Charlotte, NC 28204
888-MOREHEAD • 704-376-3357 • Fax 704-335-1110
reservation@moreheadinn.com

Rooms/Rates
6 Rooms $120/$155, 6 Suites $160/$190. All rooms are elegantly appointed with period antiques and private baths. Open year-round

Cuisine
Full breakfast consists of fresh-baked breads and pastries, waffles, eggs & fresh fruits. Full bar is service available with a substantial wine list.

Nearest Airport(s)
Charlotte-Douglas Int'l

Directions
From I-77 S: Exit at Morehead St. Take L onto Morehead St., Inn is on R, one and one half miles. From I-85: Take I-77 S. From I-77 N, take I-277, Exit Kenilworth Ave. Take R onto Kenilworth. Take R onto Morehead St. Inn will be on L, 200 yards.

Located in Charlotte's oldest neighborhood, known as Dilworth, the inn is one mile from the center of the uptown business district. The historic home was built in 1917, by a businessman who required a wonderful place in which to entertain. Today, the inn stands as Charlotte's finest example of Southern hospitality. The Morehead Inn offers six suites and six guest rooms, each with luxurious private baths, color cable TV, and period antiques. The inn's public areas feature intimate fireplaces and grand twelve-foot ceilings. Guests may walk or jog the quiet, stately streets of our affluent community, or walk to an array of wonderful dining. Our guests are also afforded complimentary access to the fitness center and pool of the YMCA, which is located six blocks from the inn. You will discover why Charlotteans refer to The Morehead Inn as 'Charlotte's most unique southern estate.'

Member Since 2002

"Everything was perfect--the room, the breakfast and, most of all, the staff!"
"The Morehead Inn is the only place I'll stay when I'm in the Carolinas."

The Duke Mansion

www.srinns.com/dukemansion
400 Hermitage Road, Charlotte, NC 28207
888-202-1009 • 704-714-4400 • Fax 704-714-4435
frontdesk@tlwf.org

General Manager
Tim Miron

Historic Inn and Meeting Place

The Duke Mansion, built in 1915 and listed on the National Register of Historic Places, offers 20 unique guest rooms in true Southern splendor with a full breakfast. The rooms are residential in their décor, and appointed with beautiful artwork and furnishings, giving you a breathtaking image of what it was like to be a member of the prestigious Duke family who made The Mansion their home. All rooms have queen or king sized beds, private baths, exquisite linens, luxurious robes, and a gourmet goodnight treat. The Mansion is an integral part of Charlotte's most prestigious and beautiful neighborhood, and is situated on four and a half acres of beautiful grounds. Its professional culinary staff and beautiful public rooms can accommodate family or business celebrations of 10-300 guests. When you select The Duke Mansion, you are supporting a nonprofit where all of the proceeds are used to preserve and protect it.

Rooms/Rates
20 Rooms. $169/$249, including breakfast, plus tax. Special seasonal rates also available.

Cuisine
Full-time onsite professional culinary staff featuring New South cuisine.

Nearest Airport(s)
Charlotte-Douglas International Airport, 20 minutes

Directions
From Brookshire Freeway, take 3rd Street exit, turn left. 3rd turns into Providence. Follow Providence to Hermitage Road, turn R. Take second entrance into The Mansion is on the left.

Member Since 2005

   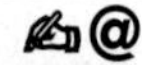 

"We truly felt like we were guests in an elegant Southern home."

Arrowhead Inn

www.srinns.com/arrowheadinn
106 Mason Road, Durham, NC 27712
800-528-2207 • 919-477-8430 • Fax 919-471-9538
info@arrowheadinn.com

Innkeepers/Owners
Gloria and Phil Teber

Elegant In Town
Breakfast Inn

AAA ◆◆◆◆

Rooms/Rates
9 rooms & suites including Cottage and Cabin $130/$295. Whirlpools, steam showers & fireplaces. Corporate & mid-week rates. Specializing in peaceful getaways, small weddings, family gatherings, business retreats.

Cuisine
Our delicious homemade breakfasts offer puffed pancakes, blueberry french toast, fresh herbed frittatas, glazed scones, and baked fruits. Our chef/owner will prepare five-course gourmet dinners served in lovely romantic setting.

Nearest Airport(s)
Raleigh/Durham

Directions
Take I-85 to Exit 176 and turn north. Travel 7 miles on Rt.501 North to Mason Rd and turn left.

Relax in the quiet comfort of our 18th century plantation home. The Arrowhead Inn rests on six acres of gardens and lawns amid venerable magnolia and pecan trees. Each of our elegant guest rooms, Log Cabin, and Garden Cottage provide a serene respite with the amenities of a fine hotel. The Arrowhead Inn, built circa 1775, has been carefully renovated retaining original moldings, mantelpieces, and heart-of-pine floors. Watch hummingbirds flutter on flowering hibiscus while relaxing with friends on our sun-warmed patio. Drift off for an afternoon nap next to your cozy fireplace. Unwind in your private whirlpool while enjoying fine wine and savory delicacies. Refresh yourself in your soothing steam shower. Awake to the delight of our abundant breakfast feast. Enjoy fine wines and a dinner feast at the Inn.

Member Since 2003

"Everything was superb-from the furnishings and service to the gourmet food...compliments to you on the right blend of class & warm hospitality!"

The Lords Proprietors' Inn

www.srinns.com/lordsproprietors
300 North Broad Street, Edenton, NC 27932
888-482-3907 • 252-482-3641 • Fax 252-482-2432
stay@edentoninn.com

Innkeepers/Owners
Arch & Jane Edwards
Traditional Village Inn

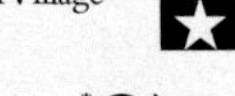

The Lords Proprietors' Inn comprises three restored homes on over an acre of grounds in the Historic District of Edenton with sixteen fully equipped and beautifully decorated guest rooms, and two luxury suites. Three spacious parlors with fireplaces, a library, and wonderful big porches are inviting places where guests enjoy our homemade cookies and tea in the afternoon, or a cordial in the evening. The Whedbee House dining room provides the setting for truly fine dining. Chef Kevin's cuisine is sophisticated, with a distinct taste of the region. A gratifying number of guests leave their table saying their supper was one of the very best they have ever enjoyed.

Rooms/Rates
Rates for our sixteen rooms are $155, $170 or $190 plus tax, for double occupancy. The rate for our two suites is $260. Single occupancy rates are available. Special package rates are described on our website.

Cuisine
A full country breakfast is served seven days a week, and is included in your rate. A fabulous four-course dinner is served by reservation only Tuesday through Saturday.

Nearest Airport(s)
Norfolk, Virginia (ORF). Approximately 1.5 hours.

Directions
From Raleigh - US 64 E to US 17 N; Norfolk - US 17 S; Washington, DC - I-95 S to US 460-E to Virginia/NC 32 S; Wilmington - US 17 N.

Member Since 1990

"We were wowed by everything here, including the wonderful food! My husband felt that his dessert was the best thing he has ever eaten."

Proprietors
Bebe & Robert Woody
General Manager
Beth Gallagher
Elegant Village Breakfast Inn

AAA ◆◆◆

White Doe Inn

www.srinns.com/whitedoeinn
319 Sir Walter Raleigh Street, Post Office Box 1029, Manteo, NC 27954
800-473-6091 • 252-473-9851 • Fax 252-473-4708
whitedoe@whitedoeinn.com

Rooms/Rates
8 Rooms. $150/$250. All rates are per night, per room.

Cuisine
An important part of the Bed & Breakfast experience is the food. The White Doe Inn is pleased to provide outstanding service and a delicious full four-course seated and served breakfast that will delight your palate and be pleasing to the eye.

Nearest Airport(s)
Norfolk International Airport, VA

Directions
Go South on VA-168 to the NC border. Once in North Carolina, US-168 merges into US-158 East. Stay on this road. Follow US-158 East to the Outer Banks. At Mile Post 16 turn West on US-64/264 crossing the George Washington Baum Bridge to Roanoke Island and Manteo.

As one of the most photographed historic homes on Roanoke Island, The White Doe Inn Bed & Breakfast has been welcoming guests since the turn-of-the-century. For years, visitors have admired its beautiful architectural details and old world charm. Now guests come from near and far to experience gracious hospitality in this lovely old home. Located in the heart of the Outer Banks, just minutes from the Atlantic Ocean and its beautiful beaches. The White Doe Inn is listed on the National Register of Historic Places and is noted for its historic and architectural significance. The Inn has been awarded the AAA Three Diamond Rating, and we are also members of the North Carolina Bed & Breakfast Inns and the Professional Association of International Innkeepers.

Member Since 2005

"This is a place of what the Italians call laniappe, the extra touch, the exquisite detail, they know what you need before you do..."

The Verandas

www.srinns.com/theverandas
202 Nun Street, Wilmington, NC 28401
910-251-2212 • Fax 910-251-8932
verandas4@aol.com

Towering above a quiet tree-lined street in the historic district stands this grand antebellum mansion. Built in 1854, the award-winning Inn is a blend of history, luxury, charm and hospitality. Guest space abounds with wonderful colors, original art, French and English antiques. Four verandas, garden terrace and cupola offer hideaways. Professionally decorated guestrooms have sitting areas, telephone, cable TV, PC jacks. Hand-ironed linens dress comfortable beds. Baths have soaking tubs, showers, marble floors, luxury amenities and robes. French pressed coffee with a gourmet breakfast. Complimentary beverages and snacks and social wine hour.

Member Since 2001

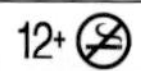

Owners
Dennis Madsen and Chuck Pennington

Elegant In Town Breakfast Inn

Mobil ★★★
AAA ◆◆◆◆

Rooms/Rates
8 Corner Rooms, $150/$250, two-night weekends. Open year-round except December 24-26.

Cuisine
Included with the room is a full gourmet breakfast with French pressed coffee served in our beautiful dining room. Complimentary beverages are always available and white wine is served each evening.

Nearest Airport(s)
Wilmington International

Directions
I-40 to exit 8 L on Rte. 17 for 4.5 miles L on 3rd. St. for 4 blocks R on Nun St. next corner. Rtes. 17, 74, 76 going North: cross drawbridge L on 3rd St. for 4 blocks, L on Nun St. next corner.

"Our thirty-eigth visit was as wonderful as our first. Thanks Chuck and Dennis!"

Ohio

"The Buckeye State"

Famous For: Cincinnati Zoo, Cincinnati Union Terminal, Taft Museum, Neil Armstrong Air and Space Museum, Put-in-Bay Village and Perry Memorial (largest Doric column in the world), Rolling Hills, Farmlands, Burial Mounds, Steel Mills, Automobile Factories, Rubber, Plastics, Chemicals

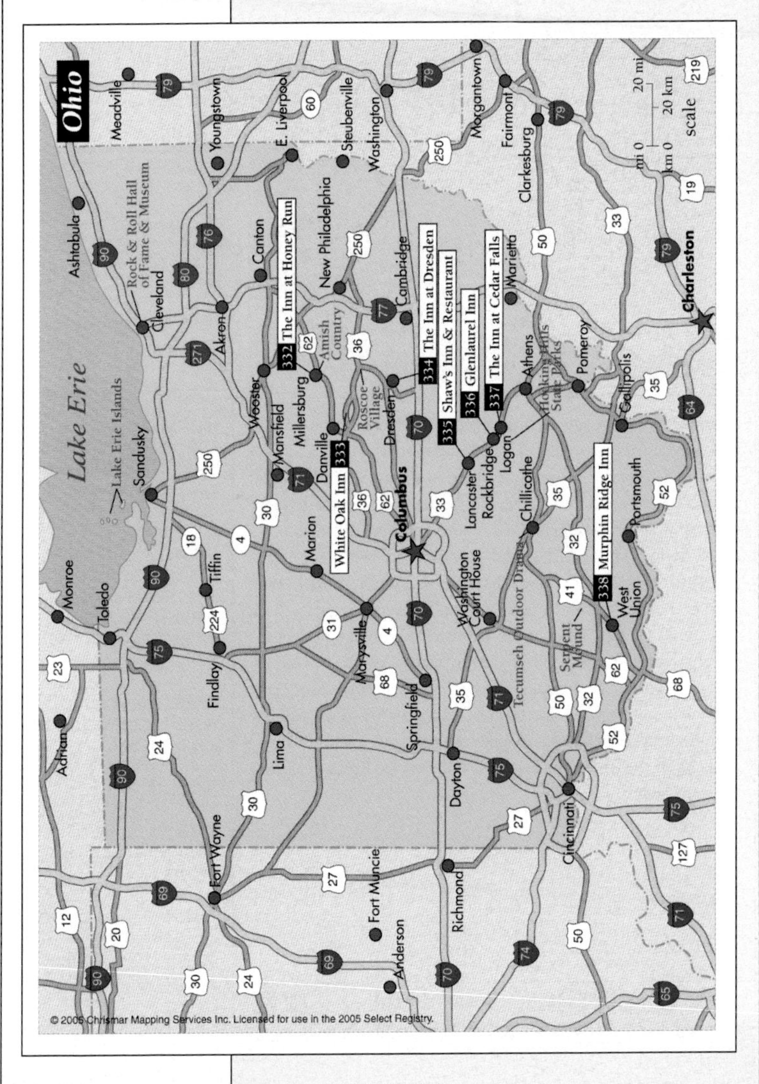

The Inn at Honey Run

www.srinns.com/honeyrun
6920 County Road 203, Millersburg, OH 44654
800-468-6639 • 330-674-0011 • Fax 330-674-2623
info@innathoneyrun.com

Innkeeper/Owner
Phillip Jenkins

Contemporary Country Inn

A prize-winning contemporary Inn located amidst the world's largest Amish community. The Inn at Honey Run provides a chance to recharge batteries and refresh souls. Located on 60 acres of woods and pasture, the Inn offers privacy and serenity in various accomodations. 24 uniquely decorated rooms in its Main Lodge; 12 earth-sheltered Honeycombs with stone fireplaces, patios and shower/whirlpool tubs; 2 guest cottages each with two bedrooms and a honeymoon/anniversary cottage with jacuzzi. Three VIP suites at the Monarch House are perfect for private getaways! Watch birds from picture windows, read by blazing fireplaces, and explore the sights and backroads of Holmes County. Enjoy seasonal educational symposiums, Sunday evening fireside presentations, hike on our private trails or enjoy cocktails in the Pheasant's Lounge. Full Service Executive Conference Center.

Rooms/Rates
43 Rooms, $99/$310 Full Service; including 3 Guest Cottages and VIP Suites. All include continental breakfast buffet.

Cuisine
Breakfast served daily. Lunch and dinner reservations required. Fine wine and beer served in dining room. Cocktails served in the lounge.

Nearest Airport(s)
Local airport in Millersburg. Just a few hours away.

Directions
From Millersburg: Rts 62/39 (E) for 2 blocks, L on Rt 241 N for 1.9 miles R (E) on County Rd 203 for 1.5 miles.

Member Since 2003

"WOW! The world and all the stress disappeared the instant I turned into your drive."

The White Oak Inn

www.srinns.com/whiteoakinn
29683 Walhonding Rd (SR715), Danville, OH 43014
877-908-5923 • 740-599-6107
info@whiteoakinn.com

Innkeepers/Owners
Yvonne & Ian Martin
Traditional Arts and Crafts Country Inn 

We invite you to visit our turn-of-the-century farmhouse in a quiet wooded country setting. The inn has ten comfortable, antique-filled guest rooms and two luxury log-cabin cottages. Enjoy a candlelit dinner in the inn's dining room, or a romantic dinner basket delivered to your room. Visit Ohio's Amish area, Roscoe Village, or Longaberger baskets. Tour local wineries. Hike the local trails, or go golfing or canoeing. Or simply spend your time soaking up the peace and quiet. Let us entertain you at a Murder Mystery, Theater event, Coffee and Chocolate tasting or a Nature weekend. Facilities are available for weddings, retreats and parties. The inn has received three major awards from *Inn Traveler* Magazine, including "Best Weekend Escape" for 2004. Come join us soon. The cookie jar is always full.

Rooms/Rates
10 Rooms and 2 cottages, $110/$195 B&B. Fireplaces and whirlpool tubs in some rooms. Weekend packages including dinners from $315 a couple.

Cuisine
Generous country breakfast included in room rate. Inn guests can enjoy candlelit dinners featuring heartland cuisine, or dinner picnic baskets delivered to the room, by advance reservation. BYOB.

Nearest Airport(s)
Columbus - 55 miles

Directions
From I71: Rte 36E or Rte 13S to Mount Vernon. Then Rte 36E 13 Mi to Rte 715. The inn is 3 miles East on SR715. From I-77: Rte 36W 35 mi to Rte 206N. 2 mi to Rte 715. The inn is 4 miles W on SR715.

Member Since 1989

"We loved the peaceful country setting and charm of the inn. The meals were delicious."

The Inn at Dresden

www.srinns.com/innatdresden
209 Ames Drive, Dresden, OH 43821
800-373-7336 • 740-754-1122 • Fax 740-754-9856
info@theinnatdresden.com

Innkeeper/Owner
Patricia Lyall
Village
Breakfast Inn

Tucked away among the rolling hills of southeastern Ohio, The Inn at Dresden provides the perfect setting for a relaxing getaway with family and friends, or a quiet weekend with someone special. Originally built by Dave Longaberger, founder of Longaberger Baskets, this elegant Tudor home offers guests a panoramic view of Dresden and the surrounding countryside. Guests at the Inn enjoy an evening social hour and a full buffet breakfast. Individually decorated rooms feature VCRs, CD players and special ammenities such as wraparound private decks, two person Jacuzzi tubs and gas-log fireplaces.

Rooms/Rates
10 Rooms $85/$170 per night. Each room is individually decorated to depict the area. Many rooms have fireplaces, decks and Jacuzzi tubs.

Cuisine
The Inn provides an evening social hour and full breakfast. Menus are available for all restaurants in the surrounding area.

Nearest Airport(s)
Columbus Airport

Directions
The Inn may be reached by SR 60N or Northpointe Dr. from Zanesville, or SR 16 from Newark or Coshocton.

Member Since 2000

"This is our ninth visit. We thank you for all the beautiful hospitality, the wonderful food, and the bluebirds."

Shaw's Restaurant & Inn

www.shawsinn.com
123 North Broad St., Lancaster, OH 43130
800-654-2477 • 740-654-1842 • Fax 740-654-7032
shaws@greenapple.com

Innkeepers/Owners
Bruce & Nancy Cork
Classic In Town
Small Hotel

Mobil ★★★
AAA ◆◆◆

Rooms/Rates
24 Rooms. Whirlpool Rooms $145/$198
Deluxe Rooms $120
Standard Rooms $83
Double Occupancy
Full Breakfast is Included.

Cuisine
Known for Steaks, Prime Rib, and Seafood. Pasta, Small Plates. Changing Seasonal Menu-- Holiday Dinners. Wine Spectator Award of Excellence.

Nearest Airport(s)
Port Columbus Airport

Directions
From Columbus: Rt. 33 East to Lancaster. Left on Main. Two blocks, Left on Broad.

From Hocking Hills: Rt. 33 West to Lancaster. Right on Main, Left on Broad.

Located on a tree-shaded square in historic downtown Lancaster, Shaw's has been described as "A unique blend of country freshness and well traveled sophistication". Just minutes from Hocking Hills, Shaw's Inn offers nine individually decorated theme rooms with large in-room whirlpool tubs, including the Napa Valley, The Pearl, The Caribbean, and Louis XIV. Full breakfast in the restaurant is included with all rooms. Shaw's Restaurant has a reputation for New York Strip, Filet Mignon with Bearnaise Sauce, Prime Rib, and Fresh Seafood. The Chef creates a constantly changing menu with seasonal items--Spring Lamb, Soft Shell Crab, Fresh Walleye, 4-pound Lobster, and many others. Add to your Holiday Festivities with four weeks of Christmas Dinners. Cork's Bar, serving every day (Sunday after 1:00), has a warm setting of dark wood and brass. Free High-Speed Wireless Internet Access Throughout. Nearby attractions include: The Sherman House, The Decorative Arts Center of Ohio, The Georgian, and The Ohio Glass Museum.

Member Since 2005

"..a uniquely pleasant experience...rooms are a delight...staff attentive"
"..fresh and creative menu.." "..relaxed environment, yet elegant.."

Glenlaurel - A Scottish Country Inn

www.srinns.com/glenlaurel
14940 Mt. Olive Road, Rockbridge, OH 43149-9736
800-809-REST • 740-385-4070 • Fax 740-385-9669
Info@glenlaurel.com

Innkeeper
Michael Daniels

Elegant Old World
Country Breakfast Inn

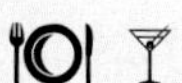

Sometimes at dinner, the story is told of how Glenlaurel was first imagined—300 years ago in the heart of the Scottish Highlands. Today, the heavily wooded 140 acre estate has a look of the old world, a veil of romance, a pace of times gone by and a quiet, almost forgotten. Whether in the stately Manor House, the nearby Carriage House or one of the wee cottages on Thistle Ridge, Glenlaurel defines pampering as lazy kidless afternoons, sumptuous fine dining for two, hot tub frolics, intimate fireside secrets, sleeping past 7, hearty breakfast choices and a morning walk through Camusfearna Gorge with ne'er a soul in sight. The Anniversary Club honors a successful marriage--year after year. Labeled the premier romantic getaway in the Midwest, every BODY deserves a wee bit o'Glenlaurel.

Rooms/Rates
3 Suites $189/$239 B&B,
4 Rooms $119/$199 B&B,
7 Crofts $219/$269 B&B,
6 Cottages $269/$319 B&B.
Always Open.

Cuisine
Dinner is "a private invitation to dine at an estate house in the country" with social hour, greetings from your host and a candlelit culinary adventure "in the European tradition."

Nearest Airport(s)
Port Columbus

Directions
From N, take 33 thru Lancaster 12 mi to 180 exit, R onto 180, 4.8 mi, L at sign for .5 mi. From W, take 180 thru Laurelville 10 mi. From S, take 33 around Athens 30 mi to 180 exit, L onto 180, 4.8 mi. From E, use 33.

Member Since 1998

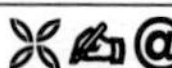

Named one of "our 25 favorite destinations" by *Midwest Living* Magazine in July 2003.

Innkeepers/Owners
Ellen Grinsfelder and Terry Lingo

Rustic Country Inn 

AAA ◆◆◆

The Inn At Cedar Falls

www.srinns.com/cedarfalls
21190 State Route 374, Logan, OH 43138
800-653-2557 • 740-385-7489 • Fax 740-385-0820
info@innatcedarfalls.com

Rooms/Rates
9 Rooms,$89/$119 B&B;
12 Cottages,$139/$209 B&B;
6 Cabins, $159/$259 B&B

Cuisine
Watch meals being created in the open kichen. Hearty country breakfasts, delectable lunches, sumptuous dinners by candle-light. Patio dining in the warm months. We offer an array of fine wines, beers and after dinner drinks.

Nearest Airport(s)
Columbus which is 50 miles.

Directions
From Columbus, U.S. Rte. 33S to Logan-Bremen Exit 664S, R on 664, 9.5 miles, L on St Rte. 374, Inn is 1 mile on L. From Cincy, 71N to Washington CH, take 35E to 22E. In Circleville, access 56E to St. Rte. 374, turn L, Inn is 2 1/2 miles on R.

The restored and comfortably rustic 1840 log houses are an open kitchen-dining room, serving the most refined of American cuisine. Antique appointed guest rooms in a barn-like structure have rockers and writing desks and offer sweeping views of meadows, woods and wildlife. We have quaint cottages ideal for two, or secluded, fully-equipped 19th century log cabins accommodating up to four. Casual fine dining for lunch and dinner is served on the patio or the 1840's log cabins. The rugged and beautiful Hocking Hills State Parks with glorious caves and waterfalls flanks the Inn's 75 acres on three sides. Casual and avid hikers will enjoy Old Man's Cave, Cedar Falls, Ash Cave and Conkle's Hollow. A variety of cooking classes, wine tastings, BBQ patio parties and hikes like morel hunting are scheduled year round. Call for a calendar of events and off season rates and specials.

Member Since 1989

"Could there be any better place to recharge and reconnect?" "The Inn made magic happen." "Meals were delicious and beautifully served."

Murphin Ridge Inn

www.srinns.com/murphinridge
750 Murphin Ridge Rd., West Union, OH 45693
877-687-7446 • 937-544-2263 • Fax 937-544-8151
murphinn@bright.net

Innkeepers/Owners
Sherry & Darryl McKenney
Traditional Country Inn

AAA ◆◆◆

Selected by *National Geographic Traveler* as one of the top 54 Inns in the U.S. and achieving a prestegious spot on the National Geographic Geotourism MapGuide—this prize-winning Inn welcomes you to 142 acres of four-season beauty. The Inn showcases the Guest House with spacious rooms, some with fireplaces or porches, and nine romantic cabins, as shown above, each with fireplace, two person whirlpool, two person shower and porch. All are decorated with David T. Smith Early American and Shaker reproduction furniture. The 1828 farmhouse features four dining rooms with original fireplaces, and gift shop. Enjoy award winning regional cuisine, in season, gathered from the Inn's gardens. View the Appalachian foothills, enjoy the night sky by the bonfire, and visit local Amish Shops, the Edge of Appalachia Preserve, the Serpent Mound State Memorial, and the Highlands Nature Sanctuary. The Inn has an outdoor pool, hiking, bird-watching, tennis, lawn games and more. Golf is nearby. Perfect for retreats, reunions, and conferences.

Member Since 1992

Rooms/Rates
10 rooms, $104/$135. 9 cabins, $170/$225. All with private baths.

Cuisine
Award-winning country inn fine dining. Full breakfast. The chef and staff make dining a charming experience that brings guests back time and again. Selected fine wine and premium beer available in the Dining House. Inn Guests Dine Nightly.

Nearest Airport(s)
Cincinnati/Northern Kentucky Int'l

Directions
FROM CINCINNATI: SR 32E., Right on Unity Rd. 2-1/2 mi. to Stop Sign turn Left on Wheat Ridge Rd. 2-7/10 mi. to Left on Murphin Ridge Rd. FROM COLUMBUS: SR 23 to 32W. Left on 41S to Right on Wheat Ridge Road at Dunkinsville. 1-1/2 mi. to Right on Murphin Ridge.

"R&R for the soul! Great hosts, accommodations, food, and trails worthy of frequent visits."

Oklahoma

"The Sooner State"

Famous For: Will Rogers Memorial, Alabaster Caverns State Park, National Cowboy Hall of Fame, Pioneer Woman Statue, Cattle Ranching, Oral Roberts University, Oil, Plastics, Rubber, Cotton.

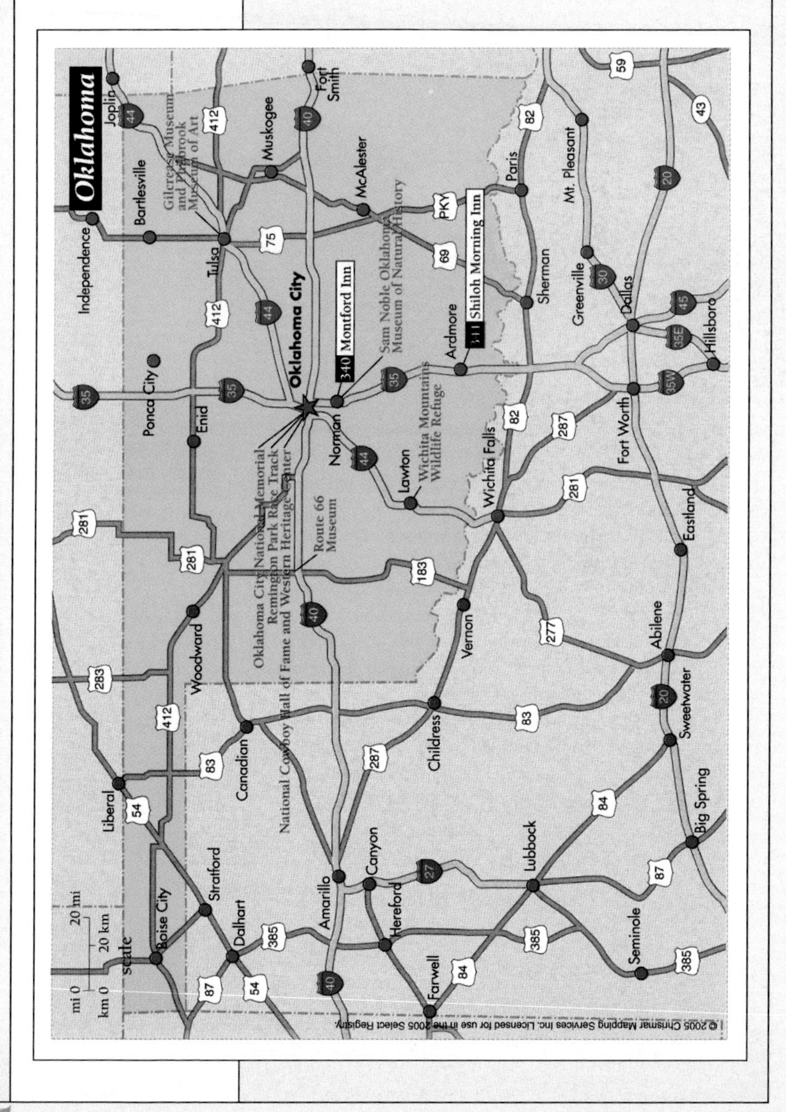

Montford Inn & Cottages

www.srinns.com/montford
322 W. Tonhawa, Norman, OK 73069
800-321-8969 • 405-321-2200 • Fax 405-321-8347
innkeeper@montfordinn.com

Innkeepers/Owners
Phyllis & Ron Murray, William & Ginger Murray

Traditional In Town Breakfast Inn

Mobil ★★★
AAA ◆◆◆

Celebrating their 11th year of operation, the Murrays welcome you to the award-winning Montford Inn and Cottages. With its ten uniquely decorated rooms in the main house, and the six incredible cottage suites, the Montford Inn has everything the discriminating inngoer is looking for in lodging. Located in the heart of Norman's Historic District, this Prairie-style inn envelopes travelers in a relaxing atmosphere. Antiques, family heirlooms and Native American art accent the individually decorated guest rooms and suites. Awaken to rich coffees and a gourmet counry breakfast served in the beautifully appointed dining room or in the more intimate setting of the suites. Relax in private hot tubs. Escape in luxurious whirlpool bathtubs. Unwind in elegant cottage suites. Stroll through beautiful gardens. Find your heart... at the Montford Inn and Cottages! Featured in *Southern Living, Country, Holiday, Fodor's, Oklahoma Today*.

Member Since 1997

Rooms/Rates
10 Rooms, $90/$169 B&B; 6 Cottage Suites, $120/$219 B&B. Open year-round, main inn closed Christmas Eve and Christmas Day. Cottage suites open all year.

Cuisine
Gourmet Breakfast served in cottages and dining room. Complimentary wine and refreshments early evening.

Nearest Airport(s)
Will Rogers World Airport in Oklahoma City

Directions
20 minutes S of Oklahoma City. From I-35, take Main St., Downtown exit 109. Turn L on University (about 2.2 miles from I-35). Go 2 blocks, turn R 1/2 block on Tonhawa.

"Hospitality at it's finest! The Murrays and the Montford staff made us feel so welcome."

Innkeepers/Owners
Bob & Linda Humphrey

Elegant Country Inn

Shiloh Morning Inn & Cottages

www.srinns.com/shilohmorning
2179 Ponderosa Road, Ardmore, OK 73401
888-554-7674 • 580-223-9500 • Fax 580-223-9615
innkeepers@shilohmorning.com

Oklahoma's premier country inn, Shiloh Morning Inn is located on 73 beautifully wooded acres, just minutes off I-35, yet a world away. Uniquely designed suites and cottages offer large luxurious baths, king beds, fireplaces, TV/VCR/DVD, private hot tubs or jetted tubs for two, and a private balcony, patio, or deck. Guests choose from an extensive library of movies and books. Walking trails are dotted with hammocks and park benches. Wildlife abounds. Privacy is a number one priority. Two new cottages take luxury to a new level. Roadrunner Hideaway is so secluded, its occupants are furnished with a personal golf cart. They will enjoy watching deer, or soaking in a hot tub on a deck cantilevered into the trees. The Villa at Shiloh is a two story cottage for the ultimate quixotic experience including an upstairs jetted tub for two, a spa shower, and a downstairs outdoor room with hot tub. The perfect romantic getaway for couples seeking the quiet seclusion of a rural countryside, Shiloh Morning Inn is truly a "Place of Peace & Rest."

Rooms/Rates
5 luxurious suites and 4 very private cottages. $139/$269. Two night minimum on weekends. Some holidays three night minimum. Closed Thanksgiving and Christmas.

Cuisine
Three course gourmet breakfast at tables for two in the dining room is included. Dinner by advance reservation available for intimate in-room dining.In-room complimentary soft drinks, juices, bottled water, coffees, and teas. Late afternoon wine & cheese available on weekends.

Nearest Airport(s)
Dallas (DFW)

Directions
Map sent with reservation confirmation. Gated Entry.

Member Since 2004

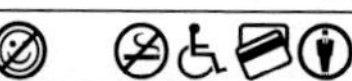

"Shiloh Morning Inn is the Gold Standard for what a B&B should be."

Oregon

"The Beaver State"

Famous For: The Oregon Trail, Mount Hood, Flowers, Lumber, Wineries, Rose Festival, Crater Lake, Painted Hills National Monument, Columbia River Gorge, Coast Range, Cascade Range, Redwoods, John Day Fossil Beds National Monument, Hart Mountain National Wildlife Refuge

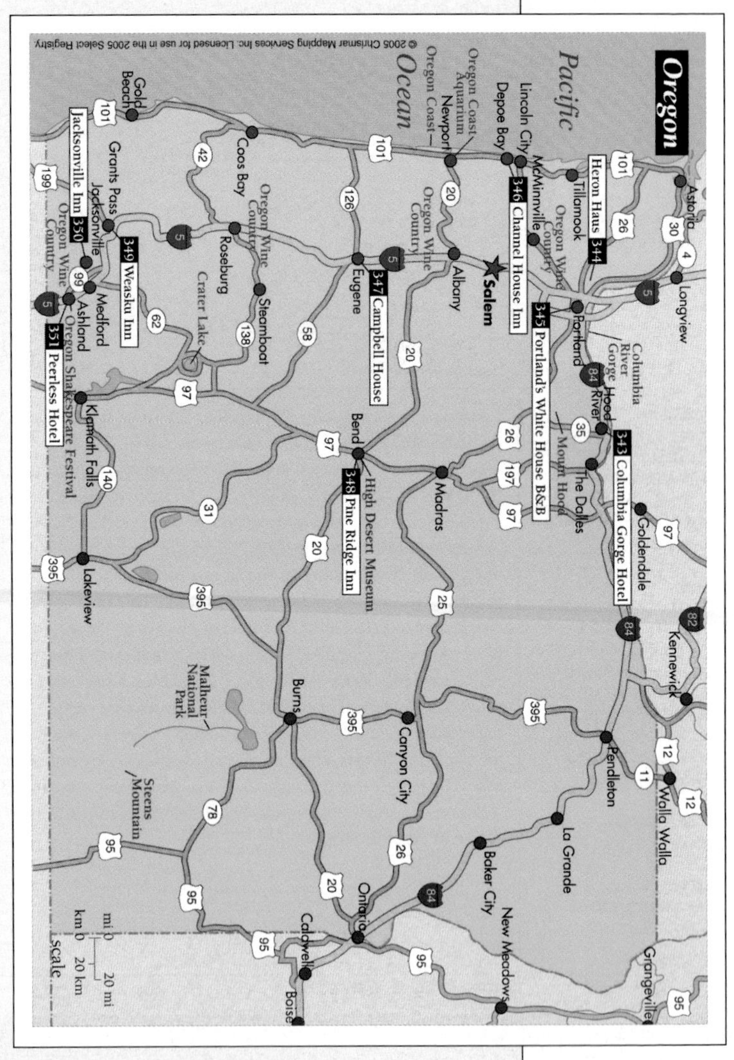

Columbia Gorge Hotel

www.srinns.com/columbiagorge
4000 Westcliff Drive, Hood River, OR 97031
800-345-1921 • 541-386-5566 • Fax 541-386-9141
cghotel@gorge.net

Owners
Boyd and Halla Graves

Elegant Waterside Hotel

Mobil ★★★
AAA ◆◆◆

At the top of a 210-foot waterfall, overlooking the majestic Columbia River Gorge, the Columbia Gorge Hotel, 60 miles east of Portland, has a national reputation for fine cuisine, warm service and elegant surroundings. In the heart of the Columbia Gorge National Scenic area, this historic property has been lovingly restored and boasts 40 fully-appointed guest rooms, an award-winning dining room, full-service lounge, outdoor seating, and exquisite wedding and meeting facilities on 6 beautifully landscaped creek-side acres. Overnight stays include a champagne and caviar hour and the 5-course "World Famous Farm Breakfast." Pets gladly accommodated.

Rooms/Rates
40 Rooms, $199/$279, 2 rooms with gas fireplaces, 5 with electric fireplaces. Rates include nightly champagne and caviar social and the five-course "World Famous Farm Breakfast." Pets welcome with a $25 charge.

Cuisine
Exceptional Northwest continental dining, 'World Famous Farm Breakfast'®. Outdoor dining on the terrace (seasonal). *Wine Spectator Award of Excellence* winner.

Nearest Airport(s)
Portland International Airport (PDX) is an hour away.

Directions
One hour E of Portland on I-84. Take exit 62, turn L. Take next L, hotel on R.

Member Since 1998

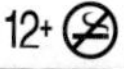

"Oregon's Finest Country Inn"
Northwest Travel Magazine

Heron Haus

www.srinns.com/heronhaus
2545 NW Westover Road, Portland, OR 97210
503-274-1846 • Fax 503-248-4055
julie@heronhaus.com

Owner
Julie Beacon Keppeler

Elegant In Town
Breakfast Inn

This elegant three-story turn-of-the-century tudor sits high in the hills, offering accommodations for both the business traveler and romantic getaways for couples. Each room has sitting areas, work areas, phones with computer hook-ups, and TVs; all have fireplaces. All have queen or king-sized beds. The baths offer special extras—one has a spa on a windowed porch; another has a shower with seven shower heads. Off-street parking is provided. Two and one half blocks down the hill is the Nob Hill area with boutiques, specialty shops, and some of the best eating places in Portland.

Rooms/Rates
6 Rooms, all with fireplaces, TV, sitting areas, phones, wireless/DSL hook-up, work areas, parking, AC: $95/$185 Single; $135/$350 Double. Open year-round.

Cuisine
Continental breakfast.

Nearest Airport(s)
Portland Airport - 20 minute drive lite-rail access

Directions
On website.

Member Since 1994

"An inviting sitting garden provides a quiet and relaxing getaway for the weary visitor."

Portland's White House B&B

www.srinns.com/portlandswhitehouse
1914 NE 22nd Ave., Portland, OR 97212
800-272-7131 • 503-287-7131 • Fax 503-249-1641
pdxwhi@portlandswhitehouse.com

Innkeepers/Owners
Lanning and Steve Holden
General Manager
Trevor Lengle
Historic In Town Mansion

Mobil ★★★
AAA ◆◆◆

Rooms/Rates
8 Rooms. $125/$225. Spa suites include Champange, Moonstuck Chocolate gift box and flat screen televisions.

Cuisine
Fresh, local Breakfast, using SLOW FOODS served in the Main Dining room by candle light. Always vegeterian with Carlton Farms hormone-free breakfast meats. Bread Pudding French Toast. Full Espresso bar.

Nearest Airport(s)
Portland International Airport, within 20 minutes.

Directions
1-5 to Weilder street to NE 22nd, north to NE Hancock. Highway 84 to Llyod Center, right at light, right on Multhnomah, 21st left to NE Hancock.

Situated in Portland's North East Historic Irvington District Portland's White House was built as a summer home in 1911 by Robert Lytle, a wealthy lumber baron. The house was billed as the most expensive home built in the district for the period. This Greek Revival Mansion boasts a lifestyle of past years with 14 massive columns, circular drive and fountain to greet you. Summer days show impressive hanging baskets and wonderful flowers to warm your senses. Restored to its original splendor by Lanning and Steve with sparkling European Chandeliers, formal linened Dining Room, Large Parlor, grand staircase, magnificent leaded glass windows, gilt-gold ceilings, Trompe loiel and Grande Ballroom. Extensive collections of European and Continental Porcelains, 18th and 19th Century oil paintings. Guests rooms appointed with period antiques, paintings, king or queen feather beds and exquisite linens.

Member Since 2004

"Warm and hospitable, beautiful room and charming atmosphere! We'll definitely be back!" Tokyo

Channel House Inn

www.srinns.com/channelhouse
35 Ellingson Street, P.O. Box 56, Depoe Bay, OR 97341
800-447-2140 • 541-765-2140 • Fax 541-765-2191
cfinseth@channelhouse.com

Owners
Carl & Vicki Finseth
Innkeeper
Bart Barrowclough

Contemporary Village
Breakfast Inn

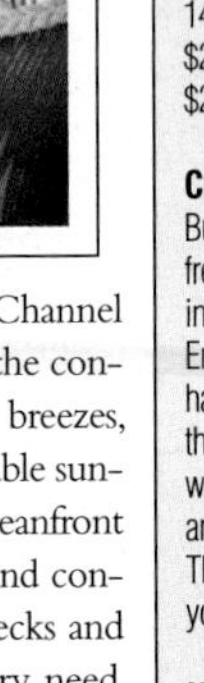

Rooms/Rates
14 Rooms, 3 Oceanfront Rooms $210/$240; 9 Oceanfront Suites, $220/$295.

Cuisine
Buffet-style breakfast featuring fresh-baked goods is served in our oceanfront dining room. Enjoy a morning repast while having one of the best views on the coast. We have a significant wine selection available and there are many fine restaurants nearby. The friendly staff will attend to your every need.

Nearest Airport(s)
Portland International (PDX) - 2.5 Hours

Directions
Just off Hwy 101, one block South of Depoe Bay's only Bridge. Turn West onto Ellingson Street, 100 feet to our parking lot.

Nestled in the Oregon Coast's magnificent scenery, Channel House combines the comforts of a first-class hotel with the congeniality of a small country Inn. Imagine fresh ocean breezes, sweeping panoramic views, powerful surf, truly unbelievable sunsets and whales within a stone's throw. Perched on an oceanfront bluff, guestrooms have an understated natural elegance and contemporary decor, including whirlpools on oceanfront decks and gas fireplaces. The friendly staff will attend to your every need. One of the West Coast's most renowned and romantic inns, it has been listed by Harry Shattuck among "a baker's dozen of world's (sic) most delectible hotels" and by Sunset Magazine as one of the 20 best Seaside Getaways on the West Coast.

Member Since 1997

"Too many accolades to count. Relax & enjoy the peace and tranquility, listen to the sound of the ocean and enjoy a truly unforgettable experience."

Proprietor
Myra Plant
General Manager
Lydia Lindsay
Elegant
In Town Country Inn

Mobil ★★★★★
AAA ◆◆◆◆

Campbell House, A City Inn

www.campbellhouse.com
252 Pearl Street, Eugene, OR 97401
800-264-2519 • 541-343-1119 • Fax 541-343-2258
campbellhouse@campbellhouse.com

Rooms/Rates
Total 19 Rooms: 12 Rooms, $92/$189; 5 Luxury FP/Jacuzzi $239/$269; 12-room Luxury Suite FP/Jacuzzi, $289/$349; 1 Guest Cottage $245/$289 with 2 rooms $345.

Cuisine
The Dining Room offers an every changing dinner menu utilizing the freshest local ingrediants. Complimentary full breakfast Dinners ranging from $16-$55 Room Service available.

Nearest Airport(s)
Mahlon Suite/Eugene Airport

Directions
From Airport: Hwy. 99 becomes 7th Ave, L on High, L on 5th, R on Pearl. From I-5, take I-105 to Eugene (exit 194B), to Coburg Rd (exit 2), stay L, merge onto Coburg Road, cross over River, take the second R (6th Ave), R on Pearl.

Built in 1892 and restored in the tradition of a fine European hotel, the Campbell House is surrounded by beautiful gardens. It is located in the historic district, within walking distance of downtown, restaurants and the theater. Hike Skinner's Butte or use over ten miles of riverside jogging and bicycle paths. Elegant guest rooms have private bathrooms, hidden TV with VCR, telephones and luxury amenities. Luxury rooms feature gas fireplaces, four-poster beds and Jacuzzi tubs. Enjoy complimentary wine in the evening and a full breakfast with newspaper in the morning. The Dining Room serves dinner Thursday through Saturday during winter months and nightly during the summer months. "Top 25 Inns in the nation," *American Historic Inns*. Weddings, receptions, meetings.

Member Since 2003

"A change in pace, place and a break in routine, for the weary business traveler."

Pine Ridge Inn

www.srinns.com/pineridge
1200 SW Century Drive #1, Bend, OR 97702
800-600-4095 • 541-389-6137 • Fax 541-385-5669
pineridge@empnet.com

Owners
Judith & Don Moilanen
Innkeeper
Addie Rehberg
Elegant Boutique Hotel/Inn

In an area known for its natural beauty, Pine Ridge Inn is distinguished by its spectacular location above the scenic Deschutes River Canyon. Cozy suites feature king sized poster or library beds, valuted ceilings, and living room areas. The Inn's spa suites feature two person Jacuzzi spa tubs in the bathing area and living room with decks overlooking Deschutes Canyon and trendy Old Mill District. Combining the ambiance of a small country inn and the amenities found only in a select number of luxury boutique hotels, Pine Ridge Inn offers unequaled comfort.

Member Since 2004

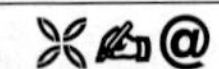

Rooms/Rates
13-Mini-suites $145/$185
7-Suites $210/$250/$325

Cuisine
Afternoon wine and local brewed beer with seasonal snacks. Evening turndown with refresh service including ice, bottled waters and a homemade pillow treat. The daily breakfast consists of a casual and friendly buffet of fruits, juices, homemade granola and hot porridge, bread goods and a plated hot special.

Nearest Airport(s)
RDM 15 miles

Directions
From HW 97, take the Bend Parkway, Exit #138 onto Colorado Ave. Follow to the 2nd traffic circle and take 3rd R onto Century Drive. Take the first L and an immediate L into drive.

"Anyone who changes their personal commitments to accommodate others shows a service level above and beyond." Dennis and Patricia Digman, Portland.

Owner
Vintage Hotels
Director of Operations
Charmaine Brown

Historic Waterside
Retreat/Lodge

Weasku Inn

www.srinns.com/weaskuinn
5560 Rogue River Hwy., Grants Pass, OR 97527
800-493-2758 • 541-471-8000 • Fax 541-471-7038
info@weasku.com

Rooms/Rates
5 Lodge Rooms, $160/$285; Jacuzzi Suites, $305; 12 River Cabins with fireplaces, $205. Open year-round.

Cuisine
Complimentary wine and cheese reception and continental breakfast are provided each day. BBQ on lodge deck for minimum fee, weekends May-September. Several restaurants are within minutes.

Nearest Airport(s)
Medford Airport

Directions
Located 51 miles north of the California and Oregon border. Take I-5, exit 48. Turn W, go across the bridge to the stop sign. Rogue River Hwy. Turn R. Go 3 miles. The Inn is on your Right.

The Weasku Inn was recently named as 'One of the country's greatest inns' by *Travel + Leisure,* and rests on the banks of the famous Rogue River, in southern Oregon. This secluded fishing lodge was a favorite vacation spot of Clark Gable during the 1920s and '30s. A complete remodeling took place in 1998, restoring the Inn to its former glory. The warm log exterior, surrounded by towering trees and 10 private acres, provides a tranquil setting ideal for an intimate getaway or corporate retreat. The lodge houses five guestrooms, and there are an additional 12 riverside cabins. A wine and cheese reception and deluxe continental breakfast are served each day.

Member Since 2001

"Top 25 Great American Lodges" - *Travel + Leisure*

Jacksonville Inn

www.jacksonvilleinn.com
P.O. Box 359, Jacksonville, OR 97530
800-321-9344 • 541-899-1900 • Fax 541-899-1373
jvinn@mind.net

Innkeepers/Owners
Jerry and Linda Evans & Mike and Jennifer Higgins

Elegant In Town Inn

Mobil ★★★
AAA ◆◆◆

Wine Spectator
BEST OF AWARD OF EXCELLENCE

The Inn offers its guests luxury and opulence, and its honeymoon cottages cater to romance and privacy of special occasions. Each has a king-sized canopy bed, whirlpool tub, steam shower, entertainment center, wet bar, fireplace, sitting room, computer with high-speed internet accessibility, and private patio with lovely surrounding gardens and waterfall--perfect for intimate weddings, receptions, and private parties. Nestled in a National Historic Landmark town, the Inn was featured on CNN and the Learning Channel's "Great Country Inns." Its restaurant is one of Oregon's most award-winning restaurants and features a connoisseurs' Wine Cellar and private catering. Five-star Diamond Academy Award of the Restaurant Industry. Recipient of "Readers' Choice Award--Best Restaurant" by Medford's *Mail Tribune* newspaper.

Rooms/Rates
8 Rooms, $149/$189 B&B;
4 Honeymoon Cottages, $250/$375 B&B.

Cuisine
Restaurant with International Cuisine; Both formal and bistro dining; Sunday brunch; Patio dining; Wine and Gift Shop featuring over 2,000 wines.

Nearest Airport(s)
Medford Airport

Directions
From I-5 N - Exit 40: S on Old Stage Road, follow signs to Jacksonville. L on California Street. From I-5 S - Exit 27: L on Barnett Road, R on Riverside Avenue, L on Main Street to Jacksonville, R on California Street.

Member Since 2003

"A destination for relaxing and pampering."

Peerless Hotel and Restaurant

www.srinns.com/peerlesshotel
243 Fourth Street, Ashland, OR 97520
800-460-8758 • 541-488-1082 • Fax 541-488-5508
reservations@peerlesshotel.com

Innkeeper/Owner
Crissy Barnett

Historic In Town Hotel

Rooms/Rates
$78/$242 (not including 8% lodging tax). Each room is uniquely decorated. Rates include breakfast, coffee service, morning newspaper, nightly turndown service, handmade Peerless chocolates and Lobby port wine service. Packages available.

Cuisine
Creative interpretation of sustainable seasonal Pacific Northwest cuisine to perfection. Wine Spectator's Award of Excellence. Dinner from 5:00 June-Oct: Tues-Sun. Nov-May: Tues-Sat Reservations: 541-488-6067 (Breakfast 8:30-9:30 a.m.)

Nearest Airport(s)
Medford Airport

Directions
Ashland's Historic Railroad District.

An intimate luxury inn built in 1900 and listed on the National Register of Historic Places, The Peerless today offers uncompromising style and service. Located in Ashland's Historic Railroad District, just steps from downtown and Oregon Shakespeare Festival. Uniquely and whimsically decorated with hand-painted murals, fine art and an eclectic mixture of furnishings from New Orleans to Hawaii. Guests are pampered with Italian bed linens, English silk and cotton towels, Aveda bath products, spa tubs, and a sumptuous complimentary breakfast. The restaurant creatively interprets flavors of the Pacific Northwest and offers a *Wine Spectator's* Award of Excellence wine list.

Member Since 2003

"Thank you for the 'The Peerless' fix." Parents of two-year-old twins.

Pennsylvania

"The Keystone State"

Famous For: Liberty Bell, Declaration of Independence, Articles of Confederation, Constitution, Gettysburg Address, Valley Forge National Historical Park, Poconos, Hershey Chocolate World, Amish Homestead, Steel, Pumpkins, Glass

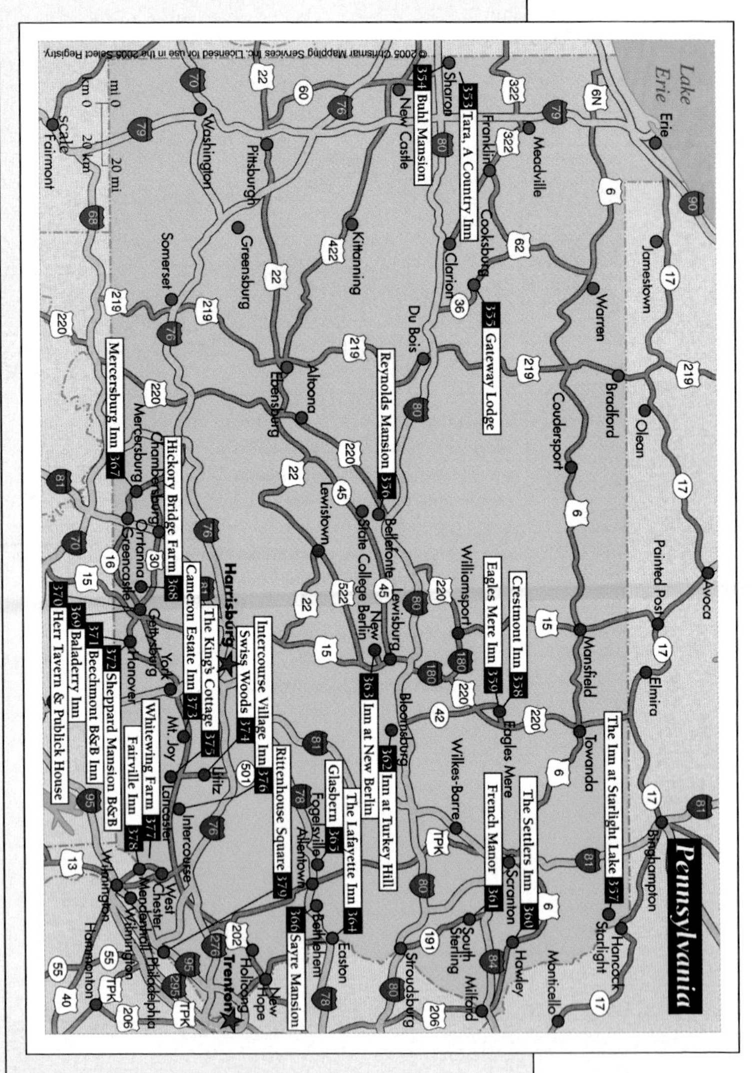

Innkeepers/Owners
Donna & Jim Winner
General Manager
Deborah DeCapua

Elegant Waterside Country Inn

AAA ◆◆◆◆

Tara - A Country Inn

www.srinns.com/taracountryinn
2844 Lake Road, Clark, PA 16113
800-782-2803 • 724-962-3535 • Fax 724-962-3250
info@tara-inn.com

Rooms/Rates
27 rooms. $250/$425 *Gone With The Wind* Getaway Packages; $195/$350 Standard Rate.

Cuisine
AAA ◆◆◆◆ Ashley's Gourmet Dining Room offers the finest in 7-course white-glove and candlelight service while Stonewall's Tavern boasts a casual atmosphere with a wide array of hearty lunch or dinner selections. Tara offers an extensive wine list and an expertly stocked lounge. Afternoon Tea is a daily opportunity for houseguests to mingle and enjoy.

Nearest Airport(s)
Youngstown, OH - 20 minutes

Directions
From I-80 take Exit 4-B to Sharon/Hermitage Follow Rt. 18 North – drive approx 7 miles to exit PA 258.

Inspired by the greatest movie of our time, Gone With the Wind, Tara recreated is in a real sense an embodiment of the Old South. Tara – although located in the "North" – offers you a lasting impression of Southern Hospitality and a chance to enjoy the luxuries of days gone by. Tara is a virtual museum of Civil War and Gone With the Wind memorabilia and antiques. Indulge in our magnificent guest rooms complete with fireplaces and Jacuzzis and enjoy the finest in gourmet or casual dining. Take a leisurely swim in either our indoor or outdoor heated pools, or stroll through formal gardens overlooking the beautiful 450-acre Shenango Lake. AAA Four Diamond lodging and Four Diamond fine dining for nearly 20 years running. Tara is the ultimate in World Class Country Inns, devoted to guests who expect the exceptional and appreciate the best.

Member Since 2005

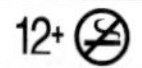

"The owners have succeeded in capturing the essence of the grand mansion that was the cynosure of *Gone With The Wind*." Dallas Morning News.

Buhl Mansion Guesthouse & Spa

www.srinns.com/buhlmansion
422 East State Street, Sharon, PA 16146
866-345-2845 • 724-346-3046 • Fax 724-346-1702
laura@buhlmansion.com

The Buhl Mansion Guesthouse & Spa was built in 1890 as a castle for Frank Buhl's wife, Julia. Steeped in history and romance, this elegant property, once the object of neglect and abuse, has been the proud recipient of AAA's highest award in hospitality. Superior gardens and an original Victorian solarium surround the magnificent Guesthouse. The moment you enter the castle you are immediately enveloped in unsurpassed hospitality and opulence. Lavishly appointed guestrooms with fireplaces and Jacuzzis, and a world-class spa offer the ultimate in luxury and pampering, royal service and grand memories of a lifetime. The full-service spa offers the epitome of indulgence with dozens of massage, body treatment, facial, nail and beauty services from which to choose as well as a sauna, steam room and monsoon showers.

Member Since 2002

Owners
Jim and Donna Winner
General Manager
Laura Ackley

Elegant Victorian In Town Breakfast Inn

Rooms/Rates
10 Rooms, $350/$475 Package Rate; $325/$400 Standard Rate.

Cuisine
Indulge with a full breakfast delivered to your room or dine in the picturesque breakfast room. Afternoon tea is served daily, champagne reception Fri & Sat. Packages include a luxurious 7-course meal at ◆◆◆◆ "Ashley's Gourmet Dining Room" or a more casual dinner at "Stonewall's Tavern" both located at nearby Tara-A Country Inn. Transportation provided on weekends.

Nearest Airport(s)
Youngstown, Ohio

Directions
From I-80: Take Exit 4-B to Sharon/Hermitage; Rte. 18N to East State St. L onto E. State. Go 3 miles. Mansion is on the Left.

"Here in the westernmost part of Pennsylvania sits one of the most elegant, romantic properties in the United States." *The Washington Post*

Gateway Lodge - Country Inn

www.srinns.com/gatewaylodge
14870 Route 36, P.O. Box 125, Cooksburg, PA 16217
800-843-6862 • 814-744-8017 • Fax 814-744-8017
info@gatewaylodge.com

Innkeepers
Joe and Linda Burney
Rustic Log Cabin
Inn & Restaurant

AAA ◆◆◆

Pennsylvania's 2004 Innkeepers of the Year. Amid some of the most magnificent forest scenery east of the Mississippi, this rustic log cabin inn has been awarded one of the top 10 best inns in the U.S. also Money Magazine's Top Travel Pick. The Inn features 2 large stone fireplaces, home-cooked meals by candlelight, indoor heated pool and sauna, afternoon tea, nightly turn-down, AC. 22 Suites with king-beds, each with a 2 person fireside whirlpool tub. 7 historic rooms with double bed, 7 Cottages with fireplaces. Customized small weddings, retreats and meetings. Conference complex. Gateway buildings are non-smoking.

Rooms/Rates
7 small historic Rooms, $95/$125; 8 Cottages, $145/$215; Suites, $225/$250 Ep. Mid-week and weekend packages. Closed Thanksgiving and Christmas day.

Cuisine
Breakfast,lunch, dinner served daily, featuring homemade french toast, catfish and omelets to Prime Rib and lobster tail.Over 300 selective wines to choose from.

Nearest Airport(s)
DuBois Regional

Directions
I-80 E:Exit 78(Brookville)R on Rte.36 N,17 miles.Lodge on R.I-80 W: Exit 62(Clarion)L on Rte.68,go thru 4 stop lights to Main St. continue 10 mi.to Rte 36 At stop sign turn R,go S 4 miles cross river Go 1/2 mile farther,Lodge is on L.

Member Since 1983

"The in 'INN' if you're looking for a way to escape from stress and pressure of everyday life."

Reynolds Mansion

www.srinns.com/reynoldsmansion
101 West Linn Sreet, Bellefonte, PA 16823
800-899-3929 • 814-353-8407 • Fax 814-353-1530
innkeeper@reynoldsmansion.com

Innkeepers/Owners
Charlotte and Joseph Heidt, Jr.
Innkeepers
Joseph Heidt III and Marisa August
Victorian Village Breakfast Inn

Escape to the Reynolds Mansion and enter a romantic atmosphere of Victorian elegance and luxurious comfort. Enjoy a game of pool in the billiard room or curl up by the fire in the snuggery with your favorite book. Relax in four common rooms, each with a unique wood-carved and tiled fireplace. Built in 1885, the mansion is a blend of the Gothic, Italianate and Queen Anne styles. Interior details include a marble vestibule, classic mirrors, Eastlake woodwork, stained glass windows and inlaid parquet floors. Come and experience the architectural wonders of Bellefonte's Victorian days. Flyfish in "Class A" trout streams, attend top-notch concerts and legendary sporting events. Go antiquing or golfing. If you are looking for a romantic getaway, or a retreat from the stress of daily life, come visit us. A warm welcome awaits you. The Reynolds Mansion has been featured on the cover of "County Victorian" and voted "Best in the US near a University." Penn State is only 10 miles away.

Member Since 2001

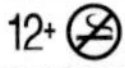

Rooms/Rates
6 Suites, $115/$275. Spacious rooms feature private baths with showers, fireplaces, Jacuzzi or steam shower, air conditioning, TV/VCR/DVD. Open year-round. Closed December 24 and 25.

Cuisine
Full breakfast included. Fine dining within walking distance. Award-winning French cuisine nearby. Complimentary Brandy

Nearest Airport(s)
University Park (SCE)

Directions
I-80 exit 161. Take Rte. 220 S. toward Bellefonte to 550. Go right at bottom of ramp and follow 550 into town. At 3rd light, turn right onto Allegheny St. At 2nd light turn left on Linn. Enter through iron gates on right.

"A night or two at The Reynolds Mansion is a week's worth of vacation relaxation."

Innkeepers/Owners
Sari & Jimmy Schwartz, Joan Roy

Traditional Waterside Inn

The Inn at Starlight Lake

www.srinns.com/starlightlake
P.O. Box 27, Starlight, PA 18461
800-248-2519 • 570-798-2519 • Fax 570-798-2672
info@innatstarlightlake.com
www.innatstarlightlake.com

Rooms/Rates
24 Main House and Cottage Rooms, $100/$195 B&B; Suite, $205/$255 B&B. Open daily for overnight guests and public dining.

Cuisine
Lakeside dining offers variety of fresh-made entrees, fresh-made pastas and pastries. Children's menu available. Full wine, beer, and liquor service.

Nearest Airport(s)
Scranton/Wilkes Barre, Stewart Airport

Directions
From N.Y., Rte. 17 exit 87- Hancock N.Y. on Pa. Rte. 191 S. 1 mi. to Rte. 370W turn R 3 mi. to sign on R; From I-81, exit 202, Rt. 107 e. to Rt. 247 N. to Forest City. Main St. 171 N. to 370 E. to inn sign.

Since 1909, guests have been drawn to this classic Country Inn on a clear lake in the rolling hills of northeastern Pennslyvania. The atmosphere is warm, congenial and informal. Twenty-four main house and cottage rooms, one with fireplace, and a suite with whirlpool, complete this delightful little universe. Smoking is allowed in the bar area or outside only. Activities for all seasons are at your disposal. But most important is the opportunity to get away from it all, and enter into the comfort and quality of hospitality that Joan, Sari and Jimmy provide.

Member Since 1976

"Loved the jaegerschnitzel, swam early this morning with the loon, a home away from home."

Crestmont Inn

www.srinns.com/crestmontinn
Crestmont Dr, Eagles Mere, PA 17731
800-522-8767 • 570-525-3519 • Fax 570-525-3534
crestmnt@epix.net

The Crestmont Inn is nestled in the woods on the highest point in Eagles Mere, a quiet historic mountaintop town surrounded by a pristine lake, State Parks and State Forests. Our Restaurant is well known for delicious cuisine, romantic fireplaces, original art and warm hospitality. Our suites include king or queen beds, large private baths with clawfoot tubs, whirlpool tubs, spacious sitting areas with cable TV/HBO, and refrigerators. Our family suites can accomodate 4 to 6 people. Enjoy nature walks, hiking, biking, tennis, lake activities, cross country skiing, ice skating, antiquing, shopping or simply relax. Crestmont Inn "Romance and Nature at its Best"!

Member Since 1989

Innkeepers/Owners
Elna & Fred Mulford
Traditional
Mountain Inn

Rooms/Rates
Rates range between $128 and $218 per night Bed & Breakfast. MAP Rates are available. Standard Rooms, Suites, Honeymoon Suites, and Family Suites each with private bath, Cable TV/HBO and telephone.

Cuisine
Traditional country breakfast included. Fine dining and casual dinners available weekends in off season and 6 nights per week in season. Cocktail lounge with fine selection of spirits, wine and beer.

Nearest Airport(s)
Williamsport, PA

Directions
From Interstate 80, exit 232 to 42(N) for 33 miles to Eagles Mere Village. Turn left onto Lakewood Ave, then first right onto Crestmont Drive.

"Your hospitality made us feel like treasured friends visiting in your home."

Eagles Mere Inn

www.srinns.com/eaglesmere
Box #356 Corner of Mary & Sullivan Avenues
Eagles Mere, PA 17731
800-426-3273 • 570-525-3273 • Fax 570-525-3731
relax@eaglesmereinn.com

Innkeepers
Susan & Peter Glaubitz

Traditional Victorian Mountain Inn

Eagles Mere, 'the last unspoiled resort,' sits on a mountain with a pristine lake surrounded by giant hemlock, rhododendron, and mountain laurel. Restored in 2000, we are the last full service Historic Inn remaining from the 1800s. Incredible waterfalls, sunsets, hiking trails, birding, covered bridges, fishing, golf, tennis and swimming. Featured by numerous travel writers. Guests enjoy genuine hospitality and personal attention. We loan our bikes, xc skis and canoe. If you want a quiet, relaxing place to spend time together while enjoying warm hospitality and gourmet meals, visit our web site or call for reservations. "The LAST UNSPOILED RESORT" now waits for you!

Rooms/Rates
16 rooms/3 suites $169/$279 includes five course Gourmet Dinner & Breakfast for two.

Cuisine
Selected as a "Top Ten" Pennsylvania Inn, our experience is in 3-and 4-star restaurants. Meals included in rates. We have the area's best reputation for excellent 5-course candlelit gourmet dinners. Wine List. Enjoy cocktails, beer & wine in our Pub. We serve ample full Country breakfasts.

Nearest Airport(s)
Williamsport Regional Airport (IPT)

Directions
Print directions from our website. I-80 to Exit #232 to Rt# 42N. I-99/15 take Rt. 220 east to Rt. 42N. From Rt 6 go south on 220 to 42S. In Eagles Mere turn on Mary Avenue.

Member Since 1993

"Wonderful Food; Accomodating Staff; Ultimate Relaxation; A Nature Photographer's Dream"

The Settlers Inn at Bingham Park

www.srinns.com/settlersinn
4 Main Ave., Hawley, PA 18428
800-833-8527 • 570-226-2993 • Fax 570-226-1874
settler@thesettlersinn.com

Innkeepers/Owners
Jeanne and Grant Genzlinger

Traditional Village Inn

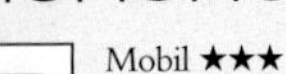

Mobil ★★★

The Settlers Inn is a place to gather. Relax, play, and rejuvenate at this artfully restored arts and crafts inn. Stroll the extensive grounds and discover colorful flower and herb gardens, a quiet reflecting pond, or sit along the banks of the meandering Lackawaxen River. Our guest rooms, thoughtfully appointed in a variety of styles and tones, feature amenities such as fireplaces, whirlpool tubs and wireless Internet access. The cornerstone of the inn is the chef-owned farm-to-table restaurant highlighting artisan bread and menus influenced by the season. The Dining Room and Chestnut Tavern reflect the style of William Morris, which is carried throughout the building. After a day of hiking or cross-country skiing, bask in the warmth of the bluestone fireplace. Summer offers dining alfresco on the terrace overlooking the grounds and The Potting Shed, our gift shop in the garden. AAA Three Diamond-rated.

Rooms/Rates
21 Rooms and Suites, $126/$212 B&B. Open year-round.

Cuisine
The seasons and cultural history of the area shape both our ever-changing menu and the preparation of each dish which highlight products of local farmers and producers. In addition to the dining room, the Chestnut Tavern is the perfect place for conversation and a flavorful microbrew. In season, alfresco dining is available on our Terrace overlooking the gardens.

Nearest Airport(s)
Scranton (AVP) Allentown (ABE)

Directions
I-84 West to Exit 26. Route 390 N to Rt. 507 N. At light, turn left onto Rt. 6 West. 2 1/2 Miles to the Inn.

Member Since 1992

Visit this Inn's website at www.thesettlersinn.com

The French Manor

www.srinns.com/frenchmanor
P.O. Box 39, Huckleberry Road, South Sterling, PA 18460
800-523-8200 • 570-676-3244 • Fax 570-676-9786
info@thefrenchmanor.com

Innkeepers/Owners
The Logan Family

Elegant French Chateau Mountain Inn

AAA ◆◆◆◆

Rooms/Rates
6 Rooms, $155/$245 B&B;
9 Suites, $230/$325 B&B.
8 Suites w/ fireplace & Jacuzzi.
Rates are per couple.

Cuisine
Gourmet breakfast. Room service available. Nouvelle & authentic French cuisine for dinner, semi-formal attire. An extensive wine list is available & top-shelf liquors.

Nearest Airport(s)
Scranton/Wilkes-Barre

Directions
From NY & NJ: I-80 W to PA exit 307. Follow 191 N 28 miles, to South Sterling, turn L on Huckleberry Rd; From PA tpke (NE Extension): take exit #95, 80E to 380N to Exit #8 for Route 423 N for 8 mi to Route 191 N, 2 miles and turn L on Huckleberry Rd.

Modeled after his chateau in the south of France, Joseph Hirshhorn created a private retreat where he could enjoy the solitude of the mountains and the serenity of "Mother Nature." Having breakfast or tea on the veranda with a view to the surrounding hilltops gives our guests this same feeling.

The accommodations and cuisine are unmatched in the area. At the French Manor, old world charm and furnishings are seamlessly joined with all the modern conveniences. All guests enjoy triple sheeting, complimentary sherry, cheese and fruit plate on arrival, and turn-down service with Godiva chocolates. Travelers can also enjoy our midweek 'Enchanted Evening' package. Add to the romance with Massage Therapy in the privacy of your own room or suite. Enjoy miles of trails for hiking, mountain biking, picnicking, snowshoeing, and cross-country skiing.

Our sister Inn, just 2 miles away, offers boating, fishing, hiking, nature programs, tennis, winter sports, indoor pool and Jacuzzi.

Member Since 1991

"Everything was exceptionally wonderful! Congratulations on this 'Paradise on Earth.'"

The Inn at Turkey Hill

www.srinns.com/turkey
991 Central Road, Bloomsburg, PA 17815
570-387-1500 • Fax 570-784-3718
info@innatturkeyhill.com

Innkeeper/Owner
Andrew B. Pruden
Historic Country Inn

Mobil ★★★
AAA ◆◆◆

Wine Spectator
AWARD OF EXCELLENCE

From romantic couples looking for a weekend diversion, corporate travelers seeking a tranquil place to rest, to visiting celebrities and dignitaries seeking quiet anonymity, the Inn is a casually elegant and comfortably appointed escape of charm and class. Among the rolling hills and farmlands of rural Pennsylvania, The Inn at Turkey Hill is considered "an oasis along the interstate." Just a moment off Interstate 80 and minutes from downtown Bloomsburg, guests are treated to a hospitable atmosphere of towering trees and friendly ducks waddling about the courtyard. Rejuvenate yourself in one of our guest rooms attractively furnished with reproduction pieces or give in to the alure of a whirlpool bath and fireplace or take advantage of some of our amenties such as complimentary high speed Internet and DVD/CD players. An award winning restaurant is located on the property featuring creative, world class cuisine and a critically acclaimed wine list along with a friendly and accommodating staff. A warm welcome awaits you.

Member Since 2002

Rooms/Rates
14 Standard rooms $109/$120; 2 Inn rooms $115/$125
5 Stable Rooms $145/$179; Deluxe King $165/$205; King Supreme $172/$225.

Cuisine
Complementary continental breakfast including hot entree. Afternoon refreshments. American-Continental cuisine featured nightly. Full service tavern.

Nearest Airport(s)
Wilkes-Barre

Directions
Conveniently located at Exit 236 of I-80. If traveling W on I-80, take Exit 236A. At the first traffic light, turn L, and the Inn will be on your L. Traveling E on I-80, take Exit 236. Turn L at the off-ramp stop sign. Turn L at the first light. The Inn will be on your L.

"How nice to find an enclave of good taste and class." Art Carey, Philadelphia Inquirer "Exquisite flavors seem to be the trademark." Times Leader

The Inn at New Berlin

www.innatnewberlin.com
321 Market Street, New Berlin, PA 17855
800-797-2350 • 570-966-0321 • Fax 570-966-9557
stay@innatnewberlin.com

Innkeepers/Owners
Nancy & John Showers
Traditional Victorian & Federal Village Inn

Mobil ★★★
AAA ◆◆◆

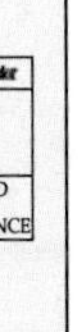

Rooms/Rates
11 rooms in 2 historic buildings, $139/$209 B&B. Whirlpool, fireplace & suite rooms available.

Cuisine
Acclaimed Gabriel's Restaurant: brunch & dinner Wed. through Sun. Contemporary American cuisine. *Wine Spectator* Award of Excellence.

Nearest Airport(s)
Harrisburg, PA

Directions
In central PA, exit 210A (Lewisburg) off I-80. Rt 15 south 11 miles to Rt 304W 8 miles to New Berlin. (OR) Rt 15 north from Harrisburg to Selinsgrove exit Rt 35. In Selinsgrove, R on Market St and L on Rt 522. R on Rt 204W 9 miles to New Berlin. The Inn is a stone's throw from the intersection of Rts 204 & 304.

The *Philadelphia Inquirer* purports, "A luxurious base for indulging in a clutch of quiet pleasures." A visit to central Pennsylvania wouldn't be complete without a stay at The Inn at New Berlin. In the heart of the pastoral Susquehanna Valley, this romantic getaway offers an abundance of life's gentle pursuits. Bike country roads and covered bridges less traveled; explore charming downtowns and mountain hiking trails; shop antique coops, Amish quilt shops, and artist's galleries. Meanwhile, back at The Inn, Innkeepers Nancy and John Showers invite guests to relax on The Inn's front porch, savor an exquisite meal and a glass of fine wine, and rediscover the nourishing aspects of simple joys and time together. The Inn offers gracious accommodations in two restored historic homes, fine casual dining at Gabriel's Restaurant, and a treasure trove for shopping at Gabriel's Gifts. Guests relay they depart feeling nurtured and relaxed, and most of all inspired...especially after indulging in The Inn's massage and yoga offerings.

Member Since 1997

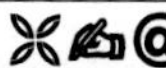

"A feast for the soul. Your chef is a treasure and your gift shop is dangerous. An uptown experience in a rural setting!"

The Lafayette Inn

www.srinns.com/lafayette
525 W. Monroe St., Easton, PA 18042
800-509-6990 • 610-253-4500 • Fax 610-253-4635
lafayinn@fast.net

Innkeepers/Owners
Scott and Marilyn Bushnell

Traditional In Town Breakfast Inn

Close your eyes...imagine the hot water in the oversized soaking tub up to your neck. Feel the bubbles? Relax with your partner in front of the fireplace and play a second game of Scrabble. Feel the warmth of the fire? The entire inn is wireless to high-speed internet access, so, go ahead, borrow our laptop and surf the net or check your e-mails. Sure, it's OK to have a second brownie! Whether visiting the colors of the Crayola Factory with the kids, riding the historic, mule-drawn canal boats, hot air ballooning above the countryside, exploring underwater diving excitement, or just watching the world go by from the wrap-around porch, The Lafayette Inn makes a great base for your getaway. Our lounge, sunroom, garden patio, and porch are ideal for a festive party, celebrating a special event, having a business meeting, or just relaxing with friends. Welcome to our inn!

Rooms/Rates
18 Rooms/Suites $125/$250. Antique-filled rooms, private baths, TV/VCR, phones. Premier rooms and suites with gas fireplaces, whirlpool or soaking tubs, balcony, gas fireplaces. The entire inn is high-speed wireless. Open year-round. Usually no two-night minimums. Children welcome.

Cuisine
Full breakfast daily, complimentary soft drinks, coffee, fruit, and pastries available all day. Excellent restaurants within walking distance. No liquor license.

Nearest Airport(s)
Lehigh Valley International

Directions
I-78, Easton exit North to Third St. toward Lafayette College. Up hill to corner of Cattell and Monroe Sts.

Member Since 2000

"What a great place for our weekend.
And the orange marmalade croissant French Toast...!!"

Glasbern

www.srinns.com/glasbern
2141 Pack House Road, Fogelsville, PA 18051
610-285-4723 • Fax 610-285-2862
innkeeper@glasbern.com

Executive Innkeeper
Michael Pinkston
Traditional Country Inn

Rooms/Rates
Four rooms, $153/$259. Six whirlpool rooms, $170/$291. Fifteen whirlpool/fireplace rooms, $186/$410. Ten whirlpool/fireplace suites, $208/$460. One whirlpool/fireplace cottage, $296/$461. Open year round.

Cuisine
Breakfast and dinner in Barn dining room year round. Breakfast buffet and entree selections from kitchen. Seasonal as well as classic year-round choices available daily. Fully licensed.

Nearest Airport(s)
Lehigh Valley International, 15 miles

Directions
From I-78 take Rt. 100 (N) for .2 mi. to L. at light for .3 mi. to R. on Church St. (N) for .6 mi. to R. on Pack House Rd. for .8 mi. to the Inn.

At the edge of Pennsylvania Dutch Country, a 21st century Country Inn has evolved from a 19th century family farm.You are welcome to explore our many pastures, gardens, and greenhouses that flourish amidst 100 acres of paths, streams, and ponds. Inside, whirlpools and fireplaces enhance most guest rooms.All have private baths, phones, high-speed Internet access, TVs and DVDs. Some luxury suites include wet bars, Jacuzzi shower systems and CD music systems. Canine friendly suites available with limitations for our four-legged friends. For the physically ambitious guest, an outdoor pool, bicycles, hiking trails and an indoor fitness center are available. Contemporary American Cuisine is offered under the Barn's timbered cathedral ceiling. Much of the food comes from the gardens and pastures of the Inn. The magic of Glasbern provides a romantic glimpse of the past couched within an invitation to enjoy the pleasures of now mingled among visions of the future.

Member Since 2002

12+

"Unbeatable-so relaxing and warm-we'll be back."

Sayre Mansion

www.srinns.com/sayremansion
250 Wyandotte Street, Bethlehem, PA 18015
877-345-9019 • 610-882-2100 • Fax 610-882-1223
innkeeper@sayremansion.com

Proprietors
Jeanne and Grant Genzlinger
Innkeeper
Tom Snoddy

Historic Gothic Revival
In Town Inn

Timeless Elegance in a Distinguished Guest House. The Inn offers luxury and comfort in eighteen guest rooms each preserving the architectural details of the Mansion. Amenities include: fine linens, private baths, highspeed wireless internet access and voicemail telephones. Robert Sayre's Wine Cellar offers guests an opportunity to sample a selection of wine. Personal Service is the cornerstone of the guest experience. The Asa Packer Room, our unique conference center is ideal for business meetings. Gatherings and special events are held in a pair of elegant parlors, each with its own fireplace. Century old trees adorn the two acres of picturesque grounds which provide a beautiful setting for outdoor affairs under our tent covering a 30 by 60 patio area.

Rooms/Rates
18 rooms and suites, $120/$250 B&B Open Year-Round.

Cuisine
Breakfast highlights homemade artisan breads, pastries, house specialties including french pudding, stratas and quiche, fresh juices and coffee ground to order. Excellent restaurants serving lunch and dinner are located within one mile of the Inn.

Nearest Airport(s)
Lehigh Valley International Airport is a five minute drive.

Directions
Located within blocks of Lehigh University, St. Lukes Hospital and Historic Bethlehem. See the website for door-to-door driving directions.

Member Since 2003

"Most enjoyable!"

Mercersburg Inn

www.mercersburginn.com
405 South Main St., Mercersburg, PA 17236
717-328-5231 • Fax 717-328-3403
Lisa@mercersburginn.com

Innkeepers/Owners
Lisa and Jim McCoy
Traditional Georgian
Village Inn

Mobil ★★★

In 1909, Ione and Harry Byron had a magnificent dream, to build a home that brought comfort and entertainment to those that entered. From that dream, the 24,000 sq. ft Prospect, with 11 ft ceilings throughout, was born. The mahogany-paneled dining room and the sun-filled enclosed porch invite our guests to a culinary experience that will not be soon forgotten. The double-curving staircases lead you to our luxuriously appointed guest rooms. Draw yourself a nice warm bath in one of our antique soaking tubs, dry off with the softest of towels, slip on a fine robe, and drift away to sleep on your feather-bed. Awake in the morning to the smell of fresh baked morning goods, and our delicious 3-course breakfast. If the season permits, stroll through the flower and herb gardens that appoint the 5.5 acre property. If golfing, hiking, fly-fishing, or skiing are on your to-do-list, let our staff make the arrangements for you. All these activities and more are only a few minutes from the Inn. We look forward to having you in our home.

Rooms/Rates
17 Rooms, $135/$275 B&B. Three with fireplaces, One with clawfoot whirlpool tub, two with Jacuzzi and TV, Three with antique baths. Kings and Queens. Open year round except Christmas Eve and Christmas Day.

Cuisine
Full gourmet breakfast, afternoon tea and scones on weekends, evening refreshments. Fine dining, seating from 5:30 till 8:30 p.m. Thurs. Fri. and Sat. and 5:00 till 8:00 p.m. on Sunday. Reservations are recommended. Full bar service.

Nearest Airport(s)
BWI, Dulles

Directions
I-81, PA exit 5 (Greencastle), W on 16; twelve miles to historic Mercersburg. Located at junction of 16 and 75.

Member Since 1998

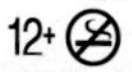

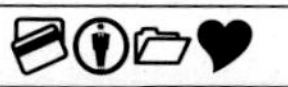

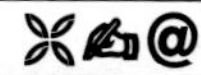

"Absolutely Wonderful! Great food, great service! The Inn and our room was so elegant. We felt so at home. Thank you for a beautiful and relaxing stay."

Hickory Bridge Farm

www.srinns.com/hickory
96 Hickory Bridge Road, Orrtanna, PA 17353
800-642-1766 • 717-642-5261 • Fax 717-642-6419
hickory@pa.net

Innkeepers/Owners
Robert and Mary Lynn Martin

Traditional Country Breakfast Inn

AAA ◆◆◆

A quaint country retreat offering 5-bedroom farmhouse (circa 1750's) accommodations (some with whirlpool baths), and four private cottages with fireplaces along a mountain stream. Dinner is served in a beautiful restored Pennsylvania barn decorated with hundreds of antiques. All meals are farm-fresh & bountiful. Full breakfast is offered to overnight guests at the farmhouse and is taken to their cottages on Sunday morning. The farm is located 9 miles west of Gettysburg, Pennsylvania, on 75 beautiful acres-a wonderful place to relax while visiting Gettysburg or antiquing in the nearby area. Featured in *Taste of Home* magazine. Serving guests since 1977.

Rooms/Rates
9 Rooms, Cottages and Farmhouse, $85/$145 B&B.
Open year-round.

Cuisine
Fine country dining in a beautiful restored Pennsylvania barn—Friday, Saturday, and Sunday. No spirits are served; you may bring your own.

Nearest Airport(s)
Harrisburg

Directions
Gettysburg, Rte 116 W to Fairfield and R 3 mi N to Orrtanna. Or Rte 997 to Rte 30 E for 9 mi turn S at Cashtown for 3 mi.

Member Since 1976

"What a special retreat from life's demands! Thank you." K. Shull

Baladerry Inn at Gettysburg

www.srinns.com/baladerry
40 Hospital Road, Gettysburg, PA 17325
800-220-0025 • 717-337-1342
baladerry@blazenet.net

Innkeeper/Owner
Suzanne Lonky

Traditional Federal Country Breakfast Inn

Mobil ★★★
AAA ◆◆◆

Baladerry Inn is located five minutes from downtown Gettysburg on four acres at the edge of the Gettysburg Battlefield near Little Round Top. This brick Federal-style home (circa 1830), served as a field hospital during the War Between the States. A large two-storied great room dominated by a massive brick fireplace is both a dining and gathering area. A brick terrace provides an outdoor area for breakfasting and for socializing. A garden gazebo offers tranquil privacy. Private and spacious, the Inn is an excellent choice for history buffs, leisure travelers, bicyclists, small business meetings, weddings and reunions.

Rooms/Rates
9 Rooms, $130/$225 B&B; $20 extra person in room. Open year-round. Smoking permitted outdoors only. No pets.

Cuisine
Full country breakfast. Guests are welcome to bring their own spirits.

Nearest Airport(s)
Harrisburg

Directions
From U.S. 15, exit at Taneytown Road. N 1 mile, R at Blacksmith Shop Road, R onto Hospital Road.

Member Since 1998

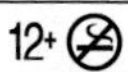

"Beautiful site and accomodations. Great breakfast. We love it. A warm place like home."

Herr Tavern & Publick House

www.srinns.com/herrtavern
900 Chambersburg Rd., Gettysburg, PA 17325
800-362-9849 • 717-334-4332 • Fax 717-334-3332
info@herrtavern.com

Innkeeper/Owner
Steven Wolf

Historic Country Inn

Mobil ★★★
AAA ◆◆◆
Wine Spectator AWARD OF EXCELLENCE

Located in the western outskirts of Gettysburg, the Tavern sits atop a ridge overlooking the Gettysburg Battlefield. The Main House, built in 1815, has a storied past becoming the first Confederate hospital during the battle. It is beautifully restored and proudly listed in the National Register of Historic Places. Guestrooms include queen beds, gas fireplaces and private Jacuzzi baths. Each room is tastefully decorated in its own unique character. Extensive *Wine Spectator* award winning wine list and premium spirits served from our full service bar. All guests enjoy a sumptuous breakfast. Elegantly appointed dining rooms have fine German china and glassware. A private downstairs dining room is available within full view of windowed wine cellar.

Rooms/Rates
16 rooms $129/$209.
Open year-round.

Cuisine
New American cuisine with regional and ethnic influences. All served with dramatic flair. On premises banquet facility.

Nearest Airport(s)
Harrisburg Airport

Directions
From Gettysburg square, Proceed on Route 30 west, 1.5 mile. Tavern is on left at Herr Ridge.

Member Since 2004

"...we can't say enough to truly explain how happy we are with the beautiful room and excellent staff."

Innkeepers/Owners
Kathryn and Thomas White

Georgian In Town Breakfast Inn

Mobil ★★★

The Beechmont Bed & Breakfast Inn

www.srinns.com/beechmont
315 Broadway, Hanover, PA 17331
800-553-7009 • 717-632-3013 • Fax 717-632-2769
innkeeper@thebeechmont.com

Rooms/Rates
Three suites, $139/$169 Four rooms, $94/$119 Corporate rates Sunday - Thursday. All rooms have A/C, televisions and telephones. Some have fireplaces/ whirlpools. Open year round.

Cuisine
Sumptuous breakfast. Help yourself cookie jar. Complimentary soft drinks and bottled water. Excellent restaurants nearby.

Nearest Airport(s)
Baltimore Washington International (BWI)

Directions
From Baltimore: I-695 to I-795 to MD 30/PA 94. Turn right at the square on Broadway (PA 194). Inn is 3.5 blocks from square on the right; guest parking in the rear of the inn. From DC: I-495 to I-270 to Rt. 15 north to Rt. 116 east.

Located on a tree-lined street of stately historic homes, The Beechmont has welcomed business and leisure travelers since 1986 with exceptional hospitality and thoughtful extras designed to meet your needs. Strolling through the garden guests are awed by its centerpiece, a 130-year-old Magnolia tree. A well-stocked library and parlor offer a backdrop for relaxed conversation, while well-appointed, spacious guest rooms assure a comfortable stay. High speed wireless internet access is available, or use our guest internet station. Guests often explore Gettysburg (just 14 miles west of Hanover), and roam through numerous antique malls, enjoy golf outings on championship courses, and discover vibrant fall colors in the hills of southern Pennsylvania. The innkeeper's sincerest wish is for The Beechmont to be a memory that lingers joyously long after your visit has ended.

Member Since 2003

"Friends couldn't treat us better." "Wonderful time. Breakfast was great!"

Sheppard Mansion Bed and Breakfast

www.srinns.com/sheppardmansion
117 Frederick St., Hanover, PA 17331
877-762-6746 • 717-633-8075 • Fax 717-633-8074
reservations@sheppardmansion.com

Innkeepers
Kathryn Sheppard-Hoar
General Manager
Timothy Bobb
Historic In Town Inn

Nestled in the heart of Hanover's Historic District stands a grand 3-story brick and marble Mansion built in 1913 by Mr. and Mrs. H.D. Sheppard, co-founders of The Hanover Shoe. Their descendants have restored the Mansion to its original splendor, now operating as an elegant Bed and Breakfast Inn and event facility, featuring the original furnishings enhanced by modern amenities. Guests enjoy numerous public rooms, bedrooms and suites featuring oversized soaking tubs in the private marble baths. After a peaceful night's slumber, aromas of coffee and baking summon guests to a gourmet breakfast served in the sunroom. Days can be spent exploring nearby Gettysburg, antique hunting or day tripping to Lancaster, Baltimore, Washington, DC or Hershey. For ultimate relaxation, in-house spa treatments are available by advance arrangement. Our recently renovated gardens provide the ideal setting for elegant large weddings or simply enjoying the grounds during an evening stroll.

Member Since 2002

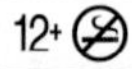

Rooms/Rates
9 rooms and suites, King, Queen and Twin Beds, $140/$350 per night. 2 BR Guest Cottage on property available weekly. Corporate rates available. All rooms have private baths, A/C, Data Port, TV, Telephones and in-room coffee.

Cuisine
Full gourmet breakfast included. Complimentary soft drinks, sweets, sherry, guest refrigerator and ice. Many fine restaurants a short drive away.

Nearest Airport(s)
BWI 1hr, MDT 1hr

Directions
One block S of Center Square in Hanover, at the intersection of Frederick St. (Rt 194) and High St. (Rt 116). Minutes from US Rt 15, I-83, I-270, I-795 and the PA Turnpike.

"Sinking into the cloud-like beds provided our best night's sleep ever!"

Innkeepers/Owners
Randy Wagner
John Jarboe

Elegant Country Inn

Cameron Estate Inn & Restaurant

www.srinns.com/cameronestate
1855 Mansion Lane, Mount Joy, PA 17552
888-422-6376 • 717-492-0111
info@cameronestateinn.com

Rooms/Rates
16 elegant guest rooms and suites and a two bedroom cottage. Private baths, A/C, fine European antiques, Ralph Lauren linens. Some have fireplaces and Jacuzzi tubs. $119/$249. Open year round. Corporate Rates Available. Elegant outdoor wedding venue.

Cuisine
Daily country breakfast included. Fine Dining Restaurant Wed. - Sun. Contemporary American Cuisine with full liquor lic.

Nearest Airport(s)
Harrisburg (MDT)
Philadelphia (PHL)
Baltimore (BWI)

Directions
Midway between Harrisburg & Lancaster, Hershey & York. Detailed directions online at http://www.cameronestateinn.com/directions.htm

The Cameron Estate Inn is the former summer estate of Secretaries of War to Lincoln and Grant. It is the largest historic Inn in the Pennsylvania Dutch and Hershey regions of the Susquehanna Valley. This grand 1805 Federal style mansion is secluded on 15 acres of lawn and woodland with two trout streams and provides the perfect venue to relax and unwind in an unspoiled country setting. Step back in time and let us pamper you with our historic, yet sumptuous guest accommodations featuring authentic European antiques. Allow us to tantalize you with our refined culinary expertise, full liquor license and extensive wine list. Well-situated out-of-the-way location ideal for exploring Lancaster, Hershey, Harrisburg, York, day trips to Gettysburg or Longwood Gardens, and all major tourist activities that include Amish/Pennsylvania Dutch, Lancaster, Hershey Park and Spa, golfing, theaters, fine dining, museums, antiquing, hiking and biking. Physically located midway between Hershey and Lancaster, but truly located....A WORLD AWAY! Visit us on the web at www.cameronestateinn.com.

Member Since 2005

"What a treasure! Lovely house, beautiful guest rooms, charming hosts! The restaurant rivals any in New York or Philly. Highly Recommended! Simply the best!"

Swiss Woods

www.srinns.com/swisswoods
500 Blantz Road, Lititz, PA 17543
800-594-8018 • 717-627-3358 • Fax 717-627-3483
innkeeper@swisswoods.com

Innkeepers/Owners
Werner and Debrah Mosimann

Traditional Swiss Style Country Breakfast Inn

Mobil ★★★
AAA ◆◆◆

Surrounded by meadows and gardens, Swiss Woods is a quiet retreat on 30 acres in Lancaster's Amish country. All rooms feature patios or balconies, some with lake views, and are decorated with the natural wood furnishings typical of Switzerland. Fabulous breakfasts, complemented by our own blend of coffee, are served in a sunlit common room. Convenient to Lancaster's famous farmers markets and wide variety of activities, Hershey is also just a short drive. After a day of antiquing, shopping or visiting quilt shops, enjoy the views of extraordinary gardens, landscaped with a wide variety of annuals and perennials. Take a relaxing hike through the woods, watch the birds, or enjoy a drink on the garden swing with a good book and a sweet treat from our kitchen. In winter settle in to read next to the inn's handsome sandstone fireplace. We offer a quiet, restful place for you to reconnect and refresh. German spoken.

Member Since 1993

Rooms/Rates
6 Rooms (2 with Jacuzzi), all with patios and balconies. $125/$190. 1 suite $155/$190.

Cuisine
Inn breakfast specialties may include garden fritatta, freshly-baked breads from old world recipes, honey apple french toast, or a potato quiche. The afternoon boasts sweets on the sideboard. Don't miss the biscotti!

Nearest Airport(s)
Harrisburg & Philadelphia

Directions
From Lancaster: 11 miles N on 501 thru Lititz. L on Brubaker Valley Rd 1 mi to lake. R on Blantz Rd. Inn is on the L. From NYC: Rt 78/22 West to exit 13-Bethel. S on Rt 501 1 mile beyond Brickerville. R on Brubaker Valley Rd. 1 mi to lake.

"Truly a haven of rest" ..."Spectacular--I didn't want to leave!" ... "beautiful grounds!"

The King's Cottage, A Bed & Breakfast Inn

www.srinns.com/kingscottage
1049 East King Street, Lancaster, PA 17602-3231
800-747-8717 • 717-397-1017 • Fax 717-397-3447
info@kingscottagebb.com

Innkeepers/Owners
Janis Kutterer and Ann Willets

Elegant In Town Breakfast Inn

Mobil ★★★

In the midst of historic Lancaster, The King's Cottage is an oasis of comfort and hospitality. The elegant decor, original crystal chandeliers and romantic fireplaces will warm your heart. Each luxurious room is fit for royalty with polished hardwood floors, canopy, brass or carved beds, antique armoires and private baths with soaking tub or whirlpool. After a gourmet breakfast, visit scenic Amish farmlands, tour historic sites or shop for handmade quilts and crafts. Relax with afternoon tea and treats while the innkeepers make plans for fine dining or dinner with an Amish family for you. On National Register. Awarded 'Top 10 Most Romantic Inn' by American Historic Inns. For business travelers, we provide a refreshing alternative to hotels with complimentary wireless high speed Internet access, full gourmet or continental breakfast times to fit your schedule, late check in, billing options, corporate rates, massage room on site and resident nationally certified massage therapist.

Rooms/Rates
7 rooms, 1 Honeymoon Cottage $150/$260. Fireplaces, Whirlpools, Hot Tub, DVD/VCR, Wireless High Speed Internet, Business rates available. Closed for Christmas

Cuisine
Gourmet breakfast with fresh local fruit & meats. Request dietary restrictions in advance. Near many fine & casual restaurants. Guest kitchen w/ice, bottled water, snacks, coffee, tea. Afternoon tea & evening cordials

Nearest Airport(s)
Harrisburg, PA - 35 minutes.

Directions
Rt. 30 to Walnut St. exit. At second light turn L. At 2nd stop sign turn L. Go 1 block & turn R onto Cottage Ave. Inn is last building on R. Parking: turn R before white wall.

Member Since 1995

"We loved the King's Cottage. We stayed in the Majestic Chambre. The room was beautiful, innkeepers friendly & breakfast excellent. Rose petal bath is great."

The Inn & Spa at Intercourse Village

www.srinns.com/ivbbs
Rt 340 - Main St - Box 598, Intercourse, PA 17534
800-664-0949 • 717-768-2626
innkeeper@inn-spa.com

Innkeepers/Owners
Ruthann & Elmer H. Thomas, CHA
Elegant Village Breakfast Inn

AAA ♦♦♦♦

Surround yourself in luxury, comfort and pleasures for the body and spirit at our inn and spa. Enjoy elegance in a quiet village setting that entreats you to a place of peace, beauty and comfort. Travel through time as you enter the 1909 Victorian Inn filled with period furnishings and antique treasures. Its refinement and sophistication deliver high-class accoutrements for those of discerning tastes. If upscale country is more your style, then reserve one of our rustic Country Homestead suites with private entrances and over 400 sq. ft. of space to relax in and forget the world around you. Our suites include ensuite baths, jet tubs, steam showers, sitting areas with love seats, fireplaces, wet bars and many other special treats which await you. For the ultimate escape in luxury, for divine romance and relaxation, find yourself engulfed in sumptuous grandeur in our Grand Suites complete with Jacuzzi and fireplace. Arise to a full five course gourmet candlelit breakfast and then indulge yourself in a delightful diversion to our on-site spa.

Member Since 2005

18+    @ 

Rooms/Rates
9 Suites - All suites have king/queen beds, ensuite bath, gas log fireplace, loveseat, microwave, refrigerator, coffee maker, CTV, CD player, phone, data port, AC.
Grand Suites $239/$339
Homestead Suites $149/$199
Victorian Rooms $139/$189

Cuisine
Full five course gourmet candlelit breakfast, prepared by our chef and served on fine English china in our formal dining room

Nearest Airport(s)
Harrisburg 1 hr, Philadelphia 1 1/2 hrs, Baltimore

Directions
Located on Pa Route 340 in the Historic Village of Intercourse. 11 miles East of Lancaster, Pa.

"For your Serenity, Enjoyment and Relaxation, OUR NEW SPA offers therapeutic massages, spa pedicures, signature manicures, & deep cleansing facials."

Innkeepers/Owners
Edward & Wanda DeSeta
Manager/Pastry Chef
Cathleen L. Ryan

Elegant Country Breakfast Inn

Inn at Whitewing Farm

www.srinns.com/whitewingfarm
P.O. Box 98, Kennett Square, PA 19348
610-388-2664 • Fax 610-388-3650
info@whitewingfarm.com

Rooms/Rates
7 Rooms $135/$199, 3 Suites with fireplaces $235/$279. Open year-round.

Cuisine
Full country breakfast, afternoon tea. Guests are welcome to bring their own spirits.

Nearest Airport(s)
Philadelphia

Directions
9 1/2 mi N on Rte 52 from I-95 (exit 7) Wilmington DE at Rte 1 turn L 8/10 mi to red lt. Turn N on Rte 52 1 1/3 mi to Valley Rd to Whitewing Farm.

Whitewing Farm is a 1700s Pennsylvania farmhouse with greenhouses, flower gardens, a barn and carriage house, all situated on 43 rolling acres in historic southern Chester County. Whitewing Farm is adjacent to Longwood Gardens. Breakfast is served in our recently renovated Haybarn. Refreshments are also available 24 hours in the Haybarn Gathering Room where guests can relax and mingle in the library, or read a book in front of the fire during the winter months. Guests are welcome to play tennis or a round of golf on our 10 hole chip-and-putt course, or relax in the pool or heated Jacuzzi. All rooms have marble-floored private baths and are decorated in Hunt Country Elegance.

Member Since 1998

"...the farm is so much more than we expected."

Fairville Inn

www.srinns.com/fairville
506 Kennett Pike (Rte. 52), Chadds Ford, PA 19317
877-285-7772 • 610-388-5900 • Fax 610-388-5902
info@fairvilleinn.com

Innkeepers/Owners
Noel and Jane McStay
Traditional Federal
Country Breakfast Inn

Mobil ★★★
AAA ◆◆◆

Located in the heart of the Brandywine Valley, the Fairville Inn, listed on the National Register of Historic Places, echoes the pastoral scenes of the Wyeth Family paintings. The allure of the Brandywine Valley, which reaches from all directions in Chadds Ford, comes primarily from the enchanting landscape and the close proximity to distinguished museums, such as Winterthur, Longwood Gardens, and the Brandywine River Museum. Accented with barn wood, beams, and occasional cathedral ceilings, the Inn is the embodiment of elegant comfort. Most rooms feature rear decks/balconies overlooking acres of gentle grassy meadows rolling toward a serene pond. Rooms in the Main House (circa 1857), Carriage House, and Springhouse have a private bath, satellite TV, telephone, and individually controlled heat/air conditioning. Most rooms have a canopy bed. Eight rooms with fireplaces in season. Fresh flowers gracefully welcome you. Your room has all the comforts of a country house inn! The inn is especially suited for adult family gatherings.

Member Since 1995

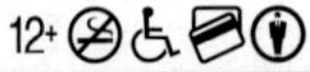

Rooms/Rates
13 Rooms and 2 Suites, $150/$250 B&B Open year-round.

Cuisine
Full breakfast (Mon-Fri 7-9 am) (Sat., Sun. and holidays 8-10 am) of refreshing beverages, cereal, fruit, yogurt, homemade 'sweets,' and hot selection(s) of the day. From 4-5 cheese, crackers, and homemade cookies compliment our afternoon tea. Guests are welcome to bring their own wine or spirits. Special diets upon request.

Nearest Airport(s)
Philadelphia International airport, 28 miles from the Inn.

Directions
Located on Rte. 52, 8 miles N of I-95 (exit 7 Wilmington DE.), 1 1/2 mi. S of U.S. Rt. 1 (Mendenhall/ Longwood Gardens area), PA.

"There are very few innkeepers who make their guest feel at home as you have. Splendid in everyway! We'll be back. Delightful and elegant."

Rittenhouse Square Bed & Breakfast

www.srinns.com/rittenhousesquare
1715 Rittenhouse Square Street, Philadelphia, PA 19103
877-791-6500 • 215-546-6500 • Fax 215-546-8787
innkeeper@rittenhousebb.com

Innkeeper/Owner
Harriet Seltzer
Elegant In Town Breakfast Inn

Rooms/Rates
8 Rooms from $239/night. 2 Junior Suites from $289/night. Open all year except Christmas Eve and Christmas Day.

Cuisine
Lavish European Continental Breakfast; Complimentary Wine Reception every evening. Turn-down service includes chocolates and bottled water.

Nearest Airport(s)
PHL

Directions
The Rittenhouse Square Bed & Breakfast is located in the Rittenhouse Square section of Philadelphia. We are on a small street located between Locust and Spruce Streets; between 17th and 18th Streets. We are a few steps away from Rittenhouse Square. Visit website for detailed directions.

From celebrities retaining their anonymity, executives returning from a high-powered meeting, to couples enjoying a quiet weekend, the Rittenhouse Square Bed & Breakfast is an intimate retreat with an enchanted setting of culture and romance. Privately positioned off Philadelphia's world-renowned Rittenhouse Square and built by famed architect Walter Cope in 1911, this stately, ten-room mansion was meticulously renovated in 2000 into a refined, petite hotel. Each morning in the Parisian-like breakfast room, artisan breads and pastries from Philadelphia's finest bakeries are served. Upscale boutiques, alluring galleries and gourmet restaurants line the pristine neighborhood. Ten elegantly appointed guest rooms including two Junior Suites add to the charm of this boutique hotel.

Member Since 2002

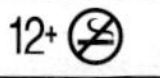

"We loved our stay. The staff was exceptional, property was lovely, location was the best!"

Rhode Island

"Little Rhody"

Famous For: Jazz Festivals, Seaside Victorian Mansions, "Mile of History," Cliff Walks, Beaches, Sailing

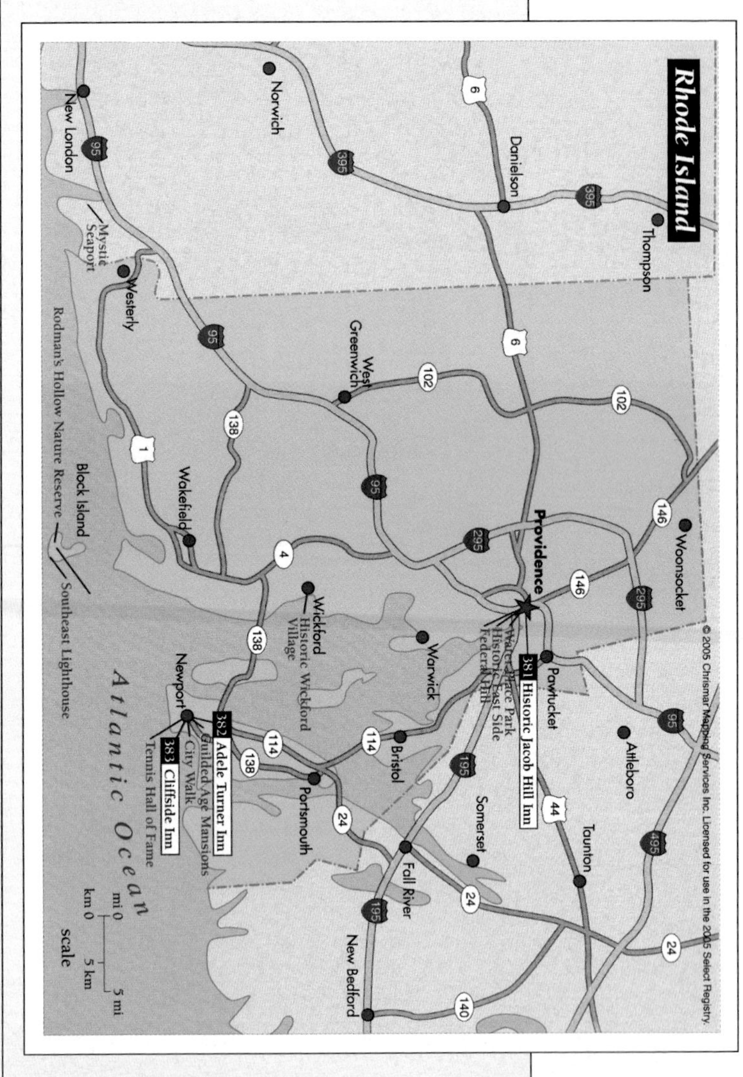

Historic Jacob Hill Inn

www.srinns.com/jacobhill
P.O. Box 41326, Providence, RI 02940
888-336-9165 • 508-336-9165
host@jacobhill.com

Innkeepers/Owners
Bill and Eleonora Rezek
Traditional Country Breakfast Inn

AAA ◆◆◆◆

Rooms/Rates
10 unique guestrooms, w/private bathrooms $199/$359. Phones, TV, AC, Internet Access. Open year-round. Pool, tennis, billiard room with large plasma TV, meeting room, and gazebo to view the beautiful sunsets. Spa services available.

Cuisine
Award-winning breakfast, complimentary beverages, cocolate chip cookies and cheese plate on arrival. Many fine restaurants nearby for lunch and dinner.

Nearest Airport(s)
Providence T F Green

Directions
From I-95: exit 20 Rte. 195 E Massachusetts exit 1 Seekonk Rte 114A. Turn L follow to Rte 44 E. Turn R follow 2.5 miles. Turn L on Jacob St. 120 Jacob St. on L.

Located on a peaceful country estate, just a ten-minute drive from downtown Providence, The Convention Center, Brown University or the Historic East Side. Built in 1722, Jacob Hill has a long history of hosting America's most prominent families, including the Vanderbilts. Recently updated rooms are spacious, all with private bathrooms; most have Jacuzzi tubs. King-and queen-sized canopied beds blend with hand-picked antiques, period wall coverings and Oriental rugs. The gleaming wood floors mirror the romantic flames from the original fireplaces. The elegant surroundings are complemented by the genuine warm hospitality that will make you feel at home. Central to several major day trip attractions: Newport, Boston, Plymouth Cape Cod, and Mystic. Awarded "Best Hotels on the Web 2004" and Best Guest accommodations 2005" "Ten best Urban Inns" Forbes.com "Room of the Year" *North American Inns* Magazine.

Member Since 2000

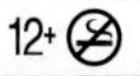

"Attention to every detail, exceptional service, delicous breakfast and elegant decor."

Adele Turner Inn

www.srinns.com/adeleturner
93 Pelham Street, Newport, RI 02840
800-845-1811 • 401-847-1811 • Fax 401-848-5850
reservations@legendaryinnsofnewport.com

Innkeeper/Owner
Winthrop Baker

Elegant In Town Inn

This elegant and romantic Victorian sits quietly tucked-away in one of Newport's most historic neighborhoods, filled with two and three-century old homes on the first gas-lit street in America. The inn has been named one of America's "Top 10 Most Romantic" and is on the National Historic Register. Built in 1855, it is framed by 27 magnificent arched windows. All guest quarters have fireplaces, king or queen beds, fine linens, antiques and artwork, TV, DVD or VCR, CD. Some rooms have Newport Harbor views, whirlpools for two, or steam bath. Perhaps the most unique room in Newport is the Inn's Harborview Spa room. French doors open out onto a private rooftop deck and hot tub, with commanding, panoramic views of Newport Harbor and Narragansett Bay. Guests enjoy daily wine and food pairing events and tasting menus, acclaimed afternoon tea, twice daily maid service and evening turndown. The inn is centrally located just two blocks from Newport's picturesque harbor and downtown restaurants, shops and famous mansions.

Member Since 2002

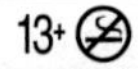

Rooms/Rates
13 Guest Quarters on 3 Floors: 10 Deluxe Rooms, 3 Luxury Suites $195/$575.

Cuisine
Morning in-room coffee service. Multi-course breakfast. Afternoon tea service. Daily wine and food events pair the best regional wines with artisan cheeses and other fine foods. Dining and wine tasting in the elegant parlor or in warmer weather on the veranda and outside tables.

Nearest Airport(s)
TF Green Providence, RI

Directions
NY: 95N to Rte. 138E, first exit off Newport Bridge to America's Cup, 3rd light L on Memorial, 2nd light L on Bellevue, 1 block L on Pelham. Boston: 95S to Rte. 24S to 138S to Memorial.

"As romantic as a Valentine" *Yankee Magazine* Editors Choice. "Sumptuous" Frommer's. *Connecticut Magazine's* Top RI B&B. *Country Living* "Inn of the Month."

Innkeeper/Owner
Winthrop Baker
Inn Manager
Daniel Coggins

Elegant Victorian
Oceanside Luxury Inn

AAA ◆◆◆◆

Cliffside Inn

www.srinns.com/cliffsideinn
2 Seaview Avenue, Newport, RI 02840
800-845-1811 • 401-847-1811 • Fax 401-848-5850
reservations@legendaryinnsofnewport.com

Rooms/Rates
Manor House - 13 Rooms:
5 Luxury Suites, 8 Deluxe Rooms.
Seaview Cottage: 3 Luxury Suites.
$250/$625

Cuisine
In-room morning coffee service. Multi-course breakfast. Legendary Newport Afternoon tea (named one of America's 20 best) features seasonal menu of tea sandwiches, scones, Devon Cream & curds, tarts, other sweets & savories.

Nearest Airport(s)
TF Green Providence

Directions
From NY: 95 N to RI exit 3 for Rte. 138, follow into Newport. America's Cup Blvd to Memorial Blvd. R on Cliff Ave. L on Seaview Ave. From Boston: 93 S to Rt. 24 S to 114 S to 214 S to Newport. L on Cliff Ave. L on Seaview.

The celebrated Cliffside Inn, home of former legendary artist Beatrice Turner, has earned a worldwide reputation as one of America's favorite boutique luxury Inns. Seamlessly blending today's most luxurious amenities--whirlpools, steam baths, fireplaces, grand beds, fine linens, LCD TVs--with exquisite design and decoration, this elegant Victorian Manor House is a one-of-a-kind place, in a unique setting near Newport's renowned Cliff Walk, beaches and Gilded Age Mansions. Beatrice Turner painted more than 3,000 works at Cliffside at the turn of the 19th century—more than 1,000 of which were self-portraits. Her remarkable story has been told by the New York Times, ABC-TV, Discovery Channel, and LIFE magazine among others. Some 100 surviving artworks are displayed throughout the Inn. Cliffside is also well known for having some of the most luxurious bathing salons and suites in New England, and a stunning collection of antique beds. Named one of the 20 Great Tea Rooms of America, afternoon tea is not to be missed.

Member Since 1997

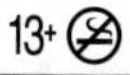

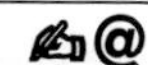

Frommer's Top RI Inn. AAA Top 10 Four Diamond Inn. "One of America's most elegant B&Bs," Getaways for Gourmets. Bride's Magazine Coastal Honeymoon Pick.

"The Palmetto State"

Famous For: Congaree Swamp National Monument, Hilton Head Island, Myrtle Beach, Plantations, Charleston, Blue Ridge Mountains, Fort Sumter, Tobacco, Corn, Peaches, Cotton, Textiles

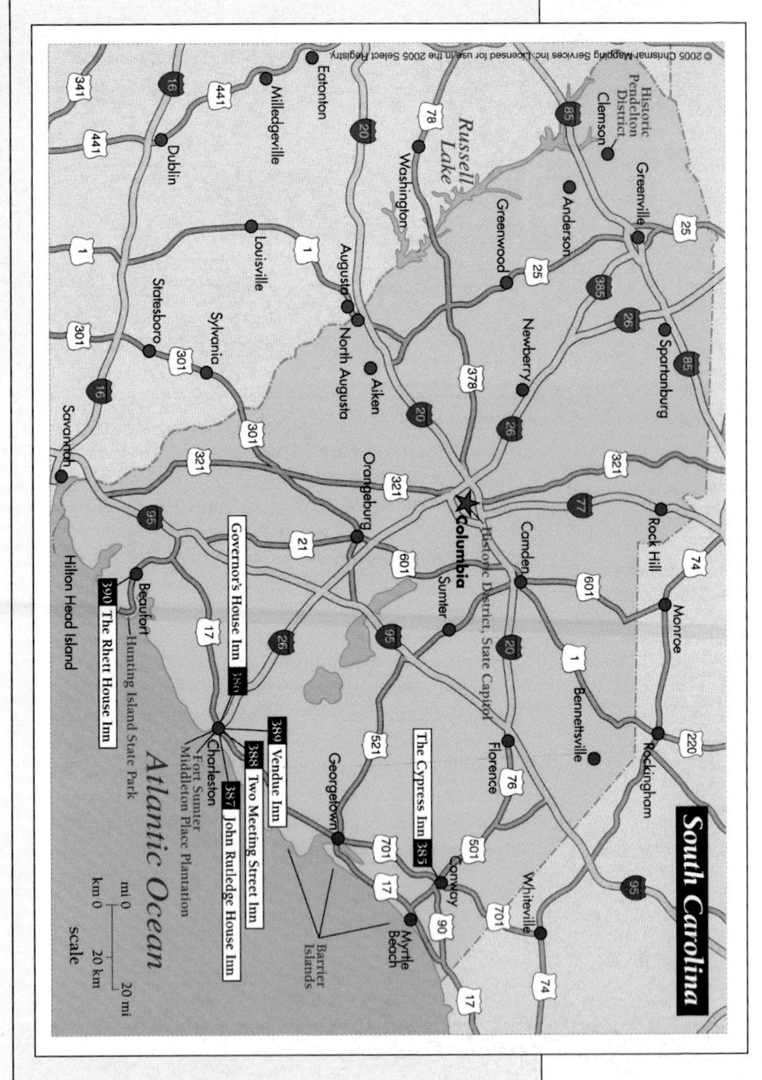

The Cypress Inn

www.srinns.com/cypressinn
16 Elm Street, Conway, SC 29526
800-575-5307 • 843-248-8199 • Fax 843-248-0329
info@acypressinn.com

Innkeepers/Owners
Carol and Jim Ruddick
Traditional In Town Breakfast Inn

Mobil ★★★

Rooms/Rates
11 Rooms, $120/$210 B&B. Open year-round. Corporate rates available.

Cuisine
A wonderful hot breakfast is served each morning. There are fine restaurants within walking distance. A small guest refrigerator is stocked with lemonade, sodas, iced tea, bottled water. Complimentary sherry, cookies and other treats.

Nearest Airport(s)
Myrtle Beach

Directions
From Hwy. 501: Take Bus. 501. W on 3rd Ave. L on Elm St. Inn is on L. From Charleston, SC: Use Hwy 701. R on Elm St. Inn is on L. From Wilmington, NC: Use Hwy. 90 R on Bus. 501. L on 3rd Ave. L on Elm St. Inn is on L.

Overlooking the Waccamaw River, tucked away in the historic town of Conway, this luxury Inn is near, but distinctly apart from the golf mecca of Myrtle Beach. Located 2 blocks from the downtown area of Conway, the Inn is within walking distance of charming shops, historic homes and stately live oak trees. Eleven unique guestrooms offer comforts such as en-suite private baths with Jacuzzis, plush robes, individual heat/air, TV/VCR with video library, high speed internet (Wi-Fi) & some fireplaces. We also have an on-site massage therapist. The Inn offers the privacy of a hotel with the personal service of a bed and breakfast. Enjoy the pristine beaches of the South Carolina coast or the peacefulness of an ancient river; an outstanding sculpture garden, or fun shows. Sample the many extras such as massages, a day at the spa or canoeing the beautiful Waccamaw River. Wonderful restaurants within walking distance of the Inn. In addition to being a destination, the Inn is great for those traveling north or south along the southeastern coast.

Visit us at www.acypressinn.com.

Member Since 2001

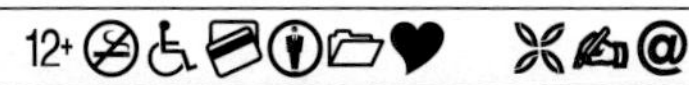

"The Carolina Coast at its best."

Governor's House Inn

www.srinns.com/governorshouse
117 Broad Street, Charleston, SC 29401
800-720-9812 • 843-720-2070 • Fax n/a
governorshouse@aol.com

Innkeepers/Owners
Karen and Rob Shaw
Elegant In Town Breakfast Inn

Governor's House is a magnificent National Historic Landmark (circa 1760) reflecting the Old South's civility and grandeur. Praised by one national publication as "Charleston's most glamorous and sophisticated inn," the former Governor's mansion is the perfect blend of historic splendor and romantic elegance. During the American Revolution, Governor's House was the home of Edward Rutledge, youngest signer of the Declaration of Independence. Today, the Inn has been acclaimed as "a flawless urban hideaway" by *Southern Living*.

www.governorshouse.com

Member Since 2000

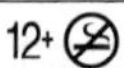

Rooms/Rates
Governor's House offers 11 elegant guest rooms and suites. Rates are $229/$475 in season. Guests enjoy high antebellum ceilings, crystal chandeliers, fireplaces, antiques, a glorious double verandah, and personal concierge service. Stroll to the Battery, the Old Market, historic homes, art galleries, and antique shopping.

Cuisine
Southern continental breakfast, Lowcountry afternoon tea. Premier restaurants nearby.

Nearest Airport(s)
Charleston

Directions
Take Meeting St. or Lockwood Blvd. S to Broad. Inn at corner of Broad and Orange Streets, 2 blocks W of Meeting St., 1 block N of Tradd.

"A glorious Inn. I consider myself so fortunate to have stayed there."

John Rutledge House Inn

www.srinns.com/johnrutledge
116 Broad Street, Charleston, SC 29401
800-476-9741 • 843-723-7999 • Fax 843-720-2615
kleslie@charminginns.com

Owner
Richard Widman

Elegant In Town Breakfast Inn

AAA ◆◆◆◆

Rooms/Rates
16 Rooms, $190/$315 B&B;
3 Suites, $330/$385 B&B.
Open year-round.

Cuisine
Continental breakfast included, full breakfast available. Afternoon tea with refreshments.

Nearest Airport(s)
Charleston International

Directions
From Charleston Visitor's Ctr.: (R) on John St., then (L) on King St., 1 mile then (R) on Broad St. The John Rutledge House Inn is 4th house on right.

Built in 1763 by John Rutledge, a signer of the U.S. Constitution, this antebellum home is now an elegant B&B Inn. Located in the heart of the Historic District, the Inn is a reminder of a more gracious time. Guests enjoy afternoon tea, wine and sherry in the ballroom where patriots, statesmen and presidents have met, evening turn-down service with chocolates at bedside and pastries delivered to the room each morning. A charter member of Historic Hotels of America, designated a National Historic Landmark.

Member Since 1992

2004 Gold List - "World's Best Places to Stay" - *Conde' Nast Traveler*

Two Meeting Street Inn

www.srinns.com/twomeetingstreet
2 Meeting Street, Charleston, SC 29401
843-723-7322
innkeeper2meetst@bellsouth.net

Two Meeting Street Inn is the city's oldest inn welcoming guests for over half a century located in the heart of the historic district. The Queen Anne Mansion was given as a wedding gift by a bride's loving father in 1890. Elegant from head to toe, the inn features a carved English oak stairwell and Tiffany windows, as well as the Spell's collection of antiques and silver. The softly curved, two tiered verandahs overlook the manicured landscaped garden and Charleston's harbour. Guests enjoy a Southern continental breakfast and gracious afternoon tea in the dining room or on the piazza. "Never have we stayed in a place so beautiful or so lovingly cared for, nor have we ever felt as pampered. Thank you for making our stay both comfortable and memorable."

Member Since 1992

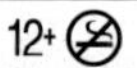

Innkeepers/Owners
Pete and Jean Spell, Karen Spell Shaw

Elegant Victorian In Town Breakfast Inn

Rooms/Rates
9 Guest Rooms, $175/$375 B&B; Victorian Rooms with 12' ceilings, canopy beds, and private baths. Closed 3 days for Christmas.

Cuisine
A gracious continental breakfast; afternoon tea; evening sherry. No bar in the Inn.

Nearest Airport(s)
Charleston International Airport 12 miles from downtown.

Directions
From I-26, exit Meeting Street/Visitor Center. A left-hand exit. When Meeting Street dead ends into the park, we are the last house on the Left.

People's choice for the City's Best Bed and Breakfast in Charleston City Paper - Seventh Year. Featured in *Southern Living* Magazine, October 2004.

General Manager
Pierre Estoppey

Historic In Town Inn

Vendue Inn

www.srinns.com/vendueinn
19 Vendue Range, Charleston, SC 29401
800-845-7900 • 843-577-7970 • Fax 843-577-2913
info@vendueinn.com

Rooms/Rates
40 Rooms, $169/$239; 25 Suites, $259/$299. Period decor; suites have fireplaces, large marble baths. Open year-round.

Cuisine
Complimentary full, Southern breakfast buffet. The Rooftop Bar and Restaurant serves lunch and dinner 7 days. Outside dining available; entertainment. The Library Restaurant is open Tuesday through Saturday from 5:00 PM until 10:00 PM.

Nearest Airport(s)
Charleston

Directions
I-26 E to East Bay Exit. Continue S on East Bay approximately 3 miles. L onto Vendue Range. Check-in is halfway down the block on R at 19 Vendue Range.

From the moment you enter the Vendue Inn, you will know you are somewhere special. Located in Charleston's French Quarter, the Vendue Inn is a place rich in the European elegance of early Charleston. Antiques and eighteenth century reproductions decorate each charming guest room and suite. There is, however, more to the Vendue Inn than the world within your room. Charleston's finest shopping and restaurants, as well as historical sights and the waterfront are within walking distance. The Vendue Inn Rooftop Bar and Restaurant, a favorite with locals, offers a view of Charleston Harbor, as well as dramatic views of historic Charleston. Join us in the newly re-opened Library Restaurant, located on the first floor.

Member Since 2002

Recipient of the Carolopolis Award, recognizing "sensitive rehabilitation of historic buildings."

The Rhett House Inn

www.srinns.com/rhetthouse
1009 Craven Street, Beaufort, SC 29902
888-480-9530 • 843-524-9030 • Fax 843-524-1310
info@rhetthouseinn.com

Owners
Steve & Marianne Harrison

Elegant Greek Revival
In Town Breakfast Inn

Mobil ★★★★
AAA ◆◆◆◆

Located in historic Beaufort. The Rhett House Inn is a beautifully restored 1820s plantation house, furnished with English and American antiques, oriental rugs, fresh orchids, fireplaces and spacious verandahs. Lush gardens provide the perfect setting for weddings and parties. Our town was the film site for "Forrest Gump," "Prince of Tides," "The Big Chill" and "White Squal." History-laden Beaufort, Charleston and Savannah offer rich exploring.

Rooms/Rates
17 Rooms $175/$315, 8 with fireplaces and whirlpool baths. Open year-round.

Cuisine
Breakfast, afternoon tea, evening hors d'oeuvres, picnic baskets, desserts.

Nearest Airport(s)
Savannah/Hilton Head International Airport

Directions
From the North, take I-95 to Exit 33, then follow the signs to Beaufort. From the South, take I-95 to exit 8 and follow the signs.

Member Since 1991

"Beautiful rooms, lovely grounds, exquisite desserts - what an enchanting place."

"The Volunteer State"

Famous For: Cumberland Gap National Historic Park, Cumberland Caverns, Fall Creek Falls, Grand Ole Opry House, Great Smokey Mountains, Graceland, Guinness World Records Museum, Country Music Hall of Fame, Tennessee Valley Authority, Zinc, Marble

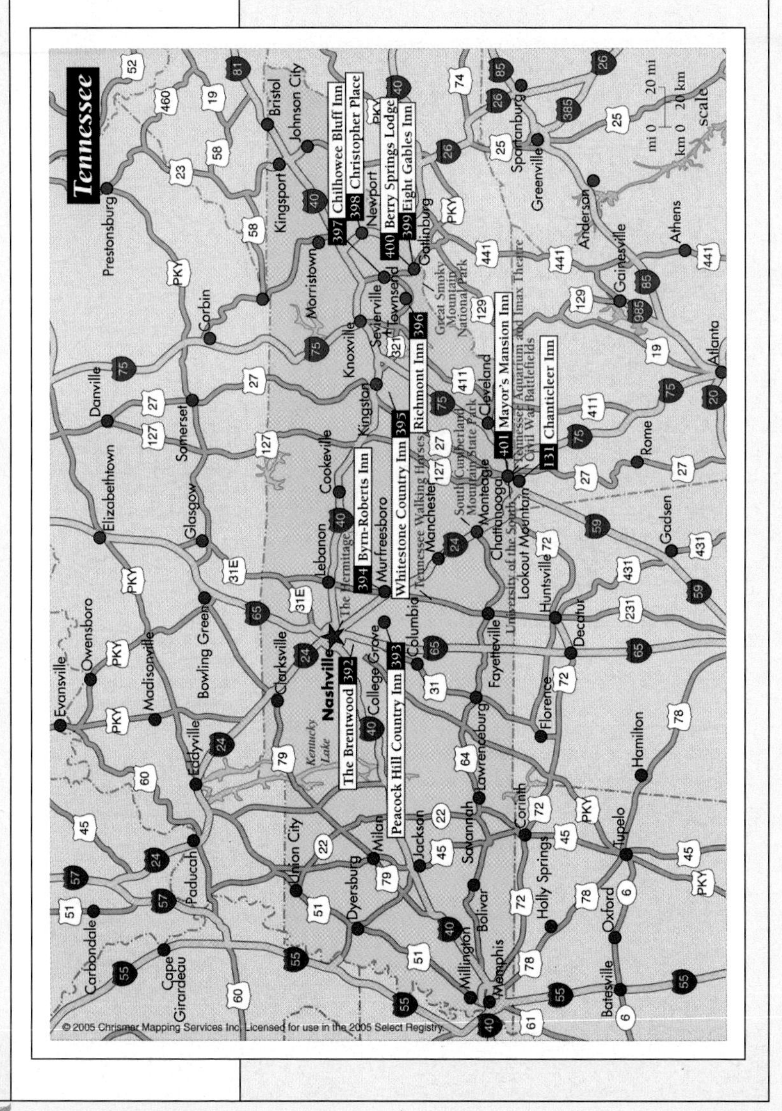

The Brentwood, A Bed & Breakfast

www.srinns.com/thebrentwood
6304 Murray Lane, Brentwood, TN 37027-6210
800-332-4640 • 615-373-4627 • Fax 615-221-9666
info@brentwoodbandb.com

Innkeeper/Owner
Ly Anne & Dick Thorman
Elegant Country Breakfast Inn

The luxurious Brentwood estate is located in one of the finest sections of greater Nashville. The drive over the stream, through the trees and up to the white columns welcomes you to our "Classic Hospitality." The casual elegance of the interior and eclectic combination of traditional furnishings, family and European antiques and objects 'd arte creates an atmosphere of quiet relaxation. Private decks overlook the rolling hillside and fireplaces warm the cool evenings. Private tours of Civil War sites, Grand Ole Opry, Country Music Hall of Fame, The Ryman, The Hermitage and Antebellum mansions can be arranged.

Member Since 2003

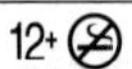   

Rooms/Rates
6 Elegant Rooms & Suites
Rooms $135/$165
Suites $175/$250
All suites have custom Jacuzzi tubs, some with fireplace and decks. Data ports, DSL, TV, phone, VCR library, terry robes.

Cuisine
Full breakfast and afternoon refreshments. Special dietary menus with notice. Minutes from fine dining and the historic attractions of Nashville, Belle Meade and Franklin.

Nearest Airport(s)
Nashville Int'l - 20 Minutes

Directions
From Nashville on I-65 S exit on Concord and turn R. At Franklin Road turn R. At Murray Lane turn L and proceed 1 mile past Granny White Pike. The Brentwood is on your right.

"Where Classic Hospitality Lives!"

Proprietors
Anita and Walter Ogilvie
Elegant Country Ranch

AAA ◆◆◆◆

Peacock Hill Country Inn

www.srinns.com/peacock
6994 Giles Hill Road, College Grove, TN 37046
800-327-6663 • 615-368-7727 • Fax 615-368-7933
peacockhillinn@yahoo.com

Rooms/Rates
7 Rooms $135/$185, 3 Suites $195/$245. All rooms and suites have king beds and large private baths. Some with woodburning fireplaces, whirlpools, European showers, private decks,screened porches. Open year round.

Cuisine
Full breakfast with individual table service between 8 and 10AM. Box lunches and romantic candlelight dinners with reservations.

Nearest Airport(s)
Nashville

Directions
From Nashville, I-65 S to Franklin exit #65, E on Hwy 96 1.5 miles, R on Arno Rd., 13.7 miles to Giles Hill Rd., R 2.8 miles to Peacock Hill Country Inn on the left. See website for detail map.

This quiet 1000-acre retreat is nestled deep in the rolling hills of Tennessee, less than 30 minutes from Franklin and 45 minutes from Nashville. The inn is on a cattle farm with peacocks, deer, wild turkey, a creek and miles of trails in the woods for hiking. A heated swimming pool, spa and lighted tennis court are on premise. The main farmhouse pampers guests in five rooms, each with its own distinct decor. The rustic log cabin and granary offer private hideaways for romance. The historic McCall House, one mile away in a hollow on the farm, has two guest rooms with screened porches and The Grand Suite with a spacious log dining/living room.

The Inn is located within 30 minutes of five surrounding county seat towns with their unique antebellum homes, antique shops, historic Civil War sites, champion golf courses and restaurants. Free tours of Jack Daniels Distillery and Tennessee Walking Horse Show Farms are favorites of our guests. Nonsmoking.

Member Since 2000

"The music, books, fireplaces, and food on the table ALL said to me, 'Welcome Home.'"

Byrn-Roberts Inn

www.srinns.com/byrn-roberts
346 East Main Street, Murfreesboro, TN 37130
888-877-4919 • 615-867-0308 • Fax 615-867-0280
byrnrobert@aol.com

Innkeepers/Owners
David & Julie Becker

Elegant In Town Breakfast Inn

Welcome to the "Heart" of Tennessee and Southern Hospitality complimented by our travel experiences! Luxury, concierge service and spa amenities greet you. Fully restored, our elegant mansion (Circa 1900) is nestled in the Historic District of a quaint college town 30 minutes SE of Nashville. All of our guests rooms include luxurious linens, king beds, fresh flowers and private baths including showers (in addition some w/double whirlpools.) Each guest room has TV, VCR, DVD, CD, cable, phones and wireless high speed Internet. Visit our web site to view our entire list of amenities. Enjoy our extensive gardens and pond with a magnificent waterfall or walk 3-4 blocks to quaint shops and restaurants. We are here to assist you plan side trips such as: Stones River Civil War site, antebellum homes, golf, antique malls or ride our tandem bike. Visit downtown Nashville to see the splendor of "Music City." Other day trips include sites such as: Jack Daniel's Distillery, Fall Creek Falls, Franklin, Chattanooga and Tennessee Walking Horse Country.

Member Since 2002

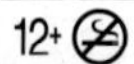

Rooms/Rates

5 upscale extra large rooms, working fireplaces $135/$235.

Cuisine

Elegant breakfasts. Complimentary beverage and snack bar. Guests welcome to bring spirits. Local menus on site and 3 fine restaurants are located within 4 blocks of the Inn.

Nearest Airport(s)

Nashville-Jet service, Murfreesboro-Prop service

Directions

Located south and east of the Nashville airport. Take I-24 to Exit 78B. Travel E 2 miles. Turn R on NW Broad Street. Go 1 block, turn L on W Main Street. Circle around the Courthouse. Go R on E Main Street. We are on the R 3 blocks from the Courthouse.

"We were greeted with dynamism, poise and dignity. Then we were bathed in tasteful opulence. Our visit was almost surreal...."

Innkeepers/Owners
Paul Cowell and Jean Cowell

Elegant Waterside Inn

AAA ◆◆◆◆

Whitestone Country Inn

www.srinns.com/whitestone
1200 Paint Rock Rd., Kingston, TN 37763
888-247-2464 • 865-376-0113 • Fax 865-376-4454
moreinfo@whitestoneinn.com

Rooms/Rates
21 Rooms/Suites, $160/$270 per night. Each room and suite has fireplace, king bed, spa tub, TV/VCR, and refrigerator.

Cuisine
The very best classic cuisine. Enjoy elegant meals in one of our three dining rooms, two overlooking the lake. For between-meal snacks, sample from the cookie jars in our great room.

Nearest Airport(s)
Knoxville, Mcghee/Tyson airport

Directions
From I-75, exit 72. Turn W on Hwy 72, go 9 miles. R on Paint Rock Rd., just after Hwy. 322 jct. Entrance is 4 miles on R. - From I-40, exit 352. S on Hwy 58. Go 6 miles to L on Hwy 72E, then 5 miles to L on Paint Rock Rd. 4 m

A spectacular 360 acre Country Estate with views of the Smoky Mountains provides you with a serene combination of natural woods and landscaped gardens. Whitestone's rolling hillsides and peaceful surroundings are guaranteed to soothe your soul and calm your spirit. We serve three lavish meals a day and you can nibble on home baked cookies and other delectable treats anytime. Many of our rooms are equipped with the sensuous delight of waterfall-spa showers and private decks. You will be surrounded by 5,400 acres of wildlife-waterfowl refuge and 39,000 acre Watts Bar Lake with opportunities for birding, fishing, kayaking, canoeing, paddle-boating or just rocking on our many porches and swinging in our hammocks. This is the perfect place for vacations, retreats, meetings, weddings or honeymoons. Whitestone Country Inn is one of only six AAA, four-diamond inns in Tennessee, and was named one of the '10 Most Romantic Inns in America!' Find a Sanctuary for your Soul.

Member Since 2000

"Just a brief note to say that at Whitestone we found a true 'Sanctuary of the Soul.' Your hospitality has demonstrated extraordinary grace."

Richmont Inn

www.richmontinn.com
220 Winterberry Lane, Townsend, TN 37882
866-267-7086 • 865-448-6751 • Fax 865-448-6480
richmontinn@aol.com

Innkeeper
Nancy Schimmick
Innkeepers/Owners
Susan and Jim Hind

Elegant Mountain Inn

Escape to the Great Smoky Mountains and refresh your body and soul. Relax in our historic Appalachian cantilever barn, elegantly furnished with 18th Century English antiques and French paintings. Breathtaking views, private balconies, spa tubs and wood-burning fireplaces. Rated "Top Inn" by *Country Inns* and awarded grand prize by *Gourmet* for our signature dessert. "...just might be the most romantic place in the Smokies"—*Southern Living*. "A wonderful place to recharge your batteries"—*Country*. "Appalachia with style," selected as "one of the top 25 authentic hotels across the United States"—*National Geographic Traveler*. "Romantic getaway"—*HGTV*. Ten minutes to Great Smoky Mountains National Park.

Rooms/Rates
9 Rooms, $135/$175, 5 Luxury Suites $185/$245 King beds/spa tubs/firepl/balconies/fridge/coffee.

Cuisine
Full French and Swiss style breakfasts. Also complimentary gourmet desserts and flavored coffees by candlelight. Evening dinners by reservation - classic four course Swiss fondue.

Nearest Airport(s)
Only 30 mins. from McGhee Tyson (Metro Knoxville) airport.

Directions
Enter Townsend (after mile marker 26), from Maryville on US 321 N. 1st R on Old Tuckaleechee Rd., R on next paved rd. (Laurel Valley), .8 mi. thru stone wall entry. Crest hill, turn L.

Member Since 1997

Located on the "Peaceful Side of the Smokies."
Visit www.richmontinn.com

Chilhowee Bluff Inn

www.srinns.com/chilhowee
1887 Bluff Mountain Road, Sevierville, TN 37876
888-559-0321 • 865-908-0321 • Fax 865-774-3308
reservations@chilhoweebluff.com

Innkeeper/Owner
Judy and Joe Hudak
Mountain Country Manor

Rooms/Rates
4 Rooms. $125/$169 per night, double occupancy.

Cuisine
Three course Gourmet Breakfast every morning. Chef-owned on-site casual Fine Dining Restaurant with creative Menu. Beautiful Mountainside Outdoor Dining. Weddings, private parties, meetings up to 50 people.

Nearest Airport(s)
McGhee-Tyson, Knoxville, TN

Directions
I-40 East of Knoxville, Exit 407/ Rte. 66/441; South into Pigeon Forge to light #3; Right onto Wears Valley Road/Rte. 321; 2.5 miles - right on Walden Creek Rd; 1/2 mile - right on Goose Gap; 1/2 mile - left on Bluff Mountain Rd.; 1 mile up Bluff Mountain on the left.

Distinguished Accommodations ~ World Class Cuisine ~ Created to pamper the weary and inspire the romantic, this four room Inn welcomes guests to a secluded mountainside plateau conveniently located to The Great Smoky Mountains National Park and all area attractions and activities. The Inn offers amenities to make you comfortable, views to help you relax, and excellent cuisine for you to enjoy! The CIA trained Chef-owner pampers guests with a delicious three course breakfast each morning. A diverse and creative menu is available at the on-site Bistro every Tuesday thru Saturday evening. Whatever others see in us that set us apart, our goal is to attain recognition from our Guests for the best quality accommodation, the highest quality cuisine, and the most attentive personal service without pretension or attitude. We offer our Guests the opportunity to relax, be pampered, and be comfortable, whether on a brief getaway, a birthday or anniversary celebration, or an extended vacation.

Member Since 2004

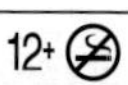

"It is said that the little things in life mean the most. You have maximized those 'little things' and created a wonderful haven from the "real" world."

Christopher Place, An Intimate Resort

www.srinns.com/christopherplace
1500 Pinnacles Way, Newport, TN 37821
800-595-9441 • 423-623-6555 • Fax 423-613-4771
stay@christopherplace.com

Innkeeper/Owner
Marston Price

Elegant Mountain Inn

AAA ◆◆◆◆

Secluded in the scenic Smoky Mountains on a 200-acre private estate, Christopher Place is the ideal inn for a romantic, relaxing getaway. An elegant setting is coupled with friendly, unpretentious service and unspoiled, panoramic views. The hosts know your name and greet you with a warm smile. You can fill your days with activities, or with none at all, as the inn is centrally located to most of the sights and attractions of the Smokies and offers many resort amenities of its own. Casual fine dining completes your romantic retreat. Special requests are encouraged. Voted the area's Best B&B. Named one of the 10 most romantic inns in America.

Member Since 2000

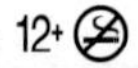

Rooms/Rates
4 Rooms, $150/175; 4 Suites, $250/$325. Spacious and romantically appointed. Most have double whirlpools, woodburning fireplaces and/or scenic views. Open all year.

Cuisine
Hearty mountain breakfast served at your leisure. Picnics. Intimate 4-course candlelit dinners by reservation at tables set for two. Some seats available to non-inn guests. Light afternoon snacks in game room. Feel free to bring your own spirits.

Nearest Airport(s)
Knoxville

Directions
I-40 to exit 435. Go Sout 2 miles on Hwy 32. Turn Right on English Mountain Rd. Go 2 miles. Turn Right on Pinnacles Way. Follow to the top.

"Thanks for providing a place for people to experience life the way they wish it was."

Eight Gables Inn

www.srinns.com/eightgablesinn
219 North Mountain Trail, Gatlinburg, TN 37738
800-279-5716 • 865-430-3344 • Fax 865-430-8767
inquiries@eightgables.com

Owners
Donald W. and Kimberly K. Cason
Casually Elegant Mountain Inn

AAA ◆◆◆◆

Rooms/Rates
10 Rooms $119/$249; 9 Suites $179/$299. Luxurious rooms, TV/VCR/CD, some with King beds, fireplaces, Jacuzzis. Open year-round.

Cuisine
Full served breakfast; Picnic baskets available for intimate excursions; Homemade soups, sandwiches & desserts served Tues- Fri in Magnolia Tea Room Cafe; 3 and 4 course candlelight dinners on Tues, Thur & Sat - RSVP; Afternoon English Tea

Nearest Airport(s)
Knoxville TN

Directions
From Hwy. 441, one mi. N of Gatlinburg, turn on Little Smoky Road. Go to stop sign, road turns into North Mountain Trail (directional sign posted). First drive on L.

Eight Gables Inn, The Smoky Mountains' Premier Country Inn, offers 19 luxurious rooms and suites. All rooms have private baths, cable TV, feather top beds, plush bathrobes, telephones, personal amenities and several feature the warmth of fireplaces and whirlpool tubs. Our rates include a full served breakfast, afternoon tea, evening desserts and coffee. Elegant candlelight dinners are available on Tuesday, Thursday and Saturday evenings with reservations. Conveniently tucked away minutes from Gatlinburg and Pigeon Forge, our casual elegance and charm will win you over. Eight Gables is easily accessible to all the area attractions and Knoxville is just 30 miles away. AAA Four Diamond rated.

Member Since 2002

"An excellent getaway from the everyday world! Your Inn has nourished both body and soul!"

Berry Springs Lodge

www.srinns.com/berrysprings
2149 Seaton Springs Road, Sevierville, TN 37862
888-760-8297 • 865-908-7935
info@berrysprings.com

Innkeepers/Owners
Patrick & Sue Eisert

Rustic Mountain Retreat/Lodge

Perched on a 33 acre secluded scenic ridge top in the Great Smoky Mountains, this lodge offers the perfect picture of solitude and romance. Take a leisurely walk down to the bass or catfish ponds and try your luck. Ride bikes, play horseshoes, relax in a hammock or just sit back and enjoy the beautiful views of the Smoky Mountains from your rocking chair on the main deck of the lodge. With this remote setting, one would not guess the lodge is within a 15-minute drive of most area destinations, including Gatlinburg, Pigeon Forge and Sevierville. Named best inn for mountain views and rest and relaxation.

Rooms/Rates
9 rooms. $149/$189, 2 Suites $209/$229. Includes breakfast and evening desserts. King Beds, Fireplace, Whirlpool Tubs TV/VCR/CD. Open year-round.

Cuisine
Country gourmet breakfast. Lunch & dinner picnic baskets are available upon advanced request. Local restaurants within 15 minutes. Nightly signature desserts.

Nearest Airport(s)
Knoxville

Directions
Interstate 40 exit #407.Go 8 miles turn left on Rt 411. Go 1.2 miles right at Middle Creek road. Go 3.9 miles left on Jay Ell Rd. Go 1.6 right McCarter Hollow Rd go 1/4 mile left on Seaton Springs Road. Lodge is first drive on left.

Member Since 2005

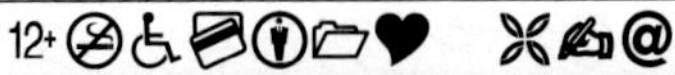

"Not enough words to describe how lovely this place is. We will be back."

Owners
Gene & Carmen Fenn Drake
General Manager
Stephanie Meents
Inn Princess
Savannah, Chocolate Lab

Elegant In Town Inn

AAA ◆◆◆◆

Mayor's Mansion Inn

www.mayorsmansioninn.com
801 Vine Street, Chattanooga, TN 37403
888-446-6569 • 423-265-5000 • Fax 423-265-5555
info@mayorsmansioninn.com

Entering the Fort Wood neighborhood, Chattanooga's premier historic district, you are immediately greeted by a magnificent mansion, built in 1889 by the city's Mayor. Picture majestic oaks sheltering this massive stone Victorian treasure that carries a prestigious award for historical preservation from The National Trust. Find yourself exploring lazy porches, 16-foot ceilings, carved pocket doors, hand-painted murals, as well as breathtaking mountain views. Hidden among the treasures of yesteryear, you suddenly discover subtle modern conveniences of 300-gallon soaking tubs, televisions, VCRs, and modem connections. Most importantly, you will rest easy always knowing our dedicated hospitality team eagerly awaits every opportunity to make your stay as unforgettable as your surroundings.

Rooms/Rates
4 Suites, $195/$275; 7 Rooms, $150/$175. Open all year.

Cuisine
Full breakfast, dinner served on Friday and Saturday evenings by reservation. Many fine restaurants a short distance away. Wines, liquors, brews, and spirits available.

Nearest Airport(s)
Chattanooga Metro Airport

Directions
From Atlanta or Knoxville I-75 to I-24W. 27N to exit 1C. 1mile straight, R on Palmetto St. 1 block to Inn. From Nashville I-24E to 27N, then same.

Member Since 1996

"Thank you for your grand southern hospitality. Grounds are immaculate and the service is outstanding. This is the finest B&B in which we have ever stayed."

"The Lone Star State"

Famous For: The Alamo, San Antonio Missions National Historic Park, Enchanted Rock, Big Bend National Park, Padre Island National Seashore, Marfa Lights, Guadalupe Mountains National Park, Lyndon B. Johnson Space Center, Armadillo, Oil, Cattle, Cotton

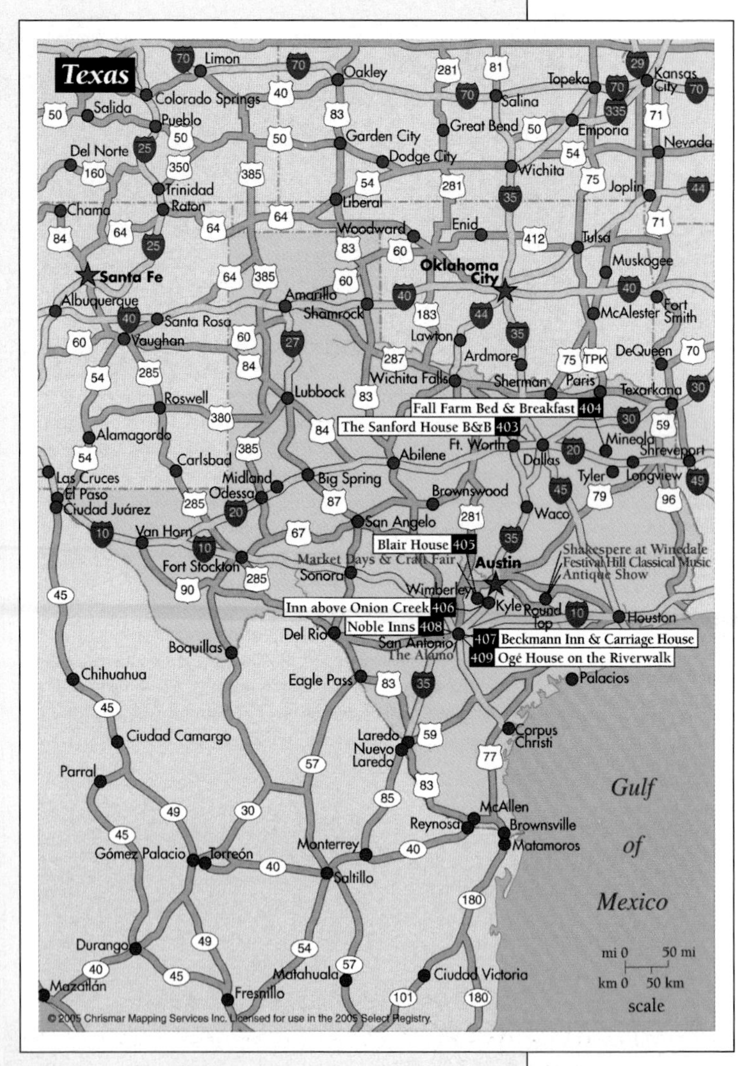

Director
Cheryl Allgood
Owners
Drs. J. Bergstrom & J. McDonald

Victorian Inn & Spa

AAA ◆◆◆

The Sanford House Inn & Spa

www.srinns.com/sanfordhouse
506 N. Center St., Arlington, TX 76011
817-861-2129 • 817-861-3624 • Fax 817-861-2030
info@thesanfordhouse.com

Rooms/Rates
7 Rooms, 4 Private Cottages. Rates from $99/$250.

Cuisine
Breakfast is included with your night's stay and varies from bagles to our delicious Belgian Waffles. Dinners, lunches, high teas and a vast array of other offerings are available with 48 hours notice. Dinners are delivered to your private cottage or served in our formal dining room.

Nearest Airport(s)
DFW Airport

Directions
From Dallas: I-30 to Cooper St Left to Randol Mill Rd Left to Center St Right to Sanford St. From Fort Worth: I-30 to Cooper St. Right to Randol Mill Rd Left to Center St Right to Sanford St.

Discover tranquility, comfort and romance nestled in the beauty of our Victorian inn, gardens and spa. Let us care for your every need as you enjoy our luxurious rooms and cottages with private baths and whirlpool tubs, grounds filled with lush vegetation, inviting pool and gazebos, or an indulgent facial, massage or other spa service. Offering a delightful complimentary breakfast, all Sanford House meals are meticulously prepared by our gourmet chef and dining is available by reservation for individuals and groups, large or small. Located in central Arlington, just minutes from DFW Airport, Six Flags and The Ballpark in Arlington, the Sanford House Inn & Spa is only a short drive away from the museums and other attractions of Dallas and Fort Worth.

Member Since 2003

Dear Cheryl - "....It was definitely a pampered and spiritual uplifting retreat. Thank you."

Fall Farm, A Fine Country Inn

www.srinns.com/fallfarm
2027 F.M. 779, Mineola, TX 75773-3287
877-886-7696 • 903-768-2449 • Fax 903-768-2079
info@fallfarm.com

Innkeepers/Owners
Mike and Carol Fall
Traditional Country Breakfast Inn

Escape to this tranquil, ten-acre retreat in the scenic piney woods of East Texas and be drawn into a luxurious country farmhouse with unique personality, reflecting Mike and Carol's history and welcoming spirit. The inviting atmosphere conveys a familiar feeling of home, yet transforms you with beautifully decorated rooms filled with color and whimsical details. Enjoy the sparkling pool in the afternoon, as well as stargazing in the soothing spa after dark. Professional massages are available in the spa room, a perfect way to end the day. A bountiful breakfast assures that no one leaves hungry. Quiet moments and total relaxation are inevitable...our hospitality awaits!

Rooms/Rates
2 Rooms/3 Suites $135/$175. Cottages $200/$250. Guest House $400. Conference Ctr. $175. Elegantly appointed rooms with comfortable sitting areas, fine linens and lovely views. Open year-round.

Cuisine
Full gourmet breakfast, afternoon refreshments, fresh fruit, cold drinks. Complimentary evening wine. Fine and casual dining in and around Mineola.

Nearest Airport(s)
Tyler or Dallas

Directions
Mineola is approx. 80 miles from both Dallas and Shreveport. From I-20, take Hwy 69 N to Mineola. When Hwy 69 forks, take Hwy 37 N for 6 miles and turn L on FM 779. Fall Farm is 2 miles on L.

Member Since 2000

"Every room and view is a warm profusion of color and pattern."

Innkeepers/Owners
Mike and Vickie Schneider

Traditional Southwestern Country Inn

Mobil ★★★
AAA ◆◆◆

Blair House

www.srinns.com/blairhouse
100 W. Spoke Hill Drive, Wimberley, TX 78676
877-549-5450 • 512-847-1111 • Fax 512-842-1147
info@blairhouseinn.com

Conveniently located just minutes from the Wimberley Square, Blair House Inn is situated on 22 peaceful acres featuring breathtaking hill country vistas. Meticulous service, warm hospitality, delectable food and luxury amenities provide the ultimate in comfort. This inviting inn is light and airy and features one of the best art galleries in Wimberley. A pool and whirlpool spa set in the hillside allows for spectacular views while relaxing. Blair House also provides spacious and attractive common areas including a living room with a fireplace, a television/game room, a library, plus a front porch with beautiful sunset views and a patio by the herb garden. Guests can enjoy a massage, use the sauna, hike the grounds, venture out on one of the bicycles or just nap in a hammock. Rated third nationwide as "Best Evening Cuisine" and "Best B&B for Relaxing and Unwinding," by *Inn Traveler* Magazine and the "Best Breakfast in Texas" - *Southern Living*.

Member Since 1998

Rooms/Rates
3 rooms, main house, $135/$165. 8 rooms or exective suites, $185/$275. All individually decorated guests rooms have luxurious linens, lovely views, Direct TV/VCR, CD players, and private baths, most with whirlpool tubs. Open year-round.

Cuisine
Full breakfast, evening dessert, 5-course, fixed menu gourmet dinner on Saturday evenings. Other times by request, special occasions. Complimentary beverages.

Nearest Airport(s)
Austin/San Antonio

Directions
From Austin take I-35 S to Kyle Exit; continue W to Wimberley; 1.6 miles S of Wimberley Square on E side of Ranch Road 12.

"We have spent just 48 hours with you. We thank you now for a lifetime of wonderful memories."

The Inn Above Onion Creek

www.srinns.com/onion
4444 Highway 150 West, Kyle, TX 78640
800-579-7686 • 512-268-1617 • Fax 512-268-1090
info@innaboveonioncreek.com

Owners
John and Janie Orr
Innkeeper
Amy Dolan
Elegant Texas Country Inn

The Inn Above Onion Creek is a replica of a late 1800s homestead set on a 100-acre Hill Country plot with panoramic views. The Inn was built to remember the past with all of the present day amenities, each of the nine rooms meticulously decorated to tell its own story about its namesake. The first of two buildings is built of rustic cedar with sawn cedar posts, while the second building is finished in white stone and supported by white pillars. The entire Inn features classic antique pieces, comfortable furnishings and feather beds. The character of the Inn as a whole is unlike anything else, providing a tranquil setting that makes it easy to unwind and appreciate the surrounding beauty. The Inn sits about five miles from the closest town and one mile off any main road. Included in each night's stay is a full breakfast and a three-course dinner, prepared using the freshest seasonal ingredients available. Hosted by a friendly staff, The Inn Above Onion Creek is the Hill Country's answer to southern hospitality.

Member Since 2003

Rooms/Rates
9 rooms, including 2 suites: $180/$295, double occupancy. All with fireplace and porch, 6 with whirlpool bath. Breakfast and dinner included in room rate. 15% discount Sunday through Thursday.

Cuisine
Upscale cuisine served in a casual rustic dining environment. Full breakfast served from 8:30-10:00 each morning. Three-course dinner served at 6:00 each evening. Complimentary coffee, tea, cold drinks, homemade cookies and fruit.

Nearest Airport(s)
Austin Bergstrom

Directions
25 miles S.W. of Austin. Exit 213 off I-35 and head W. to last stop sign in Kyle. Turn right onto Hwy. 150 W. and travel 5.3 miles.

"...beautiful sunrises and sunsets, rolling hills, flowers, butterflies, wildlife... excellent food and service...simply magnificent!"

Innkeepers/Owners
Paula & Charles Stallcup
Historic In Town Breakfast Inn

Mobil ★★★
AAA ◆◆◆

A Beckmann Inn and Carriage House

www.srinns.com/beckmanninn
222 E. Guenther Street, San Antonio, TX 78204
800-945-1449 • 210-229-1449 • Fax 210-229-1061
beckinn@swbell.net

Rooms/Rates
5 rooms $109/$159. Open year-round.

Cuisine
Full gourmet breakfast, with a breakfast dessert.

Nearest Airport(s)
San Antonio International

Directions
From airport, take 281 South to 37 South, exit Right on Durango, Left on South St. Mary's St., then immediately take Right on King William St., Left on E. Guenther St.

Experience warm and gracious hospitality at its very best, in a beautiful Victorian home and carriage house in the picturesque, downtown, King William Historic District. The perfect location for business or leisure travel accommodations. The "hidden treasure" of San Antonio, across from the landscaped Riverwalk and minutes to the Alamo by trolley. The wonderful wraparound porch welcomes guests to spacious antique filled rooms, ornately carved queen size beds, private bathrooms, robes, TVs, phones, refrigerators, hair dryers, and irons/ironing boards. A gourmet breakfast, with a breakfast dessert, is seved in our formal dining room with china, crystal and silver.

Member Since 1997

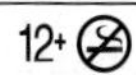

"Warm and personal hospitality, gourmet breakfast, artisitcally served, best location!"

Noble Inns

www.srinns.com/nobleinns
107 Madison Street, San Antonio, TX 78204
800-221-4045 • 210-225-4045 • Fax 210-227-0877
stay@nobleinns.com

Owners
Liesl and Don Noble
Innkeepers
Megan Macdaniel, Muffy Weyman
Elegant In Town Breakfast Inn

Mobil ★★★
AAA ◆◆◆◆

Don and Liesl Noble, sixth-generation San Antonians, invite guests to experience the rich history and ambiance of San Antonio. Noble Inns comprise The Jackson House (JH) and Pancoast Carriage House (PCH), two 1890s-era historic landmarks, located four houses apart in the King William Historic District. Both provide Victorian elegance with modern luxuries and superior amenities for the discerning business or leisure traveler, and are just off the Riverwalk near all downtown sites, including the Alamo, convention center and Alamodome. All rooms include private marble bath, gas fireplace with antique mantel, antique furnishings and elegant fabrics. Complimentary high-speed internet. Gardens feature two pools and heated spa. Two-person whirlpool tub in bath, canopy bed, and transportation in our classic 1960 Rolls Royce Silver Cloud are available.

Member Since 2001

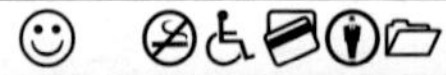

Rooms/Rates
7 Rooms, $120/$225; 2 Suites, $175/$275. Special weekday rates. Cable TV, phone w/VM, high-speed internet, robes, Central A/C.

Cuisine
The Jackson House features a full gourmet breakfast, afternoon refreshments, evening sherry. Pancoast Carriage House features an expanded continental breakfast and full kitchens en suite.

Nearest Airport(s)
San Antonio International

Directions
From airport to JH: US 281 South to Durango/Alamodome exit downtown. Rt on Durango. Left on S. St. Mary's. Rt on Madison. To PCH: same as above, then continue Rt on Turner. Left on Washington. Enter gates at 202 Washington.

"Your inn is gorgeous!—our room cozy, spacious bath, delightful spa, delicious breakfast!"

Owners
Liesl and Don Noble
Senior Innkeeper
Megan Macdaniel

Elegant In Town
Breakfast Inn

Mobil ★★★

The Ogé Inn on the Riverwalk

www.srinns.com/ogeinn
209 Washington St, San Antonio, TX 78204
800-242-2770 • 210-223-2353 • Fax 210-226-5812
ogeinn@swbell.net

Rooms/Rates
10 Rooms & Suites on 3 floors, $155/$350 B&B. Corporate weekday rates for single business travelers. All rooms include cable TV, phone w/VM, high-speed internet, robes, individual heat & A/C, guest refrigerator.

Cuisine
Full gourmet breakfast, afternoon refreshments, evening sherry.

Nearest Airport(s)
San Antonio International

Directions
From airport: US 281 South (IH 37) to Durango/ Alamodome exit downtown. Rt on Durango & go thru 3 stoplights. Left onto Pancoast St. and angle right onto Washington St. Inn is 1st house on Right. Historic marker and address plaques (#209) in front.

Boasting 1.5 landscaped acres directly on the famous Riverwalk in the King William Historic District, this 1857 Antebellum Mansion is one of Texas' historic architectural gems. With its grand verandas and spacious rooms, it is known for its elegance, quiet comfort and luxury. Furnished in European and American antiques, all rooms have a king or queen bed, private bath, cable TV, phone and guest refrigerator, and include delicious full breakfast. Several rooms have fireplace, porch and/or flat panel TV w/ DVD player. Two newly remodeled suites feature luxurious granite baths with double Jacuzzi tub and separate multi-spray shower. Conveniently located downtown near the Alamo, convention center, Alamodome, shopping, dining and entertainment. Amenities for business travelers include complimentary high-speed internet.

Member Since 1994

"Wonderful location, excellent and warm staff.
Fabulous Breakfasts. 4 stars, in my opinion."

Utah

"The Beehive State"

Famous For: Mormon Tabernacle, Great Salt Lake, Bridal Veil Falls, Arches National Park, Nine Mile Canyon, Dinosaur National Monument, Kodachrome Basin State Park, Bryce Canyon, Coral Pink Sand Dunes, Natural Bridges National Monument, "Newspaper Rock" (ancient news reports written on walls of caves), Zion National Park.

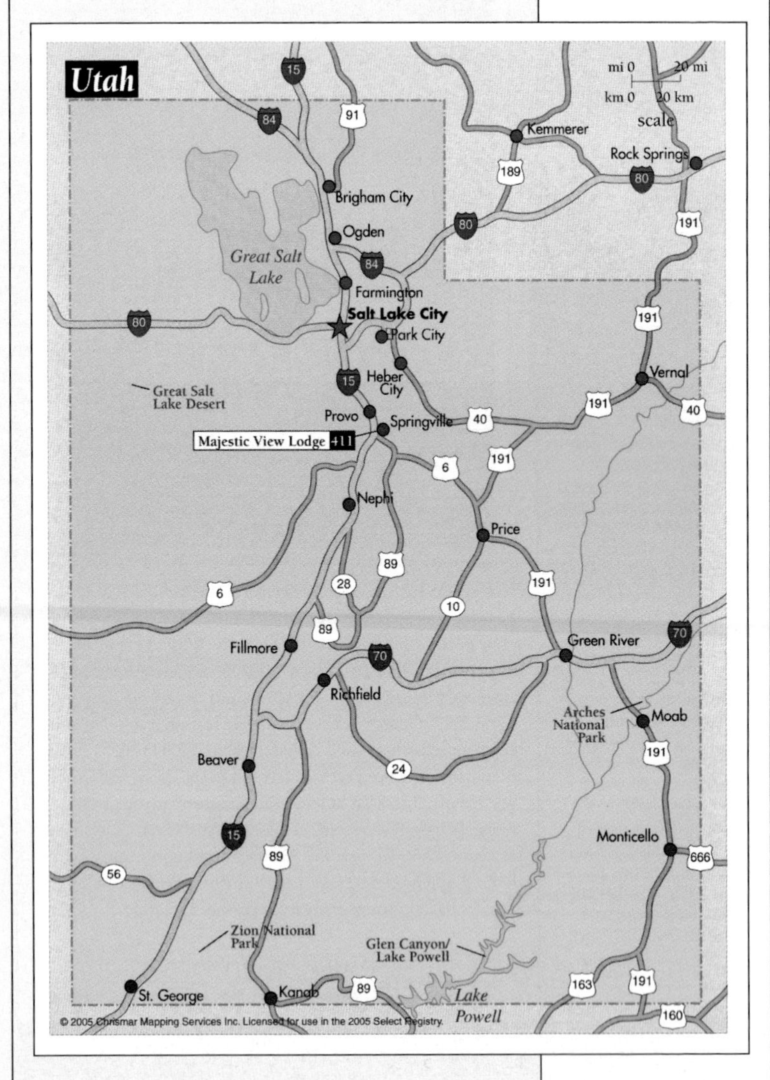

Innkeeper/Owner
John Lonetti
General Manager
Jennifer Withers

Deluxe Rustic Lodge

AAA ◆◆◆

Majestic View Lodge

www.srinns.com/majesticview
2400 Zion Park Blvd., Springdale, UT 84767
866-772-0665 • 435-772-0665 • Fax 435-772-0308
info@majesticviewlodge.com

Rooms/Rates
70 Rooms. $79/$209.

Cuisine
Coming into Majestic View to enjoy a meal in our restaurant will quickly introduce you to our friendly staff and pleasant atmosphere,with a menu of Steak, Seafood and Pasta thats sure to please. Open Daily for Breakfast, Lunch and Dinner $8.00 to $25.00.

Nearest Airport(s)
St George Airport UT, McCarren Airport NV

Directions
I-15 Exit Take the UT-9 exit- EXIT 16- toward HURRICANE/ZION NATL. PARK. Follow the signs to Zion Natl. Park as you enter Springdale. We are the large log buildings. Please enter on the L side of the road for registration.

Conveniently located at the entrance to Zion Canyon, Majestic View Lodge offers the discriminating traveler deluxe accommodations in a delightful, comfortable, rustic setting. Every room features wonderful views. Enjoy a meal in our restaurant and you'll be pleased with the quality of your meal and our outstanding service. The spectacular lodge-style interior design of our restaurant is complemented by the dramatic and unsurpassed views of Zion National Park just outside your window. The relaxing sound of our indoor waterfall completes the mood. Our Trading Post is proud to be one of the largest and finest gift shops in southern Utah. Our North American Wildlife Museum is one of the finest in all of the American Southwest. The 3000 square feet of displays were designed by an internationally-known wildlife habitat display company. It was our goal to present the wildlife in highly-accurate, natural surroundings accurate down to the finest, and sometimes amusing, detail.

Member Since 2005

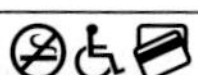

"Every room has a balcony with breathtaking view. The staff is very friendly. It is the best place I have ever stayed."

Vermont

"The Green Mountain State"

Famous For: Maple Syrup, Dairies, Lakes, Forests, Mountains and Skiing

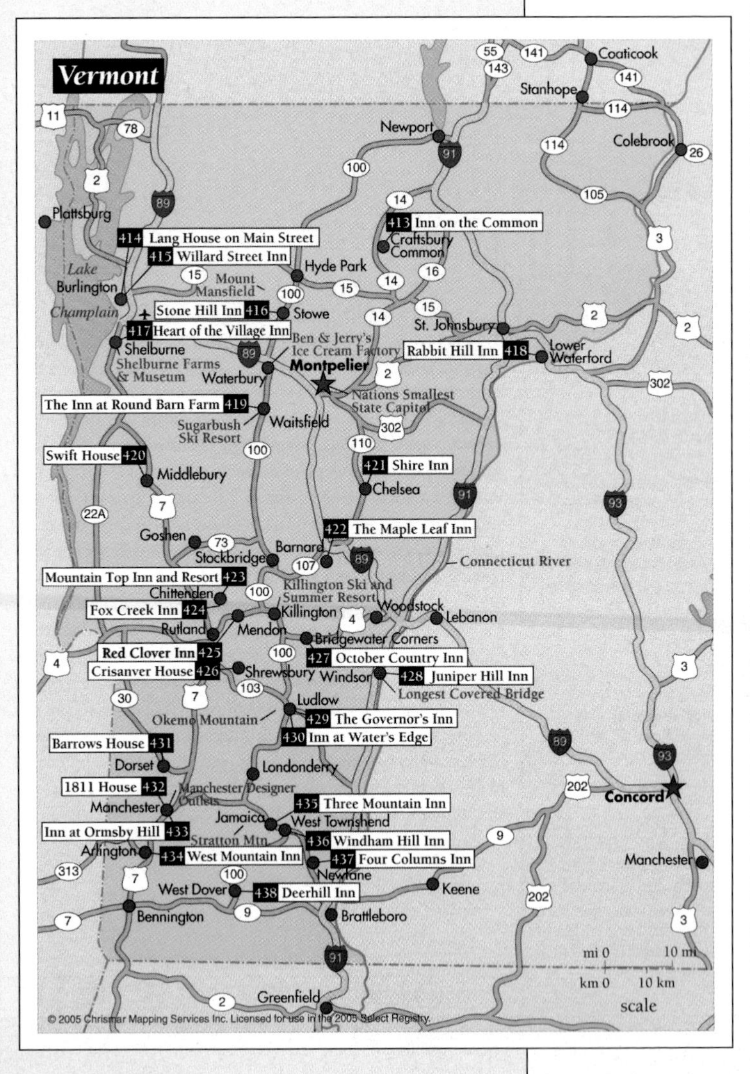

Innkeepers/Owners
Jim and Judi Lamberti, Vermont Innkeeper of the Year 1994

Elegant Federal Country Inn

Mobil ★★★
AAA ◆◆◆

Inn on the Common

www.srinns.com/innonthecommon
P.O. Box 75, 1162 N. Craftsbury Road
Craftsbury Common, VT 05827
800-521-2233 • 802-586-9619 • Fax 802-586-2249
info@innonthecommon.com

Rooms/Rates
16 Rooms. $135/$299 B&B (for one or two people per night including refreshments and full breakfast). Dinner Meal Plan (4 courses) additional, available Wed.-Sun. Rates adjusted seasonally. Rooms available with wood-burning fireplaces and/or whirlpool tub. Vermont tax and service additional. Open year-round.

Cuisine
On-site Trellis Restaurant offers innovative country cuisine. Guests enjoy a full country breakfast, candle-lit romantic dining, afternoon refreshments and our complete wine cellar.

Nearest Airport(s)
Burlington, VT

Directions
Call or visit www.innonthecommon.com.

Dreaming of a classic Vermont country inn experience? Visit Inn on the Common in scenic Craftsbury Common, one of the state's most photographed hill towns. Profiled on NBC's famous *Today Show*, the Inn has been showcased in many national and international publications. Nestled in the Northeast Kingdom's pristine countryside, this jewel of an inn offers a quiet, sophisticated retreat from today's hectic lifestyle. Surrounded by manicured gardens and the legendary Green Mountains, the Inn's lovely campus is home to three meticulously restored Federal houses. Guestrooms feature private baths, hand-stitched quilts, beautiful artwork and heirloom antiques. This is THE vacation getaway that you'll be telling all your friends and family about! Come stay a while, enjoy our gracious hospitality and superb customer service, and take home a wealth of warm, happy memories!

Skiers: Our area offers some of the best cross-country skiing in the East. Corporate, groups and weddings welcome. Check our website for specials. Gift Certificates available.

Member Since 1976

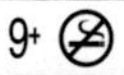

"After an incredible scenic drive, we pulled into the Inn and it was just… 'wow.' It feels like how life is supposed to be…beautiful, tranquil, inspiring."

Lang House on Main Street

www.srinns.com/langhouse
360 Main Street, Burlington, VT 05401
877-919-9799 • 802-652-2500 • Fax 802-651-8717
innkeeper@langhouse.com

Built as a private residence in 1881, the Lang House was converted in 2000 to an 11-room bed and breakfast inn. The renovation preserved the house's historic nature and added a number of contemporary amenities. The Lang House features qualities guests expect in a 19th c.Victorian home--antiques, soaring ceilings, stunning woodwork, stained glass windows, and the rosette pattern repeated throughout the house. The inn is situated in Burlington's Hill Section, which is known for its remarkable residential architecture and proximity to the University of Vermont and Burlington restaurants, shopping and cultural and waterfront venues. The Lang House innkeepers and staff provide genuine hospitality and personalized attention to leisure and business travelers.

Member Since 2003

Innkeepers
Kim Borsavage

Victorian In Town
Bed & Breakfast Inn 

Rooms/Rates
$135/$225

Cuisine
Gourmet Breakfast.

Nearest Airport(s)
Burlington International (BTV)

Directions
Located on Main Street (Rte 2), approx. 1.5 mi. from I-89 and just E of Rte 7. From I-89, exit 14W, Rte 2, which turns into Main Street. As you come down the hill into Burlington, the Lang House is on your R, just before the traffic light. If you are coming from across the Lake via the Lake Champlain Ferry, take a L at the first light onto Battery St. At the first traffic light, take a R and head up Main Street (or Route 2 E). We are located approximately 1/2 mi. up Main, on the L side of the street.

"We love the Lang House! Our room was lovely, the food great and the staff were the best. Thanks for making this such a memorable trip for us."

Owners
Beverly and Gordon Watson
General Manager
Jocelyn Potvin
Traditional In Town Bed and Breakfast

Willard Street Inn

www.srinns.com/willardstreet
349 South Willard Street, Burlington, VT 05401
800-577-8712 • 802-651-8710 • Fax 802-651-8714
info@willardstreetinn.com

Rooms/Rates
13 Rooms, $125/$225; 1 Suite, $225. Private baths, AC, cable TV. Antiques, luxurious beds, lake views. Open year-round.

Cuisine
Full breakfast served from 7:30-10:00 AM daily. Three different entrees each day, including items such as eggs benedict, waffles, French toast, and our homemade granola with yogurt, and fresh fruit. Featuring Vermont products and summer vegetables fresh from our garden.

Nearest Airport(s)
Burlington

Directions
From I-89: take Exit 14 W. Follow Rte. 2W for 1.5 miles. Turn L onto S. Willard St. (also Rte. 7S). We are 1/2 mile down, on the R side of street.

Burlington's first historic inn is located in the city's prestigious hill section. This Georgian/Queen Anne Revival-style mansion was built in 1881, and has been lovingly restored to its original splendor. Each room has its own distinct character, with fluffy beds and beautiful antiques. In many, the view of Lake Champlain takes center stage. Our classic breakfasts are served with a delightful dash of the unexpected in our marble-floored solarium. Outside, our tranquil gardens invite you in with their glorious color, lush foliage and heavenly scents. Walk to the award-winning Church Street Marketplace and the Lake Champlain waterfront.

Member Since 2002

"A lovely place to forget what day it is. Casual, comfortable elegance galore! Inn-credible!"

Stone Hill Inn

www.srinns.com/stonehill
89 Houston Farm Road, Stowe, VT 05672
802-253-6282 • Fax 802-253-7415
stay@stonehillinn.com

Innkeepers/Owners
Amy and Hap Jordan
Elegant Contemporary Mountain Breakfast Inn

Designed and built by the innkeepers, the Inn was created to be a peaceful, romantic, one-of-a-kind getaway. Relax in your bubbling, fireside Jacuzzi for two--every room has one--along with many other thoughtful touches and indulgent amenities. Schedule a massage by the fireplace in the privacy of your room, or outside in our spectacular summer perennial gardens. In winter, glide down the hill on the toboggan, or borrow some snowshoes to explore our wooded trail. Stowe has long been known as the 'Ski Capital of the East,' but this scenic mountain village offers so much to do year-round. After dinner at one of 50 local restaurants, return to the Inn for billards, games, and puzzles by the huge stone fireplace, or select a movie from the video library (popcorn provided!). This is truly a place for couples who treasure their time together. Chosen one of the Twelve Best B&Bs in North America, Forbes.com. Recommended by the *New York Times, Boston Globe, Montreal Gazette, Washington Post,* and *USA Today.*

Member Since 2002

Rooms/Rates
9 rooms, all with king bed and fireside Jacuzzi for two. TV/VCR. $265 to $390 B&B, depending on season.

Cuisine
A memorable, full country breakfast with 3 daily choices is served from 7:30 to 10:00 AM in the sunny, window-walled breakfast room with tables set for two. Evening hors d'oeuvres and 24-hour soft drinks included. BYOB if you wish.

Nearest Airport(s)
Burlington, VT

Directions
From I-89, take exit 10. Follow Route 100 North for 10 miles to Stowe. At the 3-way stop, turn left on Route 108. Go 3 miles. Turn right on Houston Farm Road. It's the first driveway on the left.

"The food at the Stone Hill Inn is the best we have had at an inn..."
- *The Boston Globe*

Heart of the Village Inn

www.srinns.com/heartofthevillage
5347 Shelburne Road, Shelburne, VT 05482
877-808-1834 • 802-985-2800 • Fax 802-985-2870
innkeeper@heartofthevillage.com

Innkeepers/Owners
Pat Button
Traditional Victorian Village Breakfast Inn

Rooms/Rates
4 king/twins $170/$190; 3 queens $160/$180; 1 queen suite $225/$245; 1 queen room $130/$150. TV, telephone, AC, private baths, 3 w/clawfoot tub, 1 Jacuzzi. Corporate rates available; open all year.

Cuisine
Early AM coffee & tea. Full breakfast featuring home made granola, yogurt, fresh fruit, baked goods & unique hot entree each day. Fresh baked cookies. Wine/cheese available.

Nearest Airport(s)
Burlington VT

Directions
From I-89, exit 13; S on Rte. 7; 4.7 miles to the inn. From I-87, exit 20; Rte. 9 to Rte. 149 to Fort Ann, NY; Rte. 4 to Rte. 22A N to Vergennes, VT; Rte. 7 N to Shelburne.

Located in the heart of Shelburne Village, this 1886 historic inn welcomes guests with elegance and warmth. The Inn has retained its prominence as one of the centerpieces of the Village, and is listed on the National Register of Historic Places. There are five Inn rooms and four Carriage Barn rooms—each elegantly decorated with a mix of period furnishings – armoires, comfortable beds, plus linens and a sunny view of Shelburne Village. Each room has a private bath, air conditioning, phone service, cable television and a cozy reading chair. The Inn's large living room, library and wrap around porch provide comfortable chairs to relax in and enjoy morning coffee, afternoon tea, or a glass of wine. Walk to Shelburne Museum. Shelburne Farms, downtown Burlington, and the airport are closeby.

Member Since 2002

"Beautiful, comfortable Inn - a warm welcome from a gracious hostess and breakfast-to-die for."

Rabbit Hill Inn

www.rabbithillinn.com
48 Lower Waterford Rd., Lower Waterford, VT 05848
800-76-BUNNY • 802-748-5168 • Fax 802-748-8342
info@rabbithillinn.com

Innkeepers/Owners
Brian & Leslie Mulcahy
Elegant Federal
Country Inn

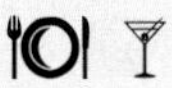

Mobil ★★★
AAA ◆◆◆◆

Even time could not change this 1795 Country Inn classic ~ an enchanting romantic hideaway in a tiny hamlet set between a river and the mountains. Our Inn features elegant and uniquely styled guest rooms, most with fireplaces, many with double whirlpool tubs and private porches. We are recognized for award-winning candlelit dining, pampering service, attention to detail, and warm hospitality unlike you have ever experienced from staff and ever-present innkeepers. Rabbit Hill Inn has been repeatedly voted one of America's Best Inns by travel writers, guidebooks, and magazines. Come experience for yourself why Rabbit Hill Inn is "a paradise for the senses, vacation for the soul!"

Rooms/Rates
19 Rooms & Suites. Classic Rooms: $185/$220 B&B / Superior Rooms w/fireplace: $225/$260 B&B / Luxury Rooms w/whirlpool & fireplace: $295/$345 B&B. All offer queen or king beds, plush robes, CD players and many fine amenities.

Cuisine
Full country breakfast and afternoon tea & pastries included. Enjoy a multi-course gourmet candlelit dinner in our romantic dining room. Beer, wine, and spirits available in our Snooty Fox Pub.

Nearest Airport(s)
Manchester, NH

Directions
From I-91 (N or S), exit 19 to I-93 S. Exit 1 R. on Rte. 18 S 7 mi. to Inn. From I-93 N, exit 44, L on Rte. 18 N, 2 mi. to Inn.

Member Since 1990

"...accommodations are incredible, meals are amazing... this just might be the most romantic place on the planet." Zagat's 2005

Innkeepers/Owners
AnneMarie DeFreest & Tim L. Piper

Elegant 18th Century Historic Country Bed & Breakfast

The Inn at Round Barn Farm

www.srinns.com/roundbarn
1661 East Warren Road, Waitsfield, VT 05673
802-496-2276 • Fax 802-496-2276
lodging@theroundbarn.com

Rooms/Rates
12 Rooms, 1 Suite $160/$315. Guest rooms are tasteful & luxurious, comforts of home, none of the demands...canopied beds, whirlpool tubs, fireplaces.

Cuisine
The Inn at the Round Barn Farm takes pride in serving creative breakfasts made with the best seasonal and local ingredients. Dinner is enjoyed at one of 15 area restaurants within 10 miles.

Nearest Airport(s)
Burlington Airport (BTV)

Directions
I-89 S exit 10, Rte. 100 S 14 miles. L on Bridge St., through covered bridge, R at fork up one mile. I-89 N exit 9, Rte. 100B 14 miles. L on Bridge St., through covered bridge, R at fork, up one mile.

We invite you to our elegant, romantic Bed & Breakfast Inn, surrounded by lush green hillsides, flower-covered meadows, graceful ponds, and extensive perennial gardens. This idyllic pastoral scene, in the heart of the Sugarbush/Mad River Valley, has offered a serene peaceful escape for travelers since 1987. The interior of the Inn is memorable; the restoration impeccable. Reconstructed timbers, refurbished floors covered in oriental rugs, walls awash in a palette of rich tones, warm, relaxing gathering rooms, and soothing music create an unpretentious atmosphere. Gracious and friendly Innkeepers await your arrival. In winter, our meadows and woodlands are covered in snow. Snowshoe trails and snowshoes are available for our guests to experience the magic of our Vermont winter wonderland.

Member Since 2000

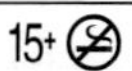

"Round Barn is the most peaceful & nourishing place on earth!"
"Enchanting views!"

Swift House Inn

www.srinns.com/swifthouseinn
25 Stewart Lane, Middlebury, VT 05753
866-388-9925 • 802-388-9925 • Fax 802-388-9927
info@swifthouseinn.com

Innkeepers/Owners
Dan & Michele Brown
Federal/Victorian
In Town Village Inn

AAA ◆◆◆

Life's most memorable moments are spent with loved ones in exceptional places. The Swift House Inn is just such a place. Located in historic Middlebury, Vermont, this 21-room former governor's mansion offers the essence of New England warmth. Inside, candlelit dinners await you. Large, comfortable rooms offer modern amenities in period decor. Relax. Sip a glass of wine by the fire, or ponder your favorite book in the library while the kids explore the garden or sled on a nearby hill. Every window frames a picture of country tranquility, yet shops, museums, and Middlebury College are a short walk away. The Inn's three buildings are on five acres with extensive lawns and fabulous gardens. Enjoy hiking just out the back door or in the nearby Green Mountains. Bike the Champlain Valley or participate in the many water activities on nearby Lake Champlain. Numerous ski areas are just a short drive.

Rooms/Rates
21 Rooms in three buildings $100/$275. Many with fireplaces and two person whirlpool tubs. All with telephone, individually controlled AC, most with TV. Sauna, steam shower, and conference room.

Cuisine
Full Breakfast. Dinner served 5 nights a week; changing menu prepared with many local Vermont products. Full bar service and extensive wine list.

Nearest Airport(s)
Burlington International Airport, 35 miles

Directions
The Swift House Inn is located on Stewart Lane just off of Route 7, two blocks north of the village green.

Member Since 2005

"Exceptional food, wonderful service..."

Shire Inn

www.shireinn.com
Main Street, P.O. Box 37, Chelsea, VT 05038
800-441-6908 • 802-685-3031 • Fax 802-685-3871
innfo@shireinn.com

Innkeepers/Owners
Karen & Jay Keller
Traditional Federal
Village Inn

Rooms/Rates
6 Rooms w/ private baths, 4 w/wood-burning fireplace, $135/$195 B&B; $215/$280 MAP. Rates include all gratuities. Open May - Oct; Weekends & Holidays Dec - Feb.

Cuisine
Vermont country breakfast. Casual afternoon tea. Romantic 5-course gourmet candlelit dinner just for guests available weekends, during the Fall colors, on Holidays, or by special request. Our wine cellar of 1,000 bottles offers a fine selection.

Nearest Airport(s)
Burlington, VT (BTV) 90 minutes via I-89

Directions
From south, I-89, VT Exit 2, L 150 yds. to STOP; R on 14, 7 mi., R on 110; 13 mi. to inn. See website for more.

Vermont before ski resorts and factory outlets? Come to Chelsea!

Dairy farms, forests, picturesque villages, trout streams, covered bridges, birds, deer, friendly folks, unbelievable starry nights. Your own bright, comfortable room with a wonderful wood burning fireplace (romantic even on the cool Vermont summer nights!) in this 1832 mansion.

Begin and end each day with fabulous meals. Enjoy our custom tours of vintage Vermont, hike the nearby hills, bike or cross-country ski this beautiful valley, swim or tube in the nearby White River, antique in the many picturesque villages -- Or... just relax by the fire, on the porch, or on our 23 acres with a rocky trout stream running through it.

Experience the simpler life... as you'd expect it to be. Come explore — come unwind!

Member Since 1986

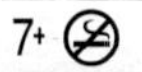

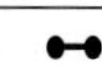

"A wonderful, relaxing place to stay with unspoiled surroundings." K. & LJ., England

The Maple Leaf Inn

www.srinns.com/mapleleaf
PO Box 273, 5890 Vermont Route 12, Barnard, VT 05031
800-516-2753 • 802-234-5342
mapleafinn@aol.com

Innkeepers/Owners
Gary and Janet Robison
Elegant Country Breakfast Inn

Mobil ★★★
AAA ◆◆◆◆

We welcome you to refresh your spirit and restore your soul in this pastoral corner of Vermont. Nestled snugly within sixteen acres of maple and birch trees, our Victorian-style farmhouse was lovingly designed and built by the innkeepers. Each spacious guest room has its own personality and charm with delicate stenciling, stitchery, and handmade quilts. Individually controlled central heating/air-conditioning, heated bathroom tile floors and a pillow library all help to add to your personal comfort. Upholstered chairs and good reading lights are provided. Woodburning fireplaces are set daily for your convenience and a collection of romantic videos awaits your viewing. An honor bar with snacks, sodas and bottled water is available at any time and room service, including delectable treats, beer and wine, may be ordered as well. "Nook and Cranny Gift Shelf". Memorable gourmet breakfasts are prepared fresh each morning and served at individual candlelit tables for two. Evening turn-down service is offered. Come share our dream.

Member Since 2002

Rooms/Rates
7 Rooms $130/$260 B&B. Spacious guest rooms with king beds, luxurious private baths with whirlpools, TV/VCR with premium satellite service, telephones, woodburning fireplaces, spa robes, hair dryers, air-conditioning. Open all year.

Cuisine
A gourmet three-course breakfast is served at individual candlelit tables for two, and light afternoon refreshments are served in the parlor at check-in. Beer and wine available.

Nearest Airport(s)
Burlington, VT

Directions
From Woodstock, VT: Go 9 miles N on Rte. 12 to Barnard. The Inn sits back in the woods on the R, just before the school.

"In all of my travels, I've never seen anything quite like the attention to detail that the innkeepers lovingly bestow on their guests." *Santa Barbara News*

Innkeepers/Owners
Steven and Lauren Bryant
Traditional Mountain Resort

The Mountain Top Inn & Resort

www.srinns.com/mountaintopinn
195 Mountain Top Road, Chittenden, VT 05737
800-445-2100 • 802-483-2311 • Fax 802-483-6373
stay@mountaintopinn.com

Rooms/Rates
6 Luxury Rooms with whirlpool tubs $245/$465. 32 Lodge Rooms and pet-friendly Cabins $130/$295. Chalets $300/$1,200. Rates include full breakfast. Open year round.

Cuisine
Unparalleled dining, New American Cuisine in the Highlands Dining Room, by the fireplace. Casual bistro fare in the Tavern. Seasonal Outdoor Terrace. Children's menu.

Nearest Airport(s)
Burlington, VT - 1.5 hours
Albany, NY - 2 hours

Directions
Easy access from Routes 91, 89, 4 and 7. Just a short drive from Killington and Rutland. From Route 4 or 7 follow the signs for The Mountain Top Inn & Resort. Visit the website for detailed directions.

Offering breathtaking natural beauty, every season for every experience, The Mountain Top Inn & Resort is surrounded by the Green Mountain National Forest and set amidst 350 acres overlooking a pristine, recreational lake. In the tradition of a mountain lodge, guests enjoy breathtaking views, unparalleled dining, warm hospitality and endless outdoor adventure. Attractive seasonal packages entice couples, families, cross country skiers, equestrian enthusiasts and nature lovers to visit the luxury Resort. Located in Central Vermont, just a short drive from Killington or Rutland, this four-season destination has something for everyone. In summer enjoy horseback riding, hiking, a private lake-front sandy beach, scenic boat rides, canoes, kayaks, fly-fishing, mountain biking, tennis and hay rides. Winter's transformation creates 80km of groomed nordic ski and snowshoe trails; as well as horse drawn sleigh rides, ice skating, and sledding. Casual, yet refined, the furnishings throughout dazzle with sophistication and comfort.

Member Since 1987

"A little piece of heaven… one of the best views in Vermont."

Fox Creek Inn

www.srinns.com/foxcreek
49 Dam Road, Chittenden, VT 05737
800-707-0017 • 802-483-6213 • Fax 802-483-2623
foxcreek@sover.net

Innkeepers/Owners
Alex and Ann Volz

Traditional Country Inn

Just the way you have always pictured a Country Inn. Here is the Vermont for which you have been searching. There are a myriad of activities: hiking, biking and water sports in Summer and alpine and XC skiing in Winter. Relaxing in front of a fireplace or sitting on the front porch with a glass of wine, these are the times when memories are made. Once the home of William Barstow, you can easily imagine the family entertaining their friends, the Fords, Firestones, and his partner, Thomas Edison. By earning our share of awards for food, wine and innkeeping, we have kept that tradition of entertaining alive. This is backwoods elegance at its best.

Rooms/Rates
9 Rooms, all w/private baths: 1 w/fp+fp in Dbl Jacuzzi; 2 w/fp + Jacuzzi; 3 w/Jacuzzi; 2 w/full bath; 1 w/Dbl. Jacuzzi; $160/$295 B&B; $190/$409 MAP.

Cuisine
Enjoy a full Vermont country breakfast and a candlelit 4-course dinner. Choose from our ever-changing menu, featuring the freshest ingredients. See the difference between eating and dining. Full bar & an award-winning wine menu with over 175 labels, many older vintages.

Nearest Airport(s)
Burlington

Directions
Chittenden is 10 miles northeast of Rutland, VT. From Rutland take Rt. 7N or Rt. 4E and follow the state hospitality signs.

Member Since 1998

"Terry and I loved staying at Fox Creek. We felt like we were guests in your home."

Innkeepers/Owners
Bill Pedersen and
Tricia Treen Pedersen

Traditional Mountain Inn

Mobil ★★★
AAA ◆◆◆

Red Clover Inn

www.srinns.com/redcloverinn
7 Woodward Road, Killington/Mendon, VT 05701
800-752-0571 • 802-775-2290 • Fax 802-773-0594
innkeepers@redcloverinn.com

Rooms/Rates
14 guest rooms: 6 with fireplace, 4 double & 1 single whirlpools, 7 with TV, all with air conditioning. $145/$290, Foliage/Holidays: $205/$360.

Cuisine
Candlelit gourmet dining complemented by fine wine from award-winning list. *Wine Spectator* Award winner since 1995. Full bar. Hearty country breakfast served in a sunlit breakfast room. Special events and celebrations welcome.

Nearest Airport(s)
Rutland State Airport

Directions
5 miles West of Killington turn Left from Route 4 to Woodward Road, 1/4 mile to Inn on Left or 5 miles East of Rutland turn Right from Route 4 to Woodward Road, 1/4 mile to Inn on Left.

Down a tree-lined country road in the Green Mountains, this rambling 1840s farmhouse estate on 13 acres offers warmth, pampering by caring staff and attentive innkeepers, and exceptional gourmet fare complemented by an award-winning wine list. Rooms are attractively furnished with thoughtful attention to detail; many offer whirlpool tubs for two, gas fireplaces and all have majestic mountain views. From the Inn, explore quaint villages and pastoral beauty or choose from many seasonal activities; Killington Resort Area is only 5 miles away; take in a round at Green Mountain National Golf Course or other fine courses nearby; explore Woodstock, Vermont; or hike the Appalachian Trail. Later dine leisurely and sumptuously from an extensive menu featuring the freshest dairy, produce and game that Vermont offers. Restaurant has been awarded *Wine Spectator* Award of Excellence since 1995.

Member Since 1998

"What a comfortable taken-care-of stay..."

Crisanver House

www.srinns.com/crisanverhouse
1434 Crown Point Road, Shrewsbury, VT 05738
800-492-8089 • 802-492-3589 • Fax 802-492-3480
info@crisanver.com

Innkeepers/Owners
Carol & B. Michael Calotta

Historic Country Inn

Central to historic places, great shopping, cultural events and year round sports, this Circa 1800s Historic Register New England Farmhouse is totally renovated. Classic country style and warm decor create comfort and charming elegance.

At 2000 ft. amid 120 acres, you are surrounded by spectacular panoramic views, a rolling tapestry of the Green Mountains and brilliantly colorful sunsets. Cottage suites provide luxuries-king bed, marble baths, his/her spun glass sinks, Jacuzzi, ceiling fans and heated towel bars.

Great fun fills your days: tennis, shuffleboard, croquet, hiking, large pristine pond, ping pong, darts, TV, VCR movies, board games, books, magazines and the porch. Meander the gardens savoring the fresh aromas. A foliage spectacle with its breathtaking colors beckons in autumn, while the Inn glows from within amidst a winter wonderland.

A boutique Inn experience-everything you imagine a Country Inn should be: fine accommodations, delicious food, magnificent views,

Rooms/Rates
6 rooms/3 suites: $110/$295. Includes served gourmet breakfast, afternoon tea, Inn baked cookies, biscotti, beverages, fruit and bedtime truffle, private bath, robes, European bath products, alarm, radio/CD, CD's, daily papers, flowers. Closed Apr/Nov. Website specials.

Cuisine
Menu of the day dinner service with linen, Wedgewood china, music, candlelight and fresh flowers. Hikers picnic lunch.

Nearest Airport(s)
Rutland - 10 min
Burlington Int'l - 2 hrs

Directions
7N or S to 103: 91S to 4W to 7S to 103: 91N to 103N: 87 to 787E to NY 7E to VT 7N to 103: From 103 to Lincoln Hill Rd to Crown Point Rd: Pickup @ Rutland Arpt or Train

Member Since 2005

12+   

"We've stayed at over 55 B&B's-But you are our TOPS! BRAVO - You are our new #1!" See our website for other guest comments.

Innkeepers/Owners
Edie and Chuck Janisse

Traditional Country Inn

October Country Inn

www.octobercountryinn.com
P.O. Box 66, 362 Upper Rd., Bridgewater Corners, VT 05035
800-648-8421 • 802-672-3412 • Fax 802-672-1163
oci@vermontel.net

Rooms/Rates
10 Rooms, $100/$165 Dbl. B&B. Dinner, $18.50 per person.

Cuisine
Full country breakfast. Internationally-themed dinners cooked to gourmet standards and served family-style. Beer and wine license.

Nearest Airport(s)
Manchester, NH

Directions
From Woodstock, follow Rte. 4 westward about 8 miles. Go 1/10 mile past Country Store at junction of Rte. 100A, turn right on Bridgewater Center Rd., and right again on Upper Rd. From Rutland, follow Rte. 4 eastward about 20 miles. Just before the Long Trail Brewery, turn left on Bridgewater Center Rd., and right on Upper Rd.

Loved for its hospitality and relaxed atmosphere, Chuck and Edie's converted nineteenth century farmhouse between Woodstock and Killington offers warmth and intimacy in the finest innkeeping tradition. The scents of baking muffins, fresh herbs and homemade desserts fill the inn as Chuck works magic in French Country, Mexican, Italian, Greek, and even American cuisines. Swim in the pool, bicycle, hike, ski, shop, sight-see or simply relax by the fire—then dine by candlelight. Away from the crowds, yet close to Killington, Okemo, Woodstock, Weston, and Dartmouth. Bridgewater Corners and October Country Inn are always just around the corner.

Member Since 1992

"Had a great time. Great food. Nice people stay here. We'll be back."

Juniper Hill Inn

www.srinns.com/juniperhill
153 Pembroke Road, Windsor, VT 05089
800-359-2541 • 802-674-5273 • Fax 802-674-2041
innkeeper@juniperhillinn.com

Innkeepers/Owners
Robert and Susanne Pearl

Traditional Country Inn

Ascend a winding driveway canopied by ancient pines to a restored Colonial Revival mansion surrounded by acres of lawns and gardens. Experience incomparable views of Lake Runnemede and Ascutney Mountain. Common areas include the spacious Great Hall, Library and Sitting Parlor. Comfortable seating, crackling fireplaces and historic elegance create a relaxing environment. All guest rooms feature antiques, decanters of sherry, chocolates, fresh flowers, robes, hair dryers, CD players. Many guest rooms also include fireplaces, private balconies or porches. Immaculate attention to detail and fine country cuisine are additional reasons Juniper Hill is awarded a Romantic Hideaway destination by *The Discerning Traveler* and featured in the *Boston Globe*. Conveniently located near popular Vermont/New Hampshire locations including Woodstock, Quechee, Dartmouth College. Enjoy skiing, canoeing, horseback or sleigh rides, bicyling, shopping, historic sites or simply relax in our beautiful surroundings.

Member Since 2002

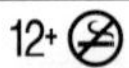   

Rooms/Rates
16 Rooms, $105/$225 B&B. Many rooms with fireplaces, porches or balconies, queen beds, antiques, woods or mountain views. All guest rooms individually air conditioned.

Cuisine
Full country breakfast menu plus daily special, afternoon refreshment from 3-5 PM. Single 7PM seating for four-course dinner by advance reservation only, Tues.-Sat. Self-serve warm beverages available 7-10PM.

Nearest Airport(s)
Manchester, NH

Directions
From I-91 North: Take exit 9. Turn R (L from I-91 S) onto Rte. 5 S. Proceed 2.7 miles, turn R onto Juniper Hill Road, stay L at fork. Driveway on R at crest of hill.

"After a fun day, it's a joy to return to our secluded mansion to savor its view, fine food & each other's company. We're ready to schedule another visit!"

The Governor's Inn

www.thegovernorsinn.com
86 Main Street, Ludlow, VT 05149
800-468-3766 • 802-228-8830
innkeeper@thegovernorsinn.com

Innkeepers/Owners
Jim and Cathy Kubec
Elegant Victorian Village Breakfast Inn

Mobil ★★★

Intimate and romantic, The Governor's Inn pampers guests with outstanding food, warm hospitality, and gracious surroundings. Afternoon tea, full breakfasts, and elegant gourmet dinners are served on antique china with silver and crystal. This late Victorian country house features extraordinary slate fireplaces and nine individually decorated guest rooms, each with its own antiques, most with gas fireplaces. Culinary Magic Cooking Seminars held on premises. Walk to nearby shops and restaurants. Take along one of Cathy's gourmet picnics as you explore Vermont. Near Okemo Mountain, skiing, golf, hiking, summer theater, bicycling, Weston Priory, antiquing.

Rooms/Rates
8 Rooms, $129/$254 B&B;
1 Suite, $244/$319 B&B.
Includes Afternoon Tea and Full Breakfast. Dinner available Sat. Ski packages. Air conditioned. Open year-round, except 2 weeks in Apr., 2 weeks in Nov., and Dec. 23-26.

Cuisine
Full, hot breakfast, afternoon tea and sweets. Extensive tea menu. Prix fixe dinner on Saturdays. Full beverage service. Specially prepared Vermont country picnics by request.

Nearest Airport(s)
Hartford - 125 miles
Boston - 144 miles

Directions
Ludlow Village is located at intersection of VT Rte. 100 & VT Rte. 103. Inn is south on Main St. (Rte 103), just off town green.

Member Since 1987

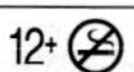   

"Everything about the inn says 'relax and enjoy'...and we did! Incredible gourmet breakfast!"

Inn at Water's Edge

www.srinns.com/watersedge
45 Kingdom Road, Ludlow, VT 05149
888-706-9736 • 802-228-8143 • Fax 802-228-8443
innatwatersedge@mail.tds.net

Innkeepers/Owners
Bruce & Tina Verdrager

Historic Waterside Inn

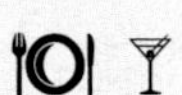

AAA ◆◆◆◆

Situated on Echo Lake and surrounded by the Black River, this 150 year old Victorian estate has been thoroughly restored and now boasts all the charm and ambiance of a truly unique Victorian Inn. Located minutes from skiing and golfing at Okemo and Killington mountains, the Inn is only a short drive to the attractions of Manchester, Weston and Woodstock. Each of our 11 rooms has a private bath, most with Jacuzzi bathtubs. Enjoy a "libation" in our English Pub, relax in an outdoor hot tub or take a swim off our private beach or curl up with a good book in our library. The Inn is completely air-conditioned. Aveeda spa packages available.

Rooms/Rates
11 rooms $125/$250 B&B. $175/$300 MAP. Golf packages starting $125/ppdo includes 18 holes of golf, lodging, breakfast and 4-course dinner. Ski Packages starting $100/ppdo includes adult lift ticket at Okemo Mt., lodging, breakfast and 4-course dinner. Reservations can be made 60 days in advance.

Cuisine
Full country breakfast. Afternoon refreshments. 4-course candlelit Dinner. Beer, wine and spirits available in Doc's English Pub and in the Dining Room.

Nearest Airport(s)
Bradley Springfield (Hartford)

Directions
4 miles north of Ludlow Village on Route 100 at Echo Lake between Okemo and Killington Resorts.

Member Since 2003

"Our 4-course dinner is not to be missed. A real Gem, don't change a thing!"

Barrows House

www.srinns.com/barrowshouse
3156 Route 30, PO Box 98, Dorset, VT 05251-0098
800-639-1620 • 802-867-4455 • Fax 802-867-0132
innkeepers@barrowshouse.com

Innkeepers/Owners
Linda & Jim McGinnis
Traditional Federal Village Inn

Barrows House is a collection of nine white clapboard buildings on 12 groomed acres in the heart of the picture-book Vermont village of Dorset. Guests have a choice of 28 rooms and suites in nine different buildings, each with a history and style of its own. All rooms and suites have as a minimum their own private bath, king or queen bed, expanded cable TV, air conditioning and private telephones. Nine also have fireplaces and two have whirlpool tubs. Dining at Barrows House is an informal and delicious adventure in American regional cuisine in our three dining rooms. Whether with iced tea in the gazebo or English garden or mulled cider in front of a warm fire and historic stenciling, Barrows House extends its welcome. Weddings and family reunions are done with a very personal touch.

Rooms/Rates
Rates range from $120 to $260 B&B double occupany for 18 double sized rooms and 10 suites, nine with fireplaces and two with whirlpool tubs.

Cuisine
Dining is relaxing and informal. The menu is Regional American in style with Continental influence. The quality of your meal will impress especially in a village of less than 1,000 people. A speciality of the Inn is Maine Crab Cakes, Chesapeake Style.

Nearest Airport(s)
Albany, NY

Directions
Boston: 3 hours
New York: 4 hours
Montreal: 4 hours

Member Since 1974

"Soft beds, wonderful food, beautiful place, best hosts —I wish I could come here every day!"

1811 House

www.1811house.com
Rt. 7A , P.O. Box 39, Manchester, VT 05254-0039
800-432-1811 • 802-362-1811 • Fax 802-362-2443
house1811@adelphia.net

Innkeepers/Owners
Marnie and Bruce Duff
Innkeepers/Owners
Cathy and Jorge Veleta

Elegant Village Breakfast Inn

Located in the heart of historic Manchester Village, the 1811 House is listed on the National Register of Historic Places. Carefully restored to its original Federal period style, the 1811 House offers unequalled ambiance with English and American antiques and decor. The inn is fully air conditioned and the 13 guest rooms offer warmth and detail with wood-burning fireplaces, oriental rugs, fine paintings and canopied beds. The British style pub, featuring a collection of over ninety single malt scotch whiskies, along with a large selection of wines, beers and liquors, is the perfect place to relax. A delicious, made-from-scratch, full breakfast is served every morning in the dining room with fine china and sterling silver place settings. The seven acres of grounds, with terraced gardens and a pond, invite you to stroll around and enjoy the exceptional views of the Green Mountains. Elegant, but casual, the 1811 House is the vacation destination you deserve for that romantic Vermont getaway.

Rooms/Rates
11 Rooms, 2 Suites $210/$280 B&B. Open year-round except week prior to Christmas and Christmas Day.

Cuisine
Elegant full breakfast, award-winning cookies and complimentary sherry. British Pub featuring over 90 single malts, English ale on tap, wine by the glass and premium liquors and cordials.

Nearest Airport(s)
Albany, New York - one hour and 15 minutes

Directions
In Manchester Center, at junction of Rtes. 11/30 and 7A, go south on Historic Rte. 7A, approximately 1 mile. The 1811 House is on the left.

Member Since 1998

"Every detail of your fine establishment was impeccable and heartwarming. I will remember always with pleasure the traditional ambiance of the 1811 House."

Innkeepers/Owners
Ted and Chris Sprague
Elegant Village Breakfast Inn

AAA ◆◆◆◆

The Inn at Ormsby Hill

www.srinns.com/ormsbyhill
1842 Main Street, Historic Route 7A, Manchester, VT 05255
800-670-2841 • 802-362-1163 • Fax 802-362-5176
stay@ormsbyhill.com

Rooms/Rates
10 Rooms, all with fireplace and Jacuzzi for two, $205/$330 B&B. Peak season premiums apply. Open year-round. See website for specials.

Cuisine
Nationally-acclaimed breakfasts served in the magnificent Conservatory with its wall of windows facing the mountains. "...a breakfast that'll knock your socks off..." *Yankee Magazine's Travel Guide.* "...perhaps the best breakfasts in Vermont," says *New England Travel.*

Nearest Airport(s)
Albany, New York

Directions
In Manchester Center, at junction of Routes 11/30 and 7A, take Historic Route 7A South. The Inn is approximately 3 miles on the left.

A distinguished, romantic, luxurious, tranquil retreat. Surround yourself with a spectacular setting. Be pampered in bed chambers with canopies, fireplaces, air-conditioning, and some with slim-line digital flat-screen televisions. Luxurious bathrooms with Jacuzzis for two. Indulge in "...the attention to detail, the romantic ambiance..." *Colonial Homes.* A patio, porch and gazebo, with breathtaking views of the Battenkill Valley and Green Mountains. A restored manor house, c. 1764, so serene you will never want to leave. Renowned for comfort, heartfelt hospitality, and profound attention to detail. "...arguably one of the most welcoming inns in all of New England." *Lonely Planet.*

Member Since 1996

"...a romantic bed-and-breakfast of the highest caliber."
Andrew Harper's *Hideaway Report*

West Mountain Inn

www.srinns.com/westmountain
144 West Mountain Inn Road, Arlington, VT 05250
802-375-6516 • Fax 802-375-6553
info@westmountaininn.com

Innkeepers/Owners
The Carlson Family
Traditional Colonial Mountain Inn

Mobil ★★★

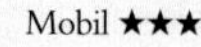

Nestled on a mountainside overlooking the historic village of Arlington and the Green Mountains beyond, the century-old West Mountain Inn has been welcoming travelers with warmth and hospitality for over a quarter of a century. Visitors are treated to spacious antique-filled guest rooms and common areas, 150 woodland acres with beautiful views, gardens, a labyrinth, and llamas providing space to relax and renew the body and spirit. Miles of hiking trails and the Battenkill River provide seasonal outdoor activities. A hearty country breakfast and an elegant 6-course dinner in front of an open hearth complement your stay. The Inn also offers private dining and meeting rooms for unique celebrations of weddings, birthdays, anniversaries, reunions or business meetings.

Member Since 1984

Rooms/Rates
12 Rooms, 3 Suites, 3 Townhouses $149/$304 B&B, $224/$379 MAP. Service charges included in all rates.

Cuisine
A full country breakfast and elegant 5-course dinner are prepared daily. Seasonal menus focus on local VT products and organic produce. Weddings and rehearsal dinners a specialty. Full bar, premium beers and exceptional wine list.

Nearest Airport(s)
Albany, NY

Directions
Vermont Route 7 N, exit 3, L off ramp, take access road to end, R on Rte. 7A into Arlington. One mile then L on Rte. 313 for .5 mile, L on River Rd., green bridge over river, Inn's driveway on the L, Inn at top of driveway.

"A wonderful ambiance where the warmth extends beyond the fireplace."

Three Mountain Inn

www.srinns.com/threemountaininn
3732 Main Street Route 30/100, P.O. Box 180, Jamaica, VT 05343
800-532-9399 • 802-874-4140 • Fax 802-874-4745
stay@threemtn.com

Innkeepers/Owners
Jennifer and Ed Dorta-Duque

Elegant Colonial Village Inn

AAA ◆◆◆◆

Rooms/Rates
15 Rooms. $145/$345.

Cuisine
This historic 1790 culinary landmark, offers an elegant dining experience, showcasing Contemporary Vermont Fresh Cuisine. The dining rooms, with wood burning fireplaces, are set in two intimate but casual rooms decorated with timeless elegance.

Nearest Airport(s)
Hartford/Springfield

Directions
Jamaica is located on VT Rt 30, 1/2 hr. NW of Brattleboro (I-91, Exit 2). Take Rte 30, North to Jamaica. The Inn is on the right. From Manchester, take VT Rte 11/30 make right to continue on Rte 30, continue on Rte 30 towards Jamaica, the Inn is on the left.

The mission of Three Mountain Inn is all about you. We await the opportunity to exceed your expectations. Our 18th Century origins are evident in the hand hewn beams and wide "King's Wood" in the Main House. The 21st Century is also evident in our amenities, Vermont-fresh cuisine in our AAA rated restaurant, extensive wine menu that has been awarded the *Wine Spectator* Award of Excellence, and our well-stocked pub. Three Mountain Inn is convenient to all of Vermont. Hiking, skiing, summer theater and the Vermont Symphony are seasonal events, while fresh air, starry nights, and mountain views are available year-round. Most of all, our staff is devoted to the fulfillment of desires you never knew existed.

Member Since 1982

"Perfect hosts, wonderful rooms with a beautiful Vermont setting."
"Jamaica Vermont...Vermont as one hoped it would be..." *Travel + Leisure*

Windham Hill Inn

www.srinns.com/windhamhill
311 Lawrence Drive, West Townshend, VT 05359
800-944-4080 • 802-874-4080 • Fax 802-874-4702
windham@sover.net

Innkeepers/Owners
Marina & Joe Coneeny
Elegant Country Inn

Windham Hill Inn, a "...place that touches your soul.." sits on 160 acres at the end of a Green Mountain hillside country road, surrounded by rock-wall bordered fields and forests, and breathtaking views. Friendly innkeepers and staff welcome you to this country estate with its sparkling rooms, memorable gourmet meals, extensive and award winning wine list, relaxing ambiance and closeness to nature. Relax in four elegantly furnished common rooms with wood-burning fireplaces, a 1911 Steinway grand piano and extensive CD library. Guest rooms feature antiques, locally crafted furnishings, hardwood floors and oriental rugs. Most rooms have soaking or Jacuzzi tubs, gas fireplaces or Vermont Castings stoves. Some have private decks. Centrally air-conditioned throughout. Close to abundant Southern Vermont events and activities. A true destination property, the Inn is "....as good as it gets, especially if you're in search of a romantic getaway." *Frommers* 2004.

Rooms/Rates
21 Rooms, $195/$380 B&B; Peak season premiums apply. Open year-round except the week prior to the 27th of December during the Christmas season, and the first two weeks of April.

Cuisine
Full breakfast and afternoon refreshments. Light Lunch avail. Dinner by reservation every evening. Wine and liquor available. Winner *Wine Spectator* award for the past 7 years.

Nearest Airport(s)
Hartford (Bradley Intl. 1.5 hrs)

Directions
I-91 N to Brattleboro exit 2, follow signs to Route 30, 21.5 miles NW to West Townshend. Turn R opposite Post Office onto Windham Hill Road, 1.3 miles, follow sign to Inn.

Member Since 1989

"Everything you would think a Vermont Inn should be!"

Innkeepers/Owners
Debbie and Bruce Pfander

Elegant Country Inn

Four Columns Inn

www.srinns.com/fourcolumns
P.O. Box 278, 21 West Street, Newfane, VT 05345
800-787-6633 • 802-365-7713 • Fax 802-365-0022
innkeeper@fourcolumnsinn.com

Rooms/Rates
15 Rooms & Suites, $150/$385 includes full breakfast. Special Packages in some seasons. 11 rooms with fireplaces, 9 suites with whirlpool/soaking tubs. Open year round.

Cuisine
Chef Greg Parks has led the culinary team for over 25 years. Awards: James Beard Foundation, Wine Spectator. Dinner nightly except Tues. Extensive wine list.

Nearest Airport(s)
Bradley, Logan, JFK

Directions
I-91 to VT Exit 2. Turn L at end of ramp. Go 1/2 mile, turn L on Cedar St. Go to the third stop sign. Turn L on VT Rte.30 N. Go 11 miles to Newfane. Village Green on the left-Inn is just behind the Courthouse.

The Four Columns Inn was lovingly built in 1832 by Pardon Kimball to replicate the childhood home of his southern wife. Today that home is an elegant country inn with 15 delightful guest rooms ranging from six charming traditional rooms to nine beautifully refurbished suites, all featuring private baths, individual heat and air conditioning, period antique furnishings, complimentary telephone usage, and afternoon tea and cookies. Gas fireplaces are the focal point in eleven rooms, and the suites deliver grand scale bathrooms with spa tubs and separate showers. Select rooms also offer high speed internet access, and televisions with DVD players plus a huge library of complimentary movies. A hearty country breakfast, complete with a selection of morning newspapers, is included for all house guests. And not to be missed is dinner in the Inn's fine dining restaurant, where Chef Greg Parks has a well earned reputation for his creative regional cuisine. Situated on the historic Newfane Green unchanged since the 1830s, the property includes 150 acres of rolling hills, an inviting stream, ponds and exquisite gardens. Guests will enjoy the lovely pool and rustic hiking trails in summer, plus access to all the seasonal outdoor activities in Southern Vermont only a short distance away. "Why go anywhere else"? - Sandra Soule

Member Since 2000

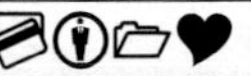

"If romance requires a stage set, Four Columns is the theater of choice!" *Country Home* "Quintessential New England!" *Daily Candy*

Deerhill Inn

www.srinns.com/deerhill
P.O. Box 136, Valley View Road, West Dover, VT 05356
800-993-3379 • 802-464-3100 • Fax 802-464-5474
innkeeper@deerhill.com

Innkeepers/Owners
Chef Michael Allen & Stan Gresens

Elegant Mountain Inn

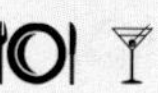

Once chosen "one of the most romantic places in the world," Deerhill Inn is nestled on a hillside overlooking the quintessential Vermont village of West Dover with panoramic views of the Green Mountains. Perfectly located in the middle of Southern Vermont, Deerhill has access to the best of Vermont and Northern Massachusetts. Museums, theaters, antiquing, shopping, hiking, boating, and of course skiing. Fourteen uniquely decorated guest rooms (including *Country Inn* Magazine's Room of the Year) with private baths, designer linens, microfiber robes, private porches and complimentary full country breakfast. Three comfortable sitting rooms, art gallery, gift shop, secluded "grotto" pool, lush gardens and the "amazing" cuisine of Chef Michael Allen complete the experience. Chef-owned and operated and only four hours from Manhattan and two and a half from Boston.

Member Since 1999

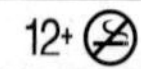

Rooms/Rates
Thirteen rooms, one suite $135/$335. Special packages and off-season discounts. Open nearly all year except late April/early May.

Cuisine
Full, made to order, Country breakfast; the "amazing" Modern American Cuisine of Chef Michael Allen; and a *Wine Spectator* awarded, New World wine list. Chosen one of the 25 best Chef-Owned Inns in the U.S. by *Conde Nast Traveler* April 1999. Full liquor license.

Nearest Airport(s)
Albany, NY - 1.5 hours
Hartford, CT - 2 hours

Directions
From I-91, Vt. exit 2 (Brattleboro); to Rte. 9W 20 miles to Rte. 100N 6 miles to Valley View Road, up hill 200 yards.

"Beautiful, charming, great touches everywhere - food incredible - just what we were looking for!! Thank you!!"

Virginia

"The Old Dominion"

Famous For: Blue Ridge Mountains, Mount Vernon, Monticello, Arlington National Cemetery, Skyline Drive, Manassas National Battlefield Park, Colonial Williamsburg, Jamestown Settlement, Virginia Beach, Yorktown, Booker T. Washington National Monument, Appomattox Court House, Chesapeake Bay, Rock of Ages Natural Bridge, Shenandoah National Park

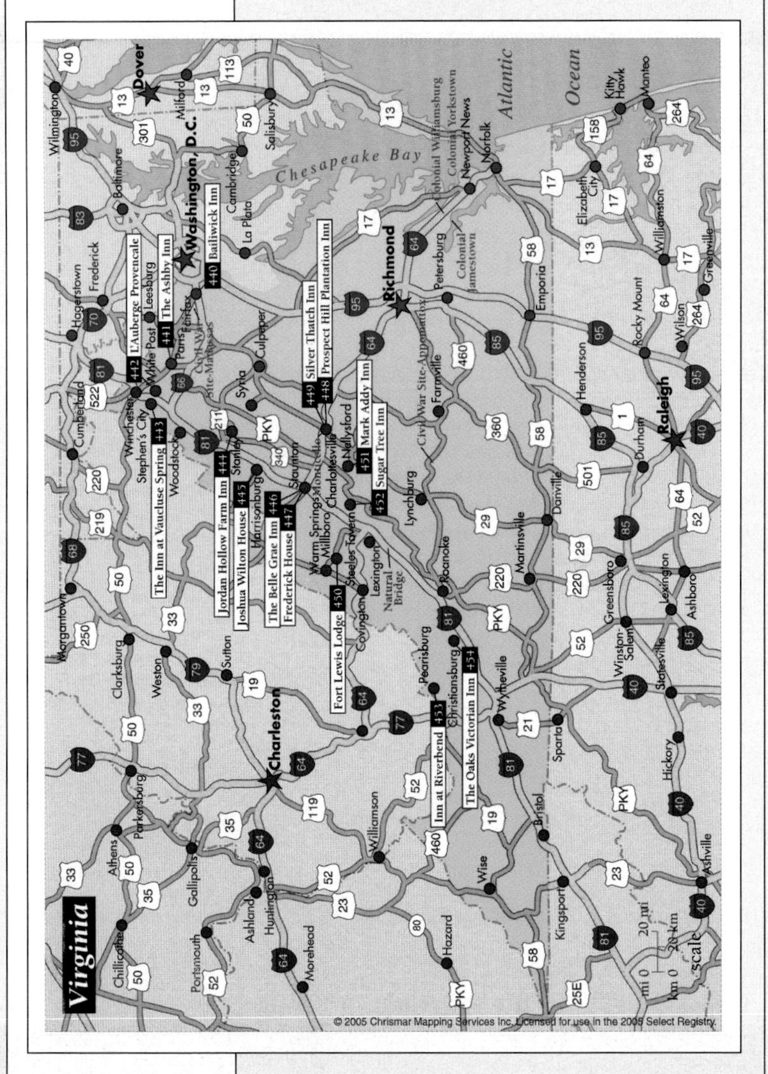

The Bailiwick Inn

www.srinns.com/bailiwick
4023 Chain Bridge Road, Fairfax, VA 22030
703-691-2266 • Fax 703-934-2112
theinn@bailiwickinn.com

Innkeepers/Owners
Bonnie W. McDaniel
Elegant In Town Inn

AAA ◆◆◆◆

This charming, elegant National Register Inn is located only 15 miles from Washington D.C. in historic Old Town Fairfax, Virginia. Luxurious guest chambers patterned after famous Virginians, with feather beds, antiques, Frette bathrobes, fireplaces, whirlpools, mini-bars, dataport phones, afternoon tea, turn-down service and gourmet breakfast. Enjoy fine dining at the Inn in its award-winning restaurant. The Inn is a wonderful place for weddings, corporate retreats,or romantic getaways. The Bailiwick has received many national awards including *Country Inns* Magazine Top 12 Inns. Featured on Food Network, Travel Network, Discovery Channel and Romancing America.

Member Since 2003

Rooms/Rates
11 Guestrooms, $170/$230; 1 Suite, $355. Afternoon tea and gourmet breakfast included in room rate. Open year-round. Packages available.

Cuisine
Elegant gourmet restaurant serving creative Continental cuisine with French and American accents in an intimate setting. Full bar service and extensive wine list available. Open breakfast, lunch, tea, cocktails and dinner.

Nearest Airport(s)
Dulles

Directions
I-66 to exit #60, Rte 123 S Chain Bridge Road toward Fairfax. Pass Main Street, Rte 236, the Inn is on the next L corner at intersection of Sager and Chain Bridge.Free parking behind building.

"Beautiful room, lovely inn, delicious food and above all, gracious service. Food is to die for. We loved it!"

The Ashby Inn & Restaurant

www.srinns.com/ashby
692 Federal St., Paris, VA 20130
540-592-3900 • Fax 540-592-3781
celebrate@ashbyinn.com

Innkeepers/Owners
John and Roma Sherman

Traditional Colonial Village Inn

Rooms/Rates
6 Rooms, $145/$185 B&B; 4 Suites, $250. Sun.-Thurs. discounts on all rooms. Closed Jan 1, July 4, Dec 24 & 25.

Cuisine
Breakfast, dinner (Wed-Sat), Sunday brunch. On-site special events. Wine and liquor available.

Nearest Airport(s)
Winchester Regional Airport
Washington/Dulles International

Directions
From Wash DC Rte 66 W to exit 23 - Rte 17 N, 7.5 miles L on Rte 701 for .5 miles or Rte 50 W thru Middleburg, L just after light at Rte. 17.

This 1829 Inn finds its character in the small village of Paris and its heart in the kitchen. The menu is guided more by tradition than trend—with great attention paid to seasonal foods like asparagus, shad roe, softshell crabs and game. Much of the summer produce, herbs and flowers come from its gardens. Guest rooms furnished in period pieces (half with fireplaces and balconies) have views stretching beyond the formal perennial gardens to the hills of the Blue Ridge. The four dining rooms are as intimate as they are distinct - from an enclosed porch, to a converted kitchen with walnut beams and fireplace, to a cozy room with booths set against faux painted walls and striking paintings. Summer dining on the covered patio overlooking the lawn attracts a wide Washington following.

Member Since 1988

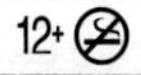

"Back here in paradise. Warm, elegant, exceptional. Don't change a thing."

L'Auberge Provencale

www.srinns.com/lauberge
Route 340, P.O. Box 190, 13630 Lord Fairfax Highway,
White Post, VA 22663
800-638-1702 • 540-837-1375 • Fax 540-837-2004
cborel@shentel.net

Innkeepers/Owners
Alain & Celeste Borel

Elegant Country Inn

A warm "South of France" breath blows over this eclectic and sophisticated Country Inn with its nationally and internationally renowned "Provencal Cuisine Moderne" by chef/owner Alain Borel and his team of chefs. Every meal here is a special and unique occasion. Three different dining rooms, each with their delightful decor, offer just the right setting for a quiet and romantic 5-course dinner and a cheerful gourmet breakfast. The Inn exudes the ambiance of Provence with warm faux painted walls, Provencale fabrics and antiques. Orchards, herbs, flowers, and vegetables are grown by the Innkeepers. Charming elegant guest rooms and suites, some with fireplaces, are all romantic. Perfect for honeymoons and special getaways. Our new Villa La Campagnette offers a swimming pool, luxury suites and privacy. The two Inns, set in Virginia Hunt Country, offer a special experience for discerning guests, with exquisite food and courteous attentive service. Weddings and rehearsal dinners are a specialty. Golfing, hiking, biking, and wineries. An Inn where Great Expectations are quietly met.

Member Since 1988

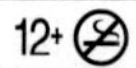

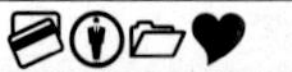

Rooms/Rates
10 Charming French Country Rooms, $150/$225; 4 Romatic Suites, $275/$325. Closed first three weeks of January. Some with Fireplaces, steam showers and Jacuzzi.

Cuisine
Elegant Five Course Dinners with Provencale flair served Wed. thru Sunday, breakfast of one's dreams, gourmet picnics and the best bistro brunch on Sunday Full extensive wine list of French Chateaux and American Wines, liquor.

Nearest Airport(s)
Dulles

Directions
1 hour W of DC Beltway. One mile S of Rt. 50 on Rt. 340, Inn is on the R. 45 minutes west of Dulles Airport. 10 miles east of Winchester in the Shenandoah Valley.

"If you're not happy about life after a meal here you haven't got a pulse." *Washington Post* "5 hearts, my top prize for Romance." *Washingtonian*

Innkeepers/Owners
Barry & Neil Myers

Traditional Country Inn

Mobil ★★★

The Inn at Vaucluse Spring

www.srinns.com/innatvauclusespring
231 Vaucluse Spring Lane, Stephens City, VA 22655
800-869-0525 • 540-869-0200 • Fax 540-869-9546
mail@vauclusespring.com

Rooms/Rates
12 Rooms/Suites: $145/$230 B&B. 3 Private cottages: $250/$285. Beautifully furnished, queen or king beds, all have fireplaces, 14 with Jacuzzis, some water/mountain views. Open year-round.

Cuisine
Full 3-course breakfast daily. By advance reservation, 3-course 'Southern Comfort' Friday night supper and romantic 4-course Saturday dinner. Wine and beer available.

Nearest Airport(s)
Dulles International

Directions
From I-66W, take exit 1B to I-81N. Go 1 mile to exit 302. Turn L on Rte 627, go .5 mile. Turn R on Rte 11, go 2 miles. Turn L on Rte 638, go 3/4 mile to Inn on L. Follow signs to check-in.

Set amidst 100 scenic acres in the rolling orchard country of the Shenandoah Valley, this collection of six guest houses is the perfect country retreat. Experience the elegance of the gracious 200 year old Manor House or the warmth and charm of an 1850s log home. For the ultimate in peace and privacy, stay in the old Mill House Studio at the water's edge, the Gallery Guest House with views of the meadow, or the Cabin by the Pond. Relax beside Vaucluse Spring's cool, crystal clear waters. Savor the region's bounty at the delicious breakfasts and weekend dinners. Ideally located for enjoying nearby activities.

Member Since 2000

Southern Living Magazine says "Perhaps The Inn at Vaucluse Spring was our best total experience. The best news? This place is an unbelievable value."

Jordan Hollow Farm Inn

www.srinns.com/jordanhollowfarm
326 Hawksbill Park Road, Stanley, VA 22851
888-418-7000 • 540-778-2285 • Fax 540-778-1759
jhf@jordanhollow.com

Innkeeper/Owner
Gail Kyle

Traditional Colonial
Country Inn

Surround yourself with spectacular mountain views, history, peace and serenity at our over 200 year-old farm. Located in the Shenandoah Valley, at the base of the Blue Ridge Mountains; you can relax in a rocking chair on a sunporch outside your room, or in front of a cozy fire. Meander through our beautiful gardens, explore the valley, vineyards, Civil War sites, historic villages, or take a hike on the five miles of trails onsite or in the nearby national park and forest. Begin and end each day with fabulous meals in our restored 1700s farmhouse restaurant. As we are a horse farm, you may bring your own horse if you like. We have 150 gorgeous acres for you to enjoy!

Rooms/Rates
14 Rooms, $190/$250 B&B; All rooms have fireplaces, hydro-thermo massage spas, whirlpool baths or soaking tubs. Closed January 2 through February 11.

Cuisine
Full restaurant dinner, breakfast, American Regional features Virginia wines and local produce (including our own "Inn-grown"). Picnic Baskets Available for Lunch. Extensive Wine List and full service bar available. Outdoor Porch and Deck Dining Seasonally with Outstanding Views!

Nearest Airport(s)
Dulles, Reagan National

Directions
Luray, VA Rte. 340 Business S for 6 mi. to L onto VA Rte. 624 L on VA Rte. 689 continue .5 mi. & R on VA Rte. 626 for .25 mi. to Inn on R.

Member Since 1985

"Unpretentious and Totally Relaxing" "Great Hospitality!"
"What a Gem!" "Super Food!"

Joshua Wilton House Inn and Restaurant

www.srinns.com/joshuawilton
412 S. Main St., Harrisonburg, VA 22801
888-294-5866 • 540-434-4464 • Fax 540-432-9525
info@joshuawilton.com

Innkeepers/Owners
Craig & Roberta Moore
Historic Victorian
In Town Inn

Located in an elegantly restored Queen Anne Victorian, the Joshua Wilton House offers guests an oasis of quiet charm and gracious living in the heart of the Shenandoah Valley. The home is within walking distance of historic downtown Harrisonburg and the campus of James Madison University. The Inn features five non-smoking bedrooms that have been decorated and furnished with beautiful antiques and reproductions. All rooms have one queen size bed, private baths, individually controlled thermostats, telephones, clock radios and hair dryers. Luxurious terry cloth bathrobes are provided for your use during your stay.

Rooms/Rates
5 Rooms, $105/$150 B&B.

Cuisine
The Restaurant offers an exquisite a la carte menu that changes with the seasons and an award-winning wine list. Featured are the food products of many small local farms and producers who supply our kitchen with high quality ingredients that simply cannot be found elsewhere. During the warmer months, seating is available on the outdoor brick patio. The restaurant is open from 5:00 PM, Tuesday through Saturday.

Nearest Airport(s)
Dulles - Washington, D.C.

Directions
412 S. Main St. I-81, exit 245, W on Port Rd. to Main St. N approx. 1 mi. To Joshua Wilton House located on R.

Member Since 1985

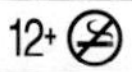   

"The best overnight we've ever had in a B&B."

The Belle Grae Inn and Restaurant

www.srinns.com/bellegrae
515 West Frederick St., Staunton, VA 24401-3333
888-541-5151 • 540-886-5151 • Fax 540-886-6641
bellegrae@sprynet.com

Innkeeper/Owner
Michael Organ
Traditional Victorian
In Town Inn

This Italianate Victorian house is the centerpiece of numerous restored 1890s homes transformed into comfortable lodging rooms in a quaint, architecturally rich residential district in Historic Staunton. The graciously furnished rooms, bistro bar, Azalea Courtyard and garden paths leading to the guest houses create a tasteful small hotel ambience. The Inn is an easy walk to the shops and museums, and an easy drive to Colonial and Civil War History. Dining is a must at Belle Grae! Each evening our Innkeeper pridefully describes the menu of the day. Shakespeare's Blackfriars Playhouse is within walking distance.

Rooms/Rates
17 Rooms, $99/$149; Suites, $139/$209 B&B, MAP available. Honeymoon Hideaway, $199. Open year-round.

Cuisine
Breakfast served daily 7:30-9 AM. Cocktails and conversation beginning at 5 PM. Dinner served Wed through Sun 5:30-9 PM. Full ABC available. Please visit website for sample menu.

Nearest Airport(s)
Shenandoah Valley Regional (Weyers Cave) or Charlottesville

Directions
I-81 exit 220, 222 or 225. Follow signs to Woodrow Wilson Birthplace. W on Frederick St. (RT 250W and 254W) to 515 W. Frederick (red brick mansion on R). Circle block for registration and off-street parking.

Member Since 1990

"Fine dining, tasteful lodging..."

Frederick House

www.frederickhouse.com
28 North New Street, Staunton, VA 24401
800-334-5575 • 540-885-4220 • Fax 540-885-5180
stay@frederickhouse.com

Innkeepers/Owners
Karen Cooksey & Denny Eister

Traditional In Town Breakfast Inn

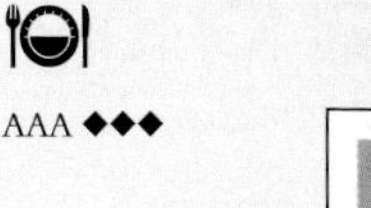

AAA ◆◆◆

Rooms/Rates
12 Rooms, $95/$165; 11 Suites, $140/$200. "Shenandoah Shakespeare Theater Package" and "Drama, Dining, Heritage & Shopping Pleasures Package" available year-round. Other packages available. Open year-round.

Cuisine
11 Restaurants available within walking distance; Fine Dining, Seafood, Steaks, American, Italian, Mexican, Ribs, Gourmet Deli, Southern Home Cooking, Casual and Coffee Shops.

Nearest Airport(s)
Shenandoah Valley Regional Airport, Charlottesville

Directions
From I-81 exit 222 follow Rt 250 West. Turn right on Coulter Ave. Turn left on Greenville. Turn right on New St.

Frederick House's five beautifully restored 19th Century residences offer 23 spacious rooms and suites in award winning buildings. The buildings date from 1810 and offer guests an escape into the relaxed atmosphere of a bygone era. All rooms are individually decorated with antiques and period furniture. All offer private bathrooms, cable TV, telephone, internet access, alarm clocks, hair dryers and bathrobes.

Frederick House is located in culturally rich historic downtown Staunton, the oldest city in the Shenandoah Valley. Staunton's historic downtown includes over 60 shops, restaurants, museums, galleries, concerts, the Shenandoah Shakespeare's Blackfriars Playhouse, Woodrow Wilson Presidential Library, Mary Baldwin College and Stuart Hall. For that leisurely getaway, park your car and enjoy strolling downtown.

From the Frederick House, explore the historical, cultural, and recreational opportunities that surround Staunton in the Shenandoah Valley. Visitors are always amazed at the variety of options to explore.

Member Since 1997

"Great romantic getaway. We will tell all our friends." "We loved being able to park our car, walk to theater & fine dining, while staying with you."

Prospect Hill Plantation Inn

www.srinns.com/prospecthill
Box 6909, Charlottesville, VA 22906
800-277-0844 • 540-967-0844 • Fax 540-967-0102
Innkeerer@prospecthill.com

Innkeepers/Owners
The Sheehan family since 1977

Elegant Plantation Country Inn

Mobil ★★★

Award-winning dining and lodging in the 1732 manor house and original 18th Century outbuildings and former slave quarters on this historic 50 acre plantation located just 15 miles East of Charlottesville, VA. Romantic 5-course candlelight dining daily. 13 rooms and suites featuring breakfast-in-bed, working fireplaces, double Jacuzzis in most rooms, private balconies, gazebo amidst manicured grounds, and swimming pool in the serenity of the coutryside near Monticello, wineries, and many other historic sites. Selected many times over the past 28 years as one of America's most romantic getaways. Come early for our complimentary pre-dinner wine reception and stroll our arboretum gardens and lawns while smelling the aromas wafting from the kitchen as we prepare the evening meal. MAP Lodging Packages include pre-dinner wine reception, candlelight dinner at table for two, full country breakfast and all gratuities. B&B and other special rates available.

Member Since 1979

Rooms/Rates
13 rms/suites from $145/$345 sgl B&B, $295/$495 dbl MAP pkgs w/gratuities included.

Cuisine
Elegant Continental-American cuisine. Wine and snacks on arrival, pre-dinner wine reception, 5-course candlelight dinner, full country breakfast-in-bed (or in dining room). All gratuities included with MAP.

Nearest Airport(s)
Charlottesville Albemarle

Directions
From Charlottesville (15 mi.) E via I-64, exit 136 at Zion Crossroads. From Washington, DC (approx. 100 mi.) I-66 W to Hwy#29 S, to Hwy#15 S to Zion Crossroads. Turn L on Hwy#250 E for 1 mile and L on Poindexter Rd. Inn is 3 mi down on L.

"Our favorite inn. Fantastic food! Coming every year for 21 years." JM, Annapolis, MD
"Wonderful food! What a GREAT inn!" LP, ChevyChase, MD

Silver Thatch Inn

www.srinns.com/silverthatch
3001 Hollymead Drive, Charlottesville, VA 22911
800-261-0720 • 434-978-4686 • Fax 434-973-6156
info@silverthatch.com

Innkeepers/Owners
Jim and Terri Petrovits
Traditional Colonial Country Inn

Mobil ★★★
AAA ◆◆◆

Rooms/Rates
7 Rooms, $145/$185 B&B.
Open year-round.

Cuisine
Breakfast for houseguests; Dinner served Tues. - Sat., specializing in contemporary cuisine, featuring local produce when available and eclectic sauces. Open to the public. Great English Pub, outstanding selection of wine and spirits.

Nearest Airport(s)
Charlottesville/Albemarle Regional Airport, 2 miles.

Directions
From S: 6 miles N of intersection of US 29 & US 250 bypass, turn R on Rte. 1520; From N: 1 mile S of Airport Rd., turn L on Rte. 1520.

This historic inn began its life as a barracks built in 1780 by Hessian soldiers captured during the Revolutionary War. As wings were added in 1812 and 1937, it served as a boys' school, a tobacco plantation, and a melon farm. It has been providing gracious lodging in antique-filled guest rooms and elegant candlelit dining since the 1970s. Relax and unwind in our intimate pub. Enjoy contemporary cuisine from our menu and wines from a list which has consistently won the *Wine Spectator* award of excellence and the *Wine Enthusiast* award of distinction.

Member Since 1986

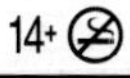

"I wanted to stay forever"

Fort Lewis Lodge

www.srinns.com/fortlewislodge
HCR 3 Box 21A, Millboro, VA 24460
540-925-2314 • Fax 540-925-2352
ftlewis@tds.net

Innkeepers/Owners
John and Caryl Cowden

Rustic Mountain
Full-Service Inn

AAA ◆◆◆

Centuries old, wonderfully wild, uncommonly comfortable. A country inn at the heart of a 3200-acre mountain estate. Outdoor activities abound with miles of river trout and bass fishing, swimming, extensive hiking trails, mountain biking, and magnificent vistas. Fort Lewis is a rare combination of unpretentious elegance and unique architecture offering a variety of lodging choices where every room has a view. Three "in the round" silo bedrooms, three hand-hewn log cabins with stone fireplaces, and Riverside House are perfect for a true country getaway. Evenings are highlighted by contemporary American-style cuisine served in the historic Lewis Gristmill.

Like most country inns, we trade in a change of pace, romance and exceptional fare. But over the years, we've come to understand that Fort Lewis has an asset that very few others have. Our wilderness - the mountains, forests, fields and streams and all the creatures that call this their home.

Member Since 1990

Rooms/Rates
13 Rooms, $175/$190 MAP;
3 Family Suites, $190 MAP;
3 Log Cabins, $225/$275 MAP.
Open April–October, closed November–March.

Cuisine
Full dinner and breakfast included in the daily room rate. Evening meals offer a vibrant mix of fresh tastes, just plucked vegetables and interesting menus. The aroma of hickoy smoke rising from the grills will leave you yearning to hear the dinner bell.

Nearest Airport(s)
Roanoke, VA (1.5 hrs.);
Charlottesville, VA (2 hrs.)

Directions
From Staunton, Rt. 254 W to Buffalo Gap; Rt.42 to Millboro Spgs.; Rt. 39 W for .7 mi. to R onto Rt. 678, 10.8 mi. to L onto Rt. 625, sign on L.

"The mountains, the river, the stars ... it's my Shangri-la."

The Mark Addy

www.srinns.com/markaddy
56 Rodes Farm Drive, Nellysford, VA 22958
800-278-2154 • 434-361-1101 • Fax 434-361-2425
info@mark-addy.com

Innkeeper
John Storck Maddox

Mountain
Breakfast Inn

Sincere hospitality based on a family legacy of gracious living awaits refreshed spirits on the sunrise side of the Blue Ridge. Vested on a verdant knoll, the inn is surrounded by magnificent mountain views and pathways redolent of lavender. History buffs explore Mr. Jefferson's country. Hot air ballooning, hiking the highest waterfall east of the Mississippi, or skiing, challenge the adventurous. Serenity awaits in the hammock or luxuriating in a Jacuzzi, or stargazing from one of five porches that envelop the home. The memorable magic of our chef edifies local bounty and harvest with classic technique and contemporary regional inspiration. We want you to be our guest!

Rooms/Rates
5 Rooms $100/$135 B&B; 5 Deluxe Rooms $135/$195 B&B. Jacuzzis, guest kitchen with complimentary snacks, beverages. Open year round.

Cuisine
Full breakfast, with an a la carte dinner menu available Wednesday through Saturday. Sunday Brunch. On/off-site catering for weddings and special affairs. Visit our website for cooking classes and special events.

Nearest Airport(s)
Charlottesville, Lynchburg

Directions
From I-64, Exit 107; turn W onto Rte. 250. After 5 miles, turn S on Rte. 151. Follow 10 miles. Turn R on Rodes Farm Drive (Rte. 613 W), first drive on R.

Member Since 2002

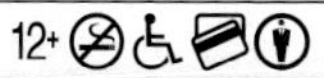   

"The most gracious hospitality we have experienced in years. The cuisine was excellent!"

Sugar Tree Inn

www.sugartreeinn.com
P.O. Box 10, Hwy 56, Steeles Tavern, VA 24476
800-377-2197 • 540-377-2197 • Fax : please call
innkeeper@sugartreeinn.com

Innkeepers/Owners
Jeff & Becky Chanter

Rustic Mountain Inn

AAA ◆◆◆

Recently featured as one of *Washingtonian* Magazine's "Most Romantic Inns" and called "Mountain Magic" by *Hampton Roads* Magazine! High above the Shenandoah Valley in the Blue Ridge Mountains, less than a mile from the Blue Ridge Parkway, is our haven of natural beauty. Set on twenty-eight wooded acres at 2800 feet, Virginia's Mountain Inn is a place of rustic elegance, peace and tranquility. Enjoy our 40-mile views, which are complimented by spring wildflowers, cool summer nights and brilliant fall colors. Each elegantly rustic room has a WOODBURNING FIREPLACE, incredibly comfortable bed, private bath, coffee maker, CD player, and is decorated with a colorful country quilt. A full breakfast is served in our glass-walled dining room and you can savor our fine evening dining by reservation.

Member Since 1998

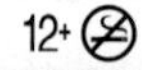

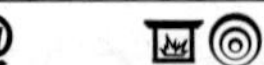

Rooms/Rates
9 Rooms, \$150/\$185; 1 Luxury Cabin, \$245; 2 Suites, \$170 & \$185; which includes our full country breakfast for two. Also our Creek House with 2 bedrooms, bath and full kitchen, \$175 excluding breakfast.

Cuisine
Gourmet four course dinners with a selection of entrees available Wednesday ~ Saturday by reservation.

Nearest Airport(s)
Roanoake

Directions
From I-81: Exit 205. East on Hwy 606 to Steeles Tavern. Turn left on Hwy 11 and then immediately right on Hwy. 56. Go up the mountain approx. 4.5 mi. to our sign. From Blue Ridge Parkway: (MP 27) West on Hwy. 56 approx. 3/4 mile to our sign.

"What a Mountain Inn should be: elegantly rustic, historic but comfortable, convenient but worlds away.... our B&B experience to date."

Innkeepers/Owners
Linda and Lynn Hayes
Assistant Innkeeper
Eric Hanson
Southern Contemporary Breakfast Inn 

Inn at Riverbend

www.srinns.com/innatriverbend
125 River Ridge Drive, Pearisburg, VA 24134-2391
540-921-5211 • 540-599-6400 • Fax 540-921-2720
stay@innatriverbend.com

Rooms/Rates
7 rooms $125/$200. Open year-round.

Cuisine
Full plated breakfast featuring fresh local ingredients. Afternoon refreshments, evening social hour with appetizers. Guests welcome to bring their own spirits.
Early hiker or business breakfast available. Picnic and candlelight dinner with prior reservation. Fine Dining at "The Bank-Food and Drink" just 3 miles away.

Nearest Airport(s)
Roanoke-70 Minutes

Directions
Located between 1-81 and 1-77,2 mi. off Hwy460. Exit 460 Business at Ripplemead/Pearisburg, left to 1st light (Walmart) and turn L. Left again at Virginia Hts, to Riverbend Dr. L at River Ridge.

Newly constructed in 2003, Inn at Riverbend sits on 13 acres on a hilltop overlooking the oldest river in the United States, the New River. Designed to view the mountains and river from the great room, TV room and each guestroom; spacious, decks and terraces provide plenty of space to enjoy the panoramic views, bird watch and even spot a deer or two in the lower meadow. The distance sound of the train sets the tone for a restful sleep. Perfect for romantic getaways, outdoor enthusiasts, retreats and family gatherings. All rooms feature private baths, large closets, pressed sheets, robes, satellite TV, wireless Internet and luxury amenities. Enjoy afternoon refreshments, the endless cookie jar, evening social hour with the other guests, turn-down service and a sumptuous breakfast. Just two miles from the Appalachian Trail. Let us help plan a hike, a trip down the river or a picnic at the Cascades Waterfalls! Dinner is available onsite Friday through Monday.

Member Since 2005

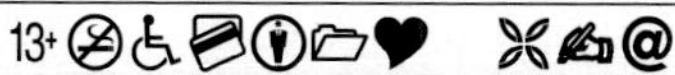

"Almost heaven, Inn at Riverbend...What a place! What a view!"

The Oaks Victorian Inn

www.srinns.com/theoaksinn
311 East Main St., Christiansburg, VA 24073
800-336-6257 • 540-381-1500 • Fax 540-381-3036

Owners and Hosts
Lois and John Ioviero

Elegant Victorian
Village Breakfast Inn

Mobil ★★★
AAA ◆◆◆◆

Warm hospitality, comfortable, relaxed elegance and memorable breakfasts are the hallmark of The Oaks, a century-old Queen Anne Victorian on the National Register of Historic Places. Set on Christiansburg's highest hill in the beautiful mountain highlands of Southwest Virginia, The Oaks delights and welcomes leisure and business travelers from around the world. Surrounded by lawn, perennial gardens and 300 year-old oak trees, the inn faces Main Street, once part of the Wilderness Trail blazed by Daniel Boone and Davey Crockett. Fireplaces and beautiful private baths with Jacuzzis for romantics. Private telephones, wireless DSL, cable TV, DVD/VCR and stocked refrigerators in all rooms. Discover the historic places of the New River, Roanoke and Shenandoah Valleys, the majestic grandeur of the Blue Ridge Parkway. Visit Virginia's wine industry or search for antiques, collectibles and crafts. The region provides the best in recreational attractions-bike trails, hiking, boating and golf...or just relax on the world class porch!

Rooms/Rates
7 Rooms, \$150/\$190 B&B; \$90 Corp. rate Sun. though Thu., Sgl. Only. Extended stay suites/7 days + (EP)(ck rates). Open year-round.

Cuisine
3-course breakfast by candlelight, excellent restaurants for dinner nearby.

Nearest Airport(s)
Roanoke

Directions
From I-81 Exit 114 (Main St.) just 2 miles on the corner of E Main & Park. From Blue Ridge Pkwy.: Take Rt. 8 (MP165) west 28 miles to The Oaks. Also near US 460. 38 miles north of I-77 and I-81 Interchange.

Member Since 1993

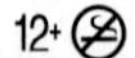

"Thank you for all you do to make our stay so pleasant.
The best breakfast we've ever had."

Washington

"The Evergreen State"

Famous For: Mount St. Helens, Redwoods, Olympic National Park, Grand Coulee Dam, Space Needle, Pike Place Market, Puget Sound, San Juan Islands, Mount Rainer, Kettle Falls, Cascade Mountains, Apples, Jets, Hi-Tech.

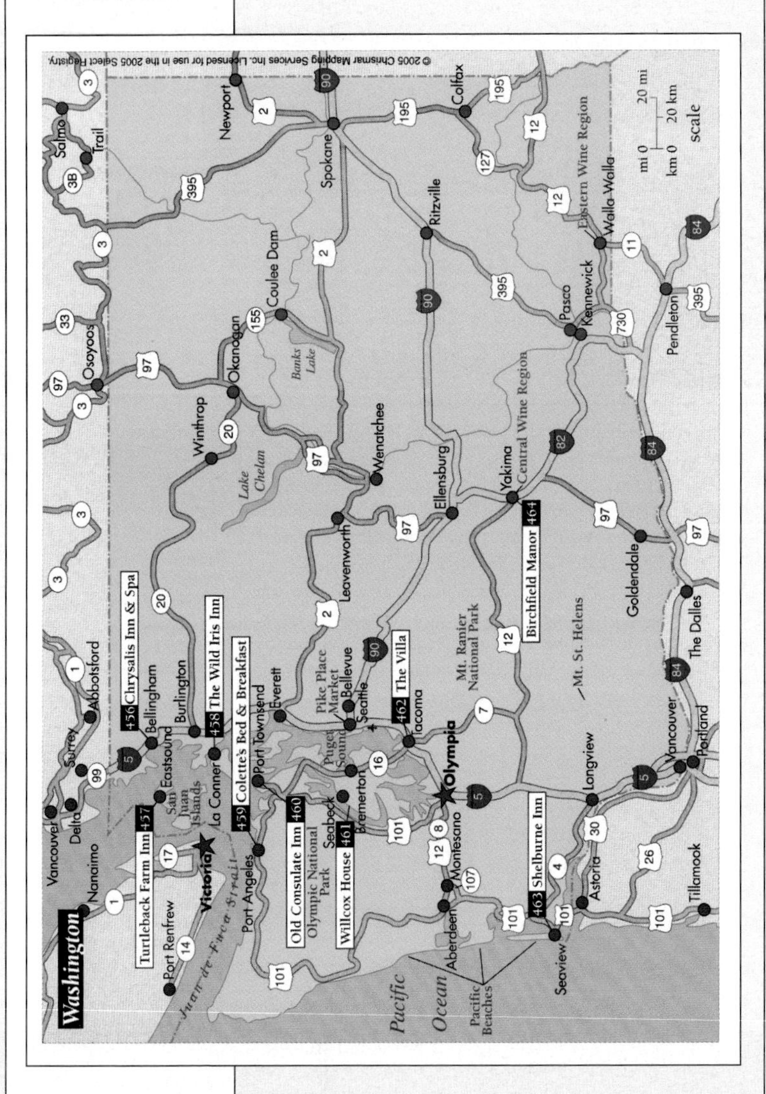

Chrysalis Inn & Spa

www.srinns.com/chrysalis
804 10th St., Bellingham, WA 98225
888-808-0005 • 360-756-1005 • Fax 360-647-0342
info@thechrysalisinn.com

Innkeepers/Owners
J. Michael and Lisa Keenan
Operations Manager
Julia Stiner
Contemporary Waterside Inn

AAA ◆◆◆

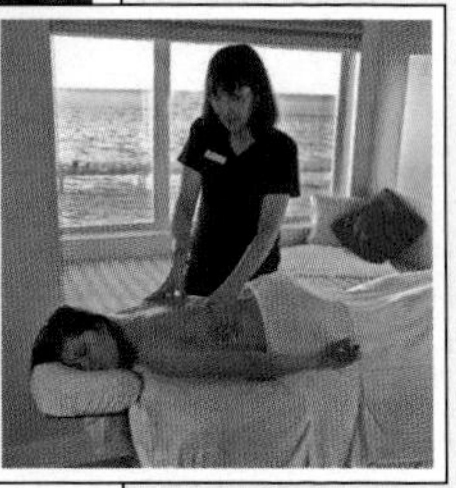

Situated on Bellingham Bay, just blocks from Historic Fairhaven, The Chrysalis invites guests to relax and unwind. From the moment you enter you sense a special place as you view the bay from the floor to ceiling windows in the living room. Enjoy the shops and restaurants in Fairhaven, stroll along the waterfront in Boulevard Park or just relax on your windowseat and watch the activity on the bay. Our spa offers massages, facials, hydrotherapy tub treatments, body treatments, maincures and pedicures, all designed to rejuvenate the body, mind and soul. Perfect for small business meetings and retreats, we can accomodate groups up to 45 in our two meeting rooms, and we offer on site catering.

Member Since 2003

Rooms/Rates
34 Deluxe Rooms, $155/$195, 9 Suites, $199/$279. All have fireplaces, window seats, 2 person tubs. Breakfast is included.

Cuisine
Fino is our full service wine bar and restaurant featuring classic foods and wines of Europe. Lunch and dinner daily, room service and outdoor dining.

Nearest Airport(s)
Bellingham Airport

Directions
Bellingham is 90 miles north of Seattle and 50 miles south of Vancouver BC, Canada. Take exit 250 off of I-5 and head west to stop light at 12th St. (about 1.2 miles). Turn right on 12th and proceed approximately 1/2 mile to Taylor, turn left. Turn right on 10th.

"What a way to celebrate life." "We love it here."
"Beautiful, indulgent, wonderful."

Innkeepers/Owners
William C. & Susan C. Fletcher

Traditional Country Breakfast Inn

Mobil ★★★
AAA ◆◆◆

Turtleback Farm Inn and Orchard House

www.srinns.com/turtlebackfarm
1981 Crow Valley Road, Eastsound, WA 98245
800-376-4914 • 360-376-4914 • Fax 360-376-5329
info@turtlebackinn.com

Rooms/Rates
11 Rooms. $100/$245 B&B. Open year-round.

Cuisine
Full breakfast, beverages anytime, fruit, freshly baked treats and complimentary sherry. Picnic baskets prepared. Luncheons and dinners catered for private parties. BYOB.

Nearest Airport(s)
Eastsound - 4 miles

Directions
From Orcas Ferry Landing: Follow the Orcas Road N 2.9mi, turn L, .9 mi to first R, continue N on Crow Valley Road 2.4 mi. to Inn.

THE FARMHOUSE and ORCHARD HOUSE is located on Orcas Island, the loveliest of the San Juan Islands. This graceful and comfortable Inn is considered one of the most romantic places in the country. Highlighted by a spectacular setting, the Inn is a haven for those who enjoy breathtaking scenery, comfortable accommodations and award-winning breakfasts. The island offers unique shopping, fine dining and varied outdoor activities: hiking, swimming, sea-kayaking, whale watching, sailing, fishing, birding, golf and bicycling. Turtleback Farm Inn is the perfect spot for the discriminating traveler to experience a step back to a quieter time.

Hideaway Report, "1000 PLACES TO SEE BEFORE YOU DIE."

Member Since 2003

"A marvel of bed and breakfastmanship full of tasteful personal touches and tender care. You are a model by which other innkeepers could use.."

The Wild Iris Inn

www.srinns.com/wildiris
121 Maple Avenue, P.O. Box 696, LaConner, WA 98257
800-477-1400 • 360-466-1400
info@wildiris.com

Innkeepers/Owners
Jill & David Britt

Contemporary Village Inn

The award winning Wild Iris Inn and LaConner, Washington, an outstanding year-round destination, are a short drive from Seattle and Vancouver, British Columbia, but "miles" away. The Inn's convenient location is perfect for your exploration of the Pacific Northwest; located just 20 minutes from the ferry terminals that lead to the San Juan Islands, Victoria, BC and points beyond. Each season brings wonderful changes to LaConner. In winter, swans and snow geese cover the fields in a sea of white. The farmlands are brightly colored with daffodils in March, world famous tulips in April, iris in May, and dahlias in August. In summer, whale watching cruises leave LaConner each day and follow magnificent orcas in the North Puget Sound. The highlight of your stay, however, will be the hospitality, service and amenities of The Wild Iris Inn. Guest suites feature spa tubs, fireplaces and decks facing the Cascade Mountains, as well as all of the amenities you would expect from a Select Registry property.

Member Since 2003

Rooms/Rates
12 Guest Suites with king beds, spa tubs, fireplaces and private decks $149/$199 B&B. 3 Casual Guest Rooms with king beds and 1 with two twin beds $109/$129 B&B. Open Year Round.

Cuisine
A full breakfast including fresh baked goods, homemade granola, hot entrees and fresh fruits is served each morning at tables for two. In-room and early departure breakfast options are also available.

Nearest Airport(s)
Seattle & Vancouver

Directions
By Land: 1 hour N of Seattle. 1 1/2 hours S of Vancouver, BC. 9 miles W of I-5. By Sea: 20 min. from the San Juan Islands & Victoria, BC ferry in Anacortes.

"It is rare to find an establishment so completely focused on their guests."

Colette's Bed & Breakfast

www.srinns.com/colettes
339 Finn Hall Road, Port Angeles, WA 98362
877-457-9777 • 360-457-9197 • Fax 360-452-0711
colettes@olypen.com

Innkeepers/Owners
Peter and Lynda Clark

Elegant Waterside Breakfast Inn

AAA ◆◆◆

Rooms/Rates
Luxury accommodations: $150/$295

Cuisine
Our chef has created an exciting variety of culinary delights. Enjoy your multi-course, gourmet breakfast served with a panoramic view of the Strait of Juan de Fuca and the San Juan Islands.

Nearest Airport(s)
Seattle and Port Angeles

Directions
Two hours from Seattle via the Bainbridge ferry. Hwy 305 to 3 to 104 to 101 around Sequim. Travel 4.8 miles past the Sequim Ave. exit, R on Kitchen-Dick Road. Drive 1.5 miles to Old Olympic Hwy, turn L drive 2.5 miles to Matson road and turn R. Drive .5 to Finn Hall Road and turn L, drive .9 miles.

Colette's is a breathtaking 10-acre waterfront estate located near Port Angeles, nestled between the majestic Olympic Range and the Strait of Juan de Fuca. This unique area is the gateway to Olympic National Park, a world of fog-shrouded coast with booming surf and wave-manicured beaches, spectacular alpine country and sweeping vistas in every direction. Each perfect day at Colette's starts with a gourmet breakfast. A luxurious king guest suite with spectacular water views, romantic fireplace, and indulgent two-person Jacuzzi tub rejuvenates guests at the end of the day. Selected for "Weekends for Two in the Pacific Northwest: 50 Romantic Getaways," "Best Places to Kiss - highest rating - 4 Kisses," and Fodor's Pacific Northwest - Top choice for the Olympic Peninsula - "considered the very best."

Member Since 2003

"Beyond all expectations...Fabulous food...Magnificent views...
An intimate Four Seasons."

Old Consulate Inn (F.W. Hastings House)

www.srinns.com/oldconsulate
313 Walker at Washington, Port Townsend, WA 98368
800-300-6753 • 360-385-6753 • Fax 360-385-2097
mike@oldconsulateinn.com

Innkeepers/Owners
Michael & Sue Delong

Elegant Victorian Waterside Breakfast Inn

Step back to a quieter more romantic time. Visit Port Townsend's award-winning founding family mansion-on-the-bluff. Warm hospitality greets you at every turn. Indulge your senses and refresh your spirit in the beauty of sweeping views of Port Townsend Bay, Mount Rainier and the snowcapped Olympics. Old-fashioned porch swings on the veranda offer views of the flower-filled gardens. Curl up with a good book by the fireside, or relax in the glass-enclosed gazebo hot tub. Enjoy afternoon tea and fresh-baked treats, evening desserts & cordials. Share a friendly game of billiards. At day's end retire to your turned down King bed with sweet treat. Awaken well-rested to our renowned 7-dish/3-course Banquet Breakfast. Come join us!

Voted "Best in the Pacific Northwest" by *Inn Traveler* Magazine.

Available for weddings, family reunions, and corporate retreats.

Member Since 1996

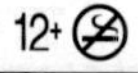

Rooms/Rates
5 King Bedrooms, 3 King Suites.
Rooms $110/$160.
Suites $160/$210.

Cuisine
Complimentary afternoon tea, cocoa and fresh baked treats. Evening desserts and cordials. Early morning coffee, tea & cocoa, 7 dish/3 course Banquet Breakfast at 9 a.m. with consideration to special dietary needs. Custom catering for groups available.

Nearest Airport(s)
Jefferson County Airport

Directions
From Seattle: Bainbridge Ferry, take Hood Canal Bridge to Hwy. 19 to P.T. From Tacoma: I-5 to Hwy. 16\3 to Hood Canal Bridge (etc). From North: Hwy. 20 to Keystone Ferry to P.T. On the bluff by the historic courthouse.

"This is what a B&B is all about!" "..never had a breakfast that good before."

Innkeepers/Owners
Cecilia and Phillip Hughes

Elegant Waterside Inn

AAA ◆◆◆

Willcox House Country Inn

www.srinns.com/willcox
2390 Tekiu Rd. NW, Seabeck, WA 98380
800-725-9477 • 360-830-4492 • Fax 360-830-0506

Rooms/Rates
5 Rooms, $139/$219 B&B. Open year-round.

Cuisine
Breakfast, afternoon wine and cheese included. Dinner available. Complimentary hot beverages. Large selection of wine and beer.

Nearest Airport(s)
Seattle

Directions
17 miles W of Bremerton on Hood Canal, near Holly.

With spectacular views of Hood Canal and the Olympic Mountains, this waterfront Country House Inn is situated in a forest setting beween Seattle and the Olympic Peninsula. The historic 1930s mansion estate offers beautiful gardens with fish ponds. Walk our oyster-laden saltwater beach. Enjoy the peace and serenity. Period pieces and antiques are featured in guest rooms, the great room, billiard room, pub, library, theater, and dining room. *Country Inns* magazine award: One of the top twelve inns in North America. Featured on *Great Country Inns* T.V. series. Golfing, birding, and hiking nearby.

Member Since 1993

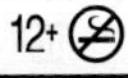   

"A jewel within an emerald forest."

The Villa

www.srinns.com/thevilla
705 N. 5th Street, Tacoma, WA 98403
888-572-1157 • 253-572-1157
villabb@aol.com

Innkeepers/Owners
Kristy and Aaron House
Historic In Town
Breakfast Inn

Mobil ★★★

Beautifully appointed and spotless, this Italian Renaissance mansion on the Historic Register is attractively furnished in Italian Country decor. The Villa overlooks the peaceful Stadium Historic District with views expanding to Puget Sound and the majestic Olympic Mountains. Amenities include European linen sheets, Egyptian cotton robes and plush towels. Artistically landscaped, The Villa features heritage rose gardens. Truly a place to relax your body and revive your spirit, yet located centrally to the most popular NW attractions. 1/2 hour from Seattle Airport. Rated 'excellent' by *Mobil, NW Best Places* and *Best Places to Kiss NW.* Full business services.

Rooms/Rates
6 Rms/Suites, K/Q, $135/$235 B&B. Fireplaces, TV/CD/stereos, soaking/spa tubs, separate showers, private verandahs, mountain/water views, phones/dataports. Open all year.

Cuisine
Three-course breakfast 7, 8, 9 AM weekdays, 8:30, 10 AM weekends. Complimentary fine wines, ale, pop, cookies and snacks all day. Award-winning waterfront restaurants nearby.

Nearest Airport(s)
Sea-Tac Airport

Directions
From I-5 N or S, take exit 133, I-705 N. Exit to Schuster Parkway, then exit to Stadium Way. At first light R on Stadium Way; at next light R on Tacoma Ave. N; then L on N 5th St., 1 block on R.

Member Since 2000

"Of all of the Select Inns we have visited, this one's attention to detail is amazing!"

Innkeepers/Owners
David Campiche and Laurie Anderson
Traditional Victorian Village Inn

Shelburne Inn & China Beach Retreat

www.srinns.com/shelburne
P.O. Box 250, 4415 Pacific Way, Seaview, WA 98644
800-INN-1896 • 360-642-2442 • Fax 360-642-8904
innkeeper@theshelburneinn.com

Rooms/Rates
13 Rooms, $125/$165 B&B; 2 Suites, $185 B&B. Additional off-site waterside B&B; two Rooms $189; 1 Suite $219. Open year-round. Wireless capabilities.

Cuisine
Gourmet Regional Cuisine features the best seasonal and local ingredients. Restaurant and Pub offer lunch and dinner featuring fine NW wines, microbrewed beer and liquor. Innkeepers' Breakfast served daily and offers creative preparations to choose from.

Nearest Airport(s)
Portland International

Directions
From Seattle, I-5 (S) to Olympia, Hwy. 8 & 12 to Montesano & Hwy. 107 then 101(S) to Seaview; From OR coast, U.S. 101N across Astoria Bridge L. to Seaview.

An unspoiled 28-mile stretch of wild Pacific seacoast is just a short walk through rolling sand dunes from this inviting Country Inn, built in 1896. Art Nouveau stained glass windows and period antique furniture highlight the Inn. A sumptuous gourmet breakfast featuring the best of the Northwest is complimentary with your room. Innovative cuisine and a discriminating wine list have brought international recognition to the restaurant and pub. Discover the western end of the Lewis and Clark trail and our China Beach Retreat with national historic sites and the Discovery Trail, which parallels the majestic Pacific Ocean. Selected as 'Best Bed & Breakfast in the Northwest', *NW Palate* Readers' Favorites. Selected as one of the 'West's Best Small Inns,' by *Sunset* Magazine, February, 2001. Featured in the January 2003 issue of, Martha Stewart *Living*. ★★★ 1/2 *NW Best Places*, the popular regional travel guide. 'Breakfast is to The Shelburne what art is to the Louvre.' *St. Louis Post Dispatch*.

Member Since 1988

"This was our first B&B experience and we felt like we started at the top."

Birchfield Manor Country Inn

www.srinns.com/birchfieldmanor
2018 Birchfield Road, Yakima, WA 98901
800-375-3420 • 509-452-1960 • Fax 509-452-2334
birchfield@ewa.net

Innkeepers/Owners
The Masset Family

Traditional Country Inn

Mobil ★★★
AAA ◆◆◆

Yakima's true Country Inn only two miles from town. We offer a relaxing getaway with award-winning multi course dinners prepared by professional chef/owners served in the casual warm atmosphere of a gracious home. Park-like grounds surround the outdoor pool. Choose from the extensive selections of Washington wines from our *Wine Spectator, Wine Enthusiast* and Northwest Wine Press award winning list—and you may find your favorite winemaker at the next table! Most rooms w/fireplace, two-person tub, panoramic views. We can personalize a tour of local wineries, direct you to roadside stands for fresh fruit and vegetables, or you may talk to Brad or Tim for tee times at the local golf courses.

Rooms/Rates
11 Rooms, $119/$219 B&B.

Cuisine
Award-winning Northwest cuisine in a casual relaxed atmosphere.

Nearest Airport(s)
Yakima Airport approx. 7 miles

Directions
I-82 to Yakima, exit 34. Go E 2 miles, turn R (south) on Birchfield Road. First house on R.

Member Since 1993

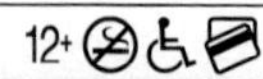   

"Restaurant of the Year" Award - Washington Wine Growers Association

"The Mountain State"

Famous For: Appalachian Mountains, Monongahela National Forest, White Sulphur Springs, Harper's Ferry National Historical Park, Smoke Hole Caverns, Apple Butter Festival, Grave Creek Burial Mounds, Country Music, Coal, Oil, Gas

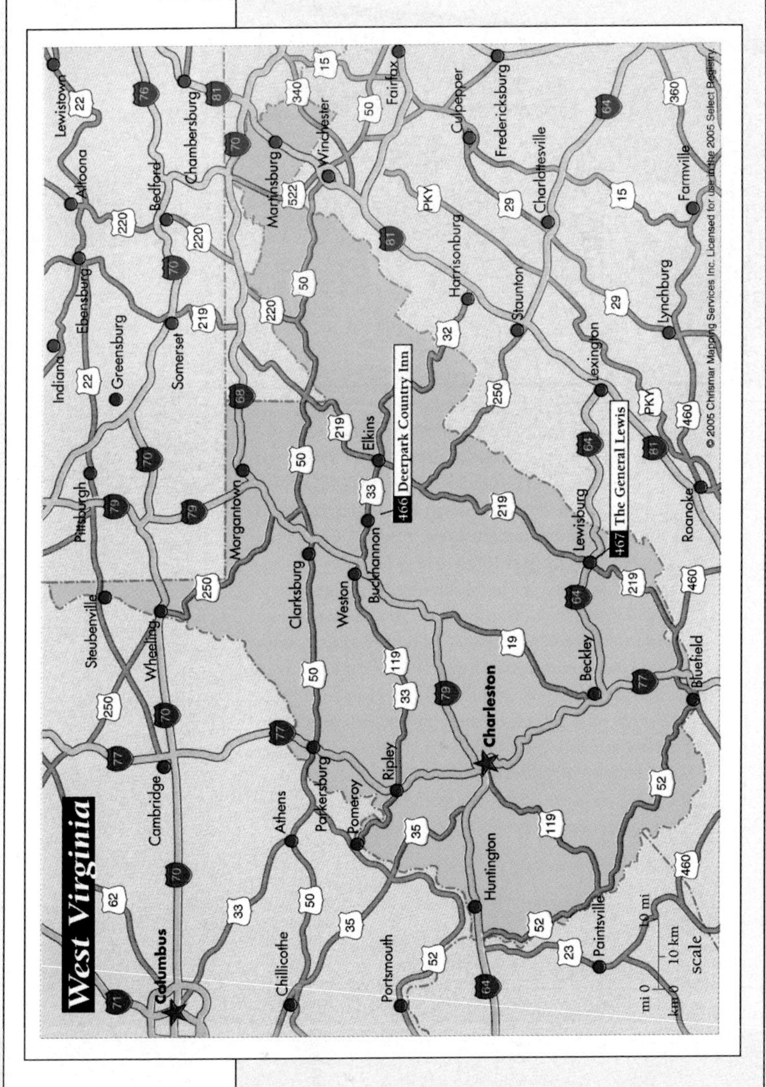

Deerpark Country Inn

www.srinns.com/deerpark
P.O. Box 817, Buckhannon, WV 26201
800-296-8430 • 304-472-8400 • Fax 304-472-5363
deerpark@deerparkcountryinn.com

Owners
Liz and Patrick Haynes
General Manager
Greg Kennedy

Traditional Country Inn

Liz and Patrick Haynes invite you to surround yourself with 100 acres of rejuvinating country ambiance that reflects a by-gone era. The inn includes an 18th Century log cabin, a post-Civil War farm house and a newly constructed Victorian wing. Detailed period architecture is featured throughout. About 400 feet from the inn is the two story lodge, a 19th Century log cabin with attached wing, offering three gracious bedrooms, a fireplace as large as a man is tall, and french doors that open onto two wrap around porches...perfect for watching fireflies or shooting stars or snowflakes falling on deep pine forests. All the rooms and suites of both buildings are richly furnished with fine antiques and collectibles, ferns and fresh flowers and crisp cotton linens; each presents its own personality as well as central air, private bath and other amenities. Mist rises from the pond that invites you to fish under the watchful eye of resident mallards and clannishly arrogant geese. Let us design a special getaway package for you.

Member Since 1999

Rooms/Rates
DBL occupancy, 4 Rooms and 2 Suites. $110/$230. B&B, private baths, phone, A/C, TV, VCR/DVD. Open year-round.

Cuisine
Gourmet breakfast daily. Full bar (honor system) on premises. Several fine dining restaurants in the area. Catered events on site -specializing in weddings and family reunions.

Nearest Airport(s)
Buckhannon Airport

Directions
From I-79: Exit 99, US 33-E, go 4 miles past Buckhannon, turn R at Keesling Mill SIGN, turn left on 151-E. When on 151-E, turn L and travel .7 mile to Heavener Grove Rd., turn R. 1.3 miles to Deerpark sign on R.

"A great discovery! Worth every inch of a 500 mile trip."

The General Lewis Inn

www.srinns.com/generallewisinn
301 East Washington St., Lewisburg, WV 24901
800-628-4454 • Fax 304-645-2601
info@generallewisinn.com

Innkeepers/Owners
The Morgan Family

Traditional Village Inn

Mobil ★★★
AAA ◆◆◆

Rooms/Rates
23 Rooms, $99/$150 EP;
2 Suites, $148/$168 EP. Open year-round. Romantic Getaway packages available December through March. Holidays and special events not available for reduced rates.

Cuisine
Breakfast, lunch and dinner. Wine and liquor available.

Nearest Airport(s)
Greenbrier Valley Airport, Lewisburg, WV, 15 minutes away.

Directions
I-64, Lewisburg exit 169, 219 South for 1.5 miles to 60 East, turn left and we are three blocks up on the right.

Come rock in a chair on the veranda of the Inn. On chilly days, dream by the fireplace, solve one of the puzzles or play a fascinating game. Enjoy Memory Hall's display of old tools for home and farm which the first family members began collecting even before they opened the Inn. Cat and dog live here. Antiques furnish every room, including canopy, spool and poster beds. Town offers antique shops, fine arts and crafts, live year round theater and music with the unique flavor of a town named as one of the best small arts towns in America. The dining room in the 1834 wing features Southern cooking. Enjoy your dining experience with specialty foods, hot homemade bread and desserts, a full service bar and wine list. Lewisburg has been designated by the National Trust for Historic Preservation as one of the "12 Most Desirable Vacation Destinations" (2004). We're located on the Midland Trail, a national scenic byway and the site of the 1862 Battle of Lewisburg. The Inn has been owned and operated by the same family since 1929.

Member Since 1973

 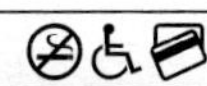  

"...a country guest house...enjoy the lovely common areas with antiques everywhere..." Frommer's

"The Badger State"

Famous For: Wisconsin Dells, Apostle Islands National Lakeshore, Lake Superior, Mirror Lake State Park, House on the Rock (a 1940s retreat built on a 60-foot rock outcropping overlooking a 450 ft drop) Dairy, Beer, Cranberry Fest, Fresh Water Fishing.

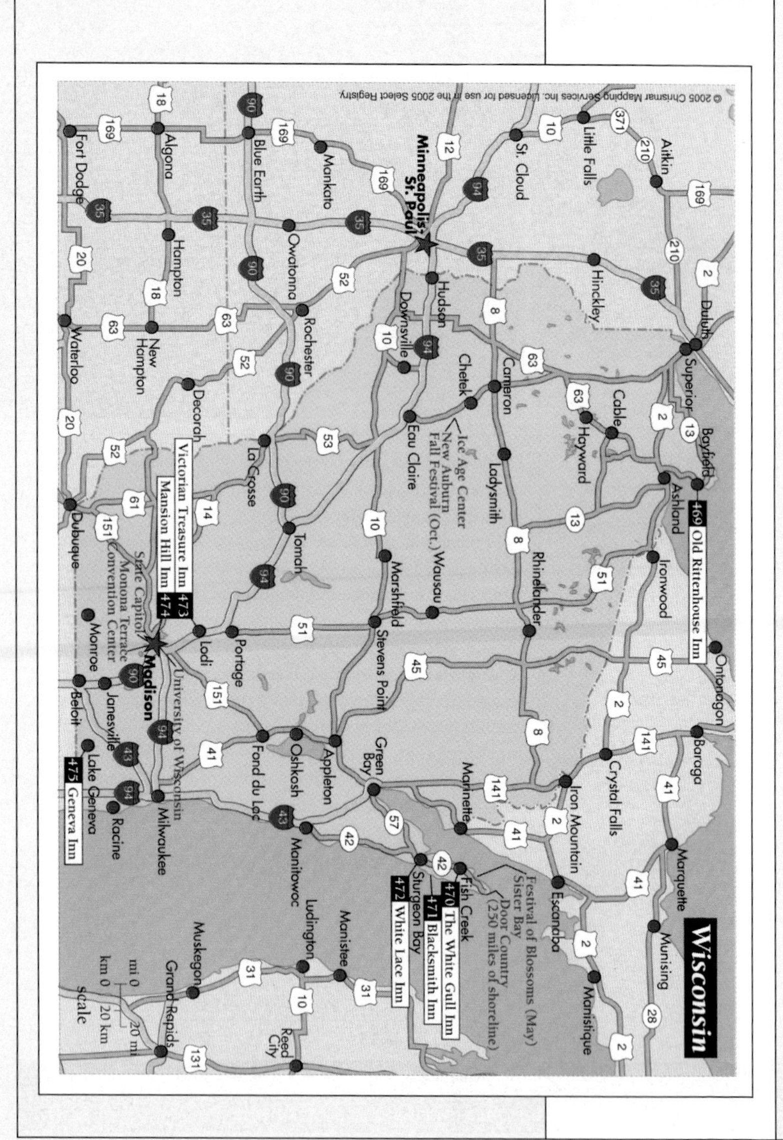

Old Rittenhouse Inn

www.rittenhouseinn.com
301 Rittenhouse Ave., P.O. Box 584, Bayfield, WI 54814
888-560-4667 • 715-779-5111 • Fax 715-779-5887
Gourmet@RittenhouseInn.com

Innkeepers/Owners
Jerry & Mary Phillips
Elegant Victorian
Village Inn

AAA ◆◆◆

Rooms/Rates
10 rooms $99/$199 B&B; 13 rooms/suites with whirlpools $139/$299 B&B; 1 Cottage, $279 B&B; All rooms have private baths. Most have fireplaces, many with lake views.

Cuisine
Serving a creative regional menu. Bayfield peninsula's freshest ingredients combined with flavorful sauces, seasonal specialties, and gourmet artistry. Serving breakfast, lunch and dinner. Featured in *Gourmet Magazine*, and *Bon Appetit*.

Nearest Airport(s)
Madeline Island - 4 miles

Directions
Duluth E on Hwy 2 for 60 miles, to N on Hwy 13 for 21 miles. Located on Rittenhouse Avenue and Third Street in the heart of Bayfield.

Victorian lodging and dining, with guestrooms in two historic Queen Anne-style mansions, guesthouse and private cottage all located within Bayfield's 52 block historic district. A stay at the Old Rittenhouse Inn combines an evening of romance and elegance with gourmet cuisine and comfortable lodging. Guestrooms are beautifully appointed with antique furnishings. Amenities include wood burning fireplaces, private baths, breath-taking views of Lake Superior, and luxurious whirlpools. Open all year offering romantic winter get-aways, wine, beer, martini, and margarita weekends, wassail dinner concerts and murder mystery weekends, antiques weekends, life-coaching weekends and spring theatre weekends.

Member Since 1980

Voted Wisconsin's Most Romantic Inn by the readers of
Wisconsin Trails Magazine.

White Gull Inn

www.srinns.com/whitegullinn
4225 Main Street, P.O. Box 160, Fish Creek, WI 54212
800-625-8813 • 920-868-3517 • Fax 920-868-2367
innkeeper@whitegullinn.com

Innkeepers
Andy & Jan Coulson

Traditional Village Inn

AAA ◆◆◆

Established in 1896, this white clapboard Inn is tucked away in the scenic bayside village of Fish Creek, on Wisconsin's Door Peninsula. Turn of the century antiques, fireplaces and meticulously restored and decorated rooms and cottages provide a warm, hospitable atmosphere. Renowned for hearty breakfasts, sumptuous lunches and candlelit dinners, the Inn is famous for its traditional Door County fish boils, featuring locally caught Lake Michigan whitefish cooked outside over an open fire. Close to summer stock theater, music festivals, art galleries, antique stores and every imaginable recreational activity, from golf to wind surfing, from hiking to cross country skiing.

Member Since 1979

Rooms/Rates
6 Rooms, $140/$205; 7 Suites, $205/$265; 4 Cottages (1,2 and 4 bedroom), $219/$425. Includes full breakfast. Winter and Shoulder Season Packages. Open year-round.

Cuisine
Hearty full breakfast included, lunches daily, and dinner from the menu or traditional Door County fish boil served nightly. Wine and beer available. Dining room open to the public.

Nearest Airport(s)
Austin Straubel Field, Green Bay (75 miles)

Directions
Milwaukee I-43 for 98 mi. to Green Bay, then Rte. 57 N for 39 miles to Sturgeon Bay; N on Rte. 42 for 25 mi. to Fish Creek, L at stop sign for 3 Blks.

"The room is lovely - fireplace, Jacuzzi, shower, sitting room. Restaurant is magnificent."

Blacksmith Inn On the Shore

www.srinns.com/blacksmith
8152 Highway 57, Baileys Harbor, WI 54202
800-769-8619 • 920-839-9222 • Fax 920-839-9356
relax@theblacksmithinn.com

Owners
Joan Holliday and Bryan Nelson

Traditional Waterside Breakfast Inn

Rooms/Rates
15 Rooms $185/$235, Cottage $275/$425; November through April, Rooms $115/$215. All rooms have whirlpool, fireplace, and balcony with view of the harbor. Open year round.

Cuisine
Guests enjoy a homemade continental breakfast from the balcony overlooking the harbor. 'There is nothing simple about the view that beckons each guest every morning.'—Jill Cordes, Food Network.

Nearest Airport(s)
Green Bay

Directions
From Milwaukee, I-43 98 miles to Green Bay. Hwy. 57 N 63 miles to Baileys Harbor. The inn is at the north end of the village on the shore.

Awaken to the sound of waves lapping the shore as the morning sunlight glistens on the water. Linger over breakfast on our sun-washed porch. Kayak in summer, snowshoe the harbor edge in winter. Step out our door to hike the nearby Ridges Wildlife Sanctuary. Bike the sleepy backroad to explore Cana Island Lighthouse. Bask in your whirlpool as you take in the warm glow of the fire. Stroll to nearby restaurants and shops. Revel in an extraordinary view of the harbor any time of year. Complete privacy with all the amenities including, water views, balconies, in-room whirlpools, fireplaces, canopied beds, fine linens, down pillows, TV/DVD/CD with in-house DVD library, phones with data ports, refrigerators and a bottomless cookie jar! Door County offers art galleries, antiquing, music, theater and miles and miles of shoreline. Experience the unrivaled pleasures of the Blacksmith Inn, located in the heart of Door County.

Member Since 2002

 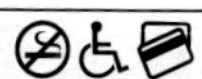  

"To fall asleep to the sound of that water is heavenly!"

White Lace Inn

www.srinns.com/whitelaceinn
16 N. 5th Ave., Sturgeon Bay, Door County, WI 54235
877-948-5223 (toll free) • 920-743-1105
Fax 920-743-8180
romance@whitelaceinn.com

Innkeepers/Owners
Dennis & Bonnie Statz

Traditional In Town Breakfast Inn

Mobil ★★★
AAA ◆◆◆

Romance and relaxation in Door County begin as you follow winding garden pathways to your beautifully appointed room or suite. Four lovingly restored historic homes are nestled in a friendly old neighborhood and bordered by a white picket fence. Guest rooms and suites are furnished for a special getaway and feature period antiques, down comforters on wonderfully ornate beds, oversized whirlpools and inviting fireplaces. Fifteen rooms have a fireplace, twelve rooms have a whirlpool and nine of our rooms/suites have both a fireplace and whirlpool. Mornings start with a delicious full breakfast served in the sunlit parlor of the Main House. Bonnie, Dennis and their staff invite you to enjoy the hospitality that has made their Inn a Door County tradition. We've had over 700 small weddings performed at White Lace Inn - usually in the Gazebo. DoorCountyNavigator.com's User's Choice Award, Best B&B in Door County, 2003. Top 10 Romantic Inns of America, 1998, 2004 & 2005, American Historic Inns.

Member Since 1988

Rooms/Rates

13 Rooms, $120/$195; 5 Suites, $200/$235. Late October-Late May, Weeknights, Rooms $70/$130, and Suites $150/$160. Open year-round.

Cuisine

A delicious full breakfast is served to our guests daily. Afternoons and evenings include hot cider, hot cocoa, lemonade, and homemade cookies.

Nearest Airport(s)

The Green Bay airport is a one hour drive.

Directions

Hwy. 42 or 57 N to Sturgeon Bay. Bus. Rte. 42/57 into town across Historic Bridge. Left on 5th Ave., 1/2 block on 5th Ave. to Inn on right.

"This Whimsical Victorian Inn doesn't merely pamper its guests, it envelops them in comfort... expected amenities are here, but the unexpected set it apart."

Victorian Treasure Inn

www.srinns.com/victoriantreasure
115 Prairie Street, Lodi, WI 53555
800-859-5199 • 608-592-5199 • Fax 608-592-7147
innkeeper@victoriantreasure.com

Innkeepers/Owners
Renee and Eric Degelau

Elegant Victorian Village Bed & Breakfast Inn

AAA ◆◆◆◆

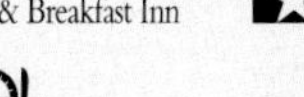

Rooms/Rates
8 Rooms; 7 Suites with whirlpools. 5 with fireplaces, $119/$279. Includes full three course gourmet breakfast and daily wine & cheese reception. Romantic Packages, Specials, Weekday Packages. Open year-round, except December 24-25.

Cuisine
Enjoy a memorable, full gourmet breakfast as featured on PBS *Country Inn Cooking with Gail Greco.* Complimentary evening wine & Wisconsin cheese reception provided.

Nearest Airport(s)
Dane County Airport (Madison)

Directions
20 miles N of Madison on I-90/94, Exit Hwy 60/Lodi W. Four miles to Main Street/Hwy 113, continue straight on 60 one block, the first R turn is Prairie Street.

Madison, Wisconsin area bed and breakfast tucked away in the scenic Wisconsin River Valley. A romantic getaway as you discover 'One of America's Top Ten Most Romantic Inns' as awarded by American Historic Inns. Gracious hospitality and casual elegance in two 1890s National Registry Victorian homes and a 1928 Craftsman bungalow featuring eight romantic, individually decorated guest rooms with private baths—including luxurious whirlpool fireplace suites with wet bars and entertainment centers including TV's, VCRs and DVDs. Caring owner-innkeepers fuss over details - meticulous accommodations, luxurious amenities, attentive service. Enjoy a gourmet full breakfast and complimentary evening reception. The inn is conveniently located in the heart of South-Central Wisconsin, four miles west of I-90/94, between Madison, WI and the Wisconsin Dells. Close to hiking, biking, skiing and wineries. Limousine service provided for dinner package and available for nominal fee to local attractions. Airport pickup available.

Member Since 1998

"Your attention to detail is WONDERFUL. Everything is so CLEAN, NEAT and great pampering!" Bob & Janet, Chicago

Mansion Hill Inn

www.srinns.com/mansionhill
424 N. Pinckney Street, Madison, WI 53703
800-798-9070 • 608-255-3999 • Fax 608-255-2217

General Manager
Jennifer Sigl

Elegant In Town Inn

Elegance, luxury and charm await you at The Mansion Hill Inn. The Inn's warm hospitality has made it a favorite of business and leisure travelers alike. Lovingly restored and lavishly decorated, Mansion Hill Inn is the American Automobile Association's only 4 diamond rated guest residence in Madison. A masterpiece of Romanesque Revival style built in 1857, it abounds in fine architectural detail and period furnishings. Each of the eleven guest suites and rooms are individually and exquisitely decorated to provide the best of antique ambience and contemporary amenities. Many rooms have marble fireplaces and balconies as well as views of the State Capitol building. The Inn is conveniently located on a quiet corner in the heart of downtown Madison and boasts sumptuous accommodations, awesome amenities, and a stellar location! There's not a sweeter spot in all of Madison, close to the campuses of The University of Wisconsin, Madison Area Technical College and Edgewood College as well as being walking distance to State Street and the Capital, Overture Center, Monona Terrace and all of Madison's best restaurants! The inn offers optional "Sweet Dreams" turndown service every night. Valet parking is also available.

Member Since 1997

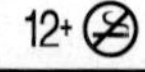

Rooms/Rates
11 Rooms including 2 Suites, $130/$340 B&B.

Cuisine
Many fine restaurants within walking distance. Complimentary refreshments, including wine tasting every evening. Continental-plus breakfast delivered to your door on a silver tray each morning of your stay.

Nearest Airport(s)
Madison

Directions
Hwy. 151 to State Capitol, turn R on Wisconsin, 4 blocks to R on Gilman 1 block to R on Pinckney.

"Madison's most gracious and intimate seclusion..."

General Manager
Richard B. Treptow
Luxury Lakeside Inn

The Geneva Inn

www.srinns.com/genevainn
N2009 S. Lake Shore Dr., Lake Geneva, WI 53147
800-441-5881 • 262-248-5680 • Fax 262-248-5685

Rooms/Rates
37 Rooms. $155/$375. Special seasonal packages offered October-May.

Cuisine
Experience the area's best American Contemporary cuisine at The Grandview Restaurant. Featuring fresh seafood, delicious daily specials, decadent desserts. Every table offers a scenic vista of Geneva Lake through large panoramic windows. Enjoy a refreshing drink at the Grandview piano lounge or lunch outdoors on a private patio during the summer months.

Nearest Airport(s)
Milwaukee-Mitchell (1 hr); Chicago-O'Hare(90 min)

Directions
2 1/2 miles south of downtown Lake Geneva, directly on Geneva Lake.

Experience distinctive European charm and exceptional luxury at The Geneva Inn located directly on the shores of Geneva Lake. Discover a truly relaxed style of comfort, intimate accommodations, breathtaking lake views, uncommon architectural craftsmanship and quiet seclusion in the peaceful atmosphere of this traditional English inn. Special touches include thick, fluffy bathrobes, bedtime bottled water and chocolates, oversized vintage or whirlpool baths, fully stocked private bars, free weekday newspaper delivery, early morning coffee available on each floor and exclusive use of the Inn's exercise facility. Guests are also treated to a complimentary, continental buffet breakfast served in The Grandview Restaurant. Fresh fruit and bakery items, flavored butters, delicious meats and cheeses, cereals and rich coffee and fragrant teas are offered. Hot breakfast specials also available.

Member Since 2004

"We love the Geneva Inn and Grandview. The rooms are comfortable, the view is beautiful and the staff is friendly and courteous. Thank you so much!"

Index by Inn

Thank you for choosing a Select Registry Inn.
You will be helping our members to uphold our Association's standards of excellence if you take a moment to fill out this card and drop it in the mail.

It is difficult for the innkeepers to know the "real" problem if you just check the boxes and do not elaborate with any additional comments. Both the Select Registry office and the Inn will make every attempt to address your concerns or your praise. It is imperative, however, that you provide your name, address, and phone number so that we can respond in a timely fashion.

— — — — — — — — — — — — — —

Name of Inn ______________________ State or Province __________ Date of visit __________

Your name and address (please print and be aware that we require a name): ______________________

____

____

____

Your phone number: ______________________

Please check ONE box in each category:	**Excellent**	**Good**	**Disappointing**	**Poor**	**Would not return**
Bedrooms/comfort/décor	❑	❑	❑	❑	❑
Public rooms/aesthetics/furnishings	❑	❑	❑	❑	❑
Food/restaurant quality	❑	❑	❑	❑	❑
Service quality	❑	❑	❑	❑	❑
Welcome/friendliness	❑	❑	❑	❑	❑
Personality/character of the Inn	❑	❑	❑	❑	❑

Additional comments: ______________________

____

____

____

____

As a discriminating traveler who wants to go to the best Country Inns and B&Bs, I recommend the following Inns (please include name, city and state/province, and tell us why): ______________________

____

____

____

Select Registry Gift Certificate Program

The perfect gift for that special person.
Select Registry gift certificates can be ordered online at:
www.SelectRegistry.com.
Our gift certificates are packaged with a copy of
this guidebook, and a message from you to the recipient.
VISA, MasterCard, and American Express accepted.
Expedited shipping is available for an additional charge.

Place Postage Here

Select Registry, Distinguished Inns of North America
501 E. Michigan Avenue
P.O. Box 150
Marshall, MI 49068

The Golden Quill Club
Loyalty Travel Program

Wherever your travels take you within the United States and Canada, you may be entitled to a $25 Loyalty Reward for repeat visits made to Select Registry properties! Start collecting stamps today while staying at our member inns. We think you'll find that some experiences are worth repeating!

Present this card to the participating Select Registry Innkeeper (or reservation desk) where you have just stayed. Ask them to place their stamp in one of the boxes signifying your stay at their inn. *Consecutive nights do not count for more than one stamp.* Be sure they validate the stay by including the Inn's name, their initials, and the date of your stay.

Required Guest Information: Guest Name ____________________

Address ____________________ Apt. # ________

Address ____________________

City ____________________ State/Province ________ Zip/PC ________

Country ____________________ [ ] Please send me the Select Registry e-newsletter.

Optional Guest Information: Phone ____________________ Email ____________________

	2nd Stay	3rd Stay
PASSPORT		
Inn		
Initials		
Date 8/22/08 Tom		
Total Amount of Invoice		

Upon collecting three separate validation stamps from three completed Select Registry stays, you are eligible to receive a $25 Loyalty Reward toward your next weeknight stay at a member property. The Loyalty Reward is our innkeeper's way of saying "thank you" for repeatedly choosing Select Registry.

When placing your reservation, inform the innkeeper of your intent to use the Loyalty Reward and, at check-in, present this card to the reservation desk.

$25 Loyalty Reward — 4th Stay

Inn ____________________

Initials ____________________

Date ____________________

Total Amount of Invoice

$ ____________________

Rules for using the $25 Loyalty Reward

- Applicable toward one night's stay at any active Select Registry member property (visit **www.selectregistry.com** for a current list of active members)
- Innkeeper may substitute a $25 invoice discount with a room upgrade, amenity, or other value-added of at least $25 for the Loyalty Reward when redeemed
- Valid Monday through Thursday nights only
- Not valid in conjunction with other discounts, special offers, or gift certificates
- Loyalty Reward not redeemable for cash
- Limit of one Loyalty Reward may be used per stay
- Not subject to replacement if lost
- Loyalty Reward will be valid for 1 year from the date of the third stay (noted above)
- Other restrictions may apply

Innkeeper: please give the guest a new Golden Quill Club Loyalty Travel Program Card and mail their completed card to the Central Office (after the 4th stay). This will ensure that each guest who has completed a series of Select Registry stays is entered into our current Vacation of a Lifetime drawing.

If you have further questions, contact the Select Registry Central Office at **800.344.5244** (269.789.0393 globally) or via email (info@selectregistry.com). You can also print a hard copy version of this card at www.selectregistry.com/goldenquillclub.

Thank you!

SELECT REGISTRY, DISTINGUISHED INNS OF NORTH AMERICA • 501 E MICHIGAN AVENUE, PO BOX 150, MARSHALL, MI 49068-0150

NO POSTAGE
NECESSARY
IF MAILED
IN THE
UNITED STATES

BUSINESS REPLY MAIL

FIRST-CLASS MAIL PERMIT NO. 19 MARSHALL, MI

POSTAGE WILL BE PAID BY ADDRESSEE

SELECT REGISTRY
DISTINGUISHED INNS OF NORTH AMERICA
501 E MICHIGAN AVE
PO BOX 150
MARSHALL MI 49068-9927

Future Destination

Please call Select Registry to discuss:

- The Register Guidebook
- www.SelectRegistry.com
- Our distinguished inns
- Becoming a member
- Quality Assurance Inspections
- Gift Certificates
- Our Loyalty Program
- Co-marketing efforts

Favorite Destination

SELECT REGISTRY
DISTINGUISHED INNS OF NORTH AMERICA

SELECT REGISTRY
DISTINGUISHED INNS OF NORTH AMERICA

Our Innkeeper's Gift to You

Thank you for choosing Select Registry, Distinguished Inns of North America! Please use this book as your guide to more than 400 of the finest Country Inns, B&Bs, and Unique Small Hotels in North America. We think you'll find that some experiences are worth repeating!

SELECT REGISTRY
DISTINGUISHED INNS OF NORTH AMERICA

800.344.5244
269.789.0393
www.SelectRegistry.com

www.SelectRegistry.com

SELECT REGISTRY
DISTINGUISHED INNS OF NORTH AMERICA

800.344.5244
269.789.0393
www.SelectRegistry.com

Notes

SELECT REGISTRY
DISTINGUISHED INNS OF NORTH AMERICA

800.344.5244
269.789.0393
www.SelectRegistry.com